Resources
for Creative Teaching
in Early Childhood
Education

Bonnie Mack Flemming / Darlene Softley Hamilton

Songs and Parodies
JoAnne Deal Hicks

Resources for Creative Teaching in Early Childhood Education

HARCOURT BRACE JOVANOVICH, PUBLISHERS
San Diego   New York   Chicago   Atlanta   Washington, D.C.
London   Sydney   Toronto

ISBN: 0-15-576624-4

Library of Congress Catalog Card Number: 76-2321

Printed in the United States of America

ACKNOWLEDGMENTS AND COPYRIGHTS

The authors and Harcourt Brace Jovanovich, Inc. thank the individuals and publishers listed below for granting permission to reproduce materials in this book. Every effort has been made to trace the ownership of each selection and to fully acknowledge its use. If any errors remain, they will be corrected in subsequent editions on notification of the publisher. Many of the selections are traditional, with the author unknown.

TEXTUAL MATERIAL

Abingdon Press, for "The Child Jesus," from *Songs for the Little Child* by Clara B. Baker and Caroline Kohlsaat. Copyright renewal 1949 by Clara B. Baker. Used by permission of Abingdon Press.

Thea Cannon, for "The Digger," from *Finger Plays and How to Use Them.* © 1952 by the Standard Publishing Company.

Ebony Jr., for material from "Kwanza Feast," by Sharon Bell Mathis (December 1973); "Gifts of Love," by Norma R. Poinsett and "Candy Maker's Kitchen: Sweet Potato Candy," by Shirley A. Searey (December 1974); and "The Seven Lessons of Kwanza," by Karama Fufuka (December 1975). Permission to adapt granted by *Ebony Jr.*

Lutheran Church in America, for "Guess What?" "Guess Who?" "Hide and Seek," "Hot Potato," "Skip-Stoop," "Together, Together," "Who Am I?" and "The Farmer Plants His Seed," from *The Bible for Three-Year-Olds* (1952); "Picture Card Guess," from *Three-Year-Olds and Jesus* (1954); "Little Friend, Little Friend" and "Look and See," from *Friends of Jesus* (1960); "Bobby Plants His Seed," from *Three-Year-Olds in Summer* (1951); "Match-'Em," "Name It," and "Scramble," from *My Storybook of Jesus* (1956); all by Darlene Hamilton, published by the Muhlenberg Press, Philadelphia. Used by permission of the Lutheran Church in America.

Standard Publishing Company, for "The Digger," by Thea Cannon, and "The Clock" and "The Turkey," by Louise M. Oglevee, from *Finger Plays and How to Use Them.* © 1952. The Standard Publishing Company, Cincinnati, Ohio. Used by permission.

ILLUSTRATIONS

Animals drawn by Ed Malsberg and Noel Malsberg.
Text illustrations and diagrams drawn by Ric Chin, Marilyn Grastorf, Elsie Halvorsen, Ed Malsberg, Steve Saxe, Bert Schneider, Vladimir Yevtikhiev.

PHOTO CREDITS

Greg Beaumont: Pages 13, 15, 17, 18, 19, 25, 26, 30, 33, 36, 46, 53, 56, 57, 71, 75, 100, 117, 130, 155, 184, 190, 213, 215, 233, 317, 332, 360, 394, 424, 477, 495, 551, 552, 605, 607, 625, 631.
Darlene Hamilton: Pages 266, 283.
Harbrace photo: Page 279.
The Nature Center for Environmental Activities, Inc., Westport, Connecticut: Page 419.
J. R. Nollendorfs: Pages 63, 64, 65, 66, 67, 68, 69, 402, 404, 502, 508, 567, 619, 632.
United Fresh Fruit and Vegetable Association: Page 547.
David von Riesen: Pages 62, 576.
Cover Photo: Bob Sanchez

To our children and our husbands, without whose love, support, and patience this tremendous task could never have been completed.

Preface

In 1969 the Curriculum Committee of the Kansas Association for the Education of Young Children compiled a resource handbook designed as a reliable compilation of curriculum ideas that could be used by student teachers, paraprofessionals, and in-service teachers within the state. The committee chose subjects that they themselves had used successfully with young children in a variety of child care facilities.

Resources for Creative Teaching in Early Childhood Education was written to continue and expand the committee's work. The book combines a quick reference for basic information about a great many subjects and a practical, scannable format. It is perforated and three-hole punched so that it can be used in a loose-leaf binder. This affords ease in handling and versatility in sequencing the sections, and allows for inserting additional ideas to tailor the book to each teacher's group and situation. A section of the book describes games, dramatic play props, music and art accessories, and playground equipment that can be inexpensively made by the teacher. Commercial games, records, and their manufacturers, as well as a concise bibliography, are also included. The book deals with a variety of subjects presented as guides and grouped under the general headings Self-Concept, Families, Family Celebrations, Seasons, Animals, Transportation, and The World I Live In. For the most effective use of the book, it is essential that a teacher become familiar with the Guide Outline, page 1, and Basic Resources for the Teacher, page 9.

Because it is an accessible reference, this book provides the teacher-aide, the substitute, student, or veteran teacher with the means to fully develop individual and group responses to various learning opportunities. A unique feature of the book is that it integrates curriculum ideas and learning opportunities for a given subject into every part of a day's program. Consequently, children can learn a concept through experiences in many different well-equipped and well-planned environments under the supervision of their teacher.

Another important factor necessary for optimum learning opportunities is a child's own feeling of worth and competence. We feel this positive self-image is fostered when the teacher accepts a child as he or she is, and allows children to grow in creativity and to express their identities without stereotyping by sex, race, religion, economic status, or level of development. We recommend that teachers honestly assess their learning centers, classroom equipment, and teaching program and behavior to minimize prejudice of any kind. It is our belief that *Resources for Creative Teaching in Early Childhood Education* will provide the basis for teachers to develop in the classroom a world of understanding for living and learning.

A special tribute is given to the Kansas Association for the Education of Young Children who sponsored the original book *Resources for Creative Preschool Teaching* and to its presidents of the past few years Barbara Bell, United Child Development Center, Lawrence, Kansas; Alice M. Eberhart; Patricia Garland, Kansas Department of Health and Environment; and Lucile Y. Paden, Ottawa University, Ottawa, Kansas, who gave their continued encouragement and support.

Special recognition must be given to our colleagues on the Kansas Association for the Education of Young Children Curriculum Committee for their creativity and commitment in writing some of the original guides for *Resources for Creative Preschool Teaching*. We would like to thank them for their permission to select from and edit their material, which provided a basic core to the guides in this edition.

Janice A. Bailey Ruth K. Nathan
Betty Christian Charlotte Trombold
Alice M. Eberhart Sue C. Wilson
Ivalee H. McCord

Our thanks go to Patricia M. Enevoldsen, Lincoln-Lancaster Child Care System; Margaret Connealy, Malone Center Head Start–Day Care; Carlene Myers, Lakeview School; Elaine Johnson, First Lutheran Church Nursery School; Nancy Gellermann, Mary Morley School; all of Lincoln, Nebraska, for testing our new material in their classrooms.

We extend special thanks for their encouragement and valuable criticism of the manuscript to Reginald Cedarface; Alita Y. Cooper, University of Kansas; Patricia M. Eggleston, Indiana University; Sylvia Frank; Margaret Haack; Paul Haack, University of Kansas; Sidney Hahn, University of Nebraska; Esperanza Hernandez, Henry Bush Child Development Center, San Marcos, Texas; Shirley Holmes, Meadow Lane Elementary School, Lincoln, Nebraska; Shirlie Hutcherson; Corina Jaimes, Head Start Child Development Center, Lockhart, Texas; Marcia L. Oreskovich, University of Northern Colorado; John Roberts and Aurora Rodriguez, Head Start Program of Hays, Caldwell, and Blanco Counties, San Marcos, Texas; Shirley K. Seevers, University of Nebraska; Robert S. Thurman, University of Tennessee; Belle Townsend, Henry Bush Child Development Center, San Marcos, Texas; Ofelia Vasquez, Community Action Inc., San Marcos, Texas; and Miriam Yeung, Omaha Public Schools.

We thank our illustrators for the original edition David Flemming; Walter Hicks; and C. N. Robinson III, Bilingual Head Start Program, La Grulla, Texas, who allowed us to adapt their drawings, and our photographers Greg Beaumont; J. R. Nollendorfs; and David von Riesen, Kansas State University. We are grateful to the staff, parents, and children of the Lancaster Child Care Center and the First Lutheran Nursery School, Lincoln, Nebraska, for allowing us to photograph them and their facilities.

Finally, each of the authors wishes to acknowledge the support and assistance of her coauthors in preparing and assembling this book into its expanded form: Darlene Softley Hamilton and Bonnie Mack Flemming for writing the manuscript and reworking all later drafts; Darlene Softley Hamilton for selecting the photographs and acting as coordinator for the authors with the publisher; JoAnne Deal Hicks for preparing the music and reading and editing the first draft of the manuscript.

Bonnie Mack Flemming

Darlene Softley Hamilton

JoAnne Deal Hicks

Contents

PART ONE   Self-Concept

PART TWO Families

PART THREE Family Celebrations

Resources
for Creative Teaching
in Early Childhood
Education

Guide Outline

Subject Titles

The order of the subject guides does not imply any prearranged teaching sequence. A logical grouping of subjects, such as Family Celebrations, Seasons, Animals, Transportation, has been made for easier reference.

Basic Understandings

Concepts children can grasp from the subject are written as statements. Choose the simplest statements for the children with the least experience and the statements with more detailed information for the children with previous experience. Some statements contain more than one concept and may be simplified as needed.

Additional Facts the Teacher Should Know

1. Carefully researched information about the subject
2. Precautions about the subject or activities
3. Care and maintenance of materials, equipment, plants, or animals

Methods Most Adaptable for Introducing This Subject to Children

A conversation, story, picture, special event, shared item, visitor, or trip may be the steppingstone to the subject. Your choice will depend on:

1. your children's previous experiences
2. your children's most recent interests
3. the season, the weather, staff skills, and community resources

Vocabulary

1. A basic list of new words to be discovered while exploring the subject
2. Add familiar words within your group's previous experiences

learning centers

Discovery Center

Firsthand experiences to help the children grasp the basic concepts include:

1. physics and chemistry experiments including cooking
2. exploring nature—plants, animals, and the five senses
3. exploring our world—sun, water, air, soil, rocks
4. books and magazines with pictures that show discovery concepts to the children

Dramatic Play Centers

Suggestions are included here for encouraging children to play out learning experiences related to this subject in the Home-Living, Block-Building, and Other Dramatic Play Centers. (See Basic Resources, p. 17.) Select ideas considering your own equipment, space, budget, community resources, and the creative interest and ability of your staff.

Learning, Language, and Readiness Materials Center

Included here are manipulative, language, and cognitive materials related to learning new concepts and to making thinking judgments such as colors, shapes, numbers, spatial relationships, and classifications. These materials are divided into two sections:

1. **commercially made games and materials for use at a table or on a mat.** Listed are puzzles, games, flannelboard aids, subject models, manipulative and cognitive materials available commercially.
2. **teacher-made games and materials for use at a table or on a mat.** Suggestions are included for teacher-made cognitive materials. Variations of learning games are described in the Basic Resources, p. 50.

Art Center

It is assumed that basic art media are offered on a daily basis in your art center. (See Basic Resources, p. 29.) Variations of the basic media and special activities related to each subject are included. Asterisks serve as a guide to the selection of experiences for your group:

  * youngest and least skilled

  ** more skilled

*** for the most experienced child

Experiences are grouped as follows:

1. creative art experiences, which include painting, crayoning, molding and sculpturing, cutting and pasting, collage, printing, mixed media.
2. other experiences in the Art Center using art media include creating objects or materials to be used for games, as dramatic play props, as gifts, or for teaching skills.

Book Center

Books here are to be explored by children individually or read to one or two children by a teacher or aide. (See Basic Resources, p. 31.) Listed alphabetically by author, the books are coded by text length, type of illustration, concept level, and the age and experience of children:

    * assumes no previous experience; brief text and simple illustrations

    ** assumes some previous experience; longer text and simple illustrations

    *** assumes many previous experiences; longer text and more detailed illustrations

    **** more informative text and excellent illustrations (often photographs); read or read-tell; use primarily in the Discovery Center or as a basis for a language or cognitive experience

planning for grouptime

The following suggestions may be used when children are gathered in small groups of three to seven, or larger groups when everyone is involved. Your group size will vary with the interest and maturity of the children, the number of children enrolled, and the size of your staff.

Music

Songs are coded to help you select those most suitable for your group.

1. Original songs will be listed by title and page number.
2. Parodies are included to supplement your music library program.
3. Copyrighted songs from Core Library music books, p. 77, are listed by title and page number for easy reference.
4. Records are listed by title, recording company, size, and speed.
5. Rhythms and singing games are listed in the same manner as songs.

Fingerplays and Poems

1. Original or traditional fingerplays and poems are written out with actions.
2. Copyrighted material from Core Library books, p. 77, is listed by title and page number for easy reference.

Stories

(To read, read-tell, or tell to a group.)

Noted here are choice picture-story books taken from the Book Center list that can be read most successfully to a group. For suggestions on storytelling see Basic Resources, p. 48.

Games

Games in this section can be played successfully with children in a small or large group at a together time. Some of these games may have been listed under Teacher-Made Games. For explanation of Games, see pp. 50–59. **Flannelboard ideas,** when used, will be noted in the appropriate sections depending on their use: to illustrate a song, under Music; to illustrate a story, fingerplay, poem, or game, in the section by that name; used with an individual child, under Learning, Language, and Readiness Materials. For instructions on how to make and use flannelboards, see Basic Resources, p. 45.

Routine Times

Suggestions are made for capitalizing on teachable moments during routine times. Appropriate activities for learning concepts related to a subject are listed to use during snacktime, mealtime, toileting, resting, dressing, transitions, or in transit (busing or walking).

Large Muscle Activities

These suggestions will primarily be used outdoors (see playgrounds, p. 61). When the weather is unsuitable, use a basement, gym, or other large space indoors (see p. 70). Circle Games, Direction Games, and Problem-Solving Games described in the Basic Resources, pp. 55–59, will be included as appropriate.

Extended Experiences

Suggestions are noted for utilizing trips, visitors, films, and other special experiences to extend children's knowledge of a subject. See Basic Resources, pp. 72–74.

teacher resources

Books and Periodicals

These are primarily teacher references.

Pictures and Displays

Ways are suggested for creating your own bulletin boards or displays. Commercial sources for suitable picture packets, mobiles, and other decorations are listed. Ideas are given for rearranging the room to best use the materials suggested.

Community Resources

This section lists possible persons, places, and things in your community that may assist you in planning your programs for the children.

Basic Resources
for the Teacher

Contents

50   learning games

60   routine times of the day

61   large muscle activities

61   large muscle activities outdoors

large mu/cle activitie/ indoor/

extended experience/

teacfier re/ource/

note/ for guiding befiavior

Basic Resources for the Teacher

good curriculum planning

1. Begin with a basic knowledge of how young children grow, develop, and learn.
2. Recognize that children learn best:
   a. when they have a good self-image and are accepted as they are by both adults and other children.
   b. if given repeated opportunities to discover, explore, be challenged, and problem-solve through direct experiences.
   c. when given diverse choices that can lead to independence, self-confidence, self-control, and a sense of responsibility.
   d. through a rich environment that considers their total development and each one's individual needs and interests.
   e. when supervised by adult facilitators who protect and ensure each child's rights without sacrificing any individual child's right to the freedom to learn.
3. Provide and allow for a balance of activities:
   a. structured/unstructured
   b. informative/creative
   c. active/quiet
   d. indoor/outdoor
   e. observing/participating
   f. alone/together
4. Capitalize on the individual strengths of the staff and the assets offered by parents and community.
5. Recognize weaknesses of each member of the staff and plan for individual personal growth. Constantly search for new ideas and for ways of improving teaching skills by encouraging the staff to:
   a. read—refer to Core Library for suggested resources.
   b. visit other centers.

c. share ideas and problems with other early childhood educators.

d. attend workshops.

e. invite resource people from the community.

f. involve parents as teachers and planners.

g. join a professional organization or an affiliate group of NAEYC (National Association for the Education of Young Children), ACEI (Association for Childhood Education International), DCCDCA (Day Care and Child Development Council of America).

Short and Long Range Planning with Staff

1. Block out a general program by the year/month/week/day:
   a. choose subject guides as aids, considering the need for repetition and the particular interests, needs, and experience of your group.
   b. study your overall plan to determine the equipment and materials most necessary for carrying out your projected plans.
   c. familiarize yourself with this Basic Resources section for ways your staff can augment your budget and extend the educational opportunities offered.
   d. expand your resources by purchasing some of the recommended Core Library books on music, songs, fingerplays, and poems, pp. 77–78.
   e. make a plan for starting or supplementing your art, music, science, fingerplay, and other idea files. Encourage input by all members of the staff and the parents.
   f. at appointed intervals evaluate your daily plans noting recommendations for the future. Modify and adapt the plans for use again with another group at another time.
   g. organize the teacher storage space and maintain it by periodic reorganization. Repair and replace or duplicate items most needed and used.
2. Make a detailed program plan for the week:
   a. consider every learning center in the classroom and each time segment of the day.
   b. make special plans for individual children; be selective in choice of materials and ideas you will present by considering each child's need, abilities, and interests.
   c. build on previous experience of the children. Cross references in this book will help you plan related experiences.
   d. gather materials needed.
   e. try out recipes, patterns, ideas, or experiments in advance, especially foods, arts, and science.
   f. be flexible—be ready to change plans, expand or substitute, as moments of readiness are identified.
   g. anticipate the need for alternative plans. Consider change of weather, shortage of staff, personal crises, limitations of plant space because of multiple uses of a facility.
   h. consider and plan for special needs requiring more staff, special equipment, materials, visitors, trips, safety supervision.
   i. define and assign specific responsibilities to staff members; outline ways in which volunteers may be enlisted to assist; encourage substitutes (volunteers and parents) to attend staff planning meetings for better continuity.
   j. each staff member should be encouraged to accept a learning center, a routine time, or a program activity for which she or he is totally responsible.
3. Make your plans unique:
   a. be selective—choose only those basic understandings and curriculum ideas that meet the needs of your children as reflected by their ability, previous experience, opportunity, ethnic culture, geographic environment, and economic situation.

b. choose ideas for development that best fit your teaching philosophy, style, and skills, and about which you can be most enthusiastic.

c. adapt to the potential and the limits of your type of program, length of school day, total physical environment, and community resources.

NOTE: This resource is not all inclusive; you should continue to add your own ideas. It is unlikely, and inappropriate, that you will use all the materials and activities suggested under any one subject with any one child or group.

learning centers

Learning Centers are areas in a school or a classroom that define a special focus or that afford a specific opportunity not otherwise possible. Centers often planned for young children may include a Discovery Center; Dramatic Play Centers including a Home Living Center, a Block-Building Center, and Other Dramatic Play Centers; a Learning, Language, and Readiness Materials Center; an Art Center; a Book Center; a Music Center; and a Center for Large Muscle Activities. Space for sleeping, resting, and eating, apart from the above or in a multiple use of the above, may also be provided as needed.

These centers divide a school or a classroom in such a way as to allow children to make choices, to move freely and independently, and to grow in areas of need. They also give opportunities for a large number of children to learn individually or in smaller groups so that the teacher can take advantage of moments of readiness, keen interest, and desire. In a more structured grouping, these activities might not otherwise be possible.

The child can be invited into the mainstream of learning in the least coercive way. The shy child may choose to enter a quiet corner and pursue learning in his or her own way, while another child, who seeks and needs companionship, can join a cooperative play group such as dramatic play or a group playing a learning game that requires several participants. A child with a keen interest and/or an ability in art or science may wish to begin the day in an area where he or she feels more confident, comfortable, and eager.

Learning Centers tend to invite a child to come and see, come and do, come and learn. A wise staff is alert to the responsibility to invite, guide, and encourage children to explore all the centers and ultimately learn in several. The staff should offer enough opportunities to learn concepts so that, whether a child selects one center or another, the end result will be the learning necessary for that particular child's growth. By helping each child find that there are alternative ways of learning the same thing, the child will discover what is the best way for him or her to learn.

Room arrangement, materials and equipment, staff, and concepts to be learned will all influence the organization of a good learning environment for young children. By setting up a series of centers within this environment you can provide opportunities:

1. for a child to make choices.
2. for discovery and learning through a direct personal experience.
3. to build a feeling of self-confidence and competence as a result of learning skills.
4. to enlarge children's vocabulary and to develop skills in communicating their ideas through the creative use of language, materials, and equipment.
5. for imaginative dramatic play through role playing.
6. to learn to think and to problem-solve by using a variety of materials.
7. to develop physical and motor skills of coordination and manipulation as the children use equipment.
8. to develop socially as children learn to relate to others.
9. to share and to be responsible to others as a member of a group.
10. to use and care for materials and equipment.
11. to complete tasks and to plan group projects.
12. to discover and expand the learning of specific information relating to a subject.

Some considerations in planning for centers include:

1. space (floor, table, display, and storage)
2. light, ventilation, heat
3. exits, entrances, and traffic patterns
4. the number of children, their interests, abilities, and needs
5. availability of enough sturdy, safe, multipurpose equipment and materials
6. size of budget for additions to basic equipment, supplementing with homemade and donated or recycled materials
7. number of staff (permanent and volunteer)
8. length of school day, program services offered, size and form of the physical plant
9. availability of an extended classroom space such as a gym, park, or outdoor yard

Remember, providing a rich environment is not enough. Adults must be facilitators, participants, and supervisors interacting with the children, other staff members, and the environment. (See pp. 83–84 for specific suggestions.)

Arrange centers in such a manner as to allow easy supervision (viewing) by staff from strategic spots without limiting the children's use of materials. There are times when a teacher may need to supervise several centers alone, such as at the beginning or the end of each day. Therefore, at times, some centers may need to be closed or "off limits." If so, make the alternatives challenging, interesting, and exciting.

Discovery Center

Guidelines for Teaching Science in the Discovery Center

1. Encourage each child to observe keenly:
   a. What do you see?
   b. What is it like?
2. Invite each child to think by posing such questions as:
   a. Why do you suppose?   c. What might happen if?
   b. What do you think?   d. How can we find out?

A table in the science corner will allow children to take information books or science materials, such as the ear of Indian corn, from the supply shelf for closer scrutiny. Note the lingerie box used as a storage box.

3. Help each child to look for explanations.
4. Encourage each child to grow and know. Invite and listen to his or her questions. Help the child to discover misconceptions.
5. Give each child a variety of experiences. Provide a well-balanced program using:
   a. living things—plants, animals—to illustrate growth and life
   b. matter and energy—heat, wind, electricity, sound, motors, fire, magnetism, cooking
   c. the earth and its elements—rocks, soil, sand, metals, water, air
   d. regions beyond the earth—sun, moon, stars, outer space
6. Give each child an opportunity to discover. Provide the necessary equipment and materials that will make experimentation and discovery possible. (See p. 14.)
7. Repeat experiences; relate to what else the child is doing and learning; give opportunities for progressive learning.
8. Use a variety of media: real specimens, models, filmstrips, pictures, resource persons, and trips that allow for direct observation and experimentation.
9. Develop in the child a respect for all living things.
10. Give cautions regarding safety in the use of equipment.

> **NOTE:** You don't need elaborate equipment. Observe nature: water, shadows, sun, sky, earth. You can do many things with only a magnifying glass, measuring cup, and a ruler.

Discovery Center Equipment

A quiet center should be planned where discoveries and exploration of materials can be made by individual and small groups of children. A closet or ample cupboard space to store equipment is needed. The center should be furnished with shelves, a variety of containers, small tables, nooks, and a few comfortable chairs or cushions. Items that will be referred to in the book include:

METRIC AND ENGLISH MEASURING DEVICES

scale—bathroom, kitchen, balance pans, and spring scales
linear—foot rule, yardstick, measuring tape (cloth and metal)
cubic—teaspoon, tablespoon, pint, quart, liter, measuring cup and spoons
thermometer—Fahrenheit and centigrade

SPECIMENS

rocks, minerals, fossils, gems	seashells	coconut shells
halite (salt in original form)	sponges	corn, wheat, other seeds
wool (raw, carded, spun, dyed)	driftwood	bird nests, eggs
cotton ball, thread, cloth	feathers	butterflies, moths
silkworms (preserved), cocoons	animals	flowers, growing plants
leaves (pressed in wax paper)	insects	

DISCOVERY AIDS

magnifying glasses (tripod and hand)	electric clock	switch box
magnets (horseshoe and bar)	color paddles	binoculars
simple machines or tools (pulleys	globe	telescope
with rope and chains, wheels,	tuning fork	flashlight
wedges, screws, levers, springs)	mirrors	microscope
dry-cell battery	prisms	stethoscope
animal cages (with exercise wheel	ant farm	telephone
or chambers and tunnels to allow	compass	terrarium
small animals exercise)	cheesecloth	vivarium
vases, pots, bowls	rubber tubing	aquarium

Storage

One key to taking advantage of a spontaneous interest in science or to responding to that teachable moment is *accessibility* of resources. Science trays, such as illustrated on p. 15, allow for stacking and compact storage. Fruit shipping cartons with rope handles are easily transported. Lids may be used to keep contents air-tight or large plastic bags may be slipped over one lid and the other half (bottom) used for another tray. Label the side for quick identification of items sought. Other suitable storage boxes for smaller items include see-through unbreakable plastic boxes, glove cartons, or hosiery cartons available in quantity from a department store. These sometimes are color-coded, which may help you with your storing by categories.

ITEMS FOR TRAY STORAGE

1. **Shapes:** circle, square, triangle, star, ellipse, oval or egg shape, rectangle, octagon.
2. **Leather and fur:** sheepskin, suede (deerskin), pigskin, kid (goat), cowhide, horsehide, mink, lamb, rabbit fur, alligator, snakeskin, and lizard. Good sources are gloves, purses, shoes, and scraps from leather shops.

3. **Color:** include prisms, colored glasses, color paddles and paint, carpet and upholstery samples in primary and secondary colors. (See Color guide.)
4. **Wood:** include crosscuts of a tree and a limb, wood shavings, shingles, sawdust, plywood, samples of various colors and grains of wood, bark, toys and utility items made of wood.
5. **Tree, flower, fruit, and vegetable seeds:** place in closed, clear, unbreakable containers (pill bottles).
6. **Nest and broken (bird) eggshells:** have donor help you label the type of bird by location of nest. Include a picture of the bird with its nest or a birdhouse.
7. **Plumbing equipment:** include faucets, elbows, T's, adapters, long and short lengths of pipe. Check with plumbing companies for supplies.
8. **Lock box:** snib lock, padlock, chain lock, cupboard latch.

NOTE: See also the specimens listed on the previous page for many more items that can be stored in trays.

Exploring and Discovery Experiences The child on the left is filling and measuring cornmeal, which is a good substitute for sand. Measuring spoons and cups are excellent additions to this discovery activity. (See Mathematics guide, p. 620.) The child on the right is discovering rock and mineral specimens hidden in a box of fine sand. Other possibilities for hidden treasures are shells and driftwood pictured under the tripod magnifying glass. Children will also enjoy using these treasures to create designs in their miniature sandbox. **NOTE:** The sandbox is contained in a second box to minimize spilling, and the cornmeal in a tight-lidded container for storage.

science opportunities are everywhere—
what can children discover?

1 **under or beside a rock or a log?**

slugs	insects	damp soil
snails	worms	mushrooms, toadstools
toads	lizards, snakes	moss
turtles	small animals	

2 **on a sidewalk?**

footprints	grass or weeds in cracks	sections to count
wet leaves / leaf prints	ice, snow, puddle of water	a game marked with chalk
ants	crevices	worms after rain

3 **on, in, or under a tree or a bush?**

nuts	crevices	small animals
fruit	holes	toadstools
birds	knots	protection from rain for
insects	branches	people and animals
flowers	twigs	designs and shapes made
pinecones	sap	by shadows and
bark	nests	formation of branches

4 **in or near a pond or a lake?**

cattails	fish	turtles
water lilies	minnows	crayfish
swans	insects	mud
ducks	leaves, seeds	rocks, stones
snakes	algae	place for birds, animals
skunks	twigs	to find water for
elephant's-ear plant	grass, moss	drinking and bathing
reflection of yourself	frogs, tadpoles	

5 **at the beach?**

sand	driftwood	crabs
seagulls	seaweed	clams
water	insects and bugs	
seashells	fish	

6 **in a pile of dirt?**

insects	worms	different colors of soil
seeds	rocks, pebbles	gravel, sand

7 **in a garden or on a lawn?**

turtles	birds	grasses
dandelion and other seeds	bunnies	feathers
anthill	bird feeder and a birdbath	worms
four-leaf clovers	kitchen garden	insects
colors	flowers	slugs

Dramatic Play Centers

Home-Living Center

1. Set up in an accessible, contained area. If adjacent to the block-building center or special dramatic play centers, it will allow interaction and cooperative play.
2. Arrange to duplicate (simulate) a real home. Set the scene by posting pictures and putting out accessories to develop interest and related play.
3. Keep orderly—clothes clean and mended and equipment repaired. Orderliness invites constructive use.
4. Equipment should be sturdy enough for group use, large enough for a child to use by himself or herself.
5. Post rules and suggestions for guiding or modifying behavior such as:
   a. Mops stay on the floor, brooms are for sweeping.
   b. It is easier to walk when the floors are clear.
   c. Food should stay on the table, in the cupboards, or in the pans on the stove.
   d. Dolls, doll clothes, dishes should be kept off the floor (except for picnics).
   e. If the family is too large, invite a child or several children to participate in another activity or encourage them to build another house, sharing the furniture.
   f. Help a child to join the group by asking if the family could use a grandmother or an uncle.
   g. All members of the family should help to keep the house clean and neat.

Home-Living Dramatic Play Center Individual servings of food have been cut from magazines and TV dinner cartons, glued to corrugated cardboard, and laminated with clear contact. Eggs are of unbreakable plastic or lathed out of wood and painted white. The plastic fruit has been filled with sawdust and glue and allowed to harden, which makes it more durable. The flower vase is made of two particle-board roll-ends glued together to hold a bouquet of artificial flowers. Roll-ends are available from small print shops, newspaper printers, and from doctors' offices.

6. Avoid or monitor the use of shared accessories that might pose a health hazard, for example, combs, wigs, pacifiers, teething rings, or silverware.
7. Rotate (remove or add) special items to renew interest in the center and encourage an expanded use of basic equipment.
8. Support the children's right to reflect a nonsexist viewpoint toward dramatic play roles chosen by themselves or others in dramatic play.

Block-Building Center

1. Allow enough space away from the classroom traffic ways.

   NOTE: Low-pile carpeting reduces the noise level.

2. Arrange blocks according to shape and size so they are accessible on the shelves.
3. Provide sufficient accessory toys to expand and develop broader use of blocks as interest development demands. Remove those not needed.
4. Station teachers near the center so they can assist with supervision.
5. Chalked boundaries on the floor will prove helpful in insuring property rights.
6. Label buildings for children so they will become interested in language.
7. To prevent hoarding, limit the number of blocks accumulated by one child before construction begins.

Boys are constructing a building using hollow cardboard blocks and plastic and rubber tools. Note their resourceful use of a lunch box as a tool kit. Hard hat in foreground is an authentic prop. The one on child's head is available commercially.

8. Pick up or help pile stray blocks that may otherwise bother the construction and/or movement of other children. Keep area clean, orderly, and all equipment in good repair.
9. Expand interests with the use of books, excursions, pictures, and other aids.
10. Post rules and suggestions for guiding or modifying behavior, such as:
    a. We build with blocks.
    b. We need an open path to the block shelves. Invite children to build away from the shelves.
    c. Put blocks that are alike together when picking them up. Remember that teachers and others can help in the clean-up task.
    d. Build no higher than your chin. (This rule keeps child visible and gives child a measurement for safety.)
    e. Encourage children to build with blocks *before* using accessories. It will encourage more constructive and creative use of both.

    NOTE: An exception might be a new, shy, or insecure child who may wish to hold an accessory while observing or before joining play.

Dramatic Play Props

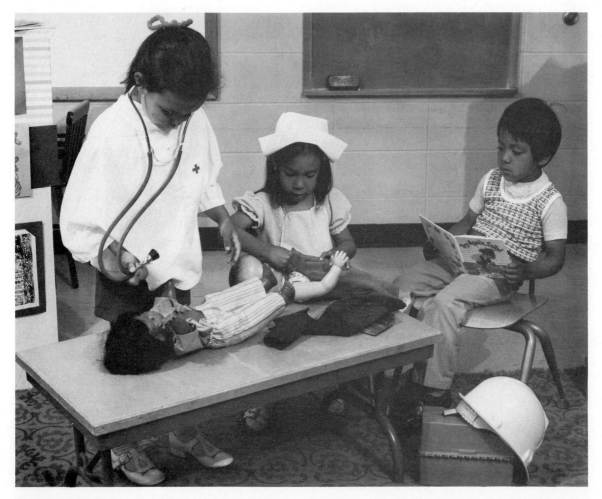

Dramatic Play Props Patterns for the girl's nurse's cap and apron may be found on pp. 22–23. A man's shirt worn backwards can be a doctor's shirt, as above, or a male nurse's outfit. Male nurses do not wear caps, they wear a pin. The pin can be made from two small pieces of press-on or iron-on red tape.

collect dramatic play props

- **Mail Carrier**
  hat (see p. 496)
  stamps
  mailbag
  mailbox
  letters
  packages
  money
  rubber stamps
  cash drawer

- **Sanitary Engineer**
  sacks
  ashcans
  wagons

- **Firefighter**
  hose
  wagon
  ladder
  rubber or cardboard
    hatchet
  hat (see p. 496)

- **Service Station**
  Attendant
  oil can
  cap
  flashlight
  rubber hose lengths
  rope (short lengths)
  sponge and bucket
  rubber or soft plastic
    tools
  cash register
  credit cards
  play money

- **Grocery Clerk**
  apron
  vendor's hat (see p. 22)
  baskets
  play money
  cash register
  food cartons, boxes
  pad and pencil
  shopping bags
  shelves
  plastic or papier-mâché
    fruits and vegetables

- **Pilot / Flight Attendant**
  cap
  airplane
  steering wheel (see p. 495)
  serving trays
  travel folders
  packing-box cockpit
  walking-board wing

- **Doctor, Nurse,**
  Nursing Attendant
  nurse's cap
  tape, cotton
  pad and pencil
  2 telephones
  kit or bag
  thermometer container
  sunglasses
    (without lenses)
  unbreakable supplies
    (pill bottles)
  bandages (strips of
    sheeting)
  stethoscope
  baby scale
  tape measure or
    height chart

- **Railroad Worker**
  (engineer, brakeman,
  conductor, porter,
  dispatcher)
  lunch bucket
  overalls
  ticket punch
  colored tickets
  lantern (without glass)
  hat (see p. 23)
  watch
  pillows
  luggage
  trays
  chef's hat
  neckerchief

- **Ranch Hand**
  hat
  chaps
  rope
  bolero
  stickhorse
  neckerchief

- **Painter**
  cap
  paintbrushes
  bucket and water

- **Police Officer**
  hat
  badge
  tickets
  license
  traffic signs
  handcuffs
  keys to jail
  pencil and pad

- **Baker**
  hat (see p. 22)
  pans
  apron
  rolling pin
  wooden spoons
  plastic bowls
  cookie cutters

- **Fisher**
  net
  cardboard for oars
  poles with string,
    spools
  paper, cardboard,
    or plastic fish
  box for boat
  styrofoam packing
    worms

- **Circus Performers /**
  Workers
  tickets
  crêpe paper
    to decorate wheels
  black hat for
    ringmaster
  crazy hats, costumes,
    and ruffled collars
    for clowns
  cardboard cartons cut
    to resemble cages
    with bars
  stands for animals
    to perform on
  white hats for
    popcorn vendors
    (see p. 22)

adapt dramatic play props

Save Accessories

- length of hose (protect nozzle or remove) (a bicycle handle grip makes a good nozzle)
- empty oil cans
- empty food containers
- paper punch or empty stapler
- buckets and brushes
- pads and pencils
- rubber stamp with handle

Make Your Own

- temporary props of paper or cardboard: hat bands, money, signs
- fishing poles, smokestacks, and oars can be made of empty upholstery rollers
- enlist aid of service or church group to sew simple cloth hats such as baker's hats, engineer's caps, scarves, stoles, shortened skirts with elastic waist bands, white bib aprons using elastic instead of ties (see patterns, p. 22)

Build Equipment

- mount laundry, fat, or flour barrels for tunnel or airplane (add wings) (see illustration, p. 67)
- use empty cartons, tote boxes, pop cartons, tile boxes, desk cartons, large florist cartons
- use discarded tires for swings, climbers, or tunnels
- mount a wheel for a multiple use vehicle

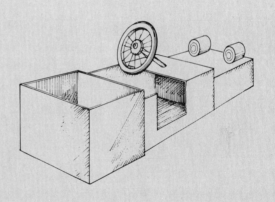

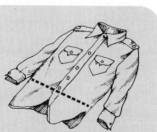

Alter Helper Shirts

- cut off sleeves
- reverse collars
- adjust neck buttons and sew on a large button
- helper shirts that are often available: mail carrier, work shirt, white or pastel shirts for doctors, orderlies, nursing attendants, lab or druggist coats or nurses' outfits (see illustration, p. 19)
- grocery or ice cream aprons can be made with elastic neck straps and an elastic waist in back (see pattern, p. 22)

Collect Real Helper Hats

- A discontinued or damaged mail carrier's cap
- a paint cap (free at a paint dealer)
- a taxicab driver's hat or sailor's hat
- a nurse's cap
- construction hard hat
- father's old felt or straw hat
- bright colored woman's hat, turban, scarf
- service station attendant's hat, cap
- a chef, firefighter, or police officer's hat

patterns for dramatic play props

NOTE: Seam allowance measurements included for all patterns on this page.

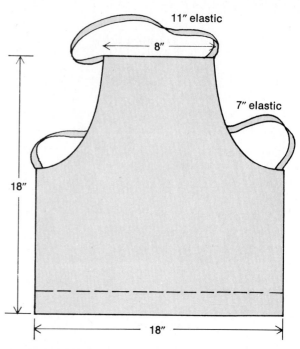

Mail Bag

Cuff open edge of large paper sack with a strip of cardboard folding top edge of sack twice over cardboard for durability. Staple ends of strap on inside of sack as shown in diagram. (See illustration on p. 190.)

NOTE: Strap must be attached to opposite side.

Grocer's Apron

Use 11 inch elastic for neck and 7 inch elastic for waist. Bottom hem is indicated by dotted lines. Attach elastic at neck and waist. Allow for other hems when cutting; measurements are finished size.

Train Engineer's Cap

Take overlapping tucks at points A-AB-B, C-CD-D, E-EF-F, and so on, and then gather remaining shape into headband. Attach bill at one of the short sides and line with dark upholstery or plastic for sturdiness.

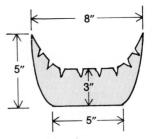

cut two 2″ x 23″ bands with ¾″ slashes on inside edge of bill (finished bill 2¼″ deep)

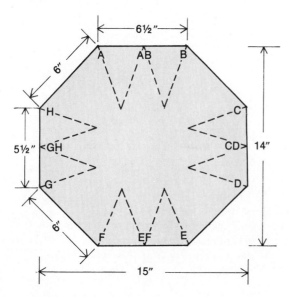

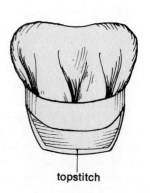

topstitch

A

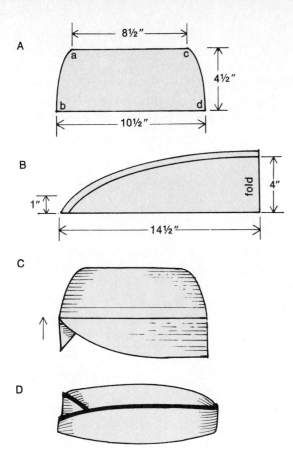

8½"

4½"

a   c

b   d

10½"

B

fold

4"

1"

14½"

C

D

Food Vendor's Hat

Sew two of part A together around curve between points **abcd** leaving straight edges at **bd** open. Sew other two part A pieces in same manner, turn inside out to form lining for first crown. Cut two of part B, open both pieces out flat. Sew together (one on top of other), bind top edges with bias tape, and leave straight edges open. Insert straight open edges of brim into open ends of both crown and lining at circumference of **bd** (headband). Top stitch, tuck in raw edges.

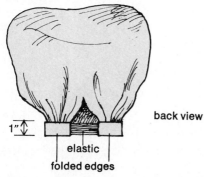

back view

1"

elastic

folded edges

Baker's Hat

Gather a circle 21 inches in diameter onto a double band about 18 inches long and 1 inch wide. When circle is completely gathered into headband, insert a 2 inch long piece of wide elastic as shown above. Allow for adjusting to varying head sizes.

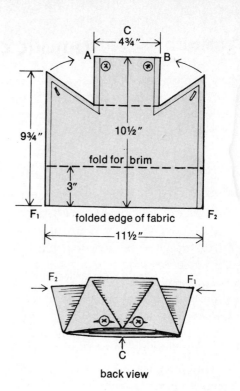

C

4¾"

A   B

9¾"

10½"

fold for brim

3"

F₁   folded edge of fabric   F₂

11½"

F₂   F₁

C

back view

Nurse's Cap 1

Cut out one pattern (above), placing F_1-F_2 on folded edge of fabric. Sew along indented stitching lines. Turn inside out, turning in open ends at AB for narrow hem. Topstitch this hem at AB (Leave no raw edges). Make button holes where indicated. See illustration, p. 19.

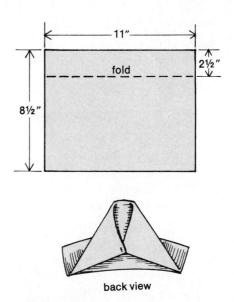

11"

fold

2½"

8½"

back view

Nurse's Cap 2

Staple an 8½ inch by 11 inch piece of stiff paper after folding as above. Overlap corner points about 1 inch when stapled. Secure to child's hair with bobby pin. Male nurse does not wear a cap. Pin identifies rank.

Cardboard and Cartons

The common box or carton can offer an endless number of possibilities for temporary equipment. Students in a Headstart Supplementary Training Program once pooled their ideas and listed 100 uses for cartons in an early childhood education center. Here are a few ideas they found helpful for use in the various Learning Centers.

Home-Living Center

1. **Stoves:** Make from sturdy rectangular boxes about 24 to 30 inches high. Paint circles for burners. Attach wooden beads or knobs on the front of the carton for heat selector dials. Secure them with plastic-coated wire and a disc of plastic on *both* sides of the cardboard to prevent tearing. Cut a three-sided opening for a door and use masking tape to reinforce the fold instead of a hinge. Insert an inverted box inside for an oven floor. To make a latch, hook a yarn loop on a button that has been secured with plastic discs on both sides of the cardboard.
2. **A Doll bed:** Make from a shallow box of appropriate size. Turn the top flaps to the inside of the carton and secure, staple, sew, or tie flaps down. Use a pillow for a mattress and cover it with sheets or a blanket.
3. **Tote box:** Make as for bed except add rope loops for handles. Paint it for greater durability and attractiveness.
4. **Partition or room divider:** Use three sides of a large desk, stereo, or cupboard carton to make a three-way play screen. Cut an opening for door or window in one section. Can be painted or wallpapered.
5. **As a mailbox:** See Road Transportation guide, p. 495.
6. **Shelves and a cupboard:** Set cartons inside other cartons.
7. **To make a desk or dressing table:** Invert carton, open end down. Cut open one side for kneehole space. Cut like a T and fold back to reinforce opening. Can also be used as a fireplace.
8. **For a television:** Cut a hole in the bottom of a carton, leaving a frame for hole, and turn on its side.
9. **To make a table:** Turn a carton upside down, reinforce, leaving two sides open.

Block-Building Center

1. **Suitbox:** Make cardboard highway sections to use with proportional blocks and cars. Use proportional double longs, Y and X shapes, arches and curves as guides and make your cardboard road segments double size for two-lane traffic. Line a median strip on each. Let children lay out these cardboard roadways and save the blocks for buildings along the highway.
2. **Tabletop play board:** Use a double section of a mattress, stereo, or pool-table carton. Hinge in the center with masking tape so that it can be stored. Paint overall surface green except where you wish to leave roadways or cement areas. Paint an irregularly shaped oval lake in the center of one section. (See p. 172 for illustration.) **Variation:** Make a cloverleaf roadway or a subdivision pattern of streets. Leave grass space for constructing houses or public buildings.
3. **Cardboard planks:** Make convenient space holders for windows in hollow-block buildings or shelves. Double sheets of corrugated cardboard are more durable than single-thickness sections. Make 11 inches by 33 or 44 inches.
4. **Rectangular carton:** Use for transportation vehicles (train, car, boat, wagon). Glue cloth or upholstery to the bottom of the box so it will pull smoothly and not scratch the floor. Attach rope pulls or use rope to link cartons together. (See p. 479 for shoebox train.)

5. **Zoo cage:** See Zoo Animals guide, p. 428.
6. **Tile boxes:** Use for hollow blocks. Reinforce inside by inserting two slotted pieces of strong corrugated cardboard that have been formed into an X-shaped partition. Tape the lids shut and paint. They will then be sturdy enough for long use.

Learning, Language, and Readiness Materials Center

This center needs good lighting, easy access to shelves, and groups of tables arranged in a manner for individual or group use. Sometimes placing a table against a dividing wall allows a child more room for activity without having to disturb or compete with another child across the table for space. Other times, center materials can be shared more easily when children's chairs are placed around the end of a table or by using a round table.

In some centers you may choose to hinge narrow tables to a wall; these can then be lifted up and braced for extended table space when needed, and used for displaying pictures when collapsed. These hinged tables allow for additional floor space when lifted.

This center, when adjacent to the Book Center, allows for the easy transition from one to another for language development experiences that may be offered in either space. (See p. 32 for preparing the Book Center.)

Directions Game Children above are playing Directions, the learning game described on page 57. Additional props may be added to develop vocabulary and understanding of such parts of speech as the following adverbs: by, besides, behind, above, beneath, under. For example with farm animals, a barn, a fence, and a trough might be used. "Susan, can you place the cow *behind* the fence? Michelle, can you place the lamb *inside* the barn in *front* of Chris? **Variation:** This game may be played using any animals in the Animal guides. With animals from woods or zoo you might want to use props such as fences, cages, trees, bushes, rocks, or hollow logs.

Language arts both in this center and the Book Center should include opportunities for:

1. **Listening:** Help the child discover and know that thoughts can be expressed aloud.
2. **Thinking:** Give opportunities for problem solving.
3. **Speaking:** Encourage the children to talk about what they are doing, will do, and can do in sharing times; to name objects; to role play in the dramatic play centers; to talk into a telephone. Accept what the children have to say as important. Listen to the children's expressed thoughts and ideas. Use fingerplays and learning games to build vocabulary and to learn nouns, adjectives, prepositions, and adverbs.
4. **Writing:** Help children discover that words and thoughts can be written down, such as labelling objects in the center, using signs, song charts with words, words lettered on bulletin boards with pictures, or lettering children's thoughts about their pictures.
5. **Reading:** Read to children. Show children that words and pictures are symbols for thoughts expressed. Relate words to pictures or objects helping children to realize the need for, and excitement of, reading signs, books, and other matter in their world. Let children see their thoughts when you have written them down, encouraging each to want to write for themselves.

Left: preparing geometric shapes for spatterpainting with a screen. *Center:* using a vegetable brush for spatterpainting with a screen. *Right:* fingerpainting on a formica square.

Art Center

An Art Center is optimumly placed where there is a washable floor, near a sink, where there is ample storage space, and out of traffic patterns. No one but the child can create the picture or idea that is in his or her mind. The creations will reflect *experience*. The *process* is more important than the *product*. Art media experiences can release emotions to allow for creation. A child often expresses feelings as well as ideas through art. When working with children in the art center:

1. introduce a variety of media.
2. be prepared
3. provide choices
4. offer support
5. it is better to ask, "Would you tell me about it?" than, "What is it?"
6. let children explore
7. provide space for drying finished products
8. supervise
9. compare only against child's previous effort
10. offer large sheets of paper, long-handled brushes, thick chalk, and pencils

Favorite Recipes for Art Materials

Nonhardening No-Cook Play Dough

2 cups self rising flour
2 T. alum
2 T. salt
2 T. cooking oil
1 cup, plus 2 T. boiling water

Mix and knead.

Salt Paint

⅓ cup salt
¼ tsp. food coloring

Spread in pan to dry before putting in shakers.

Cooked Play Dough

1 cup flour
½ cup salt
1 cup water
1 T. vegetable oil
2 tsp. cream of tartar

Heat until ingredients form ball, add food coloring.

Potter's Clay

½ cup flour
½ cup cornstarch
1 cup salt dissolved in 3¾ cups of boiling water

Blend flour and cornstarch with enough water to make paste. Boil water and salt. Add to cornstarch mix and cook until clear. Cool overnight then add 6 to 8 cups of flour and knead until you have the right consistency.

NOTE: Keep a metal salt shaker full of flour handy for the children to keep their clay from sticking.

Iridescent Soap Bubbles

1 cup of water (hard or soft)
2 T. liquid detergent
1 T. glycerine
½ tsp. sugar

Mix all ingredients.

Finger Paint

⅔ cup elastic dry starch
1 cup cold water
3 cups boiling water
1 cup Ivory Soap Flakes
oil of cloves, a few drops (preservative)
calcimine pigment or vegetable coloring

Dissolve elastic starch in cold water. Smooth lumps and add boiling water. Stir constantly. Thicken but do not boil more than one minute. Add rest of ingredients (hot or cold). Use on glazed paper, newsprint, or wrapping paper.

Sand Paint

½ cup sand (washed, dried, and sifted)
1 T. powder paint

Shake onto surface brushed with watered glue.

NOTE: Empty plastic vitamin or soap bubble bottles make excellent containers.

Sugar Flour Paste

1 cup flour
1 cup sugar
1 qt. water (2 cups cold / 2 cups hot)
1 T. powdered alum
3 drops of oil of cloves

Mix flour and sugar together. Slowly stir in 1 cup of water. Bring remainder to boil and add the mixture to it, stirring constantly. Continue to cook and stir (½ hr. in a double boiler) until fairly clear. Remove from heat and add oil of cloves. Makes 1 quart of paste. Paste keeps a long time. Keep moist by adding small piece of wet sponge to top of small jar of paste.

Soap Paint

1½ cups soap flakes
1 cup hot or warm water

Whip with an eggbeater until stiff.

Sally's Play Dough Recipe (Sally Wysong)

Below is a play dough recipe similar to the commercial type and more durable. Keep in a plastic bag or closed container when not being used.

1 cup of flour
1 cup of water
1 T. of oil
1 T. alum
½ cup salt
2 T. vanilla
food coloring for desired intensity

Mix all dry ingredients. Add oil and water. Cook over medium heat, stirring constantly until it reaches the consistency of mashed potatoes. Remove from heat and add vanilla and color. Divide into balls and work in color by kneading.

Bookbinder's Paste

1 tsp. flour
2 tsp. cornstarch
¼ tsp. alum (powdered)
⅓ cup water

Mix dry ingredients. Add water slowly, stirring out lumps. Cook in a double boiler over low heat, stirring constantly. Remove from heat when paste begins to thicken; it will thicken more as it cools. Keep covered. Thin with water when necessary.

Creative Art Tips

1. A candy box or cheese box with holes cut in its lid to hold small cans or jars makes an excellent paint-holder rack that resists tipping.
2. Rubber foam with holes makes an excellent chalk holder.
3. Old broken crayons may be shaved, and shavings spread between two thicknesses of wax paper and ironed with a warm iron. Be careful not to put colors too close together.
4. Sponge pieces may be obtained from upholstery shops and cut into various geometric shapes for sponge printing.
5. Woven baskets or solid-colored margarine tubs make good crayon holders.
6. For table use, buy white glue by the gallon and pour into small detergent bottles or permanent-wave squeeze bottles.

    CAUTION: Clear spout after each use and insert round toothpick for a stopper.

7. Discarded toothbrushes may be used for spatterpainting.
8. To make a spiral book for the children, use turkey or chicken rings available through hatcheries. Use grocery bags for pages. Remove end and slit at seam.
9. Discarded toothbrushes with a hole in one end may be cut off to about 3 inches in length and filed to make a blunt needle for sewing open-mesh vegetable bag. Thread bright yarn through the hole end of the toothbrush and tie a button at the other end of the yarn to prevent end from sliding through mesh when weaving.
10. When children are cutting paper, tape a cuffed paper bag to the edge of the table for scraps.
11. A printing shop is an excellent source for small scraps of colored paper and cardboard.
12. Mark storage box for creative art supplies on the end or top with a picture to identify its contents. Clear plastic boxes may also be used.
13. Place a piece of wet sponge inside the lid of a jar of paste to keep the paste moist between uses.
14. Crisp collage paper is a free discard from department stores; ask clerks to save lingerie and blouse inserts.

Creative Art Media

1. **Brayers:** Can be made of wooden or plastic spools and the top half of a coat hanger that has been cut and bent to form a tonglike handle. In each end of the spool, insert one of the prongs (ends). For a smooth brayer attach a piece of sponge or upholstery fabric. Use without covering to make plaid lines or stripes. (See illustration, p. 30.)
2. **Cardboard Overlay:** Allow children to glue or paste layers of geometric-shaped cardboard scraps on a surface. Children may choose to paint on top of the overlay. A print can be taken from the painted surface using a monoprint technique. (See p. 31, Nos. 9, 10.)
3. **Sewing:** Styrofoam meat and pastry trays make good contrasting forms for sewing on yarn. For the youngest children, punch holes with a nail or an ice pick at random over the tray and allow children to select hole they need for sewing. Use a threaded bobby pin for a needle. Tape prongs shut with cellophane tape. With supervision older children can use blunt tapestry needles. Bright-colored rug yarn is great.
4. **Weaving Cards:** Different shapes of notched cardboard can be wrapped with yarn then later woven with another color. When ready to weave, the best needle for young children is made by dipping the end of yarn in glue or wax. Let dry before using. A cellophane-taped end also works well.

Clockwise from lower left: plastic-spool brayer; loose-weave fabric on cardboard for needle weaving; crayons sorted by color; rolling pin with textured fabric; bent vegetable brush for spatterpainting; roll-on deodorant tubes filled with paint; sponge shapes for printing; shaker and squeeze bottles for sandpainting; crayon shavings for wax pictures; color cones, cups, and caps; corrugated cardboard for stamp printing; chalk stored in a section of upholstery foam; clothespin and sponge, Q-Tip and yarn for paint daubers; plastic screen for weaving.

5. **Crayon Sandpaper Prints:** Allow children to draw pictures with crayons on sandpaper. Place a plain piece of white paper over the crayoning and press with a warm iron. The result is a stippled-effect painting on the paper and a vivid blurred print on the sandpaper. Use discarded sandpaper belts for a free source.

6. **Color Cones:** Melt down old broken pieces of small crayons. (Scrape surfaces of light colors before melting to keep pure color, and melt crayons in sequence—light to dark—so you can use the same can.) Be sure to watch pans set in hot water. (This is a teacher-only process.) When slightly cool, pour into paper cones. Children love the result. Cone crayons can be gripped like a handle (point up), grasped by the base, or rubbed on the side for a fast sweep of color.

   NOTE: This crayon is easier for a handicapped child to grasp and move.

   Variations:
   a. **Color Cups:** Pour one inch or more of the hot crayon wax into muffin tins. These use less wax than the color cones. To remove, dip muffin tin quickly in and out of a pan of hot water.
   b. **Color Caps:** Spoon hot crayon wax into pop-bottle caps. Leave wax in lids and use for counting, collage material, or color games.
   c. **Homemade Crayon Chubbies:** Pour melted crayon wax into large, wide, or tall plastic pill bottles. When hardened, dip or roll in very hot water to remove.

7. **Imagination Paper:** Glue one scrap or shape of colored paper to a larger piece of paper. Prepare as many sheets of paper as necessary for each of the children in your group to have their own. Let children choose the piece that makes them think of a beginning for their individual picture. Using crayons and their imagination, children can complete their pictures by adding to the basic scrap or lines. **Variation:** As a starter, use a Magic Marker to make wavy, straight, zigzag, or dotted lines.

8. **Wire Sculpture:** Cast-off plastic-coated telephone or electric wire makes excellent material for wire sculpture. Offer different lengths, colors, and thicknesses.

9. **Clay Boards/Monoprint Surfaces:** May be made by cutting formica or linoleum scraps into squares or rectangles for use with clay, playdough, or fingerpaint.

10. **Monoprinting:** Children fingerpaint directly on a surface (as above); then they wash and dry their hands and place a dry piece of newsprint over painting. As it is lifted off a reverse print is revealed.

11. **Displaying children's work:** Provide a space for each child. Let child display what he or she feels is his or her best picture. Each child deserves recognition but should be measured against previous effort for optimum growth. Avoid displaying a dozen of one kind of picture together.

Book Center

Select books for young children with care. The following list provides some guidelines for choosing books.

1. The story and illustrations should be believable and give accurate information. Save fairy tales for older children. Select books with 1 to 3 characters in a story for youngest children.
2. Attractive pictures with vivid colors and simple detail appeal to children.
3. The plot should be simple and about familiar happenings.
4. Look for use of repetitious catch phrases, humor, surprise, action, rhyme, direct conversation, and a reasonable, satisfying conclusion.
5. Books should be sturdily bound and easy for children to handle.

Setting Up a Book Center

This is another center that requires good lighting, some privacy, and quiet. It should be located away from the mainstream of more active work and play. By placing this center adjacent to the science area, books are within easy reach for reference, and the aquarium, terrarium, or plants will give a homey touch to this comfortable spot for looking at or reading picture books.

When adjacent to the Home-Living Center this area may become an extended study or library. Some equipment that will aid in the use of books include:

1. a circular table with chairs and space in the center for a few selected books
2. two or three child-size rocking chairs
3. a few casually placed small beanbag chairs or a large one to share
4. a stack of upholstery or carpet squares or cushions for sit-upons
5. a small area rug with pad (so it will not slip if area is not carpeted)
6. mobiles that are more visible from a beanbag or rocking-chair position
7. a bulletin board with informational pictures relating to special books on display
8. taped background music or a record player with musical selections or story records available
9. an overstuffed divan, davenport, or chair (plastic or washable fabric is best), with legs removed so it is low enough to get on and off easily
10. murals, framed art pictures, or nature scenes
11. a flannelboard (see pp. 47–48) with figures for acting out stories
12. puppets and a puppet theater or TV box for dramatic play and story presentations
13. headsets for listening to pre-recorded stories; tape recorders for recording tapes of children's stories; individual film projectors for filmstrips with recorded stories

planning for grouptime

A part of every well-planned program for young children includes directed learning experiences in a group. These directed learning experiences are possible when children are gathered into organized small or large groups for a specific activity with one teacher. Several types of groups might include:

1. a small group when three to five children are focusing on a special need or interest interacting with an adult. This type of grouping may occur spontaneously in an existing learning center or elsewhere anytime during the day.
2. a larger group, such as a "together time," when all the children or a group of six to twelve (or more) may be gathered for a longer period of directed learning with a lead teacher (other teachers may assist). Experiences in this larger group often include the use of music, fingerplays, stories, games, poetry, and rhythms.
3. outdoors (or indoors in inclement weather) when children may be organized into a more structured group for large muscle activities, such as circle games, exercises, or practicing a motor skill.

4. routine times when all the children may be eating, resting, moving in or out of doors at one time.
5. trips or excursions that necessitate children's being in a more controlled grouping.

NOTE: See special suggestions under Planning for Grouptime in each subject guide.

Homemade circular sheer skirts with pantyhose elastic bands, commercially made tutus, and an embroidery-hoop tambourine. See instructions for making these and other homemade rhythm and music activity accessories on pp. 36–37.

Music Center

Provide a center for the exploration and creative use of music and musical equipment and accessories.

1. Let children listen to records (vocal and instrumental) for music appreciation and to increase their vocabulary.
2. Make rhythm band instruments available for exploring to encourage awareness and sensitivity to sound.
3. Record children's original songs on tape and play back.
4. Encourage children to sing songs for their own enjoyment.
5. Plan opportunities for rhythmic movement. It will encourage dramatic expression and promote growth in motor control.
6. Encourage self expression through music. Invite musicians to come and play for the children.

Music in the Child's World

Music is a part of every child's environment whether it be in the form of the song of a bird, a whistler on the street, a TV commercial, the rhythm of raindrops, a woodpecker pecking, footsteps in the hall, the staccato crack of lightning, the rumble of thunder, songs sung, or music played on instruments. By inviting children to explore instruments, to listen to nature, to participate in singing, we offer them the opportunity and experience to naturally express their feelings or ideas through music. Listen for the children's creative interpretations and encourage the spontaneous responses of your children when they are exploring sound. Tape segments of original songs or chants (with or without their instrumental accompaniment). If one of the teachers can play back on a piano or other instrument an original composition of a child, the other children will be encouraged in their musical expression and will be delighted at the recognition of their creative effort.

Listed below are several suggestions of relative sounds or emotions that may be suggested by the use of instruments as you plan music with your children.

Triangle: Raindrops, night sounds, birds, flowers, sunset, water, waterfalls, tiptoeing, dawn, snow, splashing, falling leaves, quiet, tears

Drum: Thunder, Indian dances, marching bands, heavy footsteps, anger, hammering

Tambourine and Maracas: Dancing, the word *suddenly*, fluttering, eerie Halloween sounds

Bell: Fire alarms, school or church bells, clock alarms, buoys, fire trucks

Cymbals: Garbage can lids, pan lids when mother is cooking

Finger Cymbals: Seeds, dawn, very small flowers, first raindrops

Sand Block: Feet shuffling, rustling sounds, shredding, sanding, wood in the woodshop, squirrels in the leaves, trash rattling

Rhythm Sticks, Claves, Tone Blocks, or Wood Blocks: Clocks ticking, hoofbeats, running, woodpecker, raindrops, footsteps, hammering, ascending or descending stairs

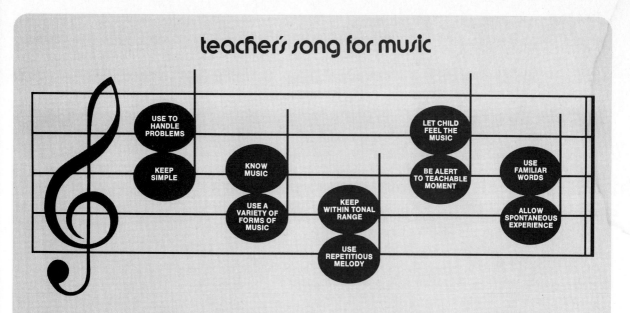

teacher's song for music

USE TO HANDLE PROBLEMS

KEEP SIMPLE

KNOW MUSIC

USE A VARIETY OF FORMS OF MUSIC

KEEP WITHIN TONAL RANGE

USE REPETITIOUS MELODY

LET CHILD FEEL THE MUSIC

BE ALERT TO TEACHABLE MOMENT

USE FAMILIAR WORDS

ALLOW SPONTANEOUS EXPERIENCE

Verse 1: Be interested in the rhythm of children's bodies. Rattles, scarves, flags, jingle bracelets, hoops with bells sewn on them, maracas, tapping sticks will all invite movement.

Verse 2: A spoken idea, a chanting rhyme and rhythm, the rhythm of a hammer or a swing, a picture, or a scarf may also stimulate movement.

Verse 3: Use music outside, especially rhythms. Try a guitar, records, or tape recordings. You need fewer limits to sound or movements as the freedom of space outdoors minimizes both. Dance can go on continuously.

Verse 4: The presence of an adult in a music area will act as a magnet.

Verse 5: Counting songs, melodies that teach information, as well as transition singing games are several other ways to use music.

Teaching Songs to Children

1. Before introducing a new song, you may wish to use it first as background music or as a segment for rhythms or accompaniment for a rhythm band if it has a strong rhythmic beat.

2. Since children learn by repetition, sing a new song to the children first. Children will soon master a short segment (one verse or just the refrain).

3. Invite children to join you, if they wish, as you sing the song again and again.

4. Use prompters such as pictures, flannelboard figures, or hand actions to help the children remember the words.

   NOTE: If you have an overhead projector, you might project selected pictures or illustrations as the children sing.

5. Use a simple accompaniment with a guitar, autoharp, or recorder. If you play the piano, use a few basic chord variations or a one-hand accompaniment since the melody should be recognizable. Elaborate accompaniment is not recommended.

6. Make certain all the teachers on your staff are familiar with the new song.

   NOTE: To aid volunteers or substitutes, post the words of the song on a wall above the lead teacher's head. This will serve as a teleprompter and aid regular staff.

7. Use the new song often until the children know it.

8. Teach one song at a time.
9. Give the children opportunities to sing songs at other times during the day. Allow and encourage them to sing at play by taping their original songs or by echoing their chants when they sing.

Music Accessories

Dance Costumes: Ask dancing schools to put up a request for discarded dance costumes or tutus to use for dress-up. Remove crotch and seam hem on costume to allow children to pull on costumes over clothes.

NOTE: Commercial tutu bands are ideal because they fit all young children without alterations. (See illustration, p. 33.)

Scarf Lengths: Gather sheer drapery scraps 6 to 8 inches wide and 24 to 28 inches long at one end. Hem other end and sides. Attach a yarn ball or a loop of discarded panty-hose elastic. Ball can be held in hand but does not need a tight grip so children's muscles are relaxed. The wristlet of soft elastic allows free movement of the wrist, fingers, and hand. When wristlet is attached to shoulder straps or belts it can simulate wings or tails, as the children may choose.

Homemade Music and Rhythm Band Instruments Clockwise from top: paddles used as bell and lid tambourines; sand blocks with drawer-pull handles; plastic bottle with stones inside for shaker; embroidery-hoop tambourine; stick bell; homemade tone block; scarf attached to elastic loop; metal cymbals; telephone-wire tambourine; baton and director's cap; scarf taped to cardboard tube, drawer-pull wood blocks.

Drapery Sheer Skirts: Ask seamstresses in drapery shops to save colorful cut-off lengths of sheer curtains. It usually takes two scraps of a width of sheer material to make a full skirt. Alternate color with white or a complementary tint or shade. Make a 1-inch casing at the top to allow for gathering with elastic. Discarded pantyhose makes an excellent free source of soft, sturdy elastic and is the right circumference for a young child. Use the selvage edges of the fabric as bottom hem. French-seam the side seams so the material will not fray. (See illustration below.)

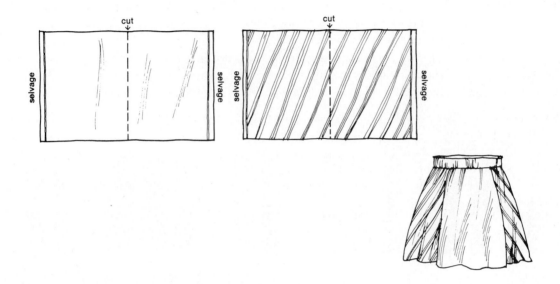

Ankle Bells: Make a 6 to 8 inch circle of elastic (from discarded panty hose). Bind two or three Christmas bells together (loosely enough so bells can jangle) with a piece of plastic-coated wire from the telephone company or an electrical shop. Then sew wire on wristlet or ankle band. This wire keeps the metal bells from cutting the thread that attaches them to the fabric.

Tambourines: Encircle an embroidery hoop on the outside edge with plastic-covered wire threaded through four large sleigh bells. Cover wire hoop with a continuous blanket stitch of rug yarn using an eleven-yard-ball of yarn. Begin between bells, make tassel when yarn meets, and attach it. Spacing opposite tassle allows surface for tapping against other wrist or hand.

Flags: Make a casing on one side of a chiffon scarf large enough and tight enough to slide over a length of cut-off hard-core upholstery pole (12 to 15 inches). Scarf can then be removed easily for laundering. Upholstery pole is sturdier and safer than doweling.

Jingle Paddles: Lace large Christmas jingle bells (available in variety stores year-round) with heavy wire through drilled holes in a discarded wooden paddle. Lightweight paddles are usually available in variety stores with a small rubber ball attached by a rubber string to the paddle.

Music and Rhythms: Use a taped sequence of appropriate music, marking the beginnings of different types or sections of music segments on the tape. Great when you cannot play the piano or cannot afford a large collection of records. Leaves the teacher free to watch and supervise the children. Also allows segment to be a predetermined, reasonable length.

Using Your Piano

How many times have you wished you could play the piano at least well enough to play simple melodies or rhythms for your children? We recognize that no crash course in music or piano will equal the preparation a musician receives through study and practice, but we feel that you should be encouraged to do what you can even though you have little or no experience at the piano.

Try the graphic instructions given below. We hope they will assist you to improvise background music on the piano to accompany children's movements for walking, running, jumping, galloping, hopping, skipping, or swaying. Suggestions are also included for tonal representations of train whistles, fire engines, clocks, raindrops, wind, and bells. The shaded sections under each heading are more difficult variations and will require using both hands and more frequent changes of the notes played. Select the version you can master most easily.

Black keys may be sharps (♯) or flats (♭)

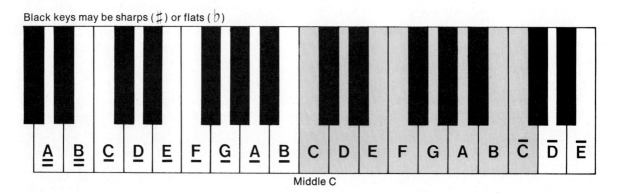

Middle C

Code:

1. **Letters** identify the keys on the piano keyboard (see illustration above). Shaded keys are the C-major scale, which has no sharps or flats.
2. **Lines** printed above or below these letters refer to their distance from middle C:

   $\bar{C}$ = one octave *above* middle C $\bar{\bar{C}}$ = two octaves *above* middle C

   $\underline{C}$ = one octave *below* middle C $\underline{\underline{C}}$ = two octaves *below* middle C

3. **Octave** is the distance between any one key on the piano and the next key above or below bearing the same name: E, $\bar{E}$ $\underline{F}, \underline{\underline{F}}$ $\bar{G}, \bar{\bar{G}}$.
4. **Numerals** correspond to the fingers and thumb used with either hand. See below.
   L.H. = left hand fingering 1-2-3-4-5 from thumb to little finger, moving *left*.
   R.H. = right hand fingering 1-2-3-4-5 from thumb to little finger moving *right*.

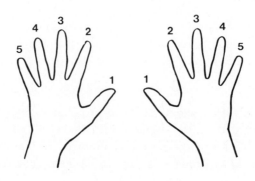

5. **Chord** (in this book) is any two or three notes played simultaneously such as CE.
   If the letters are grouped together, they will designate a chord: CEG, R.H. (1-3-5).
   If the letters are separated by dashes, they indicate single notes played in succession:
   C-E-G, R.H. (1-3-5).
6. **Sharp (♯)** is the black key above a white key of that letter (except for E♯ or B♯, when it is the adjacent white key above). Sharps raise the tone one-half step.
7. **Flat (♭)** is the black key *below* a white key of that letter (except for F♭ and C♭, when it is the adjacent white key below). Flats lower the tone one-half step.
8. **Rhythm** is the regular recurrence of grouped strong and weak beats. The terms *long* and *short* will be assigned to notes to suggest a time pattern. Accents will be identified, pauses noted, or familiar rhythmic patterns to be imitated will be cited.
9. Please read each instruction carefully, then experiment at your piano.

Walking

Using your right thumb (1) and middle finger (3), repeat any two notes alternately. Think of the left-right, left-right cadence as you strike each note. Step up the pace for a brisk walk and slow down the tempo for a leisurely stroll (C-E, C-E). Or begin with finger (4) (R.H.) on F and proceed down the scale to C and up again, using fingers 4-3-2-1, 1-2-3-4 (repeat over and over). F-E-D-C-C-D-E-F-F-E-D-C-C. Note that C and F are repeated when reversing the order sequence.

Variation: Suggested fingering: R.H. FA (1-3), FC (1-5), AC (3-5)

                                L.H. F̲, E̲, D̲, C̲ (2-3-4-5)

Play: R.H. FA FA FA FA   FC̄ FC̄ FC̄ FC̄   AC̄ AC̄ AC̄ AC̄ Repeat FA series.

       L.H. F̲   E̲   D̲   C̲   F̲   E̲   D̲   C̲   F̲   E̲   D̲   C̲

NOTE: If desired, the left hand notes can be played as octaves: F̲F, E̲E, D̲D, C̲C

Running

Play any key on the middle of the keyboard with your right forefinger (2), and then the adjacent key to the right with the middle finger (3). Repeat the separate keys rapidly: C-D-C-D-C-D-C-D or play the following notes rapidly, C-D-E-F-G-F-E-D. Then repeat. Use fingers 1-2-3-4-5-4-3-2 (R.H.). End final sequence with C.

Variation: Suggested fingering: R.H. Change with each series of 6 notes from 1 to 2 to 3 to 4 to 3.

                                L.H. Alternate (5-3-1), (5-2-1)

Play:	R.H.	C-C-C-C-C-C	D-D-D-D-D-D	E-E-E-E-E-E	F-F-F-F-F-F
	L.H.	C̲E̲G̲	B̲F̲G̲	C̲E̲G̲	B̲F̲G̲

Continue playing by returning to E, D, and C series.

Galloping

With the right hand play three consecutive notes on the keyboard using adjacent fingers and accenting the first note of each series of three. C-D-E, C-D-E (accenting the C's as when saying GAL-lop-ing). Or play E-G-C̄, E-G-C̄, E-G-C̄ accenting E and using (1-2-5) fingering.

Variation: Suggested fingering: R.H.   G-B-D̄   (1-3-5),   D̄-C̄-A (5-4-2), and G (1)

L.H.   (5-3-1),   (5-2-1),   (5-3-1),   GBD (5-3-1)

Play: R.H.   G   B   D̄   D̄   C̄   A
                    | | then | |
        L.H.   G   BD   F♯   CD

Repeat both three times and then play   G
                                        |
                                       GBD

Hopping

Think of as many animals as you can that move by hopping in a steady manner. Play G-B, G-B with your right hand using fingers 1-3. Repeat. Or play C-E-G-E-C, pause and repeat. Use fingers 1-3-5-3-1 for this rhythm exercise. Quickly release each finger from the piano keys as the children hop-hop-hop across the room.

Variation: Suggested fingering: R.H.   1-3,   then 2-4,   then 3-5, 2-4, 3-5, 2-4, 1

L.H.   5-1 (6 times) and end with 5-3-1 as a chord.

Play: R.H.   GB   -   AC̄   -   BD̄   -
               | then | then |
        L.H.   G   D   F♯   D   G   D

Repeat AC̄, BD̄, AC̄, then end with   G
                                     |
                                    GBD

Jumping

More deliberate pace than hopping. Use alternate chords of CEG and CFA played with the left hand on the lower keyboard. Suggested fingering is (L.H.) 5-3-1, then 5-2-1. Accent the thud of each jump by striking the second chord harder, such as CEG . . . **C FA**, CEG . . . **C FA**.

Swaying

Play alternately two chords (one high and then one low) very slowly and gently.

Play: R.H. (1-2-5) EG̿C̿   EG̿C̿   repeat
                         \   \   \
        L.H. (5-3-1)   CEG   CEG   repeat

Leaping

Play C and then C̄ (accenting C̄). Use a rhythmic pattern of short-long, short-long. Suggested fingering is (R.H.) 1-5.

Variation: Suggested fingering: R.H. 1-5-3-2

                                           L.H. 5-2-1 and 5-3-1

Play: R.H. C - C̄ - A - G   Play this three times, then A—F   R.H. (3 - 1)

          L.H.   CFA CEG   FF L.H. (1 - 5)

Bending and Stretching

For bending, slowly play C̄-G-E-C-G̲-E̲-C̲

               (R.H.) (5-3-2-1-3-2-1)

For stretching, slowly play C̲-E̲-G̲-C-E-G-C̄

               (L.H.) (5-3-2-1-3-2-1)

Variation: Suggested fingering: R.H. 5-2-1

                                           L.H. 1-3-5

Play: *Alternating* right and left hands, C̄-G-E   C-G̲-E   C̲-G̲-E̲   C̲ to bend
                                        (R.H.)   (L.H.)   (R.H.)   (L.H.)

Reverse the sequence for stretching.

Skipping

Using a rhythmic pattern of long, short, long, short, long, with the right hand play C-C, E-E, G-G, E-E, C-C, E-E, G-G, E-E, C-C, and so on. Suggested fingering is 1-1, 3-3, 5-5, 3-3, 1-1.

Variation: Suggested fingering: R.H. 1-3, 2-4, 3-5, 4-2, 3-1, 2-1, 2, 2

                                           L.H. 5-3-1 and 5-2-1

Play: R.H.   C - E   D - F   E - G   F - D   E - C   D - B̲   C   C

        L.H.   CEG   B̲FG   CEG   B̲FG   CEG   B̲FG   CEG   CEG

Or you may break the chords in the left hand as follows:

L.H.   C - EG   B̲ - FG   C - EG   B̲ - FG   C - EG   B̲ - FG   CEG   CEG

(Right hand remains the same.)

Fire Alarm

Play simultaneously both notes in the octave chord CC̄ four times in a series and then pause. Play: CC̄ CC̄ CC̄ CC̄ (pause) CC̄ CC̄ CC̄ CC̄. Use 1-5 (R.H.) or alternate rapidly the notes in the above sequence (left to right) C-C̄, C-C̄, C-C̄, C-C̄.

Clocks

Play alternately middle C and the higher C̄ (R.H. 1-5). Strike the notes to make an appropriate beat.

Variation: Vary the intensity and length of the interval between strikes depending upon the size of clock or watch you are duplicating: try TICK-TOCK: F-C (L.H. 1-4), tick-tock: F-C̄ (R.H. 2-5), tick-tick-tick-tick: C̄-C̄-C̄-C̄ (R.H. 5) or C̄-C̄-C̄-C̄ (R.H. 1).

Train Engine

Play with the right hand down the scale G to C and then back up to G (5-4-3-2-1-2-3-4-5). Repeat the sequence to simulate the sound of a train engine. You may wish to play the same notes with each hand separately or with the left hand only. Increase in speed and volume as the train begins to move.

Variation: Begin with two long toots on the whistle, which means Go Ahead, playing the chord F♯C̄. Have the train pull out of the station slowly. Gradually pick up speed. Three short toots on the whistle means Stop at the next station. Begin to slow the train down. One long toot means the train is approaching the station. Slow down even further and stop.

Bells

Play C (L.H. 4) then: C̄-B-A-G (R.H. 4-3-2-1) then: F-E-D-C (L.H. 1-2-3-4). Repeat same sequence holding the pedal down.

Variation: Suggested fingering: R.H. 1-2-5 (repeat for all chords)

L.H. 1-2-3-4

Play: R.H. EḠC̄ D̄FB̄ C̄EĀ BD̄Ḡ
| then | then | then |
L.H. C̄ B A G

Use the right pedal for a gong effect.

You may wish to play the chords in both hands simultaneously in different octaves or to play the right hand alone.

Raindrops

Use the black keys and play F♯ C♯ A♯ D♯ (R.H. 3-1-5-2) or C̄♯ F̄♯ D̄♯ Ā♯ (R.H. 1-3-2-5). Repeat quickly using a desired rhythm. You may wish to change hands on the keyboard as you play:

(R.H.)	(3) F♯		(5) A♯			(3) F̄♯		(5) Ā♯	
		\		\	or		\		\
(L.H.)		(2) C♯		(1) D♯		(2) C̄♯		(1) D̄♯	

Use the right pedal for a gong effect.

Or play (R.H.) C̄-Ḡ-Ā-D̿ (1-2-3-5) as separate notes for a raindrop sequence (drip-drop-drip-splash!)

Repeat quickly three shorts and then a long. For a drip-drop, drip-drop sequence use C̿-C̄ C̿-C̄ C̿-C̄ C̿-C̄ (5-1-5-1), repeat, or for a pitter-patter: C̿-C̿ C̄-C̄ C̿-C̿ C̄-C̄ (5-5, 1-1), repeat.

Heavy Wind

Begin softly and gradually play the following chords louder, then diminish to become softer again. Repeat. Use the right pedal to slur the notes.

Suggested fingering is 1-3-5.

Play: R.H. C̄EḠ D̄♭ F̄Ā♭ D̄ F̄♯Ā Ē♭ḠB̄♭ ĒḠ♯B̄. Reverse the sequence as often as desired.

Light Breeze

Suggested fingering is 1-2-3-4-5 (thumb on C̄ and progressing to the right to Ḡ). To make a bigger gust of wind use lower keys C-D-E-F-G (L.H. 5-4-3-2-1).

Playing Your Piano

Now, are you ready to try some simple improvising on your own? Chording is the secret. Play one or more of the following five chords: CEG, CFA, CEG, BFG, CEG one after the other, much like a chord sentence. These same chords may be used as accompaniment to any simple melody in the key of C (no sharps or flats) played with the other hand. These basic chords may be played anywhere on the keyboard and at whatever point in the song you choose. You do not always have to play them in sequence.

(R.H.) 1-3-5, 1-3-5, 1-3-5, 1-4-5, 1-3-5

(L.H.) 5-3-1, 5-2-1, 5-3-1, 5-2-1, 5-3-1

Usually you may play each chord whenever one of the notes within that chord is played in the melody with the opposite hand. You will find that some very simple melodies may be accompanied by the use of a single chord, while more complicated tunes may require the use of two or more of the suggested chords. Experiment and select what sounds best together. Another chord sentence, similar to the one given above, that can be used for skipping might be CEG, DFG, CEG, B̲DG, CEG.

(R.H.) 1-3-5, 2-4-5, 1-3-5, 1-2-5, 1-3-5

(L.H.) 5-3-1, 4-2-1, 5-3-1, 5-3-1, 5-3-1

Try breaking these same chords and playing them in segments as C-EG, D-FG, C-EG, B̲-DG, C-EG or as single notes C-E-G, D-F-G, C-E-G, B̲-D-G, C-E-G.

Variations to the series of notes given above to use with the key of C: if you wish to play chords to accompany a tune using any flats or sharps, use the following guide, remembering the suggestions noted for the key of C.

Key of D (2 sharps)	DF♯A	DGB	DF♯A	C♯GA	DF♯A
Key of E (4 sharps)	EG♯B	EAC̄♯	EG♯B	D♯AB	EG♯B
Key of F (1 flat)	FAC̄	FB♭D̄	FAC̄	EB♭C̄	FAC̄
Key of G (1 sharp)	GBD̄	GC̄E	GBD̄	F♯C̄D̄	GBD̄
Key of A (3 sharps)	A̲C♯E	A̲DF♯	A̲C♯E	G♯DE	A̲C♯E
Key of B♭ (2 flats)	B̲♭DF	B̲♭E♭G	B̲♭DF	A̲E♭F	B̲♭DF
Key of E♭ (3 flats)	E♭GB♭	E♭A♭C̄	E♭GB♭	DA♭B♭	E♭GB♭

NOTE: It is helpful to know that almost all songs end on the note that is the key for the song. Sometimes a song starts (the first note) on the note that is the key; however, sometimes when the song begins in the middle of a measure the first note is not the key note.

Fingerplays and Action Songs

Originally these rhyme games were written using only the fingers and hands to act out the words. They were used primarily by parents to help teach their youngest children body parts, numbers, and shapes. Some of them date back nearly 2,000 years.

In the nineteenth century, Friedrich Froebel, the man who developed the kindergarten in Germany, took adult games and songs and adapted them for children for educational purposes. He used them to integrate meanings and the emotional satisfaction of sensing relationships among parts.

Today, the best fingerplays and action songs use the *whole body* (large and small muscles) for total participation.

Value of Fingerplays and Action Songs

1. Increase manual dexterity and muscular control.
2. Develop an understanding of rhythms of speech, music, and life's activities.

3. Encourage understanding of concepts of size, shape, and place or direction.
4. Build vocabulary and aid in language development.
5. Allow for self expression, encouraging a child's own response in his or her use of body and speech for interpreting concepts.
6. Help teach number concepts, especially 1 to 10.
7. Provide relaxation (a legitimate opportunity to move and wiggle).
8. Assist the child in learning to follow directions.
9. Teach order and sequence.
10. Increase attention span.
11. Develop listening skills.
12. Give an opportunity to have fun.

Suggestions for Teaching Fingerplays and Action Songs

1. Demonstrate appropriate actions as you say or sing the words to the group.
2. Replay finger game encouraging the children to imitate only the action.
3. Do fingerplay again allowing those who wish to participate with both action and words.
4. Keep actions and movement slow enough so that children do not have trouble keeping up.
5. Repeat fingerplays often enough for children to become familiar with them.
6. Introduce variations or a new approach to an old favorite.
7. Be enthusiastic, use those songs that you enjoy.
8. Repeat old favorites. (Children enjoy repetition.)
9. Occasionally send parents the words and music to fingerplays currently being used so that they can use them at home.
10. You may wish to make a fingerplay card file for yourself to use as a prompter during group time although it is better to memorize the fingerplays you use.
11. When learning a new fingerplay or song, letter a large sign as a teleprompter and post on an adjacent wall at eye level for the staff and volunteers.

CAUTION: Select one or two fingerplays for each subject, making certain they teach *best* the concept to be learned. As with books, poems, and songs, watch for the difficulty of vocabulary, the length of verse, the concept to be learned, and the maturity level of your group. Use the simplest fingerplays with the youngest or the least mature group; increase the complexity as the group shows readiness.

Flannelboard

A flannelboard is a felt or flannel-surfaced board (can be cardboard) used as a visual teaching aid. It supports, vertically, illustrative materials that have been backed with a texture that will adhere to its surface. (See illustrations, pp. 47–48.)

Value of a Flannelboard

1. It provides for an attractive focus of attention.
2. It helps to sustain interest by providing an element of surprise or continuing suspense as materials are added to the visual screen.
3. It can be inexpensively made from a variety of available materials.
4. It can be a versatile and a flexible medium if made in various sizes and forms.

5. A flannelboard allows teachers to expand understanding through both visual and auditory means.
6. Its use (as far as what can be done on a surface) is limited only by the creativity and resourcefulness of the teacher.
7. Flannelboard props can act as a teleprompter to children as to the sequence in a game, story, song, fingerplay, or poem.
8. It can encourage children to participate verbally, thus building their vocabulary and language skills.

Using a Flannelboard

1. Select a story, game, song, poem, fingerplay, or concept to be introduced.
2. Decide subjects or pictures to best highlight sequence of events or steps in learning.
3. Gather or prepare prop materials.

Singing Games These children are using individual flannelboards (flannel is stapled to a one-foot square of heavy cardboard). As children (or teacher) sing, the child holds up the appropriate felt cut-out when his or her fruit (or animal or object) is mentioned in the song. These children are responding to the verses of "The Fruit Basket Song," p. 561, referred to in the Food guide. This idea may be adapted for use with any song, fingerplay, or action story in which a series of objects or things are mentioned.

4. Arrange parts in sequence, or number back of pieces.
5. Rehearse or test out before presenting to group.
6. Consider visibility for all who are to view presentation.
7. Eliminate prop or illustrative materials that seem contrived.

   NOTE: Manipulating prop materials should not distract you or your listeners *or* detract from the story.

8. Evaluate after use to improve your next presentation.
9. Let children participate or use flannelboard materials on their own. (See illustration, p. 46.)
10. Store flannelboard in a file where it will be readily available for spontaneous use.

Types of Flannelboards and Their Construction

Easel Flannelboard

You can make exchangeable sections, using the same base, for a painting easel or for a flannelboard. Staple, glue, or tape felt or heavy flannel to wallpaper book covers. Enamel or spray paint wallpaper book covers to make a painting easel that is washable. One book makes a double easel. Edges of carton used for base should be covered with masking tape before they are painted. Slash carton notches diagonally at the angle desired for easel. An inverted carton wedged inside box will brace easel and provide shelf space to store extra boxes of flannelgraph props. Use spring clothespin to hold paper.

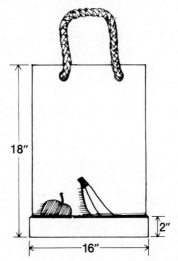

Pocket Apron Flannelboard

Pocket is handy for holding flannelgraph figures. Arms are free to place cutouts on flannelboard. To make 2-inch pocket, allow 4 or 5 inches of extra material to fold back. Make board *your* trunk length (chin to lap) when seated. Staple, glue, or tape flannel or felt to heavy cardboard. Use braided yarn for a soft strap. (See photograph, p. 619.)

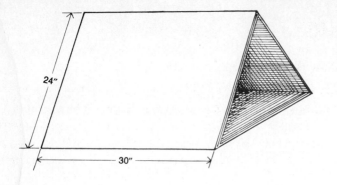

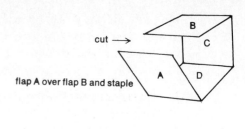

cut →

flap A over flap B and staple

Triangle Tent / Tabletop Flannelboard

Construct from masonite as freestanding flannelboard above, or cut out bottom of a square
cardboard carton, slit the side at one corner, and
overlap as shown to form a triangle. Measurements
may vary with box used.

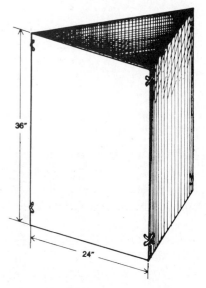

Freestanding Flannelboard

A triangle-shaped flannelboard can be braced so that it will not tip over. Lace the edges
together with plastic or leather strips threaded through holes drilled in flannel-covered masonite. This flannelboard can be placed upright on floor or tentlike on tabletop. It can simultaneously accommodate three children using different materials.

Flannelboard Tips

Magnetize your flannelboard by inserting a piece of wire screen between backing and flannel or making one side metal. Cookie sheets or metal stove protectors make good magnetic
boards. Flannel, felt, sandpaper, flocked paper, and pellon may all be used as cutouts or
backings to cutouts on the flannelboard. Coloring books of food and animals are excellent
sources of outlines for the teacher to duplicate. Coloring books are not recommended for
children's use.

Some Do's and Don'ts for Storytelling to Young Children

When You Select a Story

1. Before choosing a book, see checklist on p. 31.

   Don't use any book for a grouptime story without scanning and evaluating it.

2. Adapt it for your group. Shorten, expand, or change wording for age level, time allotted to tell story, and the occasion. Emphasize the incidents that appeal to children (sound, humor, action). Remember that for very young children three minutes is a long time.

   Don't memorize word by word and recite the story. Leave out unimportant details. Optimum delivery will be jeopardized if you concentrate on a recitation. Quote only author's choice of words that cannot be improved.

3. Evaluate and edit it. If a phrase, paragraph, or picture needs to be omitted because of insensitivity to an ethnic group, to handicapped people, or to people's economic status, paper-clip pages or write in the word change.

   Don't discard a book because of one offensive illustration or paragraph. Modify the picture or the text.

As You Prepare the Story

1. Know it. If you need prompters, clip and mark key pages where you want to read a section or be reminded of a sequence of subjects. Be sure you understand the story as a whole and the relationship of every character to the main plot so that you can better set the scene. Tell the story slowly; pause for emphasis; speed up for excitement or urgency; vary volume of voice to suggest emotion or change of character. Speak distinctly.

   Don't tack on facts you have forgotten after sequence is past. Don't forget punch line. Don't read too rapidly or mumble.

2. Rehearse the story before you tell it to the group. This will allow eye contact with children. Practice telling it aloud in front of a mirror. Tape record the story for a revealing self criticism.

   Don't extemporize unless you are an experienced and very talented teacher. Your extemporaneous rendition will only tend to insulate the child against a later encounter with the story told by someone who has planned their presentation.

3. Locate and test props. Make sure they mesh with story flow. Manipulation of puppets or flannelboard materials should not distract you or your listeners from the story.

   Don't take too long a pause locating next character or finding missing figures.

Before You Begin the Story

1. Get comfortable. Make certain the children can see and hear and are not crowded. Consider personalities and individual needs of the children. Sit where the children will be least distracted by surroundings. Be flexible. Regroup children if necessary.

   Don't allow children to sit too close to each other. Don't let yourself be driven by a time schedule.

When You Tell the Story

1. Make characters alive. Use direct conversation. Involve yourself, empathize with the feelings of the main characters. Use gestures, facial expressions, vary your voice and pace your delivery for emphasis. Maintain eye contact.

   Don't tell the story using vague characters in an obscure setting. Don't make your delivery monotonous by using the same pattern of inflection regardless of the story line.

When You Finish the Story

1. Listen for children's responses and comments. Let them think, ponder, show pleasure or displeasure. Allow the story to state its message or entertain the children. Allow children to identify with the story from their own experience.

   Answer children's questions but **don't** editorialize, moralize, or interpret.

Extended Experiences with Books

1. Use flannelboard
2. Use background music
3. Use puppets
4. Use props and pictures
5. Use tape recorder for individual listening
6. Let children dramatize
7. Talk about the story
8. Tell part of a story and let children make up a new ending

When and How to Use Poetry

1. Instead of reading a story at grouptime
2. For a plus experience to supplement another activity in the classroom
3. For active participation (fingerplays and action rhymes)
4. With background mood music
5. As a chant with a large muscle activity
6. Record a child's chant or verse recited while playing
7. Share a child's poem with the whole group
8. Make a file of poems. Place a key illustration in the corner of each card for quick identification. Illustrate one side of the card to show the children as you share the poem that is printed on the back of the card
9. Hang illustrated poems on the walls at appropriate spots in the various centers for easy reference while teaching

learning games

Value of Games

Games offer an excellent vehicle for learning while having fun. With games a child can:

1. increase vocabulary by learning to identify objects, pictures, and materials
2. develop senses of sight and hearing
3. learn to discriminate and classify
4. learn to follow directions and take turns

5. learn cause and effect
6. gain experience and social skills with other children and adults

Uses of Games

Games without props can be used at anytime and are especially useful to assist in the transition from one activity to another:

1. while children are *assembling* for a story group, singing time, or a snack time
2. while children are *waiting* for something to be prepared
3. while children are slowly *dispersing* to go home and are leaving at different times
4. while a child or children *wait* for others to finish lunch, to finish their nap, to go outside or to another room
5. while *riding* to and from nursery school or the day care center in a carpool or on a bus
6. while children are removing or putting on outdoor clothes
7. when teacher is *diverting* silly or unacceptable types of conversation or behavior
8. when preparing for a specific activity, such as an introduction of a new idea in art or science, or following a story
9. during grouptime as a tool to teach a concept

NOTE: Games with props can be planned for the whole group, with a small group, or with an individual child during a free choice time. These games extend the opportunities for learning because of the sensory properties of the props used.

Suggestions for Teaching Games

1. Young children learn best in a small group because it eliminates long waiting periods and offers more person-to-person opportunities.
2. Remember that young children's attention span for any concentrated effort is about one minute more than their age. By varying the pace and activity you may, however, keep children in an organized group for longer periods, such as grouptime, stories, songs, and games.
3. In the games, introduce only one or two concepts at a time.
4. Keep games simple, making sure instructions are clear. Try to demonstrate as much as possible.
5. Insure each child's opportunity to participate and succeed.
6. Watch for restlessness. Stop when interest wanes.
7. Rather than insist that every child participate in a game, appeal through a special interest or past experience to encourage each to want and ask to play.

   NOTE: Some young children may appear never to enjoy a group participation game but will learn the song or game by observing and will frequently use it at home. Sometimes unwillingness to follow rules is an indication that the game has gone on too long or is too structured. Perhaps those who wish to continue could do so and the others might be given an alternative activity.

8. Relays and winner games are not recommended at this age level. Children should be encouraged to compete only against their own past performances. They need many opportunities to succeed and to feel good about themselves. Too many failures can defeat this purpose. Avoid games that require waiting or inactivity by the children.

Identification Games

CAUTION: When introducing the materials to be used, always identify an object or thing as being real or just a picture, model, or toy.

Name It

A series of three or more objects is placed in a row. Identify each of them. Then let the children name them from left to right. Rearrange or scramble them and let children name the objects in their new order.

NOTE: Excellent for vocabulary building and for observation, or for developing a special interest, if you select items relating to the interest theme.

I See Something, What Do You See?

This game and its variations are excellent to play while on a walk, a sightseeing trip, an excursion, or a ride in a car. The leader simply states what he or she sees and asks the children to respond with what they see. **Variation:** Use other senses.

Look and See

Select three or more familiar objects or models. Ask children to close or cover their eyes. Hide one of the objects behind your back or under a cover. Then say to the participating children, "Look and See." Let the children guess which object is missing by noting what remains. As their skill develops, add or remove more than one object at a time. Children will enjoy hiding an object from the other children. When a child guesses successfully, let that child hide the next object. Flannelboard figures may also be used.

CAUTION: Make certain every child gets an opportunity to hide an object. If you do not select the child to be "it," suggest that a child who is eligible for a second turn choose one who has not had a turn to be next.

Sniff and Smell

Place several seasonings or spices that have a distinctive odor familiar to the children in small unbreakable containers. Film containers with punched lids are excellent. A circle of nylon cloth glued as an inner lid will prevent spills but still allow sniffing through punctured holes. Include items such as cinnamon, onion salt, coffee, cocoa, talcum, and dry mustard. **Variation:** Make a double set of the sniff and smell cans. Children can match cans with the same contents by their odor. Teacher may double-check when children have completed the matching task. You may wish to code the bottom for your convenience. Tape over lid holes to preserve odor while stored.

CAUTION: Breakable plastic bottles can be used only with careful supervision, which limits their use for exploring. Plastic is extremely dangerous when broken, especially if a piece is swallowed.

Reach and Feel

Set out a series of objects with different textures and shapes. Identify (children may assist). Discuss how the objects are alike and how they are different. Let children touch, feel, and hold the objects before you begin the game. Then place the objects inside a cloth bag or paper sack. Let children reach inside the bag and identify by feeling one of the objects inside the bag before removing it to verify their guess. **Variation:** Let the children guess by

Children are playing Reach and Feel in a Feel It Box. The child has guessed accurately that the object he was feeling in the box was grapes.

feeling through a hole or holes of a Feel It Box (see above). Leave the opposite side of the box open for children in the group to watch as one child guesses. Children can clap if child guesses correctly or shake heads or call out "Guess again!" if child's guess is wrong. If objects are different enough, children can be encouraged to guess by feeling a single object through the cloth bag. Keep bag securely closed.

Listen and Hear

Identify objects and drop or manipulate them to produce their characteristic sounds so children can see and hear. Have the children close their eyes and cover them with their hands. You may choose to produce the sound from behind a screen. Let the children recall the sound heard and identify it. **Variation:** You may tape record and play back other familiar sounds for children to guess.

CAUTION: Children resist blindfolds and they are not sanitary. Alternatives are closing eyes and covering them with hands, using a screen, having children turn their heads.

Chew, Lick, and Taste

Have toothpicks or coffee stirrers and small paper cups into which foods may be distributed and sampled. This will avoid children dipping into the main source. Identify the foods as the children taste them. Talk about differences in flavors and textures.

CAUTION: Be aware of allergic reactions or restricted foods for individuals in your group.

Can You Remember?

Show a group of children a tray of objects related to a special interest. Help identify the objects by name. Remove the tray, or cover it, and ask them to recall what was on the tray. Display five items at first, increasing the number as the children become more skillful.

Language Games

Guess Who? Who Am I?

Begin by saying, "I see somebody who is wearing a red ribbon. Guess who it is?" Eventually include each child. Continue to add clues if children can't identify the person from the first clue. When they make a mistake say "Guess again" and restate the statement as a fact, "Mary is wearing a blue ribbon and she has blonde hair, doesn't she?" (Reestablish facts in order to unlearn mistakes.) **Variation:** Describe a community helper, story book character, or animal.

Guess What? What Am I? What Can I Do?

Begin by describing something in the form of a question: "What is sometimes soft, always round, and bounces when you drop it?" Answer: a ball. Descriptions can also include sounds and uses.

What Did You Hear?

Encourage the children to duplicate (or describe) the sound of animals in the Nature Center, sounds of eating, sounds of well-known vehicles. Let them also try to duplicate a clapping rhythm or imitate a rhythm beaten on a rhythm stick or a drum.

Listening

Choose one child to be the listener. Child should be seated on the floor or on a chair in front of the group with face turned away from the group. Point to another child in the group who will become the mystery voice. She or he can say "Hi," or any other greeting. Let the first child guess who the mystery voice is. If the child cannot guess correctly, let the speaker say something else. You may wish to use two telephones while playing the game.

Who's Missing?

Select a child who is to be "it." Ask the child to hide his or her eyes. Select another child in the group to hide in a designated place. When the child is safely hidden ask the child who is "it" to look and guess "Who is missing?" You may give hints or rename all the children who are present that day.

Let's Tell a Story

Teacher may show children a picture and ask one of them to make up a story by telling what *is* happening, what *did* happen, or what *will* happen?

Show and Tell

Encourage each child to bring something from home to share with the group. Ask the child to show it and tell about it. Be ready to ask questions that will assist the children to tell about it as some children become shy in front of a group.

Problem-Solving Games

How Many?

Ask any question that demands problem solving. Use ones that allow for a variety of possible answers. For example: "How many ways can you think of to get to school?" "How can you get from one side of the room to the other without walking?"

How Can I? How Can You?

Ask a child a question on how to solve a simple problem: "How could I (you) play the record player if it were on a high table and I (you) were too short to reach it?"

Which?

Similar to game above. Often your first question, "Which?" is followed by the second question, "Why?" Select questions about things that involve a judgment or opinion.

NOTE: See also Grouping and Sorting in the next section. After the child has told you "which," ask "Why?" Objects and pictures: "Which one do you wear on your feet?" "Which one do you use to brush your teeth?" "Which animal would make a good pet?"

Why? or If?

Preface questions with the word "why?" or "if?" "Why do cows live in the country?" Let's think, "What is it that cows eat?" "Is there much grass in the city?"

Sequence or Which Comes First?

Show pictures depicting an event showing *before* and *after* to see if the child can identify the sequence. Progress to a story sequence or series of three or four pictures. Ask the child to reorder and give reasons for choices. Some pictures might be reversible: clean/dirty, chicken/egg.

Classification Games

Match-Them

Match-Them is a matching game similar to the commercial games called Perception Plaques and Match-Ems. Show and identify several sets of identical picture cards, squares, objects, or flannelgraph figures for children. Scramble the items. Let children find matching pairs. Teacher may hold the item to be matched or children may be given half of a match and take their turn to draw a match from the center of the table. If children make mistakes, call their attention to the differences. Praise their success. To vary, place draw cards facedown on the table.

Alike, Different, and the Same

Show children several items that are identical. Then introduce something different but similar, such as all alike except one is smaller, larger, a different color, or belongs to a different group. Begin with obvious differences and later progress to the more difficult as the child is ready. You may use real objects, pictures, or models.

Grouping and Sorting by Association   The girl on the left is matching the animal with the food it eats. The cut-out pictures are laminated with clear coating and glued to abstract felt shapes. When the picture is mounted on felt, the child or teacher can use it on a flannelboard for other learning games. The girl standing is grouping selected objects by color into circles of similarly colored yarn.

Grouping and Sorting by Association

Encourage children to sort and group real objects, pictures, or miniature objects into trays, boxes, or circles of yarn. Sort by content (as furniture into various rooms), by rhyme (as a goat, coat, boat, note), by type (as hat-clothes, apple-fruit), by use (as saddle with horse, cup with saucer). Begin with simple, obvious groupings like all red, all dogs, and then progress to finer differentiations such as farm animals, pets, zoo animals.

Lotto

There are many commercial lotto games available. You may also make your own lotto cards using cards and large gummed seals or cutouts. Any game played with cards divided into four, six, or nine squares with corresponding cards that are drawn to cover the squares can be considered a lotto-like game. The first child to cover all the spaces or a row on his or her card completes the game.

NOTE: For very young children, continue the game until all the children's cards are complete. Those who finish first may help the other children find the missing cards.

Ring It

Cut out the centers of plastic lids 2½ to 3 inches in diameter. Wrap each remaining circlet with bright-colored yarn until a colored ring is formed. Encourage children to use this ring to circle a matching color in any picture or on a game. This game is self-correcting.

The girl at left is playing the Ring It game. She is placing colored rings around objects of a similar color. The girl at right is counting How Many? as she plays a conservation game.

Direction Games

Directions

Fill a small, shallow carton with a number of items familiar to the children. Select a child or call for a volunteer. Give a direction to move an object to a certain place. Clap if the child succeeds. If not, assist child with, "What was it you were going to put where?"

Follow the Leader

Select a child to be the leader. Children all follow the leader doing as he or she does. An excellent game for a rainy day. Make alternate suggestions if a child can't think of an idea. **Variation:** Set up a maze to allow children to crawl under a table, step up and over a chair, walk around a pole. You may also make it more complex by having the children follow actions of the leader (changing arm, head, leg positions) as they follow.

Together, Together

This game is similar to follow the leader but can be played sitting down. The teacher says, "Together, together, let's all (do something) together." This game may be used to direct a group to another activity.

Sally Says / Sam Says

This game is similar to Together, Together. Instead of using a simple instruction to do something, you preface it with, "Sally says do _____ ." When the leader omits the statement, "Sally says," the children are instructed to stay as they were. With older children, another type of limitation might be to say, "All those wearing white may go to the table."

NOTE: The name used does not matter. Children enjoy alliteration.

Counting Games

How Many?

Set out a varying number of familiar objects. One to five for the younger children, one to ten for older children. Then ask: "How many _____ are there?" Select kind, color, or any other set of objects within a grouping.

Circle Games

Save these games for the most mature group or modify without a formal circle formation.

Play traditional action songs, such as:

"Farmer in the Dell"
"Round and Round in the Village"
"Hokey Pokey"
"This Is the Way"
"Sally Go Round the Moon"
"Did You Ever See a Lassie?" (Laddie)
"Looby Loo"
"Mulberry Bush"
"Pop! Goes the Weasel"
"Skip to My Lou"

Fly Little Bluebird
(tune: "Skip to My Lou")

Fly little bluebird, through my window
Fly little bluebird, through my window
Fly little bluebird, through my window
Um diddle um dum dey.

Hop little bluebird, in my garden
Hop little bluebird in my garden
Hop little bluebird, in my garden
Um diddle um dum dey.

Children form a circle holding hands with arms raised in VERSE 1 to make windows. One child is selected to be the bluebird. After child finishes hopping in the garden (inside the circle), teacher may select successor.

Friend, Friend from Over the Way

The children choose a friend who will come to visit to begin the game. Then they say together:

"Friend, friend from over the way,
Please come over now and play" (CHILD KNOCKS ON THE TABLE OR DOOR)

Children say:

"Come in *John* from over the way, (USE CHILD'S NAME)
What would you like to play today?"

The child chooses what he or she would like to play. Everyone pantomimes or acts out the action.

Musical Stars or Skip Squat

Set on the floor enough paper stars for all the children. Play a short interlude of music. Explain to the children that when the music stops they are to stand on a star or on designated spots. Have one less star than there are children to add excitement and an element of chance. **Variations:** blue puddles, brown rocks, snowflakes.

CAUTION: Never eliminate more than one star during the entire game. Make no emphasis on the last one down and assist each to safely land on star sometimes. Then there is never anyone out of the game but instead the child left without a star rejoins the group again as soon as the music begins.

Sally Go Round the Stars

Sally go round the stars,	F F F F G A
Sally go round the moon,	B♭ B♭ B♭ B♭ A G
Sally go round the chimney pots,	F F F F G A A A
On a Sunday afternoon. Whoops!	A A G G A G F ACF (chord)

Children make a circle with hands joined and slide to left as they sing. They drop each other's hands and with hands raised over heads, jump into the air and clap hands when they sing Whoops!

Hot Potato

Tie up a small towel, clean cloth, or nylon stocking so it is soft, light, and somewhat like a ball. Pretend it is a "hot potato." The children sit in a circle with their feet outspread and touching the feet of the child on either side. As the ball is tossed to them, they quickly toss it to someone else. Since cloth does not bounce and is soft, this is safer than a regular ball or bean bag.

Bean-Bag Toss

Select a target such as a wastebasket, carton, or innertube. (A clown face can be painted on a cardboard box with a hole for a mouth or nose.) Allow the children to toss or throw a bean bag into the container. Encourage success by offering toss (underhand flip) or throw (forceful thrust) opportunities side by side.

Singing Games Using Action Songs

There are many action songs that invite a child to respond to music. A child may even choose to sing along as he or she moves to the music. These songs will be suggested in each guide under Large Muscle Activities or Rhythms and Singing Games.

Participation Records

Some singing games and songs that describe a specific series of responses are recorded and can be used as accompaniment games if you are not a singer or do not have anyone to play the piano, guitar, or autoharp. Listed on the next page are some favorites:

Children's Record Guild

"Visit to My Little Friend"
"Nothing to Do"
"Do This, Do That"
"Skittery, Skattery"

"My Playful Scarf"
"Little Puppet"
"Indoors When It Rains"

Young People's Records

"Let's Play Together"
"Rainy Day"
"Out of Doors"

"When the Sun Shines"
"Sing Along"
"Another Sing Along"

Bowmar Records

"Singing Games" Album 1
"Rhythm Times" Record 1
"The Rainy Day Record"
"Another Rainy Day Record"

See also records put out by Romper Room, Mister Rogers, Captain Kangaroo, Sesame Street, Kimbo, Hap Palmer, and Phoebe James. (See p. 81 for addresses.)

routine times of the day

Parts of the program that vary little from day to day are considered routine and become a framework for the daily program. They give the children the security that comes with knowing what will happen next. Most often, arrival, health inspection, snacktime, toileting, mealtimes, naptime, group movement, and dismissal times are considered the routine times of the school day.

If not planned for as an integral part of the total program of the day these times may become boring and humdrum. A matter-of-fact acceptance of routine by the staff will assist children to accept the routine for their basic physical comforts and needs. There is no need for bribes, cajoling, threats, punishment, or excessive praise.

Accidents involving elimination should be handled in a matter-of-fact way.

Remember that the children's ability to accept and function within the school routines will vary considerably.

1. Some are a member of a group for the first time (an only child).
2. School routines are often quite different from home routines.
3. The school or center may have different values, rules, and limits from those of the child's home.

4. Some children are more flexible and willing to imitate, while others, who are more independent, may resist and need time and assistance to adjust.
5. Physical needs and skills will also vary with the child's age, sex, past experience, and development.

Flexibility is a valuable trait for children in today's world. The extreme conformist has as much trouble as the rebel. Therefore it is helpful if the children can become more flexible with regard to routines by:

1. giving the children a few minutes notice before making a necessary change in program
2. encouraging everyone to help so that they can all be ready sooner to participate in the next experience
3. giving reasons for routine tasks required
4. assisting children to recognize the benefits from group experience as well as individual achievement

When planning for routine times refer to the suggestions noted in each guide and take advantage of opportunities for learning and variations that will make these times more pleasant. See also Games and Fingerplays, pp. 51 and 44. Plan for a happy balance between the work activity and the rest, with opportunities for refreshments and toileting at necessary intervals.

large muscle activities

Opportunities for the development of motor skills through Large Muscle Activities should be a part of every daily program for very young children. Plans should include experiences both indoors and outdoors with specific plans for your group and those assessed as necessary for individual children in the group. Children attending an all-day program will have a greater need for these types of activities as they have less chance in the remaining portion of the day to do them in their home environment. Days of inclement weather, especially rainy days, will increase the need to implement routine opportunities for these experiences indoors.

large muscle activities outdoors

Consider Your Playground an Extension of Your Classroom

1. Provide adequate space for the size and age of your group. Enclose your play area with hedge, fence, or walls; include a gate with a lock to provide for safety from street traffic and easier supervision of the children by the staff. When there are no local required licensing standards, define boundaries by using ropes or sidewalks or other natural boundaries.
2. If limited by size of outdoor yard space available, consider scheduling playground use at different intervals during the day with fewer children in the yard at one time.

The abstract-shaped sand pit in the center of this playground is surrounded by a wide paved area that allows traffic to flow to simple and complex play units. Note climbing-tree log and sawhorses in left foreground. Cement ship in left background has multiple uses.

3. Augment and allow for alternative space by the use of adjacent parks, gymnasiums, or other play space.

4. Use space wisely, planning and evaluating the potential of every nook and corner, purchasing and making multipurpose equipment. Make certain that no less than one-third of the playground space is uncovered.

5. Build a storage unit for keeping extra equipment or accessories and for items needed for seasonal activities. If built with a flat roof and a sturdy guardrail and deck on the upper level, it can be used for a play area. Add ladders, stairs, or an incline from one level to the other.

6. Plan for your playground's accessibility to the classroom, toilet, and cloakrooms. Use large doors and a ramp for easier mobility.

7. Consider the climate and the need for protection from harsh inclement weather. Build sheltering walls and windbreaks, plan for drainage, and landscaping vegetation to provide shade and to prevent soil erosion. Plan to utilize the play yard all year 'round.

8. Arrange for open areas, equipped areas, and secluded areas with space for individuals and for groups.

9. When weather permits move some of your learning centers to the outdoor play area.

Designing Your Play Area

1. *Digging Space:* Use a sandbox or enclosed sandpile, an area of dirt for mud play, construction, and/or gardening. Remember, sand needs to be covered when not in use so that it is not used as a litter box by animals.
2. *Shade:* Use a variety of trees, shrubs, and vines of different sizes, colors, and growing cycles. Consider the use of canopies, covered patios, or terraces, and temporary shelter, such as tents, hung blankets, or beach umbrellas.
3. *Pathways:* Construct a wide curved pathway that may circle around or return to a larger paved area, allowing for group play and preventing traffic jams. When possible, include a slope and hill for variation. Hard surfaces could be blacktop or concrete. Spread redwood chips near play equipment to allow for drainage and to cushion children's falls. When paving surfaces, consider drainage to avoid standing water. Stepping-stones make interesting detours to smaller play areas.
4. *Active Play Areas:* Include low-branched trees, a large cylindrical cement tunnel under a mound of dirt, tree trunks or logs relocated in a bed of sand or wood chips, cubbies to crawl inside, bushes, play gyms, self-pumping swings, or pieces of climbing equipment made from telephone poles or tree logs cut into varying lengths and set perpendicularly in cement to form a series of stumps of varying heights. Consider need for social interaction and cooperative play.
5. *Quiet Play Areas:* Allow for areas of grass and have mushroom seats, a blanket, a shallow pool, or a single swing away from other equipment. Consider need for solitary play space.

The playground above considers the need for sun and shade, for a place to rest and dream, for a balance of free-ground area covered with a grass, sand, dirt, or cement surface. In right background note fenced-in paved area for wheeled toys. This yard provides a variety of types of play equipment, such as the motorboat, tire wall, and climbing tree.

6. *Discovery Area:* Provide places to explore and discover including space for animal cages, bird feeders, birdhouses and birdbaths, bushes and plants for insects and small animals. Have an automatic weather gauge, weathervane, thermometer, as well as space for flowers, trees, and areas where children can enjoy the snow, leaves, seeds, and water.

7. *Surfaces and Terrain:* Provide for a variety of levels and surfaces. (See illustrations in this section.)

Plan for a Variety of Play Equipment

1. Budget for the repair, replacement, and maintenance of existing equipment as well as for the addition of new equipment each year.

2. Contact members of the community for possible acquisition of an old rowboat, motor-boat, car, or van to be used for dramatic play. Take off doors, glass, and upholstery that would not weather. Be alert to hinges or apertures in which a child's hand, head, or foot might be caught. Paint with a wood or metal preservative to avoid weathering or rusting.

3. Select a few large boulders with no sharp edges to use as resting or climbing places.

4. Build your own equipment considering multiple use such as a playhouse/storage shed with stairs, railing around roof, or a cubby underneath. (See also p. 69 for a picture of climbing platforms.)

Children are walking and climbing on tree stumps secured in cement and surrounded by sand and dirt. Note varied height of stumps, which also serve to define an area.

5. Recycle discarded items into valuable, durable play equipment. (See following pages.)
6. Include play equipment that offers simple and complex challenges and meets the needs and abilities of your group. Add accessories to make more versatile.
7. If you have a square play yard, which is one of the more difficult to use, locate a sandpile, one major piece of equipment for multiple use, or a large surface area for dramatic play in the center of the playground. (See illustrations, pp. 62 and 69.) The outside corners can be smaller play areas.

Obstacle Course

Plan an obstacle course in the shape of a broken circle, square, rectangle, octagon, or U-shape that will allow the children to begin again once they have completed one cycle. This encourages a continual flow of participants, incurs less traffic confusion, and discourages haphazard sampling by children who may not wish to attempt a more difficult task. Vary skill opportunities by changing the obstacle course as group or individual needs are identified. Provide for a broad variety of motor experiences that will allow children to balance, climb, slide, jump, tumble, push and pull, and swing.

Tires

1. Tractor tires can be made into sandpile enclosures if placed on a sand-based, tiled or bricked area that will allow drainage. Cover when not in use.

Children are using this conversation swing in a variety of ways. While the swing invites sociability, it also allows children to individualize it for their own dramatic play and self-expression.

Tire wall is a sturdy, safe, economical, and versatile piece of climbing equipment. Tires are bolted together. Holes are drilled into tires to drain water.

2. Tires can be used as jumping circles. Tires slit on the worn tread line into two halves form canals for sailing boats.
3. One or more large tires can be stood upright and buried in the ground (up to the center opening) to form an archway or tunnel.
4. Large innertubes can be covered with laced canvas to form a small trampoline.
5. A series of three tires of varying circumference can be hung on three cables horizontally one above the other with space between each seat to allow for an interesting swing.
6. A series of seven or more tires can be bolted together like a flat bed mosaic and hung by cables from four poles to form a conversation swing. (See illustration, p. 65.)
7. A series of twelve tires can be bolted together standing on end one above the other in rows of three each and cabled to two posts for a climbing tire wall. (See above.) Remember to drill drain holes in each tire so that rain water will not accumulate.

Telephone Cable Spools

1. Paint and use spools as tables near the sandpile or a shady tree.
2. Smaller cable spools on wheels can be used for platforms to do tricks on if children wish to be performing clowns or animals.

Laundry barrel is placed on a wooden base to form a tunnel. Separate parts make storage easier. The barrel can also be used for skill games that involve throwing balls into a container.

Laundry or Fat Barrels

1. Cut out both ends of barrel and mount on a platform for a tunnel. Use with cleated planks for a ramp in an obstacle course.
2. Cut out one end (top) and a large hole on one side of the barrel and use it to toss in balls. The hole on one side allows the child to retrieve the ball without help. It also can suggest the more difficult feat of throwing a small ball or beanbag into the side hole.
3. Leave both ends of barrel in and cut out a door on one side to form a cozy nook for a private place.
4. Cut out a cockpit type hole on one side of the barrel for the child to crawl in when using the barrel as a spaceship. Wings and propellers may be attached if you wish to make an airplane.
5. Peepholes at various spots may be cut in the side of a barrel for other dramatic play, such as a puppet theater, window counter, or small playhouse.

Cartons or Packing Crates

1. While not very durable, cartons can afford a variety of pleasant play experiences if children are allowed to explore freely.

Duffel Bag or One Trouser Leg

1. Both can be stuffed with a pillow or foam rubber and used as a punching bag. Attach a spring or a canvas strap to the bag and hang from a hook.

Children are climbing a tree specially cultivated to allow easy access to low branches.

Tree Trunks, Logs, and Stumps

1. A solid tree trunk with many notched sturdy branches, stripped of bark and treated for weathering, makes an interesting climbing apparatus.
2. A tree that has been topped and the smaller branches removed makes another interesting climbing piece when laid on its side in sand or dirt.
3. Tree stumps or crosscuts of a telephone pole embedded in sand or cement can also be used for sitting or climbing on.
4. Screwing a plywood circle to a stump makes a low table.
5. Railroad ties used as boundaries also make steps or balance boards.

Concrete Sewer Pipe

1. Use as a tunnel, or it can be attached to other equipment in a grouping. (See p. 69.) Note in the picture the other learning opportunities when pipe is painted with symbols, signs, and numerals.
2. Makes a good base for creating both a tunnel and a small hill on a playground. To maintain the hillside on the overhead mound, turf and seed the dirt.

The play area above combines concrete sewer pipes with tree trunks, platforms of various heights, a tree, a tire, and a conversation swing. This creates a multi-use play structure for climbing, crawling, jumping, and hiding. Painted concrete sewer pipes offer additional opportunities to conceptualize numerals and directions.

Enclosure Walls, Fences, and Stair Rails

1. Paint murals or learning concepts on walls in play areas or hallways. (See illustration, p. 632.)
2. Suspend easels on fences for outdoor artists. If you dismiss your children from the play yard, use clothespins to clip take-home pictures to the fence.
3. Hang planters (can be large oil cans) on a stair rail outside to discourage sliding or climbing on it and to provide an opportunity to discover and explore while moving from one area to another.
4. If your view is desirable, plan your enclosure to allow the children to take full advantage of their surroundings.

Tips for Supervising the Playground

1. Stand (or sit) facing the children you are supervising. Position yourself near equipment where safety is a consideration.
2. Try to equalize the number of children being supervised by one teacher.
3. Remind children to bend knees when jumping and crawling.
4. Allow creative use of materials but with consideration for children's safety and for care of materials and equipment.
5. Encourage children to grasp bars when climbing or swinging with a monkey grip (thumb under, fingers over).
6. Limit turns on equipment in great demand by using a timer or counting number of turns. Encourage one-way traffic on obstacle courses to avoid collisions.

large muscle activities indoors

To individualize your program for motor development you will need to provide for large muscle activity space both indoors and outdoors. This type of indoor space will also be needed when inclement weather will not allow the children to go outside. Those rainy days need not become days dreaded by either the children or the teacher if alternative plans have been made. Below are some suggestions for providing such indoor large muscle activity areas.

1. Use center space areas (part of the regular classroom) for large muscle activities. Provide additional opportunities by equipping a Large Muscle Activity Center with one or more of the following:
   a. tumbling mat
   b. punching bag
   c. climbing gym or ladder box
   d. rocking horse or boat
2. Use converted classroom space. Move furniture out of the way or close off an area such as the Block Center and utilize that floor space to set up portable large muscle play equipment. Use a seldom trafficked doorway for hanging climbing ropes, a rope ladder, or a swing. Other portable equipment might include:
   a. balance beam or walking board
   b. ladders, sawhorses, planks
   c. swing, climbing rope, rope ladder, bar (doorway equipment)
   d. laundry or fat barrel (see p. 67)
   e. tunnel
   f. Vari-Play set available from Constructive Playthings
3. Take advantage of indoor alternative space available when weather does not permit children to go to the playgound. This might include a wide hallway, a gymnasium, or an adjacent room.

   CAUTION: Consider the need for clear trafficways in hallways and emergency exits when using these spaces. A single exit or narrow passageway should not be blocked with a swing, bar, or other equipment.

4. Plan for large muscle games and group exercises. See p. 58 and each guide for specific suggestions.
5. Provide for an expanded use of music and rhythm activities. Use the Participation Records on page 60. See the music section, pp. 39–41, for specific suggestions for rhythms.
6. Plan skill games with equipment, such as:
   a. horseshoes
   b. balls (nylon, sponge, rubber)
   c. skill-toss games
   d. wadded balls for indoor snowball fights (crumble tissue or newspaper for balls)
   e. feathers, blown to keep in midair
   f. bubbles or balloons (blow and catch them)
   g. bleach bottle scoops for catching balls
   h. many suggestions found in 1 and 2 could also be used here depending on space

Children are blowing feathers
to keep them floating in midair.

Foreground: large-muscle rainy day
activities include Color Candles for
jumping games.

extended experiences

Trips and Excursions

To Go or Not To Go? That Is the Question

1. Weigh whether the excursion is the best way to introduce children to this discovery and learning experience.
2. Is each child secure enough with the group and at the center to leave to go on a trip?
3. Is this trip best taken at this age?
4. Exactly what can the children learn, see, do on this trip?
5. Will your group be welcomed? Will young children be accepted?
6. When did you take your last trip? Remember, once a week is too often.

Have You Made Reservations?

1. Make contacts. Call ahead regarding visit or excursion.
2. Set time and date (make reservations for appointed day and time).
3. Don't forget to confirm the reservation the day you go.
4. Make suggestions to the person conducting the tour as to what the children will be interested in, might understand, and what their attention span is.

Are You and the Children Prepared?

1. Scout the area before you go. Are you knowledgeable about destination? Have you defined what is to be explored?
2. Enlist extra help: parents, volunteers, drivers.
3. Plan for extra and special means of transportation.
4. Plan with staff. Define individual teaching responsibilities. Discuss elements of concern, such as crossing a busy street.
5. Accidents may happen. Take a survival kit for assurance.
6. Make certain to include snacks and drinks, and to make provisions for toileting.
7. Watch the clock. Children have built-in timers for their needs, such as rest, eating, toileting.
8. If distance is great, you may want to stop en route for rest and/or snack break.
9. A walk in the rain might be fun, but what about a downpour?
10. You can always cancel, but have an excellent alternative plan ready.
11. Alert parents as to need for special clothing, funds for tickets, a sack lunch, boots, mittens, swimsuits. Get written permission slips and inform parents of specific plans (destination, date, time).

Keep a Travel Log

1. Take photos, make a recorded tape segment (sounds of a zoo), take notes for next trip.
2. Learn from your mistakes and build on what was positive.
3. Note signs of learning; sometimes they are not immediately evident.

Are You a Good Tour Leader?

1. Prepare the children by introducing the idea and letting them help plan the trip.
2. When plans are definite, share them with the children, but not too far ahead.

3. Brief your travelers regarding rules. Modify and make your own to meet your specific group needs.
4. Use travel time for learning as well as helping the children to pass the time.

Follow Up with Follow Through

1. Be prepared for an energetic response when you get back to your center by:
    a. having appropriate dramatic play props and dress-ups ready for use.
    b. having selected books available in Book Center before and after the trip.
    c. collecting poems, games, and songs that might be used when appropriate interest is shown.
    d. planning art activities considering the thrust of the trip.
2. Provide for instant replay. Listen enroute for children's initial responses.
3. Allow chances for verbalization of children's experiences in grouptime and small groups.
4. Treasures and souvenirs may be shared in Show and Tell.

Evaluate the Trip

1. Give children time to react and respond to the experience. Then evaluate the trip with your staff.
2. Would you do it again? What would you do differently?

Planning for Visitors

Select the Visitor

1. Choose someone who likes and is interested in young children.
2. Request educational officers from community resources or people who have very young children of their own. When invited on their day off, working parents can be more flexible about time.
3. Select members of both sexes and of different cultural groups.
4. Choose someone most knowledgeable or skilled in the resource you need. Remember grandparents, students, and retired citizens.

Interview the Visitor

1. Interview the visitor by telephone or in person. Set a specific date and time that best suits both of your schedules and plans.
2. Visit the persons at their place of work. They may then suggest other items or subjects you might want to include.

Brief the Visitor

1. List questions the children might ask or need to know.
2. Suggest items to wear or share (within children's experience).
3. Give cautions about safety in regard to tools (or other items) to be shared.
4. Describe setting visitor will be in with children.
5. Offer a few tips on ways to deal with behavior that may occur.

Preplan for Visit

1. Set the scene. Give children opportunities to discover related information from other activities before the visitor arrives.

2. Preplan some follow-through experiences for the children after the visit. Purchase or obtain equipment necessary for these experiences.
3. Encourage children to help prepare an invitation and later a thank-you note of appreciation to a visitor.

Using Films and Filmstrips

1. Preview film or filmstrip. Double check that extension cords and extra bulbs are handy.
2. Select it much as you would a book—for content, pictures, length, age level, appropriateness to interest development, and authenticity.
3. Reserve film or filmstrip, projector, and screen.
4. Edit films or, if a filmstrip, the story line to meet your needs. Make a note of sections you wish to roll past.
5. Select a room that can be darkened. Leave a small light on for children who may be frightened by darkness.
6. Mark floor for placement of screen and projector after you have focused the picture. Choose a clear wall for projection if no screen is available.
7. Have a table for projector handy so it can be placed on the marked space.
8. If the children are seated on the floor, shoot the picture so they can all see but not so high that they must sit with their necks in an uncomfortable position.
9. While viewing the film, listen and watch for children's responses (verbal, facial, and body language). When you can, encourage children to answer their own questions, if they are able, by redirecting the question with another question. If they cannot, answer them yourself or help children to discover the answers. You may wish to rerun the filmstrip.

teacher resources

Pictures, Displays, and Special Room Arrangements

1. Create your own. Start or add to a picture file. Have parents, staff, and volunteers help in the collection. Besides clipping magazines, watch for good picture sources in your community. Seasonal or topical posters in grocery stores, drugstores, department stores, travel agencies, or the post office may be available for the asking.
2. Talk to store managers about discarded cardboard shelf displays. (See illustration, p. 551.) These have many uses with little change except a coat of paint.
3. Make your own cardboard display boards or scrapbooks. (Use chickenwire rings for spiral hinges.) Pegholed fiberboard is another possibility for a sturdy surface to which pictures can be taped.
4. Screw butterfly-wing clips to the wooden frame of a blackboard to hold a section of plasterboard. This will instantly transform a blackboard into a bulletin board.
5. Make a kiosk for displaying science or art items. Use the flat surfaces to show pictures and the niches to display treasures for examination or exploration. (See illustration, p. 75.)

Mounting Pictures

1. Whenever possible mount teaching pictures using a uniform size for easier filing.
2. File smaller pictures in see-through envelopes for use with games, bulletin boards, or pasting.
3. Label pictures on the back or place in alphabetized folders.
4. If you mount pictures in color, dramatize the most important subject or object by repeating its color in the border. Always leave a wider margin at the bottom of a mat than the other three sides, which may have equal margins. Occasionally use an abstract or odd shape behind picture to mount it more attractively. Use pinking shears or tear edges for other variations.
5. Try to get a complete figure of an animal, person, or object in the picture. If mounted and displayed with other pictures choose those of appropriate sizes (relative to each other) so children will not be confused by the misproportions.

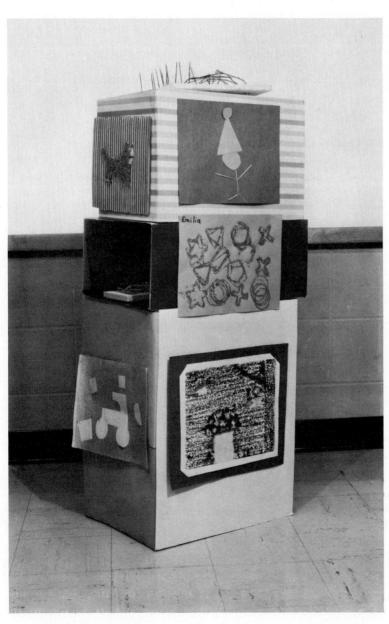

A kiosk is used to display children's art in the round. Children have chosen their best work to display. Kiosk is made by bolting cartons together. Sections may be covered with a variety of materials, such as cloth, wallpaper, or plastic, or they may be painted.

Displaying or Posting Teaching Pictures

1. Use thumbtacks at edge, *not* through picture. If you use tape, remove it after each hanging before you return the picture to the file.
2. Save some duplicate pictures for expanded use. Look for sequence pictures.
3. Use walls, hallways, stairwells as display places for children's art pieces. Change displays often. Invite a local artist to paint a mural or child-scaled wall design. (See p. 632 for illustration.)
4. Don't forget the ceiling of the restng area. Hang mobiles or pictures to suggest relaxation or pleasant memories, such as nature scenes, children holding pets, parents hugging children.
5. Use bulletin boards: at an entrance for parents' notices and messages; in the grouptime area for focus of theme or interest development or for reference; inside an entrance door for children to discover as they arrive.
6. Make a bulletin board attractive by using twisted crepe paper strips, abstract shapes of complementary colors (if you doubt your own judgment look at fabrics or paintings for shades or tints used together). Cut out colored or black letters for bolder message. Use colored yarn or string to circle related pictures.

NOTE: Suggestions are made in each guide for specific uses of pictures in games, language development, and other activities.

Core Library

General Books about Child Development

Galambos, Jeannette W. *A Guide to Discipline.* Washington, D.C.: National Association for the Education of Young Children, 1969.
> This guide invites the teacher to be self-critical and offers specific suggestions for dealing with problems that are sure to occur in groups of very young children. Techniques to avoid are also noted. It is set double space for easier reading.

Hirsch, Elizabeth S. et al. *The Block Book.* Washington, D.C.: National Association for the Education of Young Children, 1974.
> This paperback outlines the potential contributions of blocks in the early childhood curriculum. Each chapter covers a different area of learning and is illustrated by both photographs and diagrams. Arrangement and use of the Block Center, stages of block building, storage, and block accessories are included.

Hogden, Lauren et al. *School Before Six: A Diagnostic Approach.* 2d. ed. 2 vols. St. Louis, Missouri: CEMREL, Inc., 1973.
> Volume I outlines the diagnostic procedure for assessing young children's learning needs and strengths. Games, charts, forms, and checklists are included. Volume II contains directions for hundreds of activities in the areas of motor skills, language development, and social-emotional development. Helpful in planning for the individual child. Activities are organized into subsections including Art, Food Preparation, Language, Outdoors, Role Playing, Science, and Table Activities.

Leeper, Sarah Hammond et al. *Good Schools for Young Children.* 3d. ed. New York: Macmillan, 1974.
> Highly recommended for the teacher or college student in early childhood education. This book will be valuable to a Center Director or Supervisor as a one book reference.

Art

Cherry, Clare. *Creative Art for the Developing Child.* Belmont, Calif.: Fearon Publishers, 1972.

> A helpful aid that includes a variety of suggestions for the use of many art medias. Has excellent action photos of young children working with art materials.

McDonald, Pauline and Doris V. Brown. *Creative Art for Home and School.* Alhambra, Calif.: Borden Publishing, 1961.

> A concisely written book on methods and materials necessary for the use of the basic creative art media with helpful and imaginative variations. Holiday suggestions are somewhat structured.

Silverblatt, Iris M. *Creative Activities: A Manual for Teachers of Pre-School Children.* Cincinnati, Ohio: Creative Activities, 1964.

> A very inclusive handbook that has a chartlike outline of activities with methods and materials noted for use with very young children.

Language Games, Fingerplays, and Poetry

Geismer, Barbara Peck and Antoinette Brown Suter. *Very Young Verses.* Boston: Houghton Mifflin, 1945.

> This fine collection of poetry includes many old favorite poems for every occasion.

Glazer, Tom. *Eye Winker, Tom Tinker, Chin Chopper.* Garden City, N.Y.: Doubleday, 1973.

> Fifty musical fingerplays with piano arrangements and guitar chords. New and inclusive collection of traditional action songs for young children with suggestions for group participation.

Grayson, Marion F. *Let's Do Fingerplays.* New York: David McKay, 1962.

> This is one of the finest traditional and contemporary collections of fingerplays available. It is divided by subjects: The Child, Dressing Up, Things That Go, Animal Antics, The Family, The World Outdoors, Big People, Little People, Counting, Around the House, Noisemakers, and Holidays. A few sections need editing to reflect the nonsexist point of view.

Scott, Louise Binder. *Learning Time with Language Experiences for Young Children.* New York: McGraw-Hill, 1968.

> Hundreds of ideas for assisting the teachers as they work day by day with young children encouraging and developing language experiences. A subject index is helpful to teachers as they plan their program.

Scott, Louise Binder and J. J. Thompson. *Rhymes for Fingers and Flannelboards.* New York: McGraw-Hill, 1960.

> A collection of 232 fingerplays grouped into sections by subject. Subjects include: holidays, seasons, farm, home, city, zoo, field, and woods animals and others. Care is recommended in selecting fingerplays that reflect cultural awareness and sensitivity regarding sexism. We recommend that you edit and make adaptations where necessary. Some fingerplays are written in English and another language (Spanish, French, Japanese, German, Italian).

Music

Cherry, Clare. *Creative Movement for the Developing Child: A Nursery School Handbook for Nonmusicians.* Belmont, Calif.: Fearon Publishers, 1971.
    Materials offered include a broad repertoire and range of creative rhythms.

Curry, W. Lawrence et al. *Songs for Early Childhood.* Philadelphia: Westminster Press, 1958.
    This book includes a broad variety of songs and music for very young children with a simple accompaniment for the piano. Does include a few religious songs.

Eberhart, Alice M. *Swinging on a Tune.* Edited by Carol Marshall. Emporia, Kan.: Emporia State Press, 1975.
    A spiral-bound book of sixty-eight original, simple, chanty melodies on a variety of subjects. Teacher notes reflect a keen sensitivity to children. Songs show an understanding of children's spontaneity in their songs, chants, and rhymes. Scores are noted without left-hand accompaniment although three basic chords are included along with some simple suggestions when using a guitar or ukelele.

Ginglend, David R. and Winifred E. Stiles. *Music Activities for Retarded Children.* Nashville, Tenn.: Abingdon Press, 1965.
    A music handbook for teachers and parents. Describes ways all children can learn through music. Sections include: All About Me, Listen, Holidays Are Happy Days, It Can, Can You?, Let's Make Music, Things to Learn.

Landeck, Beatrice and Elizabeth Crook. *Wake Up and Sing.* New York: William Morrow, 1969.
    A fine collection of American folk songs with teaching suggestions and guitar chordings by Michael Childs, piano arrangements by Charity Bailey.

MacCarteney, Laura Pendleton. *Songs for the Nursery School.* Florence, Kentucky: Willis Music Co., 1938.
    This book has 159 songs including activities such as tone games and fingerplays for 2 to 6 year olds. Subjects include transportation, animals, water, seasons, nursery rhymes.

Music Resource Book. Philadelphia: Lutheran Church Press, 1967.
    This spiral-bound book with photographs was designed to help teachers creatively use music with children. Simply written music arrangements have notations for autoharp and included with each song are teaching suggestions. Many traditional melodies are used for action songs. Very few songs are limited by religious wording.

Planning Physical Space

Baker, Katherine Reed. *Let's Play Outdoors.* Washington, D.C.: National Association for the Education of Young Children, 1966.
    This well-organized reference describes guidelines for planning for outdoor space, equipment, and experiences to be used with very young children.

Kritcheusky, Sybil. *Planning Environments for Young Children—Physical Space.* Washington, D.C.: National Association for the Education of Young Children, 1969
    This is a helpful resource to use in planning for, organizing, and evaluating play space. Common problems are discussed and examples given of some successful uses of space. Diagrams and photographs illustrate the plans and suggestions given.

Commercial Sources for Learning Materials

NOTE: Firms with an asterisk stock early childhood materials and equipment from many individual companies. To simplify purchasing, we suggest you write for their catalogs and order from them. Books listed under Book Center in each guide can be ordered directly from the publishers (your local librarian will give you the mailing address), from a local bookstore, or from Childcraft or Gryphon House listed below.

* ABC School Supply, Inc.
437 Armour Circle N.E.
Box 13084
Atlanta, Georgia 30324

Afro-Am Publishing Co., Inc.
1727 S. Indiana Avenue
Chicago, Illinois 60616

Angeles Nursery Toys
4105 N. Fairfax Drive
Arlington, Virginia 22203

Bailey Films, Inc.
6509 DeLongpre Avenue
Hollywood, California 90028

Binney and Smith, Inc.
380 Madison Avenue
New York, New York 10017

Bowmar
P. O. Box 3623
Glendale, California 91201

* Childcraft Education Corporation
20 Kilmer Road
Edison, New Jersey 08817

Child Guidance
Questor Education Products Co.
200 Fifth Avenue
New York, New York 10010

Childhood Resources
5307 Lee Highway
Arlington, Virginia 22207

Community Playthings
Rifton, New York 12471

* Constructive Playthings
1040 E. 85th Street
Kansas City, Missouri 64131

* Creative Playthings
A Division of CBS Inc.
Princeton, New Jersey 08540

Creative Publications
P.O. Box 10328
Palo Alto, California 94303

* David C. Cook Publishing Co.
850 N. Grove Avenue
Elgin, Illinois 60120

Dennison Manufacturing Co.
67 Ford Avenue
Framingham, Massachusetts 01701

* Developmental Learning Materials (DLM)
7440 Natchez Avenue
Niles, Illinois 60648

Ed-U-Card/Ed-U-Card Corporations
Subsidiaries of Binney and Smith
60 Austin Boulevard
Commack, New York 11725

Educational Performance Associates
563 Westview Avenue
Ridgefield, New Jersey 07657

* Educational Teaching Aids Division (ETA)
A. Daigger and Co., Inc.
159 W. Kinzie Street
Chicago, Illinois 60610

Eureka Resale Products
Dunmore, Pennsylvania 18512

Fisher-Price Toys
A Division of Quaker Oats Co.
East Aurora, New York 14052

GAF Corporation
Consumer Photo Products/View-Master
140 W. 51st Street
New York, New York 10020

Gryphon House
1333 Connecticut Avenue, N.W.
Washington, D.C. 20036

Hayes School Publishing Co., Inc.
321 Pennwood Avenue
Wilkinsburg, Pennsylvania 15221

Holcomb's
3000 Quigley Road
Cleveland, Ohio 44113

Ideal School Supply
11000 S. Lavergne Avenue
Oak Lawn, Illinois 60453

Information Center on Children's Cultures
Administrative Offices
331 E. 38th Street
New York, New York 10016

Instructo Corporation
Subsidiary of McGraw-Hill Inc.
Cedar Hollow and Mathews Roads
Paoli, Pennsylvania 19301

Judy Instructional Aids
The Judy Company
Sales Office
250 James Street
Morristown, New Jersey 07960

* Lakeshore Equipment Company
P. O. Box 2116
1144 Montague Avenue
San Leandro, California 94577

Lauri Enterprises
Phillips-Avon, Maine 04966

Lego Systems, Inc.
P. O. Box 2273
Enfield, Connecticut 06082

Mab-Graphic Products Inc.
310 Marconi Boulevard
Copaigue, New York 11726

Mead Educational Services
B and T Learning
5315-A Tulane Drive
Atlanta, Georgia 30336

Milton Bradley Company
Springfield, Massachusetts 01100

National Dairy Council
111 N. Canal Street
Chicago, Illinois 60606

National Geographic Society
17th and M Streets N.W.
Washington, D.C. 20036

National Wildlife Federation
1412 16th Street N.W.
Washington, D.C. 20036

Parker Brothers Inc.
Division of General Mills
Fun Group Inc.
Salem, Massachusetts 01970

Playskool Incorporated
Milton Bradley Company
Springfield, Massachusetts 01100

* Practical Drawing Company
P. O. Box 5388
Dallas, Texas 75222

Romper Room Toys
Hasbro Industries, Inc.
Pawtucket, Rhode Island 02861

Scholastic Early Childhood Center
904 Sylvan Avenue
Englewood Cliffs, New Jersey 07632

Scott, Foresman and Company
1900 E. Lake Avenue
Glenview, Illinois 60025

Scripture Press
Victor Books
1825 College Avenue
Wheaton, Illinois 60187

Shindana Toys
Division of Operation Bootstrap, Inc.
6107 S. Central Avenue
Los Angeles, California 90001

Society For Visual Education, Inc. (SVE)
1345 Diversey Parkway
Chicago, Illinois 60614

Standard Publishing Co.
8121 Hamilton Avenue
Cincinnati, Ohio 45231

Steven Manufacturing Co.
Hermann, Missouri 65041

Sunbell Corporation
P.O. Box 7500
Albuquerque, New Mexico 87104

Thomas Y. Crowell Company
666 Fifth Avenue
New York New York 10019

Trend Enterprises
P.O. Box 3073
St. Paul, Minnesota 55165

UNICEF
U.S. Committee for UNICEF
331 E. 38th Street
New York, New York 10016

United Nations Gift Shop
New York, New York 10017

United Synagogue Book Service
155 Fifth Avenue
New York, New York 10010

Uniworld Toys
P. O. Box 61
West Hempstead, New York 11552

Vanguard Visuals
24266 Thornton Highway
Dallas, Texas 75224

Commercial Sources for Cassettes and Records

NOTE: Firms with an asterisk are retailers who stock cassettes and records from many individual companies.

AA Records
250 W. 57th Street
New York, New York 10019

* ABC School Supply
437 Armour Circle N.E.
Box 13084
Atlanta, Georgia 30324

A. B. LeCrone Company
819 N.W. 92nd Street
Oklahoma City, Oklahoma 73114

Argosy Music Corporation
Motivation Records
101 Harbor Road
Westport, Connecticut 06880

Bowmar
P.O. Box 3623
Glendale, California 91201

Camden Records
See RCA

Capitol Records, Inc.
1750 N. Vine Street
Hollywood, California 90028

* Childcraft Education Corporation
20 Kilmer Road
Edison, New Jersey 08817

Children's Record Guild (CRG)
225 Park Avenue South
New York, New York 10003

David C. Cook Publishing Co.
850 N. Grove Avenue
Elgin, Illinois 60120

Decca Records
445 Park Avenue
New York, New York 10022

Desto Records: *order from*
CMS Records, Inc.
14 Warren Street
New York, New York 10007

Disneyland Records
800 Sonora Avenue
Glendale, California 91201

Educational Activities, Inc.
P.O. Box 392
Freeport, New York 11520

Folkways Records
43 W. 61st Street
New York, New York 10023

Golden Records: *order from*
AA Records

Hap Palmer Activity Records
See Educational Activities, Inc.

Happy Time Records
8-16 43rd Avenue
Long Island City, New York 10001

* Kimbo Educational
P.O. Box 246
Deal, New Jersey 07723

KTAV Publishing House, Inc.
120 E. Broadway
New York, New York 10022

* Lyons
530 Riverview Avenue
Elkhart, Indiana 46514

Melody House: *order from*
A. B. LeCrone

Mercury Record Productions
Phonogram, Inc.
One IBM Plaza
Chicago, Illinois 60611

MGM Record Corporation
7165 W. Sunset Boulevard
Los Angeles, California 90046

Miller-Brody Productions, Inc.
342 Madison Avenue
New York, New York 10017

Mister Rogers: *order from*
Thomas Y. Crowell
666 Fifth Avenue
New York, New York 10019

National Wildlife Federation
1412 16th Street N. W.
Washington, D.C. 20036

Peter Pan Industries
88 St. Francis Street
Newark, New Jersey 07105

Phoebe James
P.O. Box 475
Oakview, California 93022

Pickwick Records
135 Crossways Park Drive
Woodbury, New York 11797

* Practical Drawing Company
P.O. Box 5388
Dallas, Texas 75222

RCA Records
1133 Avenue of the Americas
New York, New York 10036

Rhythms Productions
P.O. Box 34485
Los Angeles, California 90034

notes for guiding behavior

Suggestions for Guiding Behavior

1. Know everything you can about each child.
2. Decide what you want each child to learn.
3. Plan children's environment.
4. Establish positive, friendly relationships with each child.
5. Encourage each child in his or her growth and development of a good self-image.

Ways to Build Trust

1. Like the child. Take him or her seriously. Assure the child that you like and care about him or her.
2. Talk to the child at his or her level. Bend down, put your arm around the child's shoulder, hold hands gently, or kneel down beside the child. Eye contact is very important.
3. Be positive not harsh; gentle not weak; pleasant, calm, firm, sincere, and matter-of-fact. Be consistent about your expectations and guidance, it develops dependability.
4. Speak softly, slowly, patiently, be friendly but firm.
5. Make a suggestion rather than give a command. Save commands for emergencies.
6. Listen to child's explanation of how he or she feels. Accept his or her right to feelings.
7. Encourage child to share success, give praise, show understanding, help and learn through discovery and failure.
8. Set an example, expect cooperation, make self-cooperation possible.
9. Offer choice only when legitimate. Offer compromises or alternatives if needed.

Remember, If I Know Each Child, I Can:

1. regroup
2. protect each child's rights
3. divert
4. allow a child the opportunity to resolve his or her own problem
5. offer a compromise when rights are unknown
6. show a child how
7. ask a child a question
8. overlook certain behavior (always considering safety)
9. be flexible
10. make allowances for age-phase behavior
11. give a child a chance to rebel (within reason)
12. stop certain behavior (when safety is a factor)
13. offer duplicate materials or equipment rather than expect child to share arbitrarily

I Can Prevent Difficulties by:

1. preparing for a variety of activities, using materials and equipment in good repair that offer opportunities for every child to succeed
2. defining areas, arranging rooms attractively, and rotating activities and materials to invite challenge
3. planning for total supervision for each space with defined roles for all teachers (remembering to consider each one's abilities and special interests)
4. giving guidance and support when needed, allowing for discovery, exploration, and creativity

If I Plan I Can:

1. allow time to complete tasks
2. substitute when alternatives are needed
3. arrange equipment, space, and program to avoid accidents, overstimulation, or cross-traffic
4. set reasonable limits for safety
5. effect smooth transitions for individuals (and group) by allowing for individual differences and experiences
6. use the proximity of an adult to help modify behavior

PART ONE

Self-Concept

I I'm Me, I'm Special

basic understandings

(concepts children can grasp from this subject)

- I'm me, I'm special. **There is no one else just like me.**
- I have a special name given to me when I was born. It is on my birth certificate.
- No one has a voice just like mine; no one has fingerprints just like mine.
- I am like others in some ways; I am different from others in some ways.
- I can do some things easily; I can do some things well.
- Some things are hard to do; some things I cannot do well yet.
- I can do many things now that I couldn't do when I was a baby.
- As I get older, I will be able to do more things than I can do now.
- I do not have to be good at everything; I can make mistakes.
- I have feelings; at different times I may be glad, sad, angry, tired, or have other feelings.
- I can learn some good ways to show my feelings.
- If I know I am special, I know others can be special in their way too.
- Others need to know that I think they are special. Sometimes I need to know them better to know how special they are (in what ways they are special).
- No one can know what I think or how I feel unless I tell them or show them.
- When I share my own ideas or do things in my own way I am being creative.
- My thoughts and ideas are important. Other people have good ideas, too.
- I am likeable (loveable) to someone. I can learn to like (love) others.
- I have a right to share the materials, equipment, and the attention of the teacher and to be safe and protected in school.
- Some children are special because they have extra special needs: braces, glasses, crutches, hearing aids, a wheelchair, speech therapy.
- Each year I have a special day called my birthday. (See Mathematics guide for experiences related to birthday celebrations.)

I Have Some Things That Belong to Me

- I have a wonderful body. It has many parts: eyes, ears, nose, mouth, feet, hands, hair, skin, fingers, toes.
- I can do many things with my body. I can see, touch, taste, smell, hear, talk, move, think, and learn.
- My family (mother, father, sisters, brothers) belongs to me.
- Other things belong to me: my toys, clothes, pets, friends, treasures, things that I make.
- My thoughts belong to me. I can think, dream, wonder, wish, and enjoy just looking at things or watching others.
- Sometimes I keep my thoughts to myself and sometimes I share my thoughts with others.
- Part of my time belongs to me; I don't always need to be busy with activities.
- A place that I think is secret or special belongs to me until I share it.

I Belong to Someone

- I am someone's son/daughter (grandson/granddaughter).
- I may also be someone's brother/sister/cousin/nephew/niece.
- I can be a part of a group (my family, my class, my neighborhood).
- Someday I may choose to become a wife/husband and a father/mother.
- Someday I may become an aunt/uncle, grandfather/grandmother, or cousin to someone.
- A friend is someone who likes me just as I am.
- A neighbor is someone who lives close to where I live.
- I need to help my family (group) by caring for and sharing the things we own, helping in plans, sharing my ideas, and doing what I am asked to do or need to do.
- I am an American, that is, an Anglo-American, a Mexican-American, an American Indian (native American), an Afro-American, a Chinese-American, or other.

My Family Is Special

- My family is made up of _____, _____, _____.
- Adults in my family can be helpful because they know many things that I do not know.
- My family has certain beliefs and special ways of living and doing things. (See Families at Home and Families at Work.)
- My family celebrates days that are important to us: birthdays, Mother's Day, Father's Day, Valentine's Day, anniversaries, and graduations. (See Holiday and Seasons guides.)
- My family and I may have different customs, beliefs, and celebrations than other families. (See Holiday and Seasons guides.)
- My family and I may speak a different language from others near us.

I Live in a Special Place

- I live with my family:
  in a home ——— (what kind?)
  in a city ——— (name)
  in a state ——— (name)
  in a country ——— (name)
  in the world (on the planet Earth)

I Can Change by Growing

- I can get bigger (taller and heavier) until I am a grownup.
- I can get fatter or slimmer if I eat more than I need or less than I need.
- I need food, exercise, and rest to help me grow.
- Each year I have a birthday and become one year older until I die (stop living).

I Can Change by Learning

- When I think, remember, and decide, things can be better.
- I can learn about my body and make it work for me and for others.
- I can learn to do many things. If I try over and over again I should be able to learn to do something very well.
- I can learn by doing and discovering when I use my mind to think, eyes to see, ears to listen, fingers to feel, tongue to taste, and nose to smell.
- I can learn to do things for myself.
- I can help to keep myself clean and healthy.
- I can be thoughtful of others in what I do and what I say.
- I can learn to follow directions; I can learn to follow rules.
- I can learn to take care of, or help, other people.
- I can learn to take care of other things in my world: plants, animals, parks, streams, sidewalks, and so on.
- I can learn how to use things the right way and how to care for them properly.

I Can Change by Pretending

- I can play that I am someone else when I pretend and when I do things like that person does.
- I may wear a costume to make myself look like someone other than myself.
- I may wear a wig to change the color of my hair and to change the way it is fixed.

I Can Change by Dressing Differently

- I can get a haircut or change the way I wear my hair so that I look different.
- I can wear various kinds of clothes and look different.
- I can get cleaned up or get dirty, and I may look different.
- I may wear glasses if I need them.
- I may wear a cast if I break an arm or a leg, but . . . I am still me!

I Can Change by Getting Sick/Well

- If I skin or bruise myself, I look different until the injury heals.
- If I break a bone, I may look different until it mends.
- When I get a temperature or feel sick, I do not look the same as when I am well.
- When I am tired I look different than when I am rested; sometimes I become cross and unhappy.
- Doctors, nurses, my family, and my teachers help to keep me healthy and help me grow.

I Can Change by Acting Differently

- I can learn better ways to show my feelings: talk when I am angry, tell someone when I need help.
- I can let others know how I feel. I can listen to others and find out how they feel and what they think.
- I can work and play by myself; I can learn to work and play with others.
- I can feel good about myself when I do my share of work at home and at school.
- Sometimes I help my friends and share things. Because we are different, we sometimes argue, disagree, or even fight.
- I can learn good manners; I can learn to be polite.
- I can show others I like (love) them.
- Sometimes I am not proud of what I have done. I feel happier if I am allowed to help make things better by fixing what I have spoiled, cleaning up if I have made a mess, or being more thoughtful or friendly the next time.
- People like me better if I am friendly. I am still me, I like myself, and I am proud to be me.

Some Things I Cannot Change

- I cannot change my height, skin color, sex.
- I may not be able to change a handicap or a problem I have but I can make it better by wearing glasses, using crutches, using a hearing aid, taking medicine, not eating certain foods, or not doing some activities.
- I cannot change my family or where I live.
- I cannot solve problems that make my parents or guardians drink, argue, or fight.
- I cannot provide food, clothes, or a place to sleep for myself.
- I cannot keep my parents or guardians from getting a divorce, going to jail, leaving me, but I can tell someone else who could help me if my parents hurt me or leave me alone.
- Some things I cannot change until I am older because they are the problems or responsibilities of grown-ups.
- Until I am older I can make things better by:
  1. telling my parents or guardians I love them, if I do.
  2. avoiding accidents that may cause problems or make people unhappy.
  3. learning to do things as well as I can, and helping when I can.
  4. learning to do what I am asked.
  5. knowing (realizing) that others have handicaps and problems too.
  6. asking for help from adults to do what I can do and to become what I would like to become.
  7. staying with others in another place when people at home are unable to care for me or when it is not a pleasant or a happy place to be.

Additional Facts the Teacher Should Know

A good feeling about one's self is often considered a prerequisite to learning, or a beginning point toward achieving whatever one is capable of becoming. Each child is "special" (unique) and deserves to be accepted at whatever level of development he or she has attained physically, mentally, socially, and emotionally. Most early childhood classes are enrolling children from two or more cultural groups, and many of these children have a language other than English as their first language. Also, many classes are accepting handicapped children, such as mongoloid, cerebral palsied, deaf, blind, mute, asthmatic, epileptic, and children with heart defects, missing limbs, emotional problems. The staffs at such schools have multiple challenges and multiple opportunities.

1. They should familiarize themselves with each child and his or her family or living group. Background information gathered from a pre-enrollment interview, completed information forms, and a home visit prior to the opening of school should provide a good beginning of understanding. The staff should operate on the basis that the parents or guardians are the primary educators of the child and that they will all have to work together throughout the year for the benefit of the child.

2. The increasing number of adoptions, many of which are interracial and crosscultural, common-law marriages, single parents, divorces, separations, and foster parents makes it impossible to assume that most families are traditional, complete, or permanent units or that all children in a family have the same last name or even the same skin color. The wise teacher does not make judgments but is primarily concerned with helping children feel good about themselves, their families, and their life style, as well as helping them share their knowledge, skills, and culture with one another on a level that young children can comprehend. (See Families, Families at Home, Families at Work, and Holiday guides.)

3. All children should be assessed individually to determine their present skills and concepts, and a plan should be devised for supplementing their education regardless of their handicap or cultural background. Individual record files are important to keep, but you should not stereotype a child with an identified behavior or learning problem as being hopeless because a previous teacher recorded a lack of success. A year of maturation or a change in staff can make a great deal of difference. If a child is not making progress, assess your teaching methods instead of assuming the child is "unteachable."

4. Parents or guardians must become partners in the education of their children if real progress is to be made. The staff should try to make the parents or guardians feel welcome in the classroom. They need to share the plans they have for the particular child and should keep the parents informed as to the child's progress throughout the year by the use of conferences and written reports.

5. A rich and varied environment will help develop competence and the ability to function independently in the world. The children should be encouraged to do what they can for themselves, but they should be helped with tasks that are too difficult before frustration sets in. Provide materials and directed learning experiences that are appropriate to the age, ability, and competencies of each child in order to capitalize on their readiness, minimize frustration, and structure success.

6. At times you may wish to group children with similar needs together, such as at story time, some cognitive learning sessions, and some art experiences. At other times you should group so that children with less skills or knowledge are able to learn from those with more skills and knowledge.

7. Positive rather than negative guidance builds a positive self-image. The staff should be constantly alert for praiseworthy actions by the children in order to reinforce them with their warm approval. Artificial or unwarranted praise should not be given as children can detect insincerity. Staff members should accept the child's feelings as important.

Then they can help each one work through negative feelings to a greater understanding. Teachers should respect the dignity of each child. If corrective action is needed, it should be done quietly, firmly, and in such a manner as to avoid shaming a child in front of peers. By your manner, the child will discover that you are still friends and that it is the behavior of which you disapprove, not the child. Young children easily confuse discipline with personal rejection.

8. Children should be encouraged to share their ideas and to respect those of others. Self-concept should be an ongoing theme throughout the daily program year, not merely an aid toward getting acquainted.

9. It is now a law in most states that you must report child abuse when you have knowledge of it. The staff should see it as a symptom of a problem at home with which the family needs help. Referral to the appropriate community agencies may help to solve the problem. If you are uncertain how to help, report the incident to the nearest Child Welfare office, and they will have a member of their staff follow it up. Be assured that children are removed from the family only as a last resort.

10. Stress professionalism at all times. As staff, you will be in possession of privileged information about children and their families. Never discuss this information with others who are not professionally involved. If you wish to share a positive or humorous incident it can be done without using names. Be sure to share all these incidents with the child's family, too.

Cultural awareness is important to each child's self-image. All Americans, including the Indians and Eskimos, have migrated or immigrated to the United States from another part of the continent or another part of the world. All came here for various reasons—to seek adventure, to escape religious, political, or social injustice, as slaves or servants, by marriage or adoption, to establish a business, or to seek an education. Unfortunately there was no master plan and the influx through the years was not in equal numbers, resulting in a mainstream group and minority groups. The mainstream group not only ignored the cultural and historical contributions of the minority groups but also distorted some of the facts about them in writing our history. However, in the past decade, minority groups, including women, have gained the right to fuller consideration by the majority. Many of the minority groups now have national organizations that are concerned with cultural awareness. (See Teacher Resources, p. 113.) Colleges and universities have expanded their curriculums by adding bilingual and multicultural courses. Also, multicultural, nonsexist materials are now on the market for teachers to use in exploring with young children the diverse cultures that make up our country.

Unfortunately, space does not permit us to discuss each cultural group that inhabits our fifty states. As we researched, we soon discovered we could not generalize about any one ethnic group, as there appear to be many subgroups. Also, each cultural group has members who may be termed liberals, moderates, and conservatives. All these groups are seeking to preserve and practice their individual beliefs with differing emphasis on traditions. Further modification occurs as each succeeding generation adapts the cultural traditions to suit themselves and the ever-changing times in which they live. All these factors make it difficult to describe a single set of values or a uniform method of celebrating a special event.

As a small beginning, we wish to share some guidelines for becoming more sensitive and more culturally aware.

1. Every teacher should recognize and accept the fact that each child and each family has a cultural heritage and unique way of life. The individual family's mode of living has been shaped not only by its culture, but by its religious beliefs, education, economic circumstances, geographic location, experiences, and interpersonal relationships. Teachers should recognize that families from minority cultures are not necessarily "deficient" or "deprived." To deny or downgrade a family's culture or life style may damage a child's self-image and result in an individual with "no culture" because he or she is not happily a member of either the minority group or the mainstream group.

2. A handicapped child or one of a different culture in your class should be a matter for celebration rather than despair. The enlightened staff has the perfect opportunity to demonstrate its teaching skills and to enrich the lives of those in the class in a manner that would not be possible without that child or children.

3. The staff should not make generalizations about various ethnic groups or types of handicaps as "unteachable." They should educate themselves to a knowledgeable level about each culture, as needed, so that they can help every child develop his or her potential to the fullest. Staff meetings and in-service training should be planned to increase cultural understanding and improve teaching skills. Capitalize on opportunities to meet and make friends with others from another culture. You will be less likely to make quick judgments and broad generalizations. Ask questions, read (see Books and Periodicals, p. 111), and discuss. Avoid isolating yourself from life and the world as it really is by being concerned only with your small segment of it. "Different" can mean "unique and special" rather than "strange and threatening." It can be an exciting and rewarding adventure.

4. Staff attitudes toward those with handicaps or cultural differences will influence the attitudes of the other children. Examine your attitudes, prejudices, and behavior toward others who are "different" as honestly as you can. Try to be understanding. Ask yourself how things might look from the parents' or child's point of view. How might they feel? Why?

5. Call or refer to everyone by his or her given name, using full title for adults unless given permission to be more informal. Never call attention to an Indian child's heritage or race by calling the child "Little Chief," "Little Squaw," or "Little Brave." It is best not to insist that these children tell you their Indian names. It is wiser to let them share this information with you if the family approves and the child is willing. Otherwise it may be considered prying. "Chief," "squaw," "brave," and "papoose" are not Indian words. They are words used by non-Indians, often inappropriately.

6. First or second generation American families are often referred to by terms reflecting the country from which they come, such as Afro-American or Mexican-American. Sometimes families are identified by the larger geographic area from which they come, such as European, Asian (not Oriental), or Middle Easterner.

7. Most members of one race tend to think the members of another race "all look alike" when in fact there are many skin color variations from light to dark in each of the so-called white, yellow, red, brown, and black races. It is best to stress similarities in coloring and to describe children's skin tones with positive words like "peachy cream," "toasty tan," or "chocolate brown." There are also variations in eye and hair color and hair style within these races, making racial descriptions very difficult. Many Asians

resent the reference to being slant-eyed, preferring that their eyes be called almond-shaped.

8. Most Americans, regardless of culture, wear street clothes currently in style in this country, reserving their more traditional garments for special ceremonies and celebrations or home use. American Indians today do not wear the often-depicted buckskin clothes and feather headwear for daily living. Japanese-Americans do not always wear silk kimonos, and Chinese pant suits should not be termed pajamas as they are *not* sleepwear. If children refer to an illustration using this term, please note its inaccuracy. Mexican-Americans seldom wear sombreros and serapes except at fiestas. However, variations of the Mexican pancho and serape are popular in some parts of the country. Eskimos wear fur-lined parkas and mukluks in the coldest weather.

9. Most Americans live in wood, brick, or stone houses of one or more rooms. Some American Indians live on reservations but, except for pow-wows, they seldom live in tents or tepees as permanent dwellings. Some still live in hogans, chickees, and adobes. Eskimos once called their dome-shaped homes igloos, but only the temporary ones used while hunting were made of snow. Their winter igloos were made of stone or wood and their summer homes were tents. Many Eskimos today live in houses in villages.

10. Most peoples of the world eat foods readily available in their native country, but they can and do supplement these with imported products as needed. It is interesting to note that over 50 percent of the world's population eat rice as a main staple.

11. If you have Indians or Mexican-Americans in your class, remember they feel severely admonished or disciplined when embarrassed or shamed and therefore may not wish to participate until they have observed the situation long enough to feel confident that they can succeed. Any kind of coercion may make them bewildered, afraid, or disgusted. Further, many have been taught to show respect for adults and others who are occupied in activities and conversation and may hold back or wait so as not to intrude. You may need to assist them in entering an activity or be alert to their coming to you for a need. Indians and Mexican-Americans are taught to lower their eyes when spoken to. It is a sign of respect, not rudeness or disinterest.

12. Many Chinese-Americans still have a great respect for tradition and for their elders. Children are taught gentleness, patience, and humility. Adults are skilled in interpersonal relationships because they are taught to work around the issue, not offending, but gently and politely coming to the point in a tactful manner. Therefore, they find it difficult to excuse or accept the opposite qualities of boastfulness, impatience, and aggressiveness so common to mainstream Americans.

13. The migration of the Afro-American to America from Africa differed from other immigrants in that they were brought here in bondage, as slaves, while most people came by choice. Not only were Afro-Americans separated from their homeland and relatives, but, unlike other immigrants, their smaller family units were repeatedly broken up by many of their white owners until after the Civil War. This separation of man and wife, parents and children, made a preservation of their culture and heritage, their pursuit of independent identity, and opportunities for solidarity extremely difficult.

Black leaders emerged in the 1960s advocating racial equality. Some, like Martin Luther King, preferred to accomplish this through peaceful means, such as freedom marches and sit-ins, while others like the Black Muslims and the Black Panthers advocated Black Power through more direct confrontations.

The 1970s have found Afro-Americans continuing to collect the essence of their culture dating back to their African ancestors. Black educators are developing Ebonics, a language form that reflects the verbal and nonverbal skills of the West African, Caribbean, and United States descendants of African ancestors. These movements have resulted in an awareness by other ethnic groups of the contributions of Afro-Americans to America and have developed a pride in being Black. This improved self-image has also made possible greater unity among members of this ethnic group.

Today, through Head Start, special job training, and scholarships, young minority members (including many Afro-Americans) are being assisted in their pursuit of independence, identity, and leadership.

14. When non-English speaking children are enrolled, a competent, trained staff member who is able to communicate with these children should be available on a full-time basis. This person may speak a pure form of the language but must be willing to accept the various dialects of the families as authentic forms of communication. A child's first language should be respected and used, as necessary, while a second language is being taught. Neither language is right or wrong, each is unique. If the first language escapes a negative label, the child will learn to use each in its appropriate place and will become truly bilingual.

15. Each culture has many individuals who have made outstanding contributions to America, and each culture has traditional foods, dances, songs, games, art objects, ceremonial dress, and celebrations that can be appreciated by most young children. We have included some of these in the Season guides and Holidays and Family Celebrations. We realize this is only a beginning, and that there are many local celebrations and customs that can, and should, be included in your program. Enlist the help of local resource people and of parents as you plan your program. Every family has skills, hobbies, household articles, toys, picture books, instruments, and art objects that can be shared in some meaningful way with encouragement from an imaginative and understanding staff.

16. When children from other cultures are sharing with their classmates, avoid embarrassing them or making them feel uncomfortable. Do not expect very young children to teach the others but allow them to share when they are ready to do so. They are anxious to be part of the group and not to be isolated. They cannot be expected to know all the history of their ancestry any more than any other child of their age. It might be wise to ask yourself "What could I share about my heritage as a child?" Why then expect a member of another culture to be more informed or aware?

17. Be alert to prejudice being shown by children or their parents in car pools, on playgrounds, or at parent meetings. Give assistance and be supportive whenever possible. Focus on ways to deal with misunderstanding or ignorance. Whenever you can, disprove stereotypes and help others to do the same.
    a. Note contributions of Americans from every ethnic group.
    b. Prove that all members of another group do not look alike by examining variations within your own group.
    c. Focus on the need for equal opportunities for education and career training.

18. Try not to make misrepresentations of a culture by careless use of a phrase, a story, a song, or a joke. Guard against subtle ridicule of a group's or a class's self-image by using a garbled imitation of the language, dress, customs, gestures, or mannerisms. In a quote, always use actual words and correct pronunciation.

19. Being informed will help you to take advantage of the teachable moment. If an illustration in a storybook or painting is inaccurate, you will be able to discuss why. Offer a photograph or illustration that will portray the same object or individual more accurately.

20. Many new multicultural materials are now available. Some are very good and will be helpful; others are reactionary or inaccurate. Be selective. Good multicultural materials should meet these criteria:
    a. accurate content
    b. cultural relevancy and significance to the child
    c. if portraying the present, accurate in its representations of current attitudes and customs
    d. if portraying the past, historically accurate
    e. easily understood and interrelated with the curriculum and reflecting multicultural aspects

Space does not permit a detailed list of terms to avoid and common misconceptions. By giving you such a list we might actually be doing you a disservice in that awareness begins with your discovery and no one else can instantly sensitize you. We hope that you will be challenged to make your teaching of young children one that is truly a "small world" of living and learning, and one that will have meaning for all the families you are privileged to work with.

Methods Most Adaptable for Introducing This Subject to Children

- Introduce children and teachers to each other when they enter school. Encourage children to call each other by their first names.
- The children should wear name tags until the teacher is familiar with each child's name and then names should be used frequently.
- Names of children should be placed near coat hooks (or in cubbies) with a special picture to help children identify their things. (Names should be lettered clearly on art work but in the upper left-hand corner for left to right orientation.)
- Child may bring a special possession from home to share with the group.
- Daily health inspection provides opportunity for learning about body parts and general health care.
- Tape record children's voices or a conversation. Play it back and have the children guess who is speaking.
- Take pictures of the children and post them with their names on each.
- Use full-length or hand mirrors to help children build a positive self-image.
- Play a game or sing a song that includes everyone's name.

Vocabulary

learn	us	home	doctor
easy	they	friend	dentist
hard	his	cavity	nurse
play	hers	sick	beautician
work	ours	well	barber
help	you	healthy	examination
share	yours	checkup	neighborhood
like/love	theirs	shots	names of family members
feelings	them	wash	names of classmates
I	avenue	clean	names of ethnic groups
me	street	brush	colors of skin, hair, eyes
mine	country	dirty	names of body parts
myself	city	haircut	names for body actions
we	house	care for	names for celebrations

learning centers

Discovery Center

1. Introduce a full-length mirror or small metal hand mirrors to use to explore individual characteristics, such as eyes, skin, clothing, and hair.
2. Use a magnifying glass to explore skin, fingers, and hair.
3. Use a tape recorder to identify voice characteristics and to allow children to listen to themselves.
4. Weigh and measure children at the beginning of and regularly during the year to be aware of individual growth changes. Compare growth against the child's own previous record, not another's.
5. Take Polaroid camera pictures of the children to use in the classroom or as gifts for the parents.
6. Make hand or footprints. Compare and note differences. Notice that no two are alike. Only you can make that print. Comment about the use of footprints for identification of newborn infants, if this is done in your area.
7. Make a silhouette of each child using a flashlight to throw a shadow and tracing around the shadow. This is generally done by the teacher. Children can identify silhouettes.
8. Use a labeling machine that presses an impression on colored tape to make each child's name. You may use them in some special way.
9. With older children who live within a one-half mile radius of the school or in a small town, post a map of the city or hand draw a simplified version. Put a map pin on the street where each child lives. Around the map put pictures of the children and/or their

houses with the address printed underneath. Run yarn from the map pin to the picture. Add a picture of the school and other places the children visit throughout the year. Talk about who lives the closest (farthest) from the school, the fire station, the grocery store, and so on.

10. Prepare a display of various materials used for identification: ID. cards from a university, plant, armed forces; birth certificates, ID. bracelets, name labels in clothing, name tags, library cards, license plates, driver's license, credit cards, office name plate, monograms, personalized clothing, jewelry, pencils. Choose those most appropriate to your group. Allow children to examine these and help identify the ones they know. Discuss their uses.

Dramatic Play Centers

Home-Living Center

1. Offer a wide variety of men's and women's dress up clothes and a full-length mirror. Invite those interested to select a suitable style or color. This will help children with awareness of self, encourage them to enact home experiences, and to understand various roles of family members. (See Home-Living Center in the Families at Home guide.)
2. The addition of boy and girl dolls, dolls showing different ethnic groups with authentic features, brother and sister dolls, and drink-wet dolls gives children many concept possibilities about the self.

   CAUTION: Avoid commercial dolls where only skin color is changed. (See Commercially made games.)

Block-Building Center

1. Label with a sign any buildings made by the children, such as "Pete's Garage."
2. Take a Polaroid snapshot of a child's block building. Pin up on an adjacent wall and share with parents.
3. Add wooden, rubber, or flexible plastic people. Make an open-top play house with unit blocks.

Other Dramatic Play Centers

1. Play doctor and nurse: see patterns, p. 23. Add a stethoscope for exploring heartbeats. Encourage everyone to go for a "checkup" at the doctor's office.
2. Set up a barber shop with a chair, mirror, blunt children's scissors (or cardboard ones), hair clippers (remove cord), comb, and a sheet to tie around the neck (or make a barber's cape).
3. Play dentist: encourage everyone to have a dental checkup. Use a small hand mirror to look in mouth and a cloth napkin to put around the neck.
4. Beauty parlor encourages the building of a positive self-image through good grooming. Set out a chair, a plastic cape, cardboard scissors, plastic curlers, plastic bottles, and a mirror.
5. Play shoe store: collect shoe boxes and various kinds of shoes for men, women, and children. Set up chairs and a small stool for the clerk. Provide money, a cash register, and a foot rule or metric stick for measuring feet.
6. Play hat and wig store: set up a table with various kinds of hats and wigs. Provide a mirror and a hand mirror, a cash register, and hat boxes or paper bags.

   CAUTION: Use only plastic or washable hats and wigs for sanitary reasons.

7. Family puppets may encourage self-concepts with older children.
8. Clothing store: set up racks with a variety of men's and women's clothes. Provide a mirror, a cash register, paper bags, and clothing boxes. (Childcraft has a 3-way mirror.)
9. Department store: set up a shoe department, a hat bar, and a clothing department near each other (see 5, 6, and 8).
10. Set up a Valentine (gift) shop that sells valentines, candy (empty boxes), flowers, handkerchiefs, scarves, jewelry, and other items.
11. Sending get-well cards, Valentine's, Mother's, or Father's Day cards may lead to an interest in the post office. (See Road Transportation guide.)

Learning, Language, and Readiness Materials Center

Commercially made games and materials for use at a table or on a mat:

(See Basic Resources, p. 79, for manufacturers' addresses.)

1. Judy See-Quees: Brushing Teeth, Combing Hair, Baking a Cake, and Sliding, 4 pcs. each; Johnny Growing, Helping Mother, 6 pcs. each; A Child's Day, Building a Playhouse, Birthday Party, 12 pcs. each
2. Judy Family and Community Story Sets with teacher's guide
3. Flexible Mirror (Creative Playthings)
4. Shindana Dolls: authentic black dolls
5. Block Play People: black and white (most catalogs)
6. Fisher Price dolls: Natalie, Jenny, Audrey, Mary, Elizabeth, Joey, and baby Ann
7. Juan and Juanita: Mexican-American dolls
8. Flexible Doll Family: black and white
9. See Sex Puzzles (ABC School Supply)
10. Dressing-Undressing Puzzle (Childcraft)
11. Community Puppets: black and white (Childcraft)
12. InterPhone/The Big Line (Childcraft)
13. Drink-Wet Dolls (Constructive Playthings)
14. Just Imagine: Mini-Poster cards (Trend Enterprises)
15. Understanding Our Feelings: 28 picture photographs (Constructive Playthings)
16. My Face and Body (Instructo Flannelboard Aids)
17. Montessori Self-Help Frames (ETA and ABC School Supply)
18. ETA Best Vests: for learning dressing skills
19. Safety Everyday: mini-poster cards (Trend Enterprises)
20. Health and Safety (Instructo Flannelboard Aids)
21. Vinyl Dolls/Ethnic Dolls (ABC School Supply)
22. Lace Boot (Playskool)
23. People in the Neighborhood: Safety/Health Helpers (The Child's World)
24. Health and Personal Care: picture fold-outs (The Child's World)
25. Many Face Dolls (Uniworld Toys)
26. Color 'N Dress Dolls (Uniworld Toys)
27. Human Body Parts Flannel Aid (Milton Bradley)
28. The Family Flannel Aid (Milton Bradley)
29. The Anything Muppet (Child Guidance)
30. Tri-Lang: card game in English, Spanish, and French (Aurora Products Corp.)
31. Heritage Dolls: Indian toddler dolls (Sunbell Corp.)

Teacher-made games and materials for use at a table or on a mat:

NOTE: For detailed description of Games, see pp. 50–59.

1. Name It: use Polaroid pictures of the children.
2. Play Name It, Look and See, Reach and Feel with:
    a. nail file, comb, toothbrush, and hand mirror
    b. things we wear on our hands, such as rings, gloves, and mittens
    c. headwear: scarf, hat, helmet, bathing cap, and beret
    d. footgear: boots, rubbers, slippers, sandals, and shoes
    e. brushes that help us keep clean: nailbrush, toothbrush, bath brush, hairbrush, shoe brush, and clothes brush
    f. models of family members
    g. stethoscope, dentist's mirror, thermometer, eye chart
3. Match-Them: use pairs of socks, pairs of mittens, or pairs of shoes.
4. Alike, Different, and the Same: use items in no. 3.
5. Grouping and Sorting by Association: things we wear on our head, feet, and hands
6. Which?:
    a. have a pair of shoes for a man, woman, child, and baby. Ask which pair is worn by a baby? A man? A woman? A child? Ask which is heaviest? Lightest? Biggest? Smallest? Has the highest heel? Is brown? and so on
    b. use pictures of hands doing things, such as handshaking, waving good-by, clapping, praying, holding something, and washing

By their choice of different art activities, these children reflect their individuality. Each represents a particular racial background; each chooses to use different skills; one is left-handed; each is totally absorbed in his or her activity. Yet all are sharing the same table with one another.

c. use pictures of children doing things, such as getting a haircut, putting on shoes, brushing teeth, getting a checkup, or running, swimming, climbing, and swinging

7. Guess Who?: I'm thinking of someone who is wearing . . . describe child.
8. Listening: see Identification games in Basic Resources.
9. Who's Missing?: see Identification games in Basic Resources.
10. How Can I? or How Can You?: see Problem-Solving games in Basic Resources.
11. Find Your Name: prepare a name card with each child's first name (you may add last name later in year). Call each child's name and ask him or her to find his or her card. Clap when child chooses correctly.
12. Can You Remember?: see Identification games in Basic Resources.
13. Let's Tell a Story: see Language games in Basic Resources.
14. Boy or girl faces: make flannel faces with interchangeable parts for eyes, nose, mouth, depicting various feelings and skin tones. Use *natural* skin tones, not pink and white.
15. Paper dolls mounted on flannel representing various family members to use with Identification games or story telling. Provide a variety of clothes so the children may dress the dolls as they wish. Pattern books are a good source of multi-ethnic figures.
16. Make your own self-help frames or learning vests. Include zippers, buttons, lacings, snaps, and hooks for openings. Some may be made on pockets.

Art Center

*** 1. Paint and draw pictures of self, family, and friends (teacher must be sure to accept child's picture, not prod for more finished work that may be developmentally beyond child).
*** 2. In late part of year or with older children, have them lie on the floor and trace around them on wrapping paper. Children can *paint* figure to correspond with clothing they are wearing. Teacher can cut out figures after they are painted and display them on classroom walls. Have different skin tone paints mixed for children to choose or allow children to mix colors to match what they need.
* 3. Fingerpaint activity can end with each child making a handprint on a separate piece of paper. This helps use up excess fingerpaint before they go to wash and also gives them a concept of their own hand size. They can make fingerprints on paper and will notice that each person's are different. The teacher can use stamp pad ink for this as well as fingerpaint. **Variation:** Footprints can also be made.
* 4. Handprints made of clay dough or plaster of paris can be used as gifts for parents.
*** 5. Clay people can be made by older children. Natural clay soil in some areas is excellent and can be baked in a kiln if desired. The lump method of pulling features out of a ball of clay is more successful for baking. Pieces pulled out are less likely to break off than those put on as appendages.
* 6. A class mural can be made by putting a roll of newsprint on the floor and having each child add to the group effort by choosing the media he or she prefers, for example, paints, crayons, chalk, or charcoal. If some children choose to work with dough or clay, their creations can be displayed in a kiosk (see p. 75) or on a low shelf below the mural.
* 7. "Imagination" paper: (see p. 31 for description of materials needed and method for introducing) offer a variety of paper in all shapes, sizes, and colors. (Print scraps are excellent.) Circles, ovals, triangles, and long narrow strips make interesting pictures.
** 8. Finish the picture: paste small irregular shapes of colored paper to a piece of paper. Let children choose one that suggests an idea to them. Curved or wavy lines, dots and squares may also be penned on with a magic marker.

Other Experiences in This Center Using Art Media

*** 1. Papier-mâché puppets: make family puppets using papier-mâché. When dry, paint using skin tone paints. Collage and fabric scraps can be used for "clothes."

*** 2. Sack puppets: paint sacks with skin tones using paints or crayons. Put on facial features with paint, crayons, yarn, or collage trims.

NOTE: Throughout the year display *each* child's creative efforts frequently. Let each child select which one he or she would like to have displayed. Group a variety of media together focusing on individuality and avoiding unfair comparisons and competition. Change frequently. Use hallways, stairwalls, bulletin boards, and classroom walls for flatwork and kiosks or low shelves for sculpture and other three-dimensional pieces.

Book Center

* Adoff, Arnold. *Black Is Brown Is Tan.* New York: Harper & Row, 1973.

**** Aliki, Diogenes. *A Weed Is a Flower: The Life of George Washington Carver.* Englewood Cliffs, N.J.: Prentice-Hall, 1965 (read-tell).

** ———. *My Hands.* New York: Thomas Y. Crowell, 1962.

* Anglund, Joan. *A Friend Is Someone Who Likes You.* New York: Harcourt Brace Jovanovich, 1966.

*** ———. *Love Is a Special Way of Feeling.* New York: Harcourt Brace Jovanovich, 1960.

** ———. *What Color Is Love.* New York: Harcourt Brace Jovanovich, 1958.

* Baer, Edith. *The Wonder of Hands.* New York: Parents' Magazine Press, 1970.

** Bayer, Terry. *I Have Feelings.* New York: Behavorial Publications, 1971.

*** Bond, Jean Carey. *A Is for Africa.* New York: Franklin Watts, 1969.

* Brenner, Barbara. *Bodies.* New York: E. P. Dutton, 1973.

* ———. *Faces.* New York: E. P. Dutton, 1970.

* Brown, Margaret Wise. *The Important Book.* New York: Harper & Row, 1949.

**** Brown, Myra Berry. *Sandy Signs His Name.* New York: Franklin Watts, 1967 (read-tell).

*** Bryant, Bernice. *Let's Be Friends.* New York: Childrens Press, 1954.

** Caines, Jeanette. *Abby.* New York: Harper & Row, 1973.

**** Carlson, Bernice. *Let's Pretend It Happened to You.* New York: Four Winds Press, 1974 (read-tell).

** Clark, Ann Nolan. *In My Mother's House.* New York: Viking Press, 1941.

** Clifton, Lucille. *Don't You Remember?* New York: E. P. Dutton, 1973.

* Clure, Beth and Helen Rumsey. Bowmar Manipulative Books (set of eight) *How Does It Feel?, Me!, Things I Like to Do, Through the Day.* Glendale, Calif.: Bowmar Publishing, 1968.

*** de Paola, Tomie. *Andy (That's My Name).* Englewood Cliffs, N.J.: Prentice-Hall, 1973.

* Ets, Marie H. *Just Me.* New York: Viking Press, 1965 (paper).

** ———. *Talking Without Words (I Can, Can You?).* New York: Viking Press, 1968.

**** Evans, Eva. *All About Us.* New York: Western Publishing, 1947 (paper).

*** Feelings, Muriel. *Jambo Means Hello: Swahili Alphabet Book.* New York: Dial Press, 1974.

* Flack, Marjorie. *Ask Mr. Bear.* New York: Macmillan, 1932 (paper, 1971).

*** ———. *The Story about Ping.* New York: Viking Press, 1970 (paper).

* Freeman, Don. *Dandelion.* New York: Viking Press, 1964 (filmstrip/record).

** Fritz, Jean. *Growing Up.* Eau Claire, Wis.: E. M. Hale, 1956.

** Fujikawa, Gyo. *A Child's Book of Poems.* New York: Grosset & Dunlap, 1972.
* ———. *Let's Play.* Canada/Japan: Zokeisha Publications Ltd., 1975.
* ———. *Puppies, Pussy Cats, and Other Friends.* Canada/Japan: Zokeisha Publications, Ltd., 1975.
* ———. *Sleepy Time.* Canada/Japan: Zokeisha Publications, Ltd., 1975.
* Gay, Zhenya. *What's Your Name?* New York: Viking Press, 1955.
* Green, Mary McBurney. *Is It Hard? Is It Easy?* Reading, Mass.: Addison-Wesley, 1960.
** Grifalconi, Ann. *City Rhythms.* Indianapolis, Ind.: Bobbs-Merrill, 1965.
*** Grossman, Barney and Gladys Groom. *Black Means . . .* New York: Hill & Wang, 1970.
** Kafka, Sherry. *Big Enough.* New York: Putnam, 1970.
*** Keats, Ezra Jack. *Goggles.* New York: Macmillan, 1969 (paper, 1971).
*** ———. *Jennie's Hat.* New York: Harper & Row, 1966.
** ———. *Peter's Chair.* New York: Harper & Row, 1967.
** ———. *Whistle for Willie.* New York: Viking Press, 1964 (paper, 1969).
** Klein, Norma. *Girls Can Be Anything.* New York: E. P. Dutton, 1973.
* Krasilovsky, Phyllis. *The Girl Who Was a Cowboy.* Garden City, N.Y.: Doubleday, 1965.
** Krauss, Ruth. *A Very Special House.* New York: Harper & Row, 1953.
** ———. *The Growing Story.* New York: Harper & Row, 1947.
*** Lasker, Joe. *He's My Brother.* Chicago, Ill.: Albert Whitman, 1974.
** Leaf, Munro. *Who Cares? I Do.* Philadelphia, Pa.: J. B. Lippincott, 1971.
* Lenski, Lois. *Big Little Davy.* New York: Walck, 1956.
** ———. *Debbie Herself.* New York: Walck, 1969.
** ———. *Debbie Goes to Nursery School.* New York: Walck, 1970.
* ———. *Let's Play House.* New York: Walck, 1944.
*** Levy, Elizabeth. *Nice Little Girls.* New York: Delacorte Press, 1974.
** Lexau, Joan M. *Benjie.* New York: Dial Press, 1964.
** ———. *Maria.* Eau Claire, Wis.: E. M. Hale, 1967.
*** Mao-chiu, Chang. *The Little Doctor.* Peking: Foreign Language Press, 1965.
** Mayers, Patrick. *Just One More Block.* Chicago, Ill.: Albert Whitman, 1970.
*** McGovern, Ann. *Black Is Beautiful.* New York: Four Winds, 1969.
*** Miriam, Eve. *Boys and Girls, Girls and Boys.* New York: Holt, Rinehart & Winston, 1972.
*** Molarsky, Osmond. *Right Thumb, Left Thumb.* Reading, Mass.: Addison-Wesley, 1969.
*** Ness, Evaline. *Josefina February.* New York: Scribner's, 1963.
*** Ormsby, Virginia H. *Twenty-One Children Plus Ten.* Philadelphia, Pa.: J. B. Lippincott, 1971.
*** Rand, Ann. *I Know a Lot of Things.* New York: Harcourt Brace Jovanovich, 1956.
*** Sargent, Jessie. *Kids of Colombia.* Reading, Mass.: Addison-Wesley, 1974.
** Scarry, Richard. *Nicky Goes to the Doctor.* New York: Western Publishing, 1972.
** Schneider, N. *While Suzie Sleeps.* Reading, Mass.: Addison-Wesley, 1948.
** Scott, Ann Herbert. *On Mother's Lap.* New York: McGraw-Hill, 1972.
*** ———. *Sam.* New York: McGraw-Hill, 1967.
*** Shay, Arthur. *What Happens When You Go to the Hospital.* Chicago, Ill.: Reilly & Lee, 1969.
** Slobodkin, L. *Excuse Me! Certainly!* New York: Vanguard Press, 1959.
*** ———. *Magic Michael.* New York: Macmillan, 1973 (paper).
** ———. *Thank You, You're Welcome.* New York: Vanguard Press, 1957.
*** Sonneborn, Ruth A. *Friday Night Is Papa Night.* New York: Viking Press, 1970.
*** Stein, Sarah B. *Making Babies.* New York: Walker and Company, 1974.
** Tucker, David. *Something Special.* New York: Grosset & Dunlap, 1970.
** Wells, Rosemary. *Noisy Nora.* New York: Dial Press, 1973.
** Wilson, Julia. *Beckky.* New York: Thomas Y. Crowell, 1966.

** Wondriska, William. *The Stop.* New York: Holt, Rinehart & Winston, 1972.
 * Woodard, Carol. *It's Nice to Have a Special Friend.* Philadelphia, Pa.: Fortress Press, 1970.
** Yi, Yang and Ko Liang. *I Am on Duty Today.* Peking: Foreign Language Press, 1969.
** Zolotow, Charlotte. *William's Doll.* New York: Harper & Row, 1972.

planning for grouptime

NOTE: All music, fingerplays, poems, stories, and games listed here may be used at other times during the session as appropriate. See Core Library, Basic Resources, p. 76, for publishers and addresses. Addresses for sources of records will be found on p. 81. In parodies, hyphenated words match music notes of the tune used.

Music

Songs

GUESS WHAT I SEE?
   (tune: "I'm a Little Teapot," first 2 lines)
   Adapted by JoAnne Deal Hicks

Children take turns holding the mirror and tell others what they want sung.

Verse 1:

   Looking in a mir-ror, guess what I see?

   A _____, _____ face that belongs to me!
       (round, oval,   (brown, white, pink, tan,
       square, heart-   black if suggested by child
       shaped)   following a discussion
                                    on skin color)

Verse 2:

   Looking in a mir-ror, guess what I see?

   _____, _____ eyes that belong to me!
   (big, light, bright,   (blue, brown, green,
   round, dark)   black, gray)

Verse 3:

   Looking in a mir-ror, guess what I see?

   _____, _____ hair that belongs to me!
   (curly, long,   (blonde, black,
   straight, short)   red, brown)

Verse 4:

When I stand in sunshine, guess what I see?

A _____ black shadow that belongs to me!
  (long, short,
  depends on time of day)

Verse 5:

When I look in wa-ter, guess what I see?

A wig-gling face that belongs to me!

NOTE: Be sensitive to children's need to choose the descriptive words they like best to be sung for self-concept.

MY SPECIAL FRIEND (a parody)
  (tune: "Hi Ho—Hi Ho," the work song from *Snow White*)
  Adaptation by JoAnne Deal Hicks

My spe-cial friend, my ver-y spe-cial friend,
He (she) likes to run and play with me, I love my ver-y spe-cial friend.
He (she) has a ver-y spe-cial drum   (TEACHER SHOWS CHILDREN A TOM-TOM)
And has some silver jewel-ry, too.
I love my friend!

My spe-cial friend, my ver-y spe-cial friend,
He (she) likes to run and play with me, I love my ver-y spe-cial friend.
He (she) has a lit-tle wood-en bowl   (TEACHER SHOWS BOWL AND CHOPSTICKS)
And has a spe-cial way to eat.   (PRETEND TO EAT WITH CHOPSTICKS)
I love my friend!

My spe-cial friend, my ver-y spe-cial friend,
He (she) likes to run and play with me, I love my ver-y spe-cial friend.
He (she) has a differ-ent way to speak,
A differ-ent lan-guage all his (her) own.
I love my friend!

My spe-cial friend, my ver-y spe-cial friend,
He (she) likes to run and play with me, I love my ver-y spe-cial friend.
He (she) has a ver-y spe-cial name,
A spe-cial voice, a spe-cial face.
I love my friend!

NOTE: The parody above includes Indian, Asian, non-English-speaking children.

LOVE SOMEBODY, YES I DO

Love somebody, yes I do
Love somebody, yes I do
Love somebody, yes I do
Love somebody, but I won't tell who!

Love somebody, yes I do
Love somebody, yes I do
Love somebody, yes I do
And I hope somebody loves me too!

WILL YOU BE A FRIEND OF MINE?
  (tune: "Merrily We Roll Along")

Will you be a friend of mine,
Friend of mine, friend of mine,
Will you be a friend of mine,
And play a game with me?
(*or* And send a val-en-tine?)

Yes, I'll be a friend of yours,
Friend of yours, friend of yours,
Yes, I'll be a friend of yours
And play a game with you!
(*or* And send a val-en-tine!)

FROM *Songs for the Nursery School*, MacCarteney
  * "Activities for Two Year Olds," pp. 1–4
  * "Finger Plays," pp. 8–9
 ** "This Old Man," p. 83
*** "Resting Time," p. 91
  * "See How I'm Jumping," p. 95
 ** "Around We Go," p. 97
  * "Here I Go a Tiptoe," p. 102
*** "The Barber," p. 112
*** "I'm Skipping," p. 115

FROM *Music Resource Book*, Lutheran Church Press
  * "Sing Me Your Name," p. 8
  * "Do You Know This Friend of Mine," p. 9
  * "Here We Are Together," p. 10
  * "Sometimes I'm Very, Very Small," p. 52
 ** "Your Toes, Your Knees," p. 56
  * "Growing Up," p. 64
  * "John Has a Birthday," p. 65 (substitute name of child having birthday)
 ** "I Can," p. 68
 ** "I Helped My Daddy," p. 69
  * "Muffin Man," p. 90

FROM *Music Activities for Retarded Children*, Ginglend and Stiles
  * "Greeting Song," p. 49
 ** "If You're Happy," p. 62
  * "I Take My Little Hands," p. 63
 ** "Valentines," p. 73
  * "Pointing," p. 89

FROM *Songs for Early Childhood*, Westminster Press
 * "Love to You," p. 78
 * "Let's Make a Valentine," p. 78

FROM *Sing, Children, Sing* edited by Carl S. Miller (UNICEF, 1972). Songs, dances, and singing games of many lands and people. Choose those suitable to current interests and level of group.

Records

"Drummer Boy"/**"Let's Play Together"**/"I Wish I Were" (Young People's Record [YPR], 33⅓ RPM)

"Every Day We Grow 1-0"/"Big Rock Candy Mountain" (YPR, 33⅓ RPM)

"Me, Myself, and I"/**"My Playful Scarf"**/**"Nothing To Do"** (YPR, 33⅓ RPM)

"My Friend"/**"A Visit to My Little Friend"**/"Creepy the Crawly Caterpillar"/"Merry Toy Shop" (YPR, 33⅓ RPM)

"Sing Along"/**"Another Sing Along"**/**"Let's All Join In"** (YPR, 33⅓ RPM)

FROM *Folkways Records* (all 33⅓ RPM)
"Afrikkans Folk Songs for Children"
"Israeli Children's Songs"
"Negro Poetry for Young Children"
"Yiddish Folk Songs for Children"
"Indian Music of the Southwest"
"American Folk Songs"
"French Children's Songs"
"Negro Folk Songs"
"German Children's Folk Songs"
"Songs to Grow On"

NOTE: Any rhythm activity record you have that features development of large muscles could be used. Also any songs featuring self-concepts in record collections you already own should be used.

Rhythms and Singing Games

Body exercise songs: touch body parts as you sing. With the older children you may add other verses using other parts of the body.

(tune: "Oats, Peas, Beans")

Heads and shoulders, knees and toes
Heads and shoulders, knees and toes
Heads and shoulders, knees and toes
Let's point to them together.

(tune: "Mulberry Bush")

My head, my shoulders, my knees, my toes
My head, my shoulders, my knees, my toes
My head, my shoulders, my knees, my toes
Then we stand together.

GOOD GROOMING
(tune: "Mulberry Bush")

"This is the way we wash our face . . ."
"This is the way we put on our clothes . . ."
"This is the way we brush our teeth . . ."

Rhythms in names: when children have had some rhythm experience beat out a rhythm pattern chanting the children's names to it, for example, 1-2-3 for Tom-my Smith and 1-2-3-4 for Pedro Gar-za. Later in the year, beat out the rhythm and have children guess each person's name in the class that would fit the pattern.

The Twist: Encourage children to respond to rhythmic music in their own individual way. When space is limited, provide each with a small piece of carpet a foot square. Place on a smooth floor, nap side down. Each child may move, twist, sway anyway he or she chooses as long as his or her feet remain on the square of carpet. Children become quite skillful as they twist on the carpet. Use music with a fast beat.

FROM *Music Resource Book*, Lutheran Church Press
** "Friend o' Friend," p. 44
 * "Looby-Loo," p. 83
 * "Mulberry Bush," p. 92

FROM *Wake Up and Sing*, Landeck and Crook
** "Pick It Up," p. 18
** "Dip and Fall Back Low," p. 52

FROM *Music Activities for Retarded Children*, Gingland and Stiles
** "Ha, Ha, This-A-Way," p. 56

FROM *Creative Movements for the Developing Child*, Cherry
"Whole Body Movement," pp. 46–50
"Hand Movements," pp. 76–79
"Body Movements," p. 80

FROM *Songs for the Nursery School*, MacCarteney
 * "See How I'm Jumping," p. 95
 * "Follow Me," p. 96
** "Around We Go," p. 97
 * "Here I Go Tiptoe," p. 102
 * "Jack Jump Over the Candlestick," p. 102 (Substitute name of each child as he or she in turn jumps over the candlestick. See illustration, p. 71.)
*** "The Barber," p. 112
*** "I'm Skipping," p. 115

Fingerplays and Poems

TEN LITTLE FINGERS

I have ten little fingers   (HOLD UP BOTH HANDS)
And they all belong to ME   (POINT TO SELF)
I can make them do things
Would you like to see?   (POINT TO CHILD)
I can shut them up tight   (MAKE FIST)
I can open them up wide   (OPEN FINGERS)
I can clap them together and make them hide   (CLAP, THEN HIDE)
I can jump them up high, I can jump them down low   (OVER HEAD AND DOWN)
And fold them together and hold them just so   (FOLD IN LAP)

THIS LITTLE HAND

This little hand is a good little hand   (HOLD UP ONE HAND)
This little hand is his brother.   (HOLD UP OTHER HAND)
Together, they wash and they wash and they wash   (WASHING HANDS)
One hand washes the other.

WHERE ARE YOUR ———?

Where are your eyes? Show me your eyes—baby's eyes can see.
Where are your eyes? Show me your eyes—shut them quietly.

Where is your nose? Show me your nose—baby's nose can blow.
Where is your nose? Show me your nose—wiggle it just so.

Where is your mouth? Show me your mouth—it can open wide.
Where is your mouth? Show me your mouth—how many teeth inside?

FROM *Rhymes for Fingers and Flannelboards*, Scott and Thompson
"Con Los Manos," p. 44
"A Japanese Game," p. 47
"For My Friends," p. 71
"How Many Valentines," p. 71
"Five Little Valentines," p. 72
"Valentines," p. 72
"Rhymes for Active Times," pp. 108–13
"Rhymes for Quiet Times," pp. 114–17

FROM *Let's Do Fingerplays*, Grayson
"Make a Valentine," p. 99
"Valentine for You," p. 99

FROM *Spin a Soft Black Song*, Nikki Giovanni (New York: Hill & Wang, 1971). Select those suitable to your group.

Stories

(To read, read-tell, or tell. See Book Center for complete list.)

  * *The Important Book*, Brown
  * *Just Me*, Ets
  * *Dandelion*, Freeman
  * *What's Your Name?*, Gay
  * *It's Nice to Have a Special Friend*, Woodard
  * *Ask Mr. Bear*, Flack
 ** *While Suzie Sleeps*, Schneider
 ** *The Stop*, Wondriska
 ** *My Hands*, Aliki
 ** *Just One More Block*, Mayers
*** *Josefina February*, Ness
 ** *The Growing Story*, Krauss
*** *I Know a Lot of Things*, Rand
*** *Magic Michael*, Slobodkin

Games

(See Games, pp. 50–58, and Teacher-Made Games in this guide for directions.)

1. Identification games: Guess Who?; Who's Missing?; Listening; Look and See.
2. Circle games: Looby Loo; Hokey Pokey; Farmer in the Dell; Did You Ever See a Lassie?; Friend, Friend from over the Way.
3. Direction games: Together, Together; Sally Says; Follow the Leader; Directions.

Routine Times

1. All routines: explain to new children the reasons for inspection, resting, eating, hand washing, and teeth brushing. Throughout the year continue to teach the value of these routines.
2. Greeting children: always try to welcome each child individually upon arrival. Special attention should be given to those who have been absent.
3. Inspection: talk about keeping clean, keeping healthy, and help children to learn their body parts. Watch for healing of bruises and scrapes.
4. Children can take turns telling each other's names at snack or mealtime.
5. Children may find their place identified by a name card or place card. You might use this for snack, mealtime, or any activity time.
6. Throughout the year serve foods at snack or mealtime that are enjoyed by various ethnic groups in America and other countries around the world.
7. Handwashing: talk about importance of washing hands after toileting and before eating.
8. When toileting use correct biological terms for body parts and bodily functions, for example, penis, anus, rectum, navel, urinate, eliminate, bowel movement, and feces.

Large Muscle Activities

1. Note special progress and praise accomplishments in any skill, games, or exercises, such as using the balance beam, walking boards, and slide; pumping in a swing, running, hopping, climbing, crawling, and skipping with older children.
2. Encourage the children to try new feats. Compare their progress only against their *own* former efforts.
3. Use gym mats to do somersaults and other tumbling exercises.

Extended Experiences

NOTE: See p. 73 regarding visitors.

1. Invite a Safety Officer to come and show the children about fingerprinting.

   CAUTION: Be sure you have facilities planned so that the children can wash their fingers off after being fingerprinted. You should contact the Safety Officer ahead of time in order to discuss what you think your children will be able to understand.

2. Invite a doctor or dentist to perform any required checkups in the school if adequate space can be provided for the examinations.
3. Invite a dental hygienist to talk to the children about taking care of their teeth and demonstrate the correct method of brushing.
4. Invite a nurse to talk to the children about good health habits and to assist you in weighing and measuring the children. Record height and weight on a measuring chart. Leave up or save until the late spring or summer and measure again. Compare.
5. Invite a physical education teacher or dance instructor to assist the children in learning exercises or simple dance movements.
6. Show *Five Families* filmstrips with cassette. Includes "Chinatown," "Yah A Tat" (India), "Piñata" (Mexican-American), "Circus Family," and "Together" (Afro-American).

7. Select suitable filmstrips from the extensive *Bowmar World Cultures Program*, available with record or cassette.
8. "Children Around the World" filmstrips (Constructive Playthings)
9. A private place could be used by an individual child when:
   a. listening to records or story tapes
   b. looking at books
   c. exploring cognitive or manipulative materials
   d. thinking or resting

   This space can be created:
   a. on a raised platform—add carpet or pillows
   b. in a closet—take off door, provide a light, and a pillow or bean bag chair
   c. in a fiber barrel with top and one side cut away—add a round pillow
   d. in a quiet corner made by partitioning it off with shelves or screen—add carpet, overstuffed chairs with legs removed, or bean bag chairs
10. Show "The Many Faces of Children": filmstrip (DLM).
11. Show "Looking at Me" or "Friendly Faces": filmstrip, record, or cassette (Bowmar).

teacher resources

Books and Periodicals

1. Cooper, Terry Touf and Marilyn Ratner. *Many Hands Cooking: An International Cookbook for Boys and Girls*. New York: Thomas Y. Crowell, 1974 (also available from UNICEF).
2. Costo, Rupert. *Contributions and Achievements of the American Indian*. San Francisco: Indian Historical Press, 1974.
3. DePree, Mildred. *A Child's World of Stamps*. New York: Parents' Magazine Press, 1973 (also available from UNICEF).
4. Harrison, Barbara G. *Unlearning the Lie: Sexism in School*. New York: Liveright Publishing, 1973.
5. Joseph, Joan. *Folk Toys Around the World and How to Make Them*. New York: Parents' Magazine Press, 1972 (also available from UNICEF).
6. Kemps, C. Henry and Ray E. Helfer. *Helping the Battered Child and His Family*. Philadelphia, Pa.: J. B. Lippincott, 1972.
7. Klagsburn, Francine. *Free to Be . . . You and Me*. New York: McGraw-Hill, 1974.
8. Latimer, Bettye. *Starting Out Right: Choosing Books About Black People for Young Children*. Washington, D.C.: Day Care and Child Development Council of America, 1972 (paper).
9. Latourette, Kenneth. *China* and *The Chinese and Their History and Culture* (two volumes in one). New York: Macmillan, 1964 (also paper).
10. Martin, Patricia Miles. *Eskimos: People of Alaska*. New York: Parents' Magazine Press, 1970.
11. Parish, Peggy. *Let's Be Indians*. New York: Harper & Row, 1962. (Some illustrations portray cultural inadequacies.)
12. Pine, Tillie S. *The Africans Knew*. New York: McGraw-Hill, 1967.
13. ———. *The Chinese Knew*. New York: McGraw-Hill, 1964.

14. ———. *The Eskimos Knew*. New York: McGraw-Hill, 1962.
15. ———. *The Polynesians Knew*. New York: McGraw-Hill, 1974.
16. Peters, Margaret. *The Ebony Book of Black Achievement*. Chicago, Ill.: Johnson Publication, 1974.
17. Price, Christine. *Happy Days: Book of Birthdays, Name Days and Growing Days*. New York: U.S. Committee for UNICEF, 1969.
18. Siegel, Richard, Michael Strassfeld, and Sharon Strassfeld. *The Jewish Catalog*. Philadelphia, Pa.: The Jewish Publication Society of America, 1973.
19. Stull, Edith. *The First Book of Alaska*. New York: Franklin Watts, 1965.
20. Yellow Robe, Rose. *An Album of the American Indian*. New York: Franklin Watts, 1969.
21. Young, Ethel. *The Nursery School Program for Culturally Different Children*. Menlo Park, Calif.: Pacific Coast Publishers, 1965 (paper).
22. *American Indian Authors for Young Readers*. New York: Interbook, Inc.
23. *Sioux Indian Dictionary*. Sisseton, S. Dak.: Warcloud Products.
24. *Akwesasnee Notes*. Roosevelt Town, N.Y.: Mohawk Nations (newspaper).
25. *Ebony Junior*. Chicago, Ill.: Johnson Publication.
26. *Interracial Books for Children Bulletin*. New York: Council on Interracial Books for Children, Inc.
27. *Interracial Digest*. New York: Council on Interracial Books for Children, Inc.
28. *The Wee Wish Tree*. San Francisco, Calif.: The American Indian Historical Society (a magazine of Indian America for young people).

Pictures and Displays

(See p. 79 for addresses of firms listed.)

1. Picture packets: "Children Around the World"; "American Indians—Yesterday and Today"; "Living Together in America"; "Mainland China—Today"; "Black America—Yesterday and Today"; "Black America's Struggle for Equal Rights"; "Social Development"; "Children and the Law"; "Safety, Health, and Cleanliness" (David C. Cook).
2. Study prints: "Moods and Emotions"; "Children of America"; "Children Around the World"; "Understanding My Needs"; "Developing My Values"; "Keeping Physically Fit" (The Child's World).
3. Bulletin board displays: "Eat Balanced Meals" and "Keeping Clean and Healthy" (Instructo).
4. Picture-story study prints: "Children Around the World" and "Indians of the United States and Canada" (SVE).
5. Colors of Man Kit: includes "Colors Around Us," 12 study prints with discussion guide on back of each, Teacher's Guide to "Colors," and skin color crayons (Chicago, Ill.: Afro-America Company).
6. Pictures of each child can be taken with a Polaroid or other camera, and displayed with their names beneath.
7. Children's art work should also be displayed throughout the year with everyone having his or her work selected frequently. See Art Center, p. 102.
8. Display a group of pictures portraying children involved in various activities, illustrating many skills, such as dressing, brushing teeth, climbing a tree, riding a tricycle, and so on.
9. Fold-out charts: "Health and Personal Care" (The Child's World).

Community Resources

1. Parents of children in your classroom or friends of another culture or foreign students at a nearby college
2. Pediatrician and nurse
3. Dentist and dental hygienist
4. Speech and hearing clinic
5. Mental health clinic
6. Department of Public Welfare (Child Welfare Division)
7. Community action agency
8. Child Development Department or Early Childhood Department in local college
9. State or local chapters of these national organizations:
   a. American Association for Jewish Education, 114 Fifth Ave., New York, N.Y. 10011
   b. American Indian Historical Society, 1451 Masonic Ave., San Francisco, Calif. 94117
   c. Association for Childhood Education International (ACEI), 3615 Wisconsin Ave. N.W., Washington, D.C. 20016
   d. Bnai Brith, 1640 Rhode Island Ave. N.W., Washington, D.C. 20036
   e. Office of Early Childhood Development (OECD), Office of Education, Department of Health, Education and Welfare, 1200 19th Street N.W., Washington, D.C. 20506
   f. National Association for Retarded Citizens (NARC), 2709 Avenue E East, Arlington, Tx. 76011
   g. National Association for the Advancement of Colored People (NAACP), 1790 Broadway, New York, N.Y. 10019
   h. National Association for the Education of Young Children (NAEYC), 1834 Connecticut Ave. N.W., Washington, D.C. 20009
   i. National Congress of American Indians (NCAI), 1765 "P" Street N.W., Washington, D.C. 20036
   j. National Council for Black Child Development (NCBCD), 490 L'Enfant Plaza East S.W., Suite 3204, Washington, D.C. 20024
   k. The Day Care and Child Development Council of America (DCCDCA), 1012 14th Street N.W., Washington, D.C. 20005
10. Multicultural curriculum materials are available from these laboratories:
    a. Appalachia Educational Laboratory (AEL), 1031 Quarier Street, P.O. Box 1348, Charleston, W. Va. 25325
    b. Bureau of Curriculum Innovation, Massachusetts Department of Education, 182 Tremont St., Boston, Mass. 02111
    c. Central Midwestern Regional Educational Laboratory (CMREL), 10646 St. Charles Rock Rd., St. Ann, Missouri 63074
    d. Far West Laboratory for Educational Research and Development (FWLERD), 1855 Folsom St., San Francisco, Calif. 94103
    e. Inter-America Research Associates, National Resource Center for Bilingual/Bicultural Preschool Materials, 2001 Wisconsin Ave. N.W., Washington, D.C. 20007
    f. Mexican American Cultural Center, 3019 W. French Pl., San Antonio, Tx. 78228
    g. National Educational Laboratory Publishers, Inc., P.O. Box 1003, Austin, Tx. 78767 Spanish/English Bilingual Early Childhood Program for 3, 4, and 5 year olds. Each program level contains instructional materials for the children, in-service staff development materials, and materials for parents to use in teaching the children.
    h. Navaho Curriculum Center, Rough Rock Demonstration School, Chinle, Arizona 86503
    i. R and E Research Associates, 936 Industrial Ave., Palo Alto, Calif. 94303
    j. Southwestern Cooperative Educational Laboratory (SWCEL), 117 Richmond Dr. N.E., Albuquerque, N. Mex. 87106

2 sight

basic understandings

(concepts children can grasp from this subject)

- We see with our eyes.
- We learn things by using our eyes.
- We need light to help us to see; if it is completely dark, we can't see.
- Some animals, such as cats, can see in the dark.
- We need to take good care of our eyes so that we can see.
- Some people need glasses to help them to see.
- Some people can't see at all; they are blind. (See other senses guides.)
- Our eyes take pictures somewhat like a camera does.
- Our eyes help tell us what color something is.
- Our eyes help tell us how big or how little something is.
- Our eyes help tell us what shape something is.
- Things that are far away look smaller than when we are close to them.
- The colored part of the eye is called the iris. The color of eyes may be different. Most people have blue or brown eyes.
- The black circle of the eye, called the pupil, is really a hole to let in light so that we can see.
- If the sun is too bright, our eyes may not keep out enough light. We protect our eyes by wearing dark glasses called sunglasses.
- Eyebrows and eyelashes help protect the eyes from dust particles.
- If something gets in one of our eyes, our eyes shed tears to help wash it out.

Additional Facts the Teacher Should Know

The optic nerve relays the image viewed by the retina to the brain. Nerve fibers from the retina run through the optic nerve. It is the nerve cells in the retina that make sight possible.

The *iris* of the eye is the colored part of the eye. The *pupil* is actually a hole in the iris. The lens of the eye is located behind the pupil. The *retina* is the inner layer of the eyeball. Light enters the eye via the pupil and passes through the colorless liquid contained in the eyeball cavity. The muscles of the eye focus the lens of the eye.

Some people are nearsighted; some are farsighted. A concave lens in glasses corrects nearsightedness, a convex lens corrects farsightedness.

Some children have visual difficulties, such as seeing reverse images, color blindness, nearsightedness, farsightedness, and strabismus (crossed-eyes). Squinting, holding objects or books close to the eyes, bumping into objects, tripping, or persistently erring in color identification may indicate vision problems. Consult parent(s) and refer such children to an eye doctor for further examination and testing.

NOTE: Other guides related to this subject are: Color, Day and Night, and Festivals of Light.

Methods Most Adaptable for Introducing This Subject to Children

- Place eyeglasses, binoculars, microscope, magnifying glasses, kaleidoscope, and View Masters on a table. Talk about why some people need or use these.
- In a group setting, ask children to put their hands over their eyes. Ask, "Can you see?"
- If children are willing, put a sleepmask over their eyes. Ask, "How could you walk around if you couldn't see?" "What do you think would happen?"

  CAUTION: Wrap mask with fresh tissue for each child using it.

- If you have a doll with broken eyes, show it to the children and say, "If a doll gets an eye pushed out, we can fix the eye, but children can't get new eyes, so they need to take very good care of the ones they have."
- Use the story and/or the record of Muffin, the little dog who couldn't see for a while because he got a cinder in his eye. "What if we can't see?"

Vocabulary

glasses	eyelash(es)	vision	frames
spectacles	look	blind	nosepiece
contact lenses	see	iris	magnifying
eye(s)	sight	pupil	microscope
eyebrow(s)	sighted	lens	telescope

A giant magnifier leaves child's hands free to move objects under viewer. A dark piece of paper under a light object, or the reverse, will make viewing easier.

learning centers

Discovery Center

1. Go for an observation walk. This can be a general or a specific walk, such as "Look for bugs," or "Look for leaves." Take some binoculars, a magnifying glass, and a sack for the treasures you may find.
2. Look at objects through a magnifying glass. Have a supply of interesting specimens, such as rocks, shells, or insects. Decide which are shiny, which are dull colored. Use a magnifier to look at a telephone book.
3. Have a treasure hunt: distribute familiar articles, such as colored cubes, counters, or cardboard/artificial flowers or leaves, where they can be easily seen. **Variation:** specify the number of articles for each child to find.
4. Use cooking activities to see the difference in appearance *before* and *after*. Suggested for this:

Jell-o	bacon	pudding	scrambled eggs
gingerbread	pancakes	cupcakes	waffles

Popcorn—This one illustrates the five senses: you can *see* it pop if you have a popper with a glass or plastic lid; you can *hear* it popping; you can *smell* it; you can *taste* it; and you can *feel* the shapes of the kernels. Sing "Popcorn" song, p. 121.

CAUTION: Be sure to have all the required utensils and ingredients available before you start.

5. Have a table for the children to bring their special finds for the week.
6. Look at an object far away. Talk about how little it looks. Walk closer to it and see how much bigger it looks.
7. When you see an airplane in the sky, talk about how little it looks and how big it really is when you are close to it. Compare pictures of both instances.
8. Have an eye chart for children. Talk about the reasons some people need glasses. Recall magnifying-glass exploration.
9. If the adults in the group (or parents) wear glasses or contact lenses, ask them to show the children what they look like and how they fit.
10. Have a peep box with a small light in it. Let children look in when it is dark and when the light is on.
11. Talk about some objects that are round, big, or blue. For example, "Look at this ball, what color is it?; what shape is it?; what size is it? How did you know it was round, big, and blue? Did you hear it? Did you taste it? Did you feel it? No, you saw it with your eyes."
12. Display different things that help us to see when it is dark: a lamp, a candle, a lantern, a flashlight, a kerosene lamp.
13. Observe or "make" a rainbow—for directions see Color guide, p. 586.
14. Make a display of things people "read," such as books, magazines, Braille books, newspapers, pamphlets, and posters.

    NOTE: Choose illustrated items if possible.

15. Display items we need to read or see to help us, for example, something dirty or clean, a thermometer, a clock, a television, a filmstrip, a recipe book, travel signs, street and house numbers, maps, timetables, tour brochures, a telephone book, a picture dictionary.
16. Borrow a small animal pet (gerbil, guinea pig, turtle) to be observed by the children. Encourage children to describe what they discover by observing the pets. See chart for Animals—Pets.

Home-Living Center

1. Set out candles in candleholders on the table.
2. Have a flashlight available to look for things in dark places.
3. Have a discarded or toy camera available to take "pretend" pictures of the dolls.
4. Set out sunglass frames with the lenses removed.
5. Provide unbreakable hand and wall mirrors.
6. Place a magnifying glass and a telephone book by the toy telephone.

Block-Building Center

1. Set out road signs and traffic signals for use with road building.
2. Display pictures of people driving at night. Talk about use of headlights at night.

Other Dramatic Play Centers

1. Eye doctor: set out eye chart, doctor's coat, flashlight, mirror, and frames of glasses.
2. Set up a shop to sell eyeglasses, frames for glasses, and sunglasses. Remove lenses.
3. Make a television movie (see Art Center) and let children pretend to run a theater (picture show) or a drive-in movie.
4. Play library (after visit to a library): collect picture books, set out reading tables, and put up bookshelves. Provide librarian with a desk or a counter, stamp and stamp pads, cards, and a telephone. Paste pocket cards in books.

Learning, Language, and Readiness Materials Center

Commercially made games and materials for use at a table or on a mat:

(See Basic Resources, p. 79, for manufacturers' addresses.)

1. Lotto Games
2. Dominoes: picture or numbers
3. Judy Matchettes and See-Quees
4. Puzzles
5. Perception Puzzles
6. Fit-a-Size and Fit-a-Shape Puzzles (Lauri)
7. Kaleidoscope Puzzles (Ideal)
8. Graded Cylinder Blocks (Montessori)
9. Sorting Box Combination for Color and Counting
10. Giant Magnifier (available from most catalogs)
11. Color Paddles (available from most catalogs)
12. Flexible Mirror (Creative Playthings)
13. Microscope (available from most catalogs)
14. Guess Whose Tail?/Ears?/Feet?; What Belongs Where?; What Goes with What?; What's Part of What? (The Child's World)

Teacher-made games and materials for use at a table or on a mat:

NOTE: For detailed description of Games, see pp. 50-59.

1. Look and See: use several objects of different colors or shapes
2. I See Something, What Do You See?
3. Who's Missing?
4. Guess Who?
5. Match-Them
6. Grouping and Sorting by Association: sort by size, shape, and color
7. Alike, Different, and the Same

Art Center

* 1. Easel painting: let the children mix colors; add black or white.
* 2. Paint tempera on clear cellophane and put up in windows to let light shine through.
* 3. Paint with tempera on aluminum foil or styrofoam trays.
** 4. Drip painting: use two parts salt, one part flour, to three parts water. Add powdered tempera for desired color. Drip from a brush onto paper.
** 5. Spatter painting: place small items found on the observation walk on a piece of paper and spatter paint over it. This may include small stones, leaves, small branches, twigs, pine cones, seeds.
*** 6. Mural painting: put large lengths of paper on the wall or the floor and let the children paint or color what they saw on the walk.
** 7. Make a collage using different shapes and colors of paper, yarn, ribbon, or items found on the nature walk. (See Magic Circle Walk, p. 349.)
*** 8. Encourage the older children to make pictures about a pet. Together write a story and glue a series of pictures on a long strip of shelving paper. Thread through slots in a carton to make a movie screen.

NOTE: See Color guide for many other suggestions. When possible take easels, clay dough, carpentry workbench outdoors. If weather does not permit that, place easels nearer Discovery Center where live pets and plants may be observed while young artists are at work.

Book Center

*** Aliki. *My Five Senses.* New York: Thomas Y. Crowell, 1962.

** Anglund, Joan Walsh. *What Color Is Love?* New York: Harcourt Brace Jovanovich, 1966.

** Baum, Arline. *One Bright Monday Morning.* New York: Random House, 1962.

*** Berkley, Ethel S. *Big and Little, Up and Down.* Reading, Mass.: Addison-Wesley, 1950.

** Borton, Helen. *Do You See What I See?* Eau Claire, Wis.: E. M. Hale, 1959.

* Buckley, Helen. *Grandfather and I.* New York: Lothrop, Lee & Shepard, 1959.

** Charlip, Remy and Mary Beth. *Handtalk: An ABC of Finger Spelling and Sign Language.* New York: Parents' Magazine Press, 1974.

* Cook, Bernadine. *Looking for Susie.* Reading, Mass.: Addison-Wesley, 1959.

* Dawson, R. and R. *A Walk in the City.* New York: Viking Press, 1960.

*** Foley, Louise M. *No Talking.* New York: Bobbs-Merrill, 1970.

* Gay, Zhena. *Look!* New York: Viking Press, 1952.

** Hoban, Tana. *Look Again!* New York: Macmillan, 1971.

** Lionni, Leo. *Little Blue and Little Yellow.* New York: Pantheon Books, 1969.

** McDonald, Golden. *Red Light, Green Light.* Garden City, N.Y.: Doubleday, 1944.

* Memling, Carl. *What's in the Dark?* New York: Abelard-Schuman, 1955. Paper. New York: Parents' Magazine Press, 1971.

** Peppe, Rodney. *Odd One Out.* New York: Viking Press, 1974.

** Polland, Barbara Kay. *The Sensible Book: A Celebration of Your Five Senses.* Millbrae, Calif.: Celestial Arts Publishing, 1974.

*** Reit, Seymour. *All Kinds of Signs.* New York: Western Publishing, 1970.

** Schlein, Miriam. *Shapes.* Reading, Mass.: Addison-Wesley, 1952.

*** Shapp, Martha and Charles. *Let's Find Out What's Big and What's Small.* New York: Franklin Watts, 1959.

** Showers, Paul. *Look at Your Eyes.* New York: Thomas Y. Crowell, 1962 (Filmstrip/record/cassette).

** ———. *Mírate Los Ojos.* New York: Thomas Y. Crowell, 1968.

* Zolotow, Charlotte. *One Step, Two.* New York: Lothrop, Lee & Shepard, 1955.

NOTE: Check your library for the *Noisy Book* series by Margaret Wise Brown.

planning for grouptime

NOTE: All music, fingerplays, stories, poems, and games listed here may also be used at other times during the session as appropriate. See Core Library, Basic Resources, p. 76, for publishers and addresses. See p. 81 for record companies' addresses. In parodies, hyphenated words match music notes of the tune used.

Music

Songs

SPRINGTIME (a parody)
  (tune: "Did You Ever See a Lassie?")
  Adaptation by JoAnne Deal Hicks

My—eyes can see it's spring-time, it's spring-time, it's spring-time.
My—eyes can see it's spring-time, the grass is so green!
The green grass, the flow-ers, the sun-shine and show-ers.
My—eyes can see it's spring-time, and I am so glad!

My—ears can hear it's spring-time, it's spring-time, it's spring-time.
My—ears can hear it's spring-time, the birds sweetly sing.
The birds sing, the lambs bleat, the frogs croak, the bees buzz.
My—ears can hear it's spring-time, and I am so glad!

My—bod-y can feel it's spring-time, it's spring-time, it's spring-time.
My—bod-y can feel it's spring-time, the air is so warm.
The warm air, the breez-es, no frost and no freez-es.
My—bod-y can feel it's spring-time, and I am so glad!

NOTES: This parody may also be sung to the tune of "Ach du Lieber, Augustine." If you do, omit the pause (shown by the dash) and sing "my-eyes," "my-ears," "my-bod- . . ." on the first note, and, in the fourth line, "time and" on one note.

POPCORN (a parody)
  (tune: "Frère Jacques")
  Adaptation by JoAnne Deal Hicks

Pop, pop, pop-ping. Pop, pop, pop-ping. Our pop-corn. Our pop-corn.
Pop-ping, pop-ping, pop-corn, pop-ping, pop-ping, pop-corn.
Our pop-corn, our pop-corn . . . (or Pop, pop, pop, . . . Pop, pop, pop)

FROM *Songs for the Nursery School,* MacCarteney
 * "Have You Seen," p. 7
 * "See the Sun Shine," p. 7
 * "See My Fingers Dance and Play," p. 8
** "The Bear Went over the Mountain," p. 40
** "Who Has Seen the Wind?," p. 58

FROM *Songs for Early Childhood,* Westminster Press
** "Beautiful, Wonderful Sights to See," p. 39
** "I Went Walking Outdoors Today," p. 40
** "When It Is the Wintertime," p. 42

FROM *Music Activities for Retarded Children,* Ginglend and Stiles
 * "Did You Ever," p. 41
 * "Pointing," p. 89

FROM *Wake Up and Sing*, Landeck and Crook
** "Honey, You Look So Sweet," p. 26
 * "Come See," p. 34
 * "Twinkle, Twinkle, Little Star," p. 91

FROM *Music Resource Book*, Lutheran Church Press
** "See the Puppets," p. 45
** "I Have Two Eyes," p. 66 (Adaptation of "God Gave Me Eyes")
 * "Did You Ever See a Lassie?," p. 86

Records

"Wake Up Sleepy Eyes" and "Come See," *Songs to Grow On*, Vol. 1, Woody Guthrie
    (Folkways, 33⅓ RPM)

Rhythms and Singing Games

FROM *Music Resource Book*, Lutheran Church Press
"Blind Man's Buff," p. 85
"Did You Ever See a Lassie?," p. 86

FROM *Songs for the Nursery School*, MacCarteney
"See, How I'm Jumping," p. 95
"Follow Me," p. 96

FROM *Creative Movement for the Developing Child*, Cherry
Dramatize: "Three Blind Mice," p. 23
         "Kalamazoo, the Kangaroo," p. 37
         "Rocking Boat," p. 55
         "Circus Clown, Parade, Dancing Girls," p. 75

Fingerplays and Poems

FROM *Rhymes for Fingers and Flannelboards*, Scott and Thompson
"Monkey See, Monkey Do," p. 18
"Once I Saw a Beehive," p. 35
"What Colors Do I See?," p. 45
"I See Three," p. 51
"Hide and Seek," p. 112
"Thumbkins," p. 115

FROM *Very Young Verses*, Geismer and Suter
"Cat," p. 21
"February Twilight," p. 112
"Mirrors," pp. 150, 151
"Who Has Seen the Wind," p. 163
"Hiding," pp. 190, 191

I HAVE SO MANY PARTS TO ME

I have two hands to clap with   (CLAP)
One nose with which to smell   (SNIFF)
I have one head to think with   (TAP HEAD)
Two lungs that work quite well.   (TAKE A DEEP BREATH)
I have two eyes that let me see   (POINT TO EYES)
I have two legs that walk   (WALK IN PLACE)
I have two ears that help me hear   (CUP HANDS TO EARS)
A mouth with which to talk.   (POINT TO MOUTH)

BEAR HUNT

(LEADER GIVES A LINE—OTHERS REPEAT. PAT ON THIGHS IN RHYTHM.)

Would you like to go on a bear hunt?
Okay—all right—come on—let's go!
Open the gate—close the gate.   (CLAP HANDS)

Coming to a bridge—can't go over it—can't go under it
Let's cross it.   (THUMP CHEST WITH CLOSED FISTS)

Coming to a river—can't go over it—can't go under it
Let's swim it.   (PRETEND TO DO CRAWL STROKE)

Coming to a tree—can't go over it—can't go under it
Let's climb it!   (PRETEND TO CLIMB TREE AND LOOK AROUND)
No bears!   (PRETEND TO CLIMB DOWN)

Coming to a wheat field—can't go over it—can't go under it
Let's go through it!   (RUB PALMS TOGETHER TO MAKE SWISHING NOISE)

Oh! Oh! I see a cave—it's dark in here—   (COVER EYES)
I see two eyes—I feel something furry—   (REACH OUT HAND)
It's a bear! Let's go home!   (RUNNING MOTION WITH FEET)
(REPEAT ABOVE ACTIONS IN REVERSE USING FAST MOTIONS)
Slam the gate.   (CLAP HANDS)
We made it!

GRANDMOTHER'S GLASSES

These are grandmother's glasses   (MAKE GLASSES OVER EYES)
This is grandmother's cap   (PEAK HANDS ON HEAD)
This is the way she folds her hands   (FOLD HANDS)
And puts them in her lap.   (PLACE IN LAP)

These are grandfather's glasses   (MAKE GLASSES OVER EYES)
This is grandfather's hat   (FLAT HAND ON HEAD)
This is the way he folds his arms   (CROSS ARMS ON CHEST)
And sits there just like that.   (LOOK STRAIGHT AHEAD)

LOOK LOOK	LITTLE BOY BLUE
Look up, look down	Little Boy Blue, come blow your horn,
Look all around	The sheep's in the meadow, the cow's in the corn,
Look here, look there	Where's the little boy that looks after he sheep?
Look everywhere.	He's under the haystack, fast asleep.

Stories

(To read, read-tell, or tell. See Book Center for complete list.)

*** *My Five Senses*, Aliki (for variation use with filmstrip and/or record)
 ** *Do You See What I See?*, Borton
  * *Looking for Susie*, Cook
*** *Big and Little, Up and Down*, Berkley
 ** *Look at Your Eyes*, Showers (use with record and filmstrip)
  * *Noisy Book Series*, Brown (for variation use with the records) (See senses guides.)

Games

(See Games, pp. 50–59, and Teacher-Made Games in this guide for directions.)

Can You Remember?	Did You Ever See a Lassie?
Look and See	Sequence
I See Something, What Do You See?	Guess Who?
Who's Missing?	Match-Them
Grouping and Sorting by Association	Alike, Different, and the Same

Easter Egg Hunt: hide plastic or paper eggs, or familiar objects for the children to find.
Pin the Tail on the Donkey: older children might enjoy this game.

CAUTION: Use "Hold-it" or magnets on the tails instead of pins with magnetic flannel-board or double-sided masking tape on paper.

Routine Times

1. At snack or mealtime emphasize the use of eyes in talking about food. Teacher: "What are we having for a snack?" Child: "Carrots." Teacher: "How do you know they are carrots?" Child: "They look like carrots." Teacher: "What color are they?" (or shape or size). Teacher: "That's right, our eyes help tell us what they are."
2. When busing or walking (where crossing streets is involved), talk about how our eyes help us to drive or to walk safely. Traffic lights, road signs, median lines. Teacher: "Could you walk or drive if you were blind?" Perhaps. You *may* see a blind or partially sighted person with a cane or a dog.
3. When walking or bussing children on a sunny day, talk about the use of sunglasses and the sun visor on the car or bus. On a rainy or foggy day or late afternoon in winter discuss how the use of headlights, streetlights, and windshield wipers helps us to see.
4. At rest time talk about the eyelids and how we close them to keep the light out and give our eyes a rest.

Large Muscle Activities

1. Take a Magic Circle Walk. (See p. 349 for description.)
2. Throw a large ball into a wastepaper basket.
3. Toss bean bags into a box.
4. Try to kick a ball to a fence or other designated spot.
5. Bowling: make an alley with large hollow blocks. Use detergent bottles for pins. Plastic bowling sets are available commercially.
6. Woodworking: emphasize how we use our eyes when measuring, sawing, and hammering.
7. Try to hit a ball with a bat or small plank (for older children). Plastic bats and whiffle or cloth balls would be safest; this activity requires adult supervision at all times.
8. Johnny Can You . . . Jump the Brook?: put two lengths of rope in a parallel line about 6 inches apart and let each child "jump the brook." Increase the distance between ropes after each child has had a turn.

Extended Experiences

1. Take a sightseeing trip or walk to see what you can see.
2. Visit an optometrist or an eye doctor or have him visit the group.
3. Take slides or movies of your group and show them, or buy or borrow commercially made films, slides, or filmstrips.

   CAUTION: Leave a light on in the room or the door ajar—especially for the younger children.

4. Visit the children's section of your nearest library.
5. Use a filmstrip and/or a record of *My Five Senses* and *Look at Your Eyes*.
6. Have a blind person with a seeing-eye dog visit your center.

   CAUTION: This activity is perhaps best for older children as the children must be told they cannot touch the dog while he is visiting because he is especially trained to see for and guard his master.

7. Invite a lapidist or rockhound to bring a "black" light and some fluorescent rocks and minerals to be viewed in a dark room.
8. Invite a parent or friend (if the budget will allow) to come to the center and take candid Polaroid camera pictures. Let the children see what happens. Take a school "home movie" and view it later.

teacher resources

Books and Periodicals

Many picture books and pamphlets are published by the American Optometric Association. Often these are available from your local optometrist.

Pictures and Displays

(See p. 79 for addresses of firms listed.)

1. Display pictures of eyes or people looking at things.
2. Display pictures of a blind person with a seeing-eye dog.
3. Display an eye chart on a wall.
4. Display things we use with our eyes: mirror, magnifying glass, telescope, microscope, kaleidoscope, or View Master.
5. The Five Senses Bulletin Board Kit (Instructo)
6. Filmstrips, record, and cassette for use with books: *Look at Your Eyes, Mírate Los Ojos, My Five Senses* (Thomas Y. Crowell)

Community Resources

1. Eye doctor
2. Optometrist
3. Nurse—school nurse may lend you an eye chart
4. Local association for the blind
5. Children's librarian at nearest library
6. Check with local rock and mineral club for a lapidist or rockhound
7. Parent with a movie camera or Polaroid camera
8. Photographer

3 /ound

ba/ic under/tanding/

(concepts children can grasp from this subject)

- We hear with our ears.
- We listen to many sounds.
- We learn many things by listening.
- Sounds are made by things that vibrate.
- Sounds are air vibrations that go into the ear.
- The outside of the ear acts as a funnel to catch the vibrations that go into the ear.
- Some animals hear better than we do, for example, dogs.
- Some animals hear sounds different from those that we can hear.
- Some people can't hear at all; they are deaf. Some are hard of hearing (can't hear well).
- Most people who are deaf "hear" by *feeling* sound vibrations (waves).
- We can recognize some things by the sounds they make: dogs, birds, motors.
- Some sounds help to warn us of danger: sirens, horns, whistles, bees, rattlesnakes, growling animals, cracks of lightning, thunder.
- Some sounds help us—alarm clock bells, chimes, voices, telephone bells, doorbells.
- We can make sounds as well as hear them.
- Some sounds we like; some sounds we don't like.
- Some sounds are loud, soft, high, low, pleasant, or harsh.
- We need to take good care of our ears.

    CAUTION: When presenting this concept, avoid giving children ideas by telling them, "Don't stick things in your ears." Instead, say, "We must keep our ears clean by washing them. We must not hurt our ears or the ears of other people."

- Some people who cannot hear "talk" without making a sound. They use sign language, moving their hands in a special way. Sometimes they can read other peoples' lips and can know what they are saying.

Additional Facts the Teacher Should Know

For the sense of sound, people need nerves in the inner ear to relay vibration messages to the brain. The outer ear acts as a funnel in channeling sound vibrations to the eardrum, which separates the outer ear from the middle ear. Behind the eardrum are three small bones that carry sound to the inner ear where the organ of balance and the organ of hearing are found. Each of these organs has a nerve that connects it with the brain.

The eustachian tube connects the middle ear with the throat and ordinarily allows a balance of air pressure on both sides of the eardrum.

Some people are born deaf. Some become deaf because of injury or nerve damage; others become deaf because of repeated infections that result in scar tissue on the eardrum. This scar tissue can interrupt the flow of sound vibrations. When a cold settles in the inner ear (often due to blowing the nose too hard), medicine may be needed to stop the infection. Sometimes it becomes necessary for a doctor to lance the eardrum (puncture a small hole) to relieve the pressure of the infection and allow for drainage so that the eardrum will not burst. While the eardrum heals rapidly, a star-shaped scar may form after breaking, if the eardrum is not lanced. As scar tissue forms with repeated infections, a person may become more "hard of hearing." Surgery can repair the eardrum, allowing for improved hearing, but usually it is not indicated if the cause of deafness is nerve damage. Be alert to the need to notify a parent or a doctor if a child develops an earache at school.

Some children may have hearing disabilities. If a child repeatedly loses interest during storytime or does not respond readily to questions, the child may have a hearing loss. Consult with the parent(s) and recommend that the child go to a doctor for examination and testing.

Methods Most Adaptable for Introducing This Subject to Children

- Play a tape recorder, with previously recorded sounds, to see if the children can identify them.
- Have a variety of sound-producing objects for the children to identify without seeing or touching them—for example, drop objects or make sounds behind a screen.
- Use a piano or other musical instrument to illustrate the concepts "high," "low," "soft," and "loud." If you use a stringed instrument, demonstrate the vibrations. This can also be done with an open, empty box encircled with several rubberbands.
- A visitor might play a musical instrument or a child might bring in a music box to share.
- A siren might blow or a sudden storm with lightning and thunder might occur.
- You might obtain a telephone teaching unit from the telephone company for the children to use or bring in a homemade telephone for the home living center.

Vocabulary

ear(s)	listen	sing	high	pleasant
hear	vibration	whistle	low	harsh
deaf	talk	whisper	loud	tape recorder
sound	hum	shout	soft	telephone

NOTE: There are real phones that ring and have a dial tone or a busy signal. Children can actually hear one another through the receiver. There is often no charge for borrowing this equipment from the telephone company.

learning centers

Discovery Center

1. Pop popcorn: listen for the sounds of hot fat and popping kernels.
2. Record children talking or singing on a tape recorder. Play back.
3. Play previously taped segments of:
   a. sounds around the house—for example, a mixer, vacuum cleaner, doorbell, door shutting, toilet flushing, water running, dryer, washing machine.
   b. sounds of nature—for example, a bird chirping, cricket, dog barking, rain, wind blowing through evergreens, crunch of leaves.
   c. street sounds—for example, a police whistle, cars, bus, siren, brakes, clatter of garbage can lids.
4. Have rhythm band instruments available for exploring different sounds.
5. Tune bottles or glasses of water to various pitches. Play a tune and let the children experiment with them (with supervision for safety).
6. Make a double set of sound tubes from unbreakable plastic or metal film cans. Fill with various ingredients (in varying amounts), such as flour, rice, beans, pebbles, salt, a peachstone, and others. After shaking the containers and listening to them, the children can match those that sound alike or can arrange the containers from loudest to softest. Plastic aspirin bottles (labels removed) may be used. Glue all container lids shut when filled.
7. Go on a listening walk.
8. Set out step bells, tone blocks, and a xylophone for children to try out.
9. Use a tuning fork to help teach about vibrations.
10. Examine, operate, and make musical instruments. (See illustration, p. 130.)
11. Examine a typewriter, a see-through music box, or an alarm clock.
12. Examine a stethoscope. Let the children listen to each other's heartbeat or to the heartbeat of a guinea pig.
13. Invite the children to explore a sound tray filled with objects that can be used to make sounds. Include:

bell	coconut shell	tone block and mallet
feather	gong	eggbeater
whisk broom	triangle and striker	crisp paper
comb	alarm clock	tissue
seashell	castanet	cotton ball

Encourage children to compare the sounds of items being dropped, struck, or handled—for example, wood against wood, metal against metal, metal against wood, paper being torn and crumpled.

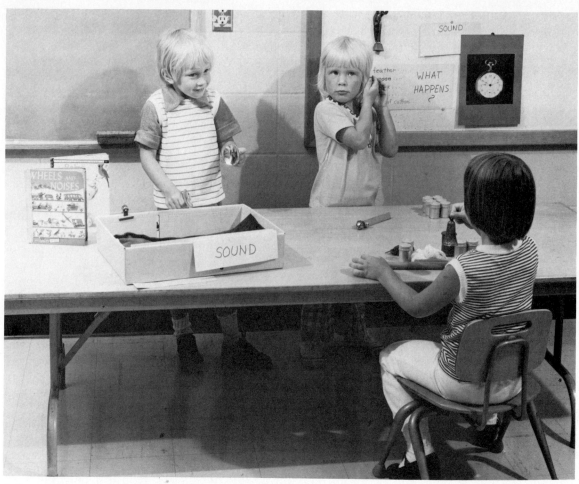

Left: reacting to sound made by drawer-pull cymbals; *right:* listening to a watch ticking; *foreground:* trying to match the sounds of different instruments.

Dramatic Play Centers

Home-Living Center

1. In this center, put an alarm clock that ticks loudly.
2. Encourage the use of the telephone. Make tin-can telephones, put one tin-can telephone in this center and another in the Block Center or in Other Dramatic Play Centers, such as a store or an office. Make certain there is more than one telephone in this center to encourage cooperative interaction. For instructions on how to make a tin-can telephone, check with your local library for the book *Toys for Fun and How to Make Them*, Walter Schutz (Beverly Hills, Calif.: Bruce Publishing).
3. Invite children to listen for kitchen sounds, such as a wooden or metal spoon stirring different kinds of foods in pans or bowls made of metal, glass, plastic, and so on.
4. Add sound-making tools, such as a toy-sized, hand-operated egg beater, a small hand sweeper, and a broom. Note sounds when used.

Block-Building Center

1. Set out small wooden, metal, or unbreakable plastic fire engines. Encourage some of the children to build a fire station, either a small one (made with wooden blocks) or one

large enough for them to play in (made with hollow blocks). Allow the children to imitate sirens.
2. Set out airplanes and encourage the making of runways for takeoffs and landings. Children can imitate the airplane motor as they use the toys.
3. Set out other motor and machine block accessories.

NOTE: Other vehicles that are often associated with a sound and that could be used include an ambulance or rescue car and a police car.

Other Dramatic Play Centers

1. Make a train from cardboard, wooden boxes, or a row of small chairs. An occasional conductor's call "All aboard" and/or piano background sounds for a train whistle or engines will add to the dramatic play.
2. Doctor's office: set out stethoscopes to give opportunities to listen to heartbeats.
3. Carpenter's shop: encourage the use of woodworking tools and invite the children to listen or describe sounds their saws, hammers, or sandpaper blocks make.

Learning, Language, and Readiness Materials Center

Commercially made games and materials for use at a table or on a mat:

(See Basic Resources, p. 79, for manufacturers' addresses.)

1. Musical instruments and sound equipment (available from early childhood materials catalogs, school supply houses, or local music or department stores):

xylophone	see-through music box
step-bells	autoharp
resonator	stethoscope
drums (tom-tom, steel, tub, bongo)	telephones (wooden and plastic)

Rhythm band sets:

wrist bells	triangles	tambourines	claves
tone blocks	maracas	rhythm sticks	drums
jingle clogs	sand blocks	hand castanets	Melodee bells

2. The Big Line and Interphone: telephones (Childcraft)
3. Note Kalimba (Childcraft)
4. See-Through Alarm Clock (Constructive Playthings)
5. Tuning Fork (Constructive Playthings)
6. Gong Bell (Childcraft)
7. Tape recorder, transister radio, alarm clock, pocket watch, typewriter, record players (available at discount stores and large department stores)

Teacher-made games and materials for use at a table or on a mat:

NOTE: For detailed description of Games, see pp. 50–59.

1. Listen and Hear
2. Listening (or Telephone): you may wish to try whispering.
3. Guess Who? or Who Am I?: imitate an animal.
4. Guess What? or What Am I?: imitate a tool or machine sound.

5. Match-Them: match sound tubes (see the Discovery Center, no. 6).
6. What Can You Hear?: recall sounds
   a. of a zoo
   b. of a kitchen
   c. of a street
7. What Did You Hear? (Echo): invite children, one at a time, to duplicate a sound, describe it, or identify it.
8. Rhyming Words: older children, especially, like to string rhyming words together. Choose words that have many possible matches: *cat, rat, mat . . .*
9. Matching Pitch: sing a child's name (high or low) and see if he or she can match the pitch.

Art Center

* 1. Offer basic media: listen for sounds when using tools and materials.
* 2. Make shakers or rattles from gourds or boxes filled with seeds, rice, or sand. These can be painted. Empty hand-size lotion bottles can be decorated with contact paper or pictures.
* 3. Make drums from oatmeal boxes or coffee cans:
     a. color or paint
     b. wind yarn around the outside or cover with wallpaper
     c. make a beater by piercing a rubber ball with a sharpened piece of doweling
** 4. Make tambourines: use bells and paper plates or throw-away pie plates. Let children paint or crayon the paper plates or glue paper or fabric scraps on the metal ones.
* 5. Make sand blocks from wooden blocks with sandpaper tacked on. Paint blocks. (See p. 34.)
* 6. Make jingle paddles and let children paint them with water base paint. (See p. 37.)

Book Center

** Blue, Rose. *I Am Here, Yo Estoy Aqui.* New York: Franklin Watts, 1971.
*** Borten, Helen. *Do You Hear What I Hear?* New York: Abelard-Schuman, 1960.
*** Branley, Franklyn. *Rusty Rings a Bell.* New York: Thomas Y. Crowell, 1957.
* Brown, Margaret Wise. *Shhhhhh-Bang!* New York: Harper & Row, 1943.
** ———. *The Country Noisy Book.* New York: Harper & Row, 1942.
** ———. *The Indoor Noisy Book.* New York: Harper & Row, 1943.
*** ———. *The Little Brass Band.* New York: Harper & Row, 1955. (Children's Record Guild and Young People's Records [story included]).
** ———. *The Quiet Noisy Book.* New York: Harper & Row, 1950.
** ———. *The Seashore Noisy Book.* New York: Harper & Row, 1941.
** ———. *The Summer Noisy Book.* New York: Harper & Row, 1940.
** ———. *The Winter Noisy Book.* New York: Harper & Row, 1947.
** Carlson, Bernice W. *Listen! and Help Tell the Story.* Nashville, Tenn.: Abingdon Press, 1965.
* Dawson, Rosemary and Richard. *A Walk in the City.* New York: Viking Press, 1960.
*** Elkin, Benjamin. *The Loudest Noise in the World.* New York: Viking Press, 1954.
** Flack, Marjorie. *Ask Mr. Bear.* New York: Macmillan, 1958 (paper, 1971).
* Frost, Marie. *Whispering Sounds: A Listening Book.* Elgin, Ill.: David C. Cook Publishing, 1967 (paper).

*** Grifalconi, Ann. *City Rhythms*. New York: Bobbs-Merrill, 1965.

* Kauffman, Lois. *What's That Noise?* New York: Lothrop, Lee & Shepard, 1965.

** Keats, Ezra Jack. *Whistle for Willie*. New York: Viking Press, 1964.

* Leher, Lore. *A Letter Goes to Sea*. Eau Claire, Wis.: Harvey House, 1970.

** Lionni, Leo. *Swimmy*. (*Nageot*, French Edition; *Suimi*, Spanish Edition.) New York: Pantheon Books, 1963.

*** McGovern, Ann. *Too Much Noise*. New York: Houghton Mifflin, 1967.

** Polland, Barbara Kay. *The Sensible Book: A Celebration of Your Five Senses*. Millbrae, Calif.: Celestial Arts Publishing, 1974.

** Showers, Paul. *The Listening Walk*. New York: Thomas Y. Crowell, 1961.

** ———. *How You Talk*. New York: Thomas Y. Crowell, 1967 (film/record/cassette).

** Simon, Norma. *What Do I Say?* Chicago, Ill.: Albert Whitman, 1967.

* Skaar, Grace. *What Do the Animals Say?* Reading, Mass.: Addison-Wesley, 1968 (paper).

** Spier, Peter. *Crash! Bang! Boom!* Garden City, N.Y.: Doubleday, 1972.

** Steiner, Charlotte. *Listen to My Seashell*. New York: Alfred A. Knopf, 1959.

* Summers, Sandra. *Bell Sounds: A Listening Book*. Elgin, Ill.: David C. Cook Publishing, 1967 (paper).

** Tresselt, Alvin. *Rain Drop Splash*. New York: Lothrop, Lee & Shepard, 1962.

planning for grouptime

NOTE: All music, fingerplays, poems, stories, and games listed here may be used at other times during the session as appropriate. See Core Library, Basic Resources, p. 76, for publishers and addresses. Sources for records will be found on p. 81. In parodies, hyphenated words match music notes of the tune used.

MUSIC

Songs

FROM *Songs for the Nursery School*, MacCarteney

* "Knock at the Door," p. 2

* "Tiptoe Aeroplane," p. 10

* "Little Engine," p. 11

*** "The Switching Engine," p. 14

** "Barnyard Song," p. 31

* "The Hen," p. 33

** "Waddling Ducks," p. 34

* "Robin Song," p. 36

** "Zumm! Zumm! Zumm!" p. 37

** "Woodpecker Song," p. 38

*** "Hear the Great Green Waves," p. 50

* "Here I Go a-Tiptoe," p. 102

** "The Clocks," p. 104

** "Ding-a-Ling," p. 108 (adapt)
 * "Cymbals," p. 109
 * "Tramp Tramp," p. 109
 * "The Bugle," p. 110
 * "Scissors," p. 114

FROM *Music Resource Book*, Lutheran Church Press
 * "Rhythm Sticks," p. 32
 * "Playing," p. 34
 * "I Have Two Ears" (adaptation of line 3, "God Gave Me Eyes," p. 66)

FROM *Music Activities for Retarded Children*, Ginglend and Stiles
 * "The Band," p. 27
** "Chiapanecas," p. 32
** "Come and Ride Our Train," p. 36
 * "Listen," p. 47
 * "If You're Happy," p. 62
 * "I Take My Little Hands," p. 63
** "I Have a Little Rooster," p. 64
 * "Sounds I Hear," p. 98
** "La Raspa," p. 126

FROM *Songs for Early Childhood*, Westminster Press
** "Popping Corn," p. 79 (adapt using name of Barbara)
** "Song of the Grandfather Clock," p. 81
 * "Do You Know the Popcorn Man?" (tune: "Do You Know the Muffin Man?"), p. 139

Records

"Child's World of Sound," "My Five Senses," and "Sights and Sounds," *Children's Literature Series* (Bowmar, 33⅓ RPM or cassette)
Creative Rhythms for Children Series (Phoebe James, 78 RPM)
"Noisy and Quiet," Tom Glazer (Lyons, 33⅓ RPM) with 16 lyric sheets
"Sounds I Can Hear," 5 records and picture cards (Scott, Foresman, 33⅓ RPM)
"Rhythm and Game Songs for the Little Ones," Ella Jenkins (Folkways/Scholastic, 33⅓ RPM or cassette)
"**Muffin and Mother Goose**"/"Musical Mother Goose"/"**Muffin in the City**"/"**Muffin in the Country**" (Young People's Record [YPR], 33⅓ RPM)
"Waltzing Elephant"/"**Penny Whistle**"/"**Shhh . . . Bang!**" (YPR, 33⅓ RPM)
"**Sing Along**"/"**Another Sing Along**"/"Let's Join In" (YPR, 33⅓ RPM)
"**Chugging Freight Engine**"/"**Little Grey Ponies**"/"**Rhyme Me a Riddle**" (YPR, 33⅓ RPM)
"**Fog Boat Story**"/"**Music Listening Game**"/"Do This, Do That" (YPR, 33⅓ RPM)
"All Aboard" (trains to the zoo, farm, and ranch) (YPR, 33⅓ RPM)
"Out Of Doors" and "Trains and Planes" (YPR, both 78 RPM)
"Little Indian Drum" (YPR, 78 and 45 RPM, and 33⅓ RPM)
"Strike Up the Band" (Children's Record Guild, 78 and 45 RPM)

Recognition of sounds in classical and semiclassical music:

Animals (cat, bird, duck, wolf): *Peter and the Wolf*, Prokofiev (Columbia, 33⅓ RPM)
Bee: "Flight of the Bumble Bee," Rimsky-Korsakov, in *American Scenes* album (Bowmar, 33⅓ RPM)

Bells, cannon, and footsteps: *1812 Festival Overture*, Tchaikovsky (Mercury, 33⅓ RPM)
Donkey: "On The Trail," *Grand Canyon Suite*, Ferde Grofé, in *American Scenes* album (Bowmar, 33⅓ RPM)
Rain: "Little April Showers," *Bambi* (Disneyland, 33⅓ RPM)

Rhythms and Singing Games

All records and songs are appropriate for listening to sound. Use your favorites and point out high sounds, low sounds, loud and soft sounds, fast and slow tempos, rhythms, and moods (happy, sad, dreamy, excited). Use a piano, xylophone, autoharp, and tone bells to show sounds, tempo, and moods.

Rhythm band: all instruments available using any good march tune

Rhythm band instruments separately:

bells: "Sleigh Ride" or "Jingle Bells," any good recordings
drums: any good march or authentic American Indian music
sand blocks: "I've Been Working on the Railroad," any recording
marching: "Little Brass Band" (Young People's Record, 78 and 45 RPM)

FROM *Major Classics for Minors* (RCA, 33⅓ RPM)

Listening and moving for an interpretation of music:

Side 1:
A variety of tempos for interpretive dancing including waltz, minuet, and tarantella. Use scarves, streamers, and tambourines.

Side 2:
wedding march—*Lohengrin*, Wagner
clowns—"The Love for Three Oranges," Prokofiev
dreamy—"Liebestraum," Liszt
march—"Marche Militaire," Schubert
spooky—"In the Hall of the Mountain King," Grieg
kingly—"Pomp and Circumstance," Elgar
pleasant—"Traumerei," Schumann

Fingerplays and Poems

FROM *Let's Do Fingerplays*, Grayson
"Clap Your Hands," p. 10
"Things That Go" (series), pp. 21–28
"Hickory Dickory Dock," p. 31
"Kitty, Kitty," p. 42
"Raindrops," p. 47
"The Finger Band," p. 86
"Noise Makers" (series), pp. 86–90
"I Am a Fine Musician," p. 87
"Hammering," p. 88
"Shake, Shake, Knock, Knock," p. 88
"Balloons," p. 89
"Pound Goes the Hammer," p. 89

FROM *Rhymes for Fingers and Flannelboards*, Scott and Thompson
"The Menagerie," p. 16
"Ten Little Ducklings," p. 27
"Once I Saw a Beehive," p. 35
"With the Hands," p. 44
"One and Two," p. 50
"Someone Is Knocking," p. 86
"Ready to Listen," p. 114
"A Readiness Game," p. 116
"Raindrops," p. 125
"My Balloon," p. 132

FROM *Very Young Verses*, Geismer
"Whistle," p. 58
"I Listen to Whistles," p. 86
"If You Look and Listen," p. 88

HERE IS A BEEHIVE

Here is a beehive   (MAKE A BEEHIVE WITH FISTS)
Where are the bees?   (PRETEND TO LOOK AROUND FOR THEM)
Hiding inside   (TRY TO SEE INSIDE THE BEEHIVE)
Where nobody sees!

Soon they come creeping,   (UNLOCK FISTS SLOWLY)
Out of the hive
One, two, three, four, five,   (EXTEND FINGERS ONE AT A TIME)
BZZZZZZZZZZZZZZZ   (FLUTTER HANDS ALL AROUND VIGOROUSLY)

Stories

(To read, read-tell, or tell. See Book Center for complete list.)

*** *Do You Hear What I Hear?* Borten
 ** *The Noisy Books*, Brown (use with records)
  * *Shhhhhh-Bang!* Brown
*** *The Little Brass Band*, Brown (record)
 ** *Ask Mr. Bear*, Flack
 ** *Whistle for Willie*, Keats
 ** *The Listening Walk*, Showers (record)
  * *What Do The Animals Say?* Skaar
 ** *Listen to My Seashell*, Steiner

Games

(See Games, pp. 50-59, and Teacher-Made Games in this guide for directions.)

1. Guess Who? Guess What?: imitate animal sounds and tool sounds
2. Listening or Telephone: use play telephones; guess who's on other phone
3. Listen and Hear: have some objects that make noise behind a screen, such as an alarm clock, bell, rattle, eggbeater, crumpled paper
4. Simon Says or Sally Says: crow like a rooster, bark like a dog
5. What Do You Hear?: a language development game for discovering sounds; ask children what sounds they could hear if they were in the country, at the seashore, in the city, in a park

Routine Times

1. At meal or snacktime serve crunchy foods like carrot sticks and celery sticks, crisp crackers, potato chips, some dry cereal.
2. At meal or snacktime talk about chewing quietly with the mouth closed and not slurping beverages and soups.
3. At pickup time suggest moving as quietly as possible without talking, and occasionally walking on tiptoe.
4. At rest time listen for sounds; when sitting or lying on blankets outside or with windows open when weather permits.
5. At rest time use one of the suggested records or play a quiet lullaby.
6. When walking or busing listen for sounds: birds, sirens, hammers.
7. When playing outside make note of sounds: a squeaky trike, a chirping cricket, an approaching helicopter, the thud of a falling block, and so on.

Large Muscle Activities

1. Take a listening walk outdoors and listen for sounds made by animals, insects, people, machines, bells, and sirens.
2. Organize a marching band.

Extended Experiences

1. Invite a parent or a musician to bring an instrument and play it for the children.
2. Visit a school during band, orchestra, or choir rehearsal. Arrange with the person in charge in advance to select two or three short pieces that the children would enjoy. Perhaps they would practice and play one or two pieces that the children know best (if music is provided in advance). An 8- to 10-minute program would be sufficient. Also ask that some of the instruments be played separately and identified.
3. Visit a church to hear an organ and the church bells.
4. Borrow the telephone company teaching unit and talk about how to answer the telephone, how to dial the telephone, and how to lay the receiver down carefully. Younger children should be taught not to play with the telephone, and older children should be encouraged to learn their own telephone number.

teacher resources

Books and Periodicals

1. *Handtalk: An ABC of Finger Spelling and Sign Language*, Remy Charlip and Mary Beth. New York: Parents' Magazine Press, 1974.
2. *Music for the Family, Childcraft*, vol. II.
3. "Making Percussion Instruments," *Creative Movement for Children*, Gladys Andrews. Englewood Cliffs, N.J.: Prentice-Hall, 1954.

Pictures and Displays

(See p. 79 for addresses of firms listed.)

1. Display pictures of ears and of things that make sounds, such as animals, clocks, machines, bells. Ask children to imitate the different sounds.
2. Display a few musical instruments.
3. Make available drinking glasses tuned to various pitches by filling with varying amounts of water.
4. My Five Senses Bulletin Board Kit, filmstrip, record, and cassette to accompany books (Constructive Playthings).

Community Resources

1. Bell Telephone Company, teaching unit
2. Local school band, orchestra, or chorus director
3. Church, carilloneur or organist
4. Hearing aid companies (often give free ear charts and pamphlets)

4 Taste

basic understandings

(concepts children can grasp from this subject)

- We taste through parts of our tongue called taste buds.
- Each food has a particular taste.
- Some foods taste sweet, sour, salty, or bitter. Some foods combine these tastes.
- We may add flavoring to a food when preparing it, to make it taste better.
- The flavor of a food or a drink is a combination of the way it tastes and the way it smells.
- Some foods taste good; sometimes we do not like the flavor.
- Sometimes we have to get used to a new taste by trying it several times. We may learn to like the taste of it.

Additional Facts the Teacher Should Know

For a sense of smell and taste, human beings need the olfactory nerves in the nose and the taste buds on the tongue. If these are not properly developed, humans will have difficulty with taste discrimination. The senses of smell and taste are based on a sensitivity to chemicals. Different nerve endings are sensitive to particular chemical stimuli—for example, salts, sugars, acids. Some children may be born without a sense of taste or smell, either of which will affect their ability to discriminate flavors.

Most young children do not have a keen sense of taste and therefore do not require as much seasoning in their food. The way the food is displayed and the size of the servings can affect children's attitudes toward eating and trying new foods. Try to serve foods from the four food groups in an attractive manner. Keep the portions small. With new foods, only one bite may be expected. If foods are served family-style, children gain independence in serving themselves and can more easily express their food taste needs. Sometimes the texture of a food can affect the child's attitude toward it.

Children can be encouraged to learn to like different foods by inviting a parent who represents a different ethnic group to come and help make a simple recipe that is a favorite food of their family. Consult your Public Health Department regarding laws regulating the preparation of foods in your center. Encourage the children to keep food preparation surfaces sanitary, to keep hands clean while cooking, and to handle equipment safely. For recipes, see book list in Teacher Resources, p. 146. (For related information and activities, see the Food, Color, sense of Smell, and sense of Touch guides.)

Methods Most Adaptable for Introducing This Subject to Children

- Prepare a favorite food that has a distinctive flavor and odor.
- Introduce a story about food like *The Carrot Seed*.
- Have a tasting party.
- Have a parent visit the school and bring or prepare a typical food from his or her traditional recipe (Jewish, Italian, Mexican, French).

Vocabulary

taste	sour	flavor	pleasant	salt
taste bud	salty	good	disagreeable	pepper
tongue	bitter	bad	delicious	cinnamon
sweet	spicy	tart	seasoning	sugar

learning centers

Discovery Center

1. Make a milkshake. Add chocolate, strawberry, vanilla, or banana flavoring.
2. Make a pitcher of lemonade. Taste it before and after adding the sugar.
3. Make popcorn. Taste with and without salt.
4. Mix cinnamon and sugar. Shake the mixture onto enriched white-bread toast or raisin toast.
5. Have a shaker full of sugar and a shaker full of salt. Let the children shake a little on their clean hands and taste it. Talk about how the tastes are alike and how they are different.
6. Melt bitter chocolate. Taste it. Add sugar. Taste it.
7. Start with strong tea or unsweetened fruit drink. Taste it. Add sugar. Taste it.
8. Bake pumpkin cupcakes, using your favorite recipe. Let children taste some of the ingredients and the final product.
9. Mix up a muffin batter. Add blueberries to some of the batter, chopped dates or nuts to some, peanut butter to some, and mashed banana to some. Identify and compare before baking.

10. Compare cooked and uncooked foods and fresh and canned foods as to flavor.
11. Have a tasting party: set out bite-size portions of a variety of foods that have distinctive flavors: salty, sweet, sour, bitter, spicy, bland. Let children match processed cheese shapes with corresponding cracker shapes. To increase the discussion about foods, consider color, texture, and odor when providing foods for the children to taste—for example, orange carrot coins, green pickle slices, yellow cubes of cheese, red radish roses, candy orange slices, shavings of bitter chocolate. Serve strong tea, grapefruit juice, pink lemonade, chocolate milk to drink.

> **CAUTION:** Before serving foods to children be aware of their allergies (chocolate, egg, milk) and special dietary needs (sugar-free [diabetics]; salt-free [high blood pressure]; or food additives [hyperactivity]).

Dramatic Play Centers

Home-Living Center

1. Encourage the preparation of foods in the housekeeping area. Comment on how delicious the food is and what good cooks the children are.
2. Collect empty cartons and cans to put on the shelves to encourage preparation, serving, and tasting of food.
3. Put up pictures in this area of people preparing and eating foods (include pictures of community helpers who serve, sell, grow, deliver, cook, prepare, or handle food or food products).
4. Allow the use of tea or a fruit drink for a tasting tea.
5. Provide utensils and ingredients to make a no-cook food—for example, rolling dates in sugar, instant puddings, no-bake cookies, or candy.

Other Dramatic Play Centers

1. At snacktime set up a bakery store and let the children "buy" their snacks. Provide a variety of cookies, rolls, or cupcakes. Provide hats and aprons for the bakers and servers, and "money" for the customers. A cash register will also be needed.
2. Set up an ice-cream stand for snacktime. Give a choice of ice creams or sherbets to be scooped into cones, or offer a choice of ice creams to be put in dishes. Offer a choice of syrups or fruits to put on top.
3. For snack or mealtime have a cafeteria with a variety of raw vegetables, crackers, dry cereals, fruits, sandwiches, and drinks available. TV trays, cash register, and "money" will be needed.

Learning, Language, and Readiness Materials Center

Commercially made games and materials for use at a table or on a mat:

(See Basic Resources, p. 79, for manufacturers' addresses.)

1. Playskool Puzzles: Milkman, Baker, Grocer, Waitress, Farmer, 14–19 pcs.
2. Judy Puzzles: Vegetables, Table Setting, Apple Tree in Seasons, 4–6 pcs.; At the Grocers, Hot Dog Vendor, 11 pcs.
3. Judy Play Trays: food set, 6 trays, 32 food cards
4. Judy See-Quees: Baking a Cake, Apple Tree in Seasons, 4–6 pcs.; Birthday Party, From Seed to Pumpkin, Story of Milk, 12 pcs. each
5. Look-Inside Kitchen Puzzle, 5 pcs. (ABC School Supply)

6. Shape Discrimination: apples, pears (knob puzzles varying in size)
7. Wooden Pop-Up Toaster (ABC School Supply)
8. Kitchen utensils, refrigerator sets, model food (available from most catalogs)
9. Food Models (available from National Dairy Council in cardboard sheets)

Teacher-made games and materials for use at a table or on a mat:

NOTE: For detailed description of Games, see pp. 50–59.

1. Name It: have a tray of fresh fruits and vegetables. Identify them by name and allow the children to taste and smell them. Blindfold each child and have each identify a fruit or vegetable by taste alone.
2. Look and See: make flannelboard figures of foods that have different tastes. Ask children which is missing—salty food, spicy, sweet, or sour?
3. Lick, Chew, and Taste: select appropriate foods to illustrate tastes.
4. Grouping and Sorting: categories could be salty, sweet, spicy, sour. Use labeled boxes, flannelboard or cardboard game board, with areas divided with a picture of a child/food identifying taste—for example, carton of salt, piece of candy, peanut, pickle—glued to each section.
5. Guess What?: describe a food; be sure to include its taste. For instance, say, "It is yellow, smaller than an orange, and tastes sour. What is it?"

Art Center

* 1. Save colored water obtained from boiling brown onion skins (yellow) and red onion skins (purple) to let the children watercolor with brushes on different sizes and types of paper.
* 2. Prepare ahead of time some colored salt (pickling, table, or ice-cream salt) by mixing with dry tempera or a mixture of liquid and tempera. When salt is dry, let children paint their picture with thinned glue and sprinkle on the desired color(s) for a textured painting.
* 3. Make a book of pictures cut from magazines of foods that taste good. Caption with what children say about their choices of pictures as they cut and paste them.

   NOTE: For younger children you may have a precut or preselected pile of pictures for them to choose for their book.

* 4. Save seeds and eggshells from food preparation to be dried out. Use as collage materials later in the week for an extended experience.
* 5. Offer a variety of the basic media (fingerpaint, clay, paint) in colors of special foods tasted or cooked that day so children will have colors they need to tell about their experiences through art.
* 6. Provide gummed colored geometric shapes for children to make a "lick and stick" picture.

Book Center

** Aliki. *My Five Senses.* New York: Thomas Y. Crowell, 1962.
*** Gibson, M. T. *What Is Your Favorite Smell?* New York: Grosset & Dunlap, 1964.
* Green, Mary McBurney. *Everybody Has a House and Everybody Eats.* Reading, Mass.: Addison-Wesley, 1961.

* Krauss, Ruth. *The Carrot Seed.* New York: Harper & Row, 1945.
** McCloskey, Robert. *Blueberries for Sal.* New York: Viking Press, 1948.
*** Polland, Barbara Kay. *The Sensible Book: Celebration of Your Five Senses.* Millbrae, Cal.: Celestial Arts Publishing, 1973.
*** Showers, Paul. *How Many Teeth?* New York: Thomas Y. Crowell, 1962.
*** ———. *Follow Your Nose.* New York: Thomas Y. Crowell, 1963.
*** Tudor, Tasha. *First Delights: A Book About the Five Senses.* New York: Platt & Munk, 1966.

NOTE: Select other stories from the Book Center list in the Food guide. Select one of the foods mentioned in the book for the children to taste before, during, or after the story as appropriate.

planning for grouptime

NOTE: All music, fingerplays, poems, stories, and games listed here may also be used at other times during the session as appropriate. See Core Library, Basic Resources, p. 76, for publishers and addresses. Addresses of sources for records will be found on p. 81. In parodies, hyphenated words match music notes of the tune used.

Music

Songs

FROM original songs in this book by JoAnne Deal Hicks
"Popcorn," p. 121
"Fruitbasket Song," p. 561
"Sing a Song of Applesauce," p. 562

NOTE: Combine the singing of the songs above with a sample taste of the food to which you are referring or, if at a time other than Music Time, sing the song as the activity is being carried out, such as popping corn or making applesauce.

FROM *Songs for the Nursery School,* MacCarteney
** "Nutting," p. 63
** "Shake the Apple Tree," p. 66
* "Hot Cross Buns," p. 75
** "Polly Put the Kettle On," p. 86

FROM *Music Resource Book,* Lutheran Church Press
* "I Have Two Eyes" (adaptation of line 2, verse 1 of "God Gave Me Eyes," p. 66)

FROM *Songs for Early Childhood,* Westminster Press
** "Beautiful Wonderful Sights to See," p. 39

WHAT FOODS DO YOU LIKE? (a parody)
(tune: "Oats, Peas, Beans")
Adaptation by JoAnne Deal Hicks

VERSE 1: Eggs and milk and ba-con strips. Eggs and milk and ba-con strips.
Do you, do you, do you, do you . . . like eggs and milk and ba-con strips?
(AS YOU SING THE QUESTION, POINT TO INDIVIDUAL CHILDREN IN THE GROUP.)

VARIATIONS FOR OTHER VERSES ARE GIVEN BELOW. REPEAT AND ADAPT AS IN THE FIRST VERSE.

VERSE 2: Dan-ish rolls and or-ange juice
VERSE 3: Pea-nut but-ter, jel-ly too
VERSE 4: Ap-ples, grapes, and can-ta-loupe
VERSE 5: Cheese and pie with cold ice-cream
VERSE 6: Corn and peas and broc-co-li

NOTE: This song may be adapted, as above, to include many combinations of foods. Encourage the children to help you select the different foods.

Fingerplays and Poems

APPLES

Away up high in the apple tree,   (POINT UP)
Two red apples smiled at me.   (FORM CIRCLES WITH FINGERS)
I shook that tree as hard as I could;   (PRETEND TO SHAKE TREE)
Down came those apples, and mmmmm, were they good!   (RUB TUMMY)

FROM *Rhymes for Fingers and Flannelboards,* Scott and Thompson
"The Baker Man," p. 24
"This Little Chick," p. 29
"An Egg," p. 41
"What Colors Do I See? p. 45 (tasting)
"Five Little Easter Eggs," p. 73
"This Little Bunny," p. 76
"Here's a Cup of Tea," p. 85
"Five Little Robins," p. 95
"The Apple Tree," p. 119 (taste)

FROM *Let's Do Fingerplays,* Grayson
"Kitten Is Hiding," p. 32
"There Was a Little Turtle," p. 33
"My Rabbit," p. 34
"This Little Calf," p. 38
"My Garden," p. 46
"Apples," p. 48
"The Teapot," p. 82
"Here's a Cup," p. 83
"Peas Porridge," p. 88
"Little Jack Horner," p. 94

NOTE: Most of the above are about food: finding it, serving it, or eating it.

FROM *Music Resource Book,* Lutheran Church Press
"I Have Two Eyes to See With," p. 67 (use as an action poem)

LUNCH
  by Darlene Hamilton

Crunch, munch
There's food for our lunch!
Today we have berries, or you may have cherries,
There's salad with peas, a sandwich with cheese.
Or—a slice of browned roast on your own buttered toast.
Crunch, munch, eat your lunch!

TASTES
  by Darlene Hamilton

Syrup and honey are sweet.
Pickles and lemons are sour.
Peanuts and crackers a treat.
For a snack most any hour!

Stories

(To read, read-tell, or tell. See Book Center for complete list.)

** *Blueberries for Sal,* McCloskey
 * *The Carrot Seed,* Krauss
 * *Everybody Has a House and Everybody Eats,* Green

Games

(See Games, pp. 50–59, and Teacher-Made Games in this guide for directions.)

1. Name It
2. Look and See
3. Listening: have one child be the baker with a plate of cookies or other baked goods. Blindfold the baker. Point to a child who says "Please may I have a cookie?" The baker says, "Yes, you may, —————." and guesses the child, who then takes a cookie. If the baker guesses wrong, he or she guesses again until he or she gets the name correct. The child whose name was guessed then becomes the baker. Continue until all have had a cookie. **Variation:** farmer with apples; squirrel with nuts.
4. Grouping and Sorting
5. Guess What?

Routine Times

1. At snack or mealtime, feature foods that can be grouped or classified.
    a. fruits: apples, oranges, fresh pineapple, bananas, cherries, berries
    b. vegetables: carrots, green pepper, cauliflower, celery, peas, corn

c. breads: enriched white, whole wheat, rye, raisin, pumpernickel
d. milk: fresh, canned, powdered, buttermilk, chocolate
e. meats: fish, eggs, weiners, hamburger, pork chops, roast lamb
2. At snack or mealtime, combine the serving of food with a Dramatic Play Activity (see Other Dramatic Play Centers, Stories, Songs, and Poems in this guide).
3. Offer snacks with different flavors, such as salty pretzels, sour lemon wedges, sweet candy orange slices, semi-sweet chocolate. Talk about putting food on the tongue to see how it tastes. Discuss how food tastes differently when seasoned or when sugar is added.

Extended Experiences

1. Visit a bakery, buy some freshly baked enriched bread rolls. Take back to the center and eat. Bake your own bread at the center. Let frozen dough rise and then let children twist their own design for their roll. Identify each child's roll by making a chart of the pan or by labeling with toothpicks.
2. Invite parents who represent different ethnic groups to come and help prepare nutritious snacks or food with the group. Make detailed preparations in advance for food/utensils needed and simplify procedures for the youngest in the group.
3. Invite a dentist to come and show the children how to brush their teeth and to discuss ways to keep teeth clean and breath fresh.

teacher resources

Books and Periodicals

1. *Food for Little People.* City of Berkeley, Department of Public Health and Berkeley Unified School District, Early Childhood Education Program. Berkeley, California.
2. *An Introduction to Educational Cooking: The Mother-Child Cookbook.* Nancy J. Ferreira. Menlo Park, Calif.: Pacific Coast Publishers.

Pictures and Displays

1. Food and Nutrition: Teaching Picture Set (David C. Cook)
2. Animals That Help Us: Fold-out Picture Charts (The Child's World)
3. Food Models: We All Like Milk; What We Do Day by Day: both models and picture sets are available from the National Dairy Council

Community Resources

1. County home economist or dairy council representative
2. Eye, ear, nose, and throat doctors
3. Dentists/dental technicians

5 ſmell

baſic underſtandingſ

(concepts children can grasp from this subject)

- We smell odors through our noses.
- We learn about some things by the way they smell.
- Some things smell good (have a nice odor) and some things smell bad (have a bad odor).
- We take baths so that we will be clean and smell nice.
- The smell of smoke tells us something is burning.
- We can tell some foods by the way they smell; we can sometimes tell what we will be eating at the next meal by the way it smells while it is cooking.
- Most animals can find things by smelling for them. It helps them find food, their friends, and their enemies.
- Flowers have a nice odor (perfume) that attracts bees and helps them find the nectar (food) they like to eat.
- Skunks give off a bad (disagreeable) odor to protect themselves and drive others away.

Additional Facts the Teacher Should Know

The senses of smell and taste are based on a sensitivity to chemicals. Different nerve endings are sensitive to particular chemical stimuli—for example, salt, sugar, acids. Because of the position of the olfactory nerve endings high in the inner back part of the nasal passages of the nose, it is sometimes necessary to sniff or smell closely to detect a delicate fragrance.

The tongue, like the fingers, has a higher number of nerve endings per square inch of surface than many other areas of the skin. Being also sensitive to chemicals makes it more highly sensitive to a variety of stimuli. Often the smell of food enhances its taste (if you hold your nose sometimes you cannot taste what you are eating). If food smells bad it may also warn you that it is spoiled. Sometimes when children have a cold or are ill their sense of smell may be hampered. The nostrils have fine hairs inside that help filter dust and particles and keep them from going into the lungs when we breathe.

Some children may be born without a sense of smell. That is, the olfactory nerve endings located in the nose are not properly developed. Children who do not have a sense of smell also have a poor sense of taste and are unable to distinguish the differences in bland foods in particular. (See guides on Food and Animals for related activities.)

Methods Most Adaptable for Introducing This Subject to Children

- Plan to cook pumpkin cupcakes (use your own favorite recipe) and ask each child to smell the ingredients before they are added.
- Children may smell an unpleasant odor, such as from a skunk, factory waste, or garbage, or a pleasant odor, such as from flowers or cooking.
- Set out smell tubes (see Teacher-Made Games).

Vocabulary

odor	aroma	fragrance	pleasant	spicy
smell	scent	perfume	disagreeable	sweet
nose	sniff	delicious	unpleasant	tongue

learning centers

Discovery Center

1. Take a smelling walk. Talk about the odors you smell and whether they are pleasant or unpleasant.
2. Cooking food is especially good for discovering smells. Bake bread, rolls, pumpkin cupcakes, peanut butter cookies, or make pancakes, waffles, or popcorn.
3. Set out a tray of fresh, cleaned fruits and vegetables. Identify the foods and let the children touch, smell, and taste them.
4. If possible, observe flowers or flowering trees or bushes nearby. Talk about how bees are attracted by the sweet smelling odor and how they carry pollen from flower to flower. Watch for bees.
5. Close windows to keep out bad odors; open windows to let in fresh air.
6. Match smelling tubes (see Teacher-Made Games).
7. Burn scented candles or incense with different fragrances. Let children guess what they think the fragrance smells like.
8. Bring in a vase of flowers or a potted flowering plant.
9. Encourage the children to explore the room to discover how different things smell, even those with no apparent odor, such as leather, rubber boots, wood, flowers, polished furniture, aquarium, pet cages, cedar chips, painted objects.

10. Collect other fragrant items for a smell tray. Include leather, fur, cedarwood, incense, perfume sachet, rubber foam, carpet, linoleum, magazine and newspaper, cotton, tissues, cork, soap, pine cones, evergreen.

Dramatic Play Centers

Home-Living Center

1. Pretend to bake and cook. Have playdough available for baking in the housekeeping corner. Teacher could comment on how good it smells.
2. Provide a dressing table with empty bottles of perfume, lotion, and creams for playing dress up.

   CAUTION: Be sure containers are unbreakable/empty.

3. Put a bouquet of real flowers on the table.
4. Set out a small carton of scented tissues.

Block-Building Center

1. Encourage fire engine play by saying "I smell smoke. I think there is a fire over here. Please come and put it out!"
2. Encourage older children to build a gasoline station. Talk about how gasoline smells.

Other Dramatic Play Centers

1. Set up a florist shop with artificial flowers, plastic corsages, and plants (add touch of perfume to articles to make them more authentic). Provide a cash register, pencil, pad, telephone table, and chairs.
2. Set up a drugstore, adding appropriate fragrant drug items.

   CAUTION: Make sure all items are unbreakable and bottles are empty.

3. Set up a bakery. (See Taste guide, p. 141.)

Learning, Language, and Readiness Materials Center

Commercially made games and materials for use at a table or on a mat:

(See Basic Resources, p. 79, for manufacturers' addresses.)

1. Judy See-Quees: Seed to Flower, Apple Tree, 6 pcs.; Baking a Cake, 4 pcs.
2. Often the senses of smell and taste are related. For additional suggestions for commercially made games and materials, see the Taste guide list.

Teacher-made games and materials for use at a table or on a mat:

NOTE: For detailed description of Games, see pp. 50–59.

1. Sniff and Smell
2. Match-Them: have two sets of smelling bottles filled with distinctive odors for the children to match. Include cloves, peppermint, coffee, cinnamon, garlic, chili, vanilla, cocoa, perfume. Small, opaque plastic bottles obtained from a pharmacy or unbreakable film tubes are best. Puncture two or three holes in each lid. Glue a circle of nylon fabric inside the lid to keep ingredients from spilling out, but allowing the odor to rise.

3. Name It: have a tray of fresh fruits and vegetables. Identify them by name and allow children to hold and sniff them. Blindfold children and have them identify the fruits or vegetables by odor alone. (See **CAUTION**, p. 53, regarding blindfolds.)

Art Center

** 1. Cook brown and red onion skins in separate pans of water. Save yellow (brown) and red (purple) liquid obtained after boiling to be used with paintbrushes in Art Center later.
 * 2. Make your own library paste; add oil of cloves or wintergreen. Use in Art Center when paste is required.
 * 3. Make a collage of pictures of things you like to smell.
 * 4. Printing with vegetables can make interesting designs if you use unedible ends, rinds, or sections of vegetables with a distinct odor used by the cook this week, e.g., green peppers, cabbage, onions. Use vegetable as you would any other printing tool, bouncing it in paint and then stamping it on a paper surface.

Book Center

*** Aliki. *My Five Senses.* New York: Thomas Y. Crowell, 1962.
*** Gibson, M. T. *What Is Your Favorite Smell?* New York: Grosset and Dunlap, 1964.
*** Polland, Barbara Kay. *The Sensible Book: Celebration of Your Five Senses.* Millbrae, Calif.: Celestial Arts Publishing, 1974.
*** Showers, Paul. *Follow Your Nose.* New York: Thomas Y. Crowell, 1963.
 ** Tudor, Tasha. *First Delights: A Book About the Five Senses.* New York: Platt & Munk, 1966.

planning for grouptime

NOTE: All music, fingerplays, poems, stories, and games listed here may be used at other times during the session as appropriate. See Core Library, Basic Resources, p. 76, for publishers and addresses. Addresses for sources of records will be found on p. 81. In parodies, hyphenated words match music notes of the tune used.

Music

Songs

FROM *Songs for Early Childhood*, Westminster Press
** "Beautiful Wonderful Sight to See," p. 39

THE SMELLING SONG (a parody)
   (tune: "Did You Ever See a Lassie?")
   by JoAnne Deal Hicks

TEACHER SINGS: Have you ev-er smelled a rose-bud, a rose-bud, a rose-bud?
                  Have you ev-er smelled a rose-bud? Oh . . . how does it smell?

CHILDREN ANSWER: (Teacher may substitute another word for rosebud. Allow the children to respond verbally.
                Adjectives and adverbs that they might use are: spicy, sweet, good, sour, badly burned.)

Fingerplays and Poems

   FROM *Let's Do Fingerplays*, Grayson
* "Flowers," a series of fingerplays, pp. 126–27

Stories

   (To read, read-tell, or tell. See Book Center for complete listing.)

*** *Follow Your Nose*, Showers
*** *What Is Your Favorite Smell?*, Gibson

Games

   (See Games, pp. 50–59, and Teacher-Made Games in this guide for directions.)

1. Name It
2. Sniff and Smell

Routine Times

1. Snack or mealtime is a natural time to talk about the odor of foods. You might want to plan some foods with distinctive odors, such as popcorn, peanut butter, bacon, cinnamon toast, chocolate milk.
2. When toileting talk about the clean soapy smell of washed hands.
3. When busing or walking talk about the smell of the earth after a rain, the smell of gasoline when stopping for a fill-up, the delicious odors from a bakery, the smell of new-mown hay or grass, the perfume of flowers or flowering bushes.

Extended Experiences

1. Take a walk and call attention to or look for things that have an odor; talk about whether it is a pleasant or an unpleasant odor.
2. Visit a bakery to see and smell the baked goods. Buy something for a snack.
3. Visit a flower shop or greenhouse. Enjoy the many fragrances and talk about the colors that you see. If possible, buy some flowers to take back to the center.
4. If the center is in a smaller town or suburb, make arrangements to visit a neighbor's flower or vegetable garden where the children would be welcome to explore.

teacher resources

Pictures and Displays

(See p. 79 for addresses of firms listed.)

1. Put up pictures of noses (people's and animals') with a picture display of good things to smell. Include pictures of flowers, perfume, and baked goods.
2. Display smelling bottles.

   CAUTION: Be certain all are unbreakable.

3. Fresh flower arrangements: choose flowers with a characteristic fragrance: mums, roses, carnations.
4. "Follow Your Nose" filmstrip, record, and cassette for use with the book (Thomas Y. Crowell).
5. "The Five Senses," LP Story Record (Bowmar).
6. "Let's Take a Walk in Spring/Summer/Winter/Fall": a series of picture charts (The Child's World).

6 Touch

basic understandings

(concepts children can grasp from this subject)

- We feel with our skin.
- We may touch things with almost any part of our body, but we usually use our fingers. (We can feel with our tongue, lips, feet, and arms.)
- Some things feel soft, hard, smooth, rough, cold, hot, wet, or dry.
- Our skin helps keep us safe. It tells us when we are near something too hot; it tells us if we are too cold, or if we are hurt.
- We can "feel" happy or sad, sick or well, sleepy or wide awake, energetic or tired.
- We can feel the sun's rays, cool shade, wind, raindrops, snow, and hail.
- We can tell if we are moving or standing still. This is called the kinesthetic sense.
- We can feel pain (or discomfort) inside our bodies. This is called the organic sense.
- When people say hello or goodbye they often touch, shake hands, kiss, or hug.

Additional Facts the Teacher Should Know

Touch is a broad term for several senses, those of pressure, pain, and temperature. The sense of touch is made possible by nerve endings scattered through the skin. Some nerve endings make our bodies sensitive to temperatures (cold or heat), others to pain, and still others to sensations from touch or pressure.

When stimulated, different nerve endings (receptors) send electrical impulses to the sensory area of the brain. When received there, the brain interprets what has happened by the kind of signal stimulus and its source. In almost a reflex chain reaction, a message is sent back to the muscles to withdraw or react to the stimuli whether pressure, pain, extreme temperature, or other. These nerve endings are also found in our mouth and inside our bodies on muscles or organs making possible sensitivity to pressure or distress internally, such as stomach pain, sore throat, earache, and others. Fingers, because of a higher concentration of nerve endings per square inch surface area, are more sensitive to stimuli (change) and therefore have a better sense of touch than most other areas of the body. Some people do not have a sense of touch and may therefore cut or burn themselves without knowing they are doing so. Some people have a very low threshold of pain, which means a little pain is very uncomfortable; others have a high threshold of pain, which means they can tolerate a good deal of pain.

Methods Most Adaptable for Introducing This Subject to Children

- Fill a box or sack with items for the child to feel and identify. Use a commercially made feel box or make your own. (See illustration, p. 155.)
- While playing outdoors encourage children to explore sand, rocks, bark, mud, water, ice and snow, twigs, fresh and dry leaves, sprouts, buds, seeds, roots, shells through touch.
- Make a feel book with different kinds of fabrics or materials: sandpaper, corduroy, satin, velvet, leather, fur.

Vocabulary

rough, smooth	many, few	furry	soapy
hard, soft	big, little	bumpy	satin
cold, hot	sleepy, awake	finger	velvet
limp, crisp	tired, peppy	feel	fur
wet, dry	sick, well	touch	corduroy
happy, sad	sticky, slick	prickly	sandpaper
thick, thin	heavy, light	skin	cardboard

learning centers

Discovery Center

1. Provide objects for the children to feel which have been warmed by a heating pad or cooled in a refrigerator.
2. Make or buy a feeling book with the animals or other figures made of various textures, such as silk, corduroy, sandpaper, smooth contact paper, cotton. Individually or in small groups identify the materials and help the children feel the differences and describe them as well. Use adjectives, such as soft, furry, slippery, shiny, smooth, rough.
3. Buy or make a feel box with two each of 4-inch squares of various types of fabrics and materials. Ask child to match samples without looking.
4. Have a tub of very warm water and one of very cold water side by side. Have children put one hand in each tub of water. Reverse hands for change in feel. Have towels available to dry hands. Add soap (liquid detergent) to warm for another feel. **Variation:** in season add ice or snow.
5. Let children explore a variety of items in a Touch and Feel tray, comparing texture, size, weight, number, and consistency by touch. Encourage them to discover how each item feels, first with bare hands, and then wearing rubber or cotton gloves. Include:

fur (soft, furry)	brushes (bristly, soft)
coil (springy, cold)	pine cone (prickly, rough)
bark (rough, bumpy)	fabrics (offer variety)
shells (smooth, hard)	wood (smooth, hard)
carpet (soft, stiff)	plastic (smooth, flexible)
cactus (prickly, sharp)	styrofoam (smooth, scratchy)
yarn ball (soft)	sandpaper (scratchy, rough)
cotton (soft, light)	rubber foam (spongy, soft)
feather (soft, stiff)	paper (crisp, soft, smooth)
rope/twine (scratchy)	metal (cold, smooth)
cellophane (crisp, thin)	

6. Encourage children to observe the different ways people greet each other, such as shaking hands, kissing, hugging, nodding. Films, pictures, and observation at home, on the street, or on TV will afford the opportunity.

7. Allow children to experiment with touch when exploring a stringed instrument or a horn with valves. Demonstrate and talk about how pianists or instrumentalists use their fingers or mouth to make their instruments play. Note that they often "feel" for these places (keys, strings, valves) without looking.

8. Put textured items into a container which conceals its contents, such as a can covered with a stocking, a bag closed with a drawstring or elastic, a closed paper sack, or a box with only a fist-sized opening. **Variations:** the task might be (a) to retrieve two like objects by feeling a concealed group of items; (b) to match one concealed item with one visible; (c) to match one item concealed with one selected from a visible group.

Children are exploring objects by touching and feeling them. See p. 14 for list of items to include in a Touch and Feel Science Tray.

Dramatic Play Centers

Home-Living Center

1. Wash doll clothes in warm soapy water and rinse in cool clear water. Talk about the temperature of the tubs of water. Feel liquid soap. How does it feel? Hang the clothes up to dry. How do they feel? Damp. Let the clothes dry. How do they feel? Dry. How do you know? They *feel* damp or dry. Talk about the various fabrics.
2. Wash dolls and dry them with big bath towels.
3. Wash dishes and rinse them.
4. Pretend the dolls are sick and have a fever. Do their foreheads feel hot? Take their temperature. Call the doctor. Give sponge baths to lower their temperature.
5. Put on blankets and sweaters when the dolls are cold.

Block-Building Center

1. Set out metal, wooden, and plastic cars.
2. Provide excelsior for hay and a piece of green indoor-outdoor carpet for grassy area.
3. Talk about how blocks feel: warm, smooth, curved, square.

Other Dramatic Play Centers

1. At woodworking bench have woods of various textures. Talk about rough and smooth. Provide sandpaper for smoothing the edges and sides of the wood of various objects made by children.
2. Set up a clothing store. Hang up the dress-up clothes on rolling clothes racks or clothes trees. Have a hat bar, shoe corner, and glove and scarf counter. Talk about the various fabrics and textures of the clothes. A full-length mirror, small mirrors, and hand mirrors would add to the discussion of the clothes—How do they look and how do they feel? Cash register, sacks, and money are needed, too. Boxes and shopping bags would also be useful. Include many textures: feathered hats, denim, satin, fur, net, velours, leather.

Language, Learning, and Readiness Materials Center

Commercially made games and materials for use at a table or on a mat:

(See Basic Resources, p. 79, for manufacturers' addresses.)

1. Sand and Water Play Table: plus sand tools (most catalogs)
2. Feel and Match Thicknesses (Constructive Playthings)
3. Montessori Graded Cylinders (most catalogs)
4. Fit-A-Space Series (Lauri)
5. Tactilmat Series (Ideal)
6. Tactile Letters/Cards, Boards: beaded, flocked, wooden (most catalogs)
7. Beamer Balance (most catalogs)
8. Bag of Feelies (Constructive Playthings)
9. Feel and Match Textures (Constructive Playthings)
10. Tactile Sensory Training Bridges Series (Constructive Playthings)
11. Flannelboard Letters/Shapes/Numbers (most catalogs)
12. Rocks/Shells/Fossils sets (most catalogs)
13. Instructor Magnetic Primary Counting Shapes: (50 three-dimensional shapes)

14. Touch and Match Kit (Childcraft)
15. Tell by Touch (Matching Textures Childcraft)
16. Autoharp (many catalogs)
17. Note Kalimba (Childcraft)

Teacher-made games and materials for use at a table or on a mat:

NOTE: For detailed description of Games, see pp. 50–59.

1. Make a feel box. Cut a sturdy cardboard box so child cannot see in but can put a hand through a hole on each side. (See illustration, p. 155.) Put pairs of matched materials of different textures, cut in 4″ squares, in the box, for example, two pieces of sandpaper, two of velvet, satin, corduroy, plastic upholstering material, cardboard, carpet (two each of several different textures and piles), formica, corktiles. Children reach in and find the two that match by feel only.
2. Name It or Scramble: use many different types of textured objects.
3. Look and See: using a screen or feel box put several articles that can be identified by touch alone out of sight, letting children see them first. Remove one article and decide, by touch alone, which one is missing.
4. Reach and Feel: use items that can be guessed by touch alone, such as pencil, crayon, ball, clothespin, string, bottle cap, blunt-nosed scissors, box, stone, spoon. Place one article in each of several sacks or sock-covered cans. Let each child select one to see if he or she can identify it. Avoid using anything sharp.
5. Grouping and Sorting by Association: have several objects made of fur, leather, plastic, or cloth, and let children group them.
6. Alike, Different, and the Same: use various squares from Match-Them. Put two alike and one different together and ask a child to show you the one that is different. Talk about the differences. Ask children to do this with their eyes closed or use a small screen or the feel box. Can be alike in color, shape, but should be different in texture.

Art Center

   * 1. Paint with tempera on corrugated paper, sandpaper, or foam trays.
   * 2. Paint eggshell halves with tempera. When dry, use a rolling pin to break them into chips. Use these later to make a collage.
*** 3. Make a sandpainting: with fingers, paintbrush, or Q-Tips, put paste or white glue on paper in the design desired. Color sand with tempera; place in containers with large holes in the top. Shake sand onto the paper with glue on it. Shake excess sand off painting onto newspaper. Fold newspaper to make a slide for returning excess sand to container if not mixed colors.
   * 4. Fingerpaint with various media: buttermilk, starch, whipped soapsuds. Add powdered tempera for color. Add rice, coffee, sawdust, salt, for different textures.
  ** 5. Dip chalk in water, buttermilk, or liquid starch, and color on sandpaper.
   * 6. Make playdough with flour and salt. Use rock or kosher salt for a grainier texture. Let children measure and feel ingredients during preparation.
*** 7. With fingertips draw designs in a tray of salt or cornmeal.
  ** 8. Use potter's clay: should be quite moist and soft.
*** 9. Gather leaves and other objects while taking a Feeling Walk. Make a crayon rubbing by placing a sheet of thin white paper over one or more objects, rubbing the paper with the side of the crayon (remove paper from used crayons for this). Any

interesting material, such as screen wire, grained wood, nylon net (open mesh), coins, or paper clips, may also be used.

** 10. Make a collage of textured materials: eggshells, yarn, corrugated paper, buttons.

** 11. Woodworking: use hammer, saw, and sandpaper to make a wood design or just experience the feeling one gets when using these tools.

Book Center

** Aliki. *My Five Senses*. New York: Thomas Y. Crowell, 1962.

** ——. *My Hands*. New York: Thomas Y. Crowell, 1962.

*** Baylor, Byrd. *Everybody Needs a Rock*. New York: Scribner's, 1974.

* Ets, Marie Hall. *Talking Without Words*. New York: Viking Press, 1968 (paper, 1970).

*** Gibson, M. T. *What Is Your Favorite Thing to Touch?* New York: Grosset & Dunlap, 1965.

* Klein, Leonore. *Mud, Mud, Mud*. New York: Alfred A. Knopf, 1962.

* Kunhardt, Dorothy. *Pat the Bunny*. New York: Western Publishing, 1962.

**** Podendorf, Illa. *Touching for Telling*. Chicago, Ill.: Children's Press, 1971.

** Polland, Barbara Kay. *The Sensible Book: A Celebration of Your Five Senses*. Millbrae, Calif.: Celestial Arts Publishing, 1974.

*** Showers, Paul. *Find Out by Touching*. New York: Thomas Y. Crowell, 1961.

*** ——. *Your Skin and Mine*. New York: Thomas Y. Crowell, paper, 1965 (film, record, and cassette).

*** Tudor, Tasha. *First Delights*. New York: Platt & Munk, 1966.

*** Witte, Eve. *Touch Me Book*. Los Angeles, Calif.: Children's Music Center, 1961.

planning for grouptime

NOTE: All music, fingerplays, poems, stories, and games listed here may also be used at other times during the session as appropriate. See Core Library, Basic Resources, p. 76, for publishers and addresses. Sources of records can be found on p. 81. In parodies, hyphenated words match music notes of the tune used.

Music

Songs

FROM *Songs from the Nursery School*, MacCarteney

* "Greeting," p. 3

* "Open, Shut Them," p. 8

* "Warm Hands," p. 9

* "Warm Kitty," p. 27

** "My Boat Is Rocking," p. 44

* "The Goldfish," p. 47

FROM *Music Resource Book*, Lutheran Church Press
* "Clap Your Hands the Way I Do," p. 43
* "This Is the Way," p. 53
* "This Old Man," p. 59

FROM *Wake Up and Sing*, Landeck and Crook
* "Put Your Finger in the Air," p. 12
* "Tap Your Foot," p. 14

FROM *Songs for Early Childhood*, Westminster Press
** "Beautiful, Wonderful Sights to See," p. 39
 * "I Love My Little Kitty," p. 48
** "My Dog Feels Soft and Silky," p. 52

Records

"Sleepy Eyes," "Don't Push Me," and "Put Your Finger in the Air," *Songs to Grow On*, Vol. 1, Woody Guthrie (Folkways, 33⅓ RPM)
"Touch Your Head," *More Singing Fun*, Vol. 2 (Bowmar, 33⅓ RPM)

Rhythms and Singing Games

Clapping: use any suitable music or record with distinct rhythm patterns. Vary the patterns by striking the hands on the thighs or on the floor as well as clapping hands together. Drums: use fast and slow tempos and vary the rhythms in patterned beats, for example, clap, clap, clap-clap or clap, clap-clap, clap or clap-clap-clap, clap, clap.

FROM *Music Resource Book*, Lutheran Church Press
* "Friend, O Friend," p. 44

Fingerplays and Poems

FROM *Rhymes for Fingers and Flannelboards*, Scott and Thompson
"Fun with Hands," p. 110
"Touch Your Nose," p. 113
"Ready to Listen," p. 114
"I Wiggle," p. 117

FROM *Let's Do Fingerplays*, Grayson
"Clap Your Hands," p. 10
"My Hands," p. 12
"Hands on Shoulders," p. 13
"Open, Close Them," p. 79

FROM *Very Young Verses*, Geismer and Suter
"Cat," p. 21   "Winter," p. 134
"Feet," p. 52   "Raining," p. 156
"Hands," p. 53   "Mud," p. 159

Stories

(To read, read-tell, or tell. See Book Center for complete list.)

** *My Five Senses*, Aliki
** *What Is Your Favorite Thing to Touch?*, Gibson
* *Mud, Mud, Mud*, Klein
*** *Find Out by Touching*, Showers

Games

(See Games, pp. 50–59, and Teacher-Made Games in this guide for directions.)

1. Together Together: find your nose, clap your hands
2. Sally Says or Simon Says: touch your head, touch your toes
3. "Did You Ever See a Lassie?": pat your knees, rub your elbow
4. Follow the Leader: touch parts of the body
5. Reach and Feel: if your group is small enough to avoid a long wait for a turn

Routine Times

1. At snack or mealtime talk about the coolness of the foods or beverages: juice, milk, ice creams, sherbets, and the warmth of the cooked foods. It feels cool to your hand when you lift the glass and cool or warm when it touches your lips, tongue, and mouth.
2. At snack or mealtime provide many different textures of food and talk about how it feels—smooth like ice cream, or rough like carrots and celery, or sticky like peanut butter, rough like nuts.
3. When washing hands talk about the temperature of the water and the slippery soap. Provide a few drops of hand lotion for children if they want it.
4. When brushing teeth talk about how brushing makes the teeth feel clean and smooth.
5. When dressing to go outside, talk about what is appropriate to wear and why. When coming inside on a cold day, talk about the warm room. When coming in on a hot day talk about the cool air-conditioning or the cool breeze from the fan.
6. When bussing the children, talk about the use of the heater or air-conditioner to make everyone feel as comfortable as possible. Also speak of the use of windows to keep out snow or rain or to let in cool breezes.

Large Muscle Activities

1. Take a Feeling Walk. Have the children select different objects because of their texture. If walk must be taken on or near private property the children may have to only look at the objects. But describe how they might feel: smooth, rough, shiny, furry, wet, dry.
2. Waterplay outdoors in appropriate season. (See the Water Around Me guide.)
3. Dig in the sand. Fill and dump sand in various containers. Allow children to dampen sand and make sand molds in various-shaped containers.
4. Dig in the mud. Make mudpies. Walk barefoot in the mud.
5. Play in the snow. (See Winter guide.)
6. Run in the wind. (For other activities on windy days, see Spring guide.)

7. Walk in the rain, with or without an umbrella. (See Spring guide.)
8. Roll down a hill or on the grass.
9. Play ball with rubber, plastic, styrofoam, yarn, or nylon stocking balls.
10. Play with horseshoes, ring toss/quoits (plastic, rubber, rope).
11. Play bean-bag toss games.

Extended Experiences

1. Some zoos have a petting farm or a petting zoo for children. Visit it.
2. Bring a live pet like a bunny, kitten, hen, or turtle for children to touch. (See Pet Animal guide.)
3. Ask a blind person to visit and bring a book written in Braille. Ask the person to explain how to read the books and how important the sense of touch is.
4. Take a feeling walk in the room or outdoors to discover how things feel by touch.

teacher resources

Pictures and displays

(See p. 79 for addresses of firms listed.)

1. Show pictures of hands doing things, people shaking hands, hugging, or kissing, and of interesting things to feel.
2. Have objects of different sizes, colors, and textures on a table for children to explore. Include a book written in Braille. Explain its use.
3. The Five Senses Bulletin Board Kit (Constructive Playthings)
4. Your Skin and Mine: film, record, and book (Thomas Y. Crowell)

Community Resources

1. School for the blind
2. Borrow some books in Braille

PART TWO

Families

Introduction
Families

basic understandings

(concepts children can grasp from this subject)

What Is a Family?

- A family is a group of people who may live together; they usually take care of one another.
- Some children are born into a family and some are adopted.
- Some families have several children, some only a few, some just one, and some none.
- Some families have two children born at one time, usually on the same day. These are called twins; three are called triplets, four are quadruplets, and five are quintuplets.
- Some children live with only one parent, guardian, or other person. This could be a father, mother, grandparent, aunt, uncle, or friend of the child.
- A person may live alone or with only a pet.
- Families may have other relatives besides those living *in* their family group, such as grandmothers, grandfathers, aunts, uncles, and cousins. Sometimes these relatives also live *with* the family.
- The family group may be changed for many reasons, for example, by divorce, death, adoption, (re)marriage, when young people leave to marry, old age, separation caused by hospitalization, military service, term in prison, or job requirements.
- Each member of a family is special. In some ways they are alike, and in some ways they are different from one another.
- Each family has a special beginning and way of life (culture), for example, Mexican, Asian, African, Scandinavian, European.
- My family is like some families but different from some others.
- A mother is a woman (parent) who has a child (or children).
- A father is a man (parent) who has a child (or children).

- Boys are called sons by their parents. Girls are called daughters.
- Boys and girls in the same family are called brothers and sisters.
- Children are called different group names at different ages, for example, infant, baby, toddler, preschooler, kindergartner, school-age, pre-teen, teenager, adolescent, or young adult.

What Is a Home?

- A home is a place where a family lives, usually where they eat, sleep, play, and work.
- Families live in many different kinds of homes, for example, a single house, apartment, row house, condominium, duplex, commune, hogan, mobile home, tent, houseboat, or chickee.
- Homes may be located in the city, town, suburbs, on a farm, in the country, on a river, on an island, in a valley, in a desert, on a mountain, or on a reservation.
- The space or ground around a home differs in size and form. There may be much space, little, or none.
- The space around a house may be surfaced, bordered by water, or may have ground that allows for grass, flowers, shrubs, or bushes to grow depending on the climate, place, and cost.
- Homes may be made from many materials, for example, wood, brick, stone, mud, grass, leaves, branches, metal, stucco, skins, canvas.
- A group of houses where families live near each other is called a neighborhood, settlement, community, barrio, or subdivision.
- Most houses have one or more rooms, each named for how it is used, for example, bedroom, living room, bathroom, dining room, kitchen.
- Often each room in a house has special furnishings to make the family more comfortable and the room more useful.
- A family needs a place to live, food to eat, clothes to wear, and people to care for them if they cannot take care of themselves.

7 Families at Home

basic understandings

(concepts children can grasp from this subject)

- Some families buy their homes, their food, and their clothes; others may build their homes, grow their own food, and make their own clothes.
- Homes and clothes may also be rented or borrowed.
- Some family members need to work to earn money to buy things the family needs, such as food, clothes, housing. (See Families at Work guide.)
- Family members can divide the work at home in many ways:
  a. sometimes mother *takes care of the children*
  b. sometimes father *takes care of the children*
  c. sometimes both parents do this at different times or at the same time
  d. sometimes another person, a friend, or a family is hired or asked *to take care of the children*

  NOTE: Insert *takes care of the house, prepares the food, does the laundry,* and other tasks in place of italicized words in a, b, and d above.

- Most families have tools and machines to help them work at home. (See Tools and Machines guide.)
- Some families own a car that they use to go to work, school, shopping, visit friends and relatives, or transport them to other places they wish to go.
- Some families own a truck, motorcycle, bicycle, boat, airplane that they may use to carry themselves or other people or objects for work or fun.
- Families each do some things in their own way, for example, customs, dress, childrearing, and lifestyle. They have certain things they believe and ways of showing them in their worship and celebrations.
- Families celebrate certain days together, with special preparations and plans for things to do. These celebrations often include parties, gifts, dinners, birthdays, weddings, Mother's Day, Father's Day, Valentine's Day, anniversaries, special religious days, and other occasions both happy and sad.

- We should try to learn about other people's ways and what they believe so that we can understand and respect them as they are.
- Some families have pets that they care for.
- Families may do many things together at home, for example, eat, sleep, cook, clean, play, work.
- Families can have good times together at home by playing games, singing, or having cookouts.
- Families may do many things together away from home, such as shopping, riding, picnicking, walking, and visiting friends, relatives, parks, zoos, and other interesting places.

Additional Facts the Teacher Should Know

Good Early Childhood centers encourage the family to share in the opportunities for learning they offer each child. At its best, the home is the primary educator of the child and programs at the centers are supplemental. Therefore teachers use interviews, home visits, and background information sheets to help them learn as much as possible about a child and his or her family that is relevant to their teaching job.

Today's society in America is made up of many cultures and many lifestyles within these cultures. Divorce, remarriages, adoptions, placement in foster homes resulting from death or illness of a parent, or child abuse are just a few of many events that may have far-reaching effects on your children. Children may not have the same last name as their parents. They may not have the same skin color, culture, or religious background as the family with whom they are currently living.

The staff needs always to be supportive of children in helping them understand themselves, their relationship with their family or the group in which they are residing, their peers, and their need to identify with their own culture grouping. (See Additional Facts in the I'm Me, I'm Special and Family Celebrations guides.)

The staff should know (1) Where each child lives and with whom; (2) How many adults are in the home; (3) How many children are there in the family and what are their approximate ages; (4) What are the blood relationships of others in the family to the child; (5) How do the children in the family relate to one another; (6) What are the child's skills and handicaps; (7) Is the child toilet trained, able to feed himself or herself, dress, communicate his or her needs; (8) What language(s) does the child speak; (9) To what ethnic and religious grouping does the child and family belong. The purpose for asking or noting this information is to aid you in assessing a child's needs and to assist you in choices relating to dealing with behavior; this information may also allow the staff to give support and understanding when it is needed.

Children should be encouraged to take pride in their culture and pride in their country. The staff should provide opportunities for children to share knowledge and experiences. The center needs to accept each child and provide opportunities for each to express his or her feelings whether happy, sad, angry, hurt, dejected, or anxious.

Other guides related to this one are I'm Me, I'm Special and Families at Work.

Methods Most Adaptable for Introducing This Subject to Children

- Individual or grouptime conversation. "Who brought you to school today?" "Does your grandmother live nearby?"
- Post pictures on the walls or on a bulletin board of families doing things together, for example, sharing, helping one another. Change the pictures or at least part of them in the presence of children. Invite them to help you. If this is not possible, take two or three children at a time on a picture walk around the room.
- When a grandparent brings the child or visits one day.
- Someone mentions that Mother's Day or Father's Day is coming soon.
- A brother or sister brings or picks up one of the children.
- You may read a story about a family or about mothers, fathers, babies, grandparents.
- A child announces that a new baby has been born in their family, or relates a family happening.

Vocabulary

mother	twins	daddy	aunt	belong to
father	grandmother	baby	uncle	love
family	grandfather	home	cousin	adoption
sister	children	husband	care for	divorce
brother	mommy	wife	live with	home

learning centers

Discovery Center

1. Invite a mother and an infant to visit. Observe the size of the baby's hands, feet, mouth, how it eats, sleeps, and dresses. Encourage the children to ask questions and offer information. Allow touching of baby's feet rather than head or hands for health and safety reasons. Talcum powder can be dusted on the baby's feet and hands and prints made on a dark piece of paper. Compare baby's prints with prints made of children's hands and feet.
2. Demonstrate use of a baby bottle and plate food warmer. This would be especially appropriate to do when a mother comes to visit with a baby and feeds the infant during snack time. Children can be allowed to taste baby foods at this time.
3. Compare the texture of pureed foods (fruit, meat, or vegetables) with the same foods that are raw or cooked whole. You may wish to puree food with a blender.
4. Put up a simple map of your area. If most of the children live within a close radius, insert a bulletin board pin and a name tag at the place each child's home is located. (See I'm Me, I'm Special, p. 97.)

5. For housecleaning see Tools and Machines guide, p. 604.

6. Borrow a pair of hamsters, guinea pigs, rats, mice, or gerbils and observe. Let animals mate and then raise a family.

   CAUTION: Do this only if you can find a home for the pets when observation is completed.

7. Talk about the animals that are monogamous, such as foxes.

   NOTE: Most large birds of prey keep the same mate each year unless one dies. Canadian geese and swans do *not* remate if their mate dies.

8. Learn names of some bird babies that are unusual, such as:

   chicken—chick   swan—cygnet   owl—owlet
   duck—duckling   pigeon—squab   eagle—eaglet
   turkey—poult   goose—gosling

   Learn names of other animal babies. (See Animal Charts.)

9. Bake cookies: If a kitchen is available, let the children (two or three at a time) help make simple drop cookies or hand-rolled cookies. If a kitchen is not available, supply plain cookies, several colors of frosting, varied decorations, and let the children decorate the cookies. Eat for party, snack, or lunch.

Dramatic Play Centers

Home-Living Center

1. Encourage adult/parent role playing by providing dress-up clothes and dramatic play props. Consider the interchangeability of props for all kinds of workers, both men and women.
   Mother/father: include aprons, hats, purses, wallets, wigs, vests, jewelry, high-heeled and low-heeled shoes, jackets, ties, keys, pull-on skirts with elastic around the waist (not long enough to trip on—shorty nightgowns and cocktail dresses do not need shortening), lunch buckets, jumbo plastic tools in a tool kit, gloves, fur stoles, white veil or piece of net curtain, and artificial flowers for bridal play.
   Grandparents: eyeglass frames, wigs, shawls, sweaters, rocking chairs, bedroom slippers, newspapers, magazines, magnifying glasses, and canes.

   NOTE: All children should be allowed to dress up, identifying with either sex role as they choose, not being limited by a stereotype as to clothes or tools used.

   Babies: Use lifesized dolls representing all the cultural groups that are available. Dress them in real baby clothes (size 6 mos. to 1 yr.). Have lots of blankets. Include a few small hand towels for bathing babies. Allow children to bring a few baby items from the display table to use in this center with supervision. A cradle, crib, bed, buggy, and rocking chair will also add to the dramatic play possibilities in this center.

2. Allow children to wash and dry doll dishes, outdoors if weather is nice. Provide tea towels dishcloths, rack, plastic dishpans, bar of soap.

3. Encourage children to clean cupboards and toy shelves.

4. Dust and sweep the Home-Living Center using dustpan, broom, mop, and dusters.

5. Encourage the children to wash and dry doll clothes. Pretend to iron when dry.

   CAUTION: Clothes and bedding may need a real washing and ironing by an adult after this.

6. Allow children to give washable dolls a bath. Provide washcloths, bath towels, and talcum powder with puff.
7. Allow a simple food to be prepared in this center today. (See Food guide.)
8. Play tea party. Take turns being hosts and visitors. For a special treat, pour water or fruit juice into cups. Cut bread, bananas, or other soft finger foods into small pieces to serve on dishes.

   CAUTION: Be sure all dishes and utensils actually used for eating and drinking are sterilized. Paper cups and plates are recommended.

9. Provide food preparation tools commonly used at home by parents, for example, eggbeater, rubber spatula, rolling pin, measuring cups, spoons. Add pudding mix or playdough to use with tools.
10. Allow opportunities for children to use rulers, measuring tape, plastic hammer, wrench, or saw to do parents' jobs around house.

Block-Building Center

1. Set out wooden or rubber family figures.
2. Add a moving van truck or label a truck as one.
3. Encourage use of blocks for building of rooms and new houses.
4. Add a camper, mobile home, tent, and boats to encourage vacation play.
5. Set out multiethnic family figures for block accessories.

Other Dramatic Play Centers

1. Set up a dollhouse adjacent to the block area with movable furniture and multiethnic rubber family figures.
2. Hand puppets of family figures (multiethnic) can be used with a threeway play screen or in connection with hollow blocks and planks.
3. Arrange for a hat bar with various types of helper hats to try on. An unbreakable hand mirror or freestanding mirror, cash register, money, and bags will encourage participation.
4. Set up a shoe store with men's, women's, and children's shoes for customers to try on. Add cash register, money, paper sacks, or boxes.
5. Arrange for a clothing store with mittens, gloves, shirts, skirts, scarves, purses, jewelry, and other appropriate items grouped into areas or on separate shelves. A small coat or hat tree is a helpful addition. Set up checkout counter similar to stores noted above.
6. Set up a grocery store. For suggested props, see Food guide, p. 550.
7. Encourage children to move (relocate) Home-Living Center or set up a second home. Provide cartons to pack, suitcases to carry clothes, and wagons to move furniture.

   NOTE: Choose any of the above or another family-related facility depending upon your children's opportunity, experience, and your community, for example, hamburger stand, café, library. (See Families at Work guide under Dramatic Play Centers.) What you highlight may reflect the visitors, trips, or interests of the children.

8. Make a tabletop or floor terrain for building a community. Duplicate a terrain similar to one familiar to children. Make more of the area cement if you are located in inner city. Illustration, p. 172, allows for yards, park, farm, lake area. Children will enjoy building homes, stores, driving with small cars or trucks on roads, adding trees, boats, animals around the lake, with endless variations. If roads are not too defined, children are allowed more alternatives in use of space. The terrain is easily stored when folded in half. Best for older children who can work together.

Cut out two sides of a stereo carton or desk carton. Tape at center to allow folding to store. Tape edges for durability. Paint with green enamel, leaving roads neutral color of cardboard or paint white. Paint lake blue.

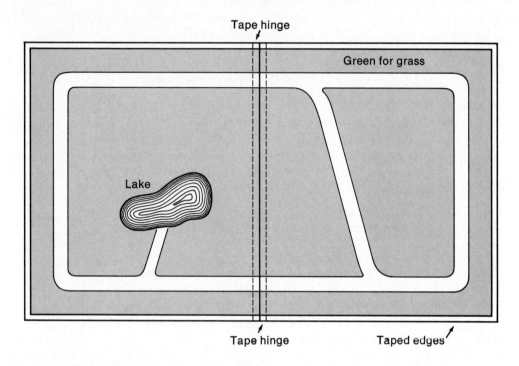

NOTE: Make a tape hinge with masking tape or paper mailing tape *before* painting surface.

Learning, Language, and Readiness Materials Center

Commercially made games and materials for use at a table or on a mat:

(See Basic Resources, p. 79, for manufacturers' addresses.)

1. Family members, multiethnic wooden and plastic figures (most catalogs)
2. Flannelboard family figures, Negro and White (Instructo)
3. Puzzle: rubber fit-in figures of family (Creative Playthings)
4. Family tree mobile material for three generations on each side of the family (Creative Playthings)
5. House and Rooms: See-Inside Puzzles, Kitchen Cupboard, Garden Scene, Toy Cupboard (Creative Playthings)
6. Judy See-Quees: Johnny Growing, Baking Cookies, Making Clothes, Helping Mother, 6 pcs. each. Brushing Teeth, Combing Hair, Baking a Cake, 4 pcs. each
7. Judy Puzzles: Black Nurse (New Baby), 13 pcs.; Doctor, 16 pcs.; At the Grocer's, 17 pcs.; The Hot Dog Vendor, 15 pcs.
8. Judy Storyboard: Building a House, At a Supermarket, Story of Milk
9. Judy Playtrays: Clothing, Food, and Currency Sets (ABC School Supply)
10. Judy Sequence Playtray Card Sets: Going Places and Planning a Party

NOTE: See lists under this heading in I'm Me, I'm Special and Families at Work.

Teacher-made games and materials for use at a table or on a mat:

NOTE: For detailed description of Games, see pp. 50–59.

1. Name It or Scramble: use diaper, bottle warmer, bottle, pacifier
2. Look and See: use rattle, pacifier, bath toy, wash cloth
3. Reach and Feel: use plastic baby bottle, rattle, pacifier, soft rubber toy, cotton ball
4. Who Am I?: describe a mother, baby, daddy, grandmother
5. If: if the baby cries what could it mean? If the milk in baby's bottle gets too hot what can you do?
6. Grouping and Sorting by Association:
   a. set out dressup clothes. Ask children to separate into various groupings: sleepwear, parents' clothes, baby clothes.
   b. set out rubber or wooden farm animals and have children find the young that belong to the adult animals; for example, cow and calf.
7. Match-Them: make sets of picture cards with two each of:
   a. family members, baby items, furniture.
   b. use several pairs of mittens, shoes, socks. Divide into two piles. Let children find the match to the one they choose.
8. Guess What?: ask child "What can a baby do?" "What can you do that a baby can't?" "What can a grownup do that you can't?"

Art Center

1. Doll cradles: precut cradles from empty oatmeal boxes. Let the children paint these with tempera.

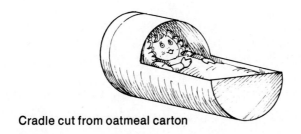

Cradle cut from oatmeal carton

2. Doll blankets: with pinking shears cut twelve-inch squares from old sheets. Thumbtack to a square of white interior insulation board and let the children decorate them with colored felt-tipped pens. When dry remove them from the board and use with oatmeal box cradles as blankets for dolls (or take them home).
3. Playdough: use rolling pins and cookie cutters with self-hardening playdough. Bake cookies in play oven and use for tea parties in the doll corner (when they become hard). See recipe in Basic Resources, p. 27.
4. Cutting and pasting: select many pages of figures from old catalogs to represent mothers, fathers, and different-aged children. If possible let the children cut around the figures they choose to represent their own family and paste them onto a shirt cardboard or other stiff backing. The figures usually need to be precut for three-year-olds.

   NOTE: An easy way for older children to cut them out is to encircle the figures with felt pen outlines and have the children try to cut on the heavy line made by the marker.

5. Encourage the children to make a collage gift or a get-well card for a child or staff member when appropriate, as an expression of caring.
6. Make a gift and greeting card for Mother's Day or Father's Day.

Book Center

* Alexander, Martha. *Nobody Asked Me If I Wanted a Baby Sister.* New York: Dial Press, 1971.

* ——. *Out! Out!* New York: Dial Press, 1968.

** Balian, Lorna. *Where in the World Is Henry?* Scarsdale, New York: Bradbury Press, 1972.

** Brown, Myra B. *Benjy's Blanket.* New York: Franklin Watts, 1962.

* Buckley, Helen. *Grandfather and I.* New York: Lothrop, Lee & Shepard, 1961.

* ——. *Grandmother and I.* New York: Lothrop, Lee & Shepard, 1961.

** Carton, Lonnie. *Daddies.* New York: Random House, 1963.

** DeRegniers, Bernice S. *Little House of Your Own.* New York: Harcourt Brace Jovanovich, 1955.

——. *The Little Girl and Her Mother.* New York: Vanguard Press, 1963.

*** dePaola, Tommie. *Nana Upstairs, Nana Downstairs.* New York: G. P. Putnam's Sons, 1973.

** Eastman, P. D. *Are You My Mother?* New York: Random House, 1960.

*** Flack, Marjorie. *Wait for William.* Boston, Mass.: Houghton Mifflin, 1935.

* ——. *Ask Mr. Bear.* New York: Macmillan, 1932 (paper, 1971).

** Fulton, Mary. *My Friend.* New York: Western Publishing, 1973.

*** Gaeddert, Lou Ann. *Noisy Nancy and Nick.* Garden City, New York: Doubleday, 1970.

*** Geisel, Theodore. *The Cat in the Hat.* New York: Random House, 1957.

*** Hawkinson, John and Lucy. *Little Boy Who Lives Up High.* New York: E. M. Hale, 1967.

*** Hoffman, Phyllis. *Steffie and Me.* New York: Harper & Row, 1970.

*** Krauss, Ruth. *The Backward Day.* New York: Harper & Row, 1950.

*** Lasker, Joe. *He's My Brother.* Chicago, Ill.: Albert Whitman, 1974.

** Marino, Dorothy. *Edward and the Boxes.* Philadelphia, Pa.: J. B. Lippincott, 1957.

** Mizumura, Kazue. *If I Were a Mother.* New York: Thomas Y. Crowell, 1968.

*** Schlein, Miriam. *The Way Mothers Are.* Chicago, Ill.: Albert Whitman, 1963.

* Schick, Eleanor. *Peggy's New Brother.* New York: Macmillan, 1970.

** Simon, Norma. *What Do I Do?* Chicago, Ill.: Albert Whitman, 1969.

** ——. *What Do I Say?* Chicago, Ill.: Albert Whitman, 1967.

*** Slobodkin, Louis. *Thank You—You're Welcome.* New York: Vanguard Press, 1957.

*** Sonneborn, Ruth. *Seven in a Bed.* New York: Viking Press, 1968.

*** ——. *Friday Night Is Papa Night.* New York: Viking Press, 1970.

*** Steiner, Charlotte. *Ten in a Family.* New York: Alfred A. Knopf, 1960.

*** Steptoe, John. *Stevie.* New York: Harper & Row, 1969.

** Stewart, Robert. *The Daddy Book.* New York: Mcgraw-Hill, 1972.

*** Stover, JoAnn. *I'm in a Family.* New York: David McKay, 1966.

*** Weber, Bernard. *Ira Sleeps Over.* Boston, Mass.: Houghton Mifflin, 1975.

** Yashima, Taro. *Umbrella.* New York: Viking Press, 1958.

** Zion, Gene. *Hide and Seek Day.* New York: Harper & Row, 1954.

NOTE: In your library, look for books about families by Russell Hoban, Ezra J. Keats, Lois Lenski, Joan Lexau, and Charlotte Zolotow, as each has several good books on this subject.

planning for grouptime

NOTE: All music, fingerplays, poems, stories, and games listed here may be used at other times during the session as appropriate. See Core Library, Basic Resources, p. 76, for publishers and addresses. Addresses for sources of records will be found on p. 81.

Music

Songs

FROM *Songs for the Nursery School*, MacCarteney
* "Shoes," p. 3. Use these words: one shoe, two shoes, tiny bright new shoes.

FROM *Songs for Early Childhood*, Westminster Press
* "Driving along the Highway," p. 80
* "Bye-Low, My Baby," p. 82
* "All Day Long as I Play," p. 82
* "My Shiny Shoes," p. 88
** "All by Myself," p. 88
* "Useful in the Family," p. 89
** "When Friends Come to Our House," p. 89

FROM *Music Activities for Retarded Children*, Ginglend and Stiles
* "He's Got the Whole World," p. 61
** "Mother Loves Me," p. 79

FROM *Wake Up and Sing*, Landeck and Crook
* "Come See," p. 34
** "Needle Sing," p. 36
** "Don't You Push Me Down," p. 54

Records

"A Place of Our Own," Mister Rogers (Pickwick International Inc. [PII], 33⅓ RPM LP)
"You Are Special," Mister Rogers (PII, 33⅓ RPM LP)
"Let's Be Together Today," Mister Rogers (PII, 33⅓ RPM, 12 inch LP)
"Let's Be Together Again," Mister Rogers (PII, 33⅓ RPM, 12 inch LP)
"Won't You Be My Neighbor?" Mister Rogers (PII, 33⅓ RPM, 12 inch LP)
"Mother Goose Songs," Frank Luther (PII, 12 inch LP)
Sounds Around Us, ("Around the House") (Scott Foresman, 7 inch, 33⅓ RPM LP)
"Every Day We Grow 1-0"/"Big Rock Candy Mountain" (Young People's Record; [YPR], 33⅓ RPM)
"My Friend"/**"Visit to My Little Friend"**/"Creepy Crawly Caterpillar"/"Merry Toy Shop" (YPR; 33⅓ RPM)
"The Sleepy Family" (YPR; 78 RPM)
"My Street Begins at My House," Ella Jenkins (Folkways; 33⅓ RPM)

Rhythms and Singing Games

FROM *Creative Movement for the Developing Child,* Cherry
"Creep," p. 22   "Walk," p. 29
Dramatize: "Little Man, Big Man," p. 30

FROM *Songs for the Nursery School,* MacCarteney
"This Is the Way We Wash Our Hands," p. 100, or as done in *Rhymes for Fingers and Flannelboards,* Scott and Thompson, p. 84

FROM *Music Resource Book,* Lutheran Church Press
"Farmer in the Dell," p. 47 (tune only)

FROM your own traditional songbook
"Rock-a-Bye Baby." Everyone sits and pretends to rock a baby while singing the song. Could also use other ethnic lullabies.

Fingerplays and Poems

FROM *Let's Do Fingerplays,* Grayson
"Five Little Girls," p. 20   "Two Little Houses," p. 70
"The Family," pp. 40-44   "Around the House," pp. 76-84

FROM *Rhymes for Fingers and Flannelboards,* Scott and Thompson
"This Is the Father," p. 78
"My Family" p. 78
"Here Is Baby's Tousled Head," p. 79
"Here Are Mother's Knives and Forks," p. 80
"Someone Is Knocking," p. 86

HERE'S A BALL FOR BABY

Here's a ball for baby, big and soft and round.   (MAKE A BALL WITH TWO HANDS)
Here is baby's hammer, my, how he can pound!   (POUND ON ONE FIST WITH ANOTHER)
Here is baby's music, clapping, clapping, so.   (HOLD HANDS WITH PALMS FACING, CLAP THREE TIMES)
Here are baby's soldiers, standing in a row.   (HOLD FINGERS STRAIGHT)
Here is baby's trumpet, Toot-too, toot-too-too!   (PRETEND TO BLOW WITH DOUBLED FIST TO MOUTH)
Here's the way that baby plays at peek-a-boo.   (HANDS OVER EYES, THEN PEEK)
Here's a big umbrella, to keep the baby dry.   (CUP ONE HAND OVER THE UPRIGHT FINGER OF THE OTHER HAND)
Here is baby's cradle, rock the baby bye.   (CUP HANDS TOGETHER, AND ROCK)

Stories

(To read, read-tell, or tell. See Book Center for complete list.)

* *Grandmother and I,* Buckley
* *Grandfather and I,* Buckley
** *Daddies* Carton
** *Are You My Mother?* Eastman
* *Ask Mr. Bear,* Flack
*** *Steffie and Me,* Hoffman
* *Peter's Chair,* Keats
*** *The Way Mothers Are,* Schlein

Routine Times

1. Let children prepare the daily snack, such as pouring their own milk or juice, peeling and slicing bananas, scraping and cutting carrots, cutting up slices of bread, washing and counting out grapes. All this must be done under close supervision. Use table knives.
2. One day for snack or mealtime serve only baby food. Provide one jar for each child of such items as apricots, plums, peaches, fruit desert. (The jars may be saved as paint containers for the easel.) You may wish to puree your own baby food.
3. For snack serve teething biscuits, milk, and baby food. A mother with a baby could be asked to bring some formula so the children could taste it.
4. You may wish to demonstrate using the bottle warmer at this time.
5. Have the children wash off the tables with a damp sponge before and after snack or mealtime. Also straighten the chairs and sweep the floor.
6. When busing or walking notice various homes you see.

Large Muscle Activities

1. Family play: take or wear dressup clothes outdoors. Set up a house of hollow blocks or large cardboard cartons, a sheet over a jungle gym, or arrangement of packing boxes. Tricycles and wagons can be family cars for going to work, shopping, or taking trips.
2. Encourage taking dolls for a walk in baby carriages or strollers.
3. Woodworking: let children use the workbench in pairs. Use hammers, soft wood, large-headed nails. *Junior Handyman* equipment in a tool box (Creative Playthings).
4. Sandplay: in hot weather use wet sand to bake cookies and cakes. Use orange crates or cardboard cartons for stoves. Have a mud picnic. Bake mudpies in the sun, mix seeds, grass, with mud, for puddings. Sprinkle with sand. Decorate with pebbles. Use leaves for sandwiches. Serve to each other or to dolls and pretend to eat.
5. Hang clothes washed in Dramatic Play Center earlier today to dry outside.
6. Set up a car and truck wash. Use a bucket of water, rags, and hose lengths.
7. Paint the outside of the center. Provide large paintbrushes and small buckets of water. Empty commercial paint cans with handles work fine!
8. Set up a simulated bowling alley with plastic pins and balls.
9. See Dramatic Play Center suggested activities for those that would be suitable to play outdoors when the weather and temperature permit.

Extended Experiences

1. Take a trip to visit someone's parent at work: police officer, firefighter, mail carrier, grocer, teacher, barber, or postal clerk.
2. If your center is in a residential area, take a walk around your block to look at and identify different kinds of housing. Consider safety and feasibility. Talk about what each home is made of, the number of floors, design, color, style. Contrast how each is different, how some are similar or the same, how the homes may differ inside—number of family members, age, number of rooms, furnishings, and so on.
3. Visit a store that sells clothes, shoes, hats, furniture, kitchenware, appliances, tools, to see where things are purchased that we need in a family. Choose a store where children can see and will be welcomed in small groups, and a time of day when there may be fewer shoppers. (See Excursions in Basic Resources, p. 72.)

4. Occasionally it is possible to plan a trip to the home of a teacher or child. Select those that are different in style or type and plan a special activity related to the trip . . . exploring a backyard, seeing a pet.
5. Invite a parent with a baby less than one year old to visit. Have children bathe the baby if possible; also feed it, change its diaper, rock it. Discuss what the baby can or cannot do—sit, walk, stand, talk, crawl. Does it have teeth? hair? fingernails? Why does it cry? What does it eat?
6. Invite grandparents to come and show pictures of themselves as children and tell interesting experiences or stories. Invite them to help with some of the center activities—read a story; help with food preparation, creative arts, or woodworking; or repair or make a piece of equipment used by the children.
7. Invite a parent, especially a father if you do not have a male on your staff, to share a special talent, such as playing a musical instrument or to show an interesting hobby collection.
8. Have a big or little brother or sister visit.

teacher resources

Pictures and Displays

(See p. 79 for addresses of firms listed.)

1. Select pictures of various family lifestyles from magazines showing as many ethnic groups as possible. Mount on colored cardboard or construction paper and hang around room.
2. Use family pictures from the teaching pictures listed under Teacher Resources.
3. Use pictures of baby animals and their parents and the homes in which they live.
4. Show some hospital-made footprints of a baby; also the bracelet that babies and mothers wear for identification.
5. Display some real baby items near the Home Living Center. Include nursing bottles, rattles, pacifiers, baby food, diapers, ointments, powder, teething rings, spoons, bottle warmer, bottles, brush, plastic pants, soft rubber toys, bath toys.

   CAUTION: Supervise closely so that the children do not actually put the nipples and spoons in their mouths. You will want to reserve the use of the bottle warmer for a demonstration by the teacher or parent. (See Extended Experiences No. 5.)

6. Teaching Pictures (David C. Cook)
7. Twelve (Present Day) Pictures (Frances Hook)
8. What We Do, Day by Day: Twelve color photographs of children, 12 inches by 15 inches. One set free to a group (American Dairy Council)

Community Resources

1. Architect
2. Carpenter
3. Plumber
4. Electrician
5. Parent with a baby
6. County home economist
7. College of home economics

8 Families at Work

basic understandings

(concepts children can grasp from this subject)

- Some family members need to work to earn money to buy things the family needs, such as food, clothes, housing.
- Family members can divide the work at home in many ways (see Families at Home).
- Some people have a special place to work in their own homes (workshops or offices); some people walk or drive, or are driven to other buildings or places to work, commuter trains, subways, buses, planes, elevated trains, trucks, monorail, jeeps, cars.
- Some people work at different times of the day and night. Sometimes their time to work changes from day to day, week to week, or month to month (shifts) or they may be on call depending on weather or need. (See Day and Night guide.)
- Some people wear special clothes or uniforms when they work to protect their clothes, to keep them safe, or to tell who they are and what they do. Other uniforms are worn to carry tools or to keep workers or what they work with clean.
- Many people use tools or machines in their work. (See Tools and Machines and Transportation guides.)
- Some people use animals or work with animals on their jobs.
- Some people grow their own food, build their own houses, and make their own clothes; others pay someone else to do these jobs for them.
- Most people are paid for their work. Some are given money and some are given checks, which they can cash for money.
- People can put checks or money in the bank to keep it safe until they need it.
- Some people may trade work to get what they want done. One person may paint a house for someone in exchange for fixing his car.
- Every job and each worker is important. We need everyone to help in his/her own way and do what he/she can do best.

- It is important that each person does his/her own job as well as he/she can and that he/she tries to do their share of the work.
- We all depend on each other for the things or services we need.
- A person who does one kind of work very well is called a "specialist."
- Most jobs can be done by either a man or a woman, if they choose to do that kind of work and have the ability and training to do it.
- Sometimes people have to go to school or take special training to learn how to do their job or to be licensed to do their work.
- Some people are taught how to do their job while they work on that job.
- Helpers in our community include:
  a. **People who help to keep us well:** doctors, dentists, nurses, druggists, health officers, sanitation engineers, foresters, florists, veterinarians for pets.
  b. **People who build things for us:** carpenters, architects, bricklayers, hod carriers, electricians, plumbers, roofers, cement workers, excavators, caterpillar operators, road, ship, and bridge builders.
  c. **People who keep us safe:** police and safety officers, fire fighters, public roads engineers and maintenance workers, weather alert staff, news and TV staff, ambulance drivers, rescue squads, inspectors.

    NOTE: An inspector is a person who makes sure things are done or made the right way for our safety and protection.

  d. **People who help us to know what is happening to others:** news, TV and radio staff, telephone operators and crew, mail carriers, telegraph operators, programmers, writers, journalists, announcers, paper carriers, politicians, city officials, librarians, legislators, teachers, ministers, rabbis, priests, readers.
  e. **People who fix things (persons who repair and maintain equipment):** TV repair personnel, utility maintenance workers, plumbers, carpenters, shoe repair persons, mechanics, electricians.
  f. **People who sell or provide things we need to buy:** farmers, salespersons, clerks, realtors, grocers, clothiers, hardware merchants, shoe salespersons, miners.
  g. **People who entertain us or provide a place for us to play:** park and recreation workers, movie projectionists, and theater owners. Miniature golf attendants, lifeguards, athletes, artists, musicians, hobby and craft shop personnel, movie stars, dancers, singers, clowns, circus workers and performers.
  h. **People who help us travel:** service station attendants, railroad engineers, stewards, conductors, bus drivers, airplane pilots, airplane flight attendants, car salespersons, persons who sell bikes, motorcycles, and other vehicles, ship and boat officers and personnel. (See Transportation guides.)
  i. **People who plan for food (grow, sell, cook, serve, deliver, prepare or handle food or food products):** milk route salespersons, farmers, grocery clerks, truckers, produce retailers, frozen food plant personnel, fishermen, harvesters, migrant pickers, caterers, restaurant managers, waiters/waitresses (tray carriers), cooks, bakers, meat packers/packagers, butchers, sackers.
  j. **People who do special things for us or others (services):** secretaries, bookkeepers, bankers, key operators, drycleaners, laundry workers, pressers, tailors, elevator attendants, dishwashers, delivery persons, movers, loaders, motel housekeepers/desk clerks, owners, cashiers, custodians.
  k. **People who make new things:** workers at manufacturing plants (paper, rubber, cars, cards, toys, garments, auto parts, steel, furniture, plastic, glass and other), dressmakers, drapers, textile mill workers, as well as artists who design and create things for beauty or utility use, locksmith or key makers, printers, writers, inventors, and explorers.

Additional Facts the Teacher Should Know

People work for many reasons: to earn money, to be able to buy necessities and luxuries, as an outlet for creativity, to be of service, for diversity of activity, to produce goods, for adventure and discovery.

In the last few years women have entered the total gamut of labor and professional markets. This has become possible with their being given the opportunity and encouragement to become trained and educated in every field with recognition for achievement.

Many women have chosen to remain single, to combine motherhood and marriage with a profession or career, to pursue a special talent, or, out of necessity, have become the breadwinner when widowed or divorced.

More and more husbands and wives work together as associates in business, as lawyers, doctors, dentists, architects, and others.

Some men, writers, musicians, artists, educators, and those with businesses in their homes, elect to share the work of the home and childcare with their wives by mutual agreement for the satisfactions that come with closer relationships within the family. If the father is a single parent, this combined role may be a necessity.

Men have also taken jobs once previously held only by women, such as nurses, airline stewards, hairdressers, teachers in early childhood education, secretaries, and telephone operators. Since both sexes may now hold almost any job, the names of some jobs need to be modified or changed to eliminate the sex differentiation where it once existed. For example, to avoid stereotypes in occupational roles remember to use:

firefighter for fireman

police officer / *safety officer* } for policeman

member of congress for congressman

business executive / *business manager* } for businessman

leader / *public servant* } for statesman

supervisor for foreman

flight attendant for steward, purser, stewardess

homemaker for housewife

professional title such as lawyer, doctor for career woman

maintenance crew member for maintenance man

logger for lumberman

newspaper carrier for newspaper boy/girl

fisher for fisherman

salesperson / *sales clerk* } for salesman, saleslady

insurance agent for insurance man

person for man, woman

humanpower for manpower

adulthood for manhood, womanhood

chairperson for chairman

camera operator for cameraman

student for coed, college boy

house cleaner / *houseworker* / *servant* } for maid, houseboy

milk carrier for milkman

practical nurse / *nurses' aide* / *orderly* / *nursing attendant* } for female/male nurse

delivery person for deliveryman

Preschool children can learn the names of various occupations and can understand a simple explanation of what each person does. It is wise to begin with jobs held by parents of the children in your center or those which your children come in contact with in their daily living. You may choose to focus on one occupational grouping at a time. See the groupings listed in Basic Understandings, p. 180.

NOTE: Until these recent changes of today's lifestyles are reflected more in the children's storybooks, poems, fingerplays, and toys that are available, you will need to edit and modify references that reflect sexism as you use otherwise suitable materials. Occasionally in telling a story you may simply change the leading character to the opposite sex to reflect this change and avoid stereotyping what boys are like or girls are like, reflecting instead what young children are like! You might also include a woman's name or man's name in a list of helpers or workers in a story to suggest that *both* might exist in that situation. Father might be barbecuing meat or fixing pancakes, bathing the baby, or doing the laundry. Mother may be fixing a chair or painting the house. We have tried to make those modifications in this book, but when referring to other books available we have been limited in such editing and therefore leave this responsibility to you.

Children can learn something of our basic economic system—that we get paid for our work and can exchange our pay for services for something we want or need and that there is a basic interdependence in our society. If given paper money and play coins to use when "shopping" and when various dramatic centers are set up to pay for services, such as service station (use of credit cards), post office (pay for stamps), or grocery store (paying for food at check-out counter) *or* in a direct, real-life experience when buying a needed item at a pet store or grocery store when group takes a trip, children get experience in purchasing goods or services.

Some occupations have been highlighted in other sections of this book where more appropriate. You may wish to refer to them: Food; Transportation; Tools and Machines; I'm Me, I'm Special; Families at Home.

Methods Most Adaptable for Introducing This Subject to Children

- On a table, display tools highlighting one kind of occupation, such as nurse's cap, stethoscope, play thermometer, empty unbreakable pill bottle, hot water bottle, or ice bag.
- Read a book about a community helper. (See Book Center list.)
- Invite a parent, dressed in the uniform or garb of his/her profession to come and show the children the "tools" of that occupation and how they are used.
- Post pictures of one grouping of community helpers on a bulletin board near entrance or cloakroom.
- Plan a trip to a place of business as part of developing an interest in another subject, e.g., grocery store—food; pet store—pets.
- The children may observe an interesting job (workers near the playground or seen when the children are on a walk).

Vocabulary

work	spend	check	names of occupations
job	buy	bank	names of businesses
pay	sell	money	task each person does
earn	trade	coins	
save	paycheck	change	

learning centers

Discovery Center

1. Talk with visitors to find out how they earn money and what they do when at work.
2. Help children discover nonsexist occupational roles by introducing children to women and men who hold similar jobs.
3. Find pictures of various jobs held by parents of your children. Put a photo of each child by a picture of his/her parent's job. Take polaroid pictures or cut from illustrative business brochures or magazines. Encourage parents and children to help collect pictures if feasible. Include in this group those who are jobless or who have nonpaying jobs, showing other kinds of jobs they do, such as caring for family.
4. Tape interviews with helpers in the community if you cannot bring the helper to the center. Show picture of the helper while listening to the tape.
5. Set up an Our Special Visitor or Work Discovery Center Area where tools of a special kind of worker are displayed and can be explored and explained each day by a parent, special community resource person, or teacher. This might be a Bake Center, special kind of Art Center, Workbench, Sewing Center. Plan for opportunities for children to pursue the activity at their level of ability.
6. Display bank books, checkbooks, and unbreakable piggy banks from your community.
7. Examine a stethoscope, simple microscope, thermometer.
8. Borrow a real telephone from the telephone company for children to explore.
9. Borrow a used typewriter for children to use. Encourage the children to find their names on a typewriter by using the letters on the keys.

Dramatic Play Centers

Home-Living Center

1. Place money in purses and billfolds so children are able to buy goods being sold in other dramatic play areas.
2. Provide lunch boxes or paper sacks and laminated food pictures or plastic fruits and vegetables for the lunch that a working person might take to work.

An indoor climbing gym can be used as a ladder when children pretend to be firefighters. The girl firefighter is using a vacuum-cleaner hose and wearing a felt hat. (See pattern, p. 496). The boy is using a cardboard tube with rope attached and wearing a real firefighter's helmet.

3. Have tricycles, wagons, or ride 'em cars for family members to drive to work or to go shopping.
4. For Work at Home suggestions see Home Living Center in Families at Home guide.

Block-Building Center

1. Set out wooden or model block accessories of community workers and family members and pictures of the job areas being emphasized to encourage the building of appropriate structures, such as Modular Community (Childcraft); Tradespeople (Constructive Playthings); families and block play people/community workers/women workers—most catalogs.
2. Set out various model toy trucks and machines. Encourage road building and building of structures to complement the occupation(s) being emphasized.
3. Use hollow blocks or large brick blocks and ride 'em cars, trucks, and machinery to encourage dramatic play on a different scale. Provide child with appropriate props. (See Basic Resources—Dramatic Play Props.)

4. When spotlighting animal doctors, set out animals (pets, zoo, woods, and farm) that a veterinarian or zoo keeper might care for.
5. Set up a tabletop terrain; see illustration, p. 172.

Other Dramatic Play Centers

> **NOTE:** Suggestions for dramatic play materials to highlight various community helpers have been included in other sections of the book. Should a special visitor, trip, or opportunity make it desirable to use one of those listed below, you will find more detailed suggestions on the pages noted. The Basic Resources sections on dramatic play props and prop patterns may also be helpful.

1. With a 3-way play screen, cash register, sacks, and money you can have a store. Vary the products sold each day, groceries, gifts, hats, shoes. (See Families at Home, p. 170, and Food, p. 550.)
2. Doctor and nurse, dentist, barber, hairstylist. (See patterns, pp. 21–23.)
3. Pilot, railroad engineer, post office clerk, firefighter, ship captain. (See Transportation guides.)
4. Grocer, truck farmer, milk route carrier. (See Food guide, pp. 550–51.)
5. Astronaut. (See Space Transportation guide, p. 524.)
6. Carpenter, painter, plumber, service station attendant. (See Tools and Machines guide, pp. 606–07.)
7. Veterinarian: set up similarly to a physician's office but have cages and pens to house animals that must remain to be cared for in the clinic.
8. Art museum or art gallery: make choice depending upon the children's past experience. Let the children plan, arrange, and rearrange their art work in a special corner in various ways. Hang pictures on a line, mount and tape to construction paper mats, or thumbtack to a bulletin board. See kiosk illustrated in Basic Resources, p. 75, for ideas on how to display wood, paper, clay, and styrofoam sculpture on surfaces or in boxes.
9. Set up a business office: telephones, small tables and chairs (to serve as desks), typewriter, stapler, paper, paper clips, pads and pencils, ink pads and rubber stamps, envelopes and postage stamps.
10. Play library: in Book Center provide a long table for checking books in and out, file cards, ink pad, and date stamp. Small, stiff stock card rectangles with child's name printed on them can be used for library cards/book cards.

Learning, Language, and Readiness Materials Center

Commercially made games and materials for use at a table or on a mat:

(See Basic Resources, p. 79, for manufacturers' addresses.)

1. Judy Puzzles: At the Grocer's, 17 pcs.; The Hot Dog Vendor, 15 pcs.; The Occupation Series, Black, 11-13 pcs. each; White, 11-18 pcs.
2. Judy Storyboard: Trip to Zoo, At the Supermarket, Story of Milk, 12 pcs. each
3. Judy Sequence Playtray Card Sets (Health Occupations)
4. Relationships: Lotto Set in wooden storage box (Childcraft)
5. Put-Together: series of four occupations puzzles, with 9 pcs. in each (Childcraft)
6. Inside Story Puzzle: Shops, Farm, Traffic (Childcraft)
7. Occupation Puzzles: Black series, 11-13 pcs.; White series, 11-16 pcs. (most catalogs)
8. Stand-up Puzzles Series: 14-20 pcs.; Everyday Puzzles Series: 10-27 pcs. (Childcraft)

9. Transportation Inlays Series: 10-12 pcs. (Childcraft)
10. Habitat: Fit-together house puzzle (Childcraft)
11. Trip to the Zoo: a scenic floor puzzle with four sections, 36 pcs. (Childcraft)
12. Upright Insets Series: Farm, Zoo, Train, Transportation (Childcraft)
13. Double Playboard Puzzles Series: Farm, Zoo, Street, Helpers (Childcraft)
14. Tools and Trades: Set 4, 10 pcs. in each puzzle (Childcraft)
15. Belonging: Zoo and Farm, 14 pcs. each (Childcraft)
16. Playskool Puzzles: Community Workers, 6 in set, 14-19 pcs. each
17. Work-a-Day Puzzles: series of simple puzzles with knobs (Constructive Playthings)
18. Community Workers and Helpers, poster cards (Milton Bradley)
19. Instructo Community Flannelboard Sets: 15-20 pcs. in each set (most catalogs)
20. Instructo Activity Kit: Community Helpers at Work, 4 helpers, 40 pcs.
21. Instructo: When I Grow Up I Want to Be, 36 occupations, clothing, accessories, and figures
22. Playskool Match-Ems: occupations with tools used, two-piece puzzles

Teacher-made games and materials for use at a table or on a mat:

NOTE: For detailed description of Games, see pp. 50–59.

1. Name It:
   a. use community helper models or pictures of people at various jobs
   b. use hats: safety officer, firefighter, baker, nurse
   c. use tools from various jobs: whistle, stethoscope, rolling pin, empty milk carton, wrench
2. Look and See: use materials listed in 1(a), (b), and (c)
3. Which: use materials listed in 1(a), (b), and (c)
4. Alike, Different, and the Same:
   a. two people wearing uniforms and one not
   b. two male safety officers, one female safety officer
   c. doctor, nurse, and letter carrier
5. Grouping and Sorting by Association:
   a. group all those who wear uniforms on the job
   b. match the tool with the helper
6. Listening: child must identify the voice of another child who cannot be seen
7. Who Am I?: describe various jobs mentioning what the person wears and does
8. Listen and Hear: typewriter, hammer, whistle, eggbeater. Sounds may be taped and replayed leaving space on the tape for the child to think and guess before final answer is given or not given
9. Let's Tell a Story: use a picture of someone at work. Choose picture with action to invite imaginative response

Art Center

* 1. Playdough: use rolling pins and baking pans from Home-Living Center. Provide baker's hats. (See patterns, p. 22.) Encourage the decoration of baked goods. Have pictures of cakes, pastries, and colorful food on plates. Children may score clay with tongue depressors, potato mashers, or other utensils.

** 2. Make a book of Families at Work. Cut out pictures of workers at various jobs and paste on construction paper. Fasten together or place in a three-ring notebook.

* 3. Artist: provide a variety of art media for several days. Expand special activities to correspond if class has a visiting artist.

4. Carpenter: set out carpenter aprons, soft wood in various shapes and sizes, hammers, saws, and nails with workbench at the woodworking center.
5. Encourage mixed media art especially for the older children: painting over a fingerpainting with an easel brush for special effects; cutting out crayon drawings and pasting on a colored piece of construction paper; painting wood/clay sculpture or paper folding products; pasting snippings and paper cut-outs to cardboard.

Book Center

* Brown, Margaret. *The Little Fireman*. Reading, Mass.: Addison-Wesley, 1952.

*** Brown, Marcia. *The Little Carousel*. New York: Scribner's, 1946.

** Clifton, Lucille. *Don't You Remember?* New York: E. P. Dutton, 1973.

*** Ets, Marie Hall and Ellen Tarry. *My Dog Rinty*. New York: Viking Press, 1946.

** Françoise. *What Do You Want to Be?* New York: Scribner's, 1957.

*** Grifalconi, Ann. *The Toy Trumpet*. New York: Bobbs-Merrill, 1968.

** Hazen, Barbara. *Froere Jacques*. Philadelphia, Pa.: J. B. Lippincott, 1973.

** Marino, Dorothy. *Where Are the Mothers?* Philadelphia, Pa.: J. B. Lippincott, 1959.

** Merriman, Eve. *Mommies at Work*. New York: Alfred A. Knopf, 1961.

*** Parish, Peggy. *Ootah's Lucky Day*. New York: Harper & Row, 1970.

* Pellett, Elizabeth, Deborah K. Osen, and Marguerite May. *A Woman Is*. Concord, Calif.: Aardvark Media, 1974.

* ———. *A Man Is*. Concord, Calif.: Aardvark Media, 1974.

** Politi, Leo. *Pedro, the Angel of Olvera Street*. New York: Scribner's, 1946 (Spanish, 1974).

** Puner, Helen. *Daddies, What They Do All Day*. New York: Lothrop, Lee & Shepard, 1969.

* Reit, Seymour. *All Kinds of Signs*. New York: Western Publishing, 1970.

** ———. *No Room for Freddy*. New York: Bobbs-Merrill (Adventures in Living Storybooks).

** Rockwell, Harlow. *My Doctor*. New York: Macmillan, 1973.

** Scarry, Richard. *Nicky Goes to the Doctor*. New York: Western Publishing, 1972.

** Schneider, Nina. *While Susie Sleeps*. Reading, Mass.: Addison-Wesley, 1968.

*** Shanks, Ann Zane. *About Garbage and Stuff*. New York: Viking Press, 1973.

*** Shay, Arthur. *What Happens When You Go to the Hospital*. Chicago, Ill.: Reilly & Lee, 1969.

** Smith, Robert P. *When I Am Big*. New York: Harper & Row, 1965.

*** Tresselt, Alvin. *Hide and Seek Fog*. New York: Lothrop, Lee & Shepard, 1965.

*** Udry, Janice. *Mary Jo Shared*. Chicago, Ill.: Albert Whitman, 1966.

*** Zaffo, George. *The Big Book of Real Trucks*. New York: Grosset & Dunlap, 1950.

NOTE: Check at your local library for a series of books by Carla Greene (Harper & Row) on professional careers.

planning for grouptime

NOTE: All music, fingerplays, poems, stories, and games listed here may also be used at other times during the session as appropriate. See Core Library, Basic Resources, p. 76, for publishers and addresses. Addresses for sources of records will be found on p. 81.

Music

Songs

FROM *Songs for the Nursery School*, MacCarteney
*   "Airplane Song," p. 10
*** "Bake a Cake," p. 107
*** "The Barber," p. 112
*** "The Steam Shovel," p. 116

FROM *Music Resource Book*, Lutheran Church Press
** "The Wheels on the Bus," p. 50
*   "I'm a Big Black Engine," p. 51
*   "I Helped My Daddy," p. 68´
*   "Muffin Man," p. 90
*   "Mulberry Bush," p. 92 (substitute words: This is the way . . .)

FROM *Music Activities for Retarded Children*, Ginglend and Stiles
*   "Come and Ride Our Train," p. 36
*   "Helping," p. 59 (adapt last verse)
** "Who Am I?" p. 105 (helpers—adapt)

FROM *Wake Up and Sing*, Landeck and Crook
** "Cleano," p. 16
** "Pick It Up," p. 18
** "Pretty and Shiny-O," p. 22
** "My Dolly," p. 26
** "Needle Sing," pp. 36–37
*** "Don't Push Me Down," p. 54
** "Rock Island Line," p. 64
** "Riding in My Car," p. 66
** "Mailman," p. 73
** "Bling Blang," pp. 74–75

FROM *Songs for Early Childhood*, Westminster Press
*   "Apples Green and Apples Red," p. 18
*   "Driving along the Highway," p. 80
** "Put the Toys and Blocks Away," p. 100
*   "Walking in the Sunshine," p. 101
*   "Springtime," p. 106
*   "Here We Go Round the Mulberry Bush," p. 108
*   "Here Comes the Postman," p. 117
*   "Do You Know the Muffin Man?" p. 118

Records

Men Who Come To My House/"**Let's Be Firemen**"/"**Let's Be Policemen**" (Young People's Record [YPR], 33⅓ RPM)

"**Build Me A House**"/"Silly Will"/"**Milk's Journey**" (YPR, 33⅓ RPM)

"**Building a City**"/"**What the Lighthouse Sees**"/"Rainy Day" (YPR, 33⅓ RPM)

"Little Fireman" (YPR, 33⅓ RPM) Use with M. W. Brown's book.
"Sing a Song of Home and Community" (Bowmar, 33⅓ RPM)

Rhythms and Singing Games

FROM *Creative Movement for the Developing Child*, Cherry
Spontaneous Movement to Recorded Music, pp. 74–75
Percussion Instruments, pp. 81–84

NOTE: See also pp. 34–37 in Basic Resources for suggestions for music, music accessories, and rhythm band instruments to be used with dancing or a band. When
using rhythm instruments let children take turns being the conductor or leader. See
also the Sound guide for a suggested list of records. If you do not own or have
access to the records listed, ask a friend to tape segments of music while playing
a piano or another instrument. You can use these tapes later with the children.

Fingerplays and Poems

FROM *Rhymes for Fingers and Flannelboards*, Scott and Thompson
"Five Brown Pennies," p. 12 (adapt to five silver dimes)
"Five Little Sailors," p. 23
"The Baker Man," p. 24
"Five Strong Policemen," p. 25 (adapt to officers)
"Five Little Firemen," p. 25 (adapt to firefighters)
"Los Maderos de San Juan." p. 43 ("The Woodmen of San Juan")
"*Eins, Zwei*," p. 47 ("One, Two")
"The Woodchopper," p. 52

FROM *Let's Do Fingerplays*, Grayson
"People," p. 50
"Ten Little Firemen," p. 53 (adapt to firefighters)
"Pat-a-Cake," p. 80

Stories

(To read, read-tell, or tell. See Book Center for complete list.)

** *My Doctor*, Rockwell
 * *A Woman Is*, Pellet, Osen, May
 * *A Man Is*, Pellet, Osen, May
** *While Susie Sleeps*, Schneider
** *Daddies, What They Do All Day*, Puner

Games

(See Games, pp. 50–59, and Teacher-Made Games, Nos. 1,2,3,7,8 in this guide, for directions.)

1. Together, Together: act out jobs: paint a house, write a book, conduct an orchestra
2. Sally Says: be a painter, a carpenter, a dancer

Routine Times

1. At snack or mealtime play restaurant. Allow children to take turns waiting on table.
2. At snack or mealtime play flight attendant and serve snack or meals to passengers on a pretend airliner.
3. At pickup time play moving van. Have children return toys to shelves using wagons, rolling platforms, or ride 'em trucks as vans.
4. When busing, children can look for people at work—trash haulers, painters, safety officers, road crews, telephone maintenance crews, mail carriers.

Large Muscle Activities

1. Athletes: play catch; toss a ball into a basket.
2. Painters: provide children with pails of water and large paintbrushes. Let children paint the outside of the center or a fence with the water.
3. Carpenters: move woodworking bench and materials outside.
4. Baker: wet some of the sand. Encourage children to bake cakes, cookies, and so on, by providing some pans, spoons, and bowls. Decorate bakery products with dry sand, pebbles, and leaves.
5. Car wash: provide sponges and pails of water near the tricycles and other wheel toy storage area.
6. Safety officer: this is a good opportunity to use safety signs with wheel toys.
7. Firefighters: take the firefighter hats and the hoses to be used with the hollow blocks for dramatic play outside.
8. Garage or service station: see Road Transportation guide, p. 502. Provide chamois or wipe rags, oil cans, hoses for gas, pumps for air in tires, and old credit cards.
9. Parking lot attendant: set aside an area for parking cars (motor toys).

Mail carrier and postal clerk are wearing regulation shirts cut down to fit them. Note the paper sack mailbag child in background is holding. For instructions on how to make mailbag, see p. 22. Children enjoy mailing and receiving used picture postcards like those shown on table.

Extended Experiences

1. Take a trip to visit a child's parent at work: telephone operator, firefighter, barber, artist, postal clerk, grocer, librarian.
2. Take a walk and look for people doing various kinds of work.
3. Ask parents to visit and to talk about their jobs. Ask them to dress as they would for their jobs and to bring one or more tools they use to share them with the children.
4. Invite someone who comes to the center on business to talk about his/her job—plumber, milk carrier, florist—or tape an interview and let the children guess who it might be. Perhaps a few interested children could be allowed to look through the door of the delivery truck. (It may not be possible for children to enter a mail truck and some other kinds of trucks.)
5. Plan to have letters delivered to children at the center by the regular mail route carrier. Address one manila envelope containing all the notes or picture postcards to the teacher so all will arrive the same day. Let the carrier hand the teacher the envelope in front of the children. Invite him to stay a moment to meet the children. Used picture postcards could be recycled by pasting a new message over the previously written note. Choose special cards to fit the interests of individual children. Parents and friends could be encouraged to save their old postcards for your center prior to this activity.
6. Show a film or filmstrip of a job which would be of interest to the children.

teacher resources

Pictures and Displays

(See p. 79 for addresses of firms listed.)

1. Put up pictures of various jobs. Be sure to include both men and women of the various ethnic groups. These can be from your personal file or the Home and Community Helpers, Community and Transportation packets (David C. Cook)
2. Athletes: display various kinds of balls—basketball, football, golf ball, baseball, tennis ball, bowling ball. Put up pictures of the various professional ball players near the display
3. Musicians: display pictures of an orchestra, a band, and musical instruments
4. Writers: display books, magazines, newspapers, paper, pencil or pen, typewriter
5. See other related guides—Food; Transportation; I'm Me, I'm Special; Tools and Machines
6. Display a city scene: Foldout Mural (Childcraft)
7. Display coins, dollar bill, bank checks, passbook, pay envelope, identification card
8. See Discovery Center and Other Dramatic Play Centers for other suggestions
9. Picture Fold-outs: People In the Neighborhood and People Who Come to My House (The Child's World)

Community Resources

1. Education officers from: department of public safety—police station; department of firefighters—firestation
2. Parents
3. Community helpers

Who's Who

A Question and Answer Song

JoAnne Deal Hicks

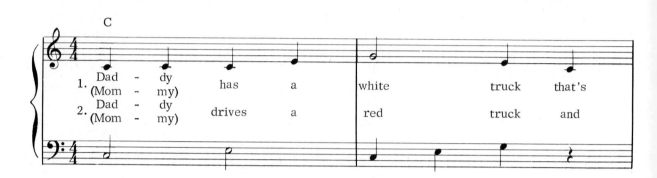

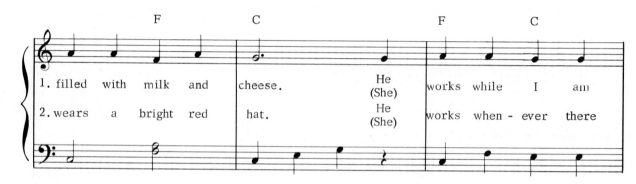

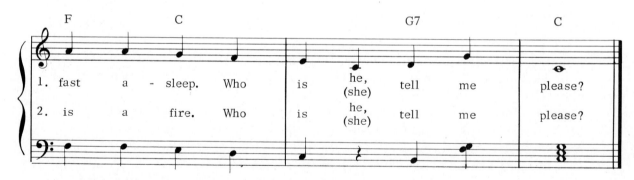

Verse 3: Mom-my drives a blue car and wears a sil-ver star.
(Dad-dy)
Her clothes are blue, her hat is blue. Who is she, tell me who?
(His)   (his)   (he)

Verse 4: Mom-my wears some white shoes, her u-ni-form is white.
(Dad-dy)   (his)
She helps the doc-tor day and night, who is she? Yes you're right!
(He)   (he)

Note:
Use with
flannelboard
figures.

PART THREE

Family Celebrations

9 New Year's Day Around the World

basic understandings

(concepts children can grasp from this subject)

New Year's Day (celebrated in the United States on January 1st) is probably the most widely celebrated holiday in the world. Many countries celebrate this holiday on a different date, but often it is the first day of their calendar year (lunar or solar). Whether New Year's Day is determined by the lunar or solar calendar, people everywhere make a similar effort to begin anew, hoping that through new resolutions made, determination, combined with good luck they will be able to make the new year ahead happier and more prosperous than the one just ended.

The custom of celebrating New Year's on January 1st began in the 1500s when the Georgian calendar was established. It is a solar calendar and is based on the time it takes for the earth to travel around the sun—365¼ days. Every four years an extra day is added to February and then that year is referred to as leap year. The twelve months in our calendar have names, and most were taken from Roman gods. January, for example, was named for the god of doors and gates; Janus had two faces, one looking forward and the other backward.

Many families in the United States have New Year's Eve parties at which there are special foods, drinks, dancing, and merriment. When the clock strikes twelve, whistles are blown, bells ring, firecrackers explode, people shout "Happy New Year," kiss, and sing, "Auld Lang Syne." The parties may be in homes, hotels, or public squares, such as Times Square in New York. (Trafalgar Square in London has such a celebration as well.) Many other families gather at churches for a Watch Night service and the New Year is begun with a religious emphasis.

Throughout the world most retail businesses are closed on this holiday. Many people traditionally visit friends and relatives and have family gatherings and serve special foods.

In the United States many people attend football games or view them on TV. Others attend or view the Rose Bowl parade in Pasadena, the Mummers' parade in Philadelphia, or the Orange Bowl parade in Miami, Florida, which are shown on TV on New Year's Eve or New Year's Day.

Noisemaking is often a part of New Year's celebrations. This practice goes back to the ancient custom of driving out evil spirits. In Scotland, men and boys parade in the streets and circle friends' homes and drown out the demons by shouting. In Denmark, they "smash in the New Year" by banging on the doors of their friends' homes and "let in the New Year" by setting off fireworks. In Japan, dancers rattle bamboo sticks. In Nigeria, drums beat and ceremonial dances are performed.

The Germans believe that the way you live the first day of the year will affect the way you live the others, so the house is made spotless. In Spain, there is a similar belief applied to food. If you eat good food the first day, you will have plenty all year long.

Some New Year's customs involve children. In Belgium, children take wafers with raised crosses on them, called "nules," to friends. In Italy, children receive gifts of coins and hang mistletoe on the door for luck. In Switzerland, children play hide-and-seek with their parents and when found shout "Happy New Year." In Portugal, children sing songs in their neighborhood, for which they receive coins and treats.

Many children's centers are closed for an extended holiday from before Christmas until after New Year's Day. Often little emphasis is made by teachers of young children on this holiday in their curriculum planning because the American New Year's celebrations seldom involve children except when they gather with or visit relatives. However, when the children return to school, invite them to recall and share how *they* celebrated the New Year's holiday. Through sharing they can learn more about the holiday and begin to recognize that children, and in fact everyone, celebrate New Year's with traditions that are sometimes similar, sometimes completely different, but always very interesting.

Extended Experiences

1. Display pictures of New Year's celebrations including parties, parades, and football games.
2. Display a new calendar. Talk about the fact that it is the beginning of a new year. Children who can recognize numbers can be shown the numbers for "last" year and for "this" year, such as 1976 and 1977. Include a lunar calendar, available from an Asian shop or import store.
3. In 1976, the United States celebrated 200 years of independence. Older children may begin to understand what this means. Display pictures of the Capitol, White House, Independence Hall, the Liberty Bell, and the Statue of Liberty. Discuss the fact that people from all over the world have come to this country to live. Because we are a mixture of peoples we have many customs and holidays that are celebrated in our country during the year.
4. Ask children to tell what they did on New Year's Day. Did they see the Rose Bowl parade on TV? Did they do something special with their family?

Not all New Year's celebrations are on January 1st. People who use a lunar calendar celebrate New Year's on the first day of the first moon, which can be anytime between January 21 and February 19. The Japanese, Chinese, Koreans, and many other Asians celebrate New Year's with the arrival of the new moon. More detailed suggestions and plans have been included for Chinese New Year because it is a New Year holiday that includes children and is observed similarly by many Asians all around the world. It begins on p. 203.

Osho Gatsu (Oh-SHOH GAHT-SOO)

The Japanese New Year's celebration is called *Osho Gatsu*. Adults stay up for the watch night gong, which is sounded 108 times to rid them of the 108 human weaknesses described in Buddhist teachings. Houses are scrubbed and families gather for a big feast. Pine branches and bamboo decorate the home in the hope they will bring the inhabitants a long life. "Strong ties" are symbolized by the hanging of a twisted rope decorated with oranges, which symbolize "roundness and smoothness" in the coming year.

In the afternoon children fly kites, play battledore (like badminton), and enjoy games with tops similar to the Jewish *dreidel*. Traditionally, in Japan, only girls play battledore and only boys play the games with the tops. As customs vary and change this may not always be true.

Extended Experiences

1. Display pictures of children and families in Japan.
2. Buy some *darumas* (wishing dolls) in an Asian or import store or make some for the children. Directions may be found in *Folk Toys Around the World* by Joan Joseph (Parents' Magazine Press).
3. Make and fly kites. (See Chinese New Year, p. 214.)
4. Play Japanese music at Rest Time.
5. Strike a gong. Experiment with making gongs from cookie sheets, piepans, and frying pans. Discover sounds made by different kinds of mallets: metal, wooden, or padded. The gong must be suspended for the best sound. Choose musical sounds.
6. Display items from Japan: tea set, dolls, battledore set, tops, and fans.
7. Read a story about children in or from Japan:
Yashima, Taro. *Umbrella*. New York: Viking Press, 1970.
————. *Crow Boy*. New York: Viking Press, 1955.
Matsuno, Masako. *A Pair of Red Clogs*. Cleveland, Ohio: Collins-World, 1960.
————. *Taro and the Bamboo Shoot*. New York: Pantheon, 1970.
8. Invite a Japanese parent or student to talk to the children about Japan. Make and serve a Japanese dish and/or bring some artifact to show.
9. Sukiyaki could be made and served for lunch or help the children make Tofu Toss. The recipe is found in the book *Many Hands Cooking: An International Cookbook* by Terry Touf Cooper and Marilyn Ratner (Thomas Y. Crowell).
10. Show the Bowmar filmstrip *Sing a Song of Holidays and Seasons* highlighting the *Japanese Rain Song*. There is a companion record or cassette, songbook, and teacher resource guide.

Many people celebrate the new year with the coming of spring when animals and dormant plants show renewed growth and activity. Most such festivals involve planting, housecleaning, buying new clothes, family feasts, and gift giving. For example, *Songkran, Baisakhi,* and *Now-Ruz* are "new year's" holidays that all begin in the spring.

Now-Ruz (Noh-rooz)

In Iran, on the first days of spring (March 20, 21, 22), families celebrate *Now-Ruz,* which means "new day." It is a national holiday in Iran and both Muslims and non-Muslims celebrate it for twelve days.

Two weeks before, dancers and musicians, called "firelighters," dance and play horns, drums, and tambourines in the streets. Other preparations include a thorough housecleaning called *khaneh takani* or "house shaking," buying new clothes, and blanching almonds for the special foods. The children place wheat, celery, and lentil seeds in bowls of water. When they are sprouted they transfer them to bowls of earth and watch them grow. On the Wednesday before New Year's each family builds a fire in front of their house. Each member jumps over the fire to bring luck and prosperity. It is not primarily a religious holiday, but the most devout go to the mosque or church at midnight.

On *Now-Ruz* the family sits around a special dinnercloth with seven articles, all beginning with the Iranian letter S. They are: a dish with a green leaf, a lighted candle for each member of the family, a bowl of goldfish, a mirror, an egg, bread, and candy. The candles and leaf represent new growth and new life, and the foods stand for the goodness of Allah. The egg is placed on the mirror, and legend has it that the earth trembles on New Year's Day and everyone holds their breath waiting to see the egg move. The fact that cannons are shot off helps! The family eats candy while a passage from the *Koran,* the Muslim holy book, is read. Then everyone embraces and says "Sad sal be in Salha!" (sahd sahl beh een sahl-HAHL), which means "May you live a hundred years!" Parents give presents, usually coins, to their children in the name of *Baba Norooz* or Father Norooz who is the Iranian Santa Claus.

In the days that follow there is much visiting of friends and relatives; a popular sweet called *bakhlava* is served. The Shah of Iran has open house at the palace for public leaders and government officials.

The thirteenth day is considered unlucky to spend indoors. Individual families plan picnics and outdoor games. The seeds that were sprouted earlier are thrown in a nearby running stream to symbolize doing away with family quarrels and starting the year with a clean slate.

Extended Experiences

1. Have a *Now-Ruz* "dinner" at snacktime. Set out a tray with the seven items. The eggs should be hard-cooked. Have one egg and one slice of bread for each child. These may be eaten as part of the snack or made into egg salad sandwiches. The sweet could be *bakhlava,* which is available from some health food stores or from an international shelf in some grocery stores. Divide into bitesize pieces.
2. Scatter wheat, celery, or bean seeds in a bowl of water. When sprouted, transfer to small pots of earth and care for them and watch them grow. Transplant to outside when all danger of frost is past or allow each child to take a plant home.

3. Watch and care for goldfish. Aquariums with aerators and filters are better than bowls if you plan to keep more than two weeks.
4. On the thirteenth day after spring begins, have a picnic. Play outdoors if weather permits. Foods enjoyed by Iranians are almonds, pistachio nuts, dried dates, and apricots.
5. Invite a parent or student from Iran to explain *Now-Ruz* to your group. Ask him or her to write the Iranian letter S on a blackboard or sheet of paper.
6. Display pictures or items from Iran. They are famous for inlaid silver jewelry, brass and copper dishes, printed cloths, and Persian rugs. Iranians today wear clothing similar to that worn in the United States.

Song Kran (Sohng-krahn)

In Thailand, the Buddhist New Year *Song Kran* comes in the middle of April and lasts three days. The statues of Buddha are washed and the Buddhist pictures are cleaned in the temple. There are parades and much throwing of water on one another, the Thai way of blessing friends and relatives. Also it is a time of kind acts. Birds are bought in order to release them on *Song Kran* and bowls of fish are freed by dumping them into ponds and streams.

Extended Experiences

1. Display pictures and artifacts of Thailand.
2. Ayer, Jacqueline. *The Paper Flowertree*. New York: Harcourt Brace Jovanovich, 1962 (read-tell).
3. Invite a parent or student from Thailand to tell about *Song Kran* and share a song, poem, or item of interest with the children. Ask if they will play a reed mouth organ for them.
4. Water play. (See the Water Around Me guide.)

Baisakhi (Bi-e-SAH-kee)

In India, the Hindu New Year, *Baisakhi*, comes in April or May. Hindus believe that bathing in the Ganges will protect them from evil. Then they go to the temple and listen to the reading of the calendar of the New Year. Women and girls wear colorful saris on this day. Elaborate feasts are held; gifts are exchanged, prayers are offered to family gods.

Extended Experiences

1. Display pictures or artifacts from India.
2. Invite a mother or student to show the children how to wrap a sari.
3. Ask the parent or student if they would play the sitar, bells, cymbals, or tabla for the children.

Rosh Hashanah (ROHSH-hah-SHAH-nah)

The Jewish New Year, *Rosh Hashanah*, is celebrated on two days in September or early October. The day is marked by the blowing of the *shofar* (ram's horn) calling the people to prayer. The *shofar* was blown when the people were called together to be told of the Ten Commandments by Moses. It is the opening of the most important time of the Jewish religious year, the ten-day period leading to the Day of Atonement, called *Yom Kippur* (YOHM kip-POOR).

At sundown on New Year's Eve the family eats a special meal. The *challah* (bread) for this meal is shaped like a ladder symbolizing prayers ascending to God on its rungs or indicating that people can go up or down in the world, the choice depends on them. However, the twisted-shaped (braided) *challahs* (plural) are eaten on the Sabbath as well as other Jewish holidays.

On this day, by tradition, the life of every man is judged by the Lord and is written in the Book of Life or the Book of Death. Therefore it is the custom for friends to greet each other with the words "May your life be inscribed for a happy New Year" or "May a good year be recorded for you." The ten days starting with *Rosh Hashanah* are known as the "days of repentance." It is a time to examine one's deeds for the last twelve months and resolve to do better. Those who are truly sorry can ask God's forgiveness and thereby be inscribed in the Book of Life on *Yom Kippur*. During the "days of repentance" Jews call on those they have wronged and ask for forgiveness.

Nine days after *Rosh Hashanah* is the "Day of Atonement," which is marked by twenty-four hours of prayer, fasting, and asking God to forgive sins. At sundown the night before *Yom Kippur* the family gathers for a festival meal. Candles are lit (one is in memory of departed ones) and the family members ask each other to forgive any wrongdoings. After the meal the family goes to the synagogue to pray. White, symbol of purity, is worn by the officials and white cloths cover the altar and the Ark, the holy chest which holds the scrolls of the *Torah*, a part of Jewish sacred scriptures. The men and boys wear white skull caps. Often white flowers are placed on the altar. From early morning the next day until sundown a service is held at the synagogue. People fast, pray, and ask God's forgiveness. At sundown the *shofar* is blown again, marking the closing of the gates of judgment for another year. Yom Kippur is the holiest day of the Jewish year. It is reverently called "The Sabbath of Sabbaths."

Extended Experiences

1. Eat apple wedges dipped in honey. Talk about sweet things. Taste some. Talk about sour things. Taste some. (See the Taste guide.)
2. Buy a loaf of *challah* bread. It is usually a special braid-shaped loaf eaten by families on the Sabbath and other special holidays, but may now be available in the shape of a ladder or round loaves that are more customary during this holiday. If neither is available, ask a Jewish friend or parent to bake several small loaves of the different shapes for you to share with the children.
3. Taste *tayglach* (honey balls) or honey cake made by a Jewish parent or a bakery. Make cans of cinnamon, ginger, allspice, and nutmeg available for the children to smell. Have the children guess which one is in the honey balls by smelling and tasting.
4. Record the sound of the *shofar* (difficult to play) on a tape recorder as well as the sounds of other kinds of horns—car, trumpet, tuba, French horn. Have pictures of instruments, or real ones, to show as you play the tape. When children are familiar with the sounds play the tape without the pictures and let the children guess which is which.

5. Read-tell any of the following stories:
   *** Cone, Molly. *The Jewish New Year*. New York: Thomas Y. Crowell, 1966.
   **** Simon, Norma. *Rosh Hoshanah*. New York: United Synagogue Book Service, 1961.
   **** ———. *Yom Kippur*. New York: United Synagogue Book Service, 1959.
6. Invite a Jewish parent or Israeli student to visit and tell about *Rosh Hoshanah* and *Yom Kippur*. Bring a *shofar* to blow.
7. Visit a synagogue and see the *shofar* there.

teacher resources

Books and Periodicals

1. Cooper, Terry Touf and Marilyn Rutner. *Many Hands Cooking, An International Cookbook for Girls and Boys*. New York: Thomas Y. Crowell, 1974.
2. Spiegelman, Judith. *UNICEF's Festival Book*. New York: United States Committee for UNICEF, 1966.
3. Joseph, Joan. *Folk Toys Around the World and How to Make Them*. New York: Parents' Magazine Press, 1972.
4. Haywood, Charles. *Folk Songs of the World*. New York: John Day, 1966.
5. Morrow, Betty and Lewis Hartman. *Jewish Holidays*. Champaign, Ill.: Garrard, 1967. (Holiday Book Series)
6. Goldman, Alex J. *A Child's Dictionary of Jewish Symbols*. New York: Philipp Feldheim, 1965.
7. Siegel, Richard, Michael Strassfeld, and Sharon Strassfeld. *The Jewish Catalog*. Philadelphia: Jewish Publication Society of America, 1973.

Pictures and Displays

1. Living Together in America, Children Around the World: Picture Packets (David C. Cook)
2. Children of Europe, Children of Asia: SVE Picture Story-Study Prints (Singer)
3. Children of America, Children Around the World: Study Prints (The Child's World)
4. A UNICEF calendar (UNICEF)

Community Resources

1. Students from countries where holidays highlighted here are celebrated
2. International food centers in supermarkets
3. Asian and import-export stores
4. Hebrew bookstore or synagogue gift shop

10 Chinese New Year

basic understandings

(concepts children can grasp from this subject)

- This holiday has been celebrated for many, many years.
- It has always been a most important and happy Chinese holiday.
- The celebration of the Chinese New Year once lasted as many as fifteen days; now it lasts for only a few days.
- The holiday begins on their New Year's, *Yuan Tan* (Wahn Tahn), Eve, with a special family dinner, which includes fish (the symbol for prosperity and surplus), pork, eggs (symbol for well-being, rebirth), and many vegetables (at least ten in one dish). This dish is called *schu-chieng-tzi* (szhoo-jing-tsi) in Mandarin.
- For us, the date of the Chinese New Year's Day changes each year because it is the first day of the lunar calendar, and we use the solar calendar. (It varies from January 21 to February 19.)
- Red is the symbol of happiness to all Chinese. This color is always used for New Year's decorations, candles, and gift wrappings.
- On this holiday, children receive gifts of money from older people, such as their grandparents, parents, aunts, uncles.
- The gift money is given in red envelopes, often with gold lettering or pictures on them. If grandparents or relatives live too far away, children may find their envelopes under their pillow when they awaken.
- Even numbers are considered lucky, especially the numbers two and ten. Therefore, two oranges, tangerines, or apples are often given and eaten on this day. Ten different dishes are often served for the New Year's feast.
- Other special foods (sweets and desserts) are baked and cooked for the occasion, such as watermelon seeds baked with cinnamon and salt, rice cakes, and dried fruit.

- Homes are decorated with brightly colored good luck scrolls or banners that are usually hung in pairs on doorways or windows.
- These good luck greetings are often written in couplets and hung in pairs on each side of the front doorway. (See p. 213, No. 10.)
- It is important to Chinese children and their parents to wear new clothes, especially new shoes, on New Year's Day to bring them good luck.
- *Kung-Hi, Fot-Choy* (Cantonese) or *Kung-Hsi, Fah-Tsai* (Mandarin) is the most common New Year's greeting, meaning "Have a happy, rich, and prosperous New Year!" Sometimes children say *Kung-Hi* or *Kung-Hsi,* "I wish you joy" and adults then say *"Sui Hi"* or *"Sui-Hsi,"* "May joy be yours!"
- The New Year's holiday usually includes a big parade the night of the first full moon of the New Year. Many firecrackers are fired.
- A lion dance or dragon dance performed by adults is an important part of this New Year's parade. Children often carry fish or flower lanterns.
- During the parade, the sound of drums, gongs, cymbals, and fireworks can be heard. It is very noisy and colorful. People cheer, set off fireworks, and tease the dragon, who pretends to bite the teasers. Dragons are make-believe animals and to the Chinese they are friendly beasts and mean good luck.
- In American cities where many Chinese live, such as New York, San Francisco, and Chicago, special festivals, celebrations, and parades are held every year on this holiday.

Additional Facts the Teacher Should Know

Nearly a half-million persons of Chinese ancestry live in the United States today. There are some highly concentrated areas of this population in San Francisco, Chicago, and New York that are called "Chinatowns." These sections are actually a city within a city. In these cities, New Year's celebrations, including parades and special traditional festivities, are still common. In other parts of the United States or where there are more second- and third-generation families, the traditional celebrations are modified. In most localities where there are Chinese restaurants, special festivities are often planned for customers. Most Chinese, however, continue to observe their traditional New Year's Day on its lunar calendar date. Many Chinese also refer to an astrological calendar that is a combination of mathematical cycles and symbolic tradition. To record time, the Chinese developed a six hundred-year cycle based on smaller cycles of sixty years each. Within the smaller cycles, each year is given an animal's name as well as an element. According to one legend, the twelve animals were selected on the basis of a cross-country race. The twelve, in order of finish, were: rat, ox, tiger, hare (rabbit), dragon, serpent (snake), horse, ram, monkey, rooster, dog, and boar. The five elements symbolically connected to the calendar are: water, wood, fire, earth, metal.

Many Chinese call each year in this cycle by its animal name, such as the Year of the Horse; some believe that all people born in that year, and other years bearing that name, have traits in common. This is similar to the widespread belief in America in the signs of the zodiac. The Chinese calendar, like the Hebrew, is lunar, and each month has twenty-nine to thirty days. Every thirty months a double month is added. The Chinese calendar does not have the Christian B.C. and A.D. but recorded Chinese culture dates back over 4500 years. It is said that a primitive society on the Asian continent existed as far back as 600,000 years ago. The Chinese New Year begins on *Yuan Tan,* the first day of the first moon, which can occur anywhere from January 21 to February 19. The festival once lasted until the full moon, about fourteen or fifteen days. Each day had its special activities, but today a family or community may shorten the celebration because of work and school schedules. On the

CHINESE FORTUNE CALENDAR

YEAR OF RAT	1972	1984
YEAR OF OX	1973	1985
YEAR OF TIGER	1974	1986
YEAR OF HARE	1975	1987
YEAR OF DRAGON	1976	1988
YEAR OF SNAKE	1977	1989
YEAR OF HORSE	1978	1990
YEAR OF SHEEP	1979	1991
YEAR OF MONKEY	1980	1992
YEAR OF COCK	1981	1993
YEAR OF DOG	1982	1994
YEAR OF BOAR	1983	1995

RAT	1	3	5	2	4
OX	2	4	1	3	5
TIGER	3	5	2	4	1
HARE	4	1	3	5	2
DRAGON	5	2	4	1	3
SNAKE	1	3	5	2	4
HORSE	2	4	1	3	5
SHEEP	3	5	2	4	1
MONKEY	4	1	3	5	2
COCK	5	2	4	1	3
DOG	1	3	5	2	4
BOAR	2	4	1	3	5

Series of elements:
1. metal
2. wood
3. water
4. fire
5. earth

24 years of a 60-year cycle;
5 of the series of 12 = 60 years.

Each combination of animal with element
occurs only once in a 60-year cycle.

Feast of Lanterns, or Feast of the Full Moon, a huge parade is staged with fireworks, gongs, drums, and people dressed in costumes carrying lighted lanterns; the parade features a golden dragon and a lion dance.

At one time some Chinese believed their activities were ruled by the *Yang* and *Yin* principle: the positive and the negative, the male and the female, life and death, the rebirth of spring and the dormancy of winter. The noise and the light created on the Feast of the Lanterns are thought by some to demonstrate the *Yang* forces driving out the evil spirits that have accumulated during the past year. The dragon is one of the four divine creatures that the Chinese also believe dispel spirits. It is also worshipped as the ruler of rivers, lakes, and seas. Its legendary appearance combines the head of a camel, horns of a deer, neck of a snake, claws of a hawk, belly of a frog, and scales of a fish. The dragon is the symbol of goodness and strength and it virtually leads the way into a good year.

In preparation for this holiday the house is thoroughly cleaned, new clothes are purchased, and special sweets are baked. Doors or gates are often lacquered red to keep out evil spirits and to bring the family joy and happiness. Red is the featured color of this holiday. Five signs of happiness are printed or written on red paper and hung by windowsills and door frames for luck. Two is considered the perfect number, so they are often hung in pairs; poems are written in couplets, double portions of food are served, and two presents are given at one time.

Characters representing Chinese words are written from top to bottom and right to left, although now this is beginning to change. If you decide to make a scroll or card with the New Year's greeting *Kung-Hi, Fot-Choy*, be sure to write it in a single column with the character for *Kung* on the top.

Good luck for the new Spring!	May you have prosperity!	Have a happy New Year!

MANDARIN:	Hsin-chwun-dah-jee	Kaw-ng hsee fah tsai	Hsin nee-an quai loh
CANTONESE:	Sahn chee-un dai-gaht	Gaw-ng hay faht choy	Sahn nee-in fai lohk

The industry and science of silk weaving is attributed to the Chinese. They are also credited with inventing the compass, paper, printing, gunpowder, firecrackers, fingerplays, and the use of herbs as medicines. The Great Wall of China is an astonishing architectural and engineering feat. The Chinese have developed the arts of lacquering, calligraphy, painting, printing, weaving, knot tying (macramé), embroidering, paper folding, and paper cutting. They have also made outstanding use of bronze and of porcelain chinaware. We have woven into this guide suggestions for using some of these contributions, which will help the children have a broader knowledge of the Chinese culture.

Methods Most Adaptable for Introducing This Subject to Children

- A display of Chinese art or artifacts, such as chinaware, sculpture, jade, rings, greeting cards, paper cuts, silk, fans, masks, Chinese characters written on a banner, five signs of luck, firecrackers, or a Chinese flag.
- A Chinese or Korean calendar that has the Chinese New Year dates circled.
- News clippings, postcards, or a colored portfolio about the Chinese New Year.
- Display and show how to use an abacus or chopsticks.

- Following the return of children after our New Year's holiday, talk about the New Year's parade on television that often will have included drums, colorful costumes, and music. Invite a Chinese parent or an Asian student from a nearby university or college to come and make a Chinese New Year's treat that the children can eat. Encourage the visitor to demonstrate the use of chopsticks or to share some artifact or treasure.
- A child may share new shoes or clothes.
- Introduce a Chinese game like Chinese Checkers, Pick-Up Sticks, or the "seven-piece puzzle" to the children. (See Games and talk about where the "7-piece puzzle" originated.)
- Introduce silkworms on mulberry leaves to the Discovery Center.

Vocabulary

Animals used to name years.

Chinese	firecracker	first	tease	tea
holiday	chopsticks	fifteen	lacquer	rice
lantern	wind chimes	compass	abacus	jade
dance	lunar, moon	gong	embroidery	incense
celebrate	solar, sun	cake	lucky	chow mein
festival	calendar	banner	sign	dragon
feast	parade	debt	above	chinaware
fireworks	almanac	red	fan	silk

Kung-Hi, Fot-Choy (Cantonese) pronounced Gaw-ng HAY, FAHT-choy = "Have a happy and prosperous New Year!"
Kung-Hsi, Fah-Tsai (Mandarin) pronounced Kaw-ng HSEE, FAH-tsai (as in sigh) = "Have a happy, rich, and prosperous New Year!"
Kung-Hi (Cantonese) pronounced Gaw-ng HAY = "I wish you joy"
Kung-Hsi (Mandarin) pronounced Kaw-ng HSEE = "I wish you joy"
   and usually followed by:
Sui-Hi (Cantonese) pronounced soo-ee-HIGH = "May joy be yours!"
Sui-Hsi (Mandarin) pronounced soo-AY-see = "May joy be yours!"
Yuan Tan (Cantonese) pronounced Ywahn Dahn = New Year
Yuan Tan (Mandarin) pronounced Yuhn DAHN = New Year
Hsin Nien (Mandarin) pronounced SYIN nee-an = New Year
Hsien Nien (Cantonese) pronounced SAHN nihn = New Year

Chinese words used in English:
   kowtow, to bow down to another person
   catsup *(keh-chop)*, tomato juice (sauce for meat)
   typhoon *(dai-fong)*, big wind
   chop suey, bits and pieces (miscellaneous)

NOTE: Chop suey is not a traditional Chinese food. According to one legend, it was first prepared from leftovers for a group of miners in California. It means "bits and pieces." Now it is available in most Chinese restaurants. Fortune cookies are probably a commercialized American product, too. Rice Krispies Squares or crunchies made from marshmallows, butter, and Rice Krispies or syrup, brown sugar, and peanut butter are actually American versions of an Asian confection called Rice Puff Squares. In Korea and China they are made from rice syrup and puffed (popped) rice. Sometimes roasted peanuts are added to the rice puffs or popped corn to add a nutty flavor. Soybeans are also popped and combined with rice syrup. Sesame seeds are browned and mixed with rice syrup to make a delicious chewy bar.

learning centers

Discovery Center

1. Silkworms in their various stages of development are a fascinating adventure for children.
2. Examine mulberry leaves. Use a magnifying glass.
3. Display Chinese chinaware, glassware, a *wok*, and chopsticks. Compare likenesses and differences with our own utensils. Notice that the chinaware is transparent when held up to the light.
4. Taste sweet-and-sour sauce and soy sauce. Smell ginger root and star anise. (The latter smells and tastes like licorice. It grows in southwest China on an evergreen tree and the fruits blossom into a star shape.)
5. Brew and taste several Chinese and American teas. One heaping teaspoon of Chinese tea will make six small cups of tea. Brew for ten to fifteen minutes in a porcelain pot. Orange pekoe tea should be brewed for only one minute and twice the amount of tea used. Many Chinese drink only hot plain tea. Americans and Europeans may add sugar, lemon, milk, or ice to their tea. If you can find a metal tea ball show children how this is used. Compare wet and dry tea leaves.
6. Examine a block print and show children how to use it.
7. Burn incense so children can smell and experience what it is like.
8. Examine a compass: let children hold it and move around the room with it in order to watch the needle move. Tell them the Chinese invented it a very long time ago.
9. Experiment with sound: tap gongs or finger cymbals, bells of various sizes, listen to wind chimes, or hit blocks of wood. (See Sound guide.) Teacher might thumb-strike a piece of crystal.
10. Explore authentic Chinese paper lanterns, kites, and paper cuts so children can discover how they are made.
11. Let children examine Chinese scrolls, children's books, silk paintings, paper kites, greeting cards, pieces of jade, paper cuts, banners, fans, masks, costumes, and authentically dressed dolls. These may be borrowed from friends or purchased from an Asian or import store. This will need to be supervised closely as items are quite fragile.
12. Bamboo pen: show hole for gluing goat's hair or camel's hair.

NOTE: There are camels in northern China.

13. Display a tea set from China and one from the United States. Look for likenesses and differences.
14. Make egg drop soup and taste it.

Egg Drop Soup (Egg Flower Soup)

1 tbsp. cornstarch
2 tbsp. cold water
1 egg
3 cups clear chicken broth
  (can use bouillon cubes or strained chicken noodle soup)

Optional: 1 tsp. chopped parsley or scallion to suggest leaves.

DIRECTIONS:

1. Pour broth into or prepare broth in a metal saucepan, bring to a boil;
2. measure water and cornstarch into a baby food jar, cover with a lid and shake vigorously;
3. open jar, pour cornstarch mixture into the broth, stir with fork until smooth;
4. break an egg into a small bowl and beat with a fork;
5. slowly pour the beaten egg into the broth.

Allow children to watch and take turns helping to pour the egg into the broth. Then they can see the flowers formed when the egg cooks in shreds as it is dropped into the broth. It sinks and then rises to float on the surface in budlike pieces. Stir until all egg has been added and cooked, remove from heat, and serve. Make sure each child gets some flowers spooned into his or her cup.

Dramatic Play Centers

Home-Living Center

1. Have two separate yard lengths of cotton or nylon with ties attached at each corner to wrap dolls to be carried (on a child's back).
2. Quilted jackets, mandarin collars, frog closings, silk scarves.
3. Provide a low table or cut off the top of a large carton.
4. Tablecloths and tea sets for tea party might be available. (A red tablecloth would be especially appropriate.)
5. Set out place mats of straw or woven paper.
6. Set out chopsticks and bowls on the cupboard shelves.

   NOTE: Allow spoons. Chinese children also use spoons until they are skilled in using chopsticks.

7. Set out plastic flowers in a simple wooden or metal vase.
8. Remove chairs and set out cushions.
9. Include a feather duster, feather hats, and feather fans.
10. Sturdy (or replaceable) lanterns or scrolls may be hung around the room by the children.

Block-Building Center

1. Add a Pagoda Tower Builder. Available from Childcraft.
2. Add boats and freeform shapes of blue construction paper for lakes, rivers, and ponds.
3. Discuss how sailors know what direction to sail when they cannot see the land. Let children use the compass in this center.

   NOTE: An inexpensive directional compass (available at variety stores) makes an ideal accessory in the block center when children have assembled boats of large wooden and/or cardboard hollow blocks.

4. Post pictures of Chinese architecture as well as of the Great Wall of China.
5. Set out animals representing the Chinese calendar years, such as rat (mouse), ox, tiger, rabbit, dragon, snake, horse, sheep, monkey, cow, dog, and boar. (Americans prefer the Year of the Mouse to the Year of the Rat.)
6. Set out proportional block arches.
7. A large rectangular empty box makes a good boat. (For other suggested ideas see Dramatic Play in the Water or Water Transportation guides.)

Learning, Language, and Readiness Materials Center

Commercially made games and materials for use at a table or on a mat:

(See Basic Resources, p. 79, for manufacturers' addresses.)

1. Pick-up Sticks (available at toy counter in most stores)
2. Chinese Checkers (available at toy counter in most stores)
3. Abacus (most stores and catalogs)
4. Tea Sets (most stores and catalogs)
5. Magnetic Tic-Tac-Toc (Constructive Playthings)
6. Judy Tangram Puzzle and Patterns
7. International Many Face Doll (David C. Cook)
8. Playskool Fish Puzzle
9. Lauri Crepe Foam Picture Puzzle: Fish, 15 pcs.
10. Weaving Mats (Ideal)
11. Large Parquetry and Patterns (Ideal)
12. Fish Puzzles (Creative Playthings)
13. Uniworld Toys (large discount stores)
14. Cup and Ball: game of skill (available in toy and variety stores)
15. Chinese Animal Year Figures (United Nations Gift Shop, New York 10017)
16. Pagoda Tower Builder (Childcraft)

Teacher-made games and materials for use at a table or on a mat:

NOTE: For detailed description of Games, see pp. 50–59.

1. Tic-Tac-Toe (called Circles and Squares in China): draw nine equal-sized squares on a piece of white or light-colored cardboard. Give each child five round counters or cubes to place on the cardboard, one at a time, alternately. The object of the game is to get three in a row first. Each child should have a different color or shape.

   NOTE: Children might be encouraged to make their own game if the larger and smaller squares of cardboard can be precut and made available. Teacher may provide commercial sets or make them.

2. Match-Them: make up sets of two each of the twelve animals for which the Chinese years are named. Let children find the two that match.
3. Alike, Different, and the Same: use sets made in No. 2. Compare other characteristics.
4. I See Something Red: each child finds something red.
5. Toothpick Puzzlers: arranging colored toothpicks can be an interesting and challenging discovery. Children may even wish to glue down their creations on a piece of paper after exploring the material on a piece of dark felt or dark paper. See illustration below.

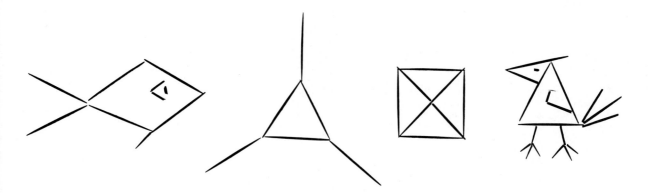

6. Pick-up Sticks: a rather difficult game for the very youngest; requires blunt or sanded ends on the pick-up sticks (sometimes available in a thicker stick). Requires great patience.
7. Seven-piece Puzzle: children fit the pieces together to make a square. Other designs and shapes can be made with the pieces. You can make your own out of poster board. For youngest children draw pattern on another cardboard and let them match the shapes to it.
8. Chinese Checkers: older children may be able to grasp the concept of how this game is played.
9. Toteetum: small cube has a dowel inserted into one end and either numbers or picture characters are painted on each side. The child spins the toteetum and predicts what side will come up. Similar to a dice game of chance. Flipping coins is also a somewhat universal game. Spinning a wooden plate on its edge and predicting which side will come up is still another pastime. These games of chance may not be acceptable by some measures of judgment.

Art Center

** 1. Blow art: older children will enjoy blowing into a straw to shoot or push the paint into a spidery branchlike painting. Give children only brown or black paint. Then by sponge-daubing bright colors on these creations they can be made to look like flower blossoms or leaves on a bush or tree. Blow art sometimes resembles skyrockets bursting in the air.

   CAUTION: Children should be advised to hold the straw above the paper.

* 2. Create a picture with shapes: begin with Chinese puzzle shapes or parquetry.
* 3. Clay work: relate the beginning of all pottery and chinaware to the use of clay and/ or the materials used to make porcelain. Encourage the children to expand their use of clay by making available some simple tools such as palate sticks, cuticle sticks, or coffee stirrers in designing their creations.

* 4. Paper folding: below are some simple plans for paper folding. (*Origami* is the Japanese term.) Show children how to fold and pleat the paper and let them make what they choose. Simple books of *origami* are available (see Teacher Resources) that may suggest other possibilities.

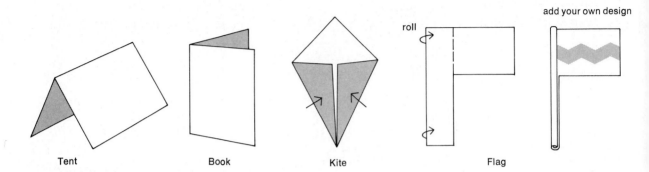

Tent   Book   Kite   Flag

** 5. Paper cutting: use after seeing some examples of paper cuts. (See Teacher Resources.) Encourage the children to cut a picture or explore the use of paper and scissors. Give them paste or glue if they need it to complete their creations. Some may also wish to continue with the use of the materials by asking to paint their cut-outs.

*** 6. Make lanterns for decorations. Use lightweight construction paper (cutting paper). If a piece of paper is 9 inches × 12 inches or 8½ inches × 11 inches it can be folded lengthwise and cut by slashing along the folded edge. When opened and rolled lengthwise into a diamondlike cylinder, it appears to be a colorful lantern. Wallpaper makes an interesting patterned lantern, although children may wish to color or paint a plain piece of paper and then cut as described, as the Chinese do. Finger-painting (monoprint), using crayons, or painting a design on a rectangular piece of paper can also be done. This may be rolled into a cylinder (without cutting) to make still a different type of lantern. Add a strip of paper to form a handle as shown in the diagram below. Two paper cups attached mouth to mouth with paper clips is another kind of lantern.

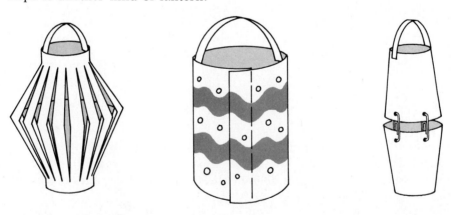

** 7. Charcoal and chalk: it is interesting to observe and to discover that if the Chinese ink stick is rubbed in a porcelain dish with a drop or two of water, it forms ink for the brush that is used to write Chinese characters. This stick is made from charcoal and oil mixed into a kind of crayon.

** 8. Printing: show children some wood-block designs and prints. Let children print some with blocks that you have made or use those that are commercially available.

During a celebration of the Year of the Dragon, toys, books, and cards from China are displayed. The woman is showing the children how to make objects by paper folding.

*** 9. Weaving: the Chinese are masters in the use of bamboo, rattan, flax, and, of course, silk. Simple weaving may be done on a weaving frame (with rug yarn), or with a slashed piece of paper by lacing other colored paper strips through the paper frame. Mesh bags or loosely woven pieces of drapery offer still other possibilities for weaving yarn. For a needle use a filed-off toothbrush with a hole in one end for the eye.

*** 10. Make good luck signs: let the children design their own good luck picture to hang like a scroll.

福　祿　壽　喜

Good Fortune	Prosperity	Long Life	Happiness

MANDARIN:　Foo　　Loo　　Hsiao　　Hsi

CANTONESE:　Fulk　　Luk　　Sow　　Hay

Other Experiences in This Center Using Art Media

1. Make a Chinese kite: Below are several kites ranging from the very simple to the more complex. The carp kite is typically Japanese but the box- and egg-shaped hollow kites are also representative of Chinese kites. They are often made with silk or paper and may be made into many shapes other than fish, such as butterflies, box shapes, and dragons. Note some of the pictures in the books listed in this guide.

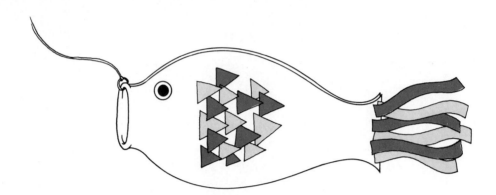

   ** a. Carp kite: Cut two matching fish shapes of lightweight paper and glue together along the outside edges to form a hollow fish. Glue a ring of pipecleaner around the mouth edge. Overlay tissue triangles and glue to the body of the fish. Glue streamers to the tail. Attach a string to the mouth so that when the kite is pulled the wind will pass through the fish.

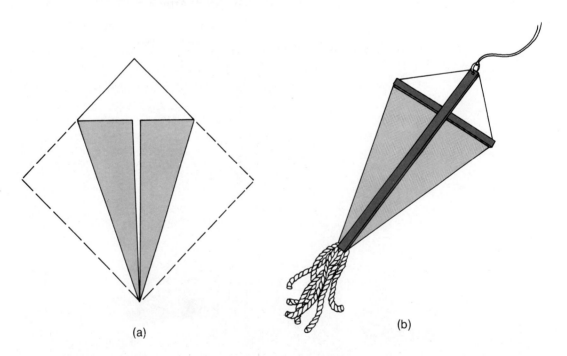

(a)   (b)

   ** b. Paper-fold kite: Use a square of lightweight paper and lay it flat with one corner pointing up. Fold in left and right corners to center (see *a* above). Add tassels or tails to lower corner. Attach a crosspiece of cardboard or wood for support (see *b* above).

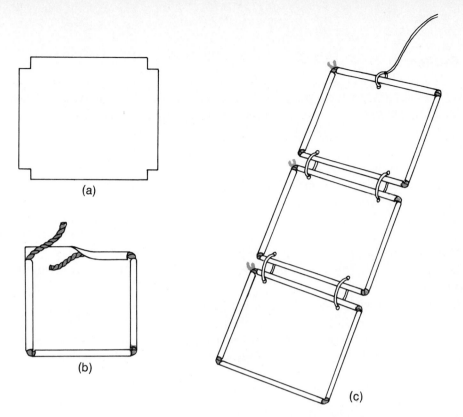

(a)

(b)

(c)

*** c. Flat kite: Begin with a rectangular piece of paper. Notch each corner as shown above, *a*. Role each edge of the paper to form a tube. Thread one length of yarn through all four tubes and secure the ends with a knot. The resulting shape is square. Punch four holes in the square, two on one side and two on the parallel side. Make several of these squares and connect them by slipping yarn through the holes. Each section of the kite can be decorated. Attach a string to one end.

Carp kites:
Directions for making a
simple version of these kites
will be found on the opposite
page.

Book Center

*** Ayer, Jacqueline. *A Wish for Little Sister.* New York: Harcourt Brace Jovanovich, 1960.

*** ———. *Little Silk.* New York: Harcourt Brace Jovanovich, 1959.

**** ———. *Nu Dang and His Kite.* New York: Harcourt Brace Jovanovich, 1959 (paper, 1975).

*** Flack, Marjorie. *The Story about Ping.* New York: Viking Press, 1970.

**** Fleischman, Sid. *The Wooden Cat Man.* Boston: Little, Brown, 1972.

**** Handforth, Thomas. *Mei Li.* Garden City, New York: Doubleday, 1938 (paper).

*** Ipcar, Dahlov. *The Biggest Fish in the Sea.* New York: Viking Press, 1972.

*** Lattimore, Eleanor. *Little Pear.* New York: Harcourt Brace Jovanovich, 1968 (paper).

** Politi, Leo. *Moy Moy.* New York: Scribner's, 1960.

*** Sendak, Maurice. *Chicken Soup with Rice.* New York: Scholastic School Book Service, 1960 (paper).

*** Wiese, Kurt. *Fish in the Air.* New York: Viking Press, 1948.

*** Wolkstein, Diane. *8,000 Stones.* Garden City, New York: Doubleday, 1972.

*** Wright, Mildred Watley. *A Sky Full of Dragons.* Austin, Texas: Steck Vaughn, 1969.

*** Yoshiko, Samuel. *Twelve Years, Twelve Animals.* Nashville, Tennessee: Abingdon, 1972.

planning for grouptime

NOTE: All music, fingerplays, poems, stories, and games listed here may also be used at other times during the session as appropriate. See Core Library, Basic Resources, p. 76, for publishers and addresses. Addresses for sources of records will be found on p. 81.

Music

Songs

Folk Songs of China, Japan, Korea by Betty Warner Dietz

Folk Songs of the World by Charles Haywood

FROM *Wake Up and Sing,* Landeck and Crook
* "Mary Was a Red Bird," p. 15
** "Pretty and Shiny-O," p. 22
** "Birthday Song," p. 24

FROM *Music Resource Book,* Lutheran Church Press
* "John Has a Birthday," p. 65
* "Growing Up," p. 99

Records

"Puff, the Magic Dragon," any children's recording
"Song of Fong-Yang," "Song of the Hoe," and "Flute Song," *Folk Songs of Our Pacific Neighbors*   (Bowmar, 33⅓ RPM or cassette and filmstrip)

Rhythms and Singing Games

1. Use drums and have a dragon dance: make a dragon head out of papier-mâché or a paper sack. Use a tablecloth or a bedspread to cover dragon's body. Attach a tail.
2. Play Asian music: use finger cymbals, tone blocks, gong, bells, or guitar.

Fingerplays and Poems

Chinese Mother Goose Rhymes by Robert Wyndham (Cleveland: World Publishing, 1968). Choose those that suit your group's age, interests, and previous experiences.

NOTE: Share with the children the fact that the Chinese are credited with using finger-plays hundreds of years ago. Show children how to make shadow pictures using their fingers. For example, make a bird, a dog, or a rabbit.

FROM *Rhymes for Fingers and Flannelboards*, Scott and Thompson
"Here's a Cup of Tea," p. 85
"Making Kites," p. 124

FROM *Let's Do Fingerplays*, Grayson
"Old Shoes, New Shoes," p. 18
"Shiny Shoes," p. 19

Stories

(To read, read-tell, or tell. See Book Center for complete list.)

*** *8,000 Stones*, Wolkstein
 ** *Moy Moy*, Politi
*** *Little Pear*, Lattimore
*** *Twelve Years, Twelve Animals*, Yoshiko
**** *Nu Dang and His Kite*, Ayer
*** *A Sky Full of Dragons*, Wright

Games

(See Games, pp. 50–59, and Teacher-Made Games in this guide for directions.)

1. Look and See: use animals of the Chinese fortune calendar year.
2. Scramble: use animals of year; also chopsticks, *daruma* doll, kite, fan, Chinese picture-book, and so on.
3. I See Something Red game

Routine Times

1. Serve rice and chicken, pork or shrimp with broccoli for mealtime.
2. Sometimes foreign foods are offered in specialty stores or international food sections of grocery stores. Inquire about what is available in your city or community and plan to serve some at snack or mealtime.

   NOTE: Expanded travel by armed forces personnel, students, business people, and tourists has broadened the opportunities for tasting and learning about food that is prepared and eaten in different parts of the world. It has also developed in many people an appreciation and a desire to eat these foods as a regular part of their diets.

3. At snack or mealtime eat some of the food that has been prepared earlier by a Chinese visitor or a parent. Observe as the food is made or help to make it.
4. Give each child a double portion or two of everything at snack or mealtime since even numbers are considered lucky in the Chinese tradition. Two of anything means double happiness. Two sections of a mandarin orange or tangerine would be especially appropriate.
5. If possible, buy some dried fruits for the children for snack or mealtime, such as dried apples. One student interviewed remembered a particular octagon-shaped tin that was always brought out for the New Year and the divided sections were filled in with different dried fruits and foods.
6. Play some Chinese music for rest time or play it as background music when the children are using art materials and participating in free-choice activities.

Large Muscle Activities

1. Flip-a-Stick: children count the number of lengths of their stick that make the distance they have flipped. First to get to an attainable score wins. Actually better just to let each take a turn and continue to practice.
2. Marble Game (needs careful supervision): in China, children used to toss marbles, stones, or seed pods into the air and catch them before they fell in a game similar to Jacks. Quite difficult, but interesting to note origin of our game.
3. Coordination Games (very difficult): pat stomach as you circularly stroke your head or vice versa. Have children cross hands and wrists and see if they can lift the finger pointed to.
4. Chinese Jump Rope (another game with many variations): one variation involves raising the rubber band rope higher and higher to see how high children can jump. Ask a Chinese-American primary-age child to demonstrate some of the basic movements.
5. Paper, Scissors, and Stone (two can play): on the count of three, both players show one of the following:

   Paper will cover a stone (HAND EXTENDED FLAT FOR PAPER)
   Scissors will cut paper (INDEX AND MIDDLE FINGER EXTENDED TO FORM V, WIGGLE AS IF CUTTING WITH SCISSORS)
   Stone will dull scissors (HAND MAKES A FIST FOR A ROCK)

   The child showing the most powerful subject wins or scores a point.

   NOTE: Sometimes called Cloth, Scissors, and Stone.

6. Blowing Game: by paper folding, children in China make little frogs. They place them

on a tabletop, and blow them across the table to see whose frog gets there first. If the tabletop can have a ledge made along the sides, Ping-Pong balls can be blown across the surface instead.

7. Flip Ball: perhaps you have a parent with craft skills. If so ask this person to make you a flip ball using the instructions in *Folk Toys Around the World* (see Teacher Resources).

Extended Experiences

1. Visit a Chinese restaurant. There are usually authentic items to enjoy.
2. Invite a parent or a Chinese student to visit and bring a Chinese treat to share with the children. If the recipe is simple enough and there is no danger involved with hot grease, knives, or cleavers, the children might help to make it. Sometimes part of the preparation can be done beforehand and described to the children when completing the final steps.
3. Children will enjoy learning the skill of manipulating chopsticks. Soup crackers or miniature marshmallows make good items to be picked up and eaten by children.

    NOTE: Many Chinese children are nearly six before they can manipulate chopsticks adroitly. Younger children in China are given spoons.

4. View "Things That Are Red" (Bowmar Art World filmstrips, record, or cassette, posters, art visuals, and teacher's manual).
5. View "Folksongs of Our Pacific Neighbors" (Bowmar World Cultures program, filmstrip and record or cassette).
6. "Five Families" (one of five filmstrips from Scholastic Films, filmstrip with cassette).

teacher resources

Books and Periodicals

1. Latourette, Kenneth. *China*. New York: Macmillan, 1964 (paper).
2. ———. *The Chinese and Their History and Culture*. New York: Macmillan, 1964 (paper).
3. Joseph, Joan. *Folk Toys Around the World and How to Make Them*. New York: Parents' Magazine Press, 1972.
4. Temko, Florence and Elaine Simon. *Paper Folding to Begin With*. Indianapolis: Bobbs-Merrill, 1968.
5. St. Tamara. *Asian Crafts*. New York: Lion Press, 1970.
6. Pinkwater, Jill. *Chinese Cooking for Beginners*. New York: Dodd Mead, 1974.
7. Wiese, Kurt. *You Can Write Chinese*. New York: Viking Press, 1945 (paper, 1973).

    NOTE: Helpful for content, but illustrations of Chinese people are inaccurate.

8. Wyndham, Robert. *Chinese Mother Goose Rhymes*. Cleveland: Collins-World, 1968.
9. Quong, Rose. *Chinese Written Characters: Their Wit and Wisdom*. Boston: Beacon Press, 1973.

10. *China: Books and Periodicals on China*, Midwest Center, 210 W. Madison Street, Chicago, Illinois 60606 (source for current books and artifacts).
11. *National Geographic* magazines.
12. Gaer, Joseph. *Holidays Around the World*. Boston: Little, Brown, 1953.

Pictures and Displays

(See p. 79, for addresses of firms listed.)

1. Note display items suggested in the Discovery Center. Write to your China bookstore (see Books and Periodicals) and check your nearest city for an import-export store.
2. Check with discount stores for toys from UNESCO or toys marked UNIWORLD. Be selective, as some are better than others.
3. Seek out and collect artifacts from your children's parents, friends, or persons who may have traveled extensively. Teachers in the public school systems with a particular interest in cultural awareness may prove helpful. When possible invite them to bring these artifacts so that they can supervise the exploration of them and be available to answer questions about them. See Basic Resources, pp. 73–74, about visitors in the classroom.
4. Obtain an Asian Lunar Calendar from an import-export store.

Community Resources

1. Art museums for Chinese artifacts
2. Parents, teachers, students, armed forces personnel, or other persons who have lived or visited in an Asian country or who may themselves be Asian
3. An import-export store
4. A Chinese or Asian restaurant and its staff
5. A university group of Asian students who may serve a traditional New Year's dinner on their New Year or participate in an International Night displaying artifacts and sharing dances, dress, or drama
6. Other special celebrations, such as parades or festivities planned in restaurants for the Chinese New Year

II Halloween

basic understandings

(concepts children can grasp from this subject)

- In the United States and Canada, Halloween is celebrated on October 31.
- Pumpkins are commonly used to make jack-o'-lanterns.
- Halloween colors are orange, black, and white.
- On Halloween children dress up to disguise themselves (hide who they are) from their friends and visit them to get a treat, or else they play a trick on their friends.
- Halloween is celebrated during the time of harvesting apples, corn, pumpkins, and nuts, and when leaves change color. These foods and materials are often used as decorations and for games at parties.

Additional Facts the Teacher Should Know

History of Halloween:

The night of October 31 is Halloween. "Hallow" means "saint." November 1 is a church festival, All Saints' Day. Thus the word "Hallowe'en" is short for "All Hallows Evening." On this date the Roman Catholic Church celebrates the feast of all those who were known to have lived a good life but who were not included on the church's calendar of saints. October 31 was believed to be the one night during the year when ghosts and witches were most likely to wander about. In the early years of Britain, October 31 was the last day of the year and celebrations were similar to our New Year's Eve.

Legend says that some thought this was the date when the souls of the dead were liberated from purgatory, which according to Roman Catholic theology is a place or state after death for making amends (or to atone) for sins. It was believed the released souls were allowed to visit their homes, and thus has evolved the present-day custom of "trick or treaters" coming to neighborhood homes dressed as skeletons. The carved pumpkin was another symbol of death.

Another legend says there was once a miserly man named Jack, who was consigned to roam the earth until Judgment Day, because he was too stingy to get into heaven and too prone to playing practical jokes on the devil to go to hell. So, Jack carried his lantern (jack-o'-lantern) as he roamed.

Still another legend concerns a circle of dough, better known as the doughnut. According to this story, an English cook invented this "soul cake" to remind English beggars about eternity. The cook cut a hole out of a piece of dough and then dropped the dough into a pan of deep fat. Its circular shape was to be a reminder of the constancy of eternity. The people who received this doughnut were supposed to pray for the dead of the family who gave it to them.

Some say that the Halloween customs of bonfires, pranks, tricks, and jack-o'-lanterns were first introduced to America in the early 1900s by the Irish immigrants. In recent years, schools, parents, and communities have encouraged parties and parades to discourage the pranks of the past and now many children and teenagers collect funds for UNICEF on Halloween. Their younger brothers and sisters dress up in costumes and masks and only ring doorbells where porch lights are lit to invite children to stop. Treats are prepared at such homes and given in return for the children's performing a trick or feat. Some communities, through the schools, encourage children to learn a trick to perform for a treat, for example, a poem, riddle, song, or physical feat, deemphasizing malicious mischief and calling it a "trick *for* a treat."

About preschool celebrations of this holiday:

Small children should be helped to realize that Halloween is a time for fun and surprises rather than a time for superstition and fright. "Casper the Friendly Ghost" cartoons, the "Bewitched" television program with Samantha and Tabitha, and the Georgie books have made witches and ghosts less frightening. However, for young children perhaps the main emphasis should be on pumpkins and their uses, jack-o'-lanterns, tricks, and disguises (guess who?) with suggestions to paint faces, wearing hats or animal costumes rather than wearing masks, or portraying skeletons, witches, or goblins. A two-year-old feels disguised wearing a lampshade (as one author put it). Save the witches and ghosts for the older children who, it is hoped, will be better able to tell what is real or unreal, fantasy and fiction or fact.

Many children will enjoy making masks but refuse to wear them. For this reason, masks that can be held in front of them are often better. Stress the fun of surprise in guessing who is who.

In recent years this holiday has been marred by vandalism as well as by the poisoning of children. Children should be encouraged to visit only the friends and neighbors that their parents suggest.

Methods Most Adaptable for Introducing This Subject to Children

- A trip to a farm where pumpkins are raised
- A trip to the store to buy apples, nuts, and several pumpkins
- Read or tell a story about Halloween or a pumpkin
- Pictures on the bulletin board of pumpkins growing, a jack-o'-lantern, or a pumpkin pie
- Bring several pumpkins to be cut and scooped out by the children

Vocabulary

pumpkins	seeds	cat	eyes	joke
jack-o'-lantern	treat	owl	nose	scare
candle	orange	mask	mouth	surprise
trick	black	costume	witch	guess
grin	pie	riddle	ghost	harvest

learning centers

Discovery Center

1. Bake sugar cookies, cutting pumpkins or other related shapes. (Tupperware has a jack-o'-lantern cutter.) Children may frost these or prebaked cookies with orange frosting. Chocolate chips and raisins or small marshmallows also can be made available for decorating.

2. Make pumpkin custard from the meat of a pumpkin. Use recipe for pumpkin pie filling, but pour in custard cups and bake. Place custard cups in baking pan. Fill pan with 1 inch of hot water. Bake at 350° for 30 min. (or until knife inserted comes out clean).

3. Make orange Jell-O or chocolate Shake a Pudding or orange Kool-Aid.

4. Observe pumpkins growing on the vine. Note variations in color, size, shape, quality, weight, and how pumpkins differ from squash.

5. Make jack-o'-lanterns from pumpkins. Let the children draw on the eyes, nose, and mouth shapes they want with a wax marking pencil. Teacher does the cutting. Children can take turns scooping out the seeds. For a special treat darken the room and light a candle inside a pumpkin. An adult should always be present, careful to watch children nearest the jack-o'-lantern. Short candles smoke less than tall ones. Drip candle wax into the pumpkin to secure the candle or nail from the underside of the pumpkin to hold the candle.

6. Wash and dry pumpkin seeds for planting, baking, frying, or dyeing for use in making collages. When making the jack-o'-lantern, notice how the seeds grew inside the pumpkin.

7. Discover differences between raw and cooked pumpkin. Taste some of each.

8. Discover uses of pumpkins—puddings, pies, decorations, Halloween jack-o'-lanterns.

9. Observe difference between cut apples and carrots that are dipped in lemon juice (prevents browning) and those that are not.

10. Display masks used by community helpers in their work. Include picture books and mounted pictures that illustrate how and why they are worn. Include some of the following: oxygen mask, ski mask, football helmet with face guard, motorcycle goggles, face shields or goggles for welders or sanders, airpacks worn by firefighters, a sleep mask, a hospital-type mask, dark sun glasses, a gas mask. Let children try on some of the masks and see if they can guess or think why each is worn.

Dramatic Play Centers

Home-Living Center

1. In this center or behind a three-way play screen, have a costume shop with a mirror, or buy Halloween costumes and accessories like those listed:
   a. Disguises for younger children:
      Hats, these are often enough for the youngest children
      Mail carrier, mail carrier's hat and bag
      Safety officer, police officer's hat and tickets
      Cowboy/cowgirl, felt hat and stick horse
      Mother or lady, colored or veiled hats with flowers, women's high heels, purse
      Father or man, vest, tie, wallet, hat, car keys, shoes
   b. Disguises for older preschoolers:
      Scarecrow, patchy blue jeans, pants and shirt, fringe sleeves, collar, and pant legs, battered hat, old pair sneakers (cut so toes show)
      Bride, white dress (gathered or gored skirt with elastic waist), veil, lace curtain train, artificial flowers for hair and bouquet, rings
      Animals, dyed "sleepers," stuffed tails with loop to fasten to belt, ears attached to skull cap
      Ballerina, a tank top, sleeveless T-shirt top, or a body suit, with a ruffled tutu to tie around waist, pipe cleaner tiara, ribbons to tie around shoe and ankle
      Man, black mustache (can be painted on with mascara), old hat, black tie
      Pirate or Buccaneer, tie a bandana around head, attach curtain rings to ears with tape, notch pair of old blue jeans, wrap waist with a sash, wear a bolero and add a cardboard or rubber knife
      Clown, pointed hat, crepe paper, or cloth ruffles to tie around neck, wrists, and ankles or button on to a clown suit
      Queen or king, gilt cardboard crown covered with sequins and beads. Use same materials to make a tiara for a queen. Old lace tablecloth or velvet curtain can be draped or pinned for a cloak or robe. King needs cardboard sword or scepter

Block-Building Center

1. Set out farm helper figures with wooden or rubber family, tractors, trucks, and wagons.
2. Encourage farm play. Supply spools and colored cubes or small plastic vegetables to be harvested, loaded into trucks, and driven on the road to market.
3. Talk about how you get to the biggest city near you (if you live in a small town), such as up and down hills, over bridges, and through tunnels. (See Road Transportation guide.)

Learning, Language, and Readiness Materials Center

Commercially made games and materials for use at a table or on a mat:

(See Basic Resources, p. 79, for manufacturers' addresses.)

1. Family Face Puppets: to hold in front of the face, white and black (Instructo)
2. Animal Face Puppets: six masks to hold in front of the face (Instructo)
3. Face Puppets: six masks to hold in front of the face (Ideal)
4. Plastic Hats: six heavy gauge vinyl hats (Childcraft)
5. Play Hat Set (Constructive Playthings)
6. Fantasy Play Hats for boys and girls (ABC)
7. Puppet Playmates: community helpers and space explorers (ABC)

8. Judy See-Quees: From Seed to Pumpkin, 12 pcs.
9. Face Matching: 12 pairs of matching faces (Creative Playthings)
10. Farm Lotto (Ed-U-Card)
11. Clown Perception Plaques: 12 pairs (Creative Playthings)
12. Judy Puzzle: Halloween, 22 pcs.
13. Fruits I Like: beginners inlay puzzle, 4 pcs. (Playskool)
14. Fall and Halloween gummed back stickers (Dennison, Hallmark)
15. Holiday Felt Cut-outs: jack-o'-lanterns (Milton Bradley)

Teacher-made games and materials for use at a table or on a mat:

NOTE: For detailed description of Games, see pp. 50–59.

1. Name It: use Halloween objects: mask, owl, black cat, pumpkin.
2. What's Missing?: use hats, masks, or Halloween objects.
3. I See Something: I see something about Halloween in the room and describe what it is. Let the children guess and do the same for you.
4. Grouping and Sorting: have a group of orange and black objects and sort by color.
5. Guess Who?: describe a child in the group by saying, "I see someone who is wearing a blue dress and has brown eyes." A variation is to describe a community helper or a story character.
6. Listening: tell the children that it is hard to guess who is visiting us if they're dressed up, but sometimes you can tell who they are by listening to their voices. The child pointed to may say, "Hello," or "trick for a treat."
7. Alike, Different, and the Same: Cut several orange pumpkins and black cats out of felt, cardboard, or upholstery plastic. Vary the size, shape, and form of those made. Ask children to match two that are identical, to select one that is different, or to find several that are similar.
8. Make a felt pumpkin plus black felt triangles, circles, crescents, ellipses, and squares to arrange a variety of jack-o'-lantern faces. See p. 226 for shape suggestions.
9. Cut a pumpkin out of orange upholstery plastic or other heavy fabric. Use a satin zigzag stitch to secure the edges and make pumpkin crevice lines. Sew on buttons (at least ½" in diameter) where the eyes, nose, and mouth could be. Children can then button on felt or plastic shapes to create their own jack-o'-lanterns. Sew buttons as if for a coat, leaving a long shank for easier buttoning. Sew buttons on both sides of fabric to make it sturdier and reversible! For illustration of pumpkin and face pieces see p. 226.

    NOTE: The felt pumpkin invites the most creative use. The button-on pumpkin combines the possibility of another learning skill to the child's creative use, and is best for older children. The very young will want to keep theirs, so you may explain that it belongs to the Center, but after they have experimented with this one they can make one like it out of paper shapes to take home.

10. How Many?: Children may need to talk about how many eyes, noses, mouths are needed for a face in above activities or during creative experiences in the Art Center.

Art Center

* 1. Use orange and black paint at the easels to encourage Halloween art.
* 2. Fingerpaint in orange or make monoprint. When dry cut into pumpkin shapes.
* 3. Tint playdough with orange tempera. (For basic recipe of playdough, see p. 27.)
    Variation: Allow children to knead red and yellow powdered paint or food coloring into the playdough.

Button-on Pumpkin

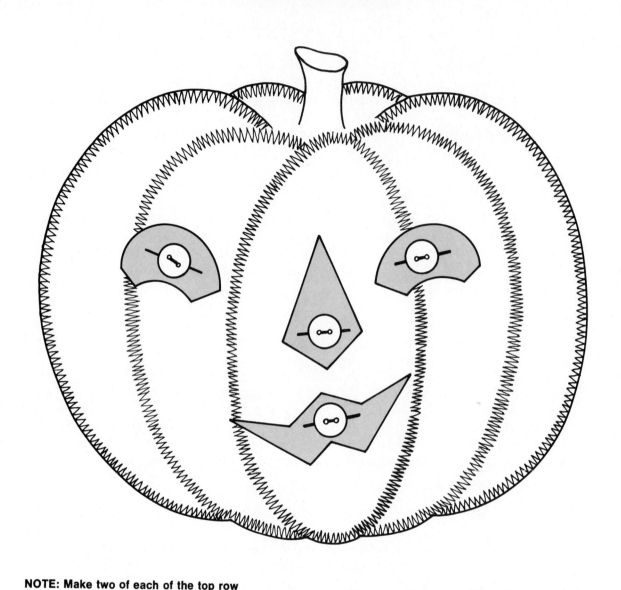

NOTE: Make two of each of the top row

EYE shapes:

NOSE shapes:

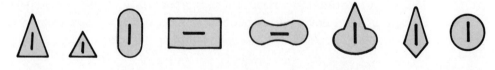

MOUTH shapes:

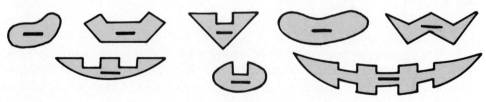

Other Experiences in This Center Using Art Media

*   1. Create a paper jack-o'-lantern: allow child to select a paper pumpkin from a variety of sizes, shapes, shades of orange. (These may be precut or predrawn for the youngest.) Child attaches snippings or precut geometric shapes for eyes, nose, and mouth. Identify shapes: crescents (moonshaped), triangles, squares, circles, and half-circles as you give them to the children. Features for the jack-o'-lantern may be precut from black gummed paper for the youngest to stick on. Talk about how many eyes, noses, and mouths we have and show on a felt pumpkin a variety of faces possible by inverting and reversing the same shapes. DO NOT POST OR MAKE A SAMPLE as it may limit their creativity. The older children may be able to draw their own pumpkins, to cut them out themselves, and to cut the desired feature shapes.

***   2. Make a "handle mask": let the children cover a bent wire clothes hanger with an old top to a nylon stocking or panty hose. Precover for the youngest child. Have children create a face by gluing on scraps of felt, cloth, and yarn. (See below.) Child can hold in front of face. For fun, the teacher may make wild guesses as to who the child is: for example, Robbie the Rabbit, Freddie the Frog. The child is always identifiable behind the mask although he may think he's hiding.

       CAUTION: Be sure to bend the open end hook back on itself to form the handle and eliminate a sharp point. (See illustration below.)

***   3. Make a paper plate mask: attach a tongue depressor or popsicle stick to the bottom of a paper plate with tape or staples and let child decorate a face (similar to idea No. 2). Guess person by clothes or exposed hair. (See above.)

**   4. Make a seed collage picture: arrange pumpkin seeds on dark-colored paper. To add variety you may also dye seeds different colors, using food coloring of desired intensity and one teaspoon vinegar to a cup of water. Spread on paper towel to dry before using.

**   5. Make a trick or treat bag: prefold a cuff around a large-size sack, inserting a thin strip of cardboard. On opposite sides staple an orange or black strip of bias tape, rope, string, ribbon, or cord for a handle. Encourage children to cut or tear Halloween shapes, such as pumpkins, owls, cats, cornstalks, or nuts, out of construction paper and glue onto sack. Crepe paper streamers, strips of black and orange paper, fringed borders, or yarn also make attractive decorations.

***   6. Make Halloween banners for a parade: use crepe paper streamers or tissue taped to the end of a small upholstery cardboard core or tube (available free at any upholstery shop). Glue or tape on the face of a pumpkin, clown, cat, or any other nonfrightening face.

***   7. Make rattles or noisemakers out of small empty boxes. Put in a few stones or spools, tape shut, paint or decorate, fasten to stick or carry in hand.

* 8. Make sack pumpkins: fill a small white or brown paper sack with torn newspapers. Have some pretorn as children tire of tearing and want to proceed. Twist top and secure with a rubber band. Then let children paint all sides of the pumpkin orange and the twisted stem green. When dry you may let older children add eyes, nose, and mouth by gluing on shapes to create a fat sack jack-o'-lantern. Some may wish to twist a strip of green crepe paper around the top for a gay stem. Youngest may leave plain to make a pumpkin patch prop to play "Halloween Pumpkin Patch," p. 230.

** 9. Make a pumpkin patch picture: this activity is fun following a trip to a pumpkin patch. Let the children paint a piece of brown or beige construction paper with glue. Give each child several cotton balls to roll in a shallow pan of *dry* orange tempera for use as pumpkins and supply several lengths of green yarn to be twisted around among the pumpkins like a creeping vine.

CAUTION: Be sure the children wear aprons for this activity.

*** 10. Make Halloween Sack Puppets (for most mature young children): a two-step process. Paint sacks orange for a pumpkin, black for a cat, or leave brown or beige for an owl. Precut appropriate shapes children might choose or need. You may let children snip their own snippings. (See illustration below.)

Book Center

*** Balian, Lorna. *Humbug Witch*. Nashville, Tenn.: Abingdon Press, 1965.

*** Bridwell, Norman. *Clifford's Halloween*. New York: Four Winds Press School Book Service, 1967.

**** Foster, Doris. *Tell Me Mr. Owl*. New York: Lothrop, Lee & Shepard, 1957 (read-tell).

** Keats, Ezra Jack. *Hi Cat!* New York: Macmillan, 1970 (paper, 1972).

* Kravetz, Nathan and Muriel Farrell. *Is There a Lion in the House?* New York: Henry Z. Walck, 1970.

*** Miller, Edna. *Mousekin's Golden House*. Englewood Cliffs, N.J.: Prentice-Hall, 1964.

**** Slobodkin, Louis. *Trick or Treat*. New York: Macmillan, 1967 (paper, 1972).

** Unwin, Nora. *Proud Pumpkin*. New York: E. P. Dutton, 1953.

** Yezback, Steven. *Pumpkin Seeds*. New York: Bobbs-Merrill, 1969.

*** Zolotow, Charlotte. *A Tiger Called Thomas*. New York: Lothrop, Lee & Shepard, 1963.

planning for grouptime

NOTE: All music, fingerplays, poems, stories, and games listed here may be used at other times during the session as appropriate. See Core Library, Basic Resources, p. 76, for publishers and addresses. Addresses for sources of records will be found on p. 81. In parodies, hyphenated words match the music notes of the tune used.

Music

Songs

THE HALLOWE'EN PARTY (a parody)
(tune: "Mary Had a Little Lamb")
Adaptation by JoAnne Deal Hicks

Pump-kins have such hap-py grins, hap-py grins, hap-py grins.
Pump-kins have such hap-py grins. It's Hal-low-e'en at last.

Cats have come with long, black tails, long, black tails, long, black tails.
Cats have come with long, black tails. It's Hal-low-e'en at last.

Ghosts have come to school to-day, school to-day, school to-day.
Ghosts have come to school to-day. It's Hal-low-e'en at last.

Witch-es have their witch-es' brooms, witch-es' brooms, witch-es' brooms.
Witch-es have their witch-es' brooms. It's Hal-low-e'en at last.

HALLOWE'EN (a parody)
(tune: "This is the Way")
Adaptation by JoAnne Deal Hicks

I saw a pump-kin face so *glad*, face so *glad*, face so *glad*.
I saw a pump-kin face so *glad*,
It's Hal-low-e'en in Oc-to-ber!

Variations: 1. Repeat verse 1 inserting "face so *mad*," or . . . "face so *sad*."
2. Repeat the same sequences (three verses), including the above variation of emotions, but substitute "ghost with" or "cat with" for the word pumpkin.

NOTE: Flannel cut-outs depicting these emotions or things could be displayed on a flannel-board as the song is being taught.

HALLOWE'EN PUMPKIN PATCH (a parody)
(tune: "Farmer in the Dell")
Adaptation by JoAnne Deal Hicks

Several children are selected to sit in the center of the room to represent pumpkins in a pumpkin patch. Each child holds a cut-out of a particular pumpkin shape. Some are tall and thin, short and fat, round, oblong, flattop, and so on. Also, colors should vary from bright orange to light orange to green-tinged orange.

NOTE: Real pumpkins may be used if you caution the children to "Handle with Care!"

The other children are told, "When the song begins, one of you will be selected to go to the pumpkin patch and choose the pumpkin shape you like best! When you have made your choice, you and the person holding the pumpkin shape will rejoin the circle and sing along with the rest of the group as we walk around the pumpkin patch.

Verse 1: We see a pump-kin patch. We see a pump-kin patch.
Hi-ho, it's Hal-low-e'en, we see a pump-kin patch.

Teacher selects child who is to choose a pumpkin. When he/she makes the selection, rest of group sings:

Verse 2: He'll (She'll) take that pump-kin home. He'll (she'll) take that pump-kin home.
Hi-ho, it's Hal-low-e'en, he'll (she'll) take that pump-kin home.

The two children now rejoin the group and all walk around the pumpkin patch singing verse 1.

Repeat until every child has had an opportunity to select a particular pumpkin . . . or until interest lags.

NOTE: Farmers usually give children pumpkins to take with them after a group visits on a tour. If not, explain that we would need to pay the owner for pumpkins chosen as we do in a store.

FROM *Songs for the Nursery School*, MacCarteney
* "Pumpkin Mellow," p. 64
* "Hallowe'en," p. 65

FROM *Music Activities for Retarded Children*, Ginglend and Stiles
*** "Hallowe'en Is Coming," p. 58
* "Jack o'Lantern," p. 70

FROM *Music Resource Book*, Lutheran Church Press
* "Mister Clown," p. 50
* "Hallowe'en," p. 74

Records

"Halloween Rhythms" (Phoebe James, 78 RPM)
"Halloween Sounds," "I'm a Witch," and "Three Black Cats," *The Small Singer*, Record 1 (Bowmar, 33⅓ RPM)
"March of the Ghosts," *The Small Player* (Bowmar, 33⅓ RPM), also cassette and filmstrip

"This is Halloween," *Sing a Song of Holidays and Seasons* (Bowmar [cassette and filmstrip with 20 minibooks and teacher's resource guide priced separately], 33⅓ RPM)
"Tonight is Halloween," "Smallest Witch," and "I'm Not Scared," *More Singing Fun,* Record 1 (Bowmar, 33⅓ RPM)
"Trick or Treat" (Disneyland, 33⅓ RPM)

Rhythms and Singing Games

FROM *Songs for the Nursery School,* MacCarteney
"Chase Your Tail Kitty," p. 25 (Halloween kitty, of course!)
"Little Mouse Creeping," p. 26 (adapt to "Creeping Pumpkin Vines," suggesting to children they may be pumpkin vines creeping across the pumpkin patch)

Costume parade: use any good marching record and parade around the room, or if more than one room in your Center, parade through building.

Fingerplays and Poems

FROM *Rhymes for Fingers and Flannelboards,* Scott and Thompson
"Halloween," p. 59

FROM *Let's Do Fingerplays,* Grayson
"I've a Jack-o'-Lantern," p. 95 (See others on pp. 95–98)

MY PUMPKIN
by Darlene Hamilton

Here's my orange pumpkin (HAVE HANDS OUTSPREAD)
Big and fat and round (MAKE CIRCLE WITH HANDS)
It's the very best one (HOLD UP ONE FINGER)
I could find downtown (POINT IN THAT DIRECTION)

Now I need to make a nose ("CUT" NOSE ON YOUR FACE)
A mouth . . . some eyes (CIRCLE EYES LIKE GLASSES)
Or mother will use it (MOTION TO REMOVE)
To cook and bake some pies (ACT LIKE STIRRING)

JACK-O'-LANTERN
by Darlene Hamilton

See my jack-o'-lantern (POINT)
Smiling right at you (SMILE)
You don't need to be afraid (LOOK FRIGHTENED)
It can't holler *Boo!*

PUMPKINS
by Darlene Hamilton

A pumpkin is big (CIRCLE HANDS OVER HEAD)
A pumpkin is round (CIRCLE ARMS IN FRONT)
A pumpkin has a great big smile (OUTLINE SMILE ON MOUTH)
But doesn't make a sound. (PUT FINGER OVER LIPS)

MY JACK-O'-LANTERN FRIEND
Anonymous

(USE APPROPRIATE ACTIONS)
All children have a happy friend, who comes just once a year.
He has two eyes, a nose, a mouth, and grins from ear to ear.
He has a light that's tucked inside. He's big and round and yellow.
And, when we light the candle bright, he's such a jolly fellow.
Now, who is he? Of course, you're right! He's jack-o'-lantern, big and bright!

PETER, PETER, PUMPKIN EATER

Use the traditional poem by Mother Goose with the picture from Nonsense Rhymes Picture Set (The Child's World)

Stories

(To read, read-tell, or tell. See Book Center for complete list.)

*** *Humbug Witch*, Balian
*** *Clifford's Halloween*, Bridwell
**** *Trick or Treat*, Slobodkin
**** *Tell Me Mr. Owl*, Foster
*** *Mousekin's Golden House*, Miller
** *Proud Pumpkin*, Unwin
*** *A Tiger Called Thomas*, Zolotow
* *Is There a Lion in the House?* Kravetz and Farrell

Games

(See Games, pp. 50–59, and Teacher-Made Games in this guide for directions.)

1. Name it
2. What's Missing?
3. I See Something
4. Guess Who?
5. Listening

Routine Times

1. At snacktime, drink orange juice through black licorice straws (cut ends to open).
2. Cheese pumpkins can be served for snack or mealtime.
   a. Cheese slices cut in shapes of pumpkins. Serve plain or on bread or crackers.
   b. Let children grate processed cheese and mold into pumpkins. Eat immediately.

   NOTE: Wash hands first!

3. Jack-o'-lanterns made of a variety of foods may be served at snack or mealtime during Halloween week:
   a. apples with raisins for eyes, nose, mouth. Use the end of the peeler to make holes in which to poke raisins.
   b. Cut out a face in an apple using sharp point of knife. Dip in lemon juice or comparable substitute.

c. Use whole peeled oranges for pumpkins. Slice out a wedge and insert a small apple wedge for mouth, raisin eyes, and a miniature marshmallow for a nose. One can be divided in halves, if flat side of each is placed down.

4. Carrot strips and raisins may be served at snack or mealtime.
5. For snack, eat Halloween cookies which the children have baked or decorated.
6. Play "Guess Who?" while waiting for snacks or meals. (See Teacher-Made Games, No. 5, p. 225.)

Large Muscle Activities

(See also Rhythms and Singing Games, p. 231.)

1. Costume Parade: march around the room (if Center has more than one group, parade through other rooms)
2. Bean Bag Game (ETA or make your own)

Extended Experiences

1. Take a trip to the store to buy several pumpkins—one pumpkin per five children. Encourage children to select their favorite one, noting color, weight, shape, flaws, size, and price. Each group of five might choose their own and give necessary coins to cashier (with supervision of teacher, volunteer, or parent). This will give all the children an opportunity to participate in the total experience. If you can walk to the store, take a wagon to carry the pumpkins back to the Center.
2. Trip to a pumpkin farm: select pumpkins for the Center and, if possible, one for each child.

Right: Felt shapes encourage a child to create different faces for a felt pumpkin. *Center:* Black cat silhouettes, in various poses, challenge the child to describe each pose and to match poses that are identical. *Left:* Child is sorting items that are orange by placing them within a circle of orange yarn.

teacher resources

Books and Periodicals

1. *Your Preschool Child* (Making Most of Years 2-4), Burnett. New York: Holt, Rinehart & Winston, 1961.
2. *If You Live with Little Children*, Kauffman and Farrell. New York: G. P. Putnam and Sons, 1957.
3. *Jack and Jill, Wee Wisdom*, and *Highlights* October issues often have activity ideas that can sometimes be simplified or adapted for young children or used by the teacher for room decorations.

Pictures and Displays

(See p. 79 for addresses of firms listed.)

1. Halloween in Holidays Packet (David C. Cook)
2. Fall Harvesting in Seasons Packet (David C. Cook)
3. Peter, Peter, Pumpkin Eater in Nonsense Rhymes (The Child's World)
4. Fruits from Vines: picture fold-outs (The Child's World)
5. Take a Walk in Fall: fold-out charts (The Child's World)
6. Halloween (Hallmark decorations)
7. Harvesting Corn and Roadside Stand: SVE Study Prints (Singer)
8. Fall and Winter Holidays: SVE Study Prints (Singer)
9. Make a mobile with Halloween symbols. Hang a mobile in room, such as pumpkin, cat, owl. You may eventually replace it with children's own creations.
10. Try to find a picture showing ingredients for a pumpkin pie—egg, milk, can of pumpkin.
11. Pictures of fields of pumpkins, tall pumpkins, short pumpkins, pumpkins in store or on truck, families making jack-o'-lanterns.
12. Put up orange and black paper chains or crepe paper streamers around the room.

Community Resources

1. Grocery store, to buy pumpkins
2. Roadside stand, to buy pumpkins
3. Farm, to see pumpkins growing
4. 4-H Club member, to see pumpkins growing

12 Thanksgiving Around the World

Many Americans think Thanksgiving Day began with the Pilgrims. One reason might be that it has been declared both a legal and national holiday commemorating the Pilgrims' first Thanksgiving feast. It is celebrated today in several ways. It has become a day for family reunions, feasting, religious services, parades, football games, turkey raffles and shoots, and, sometimes, dancing.

Giving thanks for an abundant harvest actually is one of the oldest and most-celebrated kinds of holidays in the world. The date varies with the seasonal harvest of the country in which it is celebrated.

Harvest Home Festival

One of these holidays, Harvest Home Festival, is held on October 15th in England and Canada. This is the approximate time (late September to mid-October) that the first Thanksgiving feast was held at Plymouth. It would not be surprising that these colonists from Scromby, England, should model their celebration after a traditional holiday of their homeland. However, foods prepared and eaten in America reflected what was abundantly available here.

In England, this holiday is likely a remnant of influence from the Roman Empire. The Romans celebrated their Thanksgiving in early October. It was dedicated to Ceres, goddess of the harvest, and the holiday was called Cerelia. The English often held a parade, with a queen who had been selected to ride in a carriage drawn by white horses; unlike the Romans, however, they did not wish to honor the Roman goddess but instead showed their gratitude for a fine harvest by attending church services.

In ancient times, other harvest festivals were held in Chaldea, Egypt, and in Greece. Moslems, Chinese, and Jews still celebrate the harvest of crops. Some of these holidays are listed below.

Harvest Moon Festival

This festival is held on August 15th, or in the middle of the eighth month of the lunar calendar. Traditionally this is a Chinese festival, but it is also celebrated by other Asians as a time of thanksgiving for the harvest of summer crops. According to legend this is also the moon's birthday. The moon on this night is considered to be the largest and fullest of the year. Specially decorated moon cakes are baked of pale yellow flour. Round fruits, such as oranges, are arranged on four plates that surround a fifth plate on which moon cakes are placed. Red candles and incense are burned and music is played everywhere. The holiday lasts for three days.

Extended Experiences

1. Invite an Asian mother to make moon cakes as a special treat, or to assist and supervise the children in preparing them.
2. Serve oranges and moon cakes for a snack, arranging them as described. Pre-peel oranges.
3. Burn incense and play recordings of Asian music.
4. Make night and day pictures using chalk, gummed moon and star shapes, white paint on dark paper. (See Day and Night guide, pp. 537–38.)

Sukkot (Soo-cot)

Sukkot, a Jewish holiday observed in September or October, celebrates the harvest and commemorates the forty-year period after the Exodus from Egypt, during which the Jews wandered in the wilderness and lived in huts made of branches. A hut or a booth called *sukkah* (succah) is built of boards or canvas in the garden near the house or at the synagogue. The top of the *sukkah* is made of pine branches through which the stars can shine at night. Flowers, vegetables, and fruits are woven into the branches or hung by children in the hut for decoration. During the festival, as many meals as possible are eaten in the *sukkah* and always include harvest fruits and vegetables. "Apple slice" and rolled strudel are frequently served. It is customary to invite guests, especially those who do not have a *sukkah* of their own. Some people like to sleep in the *sukkah* at night. *Sukkot* is celebrated for eight days by orthodox and conservative Jews both in and outside of Israel. On the last day of *Sukkot,* Jews thank God for the *Torah* in a ceremony called *Simhat Torah* ("rejoicing in the law"). Although associated with *Sukkot,* this is actually a separate holiday that comes after *Sukkot.* The sacred scrolls of the *Torah* are taken from the ark and carried around the synagogue. Everyone joins in. Boys and girls carry flags. On top of the flagstaffs are candles in hollowed-out apples. After the parade, the children are given nuts and candies.

NOTE: "Apple slice" is a baked dough with apples like a strudel.

Extended Experiences

1. See the Discovery and Learning Language Center sections in the Food, Fall, and Thanksgiving guides for suggestions for activities involving apples, nuts, and other harvest foods.
2. Taste Jewish "apple slice" or rolled strudel.

3. Children might enjoy building a *sukkah* out of a large refrigerator cardboard box. Cut a door in one side and wide slits in the roof to appear like slats so that children can look up through the roof. Plastic flowers, fruits, vegetables, branches, and leaves can be placed on the roof. Snacks of raisins, nuts, and citrus fruits can be eaten inside.

4. Add the following books to your Book Center to read-tell at storytime:

**** Edelman, Lily. *The Sukkah and The Big Wind.* New York: United Synagogue Book Service, 1956.

**** Morrow, Betty, and Lewis Hartman. "Sukkot, A Double Thanksgiving," in *Jewish Holidays.* Champaign, Ill.: Garrard, 1967, pp. 33–45.

**** Simon, Norma. *Our First Sukkah.* New York: United Synagogue Book Service, 1959.

**** ———. *Simhat Torah.* New York: United Synagogue Book Service, 1960.

Ashura (A-shoora)

This holiday of thanksgiving is celebrated sometime during February by Moslems to commemorate their joy in Noah and his family's survival of the Flood and the sparing of humankind. According to legend, Noah asked his wife to prepare a special pudding on the day he was able to set foot on land after the flood. She gathered dates, figs, grapes, nuts, and currants in great quantities and prepared the largest pudding ever made. The pudding was called *Ashura.* On this holiday a similar pudding is prepared and eaten by Moslems as an expression of thanksgiving.

Extended Experiences

1. Allow children to play with a toy ark (houseboat) and pairs of animals in the Block Center. Place on shelves miniature painted animal sets including models of male and female farm and wild animals.

   NOTE: Noah's Ark: pull toy, 32 pcs.; two take-apart Noah's Ark models (one has 39 pcs.) (ABC School Supply).

2. Offer the children an opportunity to make a simple pudding adding any or all of the following fruits: dates, figs, grapes, nuts, currants, and so on.

3. Judy Puzzle: Noah's Ark, 19 pcs.

4. A large cardboard box could also be set out for an ark the children may build. Hollow-block ramps can be used to march up into it.

Kwanza (Keh-WAHN-zah)

This special holiday, celebrated by some black American families from December 26th to January 1st, is in recognition of traditional African harvest festivals. In the African language Kiswahili, *kwanza* means "first fruits." In the United States, the holiday originally began as an alternative to the highly commercialized version of Christmas. It starts on Christmas Day and lasts for an entire week, with special parties on successive days, and often ends with a community-wide harvest feast and party on the seventh day. Small gifts are traditionally given on each day. The *kwanza* holiday stresses the unity of the black family. Often, homemade or homegrown gifts, such as pecan pralines, molasses peanut brittle, molasses bread, and fruit are given.

Seven lessons associated with observing this holiday and a key word for each are listed below:

1. *umoja* (unity)
   We must stand together.
2. *kujichagulia* (self-determination)
   We must decide in our own way.
3. *ujima* (cooperation)
   We must work together.
4. *ujamaca* (sharing by all)
   We must share what we have.
5. *kuumba* (creativity)
   We need to use creativity in reflecting pride in and in caring for our community.
6. *nia* (purpose)
   We must have a purpose in life to make a better world.
7. *imani* (faith)
   We need to have faith which will result in works and action.

Customs of the Traditional African Holiday

1. Lighting candles called *mishumaas* to remind people to live and build together.
2. Placing candles in the *kinara* (candleholder) on a straw mat called the *mkeka* in the center of the table.
3. Holding a feast on the last day of Kwanza during which everyone drinks from a unity cup called the *kikombe*.
4. Giving each child an ear of corn. This corn is called *mihindi*.
5. Giving gifts on the last day. These love gifts are called *zawadi*.

The following recipe is a traditional African treat. It is associated with *John Canoe,* the celebration that African slaves held at Christmas time. It also can be enjoyed by children during *kwanza*.

Sweet Potato Candy

1 lb. sweet potatoes (2 cups)   For flavoring, you may add:
2 cups sugar (1 brown, 1 white)   pineapple juice
1 tsp. lemon juice   orange juice
1 cup marshmallows (optional)   vanilla or cinnamon

1. Wash and boil sweet potatoes.
2. Cool, peel, and mash potatoes in a colander to remove strings.
3. Place in a pan and add lemon juice, sugar, and marshmallows.
4. Cook over low flame, stirring constantly until very thick.
5. Set aside to cool.
6. Add vanilla and/or other flavoring.
7. Spoon out candy into paper cups.
8. Dust with powdered sugar, or sprinkle with sugar candies such as candy beads.

Extended Experiences

1. Allow your children to make love gifts for a friend or family member.
2. Serve fruit or make sweet potato candy.
3. Mount pictures of families doing things together for the holidays from *Ebony* magazine. Include December issues of *Ebony, Jr.* magazine.
4. Eat ears of corn if meals are served at your center, light candles, and have a *Kwanza* party.
5. For further information about this holiday, write: Institute of Positive Education, 7528 Cottage Grove Avenue, Chicago, Illinois 60619.
6. Chase, William D. *Chase's Calendar of Calendar Events*. Flint, Mich.: Appletree Press, 1965.

Shichigosan (Shee-CHI-goh-sahn)

Shichigosan is also called the Feast of the Living Children. Celebrated on November 15, it is a day of thanksgiving honoring seven-year-old girls, five-year-old boys, and all three-year-old children, because they have survived three critical periods of childhood. The children are presented by their parents at a shrine. After their presentation, they have their picture taken and receive a gift of "candy for a thousand years." This is long sticks of red and white candy in a bag printed with pictures of a crane and a tortoise (symbols of good fortune and long life). The children are also given balloons.

Traditionally, this is the first time that a three-year-old girl wears her hair fully dressed in the fashion of her mother, the first time a five-year-old boy wears a long *kimono*, and the first time a seven-year-old girl puts on a stiff *obi*, or wide *kimono* belt. In America, Japanese children are more likely to wear bright-colored clothes to reflect their joy and thankfulness.

Extended Experiences

1. Allow the children to play with balloons.
2. Display some Japanese dolls in traditional dress.
3. See the Chinese New Year guide for other information regarding Asian customs, toys, and games.
4. Include a tortoise or a crane in stories read or games played, mentioning their significance to Japanese people.

13 Thanksgiving in America

basic understandings

(concepts children can grasp from this subject)

- Thanksgiving is a time to be thankful. Today, people celebrate Thanksgiving by having a big dinner with family, relatives, and friends.
- Turkey, goose, and vegetables are usually served for Thanksgiving dinner because that is what the Pilgrims and the Indians ate at their first Thanksgiving feast.

The First Thanksgiving Celebration in America

- Many years ago (in 1621), the Pilgrims at Plymouth and the Wampanoag Indians observed this first Thanksgiving feast.
- The Pilgrims were thankful for the help of the Wampanoag Indians and were grateful to Squanto, a Patuxet Indian, for sharing seeds and showing them how to use and prepare foods and plants. They were glad to have food for the winter.
- There were fifty-one colonists and ninety-one Indians at the first Thanksgiving feast. Five colonist women and a few teenage girls prepared the big feast. The Indians shared some deer meat.
- Their party (celebration) lasted about three days. The people ran races, had wrestling matches, paraded their soldiers, and played games (including stool ball, a type of croquet).
- The Indian men made popcorn for the English children and showed them how to eat it with maple syrup.

The Wampanoag (WAHM-peh-NOH-ag) Indians and the Pilgrims at Plymouth

- The American Indians lived in America before the Pilgrims came.
- The Pilgrims had come across the ocean from England to have a better life and to be able to live more as they wished.

- The Indians and Pilgrims both dressed and lived differently from the way we do today.
- The Indians, at first, were curious about the colonists from England who had landed at Plymouth, about their big ship, the *Mayflower*, and about their clothes, tools, jewelry, and food. The colonists were curious about the Indians, too.
- Massasoit was the name of the leader of the Wampanoag tribe of Indians that were friendly with the colonists at Plymouth.
- The Wampanoag Indians protected the colonists and the Plymouth colonists protected the Wampanoags from other, less friendly, Indian tribes.
- The Indians taught the Pilgrims how to grow and use many foods—corn, berries, squash, pumpkins, sweet potatoes, apples, beans, and maple syrup.
- When the Pilgrims came to America, the Indians lived in wigwams, caves, long log houses, tepees, adobe houses, hogans, and chickees, depending on their environment.
- Different Indian tribes are known for the many beautiful things they make: paintings, jewelry, pottery, baskets, blankets, rugs, leather shoes and clothing, and beadwork.

Additional Facts the Teacher Should Know

Many historical references to the first Thanksgiving as a harvest festival take their information from William Bradford's journal and his *History of Plimoth Plantation*, Mourt's *Relation* (said to be printed by G. Mourt or George Morton in London, 1622), the writings of Edward Winslow (a friend of Bradford's), and Nathaniel Morton's *New Englands Memoriall*, printed in Cambridge in 1669. Some information was also preserved in letters written by colonists to their relatives in England. Basically, most agree that in late September or mid-October of 1621, the first feast of thanksgiving for a good harvest was proclaimed in the New World. The feast consisted of venison (contributed by the Indians), wild turkey (as we call the bird today), geese, clams, boiled eels, bass, watercress, leeks, and spirits referred to as "comfortable warm water," made from green grape juice fortified with spirits brought from England and Holland.

Other foods probably eaten were dried gooseberries, strawberries, cherries, and plums as well as cornbread or "journey bread." Cranberries, pumpkin pie, puddings, celery, and sweet potatoes were added to the menu in later years.

Of the one-hundred-two colonists who arrived on the *Mayflower*, only fifty-one survived to celebrate the Thanksgiving feast at Plymouth.

Edward Winslow, a friend of William Bradford, tells how the governor, in gratitude to the Indian leader Massasoit, invited him to the feast. Massasoit gladly accepted and brought ninety fellow tribesmen. Massasoit realized that the Pilgrims would need more food to feed his men. Massasoit sent several of his men to hunt for game, and they returned with five deer. The feast was eaten outside on log tables, as no building or dwelling was large enough to hold one-hundred forty-two people.

To the delight of the Pilgrims' children, the Indians heated corn in earthen jars over a fire until the kernels burst into white puffs. Maple syrup was poured on the popped corn to make a confection somewhat like our popcorn balls.

Forks were not yet commonly available. Knives were sometimes used for cutting meat and wooden spoons were used for stirring. Wooden spoons, bowls, and mugs were likely used. People often ate with their hands when they did not have utensils.

While the Pilgrims of Plymouth were considered very devout and strict in their religious faith and practices, it is interesting that little or no mention is made of religious services being held during those three days of feasting and pleasure. It is possible this was because the occasion became a joint celebration with the Wampanoags and therefore reflected some of the customs of each group in celebrating a good harvest without reflecting the religious customs of either.

The colonists were grateful to the Wampanoag Indians and to Squanto, the sole survivor of the Patuxet tribe which had once lived in the Plymouth area. Without his knowledge of how to plant and fertilize corn and how to dry fruit, the colonists would have faced starvation, for, unfortunately, the grain they had brought from England and sown in America had produced a very poor crop. The Wampanoag Indians also gave them seed corn to add to the store they found among the remains left by the Patuxet tribe. The colonists learned that the Patuxets had been eliminated by an epidemic several years earlier.

Treaty Between the Wampanoag Tribe and Plymouth Colony

It is unlikely that the first Thanksgiving celebration for a good harvest in America would have been shared with the Wampanoag Indians without the treaty made and agreed to by John Carver, Governor of Plymouth, and Massasoit on behalf of their respective groups in March 1621.

NOTE: John Carver died the same spring, but William Bradford, who succeeded him as governor, upheld the treaty for the thirty years of his governorship. This mutually agreeable treaty, which remains a model today, was respected and upheld by both groups until after the death of these leaders.

It provided that:
1. both groups agreed not to injure the other. If one of their members did, the offender was to be sent to his or her own leader for punishment.
2. if either a colonist or a Wampanoag Indian took anything from the other group, it was to be returned.
3. if either group was attacked by another group, each promised to aid the one attacked.
4. Massasoit promised to notify all the other tribes of the pact.
5. when either group visited the other, weapons were to be left behind.

The treaty was eventually broken because:
1. there was a change in leadership of both groups.
2. there were conflicting views on the ownership of the land. Although the Indians agreed to a price for their land, the deeds meant little to them because they believed the land was to be shared and could never be owned. They did not realize that they were relinquishing their property rights forever.
3. the colonial evangelists tried to sway the Indians from their own religious faith.
4. the colonists who arrived later were not as religiously devout as the earlier group and did not respect the promises that group had made to the Indians.

All of these ill feelings culminated in Phillip's war (1675 to 1676) when Phillip, Massasoit's son, was killed. Three of the colonial towns were raided but were later restored. The six remaining towns were left untouched. Historians record that some members of the Wampanoag tribe fled north to Canada or west to the Hudson River. Those who remained were enslaved by the colonists. It is estimated that 100 Wampanoags and 100 colonists (about seven percent of the population) were killed during the war. The Wampanoag land was sold to provide for colonists who were crippled or impoverished by the war. This event is considered the end of the Wampanoag tribe, although some descendants live in New England today.

Thanksgiving Services Held Before 1621

Accounts show that there were several religious prayer services of thanksgiving earlier than 1621:
1. In Virginia in 1584, proclaimed by Captain Arthur Barlow (sent by Sir Walter Raleigh) upon landing in Virginia.
2. On August 9, 1607, when the Popham colony settlers landed on the coast of Maine and had Sunday services with a sermon and prayer.
3. In 1607, when the Jamestown colonists entered Cape Henry in Chesapeake Bay, erected a cross, and knelt to thank God for their safe arrival.
4. In 1610, the surviving 60 colonists of the original 490 held a service of thanksgiving at Jamestown because they received additional supplies.
5. On December 4, 1619, at Berkeley Hundred, up the James River from Jamestown, a thanksgiving service was held by thirty-nine settlers who had just landed. It was observed again in 1620, 1621, and 1623.
6. In 1620, soon after the arrival of the *Mayflower* at Plymouth, a thanksgiving service was held.

More Facts about the Pilgrims and How They Lived

Pilgrim clothing was very colorful. The men's breeches were cut full and were fastened below the knee by garters which had long tags called points. Their stockings were plain-knitted. Their leggings were knitted, had no feet, and came up over the thigh. The men's shoes and boots were either of natural tanned leather or black. Illustrators usually place silver buckles on the Pilgrims' shoes and hats; however, buckles were not mentioned in the original inventories. Most of the Pilgrims wore a band or white linen collar that lay flat over their coat. Long-sleeved shirts of white, blue, brown, or green were worn by men. A stomacher was worn under the laced bodice to provide a contrast in color or material, and a waistcoat, usually red, over that for warmth. The usual stocking-cap headgear for men was the Monmouth cap.

The skirt of the women's dress was ankle length and cut full, while the bodice was shaped to the figure. For headwear, women wore the coif, a white linen cap which came down over the ears. In colder weather, they wore beaver-pelt hats. Outdoors they wore a hooded cloak.

Children's clothes were like those of the adults, except that boys wore a dresslike coat until the age of six, after which they dressed like the men.

American Indian Values

Each Indian first considers himself or herself a member of his or her particular tribe, and second, an Indian. Originally, each geographic grouping of Indians differed somewhat in language, mode of dress, lifestyle, type of home, and values. Different tribes do, however, share similar values with other Indian groups. Here is a composite list of Indian values that will be helpful for planning and learning about Thanksgiving in America.

1. **A feeling for individual freedom and self-worth.** Indians believe that each man, woman, and child should be allowed to express himself or herself in his or her own way.
2. **Bravery and prowess in physical skills** with concern for the protection of nature.
3. **Nobility and pride in race and tribe** and an appreciation for tradition, which includes a respect for the wisdom and guidance of elders.
4. **Respect for the earth and a Supreme Being,** which, Indians feel, requires maintaining a balance of nature's cycles for harmony between humans and their environment.
5. **Kinship and concern for others** (patience, generosity, sharing). Indians have a heritage of true communal living and although some of them own private property, they tend to retain the feeling that wealth is not measured by what they own but by what they have that can be shared. They have a strong feeling that everything should really belong to everyone and should be shared on the basis of need. They welcome visitors as an opportunity to show hospitality. By so doing, they feel they have assured themselves of a similar kindness sometime in the future. Family ties go beyond the immediate family of relatives and tribe.
6. **Respect for everyone's right to dignity.** In their approach to life and to other people Indians are often more patient, considerate, restrained, and less aggressive than other cultures.
7. **Trust and integrity.** The feeling of community is so strong that jails, laws, and locks are not as necessary as in other cultures. It is said that an Indian who had been sentenced to death by his tribe was trusted to go back to his family and get his affairs in order before returning for execution.
8. **Indians believe that peace (among nations, families, tribes) exists** when people "walk in parallel paths," united by common purposes, causes, or mutual respect.
9. **Equality for all.** Every person has equal rights in a council regardless of age or sex.

   NOTE: Children should be told that a person is born an Indian; it is not chosen like a profession; it is *growing up* Indian.

The Thanksgiving Turkey

The turkey is a member of a bird family that includes chickens, pheasants, and peacocks and is native to North and Central America. When the settlers arrived in the New World they mistook this native bird (*Meleagrididae*) to be the African guinea hen, which had been imported into Europe via Turkey. The Europeans called the guinea hen "turkey" from the Hebrew word *tukki* meaning peacock. When the settlers saw the *Meleagrididae* they thought it was the same, so they called it "turkey."

Methods Most Adaptable for Introducing This Subject to Children

- Present a puppet show or flannelboard story of the first Thanksgiving.
- Learn a Thanksgiving song.
- Ask the children what they are thankful for.
- Talk with the children about the hunting season (direct conversation toward children whose fathers shoot or hunt game). Share what they know about hunting. Then share with them how the Pilgrims and Indians had to hunt, fish, and plant seeds to get enough food to eat and furs to keep warm.
- Display pictures of Pilgrims, Indians, food, and Thanksgiving feasts.

   CAUTION: Avoid those that show Indians as savages or warriors.

- Show pictures of foods and discuss how the Indians helped the Pilgrims find and grow food.
- Display a cornucopia with real or artificial fruit and vegetables.

Vocabulary

Thanksgiving	log cabin	sign language	hunt	pumpkin
give thanks	reservation	Indian horn	game	canoe
cornucopia	moccasins	feast	hides	tepee
bow and arrow	totem pole	dinner	rattle	wigwam
tomahawk	harvest	food	leather	gobble
tom-tom	fruit	warrior	feathers	hogan
Pilgrims	vegetable	wampum	turkey	adobe
Indians	cradle board	hominy	cranberry	chickee

NOTE: We have intentionally omitted brave, squaw, chief, and papoose. These terms are not used except by non-Indians, and often inappropriately.

learning centers

Discovery Center

1. Examine turkey feathers and eggs. Note how they differ from those of a chicken. Scramble two turkey eggs.
2. Vegetable dyeing: dip pieces of white cloth or white turkey feathers into solutions made by boiling the following plants in water and allowing to cool.

Goldenrod stalks and flowers—yellow	Spinach leaves—green
Sumac leaves—yellow-brown	Blackberries—blue
Onion skins—yellow or red	Sunflower seeds—blue
Beets—red violet	Hickory bark—brown
Dandelion roots—magenta	Walnut hulls—brown
Rhubarb leaves—light green	Cranberries—pink or red

   NOTE: If supervision is minimal, boil solutions in advance. If turkey feathers are used, wash them first in soap and water to remove oil. Rinse.

3. Cooking: prepare a food with the children that is related to Thanksgiving, using the recipes from your favorite cookbook. Make cranberry salad, Waldorf salad, popcorn balls, pumpkin pie, or sugar cookies in the shape of a turkey. Bake potatoes. Use watercress or leeks in snacks or salads. Make Indian fried bread and serve with syrup.

4. Examine dried fruits: show samples of fresh grapes and raisins (include other fruits, such as apples, peaches, plums, and apricots, if available). What happens if raisins are put in water? What happens if grapes are put in the sun to dry?

5. Sail a boat: find a picture or model of the *Mayflower*. Tell the children that this is the kind of ship in which the Pilgrims came to America. Float the model in the water table, sink, or tub of water. If a model of the *Mayflower* is not available, a stick woven through a piece of paper and implanted in a styrofoam block, a piece of balsa wood, or a floating bar of soap will do. Tell the children to blow on the sails to make the ship move. What happens when they stop blowing? If a toy motorboat is available, demonstrate how it moves. Which is faster?

6. Floating and sinking: floating boats may lead to an interest in other objects that float or sink or other water activities. (See Water guide, p. 567.)

7. Globe study: for older children with many experiences with this subject a study of the globe may add new interest. Show the children where England is and that Plymouth, Massachusetts, is below Boston, and across from Cape Cod and Provincetown, Massachusetts. What is the ocean? How can you cross the ocean? This may lead to an interest in transportation. (See related guides.)

8. Display leather moccasins, jackets, leather scraps, and fur. Allow children to examine.

9. Set out an ear of corn. Shell. Let children pop, butter, and salt the corn.

10. Display woven baskets and basket-weaving materials.

Dramatic Play Centers

Home-Living Center

1. Set out artificial fruit and vegetables. Encourage preparation of a big feast. Teacher may mount pictures of turkeys, potatoes, or pie on heavy cardboard or cut food sections from TV dinner boxes for children to use in preparing a Thanksgiving dinner.

2. Baking: provide playdough, rolling pins, cookie cutters, and child-size pans or aluminum pot-pie pans for baking pies, cookies, or bread.

3. Dressup clothes: add types used by early settlers. Ankle-length skirts, plain white aprons, pellon collars, dark dresses, long-sleeved shirts, and black jackets.

4. Teacher might make an Indian cradle board to carry dolls, using corrugated cardboard or fiberboard. Cut oval 14 inches by 8 inches. For doll, teacher may stuff small sack for head and larger bag for body, or use a regular doll. Bind Indian doll baby to board with ribbon and use narrow ribbon for carrying straps.

CAUTION: Do not use the terms papoose, squaw, or chief.

Block-Building Center

1. Encourage children to build houses to play in and to play families coming for a Thanksgiving Day visit.

2. Transportation toys: trains, planes, buses that bring visiting grandparents.

3. Build farms: set out animals, tractors, trucks. Provide spools, small rocks, and other small articles for crops to harvest and take to the market.

4. Toy logs: older children may build log cabins. Flexible plastic and rubber family figures can be dressed in Pilgrim and Indian clothing made from felt and imitation leather if teachers have skill and time. These will encourage the children to dramatize the Thanksgiving story.

5. Use unbreakable plastic tepees, spotted horses, hogans, buffalo, cattle, turkeys, and other objects that the early Indians might have used.

6. Emphasize Indians and settlers working together and helping each other; deemphasize conflicts.

   NOTE: Teachers should explain to children why the Indians were angry with the Pilgrim settlers in pioneer times. Be alert to expressions or statements by the children that reflect misunderstandings or stereotypes about Indians. Help them to realize how it might feel to have intruders take over what belongs to oneself or to have promises not kept.

Learning, Language, and Readiness Materials Center

Commercially made games and materials for use at a table or on a mat:

(See Basic Resources, p. 79, for manufacturers' addresses.)

1. Judy Puzzles: Thanksgiving, 20 pcs.; Saying Grace, 18 pcs.; Going to Church, 17 pcs.; Table Setting, 10 pcs.
2. Fractions Made Easy (Milton Bradley)
3. Judy See-Quees: From Seed to Pumpkin, 12 pcs.
4. Fruits I Like: Primary Playskool Puzzle Plaque, 4 pcs.
5. I Set the Table: Primary Playskool Puzzle Plaque, 5 pcs.
6. Instructo Flannelboard Cut-outs: primary and holiday sets
7. Vegetable and Fruit Poster Cards (Milton Bradley)
8. Thanksgiving and Autumn Decorative Seals (Eureka-Carlisle, Hallmark)
9. Farm Lotto (Ed-U-Cards)
10. Large and small beads to string
11. Threading sequence and stringing rings (Childcraft)
12. Scope, a new dimension in parquetry design (Childcraft)
13. Intarsio and Intarsio Rounds, advanced inlaid design set (Childcraft)
14. Color Cubes and Parquetry Blocks (most catalogs)
15. Shapees: manipulative toy; unbreakable colored pieces snap together (Constructive Playthings)
16. Crystal Mosaics (Childcraft)
17. Giant Mosaics (most catalogs)
18. Skin head tom-tom and rubber head tom-tom (Childcraft)
19. Rosetta Puzzles (Childcraft)
20. Colonial Quilt Maker (Creative Playthings)

   NOTE: See also Food and Fall guides for other appropriate materials related to harvest.

Teacher-made games and materials for use at a table or on a mat:

   NOTE: For detailed description of Games, see pp. 50–59.

1. Name It: identify fruits and vegetables and other Thanksgiving symbols such as Pilgrims, turkeys, *Mayflower*
2. Look and See: use fall fruits and vegetables or other reminders of Thanksgiving
3. Reach and Tell: use fruits, vegetables, or Thanksgiving symbols
4. Sniff and Smell: use fruits and vegetables. (See Food and Smell guides.)
5. Chew, Lick, and Taste: use fruits, vegetables. (See Food and Taste guides.)
6. Match-Them: use real objects or make cards using decorative seals
7. Grouping and Sorting by Association: use matching cards made for Match-Them or real fruits and vegetables to mix and sort

8. Alike, Different, and the Same: use the picture cards or real objects. Set out two that are alike and one that is different, for instance: two green apples and one red. Vary the size, such as two big pumpkins and one small one
9. How Many?: count real objects or use pictures or flannel cut-outs
10. Count turkeys, pumpkins, Pilgrims
11. Make designs on small cards to be reproduced by matching with parquetry blocks
12. Identify and match colored feathers or beads with other items in the room
13. Make patterns with beads stringing red, red, blue; red, blue, red, and so on
14. Make cards of Indian symbols to be matched; also hand signals for Indian words

> **NOTE:** Check with a native American Indian, a Cub Scout, an Indian Guide leader, or your local librarian for a book on Indian sign language.

Art Center

* 1. Sand drawing and painting: show the children how to smooth sand in a sandbox or tray using a long flat stick and then how to draw with a round stick or a finger in the smooth sand. Sand can also be washed and dried in an oven, mixed with dry tempera, and placed in shaker dispensers to be used in sand painting on a surface. After the children have drawn a picture with glue on lightweight cardboard or stiff paper, they can sprinkle on sand from the shakers. Let dry, then turn upside down and tap to remove excess sand.

** 2. Texture designs can be made by children, crayoning on newsprint over precut shapes of sandpaper or corrugated cardboard. Other textures can be introduced by the teacher for interesting effects and designs.

*** 3. Playdough Indian beads: let children help you measure and mix two cups of flour, one cup of salt, one cup of water, and one teaspoon of cooking oil. Shape into small balls or ovals and push a toothpick through the center to make a hole for stringing. These will need to dry for a couple of days before being painted. While mixing, you may wish to add food coloring. Use sturdy yarn or heavy twine for stringing.

> **NOTE:** If you make them at school on Friday they will be ready for painting the next Monday.

* 4. Paste precut pieces of various colored tissue paper onto construction paper. (Children may discover that by overlapping pieces, tissue has the appearance of feathers or fall leaves.)

** 5. Mosaics: let children make mosaic designs and pictures using Indian corn, pumpkin seeds, squash seeds, and acorn tops.

** 6. Collage: glue dried seeds, sticks, or grasses onto paper

* 7. Printing: use fruits or vegetables (teacher should prepare them in advance). Cut one-half inch from the large end of a sturdy fat carrot or celery stalk for circles and crescent shapes, or half of a grapefruit shell. Dip fruit or vegetable into desired paint color and press onto paper.

> **NOTE:** Use parts of fruit or vegetables that are ordinarily discarded or not edible.

8. Border designs: describe a border as "shapes lying in a row." Give the children an assortment of strips of colored and white paper printing scraps. Let each child select from a tray of assorted precut geometric shapes of construction paper the shapes he or she needs to design a border. Find examples in pictures of art objects or children's clothes. Allow the children to print a border, using small spools, bits of wood-molding scraps, dowels, plastic lids, rolls of corrugated paper, or bits of

sponge cut in shapes, which have been dipped into shallow pans of thickened paint. Have several colors of paint from which to choose.

** 9. Burlap pictures: cut squares from burlap bags or colorful burlap material.
    a. String embroidery large-eyed, blunt needles with fine, bright-colored yarn. Let children sew a design or picture.
    b. Duplicate "porcupine quill art" by letting the children do the above project using colored toothpicks instead of yarn.

** 10. Rugs (dollhouse or block accessory size) may be simulated by fringing loosely woven upholstery fabrics. Cut in rectangles and squares and show the children how to unravel the threads to make a fringe. See (a) below. Some children may be able to do some simple weaving with loops on a frame or with yarn lengths on a home-made frame (b). The teacher will need to secure the edges of the upholstery fabric and the weaving by stitching them on a sewing machine, so they will not fray.

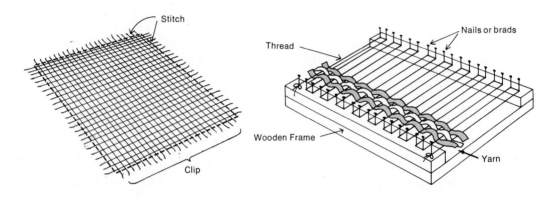

11. Necklaces: supply the children with a collage tray of odds and ends that can be strung to form a simulated Indian necklace. Geometric-shaped cardboard pieces, large-holed buttons, plastic discs cut from plastic meat trays and punched for threading, or plastic straws cut in various lengths are a few items to include. A "stringing needle" may be made on one end of a yarn length by wrapping the end with tape, or by dipping approximately one inch of yarn into the glue.

NOTE: Do not have children make feathered headdresses. Feathers are earned by achievement of a difficult feat. They are not used simply for decoration.

Book Center

*** Baker, Betty. *Little Runner of the Long House.* New York: Harper and Row, 1962.
*** Benchley, Nathaniel. *Small Wolf.* New York: Harper and Row, 1972.
*** Clark, Ann Nolan. *Along Sandy Trails.* New York: Viking Press, 1969 (read-tell).
*** ——. *The Desert People.* New York: Viking Press, 1962.
**** ——. *The Little Indian Pottery Maker.* Los Angeles: Melmont Publishing, 1955.
**** ——. *The Little Indian Basket Maker.* Los Angeles: Melmont Publishing, 1957.
**** ——. *In My Mother's House.* New York: Viking Press, 1941.
** ——. *Little Herder in Spring.* Lawrence, Kans.: Haskell Institute Publication Service, 1970.
** ——. *Little Herder in Summer.* Lawrence, Kans.: Haskell Institute Publication Service, 1970.
** ——. *Little Herder in Autumn.* Lawrence, Kans.: Haskell Institute Publication Service, 1970.

** ———. *Little Herder in Winter*. Lawrence, Kans.: Haskell Institute Publication Service, 1968.

**** Dalgliesh, Alice. *The Thanksgiving Story*. New York: Scribner's, 1954 (read-tell in segments).

*** Floethe, Louise. *The Indian and His Pueblo*. New York: Scribner's, 1960.

**** ———. *Sea of Grass*. New York: Scribner's, 1963 (pictures and references).

*** Friskey, Margaret. *Indian Two Feet and His Eagle Feather*. Chicago, Ill.: Childrens Press, 1967 (read or read-tell, depending on age of group).

** ———. *Indian Two Feet and His Horse*. Chicago, Ill.: Childrens Press, 1971 (read or read-tell).

** ———. *Indian Two Feet and the Wolf Cubs*. Chicago, Ill.: Childrens Press, 1971 (read or read-tell).

**** Hays, Wilma Pitchford. *Little Yellow Fur*. New York: Coward, McCann and Geoghegan, 1973 (read-tell about Indians long ago).

** Moon, Grace and Carl Moon. *One Little Indian*. Chicago, Ill.: Albert Whitman, 1967.

**** Wondriska, William. *The Stop*. New York: Holt, Rinehart and Winston, 1972.

planning for grouptime

NOTE: All music, fingerplays, poems, stories, and games listed here may be used at other times during the session as appropriate. See Core Library, Basic Resources, p. 76, for publishers and addresses. Addresses for sources of records will be found on p. 81. In parodies, hyphenated words match the music notes of the tune used.

Music

Songs

THANKSGIVING DINNER (a parody)
(tune: "Frère Jacques")
Adaptation by JoAnne Deal Hicks

Verse 1: We eat tur-key, we eat tur-key. Oh, so good. Oh, so good.
Al-ways on Thanks-giv-ing, al-ways on Thanks-giv-ing.
Yum-yum-yum. Yum-yum-yum.

Verse 2: Mashed po-ta-toes. Mashed po-ta-toes. Oh, so good. Oh, so good.
Al-ways on Thanks-giv-ing, al-ways on Thanks-giv-ing.
Yum-yum-yum. Yum-yum-yum.

Verse 3: Pie and ice-cream.   (REPEAT AS IN VERSE 2)

Verse 4: Home-made bis-cuits.   (REPEAT AS IN VERSE 2)

Verse 5: Tur-key dress-ing.   (REPEAT AS IN VERSE 2)

FROM original songs in this book by JoAnne Deal Hicks
*** "My Special Friend," p. 105
* "Fruitbasket Song," p. 561
* "Sing a Song of Applesauce," p. 562

FROM *Songs for the Nursery School,* MacCarteney
* "Gobble, Gobble, Turkey," p. 65

FROM *Music Resource Book,* Lutheran Church Press
* "Did You Ever See a Lassie?" p. 86 (substitute the word "turkey" for "lassie" and "strut" for the word "go")

FROM *Songs for Early Childhood,* Westminster Press
** "Brown Leaves Crunching When We Walk," p. 17 (adapt to "We Are Thankful for This Day!")

FROM your favorite traditional song book
* "Old MacDonald"

Records

"A Song of Thanksgiving," "Picking Apples," "Lifting Pumpkins," "Playing Harvest Games," *Autumn (November)* (Bowmar, 33⅓ RPM or cassette). Companion reading books and picture songbook sold separately.
"Little Indian Drum"/"Hiawatha"/"Pony Express" (YPR, 33⅓ RPM)
"Play Party Games" Records 1 and 2 (Bowmar, 33⅓ RPM)
"Singing Games" Records 1, 2, and 3 (Bowmar, 33⅓ RPM)

NOTE: Singing games and dances were popular with pioneer children.

"Seasons—Fall" (Kimbo, 33⅓ RPM or cassette and filmstrip)
"Thanksgiving," *Holiday Rhythms,* Lucille Wood and Ruth Tarner (Bowmar, 33⅓ RPM)

Rhythms and Singing Games

Dramatize: different methods of going to grandmother's (aunt's, cousin's, or friend's) house, such as walk, run, ride trike, fly, go by train, bus, car.

Strutting: children may strut like a turkey, using appropriate music.

Hop, Skip, Jump: use the record *Rhythmic Activities,* Vol. 1 (RCA).

Drums: reproduce chants or poems to music or drumbeats. Walk, jump, hop, skip to drumbeats.

Dance: toe-heel, toe-heel to Indian music.

Fingerplays and Poems

MR. TURKEY

Mr. Turkey's tail is big and wide.   (SPREAD HANDS WIDE)
He swings it when he walks.   (SWING HANDS BACK AND FORTH)
His neck is long, his chin is red.   (STROKE CHIN AND NECK)
He gobbles when he talks.   (OPEN AND CLOSE HAND)

Mr. Turkey is so tall and proud.   (STRAIGHTEN SELF UP TALL)
He dances on his feet.   (MAKE FINGERS DANCE)
And on each Thanksgiving Day,   (HANDS IN PRAYER)
He's something good to eat.   (PAT STOMACH)

FROM *Let's Do Fingerplays*, Grayson
"Our Table," p. 94

FROM *Rhymes for Fingers and Flannelboards*, Scott and Thompson
"A Thanksgiving Fingerplay," p. 62
"Thanksgiving," p. 62
"Five Little Pilgrims," p. 62

Stories

(To read, read-tell, or tell. See Book Center for complete list.)

** *Along Sandy Trails*, Clark
**** *The Thanksgiving Story*," Dalgliesh (read-tell in segments)

NOTE: Story telling is a very important part of Indian culture. Stories should be told when possible.

Games

(See Games, pp. 50–59, and Teacher-Made Games in this guide for directions.)

Play traditional circle games similar to those that Pilgrim children might have played.

1. Hokey Pokey
2. Mulberry Bush
3. Skip to My Lou
4. Oats, Peas, Beans
5. Looby Lou
6. Did You Ever See a Lassie?
7. Go Round and Round the Village
8. A-Hunting We Will Go
9. Bluebird Through My Window
10. London Bridge

Routine Times

1. At snack or mealtime have a cornucopia with real or artificial food as a centerpiece.
2. Plan a Thanksgiving dinner the last day your group meets before Thanksgiving. Serve small portions if the meal is lunch or snack.
3. In settings where it is permitted, pray or offer grace before the Thanksgiving dinner or snack.
4. Talk about table manners, especially saying "thank you."
5. Talk about food: its color, texture, size, shape, taste, and odor as you are eating during snack or mealtime. (See Color, Food, Smell, and Taste guides.)
6. At snack or mealtime use foods prepared by the children such as turkey cookies, popcorn, pumpkin pie, cranberry or Waldorf salads.
7. Serve foods for snacks or mealtime that Indians first introduced to the Pilgrims:
   Snacktime foods: popcorn, peanuts (use peanut butter on crackers), strawberries, pineapple chunks, cocoa, fresh or dried fruit (apples, figs, grapes, peaches).

Lunchtime Foods: cornbread cakes with maple syrup, corn, sweet potatoes, nuts, squash, turkey, tomatoes, beans, pumpkin pudding, barbecued meat, fish, potato cakes, succotash. For salad: apples, raisins, nuts, and celery combined, carrot sticks. For dessert: fried bread, pudding, or fruit.

8. At lunchtime, talk about what it would be like not to have forks—only hands or wooden spoons—with which to eat.
9. At pickup time, use a wagon to carry toys and equipment back to storage area or shelves. Point out that this is how the early settlers moved their things. Have a picture of a covered wagon.
10. At transition times: walk like Indians from one activity to another, quietly or single file.
11. At grouptime: sit like Indians (cross-legged). Discuss talking things over to make decisions, the way a tribal council does.
12. When you wish to call the attention of the children: use Indian sign language to share a secret message. Check with a native American, a Cub Scout leader, or an Indian Guide leader for Indian sign language for some common words you might use. Your local library will also have books on the subject.

Large Muscle Activities

1. See Rhythm Activities under Music.
2. Catch the Turkey: all the children are turkeys except one who is a Pilgrim. The Pilgrim chases the turkeys until he catches one. The child who is caught becomes the Pilgrim. This game will probably interest only a few of the older children.
3. Skill Games: include games young Pilgrims or Indians may have played.
   a. Run to a destination and back.
   b. Walk a log, balance beam, or chalkline drawn on cement or on the floor.
   c. Play follow the leader.
   d. Play with balls of various sizes.

Extended Experiences

1. Take a trip to the grocery store to look at or buy Thanksgiving foods—turkeys, pumpkins, apples, nuts, celery, onions, potatoes, cranberries.
2. Visit a turkey farm. Ask permission from owners to make a loud noise such as blowing a whistle or horn to get turkeys to "gobble." Ask permission to collect turkey feathers or ask owner to save some for you to use in Discovery, Creative Arts, and Language Arts Centers.
3. Visit a local reservation, Indian school, museum, or crafts shop where Indian wares and materials may be seen.
4. Have a grandmother or grandfather visit and tell about Thanksgiving Day when she or he was a child.
5. Invite an Indian to visit the center and share artifacts, paintings, beadwork, jewelry, leather goods, pottery, blankets, or rugs.
6. Show a film or slides of Indian homes from long ago and now. Also show the differing ways of life among the Indian tribes.

teacher resources

Books and Periodicals

1. Costo, Ruperto. *Contributions and Achievements of the American Indian.* American Indian Historical Society, 1451 Masonic Ave., San Francisco, Calif. 94117.
2. Langdon, George D., Jr. *Pilgrim Colony, A History of New Plymouth, 1620–1691.* New Haven and London: Yale University Press, 1966.
3. Dillon, Francis. *A Place for Habitation: The Pilgrim Fathers and Their Quest.* London: Hutchinson, 1973.
4. Parkes, Henry Bamford. *A Journal of the Pilgrims at Plymouth: Mourt's Relation.* New York: Corinth Books, 1963 (from original printing, 1622).
5. Gill, Crispin. *Mayflower Remembered: A History of the Plymouth Pilgrims.* New York: Taplinger, 1970.
6. Eaton, Walter Prichard. *Plymouth.* Plymouth, Mass.: Plymouth Publicity Committee, 1940.
7. Anon, Alice. *Talking Hands.* New York: Doubleday, 1968 (helpful reference for sign language).
8. Globok, Shirley. *The Art of the North American Indian.* New York: Harper and Row, 1964.
9. Parish, Peggy. *Let's Be Indians.* New York: Harper and Row, 1962 (note our reference p. 250 regarding feathers).
10. Pine, Tillie S. *The Indians Knew.* New York: McGraw-Hill, 1957 (excellent reference, tracing what Indians knew to how we use the same information today, and telling what the child can do knowing it; *inaccurate* illustrations of tribal dress).
11. ———, and Joseph Levine. *The Eskimos Knew.* New York: McGraw-Hill, 1962.
12. *The Weewish Tree.* American Indian Historical Society, 1451 Masonic Avenue, San Francisco, Calif. 94117.
13. Akwesasne Notes. Mohawk Nation, Rooseveltown, New York 13683.
14. Interracial Books for Children Bulletin, Council on Interracial Books for Children, Inc., 1841 Broadway, New York 10023.
15. Multi-Ethnic Books for Young Children. ERIC–NAEYC publication, available from NAEYC.

Pictures and Displays

(See p. 79 for addresses of firms listed.)

1. Place cornucopias filled with real or artificial foods on the tables at mealtime on a low shelf or in the Book Center.
2. Place potato, apple, or pine-cone turkeys on the tables.
3. Use a Thanksgiving table decoration.
4. Make a log cabin out of toy logs and use wax figures of Pilgrims, turkeys, and Indians that are available in novelty stores at Thanksgiving.
5. Display wall or bulletin-board pictures of turkeys, Pilgrims, Thanksgiving dinners, and other aspects of life for which we are thankful.

6. Make a November calendar using felt cut-outs on a flannelboard to mark off the days, or posterboard using gum-backed Thanksgiving Day seals.
7. Seasons, Holidays, Food, and Nutrition: Commercial picture packets (David C. Cook).
8. Thanksgiving, Pilgrim, and Indian stickers and pictures (Dennison Manufacturing Co.).
9. Display a diorama showing Indian customs.
10. Display original artwork by Indians or professional paintings depicting Indians in original settings then and now. Be selective!
11. Instructo Picture Sets: Indians of the Eastern Forest, 1, 22 inches × 17 inches; illustrations of typical shelters, dress, ways of gathering food, transportation and village activities.
12. Display blankets, rugs, jewelry, pottery, baskets, or clothing loaned by interested persons, reflecting Indian or colonial times.
13. Set up a model Indian village of a particular tribe or of models of different kinds of Indian homes.

Community Resources

1. Consult Y.M.C.A., Indian Guide leader, or Boy Scout leader for books and help with Indian crafts
2. Indian Center located in your community
3. American Indian parents or friends
4. Indians living on a reservation within commuting distance
5. American Indian Historical Society, 1451 Masonic Avenue, San Francisco, California 94117
6. National Congress of American Indians (NCAI), 1765 P Street, N.W., Washington, D.C. 20036
7. Navajo Curriculum Center, Rough Rock Demonstration School, Chinle, Arizona 86503

14 Festivals of Merriment and Light

Festivals of Merriment

Most people seem to need a time for humor and expressions of exuberance, happiness, and frivolity to counterbalance the monotony of toil, the seriousness of meditation and deep thought, and the ignorance of superstition and to alleviate fear, despair, and disappointment in life. Therefore, it is not surprising that people everywhere have holidays and celebrations that involve merriment.

Many holidays are related to the rejuvenated spirits of people and the awakening of nature in spring. Others involve masquerading, playing tricks, or making fun of others, oneself, or one's fears through stories, dramas, games, and songs. These traditions have been passed along from one generation to another. However, a great number of these holidays, which include merriment for children and young adults and *seem* only for fun, usually have much greater religious or nationalistic significance to their parents.

April Fool's Day

April 1st is known as April Fool's Day, or All Fools' Day. No one knows how it began, but it is the day people like to play tricks on one another. For example, someone ties a string to a wallet and hides out of sight. When someone else comes along and tries to pick it up, the person holding the string jerks the wallet out of reach and yells, "April fool." Also, one may be tricked into believing something is true when it is not, such as saying to someone, "You have a red spot on your chin!" When the person goes to the mirror to see for himself/herself, you say, "April fool!"

In France, a person who has a joke played on him or her is called an "April fish," and in Scotland, this person is referred to as an April *gowk*. A *gowk* is a word of Scandinavian origin meaning a fool or simpleton.

The kind of humor involved in April fool jokes is best understood by the older child. Some four- and five-year-olds can begin to understand this kind of humor.

St. Patrick's Day

On March 17th each year, the Irish and Irish-Americans celebrate St. Patrick's Day by the "wearin' of the green"; and the Irish in New York City hold a huge parade. This holiday commemorates St. Patrick who, legend tells us, went about Ireland as a missionary, preaching and using the shamrock as an illustration of the Trinity. St. Patrick also was credited with ridding Ireland of snakes. Irish-Americans like to wear shamrock pins or some article of green clothing.

Extended Experiences

1. Learn about the color green. (See the Color guide.)
2. Discover that the shamrock is the national symbol of Ireland. (The shamrock is a low-growing plant with three leaves, similar to the field clover that grows in the United States and Canada.)
3. Several weeks before St. Patrick's Day, cut a large flat green sponge in the shape of a shamrock. Dampen the sponge and sprinkle generously with grass seed. Keep moistened and by St. Patrick's Day, it will be covered with green grass.
4. Post pictures of Ireland and help older children find it on the globe. Ireland is called the "Emerald Isle" because its land is covered with beautiful green grass.
5. Post pictures you may have of a St. Patrick's Day parade.
6. Have a parade at music time.
7. Play "The Irish Washer Woman" and let the children dance or move to this fast music tempo.
8. Display the Irish flag or a picture of one. Older children may be able to cut and paste, paint, or crayon one. The flag is rectangular with three equal vertical blocks of color, which are, from left to right, green, white, and red-orange.
9. Invite a parent to bring Irish linen, a Kerry cloak, a clay pipe, or a tall hat to show the children. English and Gaelic are spoken in Ireland. Perhaps this parent could teach the children a few words of Gaelic. (Gaelic is a very unusual and difficult language, so the words should be kept simple.)
10. Oatmeal or oatmeal bread could be served for breakfast. Irish stew could be served for lunch. Although Ireland is credited with the potato, it was actually native to Peru and it was brought to Ireland by Sir Walter Raleigh when he returned from a trip to Virginia. *Broonie* (Irish gingerbread) can be served for snack or dessert. (The recipe is on p. 22 in *Many Hands Cooking;* see Teacher Resources.)

Mardi Gras (MAR-dee GRAH)

Mardi Gras is a carnival celebrated in the southeastern part of the United States from December until Shrove Tuesday, just before the fasting and more devout period of Lent begins.

Long ago, Shrove Tuesday, or Fat Tuesday, became the day to consume all meats and fats prior to Ash Wednesday. In England, pancakes were made and eaten on that day and it became known as Pancake Day. Races are still held with the competitors flipping pancakes in skillets as they run. Some rural communities in America hold similar races. In private boys' schools in England, the cook rings the pancake bell and tosses the pancakes in the air for the boys to catch, much to their delight!

In Germany, filled rolls similar to jelly doughnuts called *Fastnachtkuchen* (fast-nahkt-KOOK-han), fast night cakes, are popular. In Denmark, the Monday before Shrove Tuesday is a school holiday and is considered the merriest holiday of all. It is called *Fastelaun* (fast-eh-LAWN). The Danes dress in masks and costumes as American children do at Halloween and go from door to door singing and collecting coins for a Shrovetide feast. A Shrovetide bun called *Fastenlaunsboller* (fast-eh-LAWNS-bahl-ah) is served. The French term for Fat Tuesday is *Mardi Gras*, which accounts for the festival name in New Orleans and the South, where many French immigrants settled. In France and in the rest of Europe, the carnival usually lasts from Epiphany (January 6th) until the day before Ash Wednesday.

In New Orleans and other large cities of the South, there are men's and women's clubs whose sole existence is to plan a ball and a parade to be staged during carnival. Memberships in these clubs are limited (300 or less), expensive, and either inherited or by invitation only. One of the clubs is for Afro-Americans.

All of the clubs stage an elaborate formal ball, which is also by invitation only. Many of the clubs plan parades which have elaborately decorated floats, musical bands, and, of course, a king and queen. After a court for the king and queen is selected, the remaining club members plan and stage the parade. A theme is selected, a float built, bands invited, favors purchased, and doubloons (coins) struck with the crest of the club on one side and the theme and year on the other side. The parades usually travel a fifteen-mile route which takes about four hours to complete. Favors and doubloons are thrown from the floats to the watching crowds.

During the early stages of carnival, the parades take place on weeknights and during the afternoon of the weekends. During the last week, several parades are held each day and on the Saturday afternoon before Shrove Tuesday, all the schools participate by entering their individual floats and school marching bands.

As the carnival progresses the number of balls increases. The climax of the festivities comes with parades and formal balls held by the Rex and Comus, which are the two oldest clubs in the city.

Extended Experiences

1. View pictures of decorated floats and uniformed marching bands.
2. Those centers which are located in cities where carnival parades are held could attend a parade.
3. At music time the children might have a carnival parade. A king and queen could be selected, dressing in robes and crowns and wearing masks. They could be pulled in a decorated wagon. Crepe paper could be woven in the tricycle wheels and entered in the parade. Others could form a marching band. Uninflated balloons could be tossed as favors to those who are watching.

4. Read or tell these stories about carnival:
   *** Charlip, Remy. *Harlequin and the Gift of Many Colors*. Parents' Magazine Press, 1973.
   *** Wright, Mildred. *Henri Goes to the Mardi Gras*. Putnam, 1971, could also be read.

Purim (POOR-ihm)

For Jewish families Purim is *the* festival of merriment. It is an obligation to eat, drink, and be merry. It is a springtime religious festival and comes on the 14th day of the Hebrew month Adar, which usually falls in March. It is celebrated to mark the victory of the Jews in Persia, as written in the Book of Esther.

The story of Purim tells of Esther, a Jewish woman who was married to the King of Persia. Haman, then the Prime Minister of Persia, hated the Jews and tricked the king into agreeing that all the Jews in Persia should be killed. Esther heard of the plan and told the king how Haman had tricked him. When the king heard this, he had Haman put to death, and then gave the Jews their freedom. Purim is also called the Feast of Lots, because Haman drew lots to see which day would be best suited to enact his sinful plan.

The day before Purim is one of fasting. On the day of the holiday, the *Megillah* (Book of Esther) is read. Every time the name Haman is mentioned, the children yell, stamp their feet, and twirl a noisemaker called a *grager*.

Jewish children today have Purim parties and enjoy dressing up in biblical costumes and acting out the story of Esther. In Israel, children go from door to door singing loudly and reciting humorous poems.

Usually money and food are given to the poor. In the afternoon there is a feast with gifts of food for friends and relatives. *Hamantaschen* (Hah-mehn-tah-shen), which are three-cornered cakes with poppy seeds and honey or dried fruit fillings, are traditionally served. Some say the triangular shapes resemble Haman's hat (jailers wore tricornered hats in those days) and others say they are "Haman's pockets" because he had to pay out of his pocket for his wicked plan.

Extended Experiences

1. Listen to a story that the teacher could read or tell using any of the following books:

   *** Morrow, Betty, and Lewis Hartman. "Purim, A Springtime Carnival." In *Jewish Holidays*. Champaign, Ill.: Garrard Publishing Co., 1967, pp. 48-53.
   *** Simon, Norma. *Happy Purim Night*. New York: United Synagogue Book Service, 1959.
   *** ———. *Purim Party*. New York: United Synagogue Book Service, 1959.

2. Sing a Jewish song or listen to Israeli music on a record. (See Music, p. 273, in the *Hanukkah* guide for suitable sources.)
3. Invite a Jewish parent to bring a *grager* to show the children or buy one at a Hebrew bookstore.
4. Display different kinds of noisemakers used at birthday parties, New Year's Eve, and Halloween. Also display a *grager* and a *shofar*.

5. Make *hamantaschen* using recipes below, or ask a Jewish parent to bake some and bring for a snack or to come and help the children make their own.

Hamantaschen

BASIC RECIPE:

Roll canned biscuits to ¼ inch thick;
brush tops with melted butter;
place a teaspoon of the chosen filling in the center;
pull up the edge to form a tricorne, pinching the corners to let some of the filling show;
brush the tops with honey or beaten egg;
bake on a greased cookie sheet for 20 min. at 350°.

FILLINGS:
a. Poppyseed filling:
   Melt 1 tbsp. of butter with 1 tbsp of honey;
   add 1 tsp lemon juice, ½ cup ground almonds, and 1 cup poppyseeds;
   stir until blended.
b. Dried fruit filling:
   In the top of a double boiler, mix ½ cup each of raisins, pitted chopped prunes, chopped dried apricots, and fresh bread or cake crumbs;
   add ½ cup honey;
   stir over boiling water until honey melts;
   if too thin, add more crumbs; cool.
c. Plum jam filling:
   Beat together 1½ cup plum jam, grated rind, and juice of 1 lemon, ½ cup chopped almonds, and ½ cup bread or cake crumbs.

Halloween

Halloween is observed on October 31st by children in the United States and Canada. We feel it is the best festival of merriment that can be explored in depth by young children. See Halloween guide.

teacher resources

Books and Periodicals

1. DePree, Mildred. *A Child's World of Stamps.* New York: Parents' Magazine Press, 1973. Latin American countries feature carnival on their stamps on pp. 86–88.
2. Joseph, Joan. *Folk Toys Around the World and How to Make Them.* New York: Parents' Magazine Press, 1972. Haman Knocker from Israel, p. 40.
3. Cooper, Terry Touf, and Marilyn Ratner. *Many Hands Cooking, an International Cookbook for Girls and Boys.* New York: Thomas Y. Crowell, 1974.

4. Siegel, Richard, Michael Strassfeld, and Sharon Strassfeld. *The Jewish Catalog.* Philadelphia, Pa.: Jewish Publication Society, 1973. Includes instructions for making a Franklin *grager.*
5. Spiegelman, Judith. *UNICEF's Festival Book.* New York: United States Committee for UNICEF, 1966.

Pictures and Displays

(See p. 79 for addresses of firms listed.)

1. Children of America, Color Study Prints including Jewish children (The Child's World)
2. UNICEF Wall Calendar, United States Committee for UNICEF, 331 East 38th St., New York 10016

Community Resources

1. Synagogue or temple
2. Hebrew bookstore
3. Food store with international food section

Festivals of Light

Candles were one of the first sources of man-made light. Therefore, it is not surprising that they have been used extensively in religious ceremonies and festivals not only for the light they provide but for the beauty and symbolic meanings they have acquired throughout the world. Many families use candles in their daily or weekly religious observances at home and in their houses of worship.

Candle lighting is a very real part of family celebrations in the United States. Birthdays are usually celebrated by giving presents and serving birthday cake lighted with one candle for each year of life. Weddings, anniversaries, showers, and dinner parties often feature lighted candles. Candle making is a hobby for many. Candles are created in all shapes, sizes, colors, and scents. Candles can also serve as emergency lighting when the electricity goes off.

The Greeks and Romans, we know, used torches to light their celebrations, particularly those held after dark. The Olympic games of the ancient Greeks, held on the plains at the base of Mount Olympus, were opened with an impressive torch-lighting ceremony. The Olympic flame was lighted with a torch that was carried by hand all the way from Olympia, Greece, to Athens. This tradition is still carried on today, with the torch lit by the sun (and a magnifying glass) and carried by train, ship, or plane, then car, skis, or sled to the site of the Olympic games.

Candlemas

Candlemas is a very old church holiday. It was a Jewish custom for every mother to go to the temple forty days after the birth of her first son and "present him to the Lord." Thus the Christian Bible has recorded that Mary took Jesus to the temple on the appointed day. It also states a devout man named Simeon said that Jesus was to become a "light to lighten the Gentiles." In the Roman Catholic Church the lighting of candles and the Candlemas ceremony are held in honor of this event and also in honor of the Virgin Mary. On this day they bless all the candles that will be used in the church services throughout the year. Some Protestant churches also celebrate Candlemas in early February.

In Luxembourg, after blessing the candles, the boys and girls visit shut-ins and the elderly and sing songs about lights. In Mexico, the sacred doll that was placed in the crèche on Christmas Eve is removed. It is dressed and put on a tray decorated with flowers. In some churches the godfather and godmother (or sponsors) presiding at the last *Las Posadas* give a fiesta for the others who were present at the ceremony. (See Christmas Around the World guide.)

Extended Experiences

1. Visit a nearby church to see lighted candles or decorations with candles and flowers for a special occasion such as a wedding or Christmas.
2. Display pictures of candles used in churches or synagogues.

   NOTE: Because of the religious significance of this holiday it would perhaps suit only those school centers that are sponsored by a church.

St. Lucia's Day

On December 13th, many Christian countries in Europe celebrate St. Lucia's Day. St. Lucia was put to death by the Romans 1500 years ago for her Christian beliefs, and later was made a saint. In Italy, large bonfires are built and there are candle and torchlight processions.

In Sweden, a young girl, usually the oldest daughter, dresses up in a long white dress tied with a red sash and places a crown of evergreens adorned with glowing candles on her head. Traditionally, it is her task to serve coffee and special twisted buns with raisins to her family at daybreak. The buns are twisted into different shapes as illustrated below, the favorite being one called "Lucia cats."

| Lucia's Crown | Lucia Cats' Eyes | Star Boy | Lucia Cats' Tails |

St. Lucia is followed by her brothers, who are dressed in white and wear pointed hats with silver stars and who are called "star boys." Her sisters wear white robes, too, but have tinsel in their hair. They are called "Lucia maidens." They carry candles and the "star boys" carry additional trays of buns. This ceremony is to assure the family that beginning on this day (the shortest, darkest day of winter) the days will begin again to be longer. It also reminds them that Christmas is near.

Extended Experiences

1. If December 13th falls on a day your center is open, you may wish to tell the children about St. Lucia Day in Sweden and serve "Lucia buns" and hot chocolate for breakfast or snack. Children who arrive early may like to twist yeast dough into interesting shapes and add raisins for decorations. (See illustration, p. 263, for some traditional shapes.)
2. Make a circlet of real or artificial evergreens for a child who will play the part of "Lucia." Candles may be added but **should not be lit** (best if imitation candles are used to duplicate the battery candles used by most Swedish "Lucias" today). Cut a discarded sheet to drape around her shoulders and hang to her ankles. Let one girl at each table be Lucia and one boy be "star boy." He should wear a similar robe and a white pointed cap made of construction paper to which silver stars have been glued.
3. Candles placed in evergreen wreaths for centerpieces may be lit at each table if adequate adult supervision is available.

Divali (Dee-WAH-lee)

In India the most exciting holiday for young Hindu children is the festival of lights known as *Divali*. It is celebrated near the end of October or in early November. Garlands of flowers are hung over the outside door and good luck symbols are drawn on the door with colored powders. For days prior to *Divali* the house is scrubbed, new clothes are purchased, and special foods are prepared.

Also many *diyas* are made. These are little clay saucers filled with mustard oil with a wick inserted. At night the wicks are lit and the *diyas* placed on the windowsills, on the roofs, and along the roads leading to the houses. This is done to attract *Lakshmi*, a Hindu goddess who the Indians believe will bring them wealth and good fortune if she visits their home and blesses them.

In Ceylon (Sri Lanka) this festival is called *Deepvali*. Every house is lighted. The children especially like the sugar candy, which tastes like our maple sugar candy, and is often made in the shape of animals, flowers, and people.

In India, lighted candles in little boats made of banana leaves are floated down the river after dark. The family rises early on *Divali* and everyone dresses in their new clothes. They visit friends and relatives and exchange gifts. Later in the day there is a carnival with rides, treats, and fireworks. The *diyas* are lighted at sunset. Lakshimi, the goddess of wealth and good fortune, is believed by Hindus to be guided to earth and to their homes by the lights. It is hoped that she will leave her blessings of wealth and good fortune when she visits their homes.

Extended Experiences

1. Activities centering around *Divali* should include telling the highlights of this festival of light. The children might enjoy making *diyas* out of modeling clay. A candlewick, available at craft shops, and olive oil or a small spoonful of Sterno cooking fuel can be placed in each *diyas*. The room should be darkened and the wicks or Sterno lighted. The Sterno burns with a blue flame and will leave no residue in the *diyas*, which the children may wish to take home.

2. Perhaps the cook could serve an East Indian dish that day. Curried rice, chutney, and kabobs are popular East Indian dishes. For snacks you may wish to serve cashews, almonds, pistachios, or peanuts mixed with raisins. If your grocery has an international foods section you may find East Indian foods to share with the children.

3. Put up pictures of families in India. If you have Indian families in your center or community invite one of them to show the children how to wrap a sari, explain a caste mark, prepare a special food, and show any jewelry, art objects, or other items they may have to share.

Hanukkah (HAHN-uh-kuh)

Candle lighting is an integral part of the Jewish family's observances of the Sabbath, as well as most of their other celebrations. *Hanukkah*, traditionally spelled *Chanukah*, with its eight days of candle lighting and other festivities, has been chosen as the festival of light to be written as a complete guide in this book. See Hanukkah guide.

teacher resources

Books and Periodicals

1. DePree, Mildred. *A Child's World of Stamps.* New York: Parents' Magazine Press, 1973.
2. Cooper, Terry Touf, and Marilyn Ratner. *Many Hands Cooking, An International Cookbook for Girls and Boys.* New York: Thomas Y. Crowell, 1974.
3. Spiegelman, Judith. *UNICEF's Festival Book.* New York: United States Committee for UNICEF, United Nations, 1966.

Pictures and Displays

(See p. 79 for addresses of firms listed.)

1. Children Around the World (SVE Picture Story, Study Prints)
   Set two, Children in Europe, Sigrid of Sweden, with study sheet.
   Set three, Children in—Asia, Ranjit of India, with study sheet.
2. UNICEF Wall Calendar, United States Committee for UNICEF, 331 East 38th Street, New York, New York 10016.

15 Hanukkah

basic understandings

(concepts children can grasp from this subject)

- *Hanukkah* (HAHN-nu-kuh) is a festival of light observed by Jewish people.
- *Hanukkah* celebrates religious freedom for the Jews.
- Candles are lit each night in a special candleholder called a *menorah* (meh-NOR-ah). The candle known as the *shamash* is lit every night. In addition, one candle is lit the first night, two the second, and so on, until there are nine in the *menorah* on the last night.
- Families enjoy eating potato pancakes called *latkes* (LOT-kuhs).
- Children like to play games with a *dreidel* (DRAY-dull).
- Gifts are generally given to children—one each night. Frequently *gelt* (coins) is given. Bags of chocolate coins covered with gold foil are in favor in American families.

Additional Facts the Teacher Should Know

Hanukkah, a festival of light, comes in late November or December and begins on the 25th day of the Hebrew month *Kislev*. The Hebrew calendar is a lunar one, so the exact date of *Hanukkah* varies each year. The Hallmark Date Book, distributed free where Hallmark cards are sold, or the current UNICEF wall calendar identifies the Jewish holidays. *Hanukkah* celebrates a great victory for the Jews approximately 2100 years ago.

Antiochus, a Syrian king, drove the Jews from their temple in Jerusalem and ordered them to worship Greek gods or be put to death. The Jews fought back and under the leadership of the Maccabees finally regained Jerusalem and set about purifying their temple, which the Syrians had defiled. When it was ready they proclaimed a holiday and called it *Hanukkah*, which means "dedication." The celebration lasted eight days.

There is a legend about the first *Hanukkah* which relates how only one little jar of oil was found to light the holy lamp in the temple for the festival. It should have lasted only one day, but it miraculously lasted eight days until new oil was ready. This is probably why *Hanukkah* is celebrated for eight days.

A variety of *menorahs*.

Today, each family has a *menorah*, a candelabrum with eight branches made of wood, brass, silver, or gold. The first *menorahs* used little pots of oil, but today candles are used. There is also a place for a smaller candle called the *shamash* (SHAH-mush). It is usually in the center and a little higher than the others but can be forward, behind, or to the right of the others if on the same level. It is lit first and then is used to light the others. The candles are placed in the *menorah* beginning on the right and moving to the left each day with the required number of candles. Then the candles are lit from left to right beginning with the new candle. Forty-four small candles are needed for the eight-day festival, because each night you must use new candles.

Potato pancakes called *latkes* (LOT-kuhs) are frequently served during *Hanukkah*. They are dipped in sour cream or served with applesauce. Christians have a similar custom of eating pancakes on Shrove Tuesday. Gifts are given to Jewish children at the beginning of the holiday or one each night. The intent is to spread light and joy. Although *Hanukkah* is celebrated during the same season as Christmas and gifts are given to children as part of both celebrations, *Hanukkah* is *not* the Jewish Christmas. Christmas is a Christian holiday; and Hanukkah is a Jewish holiday. Each celebration is important to a child in his or her own faith for a very different reason. Also at *Hanukkah* time, Jewish children enjoy playing the *dreidel* game while adults play cards. The *dreidel* is a four-sided top with Hebrew letters on each side representing the words in the phrase "A Great Miracle Happened There," referring to the oil lasting for eight days during the first *Hanukkah*.

Very young children, whether Jewish or non-Jewish, do not always comprehend the history of their faith or the deeper meanings involved in their celebrations. But they can learn the name of the celebration and begin to understand some of the outward symbols for the inner meanings. Jewish children should be given the opportunity to develop a good concept of self and pride in one's family and heritage by sharing their beliefs and customs. Non-Jews can learn that not everyone believes the same thing, and we must respect each person's right to his/her own beliefs. All can learn they have some beliefs in common and some that differ.

Methods Most Adaptable for Introducing This Subject to Children

- Display of *Hanukkah* candelabra, *dreidel,* or pictures.
- Sing a song or read a story about *Hanukkah.*
- Discussion of festivals of various religions or national groups.
- Discussion of the fact that different peoples have festivals centering around the use of candles and other lights during the gray winter with its long, dark nights.
- Invite a Jewish parent to display *Hanukkah* decorations and *menorah.*

Vocabulary

candle	*shamash* (SHAH-mush), helper candle
light	*ner tamid* (nehr-TAH-MEED), everlasting light
first, eighth	*dreidel*
gelt	Maccabee (Jewish soldier-hero)
menorah	*latke*

learning centers

Discovery Center

1. Make potato *latkes*:

Latkes
2 cups raw grated potato
1 small grated onion
1 tsp. salt
1 pinch of pepper
1 tbsp. flour (matzo meal)
½ tbsp. baking powder

1. Peel the potatoes and soak in cold water.
2. Grate them and pour off the liquid. Add the grated onion, salt, and pepper.
3. Mix flour and baking powder and add to potato mixture.
4. One or two well-beaten eggs *may* be added.
5. Drop by spoonfuls onto a hot, well-greased griddle (fry pan). Spread thin with back of spoon.
6. Turn when very brown. Drain fat.

   NOTE: A potato pancake mix may also be used. *Latkes* are especially good served with applesauce or dipped in sour cream.

2. Make *Hanukkah* cookies: use your favorite sugar cookie recipe. Cookie cutters in the shapes of a candle, a *dreidel*, a lion, or a Star of David (six-pointed star) are available in Hebrew bookstores or a specialty store, or you may borrow some from a Jewish parent.

3. *Hanukkah* salad may be made by constructing a fruit candle as follows: a slice of canned pineapple for a base. Stand one-half of a banana in the pineapple for a candle. Place a maraschino cherry on top of the banana for flame (slit banana to insert).

4. Light: candles and the light they give may lead to the discovery and discussion of many different kinds of light, such as electricity (lamp), gas (yard light), fire (firelight), sun (sunlight), kerosene (lantern), and battery (flashlight). Help children find these in their environment and/or collect pictures illustrating these to put on the wall or in a scrapbook.

5. Post pictures or display often-used lights. Include small electric lamp, traffic lights, neon lights, flashlight, candle (teacher-supervised!), porch light. If you have adequate supervision light a candleholder with chimney; demonstrate how the chimney keeps the candle from being blown out. Demonstrate how a candle snuffer is used to put out a flame.

Learning, Language, and Readiness Materials Center

Commercially made games and materials for use at a table or on a mat:

(See Basic Resources, p. 79, for manufacturers' addresses.)

1. Judy Puzzle: *Hanukkah*, 12 pcs.
2. *Dreidel:* wooden or plastic (available in larger department stores and Hebrew bookstores)
3. Cookie cutters: Star of David, lion, *dreidel*, candle (department stores and Hebrew bookstores)
4. Gold coins (play money) (variety store)

Teacher-made games and materials for use at a table or on a mat:

NOTE: For detailed description of Games, see pp. 50–59.

1. How Many?: count candles on flannelboard *menorah*.
2. I See Something: find round things like a *latke*.
3. Chew, Lick, and Taste: a *latke* and a pancake.
4. *Dreidel* Game I: materials needed: *dreidel* (see pattern, p. 271) and tokens, nuts in the shell, or wrapped candies. Procedure: Everyone playing puts in a token. Children, in turn, spin the top and play for the tokens, nuts, or candies. If the letter *nun* (‏נ‎) faces up, the child gets nothing. If the letter *heh* (‏ה‎) appears, he gets half of the tokens. If the *shin* (‏ש‎) appears, he must put a token in the group pile from his stock. If the *gimel* (‏ג‎) appears, the child wins. Singing the parody "Dreidel Game," p. 273, may help the children remember. (See also Dreidel Game II, p. 274.)

How to make a *dreidel:* use oaktag or a file folder to make a cube 2 inches square (or any size between 2 inches and 4 inches). Use the pattern and example shown on the opposite page. A dowel with one end pointed can be inserted through the holes in the top and bottom of the cube. Adjust cube up or down on dowel until it is balanced enough to spin easily. Wood or cardboard can be used if you have the necessary tools.

Dreidel pattern

With paper cut-out in front of you, fold on dotted lines so flaps are inside and Hebrew letters are outside.

Cut holes to suit the dowel diameter

Reading from **right** to **left**, the Hebrew characters from the four sides of the Dreidel.

Nes — MIRACLE

Gadol — GREAT

Hayah — WAS

Sham — THERE

"A GREAT MIRACLE WAS THERE!"

Glue flap

Glue flap

Glue flap

Glue flap

Glue flap

Glue flap

Glue flap

Glue flap

Top hole for dowel

Bottom hole for dowel

Fold on dotted lines

Cut on solid lines

Finished Dreidel

Art Center

* 1. Easel paint: feature orange, white, and dark blue paint.
** 2. Paint and crayon: make enough *dreidels* for each child in the group and let each paint or crayon every side of the cube. Teacher puts letters on or children use gum-backed letters.
*** 3. Pasting *menorahs:* eight long strips of paper, straws, pipecleaners, yarn, or felt can be pasted on background paper to represent candles. One short one should be cut for the *shammash.* Pieces of cotton dipped in yellow paint, short lengths of yellow yarn, clippings of yellow paper, or Q-Tips dipped in yellow, red, or orange paint will offer a variety of possibilities for making flames. Gold or silver glitter can be used to cover a line of glue placed under the candles to represent a metal candleholder. Gold or yellow paper rectangles can be pasted on for bases.
* 4. Paper chains: use royal blue and white construction paper for making chains in the traditional manner. Teacher can precut strips or children with cutting experience can cut their own strips.
* 5. Sponge prints: cut sponges in the shape of the Star of David, *dreidel,* lion, or candle. (See patterns on p. 275.)

Other Experiences in This Center Using Art Media

1. Greeting cards:
* a. Spatter-paint *Hanukkah* symbols, using white paint on royal blue construction paper. Fold paper in half to form card before painting.
** b. Use sponge stamps to print a combination of symbols on a card. (See No. 5, in Art Center above.)
*** c. Cut and paste two triangles one inverted over the other to form Star of David (six-pointed star) or paste precut *dreidels* to a prefolded card. Encourage children to make a border and, if they are able, to letter their names inside.
*** 2. Gifts: can be made for parents, for Jewish children in local hospitals, or to exchange. Candleholders can be made of styrofoam or wooden spools mounted on a board and painted. Make eight places for candles, plus an extra one for the *shammash* which is used to light the others.

Book Center

*** Chanover, Hyman and Alice. *Happy Hanukkah Everybody.* New York: United Synagogue Book Service, 1954.
*** Garvey, Robert. *Holidays Are Nice.* New York: Ktav Publishing House, 1960.
*** Morrow, Betty, and Lewis Hartman. "Hanukkah, Feast of Lights," in *Jewish Holidays.* Champaign, Ill.: Garrard Publishing, 1967, pp. 41–47 (Holiday Book Series).
*** Simon, Norma. *Hanukkah in My House.* New York: United Synagogue Book Service, 1960.
*** ———. *Hanukkah.* New York: Thomas Y. Crowell, 1966.
**** Spiegelman, Judith. "Hanukkah" in *UNICEF's Festival Book.* New York: United States Committee for UNICEF, United Nations, 1966.

planning for grouptime

NOTE: All music, fingerplays, stories, poems, and games listed here may also be used at other times during the session as appropriate. See Core Library, Basic Resources, p. 76, for publishers and addresses. Addresses for sources of records will be found on p. 81. In parodies, hyphenated words match the music notes of the tune used.

Music

Songs

DREIDEL GAME (a parody)
 (tune: "This Is the Way")
 Adaptation by JoAnne Deal Hicks

The drei-del game is fun to play, fun to play, fun to play,
The drei-del game is fun to play, on Ha-nuk-kah in the morn-ing.

The "shin" turns up, you put one in, put one in, put one in . . .

The "heh" turns up, then you get half, you get half, you get half . . .

The "nun" turns up, then you get none, you get none, you get none . . .

"Gim-mel" turns up, then you get all, you get all, you get all . . .

FROM original songs in this book by JoAnne Deal Hicks
* "Happy Hanukkah," p. 276

FROM song books listed below, available from United Synagogue Book Service
"Songs to Share," Rose B. Goldstein, 1949
"The Songs We Sing," Harry Coopersmith, 1950
"More of the Songs We Sing," Harry Coopersmith, 1970

Records

"Children Sing on Hanukkah" (Tikva, 33⅓ RPM)
"Hanukkah," *Holiday Songs and Rhythms*, Hap Palmer (Educational Activities, Inc., 33⅓ RPM)
"Israeli Children's Songs," Ben-Ezra (Folkways, 33⅓ RPM)
"My Dreidel," *Kindergarten Songs*, Record 1 (Bowmar, 33⅓ RPM)
"O Hanukkah," *Folk Songs of Israel* (Bowmar, 33⅓ RPM, cassette and filmstrip)
"Songs to Share" (United Synagogue Book Service, 33⅓ RPM)
"Yiddish Folk Songs for Children" (Folkways, 33⅓ RPM)

Rhythms and Singing Games

"Hava Nageela," *Harry Belafonte at Carnegie Hall* (RCA, 33⅓ RPM) or *An Evening with Harry Belafonte* (RCA, 33⅓ RPM)
Children may use scarves or crepe paper streamers of orange, white, and dark blue.

Fingerplays and Poems

FROM *Rhymes for Fingers and Flannelboards*, Scott and Thompson
"Hanukkah Lights," p. 70

FROM Holidays Picture Packet, *Hanukkah*, p. 11 (David C. Cook)

Games

Dreidel Game II: Children form a circle holding hands. One child is chosen to be a *dreidel* in the center. Children walk around in a circle while child in center turns in place for first half of melody (use any Israeli music). Then both the circle and the *dreidel* stop. The child in the center chooses another child to spin by holding hands and turning together in the center while circle moves again for the last half of the melody. The chosen child stays in the center for the start of a new game and the first child rejoins the circle. Repeat until every child who wishes can be a *dreidel*. Form a second circle if time will not allow everyone a turn.

Routine Times

1. During snack or mealtime serve *latkes*, candle salad, or sugar cookies in the shape of the Star of David, a lion, a candle, or a *dreidel*.
2. When walking or busing look for a synagogue or a temple.

Large Muscle Activities

(See Rhythms and Singing Games and Games in this guide.)

Extended Experiences

1. Visit a temple or synagogue to see the eternal light (*ner tamid*).
2. Invite a Jewish parent, student, or friend to come to the classroom. Ask them to share with the children any of the following:
   a. a *menorah*: show how it is lighted and explain how it is used.
   b. a *dreidel*: show how to play the *Dreidel* Game, and explain the letters.
   c. some *Hanukkah* sugar cookies for snacktime, or bring *Hanukkah* cookie cutters and help the children make and bake cookies. Discuss the reason for shapes chosen.
   d. some *latkes*, serve with sour cream or applesauce. The visitor might be asked to help supervise and to assist the children in making *latkes*.

teacher resources

Books and Periodicals

1. Cavanah, Frances, and Lucy Pannell. *Holiday Round Up*. Philadelphia: Macrae Smith, 1968.
2. Dobler, Lavinia. *Customs and Holidays Around the World*. New York: Fleet Press, 1963.
3. Margalit, Avi. *The Hebrew Alphabet Book*. New York: Coward, McCann, 1965.
4. Mervis, Rabbi Leonard J. *We Celebrate the Jewish Holidays*. New York: Union of American Hebrew Congregations, 1953.
5. Purdy, Susan. *Festivals for You to Celebrate*. Philadelphia: J. B. Lippincott, 1969.
6. Siegel, Richard, Michael Strassfield, and Sharon Strassfield. *The Jewish Catalog*. Philadelphia: Jewish Publication Society of America, 1973.
7. United Synagogue Book Service, 155 Fifth Avenue, New York 10010. For storybooks, song books, and records listed in Book Center and Music.

Pictures and Displays

(See p. 79 for addresses of firms listed.)

1. Children Around the World: "Ziva of Israel," set of three, SVE (Singer)
2. Holidays Picture Packet: "Hanukkah" (David C. Cook)
3. Holidays of the Year: "Hanukkah" (Vanguard Visuals Company)
4. Children of America: 13 inches by 18 inches color print of Jewish children (The Child's World)
5. UNICEF wall calendar (United States Committee for UNICEF, 331 East 38th Street, New York 10016)

Community Resources

1. Jewish parents in your center; students in a nearby college or university
2. Rabbi or director of Hebrew education
3. Hebrew bookstore
4. Temple gift shop

Lion

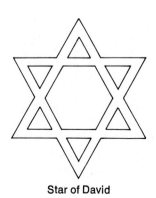

Star of David

Menorah

Happy Hanukkah

JoAnne Deal Hicks

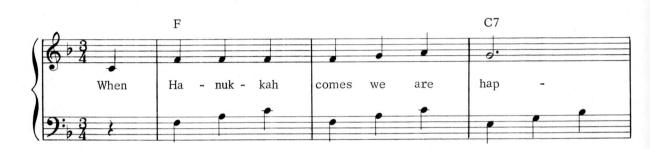

When Ha - nuk - kah comes we are hap -

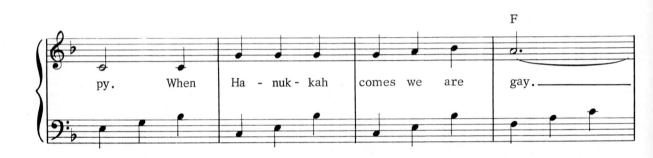

py. When Ha - nuk - kah comes we are gay. _____

_____ We light a lit - tle can -

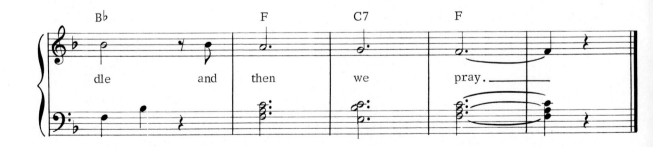

dle and then we pray. _____

16 Christmas Around the World

Christmas is one of the two most-celebrated holidays of Christians around the world. Easter is the other. Many unique Christmas customs of the United States are based on traditions brought and shared by the many immigrants to America.

People all over the world celebrate Christmas in similar ways due to the widespread travel of missionaries, service personnel, and tradespeople both in the past and present. Unfortunately, some of these customs have become highly commercialized.

An important part of the Christmas celebration is worship. Christians universally worship with music, drama, symbols, candles, and gift-giving to express their faith with love, joy, and hope, including a sincere concern for peace. Also part of Christmas celebrations are carols, cantatas, pageants of the Christmas story, candlelight services, and gifts to the needy. Christmas cards and hymns have been written in almost every language. More and more paintings of the Madonna and Child, the Holy Family, and the Flight into Egypt are being painted by artists depicting their own particular culture or race. Examples may be found in *The Faces of Jesus*, Buechner and Boltin (New York: Simon and Schuster, 1974).

Advent

In the Christian Church calendar year, this season begins four Sundays before Christmas, usually the weekend following Thanksgiving. Advent can last from twenty-three to twenty-eight days. To Christians, Advent literally means "coming" and emphasizes the threefold coming of Christ—his birth, his coming into the lives of those who believe in him, his coming on the final day of judgment.

The Advent celebration includes plans for daily personal and family worship, with special church services and other unique plans for celebrating Christ's birth at Christmastime, such as the use of Chrismon trees, Advent wreaths, and Advent calendars.

A Chrismon (Kris-mahn) tree is an evergreen tree exquisitely decorated with jewel-like monograms of Jesus Christ. Its decorations are characterized by being made only with the colors of gold and white that liturgically represent, to many Christians, purity, perfection, majesty, and glory. Beads, sequins, braids, pearls, styrofoam, wire, wood, and metals may be used in their creation. Many Chrismon trees include a children's section with lambs, butterflies, fish, mangers, stars, and other figures easily recognized by very young children. Some congregations encourage families and individual members to design and create their own Chrismons to decorate their church tree; others select small groups of artistically talented lay persons to make decorations for a tree.

Advent wreaths are made with a circle of evergreen formed to include four purple (or red) candles within its shape. One candle is ceremoniously lit each week during family worship until all four are lit on the Sunday preceding Christmas. Some Christians place a larger, white fifth candle in the center of the evergreen to be lit on Christmas Day.

NOTE: Some families light the appropriate candle or candles every day during each week in Advent while they have family devotions or worship.

Paper or cardboard Advent calendars are often a triptych (threefold) nativity picture with numbered windows on its surface. When these numbered window flaps are opened, a scripture passage is revealed inside that can be read on that day until the last is read on the 25th of December.

Extended Experiences

1. Make or buy an Advent calendar to use when counting the days until Christmas. Sing a carol or read a poem as you use the calendar.

    CAUTION: Do not mix the Santa Claus legend with the use of the calendar.

2. Visit a Lutheran Church where a Chrismon Tree has been set up for the Advent season. (Other denominations may also have such a tree.)
3. See Christmas guide to find other suggestions for this season.

Las Posadas (Lahs-poh-SAH-thas)

Las Posadas, which literally means "lodging," is celebrated in the United States during Advent by Catholics and some Protestants who are Spanish Americans or Mexican Americans. The holiday begins on December 16. It is a reenactment of Joseph and Mary's trip from Nazareth to Bethlehem to seek lodging the night before Jesus was born. Often this Catholic celebration involves the whole community; in cities it may be celebrated by a single parish or neighborhood.

Las Posadas begins in the United States when statues of Mary and Joseph are picked up from the church by *padrinos* (pah-DHREE-nohs). They are a man and wife who are chosen sponsors of that year's *Las Posadas* activities. (In some other countries women may not be allowed to perform this task.) They begin by seeing that the statues will be moved from house to house during this *novena* (nine days) by selecting eight other couples to assist them, one for each night. They also plan for a crib or crèche to be set up in the church for the Midnight Mass on Christmas Eve, at which time the figures are returned. Often candles and tree lights are used to suggest the star with the figures. In South America flowers and moss are also used. Sometimes in cities in other South American countries, such as Colombia, parades of people on Christmas Eve go from one church to another just to view the beautifully decorated crèches called *nacimientos* (nah-see-mee-EHN-tohz), or *pesebres* (pay-SAY-brayz), and then finally attend Midnight Mass at their own church. (See p. 287.)

Led by two children holding the clay figures of Joseph and Mary, families walk or march during *Las Posadas* to different unlighted houses along a preplanned route "looking for lodging," and singing traditional and original songs in English or Spanish. Many times they are accompanied by members of a *mariachi* band playing violins, guitars, and trumpets. Everyone sings traditional tunes while requesting entrance for the Holy Family.

By prearranged plan they are denied lodging until a designated couple turns on their lights and invites them in. At least two extra unplanned stops are made each night and these may be stops at non-Catholic homes. Others may join the group as they march along.

The blindfolded child in the picture is attempting to break a *piñata* with a stick. A *piñata* can be made from a large earthenware jar or a papier-mâché form in a variety of shapes, such as a bird, a donkey, a doll, or a dog.

When they finally gain entrance to a home, the guests gather around the crèche or Bethlehem scene (the *nacimiento* or *pesebre*) for praying, singing songs, and reading scripture. Following worship the host family usually serves coffee, punch, wine, and cookies for refreshment. Sometimes, especially on the last night *empanaditas, tamales, bizcochitas, tortillas,* or *buñuelos* may be served. At each of the designated nine homes a small homemade *piñata* (peen-YAH-tuh) is often suspended from a rope on a pulley or thrown over a beam indoors or over a tree limb in the patio.

Children are blindfolded, spun around two or three times, and then given chances to swing a stick to break the *piñata*. There is not always enough candy to go around and this encourages children to share. An adult or older child manipulates the rope, to keep the children from breaking the *piñata* too soon, so that every child who wishes gets a turn. Finally some lucky child breaks the *piñata* and all the children shout joyfully and scramble for the treats. In some countries this activity is accompanied by a chant in Spanish, such as "You are near, you are far, hit it, hit it, now," to assist the child who is blindfolded to find the *piñata*. On Christmas Eve, the last night of the *novena*, the *padrenos* pick up the statues at the last destination and proceed to the local church. Young boys and girls dress as shepherds and stand close to the manger. The sponsors (the *padrenos*) approach the manger, carrying a wooden or wax figure of the Holy Baby. The people kneel and sing a litany and *El Rorro* ("Babe in Arms").

At midnight, on *Noche Buena* (NOH-cheh Boo-AY-nah) as this night is called, church bells are rung, whistles blown, and sometimes fireworks fired to announce the baby's birth. Then everyone attends the Mass of the Cock or *Misa de Gallo* (MEE-suh deh GAH-yoh), at which nine "Ave Marias" are sung. After mass the people return home and eat with their extended families such foods as suckling pig and *buñuelos* (boo-NWAY-lohs), thin pancakes with brown sugar sauce. These gatherings reestablish family ties and relationships and often include godparents, who are considered as close as blood relatives.

Extended Experiences

1. Make a *piñata* for the last day before Christmas vacation. Fill it with sugarless gum, uninflated balloons, and wrapped peanut butter kisses, nutmeats, raisins, popcorn, and other nutritious snacks rather than more candy, and small unbreakable plastic block accessories or dramatic play props such as homemade paper bag or sock puppets.
2. Sing the following parody:

PIÑATA SONG (a parody)
  (tune: "If You're Happy and You Know It")
  Adaptation by JoAnne Deal Hicks

A *piñ-a-ta* can be *so* much fun to *break* . . . (CLAP, CLAP)
A *piñ-a-ta* can be *so* much fun to *break* . . . (CLAP, CLAP)

Ev-'ry-bod-y tries and tries
With a blind-fold on their eyes
'Til "CRAA-AASHH!" (SPOKEN) down
falls a won-der-ful . . . sur-prise!

3. Visit a Spanish-speaking home where a *nacimiento* or a *pesebre* may be set up for one of the nights of *Las Posadas*. Ask to see the *piñata* if one has been prepared or purchased.
4. Invite a *mariachi* band to come and play or play records by a *mariachi* band.
5. Invite a parent to come and prepare *buñuelos* for or with the children.
6. Add the following books to your Book Center:
   ** Ets, Marie Hall, and Aurora Lenastida. *Nine Days to Christmas.* New York: Viking Press, 1959.
   *** Politi, Leo. *Rosa.* New York: Scribner's, 1963 (also in Spanish).
   *** ———. *Pedro, the Angel of Olvera Street.* New York: Scribner's, 1946 (Spanish, 1974).

Epiphany

Epiphany is the season on the Christian church calendar following Christmas. It begins the Sunday after Christmas and continues until the beginning of Lent. (This date varies with the date of Easter, which falls on the first Sunday after the first full moon of spring.) Epiphany, which may include four to six Sundays, is the season celebrating the visit of the Magi to the baby Jesus. January 6th is called Twelfth Night or the Feast of the Epiphany.

Twelfth Night

This holiday, celebrated on January 6th, is also known as the Three Kings' Day, Holy Kings' Day, Little Christmas, Old Christmas, or the Manifestation of Christ to the Gentiles. It recalls the visit of the Wise Men to Bethlehem and refers to the last of the twelve succeeding days after Christmas. It usually ends the Christmas celebrations, although technically the religious Christmas celebration continues the entire season of Epiphany.

With the change of the old calendar to the Gregorian calendar by the English, eleven days were arbitrarily eliminated and this caused continued confusion as to when to celebrate certain traditional holidays. Therefore some European countries refer to Twelfth Night as Old Christmas Day.

Many Christians who display crèches do not add the baby Jesus figure until Christmas Eve nor the Wise Men until during the Epiphany season. The stable is then removed and Mary, Joseph and the baby are moved to a Palestinian home where the Wise Men are added on the twelfth night. Sometimes Wise Men are placed at a great distance from the stable and gradually moved closer until January 6th.

In Austria and Germany, young boys go about singing star songs during Epiphany, carrying a gold star on a pole. Three of the boys are dressed as kings. Sometimes they carry a crèche and when they find a home without one, they leave it.

In Europe, many English, French, German, and Dutch families serve a special fruitcake, heavily iced and decorated with gold and silver stars, flowers, crowns, dragons, and little figures of the Wise Men. Hidden in each cake is a bean and a pea. Whichever boy finds the bean is the Twelfth Night King. The girl who finds the pea is Queen. If either is found by the opposite sex they have the right to choose their own king or queen.

In the United States some communities have a public burning of old Christmas trees with festivities planned for families attending. This is a Northern European custom.

In Nigeria this holiday is called *Timkat* (TIHM-KAHT). It celebrates Christ's baptism and is a day of baptism, conducted by a priest in special robes, for all who come to a specific spring or pool for that ceremony.

In Italy on the eve of Epiphany, *La Befana* (lah-beh-FAH-nah), a legendary benefactress, brings gifts to children. She leaves gifts in their shoes and is said to come down the chimney on a broom. Children who have been bad get rocks or ashes. Children blowing paper trumpets often roam the streets on this day.

In Spain, Puerto Rico, and Mexico on Three Kings' Day the Magi are supposed to bring gifts to put in shoes or boxes that the children have filled with straw or grain. In the morning, a sweet called *turrón* (toor-OHN) (a candy loaf of roasted almonds in caramel syrup) is left and the grain is gone. The Magi's camels are supposed to have eaten the grain and straw.

In Greece, on Epiphany, the village priest throws a little cross into a body of water (sometimes with a ribbon attached to retrieve it). Other times the cross is recovered by young men diving into the water. He then may bless those assembled with droplets from the cross or go from house to house sprinkling holy water to bless homes. In some Greek communities in America, this blessing of the water includes a parade and other religious activities.

In Sweden, on Epiphany *(Trettondedag Jul)*, "Star Boys" *(Stjarngossar)* traditionally put on a pageant portraying the story of the Three Kings. They wear tall cone-shaped hats decorated with tinsel, a white robe, and carry poles with torchlike lights on their ends. Therefore star boys in America are often a part of Swedish traditional celebration festivities.

Unique Customs for Celebrating the Christmas Holidays from All Over the World

Following are some interesting customs by country, many of which are remembered and maintained by Americans in the United States today as part of their cultural heritage. On p. 289 some of the customs most easily adapted for use with young children have been listed in Extended Experiences. You may wish to select others from the material listed below or from other customs your students and their parents share with you.

Sweden—St. Lucia is a special Christmastime holiday. (See Festivals of Merriment and Light, p. 263.) Because of the long period of darkness in midwinter all kinds of lights are welcomed. Candle-making and giving is therefore an important part of the Swedish Christmas holiday. *Pepparkakor* (ginger cookie) trees, brass angel candle chimes, candles, and live green Christmas trees are other Swedish traditions related to Christmas. Evergreen trees are decorated with intricate straw figures (stars, animals, sunbursts, snowflakes, and people) and always include at least one bird in a nest. Other paper decorations include miniature flags of blue and yellow, the national colors of Sweden. Brightly painted horses, pigs, goats, and wooden figures as well as straw mobiles and straw centerpieces in the form of crowns are other decorations for this holiday.

Jultomte, an old gnome, is said to give gifts on Christmas Eve. Dipping Day, *doppa i grytan* (dip-in-the-pot), comes on the day before Christmas. The custom recalls a famine winter when the only food available was black bread and broth. Today it is an aid to a mother who is busy baking and cooking for the family gathering. Dipping dark rye bread into the broth

Cookie trees are usually wooden trees made of graduated lengths of dowels, for branches, threaded through a thick dowel trunk-post. Some are made to be flat, others are branched on all sides. A sheaf of wheat is tied to the top of the tree with a ribbon. Cookies are hung on the branches by yarn or fine twine, and small lady apples are pierced on the end of each branch like fruit growing on the tree.

of the simmering sausages assuages appetites so that the family can more patiently wait and look forward to the evening meal. The Christmas Eve family dinner includes *lutfisk* (a white fish), saffron or caraway bread, and pork of some kind (sausages and ham). All are commonly eaten before the family goes to church services. (Most Swedes, however, prefer attending *Julotta* services on Christmas morning.) The holiday ends the day after Holy Kings' Day, January 6th, with the burning of the tree or the replanting of the tree in the yard.

Denmark—Rye or wheat is placed on every gable and gateway and in the barn for the birds to eat. Rooms and windows in Danish homes are decorated with evergreen. Trees are decorated with heart-shaped woven paper baskets or baskets shaped like miniature hats, which are filled with candy. Flat linked paper chains, inverted cones, triple bells, and garlands of tiny flags are other tree decorations made from paper, using red and white, the Danish national colors, with a touch of gold. *Nisse*, a tiny bearded sprite, is said to deliver presents to children. On Christmas Eve children walk around the Christmas tree singing carols. Then they all sit down to hear the Christmas Story told to them by their parents. The legend of the Friendly Beasts (animals able to speak on Christmas Eve) is also often told in Denmark. Goose and *grød* (rice pudding) are traditional foods served at Christmas.

Norway—Norwegians say there should be different kinds of cookies for every day of the Christmas season, fourteen in all! They probably consider Christmas Eve through the Twelfth Night festival the Christmas season (Little Christmas to Big Christmas).

The Christmas tree is usually topped with a replica of the aurora borealis. Paper fishnets, cranberries, and popcorn are other decorations. Sheaves of rye and wheat are tied on posts or high buildings to feed the birds. As in other Scandinavian countries, traditional church services are held on Christmas Day with family dinners often on Christmas Eve.

England—Noted for the first Christmas cards, yule logs, fruitcake, plum pudding, mincemeat pie, mistletoe, holly, and bells. Dickens' *Christmas Carol* is commonly read during the holidays. Christmas trees are planted in tubs indoors to be returned to the garden after the holidays so they can be used again and again. Trees are topped with the British crown or an angel and may be covered with angel hair and artificial snow. Other decorations often include candy and sugarplums tucked into ribbon- and flower-decorated cornucopias or silver-filagreed doily baskets. Swags of red and gold ribbon are also used, and tiny packages wrapped in velvet, ribbons, or even brocade. Father Christmas gives gifts to children on Christmas. These are placed by the fireplace, but gifts to others are given on Boxing Day, December 26th. Bells are traditionally rung from every tower and church belfry at midnight on Christmas Eve, announcing Christ's birth. Carolers gather in town squares under the village trees. Earlier bells toll warning to the Prince of Evil that the Prince of Peace's birth will soon be announced.

Wales—Carol singing is accompanied by the harp. Each town offers prizes for the best carols composed each year. Goose is often eaten. Taffy making is an important custom for the holidays, as well as the preparation and eating of plum pudding.

Ireland—Candles burn brightly in windows to light the way of the Holy Family. All wanderers are given a meal and coins.

Greece—People sing carols while beating drums and striking triangles. Carolers are given figs, cookies, walnuts, almonds, oranges, tangerines, pomegranates, and money. *Christpsomo* (bread of Christ) is a simple cake decorated with nuts and covered with powdered sugar. When the cakes are soaked in diluted honey they are called *melomacaromas*. Christmas is primarily a religious festival with no Christmas trees or presents. Greeks give presents on St. Basil's Day, June 14th, commemorating one of the four fathers of the Orthodox church.

Italy—The crèche (or *presepio*) is the center of the Italian Christmas celebration. *Presepios* include artistically crafted figures of the Holy Family, shepherds, and domestic animals. Gifts at Christmas are for the family and thought to be brought by *Gesù-Bambino*, the Christ child, not by Santa Claus. Christmas letters or notes, written and decorated by little children as a surprise for their parents, include promises to be good, helpful, and obedient or are notes of praise. These are hidden under the father's plate or tucked in his napkin or under the tablecloth, and read ceremoniously by him when the whole family is gathered and the meal is finished. Another form of *presepio*, which is equivalent in popularity to the Christmas tree in America, is the *ceppo*, a pyramid-shaped tripod fitted with three shelves. Candleholders for fat votive candles are fastened to the tripod sections at the corner of each shelf, making nine candleholders. The top shelf of the *ceppo* contains a star or angel, and the middle shelf holds small gifts for the children, secretly placed there by the parents. On the bottom shelf are beautiful ceramic or hand-carved figures of the Holy Family and sometimes a few lambs, a donkey, and a cow. Sometimes fringes or tassels decorate the edges of the shelves. In some families each child has his or her own small *ceppo*. On Christmas Eve the candles are lit beside the *presepio* or on the *ceppo*, and the children dance around it with tambourines while singing. During the holidays children go door to door reciting Christmas selections and receive coins to buy special treats.

Spain—A *nacimiento* or manger scene is found in almost every home (literally, the word means birth). It is often lighted with candles and children dance around it with tambourines while singing. Figures included in the nativity scene are a gray donkey, a Spanish bull, shepherds, and an angel. Some include a home for Herod and others have the Wise Men approaching from the East. Festivities end on the twelfth day of Epiphany, January 6th. On this date the Magi (the Three Kings) are supposed to leave gifts for children on their way to visit the Christ child. Children leave shoes on balconies with *cebada* (barley) for the tired camels. A favorite sweet served is *dulces de almend* (a sweet almond pastry). Elaborate parades are held in big cities on that day, honoring the Three Kings.

Germany—Credited with the first Christmas tree. Crafting wooden toys and giving home-made gifts are still important customs. Such items are often used to decorate Christmas trees. Advent wreaths, candles, calendars, and other traditions are related to the religious celebration of Christmas in Germany. Tree decorations also include *lebkuchens* (layb-KOO-h'kens), gingerbread cookies shaped like men and women, animals, stars, hearts, and other hand-carved ornaments. *Christkind* (Christ child) (sometimes called "Kriss Kringle") is the bearer of gifts—nuts, apples, and sweets—to children. Some homes give each other secret homemade gifts from the Christmas Angel once every week during Advent. *Stollen* (SHTUHL-len), a fruit-studded coffee cake, is often served at Christmas.

Netherlands—St. Nicholas Day is December 6th, when St. Nicholas is said to arrive in this country by ship. He comes wearing a white bishop's robe, a scarlet cassock, a tall red hat called a miter, and white gloves. He then mounts a white horse and delivers gifts to children. On Christmas Eve, inexpensive gifts are given, each one wrapped mysteriously and elaborately. Sometimes they are in a series of boxes, one within the other. Every gift is accompanied by a verse or rhyme.

Czechoslovakia—Christmas celebrations begin on December 6th. The holiday ends with the visit of the *Tri Kralu* (Three Kings). The manger, the *jeslicky*, is always in the church or home. Young pig or goose is often served for dinner. "Good King Wenceslaus" is a traditional carol. Delicately dyed cornhusks are used to create nativity scenes. Sometimes tree ornaments are fashioned from bread dough and painted elaborately. Other ornaments are made from paper, straw, eggshells, and woven baskets. They can appear as little houses, heart-shaped windows, peasant dolls, clowns, birds, violins, or angels. Traditionally, children feed animals a portion of their Christmas dinner so the animals will give more milk, lay more eggs, and so on. It is said *Svatej Nikulas* comes down from heaven on a golden rope and leaves gifts on December 5th. On Christmas Eve, families gather around the trees and fortunes are told. In Czechoslovakia (and Austria) hand-carved, heirloom crèches called Bethlehems or cribs have been placed under Christmas trees for generations. Originally, these were carved during long winter months by miners in their slack season and sometimes had as many as 100 pieces or more. These scenes were characterized by their inclusion of entire miniature villages, reflecting both the misery and joy of the people.

France—*Crèche* is the French word for cradle and has come to be the term used for any manger scene including the figures of Mary, Joseph, and the baby Jesus. It can also include a donkey, cow, sheep, shepherds, and approaching Magi. It was popularized in the thirteenth century by monks who were concerned that people did not realize the true meaning of Christmas because they could not read and church services were held in Latin. Inspired after seeing shepherds sleeping in a nearby field with their sheep they gathered live animals and asked people to take the parts of Mary, Joseph, and the shepherds in a living portrayal of the biblical story. They invited children to come to the manger and sing lullabies to the baby Jesus. The custom became very popular and gypsies are said to have carried it throughout southern Europe. Churches in France often have a living *crèche* with real people and animals. Sometimes smaller *crèches* are decorated with holly, moss, laurel, and stones. *Santons*, or little saints, are made to be added to miniature *crèches* in the home. They are painted terra-cotta figures placed around the manger, representing families and tradespeople of a particular village. Trees are decorated with many different-colored stars. On Christmas Eve, toys, candies, and fruits are added to the tree. Most gifts are not given until St. Nicholas Day, December 6th, and then primarily to children. *Père Noël*, Father Christmas, is tall and slim and leaves gifts on Christmas Eve in shoes that have been placed before the fireplace. Drama and puppet shows are often part of the children's holiday. A special French treat is *bûche de Noël*, traditionally a yule log confection made of crushed chestnuts or cake molded into a log and decorated with plenty of mistletoe and holly. Variations today may resemble a log-type frosted cake like a jelly roll confection, but made with creamy filling and pistachio nuts. Baked ham and roast fowl are often served.

Rumania—On Christmas Eve boys carry long bags in which to pack gifts as they offer greetings to families, singing *colinde* (carols). A *steaua* (a star placed on a pole with little bells under it) announces the approach of the singers. Strings of cranberries, paper chains, cookies, pretzels, and apples are put on the Christmas tree with straw heaped beneath it.

Yugoslavia—Wheat is planted on a plate on December 10th. By Christmas Day, the resulting miniature field of wheat serves as a decoration and sits on the windowsill. Tables are strewn with straw as a reminder of the manger. Roasted suckling pig is eaten. *Kolaches*, ring-shaped coffee cakes filled with prunes or apricots, are made and three candles are placed within the ring. The first candle is lit on Christmas Eve, the second on noon of Christmas Day, and the third on New Year's Day. A *kolache* is not cut until January 6th, but then with an elaborate ceremony. Quite often the children write to Jesus and the angels, who bring gifts on Christmas morning.

Poland—Christmas is often called Little Star (*Gwiazdka*). No food is served on Christmas Eve until the appearance of the first star, in commemoration of the star of Bethlehem, a signal for the beginning of the festivities. Gilded nuts, sweets wrapped in colored paper, frosted cookies, bits of ribbon, straw, beads, eggshells, and even feathers are made into clowns, chickens, fish, pitchers, and stars to give Polish Christmas trees a special look. Straw is placed under the tablecloth because the Christ child was born in a manger. Sometimes villagers dressed as animals go about singing carols and are rewarded with food and drink. Boys, singing carols, often wander from house to house with small boxes of the manger scene or lighted stars mounted on poles.

South Africa—Christmas is a summer holiday; there is no school. Christmas greeting cards often show robins. There are open-air lunches of turkey or roast beef, mincemeat pie, suckling pig, and yellow rice seasoned with turmeric. The Christmas holiday is usually a week-long carnival. People dressed in gay, fancy clothing sing, dance, and parade in the streets, often accompanied by pipe and string bands.

Ghana—Yam and rice festivals and tribal dances are part of the cultural celebrations before Christmas. Christmas is a symbol of hope. Flowers and palm branches are used as decorations during Advent. Groups go together to buy cows, sheep, or goats to slaughter for the Christmas Day feast. Father Christmas does not come from the North Pole but from the jungles. *Egbona hee! Egbona hee! Egogo vo!* means "Christ is coming! Christ is coming! He is near!" It is a common greeting. There are also fireworks. The church has a decorated tree and candles but usually individual homes do not. Foods eaten include rice and *fufu,* which is a dish of yams pounded into a kind of paste, and stew-porridge, with bean or okra soup. Sheep, goats, cows, hogs, and chickens are served as meat for the day. Some people prefer fish. Gifts are given, Christmas cards are sent, and enemies are reconciled. Love and forgiveness are emphasized.

Japan—The Japanese tree is decorated with faintly tinted Christmas cards, finely lined woodcuts, dolls, tangerines, paper fans, wind chimes, and tiny toys and dolls. Green and red paper balls, holly, and red Japanese lanterns are other decorations used. Christmas pageants are performed in Japanese dress. Party boxes or bags of Japanese cakes are shared. It is a church-centered holiday because seldom are all family members Christian. It is often a day of caring for others in hospitals. Japanese usually decorate a "back," which is a backdrop or cloth on which is fastened a scene of the shepherds or Wise Men with the Holy Family. Cardboard banners in assorted colors quote Bible verses about the birth of Jesus. Glass wind chimes are hung on the Christmas tree (usually a pine tree). A flat cake made from pounded, cooked rice called *mochi* is a favorite Christmas treat. It was once offered at sacred shrines but as a symbol of happiness it is now eaten on other festive occasions.

Taiwan—Poinsettias bloom from November to March. Streamers and paper chains are made. Big red and gold ideographs, messages written with Chinese characters, are beautiful and magnificent. Candy like solid marshmallow is made of rice flour and sugar and decorated with Christmas symbols. Greeting cards are handpainted, often on fabric which is then glued to cards. Christmas is not a legal holiday; therefore it is usually celebrated on the weekend nearest December 25th.

China—The Christmas tree is called the "Tree of Life." It is decorated with paper lanterns and foil-covered paper that is made into fans, tassels, and chains. Glass ornaments lacquered with brilliant colors are also used for decorations, as well as Chinese lanterns, holly leaves and berries, tinsel, and mellow lights. Sending postcards or greeting card giving is more common than giving gifts. Gifts are given to Christian relatives, who may get silks, jewels, or more valuable gifts; to Christian friends or distant relatives, who might get food or cut flowers; and to the poor. *Lan Khoong* (nice old father) or *Dun Che Lao Ren* (Christmas old man) are Chinese Santa Claus equivalents. The Christmas meal is often shared with the church family, as usually few members of a family are Christians. On Christmas Eve there is a lantern parade. The biggest feast is saved for New Year's Day, which is traditionally a bigger holiday in China. Many Chinese greeting cards are exquisitely painted fabric pictures. Usually the Holy Family is painted with the features and dress of the Chinese.

Panama—*Nacimientos* (manger scenes) in churches and private homes are very elaborate and artistic. They often include houses, trees, waterfalls, and grass duplicating a small Bethlehem scene. At school Christmas gifts and greeting cards are made by hand. Plays and pageants are given. Children send letters to the baby Jesus. Straw is woven into sunbursts, birds, fish, butterflies, people, and animals and are used as tree decorations. The poinsettia plant, native to that country, is called *Flor de la Noche Buena* (flower of the Holy Night).

Mexico—Houses are decorated with colored paper lanterns, garlands, or wreaths of Spanish moss and evergreen. Pine branches and moss cover the area of the room where the table holding the nativity scene is located. The crèche or *pesebre* has shepherds, sheep, small huts, and trees. The figures of Mary, Joseph, and an empty cradle are placed in the stable. The manger is not filled with the baby Jesus figure until Christmas Eve. Santa Claus and Christmas trees are rare. Children receive toys and gifts on Epiphany. On the night of January 5th they put their shoes on a window ledge before going to sleep. On Christmas Eve they receive candies and trinkets. In many other Spanish-speaking countries of South and Central America or the West Indies, Bethlehem scenes, including the manger and the Holy Family figures, are given similar focus and emphasis for worship during the Christmas holidays. For example, in Cuba such scenes are surrounded with eggs and cookies and decorated with fruit and flowers. In Costa Rica, a special small room known as a *portal* is filled with such a scene and visitors come to view each family's manger. In Honduras, *nacimientos* are set up in almost every home and are made from materials varying from very elaborate to very rustic, depending upon the means or skill of the individual family. Families come to view portals much as they do in Costa Rica. In Ecuador, the brightly painted *pesebre* figures are often made of bread dough and placed in simple cardboard box mangers. In most such countries each child places his most valuable possession near the *nacimiento* during this season and it becomes a part of the scene.

Syria—The Christmas holiday begins with St. Barbara's Day on December 4th and ends with the Epiphany celebration on January 6th. St. Barbara is a saint honored for her goodness, faith, and love. She is a fine example to all Christian children. On the eve of this holiday special sweets are served made from wheat, nuts, honey, and sugar. Wheat is cooked with sugar and flavored with rosewater. These treats are taken to the poor or to the homes of those in whose families someone has died recently. A party is given on St. Barbara's Day that includes dancing, singing, and games. In a special ceremony, girls, one by one, go to an elderly woman who anoints their eyes with a salve. The legend of St. Barbara suggests that her miserly father did not approve of her giving to the poor. When he caught her, he threatened her with a sword and it is said that God turned the sword into a crochet hook. When her father demanded to see the food she had hidden in her lap, it had become roses. Parents hope this holiday and legend will teach children to be unselfish and to care and share with those less fortunate. Children are encouraged to do this by sharing with others. Chicken, oranges, nuts, and pastries are special foods eaten during the Christmas holidays in Syria. Children save money to give to the poor.

On January 1st presents are exchanged. It is a day for circumcision of male children.

Children go door to door to receive Turkish sweetmeats. January 2d is a woman's visiting day. It is said that in southern Syria every tree bends its trunk and inclines its branches on Christmas in homage to the Christ child. The gentle camel of Jesus is said to travel over the desert bringing presents to children. According to legend this camel was the youngest camel of those that traveled with the Wise Men. Children customarily leave water and wheat for the camel on this night. Candles are also placed in windows to guide the camel over the hills.

India—Bundled branches of rice straw are put in water and soaked, then plastered with mud. Green pieces of oleander are stuck in and candles put on the ends of the branches to form a Christmas tree. Paper chains and mica (a thin, sheetlike, fragile mineral) are scattered over the tree for decoration. Candles are put in candleholders in the windows of churches. Little candles are sometimes lighted and placed all along the roof.

Extended Experiences

1. Choose a real tree for your Center and after the holiday plant it in your school yard or in the yard of a teacher or parent as soon as weather permits. (England)
2. Plan a display of Christmas cards from other countries. Check with parents, armed forces personnel, ministers, and students from other countries, all of whom might have such cards. Examine and note how they are alike or different and notice particularly the stamps on the envelopes.
3. Plan to decorate an evergreen tree or potted branch with treats for the birds. Your favorite garden center or tree nursery will be helpful with seed suggestions.

   NOTE: Let children string, hang, or fill containers with popped corn, cracked corn, cubes of cheese, doughnuts (stale or fresh), rolled oats, melon rinds, raisins, cranberries, pork fat, crumbs, cabbage or lettuce leaves, pumpkin or watermelon seeds, grain, peanut butter (if mixed with cornmeal so it will not choke the birds), and uncooked peas. (Scandinavia)

4. Make some Danish rice pudding. (Denmark)
5. Hang colorful Swedish Christmas wall hangings over your walls. (Sweden)
6. Make and decorate some Christmas cookies. Select cookie cutters shaped like shepherds, sheep, Wise Men, donkeys, the baby Jesus and other nativity figures. (Germany, Poland)
7. Invite children to share food, mittens, and other items with those less fortunate than themselves. St. Barbara's Day (December 4th) would be a good date. (Syria, Canada, and Japan)
8. Display a hand-carved crèche borrowed from a friend. (Austria, Czechoslovakia)
9. Buy or borrow a few wooden, straw, or other unbreakable Christmas tree ornaments imported from another country. (Germany, Panama, or Scandinavian countries)
10. Invite a Japanese friend to paper-fold some fish, stars, or butterflies (symbols of Christ) for your tree. (Japan)
11. Display pictures of trees showing decorations of different ethnic groups.
12. View a *nacimiento* (crèche which usually includes a whole village scene), a *pesebre* (manger), or *ceppo* (tree-like group of shelves for gifts and crèche) in the home of a Spanish American, Mexican, or Italian family, during the *novena* of *Las Posadas*. You might try to prepare a *nacimiento* in a corner of your room with the children's help. (Mexico, Spain, Italy, South American countries)
13. Invite a harpist (student) to play Welsh carols or other Christmas music. (Wales)
14. Share simple gifts on the Twelfth Night, January 6th. (See pp. 298–99 for suggestions regarding gifts.) (many countries)
15. Borrow a *pepparkakor* tree from a Swedish friend. *Pepparkakor* is the name for ginger cookies. Hang Christmas treats on the tree and serve snacks one day. (See p. 282 for a description of the tree.) (Sweden)
16. Encourage the children to draw a picture letter for their parents. Older children might choose a piece of paper labeled "I love you because you . . ." or "I promise to help by . . ." to be folded up and sealed inside a decorated envelope to be placed by their father's plate at dinner. (Italy)
17. Make small cone-shaped containers for treats from flocked vinyl wallpaper scraps to decorate a tree. Staple on small sprays of flowers as you attach ribbon or yarn handles. Staple silver or small white plastic doilies into decorative baskets and attach twisted silver cord or braid for handles. (England)

Books and Periodicals

1. Hole, Christina. *Christmas and Its Customs.* New York: M. Barrows, 1958.
2. Ickis, Marguerite. *The Book of Festival Holidays.* New York: Dodd, Mead, 1964.
3. Kainen, Ruth Cole. *America's Christmas Heritage.* New York: Funk & Wagnalls, 1969.
4. Wernecke, Herbert H. *Celebrating Christmas Around the World.* Philadelphia: Westminster Press, 1962.
5. ———. *Christmas Customs Around The World.* Philadelphia: Westminster Press, 1959.
6. Many December issues or special Christmas issues of homemaking magazines.
7. Information Center on Children's Cultures, a service of the United States Committee for UNICEF, 331 East 38th Street, New York 10016.

17 Christmas in America

basic understandings

(concepts children can grasp from this subject)

- December 25th is Christmas Day and is a national holiday in the United States.
- Christmas is the Christian celebration of the birth of Jesus (the Christ Child).
- Christians believe God sent His Son to earth as a special gift of love, and like the Wise Men who brought gifts to Him as a token of their love, esteem, and respect, they give to others in Jesus' name.
- Christmas symbols are evergreen trees, stars, candles, crèches, bells, wreaths, holly, angels, sleighs, Christmas stockings, tree ornaments, reindeer, elves, Santa Claus.
- Colors used at Christmas come from some of the symbols we use, for example, red for holly berries, cranberries, and Santa's suit; green for evergreen trees, wreaths, and holly; and silver or gold for the bright star the Wise Men followed.
- In the United States traditional activities of the Christmas season include: carol singing, special church services, gift making and giving, family gatherings at festive dinners and special parties, sending greetings and cards to friends.
- Many children believe in Santa Claus.
  - a. Stories, songs, and poems suggest that Santa and his wife live at the North Pole and that Santa spends the whole year making and painting toys, which he delivers in a sleigh pulled by eight reindeer, to good boys and girls while they are asleep on Christmas Eve.
  - b. We may see many persons dressed like Santa Claus during the Christmas season.
  - c. Anyone can be a Santa's helper or play Santa to another person if he or she gives a gift secretly (anonymously).

Additional Facts the Teacher Should Know

Christmas is a time set aside by Christians throughout the world to celebrate the birth of their Savior, Jesus Christ. The word "Christmas" is derived from the early English term, *Christes masse*, which means Christ's Mass. No one knows when it was first celebrated except that it began in the early Roman Church.

Many Christmas customs, celebrations, and legends have a pagan beginning. When the pagans of Northern Europe became Christians they made their sacred evergreen trees a part of the Christian festival and decorated them with gilded nuts and candles to represent stars, moon, and sun.

The most popular legend about the first Christmas tree concerns Martin Luther, a German clergyman who found a small fir tree, glistening with snow, in the woods on a starry night. He took it home for his children and placed many lighted candles on it to represent the stars. Holly and mistletoe became symbols of Christmas, also. To children the Christmas tree represents much of the excitement and color of the holiday season. Children may share in its decoration. The family usually gathers around it on Christmas to open their gifts. A Scandinavian legend loved by children is "The Friendly Beasts." According to this story all dumb animals are able to speak at midnight on Christmas Eve.

Because of the length of the season (often Thanksgiving to New Year's), Christmas is more than a single holiday and it becomes a time of great joy and anticipation. Some young children may wish to share an Advent calendar, which covers the Advent season (twenty-two to twenty-eight days before Christmas). See p. 277.

Although Santa Claus is not a part of the religious celebration of Christmas, he is a very real part of the very young child's Christmas and is one of the most beloved figures in the legends of childhood. The modern mythical Santa, it is said, developed from a real person, St. Nicholas, the patron saint of school boys, who, dressed in his bishop's robes, brought gifts to them. Only American children say "Santa Claus." This jolly personage is St. Nicholas to most other children of the Christian world. Clement C. Moore's *A Visit from St. Nicholas* probably gives the best modern-day description of the saint. Reindeer appear in this poem (which is probably from a Scandinavian legend). Children seem to want to believe in Santa Claus even if they are not consciously taught this myth. This belief must be respected even if it is not encouraged. As children mature in their understanding, they begin to realize that Santa Claus is the embodiment of the wonderful spirit of Christmas and of giving gifts anonymously.

Children should be encouraged to realize that Christmas is a time to share and to give gifts, not just an occasion when they receive presents themselves. They can be helped to play Santa Claus by preparing gifts to be given anonymously to others. Surprises and secrets are especially fun (making gifts for parents, friends, or other special persons). The Christmas season is the most exciting time of all for young Christian children. In many homes, children hang up stockings on Christmas Eve that they hope to find filled with treats in the morning. The Christmas story, simply told, is suitable and easily adapted to the very young child's understanding.

CAUTION: When mentioning a specific person, place, or thing for which there are several names, be sure to clarify that they all refer to the same person, place, or thing. Very young children are often confused by duplicate references; for example, most often Jesus is referred to by that name by young children, although Christian adults may also refer to Him as Savior, Lord, Christ, Master, the Good Shepherd, or Jesus Christ.

Methods Most Adaptable for Introducing This Subject to Children

- Children may pin pictures of Christmas activities on bulletin boards, helped by a supervising adult who can discuss the pictures as they are chosen. (Use push-pins, which are much easier for children to manipulate than thumbtacks.)
- Take a picture walk during free playtime. One teacher may accompany several children to look and discuss what they see.
- A child or teacher may share or talk about a Christmas picture, book, or object.
- Children may make decorations for the room or the Christmas tree.
- Take a shopping trip to buy a tree for the room or to see a decorated store window.

Vocabulary

Christmas	inn	bells	candy cane
manger	cattle	merry	elf (elves)
crèche	cow	wreath	wrap
Christ Child	donkey	holly	Christmas tree
Baby Jesus	sheep	night	poinsettia
Mary	dove	glitter	mistletoe
Joseph	star	pine cone	Christmas Eve
shepherd	angel	evergreen	Santa Claus
Wise Men	bell	snow	St. Nicholas
(Three Kings)	carol	ornament	reindeer
Bethlehem	sing	lights	decorations
gift	sleigh	twinkle	stocking
stable	mantel	tinsel	chimney
stall	jingle	candle	present

learning centers

Discovery Center

1. Collect different species of evergreen branches and pine cones. Feel and smell. Identify and compare shape, size, color. Count. Use a magnifying glass. Note likenesses and differences—find two that are alike.
2. Remind parents that the winter sky has particularly brilliant stars that will stimulate a child's sense of wonder.
3. Christmas ornaments and wrappings have delightful sensory appeal. Discuss color, shape, size, texture.
4. Cookies may be mixed, cut with cutters, baked, frosted, and decorated. Choices may depend upon the maturity of the group or the time available.

Dramatic Play Centers

Home-Living Center

1. If children wish to dress up as Mary or Joseph, have available loose-fitting, long kimono-type robes (striped or plain), wide sashes, head scarves, and crosswise strips of nylon stocking for securing head pieces. Show them how babies were wrapped in a long cloth (swaddling clothes) when Jesus was a baby.
2. Glittered cardboard crowns might be set out for use in portraying the Three Kings.
3. A three-way play screen might be used as a manger backdrop. Stuffed toy animals could be set out to use in a manger. A long rectangular box could be filled with hay (or excelsior).
4. Add a cradle, crib, and rattles for use with dolls.
5. Children may need or request doctor or nurse dramatic play props if they are familiar with babies being born in hospitals.
6. See Art Center, No. 13, regarding a small Christmas tree for children to use in the Dramatic Play Center.

Block-Building Center

1. Children may need or request large cardboard brick blocks to make chimneys and fireplaces.
2. A large painted packing box or hollow blocks will make a fine stable. A box of hay or straw that is large enough to hold a doll or crèche figures will make a manger bed.

   CAUTION: If you have children who are allergic to hay, substitute excelsior or another similar material.

3. Provide wooden, cardboard, or unbreakable plastic crèche figures large and sturdy enough to withstand handling by the children. Very young children need figures of only Mary, Joseph, and the baby.
4. A child-size cradle 16 inches by 29 inches is available from Community Playthings or Constructive Playthings.
5. A child-size bed 15 inches by 29 inches is available from Community Playthings or Constructive Playthings.

Other Dramatic Play Centers

1. Santa: a rocking boat is an excellent prop for a sleigh. Hollow blocks can be made into stalls for the reindeer. Children can pretend to be reindeer or use stick horses as props. Provide children with a burlap sack, to be filled with small toys for their sleigh. Add sleigh bells and a red stocking cap for anyone wishing to play Santa.
2. Jack-in-the-Box: children hide in a large cardboard box one at a time and pop out while teacher and remaining group recite this poem.

   > Down in the box there is a little man
   > Who waits and waits as quiet as he can
   > Until he opens the lid of his box
   > A-n-n-n-n-nd (PAUSE) . . . UP HE POPS!

   NOTE: A box with a top that has been cut on three sides and hinged on the fourth is the best. Box may be painted or decorated.

Learning, Language, and Readiness Materials Center

Commercially made games and materials for use at a table or on a mat:

(See Basic Resources, p. 79, for manufacturers' addresses.)

1. Little Jack Horner: puzzle, 9 pcs. (Sifo)
2. Favorite Toys: puzzle, 5 pcs. (Sifo)
3. Judy See-Quees: Twelve Days of Christmas, 12 pcs.
4. Judy Puzzles: Manger Scene, 12 pcs.; Shepherds See the Angels, 22 pcs.; Wise Men Follow the Star, 16 pcs.
5. Nativity and Santa's Toy Shop: two different flannelboard aids sets (Trend Enterprises)
6. Bible Set: seven wooden crèche figures to use with unit blocks (Community Playthings)
7. Unbreakable plastic and cardboard crèche figures, Christmas story books, puzzles, and picture sets are available through denominational religious bookstores

Teacher-made games and materials for use at a table or on a mat:

NOTE: For detailed description of Games, see pp. 50–59.

1. Name It or Scramble: use Christmas ornaments or models of symbols such as tree, Santa, Christmas stocking, crèche
2. Look and See: use Christmas ornaments or symbols
3. Ponder Posters: use trees, Christmas balls, or stars with one or more different from the others in color and position (See illustration below.)

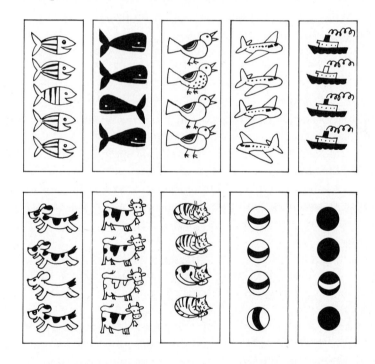

4. Alike, Different, and the Same: children can choose from felt shapes as follows: alike: all trees; different: trees of different sizes and shapes; or same: two trees exactly alike
5. Flannelboard sequence story: *Jesus Is Born*. Cincinnati, Ohio: Standard Publishing, 1958. Method: cut the needed figures from pictures that have been mounted on light-weight cardboard. Paste a piece of sandpaper or flannel on the back of each piece of cardboard. Children place the figures on the flannelboard while the teacher tells or reads the story (Children may use alone.)

6. Christmas Tree: make a large two-dimensional felt Christmas tree about one foot high. Use felt stars, balls, and bells to decorate. Yarn or trimming braid may be used for garlands. Children may decorate tree as many times and in as many ways as they wish. The felt tree can be placed on a flannelboard or laid in a flat box and the trimmings placed in the lid (See p. 302 for a song that may be used with this tree.)

7. Match-Them and Counting: count or match one, two, three, four trees, bells, pine cones, sprays of evergreens, pictures or models of cars, dolls, or toys

8. Grouping and Sorting by Association: mount Christmas stickers on small squares or circles of cardboard. Sort into a partitioned box or into separate labeled boxes

9. See also group games for Christmas, p. 305, for other teacher-made games two or three children can play with an adult at a table or on a mat

Art Center

* 1. Put out red and green easel paint *only*, to emphasize the basic Christmas colors. Another day put out white, blue, yellow . . . or blue-green, olive, red-violet for variation.

* 2. Any creative art project may be made especially Christmas-like by using red and green in such media as blotto-painting, sponge-painting, and string-painting, or by sprinkling glitter from small shakers on the finished product.

* 3. Invite children to experiment with long sprigs of evergreen as paintbrushes. Let them use a dark-colored paint on white paper or white paint on dark-colored paper. Makes a delicate painting.

* 4. Fingerpaint with red or green on large sheets of paper. When these are dry, children can, if they wish, cut Christmas designs such as big bells and trees from their fingerpaint paper as a second experience. Fingerpaintings may also be matted with a tree, bell, or Christmas tree ball shaped opening in the mat.

** 5. Spatterpaint Christmas shapes: use white paint on red or green paper or vice versa. Child may select another color.

** 6. Decorate windows: use Christmas stencils, a sponge, and Glass Wax. Invite some children to help you.

** 7. Styrofoam sculpture: invite children to use small pieces of styrofoam, precut by teacher from scraps, with colored pipecleaners or lengths of scrap telephone wire to make interesting decorations to hang on the tree or set in the room or on the tables at snacktime.

** 8. Set out wooden toothpicks with styrofoam balls. Children may wish to make 3-D stars. Color the toothpicks with food coloring, a box at a time. This is much cheaper than purchasing colored toothpicks.

*** 9. If the children are cutting out Christmas trees at a cut-and-paste table, set out paper punches, pencils, cuticle sticks, or meat skewers for anyone who may wish to punch holes in their trees. Have available variegated tissue and shiny metal-colored paper at the table. Let children discover what happens when the punched-out trees are placed over other paper. It appears as though the tree has Christmas lights in it, or is lighted with colored lights. Children may wish to paste the colored paper to the backs of their trees.

** 10. If folded blank cards are available with a collage tray of various scrap materials for additives, children will enjoy designing their own cards or tree decorations.

** 11. Let children decorate green triangles or irregular Christmas tree shapes with collage trimmings such as lace, yarn, ribbon, felt scraps, buttons. Bits of colored foil snipped by children can also be added. **Variations:** (a.) Yesterday's fingerpaintings can be cut into tree forms and decorated as described above. (b.) An egg carton lid can be used as a collage base. If children brush thinned white glue over its entire inside surface, they can then press down collage items selected to form their shadow-box picture. Dry and hang.

* 12. Children may paint their own wrapping paper by using printing tools such as sponge or wood or cork shapes precut by the teacher into Christmas designs. Older children may print on tissue paper if stamping pads are used. Usually newsprint or a plain paper shopping bag works best. Use paint sparingly in shallow trays or make pad of paint-soaked paper towels. **Variation:** A child-sized rolling pin can be covered with flocked vinyl wallpaper or a piece of textured upholstery. Secure with rubber bands. When rolled over a paint-soaked pad it can be used like a brayer to create designed wrapping paper. Other such brayer-type rollers which can be used similarly are hair rollers or spool brayers (see illustration, p. 30). The spool brayer can be used to create striped or plaid wrapping paper, greeting cards, or gift tags. Offer the children a variety of quality paper scraps from a print shop.

* 13. Provide a small artificial tree and appropriate-sized durable decorations to be used by one or two children at a time. Allow them to decorate, remove, and redecorate when and as they wish.

> **NOTE:** Move tree when children need it to expand their dramatic play, such as into Home-Living Center, or into the Block-Building Center when builders have completed a fireplace, a room, or a home and feel they need a tree to complete their furnishings.

Other Experiences in This Center Using Art Media

Tree Decorations

** 1. Gallon milk bottle lids and other small plastic lids can be used as a base on which to glue or stick small Christmas stickers. Pictures cut from old greeting cards can also be used. Punch a hole for a ribbon or yarn hanger. Invite children to lick and stick.

*** 2. Tree garlands can be made from lengths of yarn with Christmas seals stuck back to back at intervals enclosing the yarn.

*** 3. Make available compartment sections of egg cartons for the children. These individual, bell-like sections may be covered with a circle of aluminum foil, painted, or decorated with magic markers. Real jingle bells, available from variety stores, can be threaded on a pipecleaner through the bell-like sections. Several may be attached to a ribbon or a piece of yarn to hang on the tree.

* 4. Styrofoam meat trays may be cut in Christmas shapes by children (drawing around a cookie cutter or designing their own shape). A hole can be punched in the top through which a loop of yarn can be threaded to serve as a hanger to hold the ornament on the tree. Children may decorate these with glitter, paint them with felt-tip pens, or color with crayons. Adhesives do not stick well to this plastic.

** 5. Pipecleaners and colored plastic telephone wire can be twisted into wire sculptures to make candy cane ornaments and other tree ornaments.

** 6. Let children cut out decorations from playdough with cookie cutters, or older children might mold some. When dry, these can be painted with tempera and hung on the tree.

** 7. Invite children to roll, tear, cut, and crumple aluminum foil into various free-form sculptures. Set out some dowel sticks or pencils. (If a strip of foil is coil-wrapped around a pencil and slightly crumpled, it looks like an icicle.)

*** 8. Color glue by adding powder paint to white glue. Let children pour the glue into any mold they choose which has been lined with a piece of plastic wrap. Allow to dry for four days. Peel off paper. These ornaments can be hung by yarn if the teacher drills a hole in each.

*** 9. Melt plastic berry boxes by laying them upside down on a sheet of foil in a covered electric skillet. Set temperature control at 250°F. If you have a skillet with a glass lid, it is fun for the children to watch them melt. If suspended by a loop of yarn, these make interesting, lacy free-form decorations for tree or window.

CAUTION: Supervise closely. Only the teacher should raise the lid.

** 10. Children will enjoy selecting pieces of styrofoam packing to string on yarn or string for frosty garlands. Threaded bobby pins make good needles. Variation: They may wish to punch holes in bits of colored construction paper or use precut lengths of straw to alternate with the styrofoam and add color to their garlands.

*** 11. Cranberries and Cheerios can be strung to hang on trees for feeding the birds. Popcorn is frustrating for young children to string because the kernels break. Few children like raw cranberries.

CAUTION: Use blunt yarn needles. Allow adequate space and permit only one or two children to sew at a time.

*** 12. Brightly colored flocked vinyl wallpaper can be cut into shapes to be hung on a Christmas tree for decorations. To make them sturdy mount on heavy cardboard.

Gift Ideas

* 1. Children can make handprints on art paper. (A better-quality paper is more suitable for framing.) If a kiln is available, make handprints from ceramic clay. Before firing, punch one or two holes at the top through which yarn or bright ribbon can be threaded later and tied in a bow for hanging.

** 2. Show children how they can place a photo of themselves face-down in a glass caster and cover it with a round piece of cardboard. Children can then fill the caster cup with salt dough or plaster of Paris. When the dough is dry, paste or glue felt over the dough, invert with the felt side down, and use as a paperweight.

*** 3. Another paperweight can be made by filling the bottom of a milk carton ¾" deep with plaster of paris or salt dough. Children may choose different kinds of seed pods, to be pushed into the plaster as close together as possible. Gum tree seeds, pine cones, arborvitae cones, and acorns work well. When plaster is dry, tear carton to remove, spray with clear plastic or antique gold, and glue felt to the bottom.

NOTE: Felt helps protect wood surfaces against scratches.

*** 4. A simple candleholder can be molded by children using a 3" ball of sawdust dough or salt dough. (See recipes, p. 27.) Children need to flatten the bottom and to use a real candle to make the candle hole the size they wish. Allow to dry, paint white or another color, sprinkle with glitter.

CAUTION: Be sure candle hole will hold candle straight.

** 5. Pinecones are easily decorated by young children. Brush tip of each scale with glue and then sprinkle with glitter and sequins. The teacher may spray each cone with green, silver, or gold paint before the children decorate it, which will make a more ornate product or will give children greater choice in selecting the color, size, and shape of their cone tree.

** 6. Centerpieces: Children will enjoy creating their own holiday centerpieces to share with their families if given a variety of materials, such as pine cones, to be painted, glittered, or decorated. Children can use sequins, evergreen twigs or small branches, holly, discarded Christmas wrapping bows and bits of ribbon, doilies, and a container. Cardboard fruit cartons or berry boxes can be wrapped or laced with strips of yarn or ribbon. Crumpled aluminum foil or sturdy wrapping paper can also be used to cover the container.

*** 7. An abstract or "accidental" design can be made by children either by dripping or squirting streams of thinned acrylic paint (polyresin base) on a solid-colored piece of upholstery fabric, or by placing shavings from a batik crayon on the same kind of fabric and pressing with a warm iron under waxed paper. If color combinations are planned by the teacher, and not too many colors are used, the result cannot fail and may be beautiful enough to be permanently stretched over a wood frame.

Book Center

*** Aichinger, Helga. *The Shepherd.* New York: Thomas Y. Crowell, 1967.
*** Barry, Robert. *Mr. Willoughby's Christmas Tree.* New York: McGraw-Hill, 1963.
*** Bianco, Pamela. *The Doll in the Window.* New York: Henry Z. Walck, 1953.
*** Brown, Margaret Wise. *A Pussy Cat's Christmas.* New York: Thomas Y. Crowell, 1949.
** ———. *On Christmas Eve.* Reading, Mass.: Addison-Wesley, 1965.
*** Carlson, Bernice. *Listen! and Help Tell the Story.* Nashville, Tenn.: Abingdon Press, 1965, pp. 72–73, 130, 167.
*** De Brunhoff, Jean. *Babar and Father Christmas.* New York: Random House, 1946.
*** Duvoisin, Roger. *One Thousand Christmas Beards.* New York: Alfred A. Knopf, 1955.
** ———. *Petunia's Christmas.* New York: Alfred A. Knopf, 1952.
** ———. *The Christmas Whale.* New York: Alfred A. Knopf, 1945.
*** Ets, Marie Hall. *Nine Days to Christmas.* New York: Viking Press, 1959 (read for *Las Posadas*).
** Freeman, Don. *Corduroy.* New York: Viking Press, 1958 (paper, 1970; film, record, cassette).
** Jackson, Kathryn. *The Animals' Merry Christmas.* New York: Western Publishing, 1972.
** ———. *The Story of Christmas with Its Own Advent Calendar.* New York: Western Publishing, 1973.
*** Joslin, Sysyle. *Baby Elephant and the Secret Wishes.* New York: Harcourt Brace Jovanovich, 1962.
*** Karasz, Ilonka. *The Twelve Days of Christmas.* New York: Harper & Row, 1949.
*** Keats, Ezra Jack. *The Little Drummer Boy.* New York: Macmillan, 1968 (paper, 1972).
*** Kroeber, Theodora. *A Green Christmas.* Berkeley, Calif.: Parnassus Press, 1967.
* Lenski, Lois. *I Like Winter.* New York: Oxford University Press, 1950.
*** Lindgren, Astrid. *Christmas in the Stable.* New York: Coward-McCann & Geoghegan, 1962.
** Lipkind, William and Nicholas Mordvinoff. *Christmas Bunny.* New York: Harcourt Brace Jovanovich, 1953.
** Lloyd, Mary Edna. *Jesus, the Little New Baby.* Nashville, Tenn.: Abingdon Press, 1951.

*** Miller, Edna. *Mousekin's Christmas Eve*. Englewood Cliffs, N.J.: Prentice-Hall, 1965 (paper).

** Moore, Clement C. *The Night Before Christmas*. New York: Random House, 1961 (paper, 1970).

** Piper, Watty. *The Little Engine That Could*. New York: Platt & Munk, 1930.

** Politi, Leo. *Pedro, the Angel of Olvera Street*. New York: Scribner's 1972.

** ———. *Rosa*. New York: Scribner's, 1964 (also in Spanish).

** ———. *The Nicest Gift*. New York: Scribner's, 1964.

**** Rockwell, Anne. *Befana*. New York: Atheneum, 1974 (read-tell).

*** Von Jucken, Aurel. *The Holy Night*. New York: Atheneum, 1968.

* Woodard, Carol. *The Very Special Baby*. Philadelphia, Pa.: Fortress Press, 1968.

planning for grouptime

NOTE: All music, fingerplays, poems, stories, and games listed here may be used at other times during the session as appropriate. See Core Library, Basic Resources, p. 76, for publishers and addresses. Addresses for sources of records will be found on p. 81. In parodies, hyphenated words match music notes of the song used.

Music

Songs

FROM *Songs for the Nursery School*, MacCarteney
*** "The Friendly Beasts," p. 67
*** "O Christmas Tree," p. 69
*** "Patapan," p. 70
** "Now Sing We Merrily," p. 72
*** "Silent Night," p. 72

FROM *Songs for Early Childhood*, Westminster Press
*** "Away in a Manger," p. 59
*** "Softly, Tread Softly," p. 60
* "Little Baby Jesus," p. 61
** "Shepherds Leave the Hillside," p. 62
* "O Hear the Bells That Ring and Ring," p. 63
*** "O Come Little Children," p. 64
* "We Wish You a Merry Christmas," p. 76

FROM *Wake Up and Sing*, Landeck and Crook
* "Almost Day," p. 41
** "Mama Bake the Johnny Cake, Christmas Comin'," p. 42

FROM *Music Activities for Retarded Children*, Ginglend and Stiles
** "Mary Had a Baby," p. 65
** "Santa Claus Is Coming," p. 75

FROM *Music Resource Book*, Lutheran Church Press
*** "I Will Play," p. 26 (Children use various rhythm instruments to this French folk tune.)
** "O Christmas Tree," p. 76
* "We Wish You a Merry Christmas," p. 77

FROM a book of traditional songs or sheet music in your own collection
** "Twinkle, Twinkle, Little Star"
** "Jingle Bells"
*** "Up on the House Top"
*** "Here Comes Santa Claus"
*** "Santa Claus Is Coming to Town"
*** "Rudolph, The Red-Nosed Reindeer"
* "Merry Christmas to You" (tune: "Happy Birthday to You")

* * * THE DEAR LITTLE JESUS
(same tune as "O Come Little Children," *Songs for Early Childhood*, p. 64)

The dear little Jesus once lay in the hay.
He slept and He smiled and He grew day by day,
Until He could run and could play and could be
A help to His mother like you and like me.

DOWN THE CHIMNEY SANTA CAME (a parody)
(tune: "London Bridge")

Verse 1: Guess whose beard is long and white? long and white? long and white?
Guess whose beard is long and white? Dear old San-ta!
Verse 2: Guess whose suit is red and white? . . . Dear old San-ta!
Verse 3: Guess who comes on Christ-mas Eve? . . . Dear old San-ta!
Verse 4: Down the chim-ney, San-ta came, . . . Dear old San-ta!
Verse 5: With a doll that says "Ma-ma," . . . Dear old San-ta!
Verse 6: With a train that goes "Choo-choo," . . . Dear old San-ta!
Verse 7: With a truck that goes "Beep-beep," . . . Dear old San-ta!

NOTE: Repeat in each verse, as in verse 1. Encourage the children to help you think of other verses to fit the tune.

Records

"Christmas Rhythms" (Phoebe James, 78 RPM)
"Traditional Christmas Songs," *December Holidays* (Bowmar, 33⅓ RPM)
"Twelve Days of Christmas" (YPR, 78 RPM)
"We Wish You A Merry Christmas" (YPR, 78 RPM)
"Jingle Bells" (YPR, 78 RPM)
"Pussycat's Christmas" (YPR, 78 RPM)

Christmas collections are available containing traditional Christmas songs, such as:

"Jingle Bells"
"Santa Claus Is Coming to Town"
"Up On the House Top"
"Here Comes Santa Claus"
"Rudolph, The Red-Nosed Reindeer"
"Away in a Manger"
"'Twas the Night Before Christmas"

Rhythms and Singing Games

Make a felt cutout of a Christmas tree about nine inches wide by twelve inches high and tack it to a bulletin board or a heavy piece of cardboard. Also using felt, make the decorations that are mentioned in capital letters in the parody below. While the teacher and children sing the song, one or more children may add the decorations to the tree.

HERE'S OUR LITTLE PINE TREE (a parody)
   (tune: "I'm a Little Teapot")
   Adaptation by Darlene Hamilton

Here's our lit-tle pine TREE
   tall and straight.
Let's find the things
   so we can dec-o-rate
First we want to put
   a STAR on top!
Then we must be care-ful
   the BALLS don't pop
Hang on all the TIN-SEL
   shin-y and bright
Put on the CANES
   and hook them just right
Fin-ally put some PRES-ENTS
   for you and for me
And we'll be read-y
   with our CHRIST-MAS TREE!

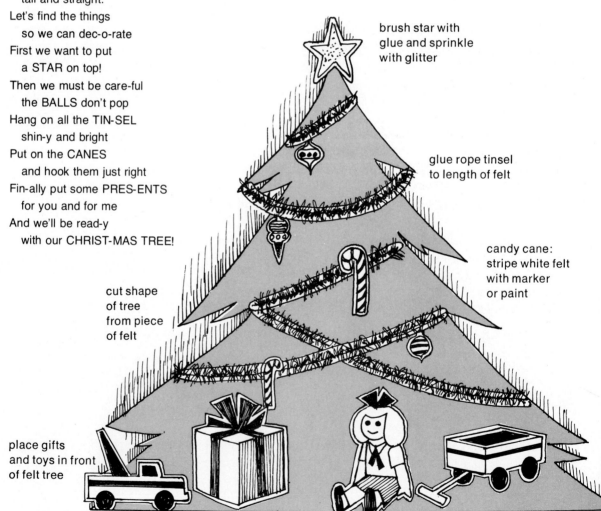

brush star with glue and sprinkle with glitter

glue rope tinsel to length of felt

candy cane: stripe white felt with marker or paint

cut shape of tree from piece of felt

place gifts and toys in front of felt tree

FROM *Songs for the Nursery School*, MacCarteney

"High Stepping Reindeer," adaptation of "High Stepping Horses," p. 38

"Little Brown Reindeer," adaptation of "Gray Ponies," p. 41

"O Christmas Tree," p. 69. Children join hands and dance around a tree.

"March of the Toys," Victor Herbert. Children may pretend they are toys in a toy shop who wake and dance when the toymaker goes to sleep. When he awakens, they freeze into immobility. Children can decide which toy they would like to imitate, and move in that manner. This will probably take some discussion beforehand.

"Jingle Bells" or "Sleigh Ride." Children pretend they are reindeer. Use sleigh bells or wrist bells.

NOTE: See also Large Muscle Activities in this guide for other musical participation games.

Fingerplays and Poems

FROM *Rhymes for Fingers and Flannelboards,* Scott and Thompson

"Dreams," p. 64

"The Angel on My Christmas Tree," p. 65

"Five Bright Stars," p. 65

"The Toy Shop," p. 66

"Eight Tiny Reindeer," p. 68

"Santa's Reindeer," p. 69

"Christmas Presents," p. 69

"Little Jack Horner," p. 106

FROM *Let's Do Fingerplays,* Grayson

"Christmas Is A-Coming," p. 92

"Santa Claus," p. 92

"Christmas Bells," p. 92

"Christmas Tree," p. 93

"Here Is the Chimney," p. 94

CHRISTMAS IS HERE

Here is the wreath that hangs on the door,   (MAKE A CIRCLE WITH ARMS OVER HEAD)

Here is the fir tree that stands on the floor,   (MAKE A TRIANGLE WITH THUMBS AND FOREFINGERS)

Here is the book from which carols are sung,   (PALMS TOUCHING AND FACING UPWARD LIKE BOOK PAGES)

Here is the mantel from which stockings are hung.   (PLACE ONE BENT ARM OVER THE OTHER BENT ARM IN FRONT OF BODY. DROP ONE ARM LIKE A HANGING STOCKING)

Here is the chimney that Santa comes down.   (MAKE AN UPRIGHT RECTANGLE WITH THUMBS AS THE BASE AND FINGERS FOR THE SIDES)

Here is the snow that covers the town,   (FINGERS FLUTTER DOWN)

Here is a box in which is hid   (CLOSE RIGHT FIST WITH THUMB INSIDE AND PLACE LEFT HAND ON TOP)

A Jack that pops up, when you open the lid.   (LIFT LEFT HAND UP AND POP OUT THUMB)

Here's the children's Christmas tree   (MAKE TRIANGLE WITH THUMBS FOR THE BASE AND THE FINGERS FORMING THE PEAK)
Standing straight and tall.
Here's the pot to put it in   (CUP HANDS TOGETHER)
So it will not fall.

Here are two balls bright and gay .   (MAKE CIRCLES WITH THUMB AND INDEX FINGER OF EACH HAND)
One ball—two balls—see?   (HOLD UP TO SEE)
And two tall candles red!   (HOLD INDEX FINGERS UP STRAIGHT FOR CANDLES)
To trim our Christmas tree.   (REPEAT TRIANGLE FOR TREE)

Stories

(To read, read-tell, or tell. See Book Center for complete list.)

** *Jesus, the New Little Baby,* Lloyd
*** *Mousekin's Christmas Eve,* Miller
** *The Night Before Christmas,* Moore
* *The Very Special Baby,* Woodard
*** *Mr. Willoughby's Christmas Tree,* Barry

** *The Nicest Gift,* Politi
*** *One Thousand Christmas Beards,* Duvoisin
** *Petunia's Christmas,* Duvoisin
*** *Christmas in the Stable,* Lindgren

A Christmas Story to Tell to Your Group

This is the story of the first Christmas long, long ago.

Once there was a woman and her name was Mary. She was going on a long journey and she rode on a donkey.

There was a man and his name was Joseph. He was going on the long journey with Mary and he walked beside the donkey.

The name of the town that Mary and Joseph were going to was Bethlehem. It was a town in Judaea (Palestine, now in Israel).

The donkey's hoofs went pat, pat, pat, pat, pat on the sandy road; and Joseph's feet went thump, thump, thump, thump on the sandy road.   (PAT HANDS ON FLOOR FOR HOOF BEATS AND FOOTSTEPS)

On and on they went until they came to Bethlehem. They stopped at a great big house and went knock, knock, knock.   (KNOCK ON FLOOR WITH KNUCKLES)   "Please may we come and stay tonight?" asked Joseph.

A woman opened the door   (MOTION FOR OPENING DOOR)   and said, "No, we don't have room for you."   (SHAKE HEAD NO)   "But you can make a bed in the stable if you wish!"

Then they went to a stable where the cattle stayed. They opened the door and looked in. The cattle said, "Moo, moo, moo,"   (IMITATE MOOING)   as if to say "Here is room for you." So Mary and Joseph went into the stable. They found some clean, sweet hay. They made it smooth   (SMOOTHING MOTIONS WITH HANDS)   and laid down on it to rest.   (PILLOW HANDS UNDER HEAD AND CLOSE EYES)   They were very, very tired.

That very night God sent the wonderful baby Jesus to live with them. Mary dressed him and laid him on the hay. She said, "My little baby, I will call you Jesus." Then she sang this little song to him: "Sleep, my little Jesus. Sleep, my baby, sleep," and the baby went fast asleep.   (ROCK IMAGINARY BABY IN ARMS)

Games

(See Games, pp. 50–59, and Teacher-Made Games in this guide for directions.)

1. Guess What? (Christmas riddles): teacher describes a Christmas symbol or a toy and the children guess; for instance, "I'm brown and white, have four legs and antlers, and pull Santa's sleigh. Who am I?"
2. Merry Christmas (variation of Listening): children are seated in semicircle. Teacher chooses one child to hide eyes by putting his or her head in teacher's lap (otherwise they can't resist peeking). Teacher points to one of the children in the semicircle, who says, "Merry Christmas to you!" or "Hi Santa!" Child who just said "Merry Christmas" then hides his or her eyes. Child must guess voice. This game requires that the children know each other well.
3. Santa and His Reindeer (or Elves): children are seated in semicircle. Teacher chooses one child to be Santa. He or she puts his head in teacher's lap. Teacher points to one of the children (reindeer or elf). This child hides. Santa is then told to look at the remaining reindeer or elves to see if he can tell who is missing. The hidden reindeer or elf then becomes the new Santa.
4. Who Am I?: describe Mary, Joseph, Jesus, or the animals included in a crèche, such as a donkey, a lamb, or a cow.

Routine Times

1. Use the fingerplays while the children are coming to the table for snacktime. Milk may be colored red or green with food coloring. (Let the children drop in the color themselves.) They may eat the cookies that they have baked or frosted.
2. When washing hands, let children make thick soap suds and make lovely Santa beards! Mirrors add to the fun if you do not normally have them on the wall by the wash basins.
3. Christmas carols may be played softly on the piano or record player during rest time.
4. When walking or busing, look for nativity scenes, Santa, and Christmas decorations.

Large Muscle Activities

(Traditional tunes are used in games 1 to 4 below. All pages noted are from the *Music Resource Book*, Lutheran Church Press.)

1. Did You Ever See a Toy? adaptation of "Did You Ever See a Lassie?" p. 86. Children watch child in the circle who acts out the motions of any toy (truck, doll, or racing car), and then they try to guess the name of the toy.
2. Here We Go Round the Christmas Tree: adaptation of "Here We Go Round the Mulberry Bush," p. 92. "This is the way to chop the tree, carry it home, stand it up, put on the lights."
3. See the Puppets, p. 45: pretend to be puppets; move with words describing an action.
4. Santa's Pack: let children all choose a toy to "be" and carry. Child who plays Santa calls out name of toy to be added to his pack in his invisible sleigh. Child joins Santa in a follow-the-leader trip around the room, leaving toys where they belong on shelves. Adapt to suit your group and space. **Variation:** Can also be played like Fruit Basket Upset with record or piano music to signal change (delivery) of toys. Santa may choose children to join him by touching them or motioning when music stops. All go to place and new Santa can be chosen.

Extended Experiences

1. Organ recital: if you are fortunate enough to know an organist, perhaps he or she will allow the children to watch and listen for a few minutes while he or she practices Christmas music at a nearby church.

2. Visit a Santa: visit a department store to see a Santa, or interesting store windows planned especially for children. Plan smaller groups for such an excursion. Extra adults will be necessary to help supervise the group. **Variation:** Have a Santa visit your group. Plan for him or her to share or bring a treat. (You may provide it!)

3. Visit a church that has a Chrismon tree and Advent wreath (many Lutheran churches do). Ask the pastor, assistant pastor, or Director of Christian Education to show these to the children.

   NOTE: See p. 278 for a description of a Chrismon tree.

   An Advent wreath is made with four purple candles (red may be substituted if purple not available) for the four Sundays preceding Christmas in the Advent season of the church year. Sometimes there is a fifth, larger candle, usually white, to burn on Christmas. Only one candle is burned the first Sunday, two the second, and so on.

4. Have a Christmas party: serve homemade cookies and a red or green powdered drink mix the children have prepared. Use decorated napkins. Gifts for parents and gift wrap made and designed by the children as well as room and tree decorations will add to your party.

Guidelines

1. Make certain every child can have one parent, family member, or friend attend the party.

2. If you plan to let parents observe children in a grouptime experience, select things to do that children enjoy: play games, sing songs, and tell or read a story just as you usually do. Make certain there is no focus on any one child! Keep it simple and unrehearsed, and follow the usual routine if possible.

3. Have parents seated behind the children or on the side of the room so children will be less aware they are being observed. (If group is small let parents and children sit together and both participate.)

4. There should be no pressure on performance.

5. Group should be only those children who are normally in the room together.

6. Hold party during regular school hours.

7. As you serve refreshments or just before, let children deliver gift packages to parents or friends attending. **Variation:** (a.) You may plan a similar parents' party for another time of the year, when the calendar may not be so filled with events, when the weather may be better, and when more parents and children can attend. In the fall, children beginning school may be coming down with the usual childhood communicable diseases, measles, chickenpox, mumps. Two or three other holidays (Valentine's Day and Mother's or Father's Day) offer similar opportunities for decorations (hearts and flowers), gifts, gift wrap, and greeting cards, as well as other decorations. (b.) You may wish to invite parents, family members, or friends for only one small group of your whole class at a time. Invite these different small groups of parents over a series of succeeding days.

teacher resources

Books and Periodicals

1. Sechrist, Elizabeth H. *It's Time for Christmas*. Philadelphia, Pa.: Macrae Smith, 1959.
2. Wilson, Dorothy. *The First Book of Christmas Joy*. Illus. by Mary Ronin. New York: Franklin Watts, 1961.

Pictures and Displays

(See p. 79 for addresses of firms listed.)

1. Birth and Boyhood of Jesus: set of twelve pictures, Richard and Frances Hook (David C. Cook)
2. Holiday Theme: teaching pictures set (David C. Cook)
3. Christmas decorative cut-outs for bulletin boards (Eureka-Carlisle)
4. Christmas cut-outs (Eureka-Carlisle)
5. Crèches: manger scene standups, about 14″ high (Standard Publishing Co.)
6. Set up a Christmas tree for children to decorate with items they have made, adding tinsel last.
7. Red and green crepe paper and evergreen branches can be placed around the room for added decoration.
8. Set up a durably made (wooden or unbreakable plastic) manger scene or crèche on a table or bookshelf.
9. Holiday Poster Set (Instructo)
10. Picture sets including the birth of Jesus, the shepherds, and the Wise Men, religious puzzles, and small cardboard, wooden, or unbreakable crèche figures are all available from denominational religious bookstores.

Community Resources

1. Department stores with special windows for young children
2. Religious bookstore or any denominational publishing house
3. Nearby Christian churches: contact the minister, pastor, vicar, rector, or director of Christian education. All of them can tell you about special displays, services, and other plans which might be of interest to young children.

PART FOUR

seasons

18 Winter

basic understandings

(concepts children can grasp from this subject)

Winter is a season that comes after fall and before spring. There are many changes in nature in winter:

Earth Changes

- When it gets very cold, water freezes (gets hard), making ice, such as snow, sleet, icicles; also, materials that contain water will freeze.
  a. Sleet is frozen raindrops.
  b. Snow is frozen crystals of water.
  c. Ice is a frozen mass of water.
- In many areas the weather is warmer and it rains instead of snowing.
- We have blizzards when a strong wind blows for a long time during a heavy snowstorm. It causes deep snowdrifts and makes it hard for people to see or move around outside.
- Daylight hours get shorter in the United States in winter. In parts of Alaska there are some days with no daylight at all during this season.
- Children have more chance to see the moon and stars before going to bed or when they wake up early. (See Day and Night guide, p. 533.)
- Usually, in the United States, the winter weather is colder, chillier, and damper, and the wind is more likely to feel cold than in other seasons of the year.
- The length of the winter season will be longer or shorter depending on the kind of weather there is where we live.

Plants

- Where it is very cold most plants stop growing for a while. (They seem to die but their seeds, roots, or bulbs often live underground, protected from the frost by dirt and a blanket of snow.)

- Where it rains instead of snowing, flowers and trees continue to bloom and grow all year round.
- Some plants and trees grow and bloom all year round and are called "evergreens."
- Some trees lose their leaves and become bare.
- Some indoor plants seldom bloom except during the winter, e.g., the Christmas cactus.
- When frozen, plants wilt and turn brown.

Animals

- Some animals hibernate (rest or sleep for a long time) during the winter.
- Animals hibernate in trees, underground, in caves.
- Birds migrate (fly away) to a warmer climate where they can find food during the winter months.
- Sometimes wild animals grow thicker fur, down, or hair in winter to keep them warm.
- Some animals' fur changes color in the winter to help protect and hide them when it snows.
- A few animals, such as ants and squirrels, store food for winter.
- Some animals enjoy playing in the snow and on the ice.
- Special care must be taken of some animals in winter, such as sweaters for short-haired pet dogs, protection for livestock against blizzards, food for birds who remain, or for those who return too early when there is a late snow in spring.

People

- Depending upon how cold it is children and adults need to wear heavier, warmer, or special clothes in winter, for play and work, such as boots, sweaters, scarves, mittens, caps, hats, coats, thermal outfits.
- Children and adults enjoy playing in snow or on ice, such as sledding, skating, skiing, or tobogganing.
- Where it is very cold people often spend more time indoors in winter—baking, using fireplaces, giving parties, dinners, playing games inside.
- People need to clear snow from sidewalks and streets in order to walk or drive safely.
- Cold weather, rain, snow, and freezing sometimes make it difficult to build or paint houses or to pour cement.
- Drivers have to put antifreeze in their cars to prevent the water in their radiators from freezing when it is very cold. They also need snow tires and chains when driving in snow or on ice.
- People are more likely to catch colds and flu in winter when we have less sunshine than in the summer.
- When it gets too cold outside we need to heat the buildings where we live, work, or play, and turn on the heater in buses, cars, and trucks.

Additional Facts the Teacher Should Know

It is difficult for young children to comprehend the full significance of any of the seasons. However, they can understand that winter is a time when certain changes take place in our environment and certain events, activities, and holidays occur. Some of the holidays that may be celebrated by young American children and their families in the United States during the winter months include:

Advent, a season varying from 22 to 28 days before Christmas
St. Barbara's Day, December 4
St. Lucia's Day, December 13
Las Posadas, December 16–24
Hanukkah, December
Christmas, December 25
Kwanza, December 26 to January 1
Epiphany, December 26 to beginning of Lent
New Year's Day, January 1
Twelfth Night (Three Kings' Day), January 6
Hsin Nien or *Yuan Tan* (Chinese New Year), begins anytime after January 21 to February 19
    (lunar calendar)
Islamic New Year, same as above
Martin Luther King's Birthday, January 15
Candlemas, February 2
Osho Gatsu, early February
Ashura (*Muharran*), 10th day of the first moon month (early February)
Lincoln's Birthday, February 12
Valentine's Day, February 14
Washington's Birthday, February 22
Mardi Gras, varies from February 3 to March 9
Purim, 14th day of the month *Adar* (February, sometimes March)
Hina Matsuri (Japanese Doll Festival), March 3
St. Patrick's Day, March 17

Winter is one of the four seasons of the year. In most of the United States winter extends from approximately December 22d to March 20th. Winter in the southern hemisphere is from June 21st to September 22d. The four seasons vary in time and length all over the world as the sun's rays strike the earth differently at any one time. These differences account not only for milder winters in the southern United States but for the short days of sunlight and long nights of darkness. Because it gets dark early in this season, winter is a good time to learn about day and night. (See Day and Night guide, p. 533.) The stars are visible in the winter while the young child is still awake. Parents should be encouraged to help the child find and enjoy them.

Each snowflake is unique—no two are alike! All snowflakes are hexagonal (have six sides). You can help children appreciate their uniqueness and beauty by providing them with magnifying glasses and enlarged photographic reproductions. The exact way in which they grow depends on what is happening in the atmosphere when they are formed. Snow that comes from very high and very cold clouds, where rapid freezing takes place, have simple crystals. Snow falling from and through warmer air builds up more elaborate patterns.

Snow festivals are celebrated in many northern countries as well as in northern states of the United States—Minneapolis and St. Paul's Winter Snow Festival and Ice Carnival, and Japan's Snow Festival. For their Snow Festival, Japanese children build snow houses in which to sit and sing. Special food treats are made and eaten. Adults parade through the villages with huge colorful banners. Farmers sell winter products and other wares, such as raincoats, buckets, minnows, snowshoes, and straw products.

Winter in the United States is also the season for bowl football games and colorful parades; both can be viewed on television by those who cannot attend. The Ice Follies' and the Ice Capade's troupes tour and perform in ice skating shows in arenas. These shows are enjoyed by whole families. Some children travel with their families to ski resorts and winter play-lands for special fun with ice and snow. All children enjoy snow if it is a part of the winter weather where they live.

Mistletoe, holly, poinsettia plants, and evergreens are the most common plants and flowers that bloom or remain green in the winter and are therefore most frequently used for decoration during this season. Both mistletoe and poinsettia plants are poisonous to humans if eaten, so if you use these plants for decoration take proper precautions. Tell the children that "some plants are good to eat and some are not good to eat and will even make us sick." If you live where it is too cold for plants to grow outside you may wish to plant bulbs or seeds indoors. This will give the children an opportunity to understand that plants need warmth and light to grow.

Birds migrate in fall or early winter because food becomes scarce, not because it is cold. Birds grow an undercoating of down that keeps them warm. However, when ponds freeze and snow covers the ground and many bugs and insects die or hibernate birds have limited sources of food. Children might enjoy helping feed birds during the winter. (See illustration.) However, if you start a bird-feeding station you should maintain it all through the winter or else the birds who remain because of your efforts may be stranded and die. The children may find dead birds, insects, and animals during the winter and will need help in understanding and accepting this part of the life cycle. Margaret Wise Brown's *The Dead Bird*, published by William R. Scott, Inc., in 1958, is very helpful in teaching what death is, and an appropriate ritual is included.

Make a bird feeder from a gallon-size plastic milk jug or an economy-size bleach bottle. Cut out two sides so the birds can fly through. Weight jug with coarse pebbles and fill it with birdseed. Wire it securely to a tree limb.

The children might enjoy making a Christmas tree for the birds. A bare bush or evergreen tree will be satisfactory for hanging food decorations. The children can string Cheerios on plastic laces, shoelaces, or yarn with a blunt needle and drape on the branches. Cranberries or popcorn can be strung by the teacher or parents and hung on the tree by the children.

Suet or bacon fat can be melted and mixed with wild birdseed in equal proportions or mixed with peanut butter for an added treat. This mixture can be poured into half walnut shells, aluminum pie tins, margarine tubs, paper cups, or on pine cones, and if holes are punched in containers to attach wire or string they may be tied to the tree. Also pine cones plastered with peanut butter and rolled in birdseed can be hung on the tree.

NOTE: Always mix birdseed with peanut butter. Straight peanut butter may cause birds' bills to stick together so they cannot get their mouths open.

Short stalks of milo can be tied to the tree. Pour melted fat over birdseed mixture in small paper cups. Insert wire or pipecleaners into the mixture with two inches or so protruding. When hardened, peel away the paper and hang on a tree. Stale bread or doughnuts can be hung on the branches or crumbled and thrown on the ground. Chicken scratch, livestock grain, and apple peelings are also appreciated by birds. If you do not have a suitable tree or bush, food can be spread out on the top of a box. A simple V-shape roof nailed to the box would provide protection from the wind while eating. Dishes holding food should be nailed or tied down because some birds push and shove while crowding around food.

Children may wish to help our small animal friends by building a shelter for them. Dead branches heaped over an old stump, a pile of rocks, logs, or rail piles make good escape cover or winter dens. Old drain tiles buried under rocks and earth make artificial burrows. Children can put nuts and seeds out for squirrels, and leafy vegetables, beans, and carrots for rabbits. Interest in animals that live well in ice and snow may be developed through pictures of polar bears, penguins, and seals. (See also Animals of the Woods.)

Citrus fruits grown in Florida, Texas, and southern California are the most prevalent ones available in the winter. Grapefruit, oranges, and tangerines are plentiful and make good snacks peeled and sectioned or squeezed and drunk. Many young children do not like grapefruit or its juice by itself, but if it is combined with other fruit or juices it is acceptable in small amounts. Cranapple juice is also available now. (Other guides related to Winter are Water and Animals.)

Hina Matsuri (HEE-nah MAT-SOO-ree)

Traditionally, peach blossoms are a symbol of wedded happiness and also of the qualities of mildness, softness, and peacefulness, prized traits for Japanese women.

Hina Matsuri, the Japanese Doll Festival or Peach Festival, begins on March 3rd. It is a time when peach blossoms are usually in full bloom. Treasured heirloom dolls are exquisitely dressed in colorful embroidered silk costumes and are arranged very carefully on a tierlike platform in a special room or place in the home. Emperor and empress dolls are placed on the top shelf and ladies-in-waiting and their attendants are arranged on lower shelves. On the bottom shelf are placed lacquered miniature furniture and little musical instruments. Peach blossoms are arranged all around them. Some little girls are given the first doll for their collection at the time they are born. The dolls (*hina ningyo* pronounced HEE-nah NIN-GEE-yaw) are highly treasured, and because of the time it takes to produce them, they become almost priceless. They are handed down from generation to generation. Girls invite their friends over on this day to see their collections and to have special treats. Often soup, fish, rice boiled with beans, special diamond-shaped cakes, and fruit-shaped candies are served with tea.

Methods Most Adaptable for Introducing This Subject to Children

- Notice when it snows for the first time.
- Take a pan of water outside on a freezing day. Observe the results.
- Observe that some trees have bare branches and some are evergreens.
- Prepare a bird feeder or animal shelter.
- Read a story about winter or the four seasons.
- Bring in a large dishpan or baby's bathtub filled with snow.

Vocabulary

winter	freeze	animals	ski	snowflake
snow	trees	feeder	sled	hockey
cold	bare	hibernate	skate	mistletoe
ice	evergreen	migrate	frost	holly
icicle	birds	temperature	sleet	poinsettia

learning centers

NOTE: Many suggestions are made for climates where there is snow. If you live in a warmer climate adapt each suggestion to rain. (See Water guide.) Or use ice or frost from freezer or refrigerator where feasible. If, however, mountains are nearby, you can take along a cooler and pack some snowballs/snow/icicles for children to see when you return.

Discovery Center

1. Take a pan of water outside when the temperature is below freezing. Observe what happens. After it has frozen bring the pan inside again; what happens?
2. Fill a juice can and a half pint milk carton with water. Staple milk carton shut. Take both outside in freezing weather or place in a freezer. Observe what happens. **Variation:** Set out a small carton of milk to freeze. When frozen give children a spoonful to taste.
3. Bring a pan of snow inside for measuring and exploring.
4. Bring icicles inside and place in a suitable container to observe as they melt.
5. Outside, observe snowflakes that fall on children's coat sleeves or catch some on a dark velvet cloth. Use magnifying glass if available.
6. Make snow cones by packing clean crushed ice in paper cups with an ice-cream scoop or large spoon and pouring fruit flavored gelatin powder or syrup over the ice. Let children choose the flavor they want. Other flavorings and diluted food coloring may also be added if you like.

If weather does not permit the children to play outdoors in the snow, bring the snow indoors for a discovery experience. If you live where there is no snow, try to get snow from a freezer locker plant when freezer room is cleaned.

7. Store some snowballs or cartons of snow in the deep freeze so that the children can discover the snow is still frozen in late winter or early spring when the snow has melted and disappeared completely outside. Discuss why.
8. Make ice cream, using your favorite recipe. Talk about why the cream freezes.
9. Let children mix food coloring with snow.
10. Look for animal or bird tracks in the snow.
11. Buy as large and as accurate a thermometer as you can and let the children explore. Indoor-outdoor thermometers: allow children to compare the two and see the similarities and differences. They can see that as it gets colder the mercury goes down.
12. Make a large cardboard thermometer. (See Discovery Activity No. 5 in Mathematics guide, p. 620.) Use extra wide cardboard and paste pictures of children in appropriate clothes beside the related temperatures: snowsuit, cap, and mittens for under 40 degrees; a warm jacket, hat, and mittens for the 40s and 50s; a light jacket or sweater for the 60s.
13. Make Jack wax. Pour two cups of maple syrup in a saucepan and boil until the softball stage is reached. Pour the hot syrup over crushed ice in a salad bowl. Twirl the wax onto forks.
14. Go outside on a cold day to see water vapor when children breathe and talk.

15. To show that plants need sunlight, force a hyacinth bulb. In the fall plant hyacinth bulbs outside in a buried pot. Dig up in January and bring inside. Put in a warm, dark place. Yellow leaves will appear. Move the plant to a sunny ledge and watch the leaves turn green and the plant grow and blossom.
16. Display the Take a Walk in Winter sequence chart (The Child's World) or listen to the cassette tape of sounds with accompanying book by the same title.

    NOTE: See Discovery Center in Water and Animal guides.

Dramatic Play Centers

Home-Living Center

1. Set out heavy blankets, sweaters, warm jackets, hats, and snowsuits for the dolls, suggesting the need for warmer clothes in the winter (if this is true in your area).
2. Put up pictures of snow, rain, and activities related to each. Include pictures of children dressed for freezing temperatures or rainy weather, using some that are appropriate to your area's climate.

Block-Building Center

1. Set out animal figures and suggest that unit blocks be used to build a barn, a stable, or another animal shelter.
2. A bulldozer can be a make-believe snowplow and dump trucks can be used to haul away the snow.
3. Lincoln logs can be set out for older children to build houses as the pilgrims did their first winter.

Learning, Language, and Readiness Materials Center

Commercially made games and materials for use at a table or on a mat:

(See Basic Resources, p. 79, for manufacturers' addresses.)

1. Judy Puzzles: Snowman, 3 pcs.
2. Judy See-Quees: Making a Snowman, 6 pcs.; Children and Seasons, 12 pcs.
3. Snowman: a size and shape puzzle with knobs, 3 pcs. (Childcraft)
4. Snow Crystals: 100 pcs. to form five different crystal patterns (Constructive Playthings)
5. Four Seasons: 4-pc. puzzle for each season (Childcraft)
6. Snowflakes: multi-colored, interlocking, polyforms (Holcomb's)
7. The Four Seasons (Dennison bulletin board aids)
8. We Dress for Weather (Instructo)
9. Rosetta Puzzles: 3-puzzle set with 36 triangular pcs. per puzzle (Childcraft)

Teacher-made games and materials for use at a table or on a mat:

NOTE: For detailed description of Games, see pp. 50–58.

1. What's Missing?: use a styrofoam snowball, plastic or paper snowflake, model snowman, pair of mittens, pair of earmuffs, ski mask.
2. Match Them: show children a styrofoam snowball. Say, "This snowball is round. Find me something else that is round." or "This plastic snowball is white. Find me something else that is white." "These mittens are red. Find me something else that is red."

3. Match-Them: scramble several pairs of mittens. Have children find a matching pair.
4. Reach and Feel: use objects similar to those in No. 1.
5. Show Me: use objects similar to those in No. 1. "Show me the one we wear on our hands." "Show me the one that keeps our ears warm."
6. Make a winter calendar for one or all of the months, making each day a two-inch square. Use decorative seals to mark the special holidays, birthdays, and other events that will have meaning for the children at your center. Surround the calendar with paper snowflakes two inches in diameter. (See Pictures and Displays.) As each day goes by cover it with one of the snowflakes. In areas where there is no snow, mark off the days with poinsettias or evergreen trees or raindrops/clouds.

Art Center

* 1. Feature white paint at the easel for painting snow pictures.
* 2. Provide white chalk and colored construction paper for making snow pictures.
** 3. Paint pine cones white or green (or any other color if used for Christmas tree decoration) and glue to styrofoam bases. Use as decorations on the snack or library table or use to add a winter effect to unit block building of houses or roads. Bare twigs stuck in styrofoam could be used as deciduous trees in the same manner.
* 4. Mix up soapflakes and water into a thick paste using a hand beater or electric mixer. Add a small amount of liquid starch and white powdered tempera for a more permanent, attractive product. Let children create designs by painting the thick mixture on with a brush or rub it on with a tongue depressor.
*** 5. Children who have had a great deal of experience with clay and dough may discover they can make snowmen with these media.
*** 6. When outdoors encourage children to mold or sculpt with snow to make free-form figures, not just snowmen, snowballs, and walls.
** 7. Paste cotton balls on construction paper to make a snowy day picture.
** 8. Make a star shape out of sponge or cut a green pepper in half around the middle. Notice the unusual star shape. Let children dip the green pepper in white paint and print snowflakes on colored construction paper.
** 9. Make styrofoam sculptures using precut free-forms cut from scrap styrofoam with styrofoam balls, toothpicks, bits of yarn, leather, feathers. Use toothpicks and pipe-cleaners with glue to assemble or to add attachments.

Book Center

* Adelson, Leon. *All Ready for Winter*. New York: David McKay, 1952.
*** Bancroft, Henrietta. *Animals in the Winter*. New York: Thomas Y. Crowell, 1963.
*** Branley, Franklin. *Big Tracks, Little Tracks*. New York: Thomas Y. Crowell, 1960.
* Brown, Margaret. *The Dead Bird*. Reading, Mass.: Addison-Wesley, 1958.
** ———. *The Indoor Noisy Book*. New York: Harper & Row, 1942.
* ———. *The Winter Noisy Book*. New York: Harper & Row, 1947.
** Buckley, Helen. *Josie and the Snow*. New York: Lothrop, Lee & Shepard, 1964.
** Burningham, John. *Seasons*. New York: Bobbs-Merrill, 1970 (paper).
*** Burton, Virginia Lee. *Katy and the Big Snow*. New York: Houghton Mifflin, 1959 (paper).
** Chaffin, Lillie. *Bear Weather*. New York: Macmillan, 1969.
*** Duvoisin, Roger. *The House of Four Seasons*. New York: Lothrop, Lee & Shepard, 1956.
** Fisher, Aileen. *Where Does Everyone Go?* New York: Thomas Y. Crowell, 1961.

*** Foster, Doris. *Pocketful of Seasons.* New York: Lothrop, Lee & Shepard, 1960.
*** Freeman, Don. *Ski Pup.* New York: Viking Press, 1963.
*** George, Jean. *Snow Tracks.* New York: E. P. Dutton, 1958.
*** Harder, Berta and Elmer. *The Big Snow.* New York: Macmillan, 1948 (paper, 1972).
*** ———. *Snow in the City.* New York: Macmillan, 1963.
 ** Hoff, Syd. *When Will It Snow?* New York: Harper & Row, 1971.
 ** Ipcar, Dahlov. *Black and White.* New York: Alfred A. Knopf, 1963.
*** Kay, Helen. *One Mitten Lewis.* New York: Lothrop, Lee & Shepard, 1955.
  * Keats, Ezra Jack. *The Snowy Day.* New York: Viking Press, 1962.
 ** Kent, Jack. *Just Only John.* New York: Parents' Magazine Press, 1968.
*** Kessler, Ethel and Leonard. *Slush, Slush.* New York: Parents' Magazine Press, 1973.
  * Lenski, Lois. *I Like Winter.* New York: Henry Z. Walck, 1950.
  * McKie, Roy and P. D. Eastman. *Snow.* New York: Random House, 1962.
 ** Marino, Dorothy. *Buzzy Bear's Winter Party.* New York: Franklin Watts, 1967.
*** Miller, Edna. *Mousekin's Woodland Sleepers.* Englewood Cliffs, N.J.: Prentice-Hall, 1970.
  * Parker, Bertha. *The Wonders of the Seasons.* Chicago, Ill.: Childrens Press, 1955.
  * Podendorf, Illa. *The True Book of Seasons.* Chicago, Ill.: Childrens Press, 1972.
*** Selsam, Millicent. *A Time for Sleep.* Reading, Mass.: Addison-Wesley, 1953.
  * Shaw, Charles. *It Looked Like Spilt Milk.* New York: Harper & Row, 1947.
*** Tresselt, Alvin. *White Snow, Bright Snow.* New York: Lothrop, Lee & Shepard, 1947.
*** ———. *The Mitten.* New York: Lothrop, Lee & Shepard, 1964.
 ** ———. *It's Time Now!* New York: Lothrop, Lee & Shepard, 1969.
 ** Welber, Robert. *The Winter Picnic.* New York: Pantheon Books, 1970.
  * Weygant, Sister Naomi. *It's Winter.* Philadelphia, Pa.: Westminster Press, 1969.
  * Zolotow, Charlotte. *Summer Is.* (all seasons) New York: Abelard-Schuman, 1967.
*** ———. *Hold My Hand.* New York: Harper & Row, 1972.

planning for grouptime

NOTE: All music, fingerplays, poems, stories, and games listed here may also be used at other times during the session as appropriate. See Core Library, Basic Resources, p. 76, for publishers and addresses. Addresses for sources of records will be found on p. 81. In parodies, hyphenated words match music notes of the songs used.

MUSIC

Songs

WINTER (a parody)
   (tune: "Pussy Cat, Pussy Cat")
   Adaptation by JoAnne Deal Hicks

Win-ter is here; it's so co-ld to-day. Win-ter is here, it's too co-ld to play.
We must stay in-side, for there's much too much snow.
We sit by the win-dow and hear the wind blow!

FROM *Music Resource Book*, Lutheran Church Press
* "Isn't It Fun?," p. 46

FROM *Songs for the Nursery School*, MacCarteney
** "Coasting," p. 54
** "It's Snowing," p. 55
** "The People's Feet Go Crunch," p. 56
** "It's Raining on the Town," p. 59 (change "raining" to "snowing" to suit your climate)
* "Falling Leaves," p. 63 (change "red leaves" to "snow flakes") Cut snowflakes out of white typing paper or construction paper. (See Pictures and Displays.) Let each child hold two, letting them fall to the ground one at a time as the song is sung
*** "O Christmas Tree," p. 69 (You may wish to change "Christmas tree" to "evergreen.")

FROM *Songs for Early Childhood*, Westminster Press
*** "We Have a Little Visitor," p. 41
** "When It Is the Wintertime," p. 42
* "Airy, Fairy Snowflakes," p. 43
*** "Snow Makes Whiteness Where It Falls," p. 44 (spoken rather than sung)
*** "Soft Little Snowflakes," p. 45
* "Tiny Little Sparrows," p. 49
** "Thumbs in the Thumb-Place," p. 105

FROM *Music Activities for Retarded Children*, Ginglend and Stiles
* "The Seasons," p. 94
** "Winter Song," p. 112

Records

"Frosty the Snowman" (any recording)
"Sleigh Ride" by Leroy Anderson (any recording; use bells to keep time)
"Jingle Bells" (YPR, 78 and 45 RPM)
"All About the Seasons" (Decca)

Rhythms and Singing Games

Snowflakes: give children white scarves or white crepe paper streamers or precut white paper snowflakes.
a. Play fast tempo music and let children pretend to be snowflakes on a windy day.
b. Play slow tempo music and let children pretend to be softly falling snowflakes.

Ice skating: play the *Skater's Waltz* and let the children pretend to be ice skaters.

Sleigh ride: using a rope as a harness and stick horses, let the children pretend to be horses pulling a sleigh through the snow. Six horses could pull at a time and the rest of the children could be sitting in the sleigh. (Line up several rows of three chairs each, as needed.) Those in the sleigh can have bells to shake in time with the music.

FROM *Creative Movements for the Developing Child*, Cherry
"Build a Little Snowman," p. 53.
"The Big Snowman," p. 54

Fingerplays and Poems

FROM *Let's Do Fingerplays*, Grayson

"Mittens," p. 18
"My Zipper Suit," p. 18
"The Mitten Song," p. 20
"Big Hill," p. 23

"Snowflakes," p. 48
"Snow Men," p. 48
"Shiver and Quiver," p. 58

FROM *Rhymes for Fingers and Flannelboards*, Scott and Thompson

"In Wintertime," p. 120
"Snowflakes," p. 122
"Ten Little Snowmen," p. 122
"I Am a Snowman," p. 123
"The Snowman," p. 123

FROM *Very Young Verses*, Geismer and Suter

"First Snow," p. 133
"Winter," p. 134
"Ice," p. 136
"Snowstorm," p. 135
"Stopping by the Woods on a Snowy Evening," p. 138
"The Snowflake," p. 139
"Galoshes," p. 140
"Snow on the Roof," p. 141
"Icy," p. 142
"White Fields," p. 143
"Snowflakes," p. 144

Stories

(To read, read-tell, or tell. See Book Center for complete list.)

  * *All Ready for Winter*, Adelson
 ** *Josie and the Snow*, Buckley
*** *The Big Snow*, Harder
  * *The Snowy Day*, Keats
 ** *The Winter Picnic*, Welber
  * *The Wonders of the Seasons*, Parker
  * *The True Book of Seasons*, Podendorf
*** *White Snow, Bright Snow*, Tresselt
  * *Snow*, McKie

Games

(See Games, pp. 50–58, and Teacher-Made Games in this guide for directions.)

1. What's Missing?
2. Match-Them
3. Reach and Feel
4. Show Me

Routine Times

1. At snack or mealtime serve fruits that are available in winter: oranges, grapefruit, tangerines; talk about the fact that these are grown where it is warmer and are brought on ship, boat, train and/or truck to stores in the city.
2. At snack or mealtime serve foods that are white in color, such as milk, marshmallows, enriched white bread, popcorn, potatoes, or rice. And talk about the relationship between the color of snow and the color of the food.
3. At rest time pretend to be hibernating animals sleeping through the cold winter.
4. When walking or busing the children to and from the center call attention to any signs of winter: frost, snow, bare trees, evergreens, people dressed warmly, frozen ponds, water vapor from nose and mouth.
5. When dressing to go outside you might talk about the weather. Look at the outdoor thermometer and decide how cold it is and what you need to wear. If you made a cardboard thermometer with pictures of the children in appropriate clothing at the various levels of degrees this might help them decide. Set the cardboard thermometer at the same position as the outdoor thermometer and see which picture is closest to it. You might recite "The Mitten Song," "Mittens," or "My Zipper Suit," from *Let's Do Fingerplays*, as the children are putting on these articles of clothing.

Large Muscle Activities

1. Provide children with child-size snow shovels and let them shovel the play yard walks, trike paths, and other paved surfaces. Show children where to put the snow. It could be loaded into wagons and carried to another part of the yard for snow sculptures or the activities suggested in No. 2.
2. Provide children with some of the sand toys or kitchen pans and utensils that would be appropriate for using with snow as they would with sand: pails, shovels, spoons, molds, pie plates, measuring cups.
3. If the snow is the wet kind that sticks together, make a snowman or mold it into interesting shapes as you would with clay or dough.
4. Show children how to make angels by lying down on your back in the snow and moving your arms up and down.
5. If you have a hill in your play yard and the snow is good for sledding, provide the children with cardboard squares from packing boxes, flying saucers, old trays, or sleds. Establish traffic patterns for going up and coming down. It is ideal to have an adult at the top and one at the bottom of the hill to help regulate traffic. However, if only one adult is available for this area it is best that she or he be stationed at the bottom of the hill, so he/she can direct those who have completed their slide where to climb back up if they want another turn. The adult could instruct the children at the top of the hill to wait until called, such as "Go, ————," allowing one child at a time to proceed, thereby avoiding rear-end collisions.
6. Throwing snowballs at others should be discouraged. Provide a suitable target for those who wish to throw snowballs. The target should be away from the general play area.
7. Children's ski-skates (available commercially) or snowshoes are fun to wear outside after a new snow.
8. Follow the Leader can be played in fresh snow by children following the footsteps in the snow made by the leader. Zigzag or circle patterns of footsteps can be made. If an adult is the leader remember to take small steps, especially if the snow is deep. Try hopping and jumping as well as walking.

9. Snowball Toss: make snowballs and see how many you can toss into the snowman's hat, a box, or a waste basket. If no snow is available, use styrofoam balls as snowballs. Count the balls. White nylon balls can be made from nurses' white discarded panty-hose scraps.

Extended Experiences

1. Take a walk and look for things that tell us it is winter: snow, ice, bare trees, icicles, frozen pond, evergreen trees, people dressed warmly.
2. Visit a site where your children could safely go sledding if your facility does not have a suitable slope.
3. Visit a frozen pond. If the ice is thick enough let the children walk on the ice. Ice skates with double runners are available for preschoolers. Sleds and flying saucers pull easily over frozen ice, so bring them along.
4. If you know someone with a horse and sleigh you might wish to arrange a ride for the children.
5. Show a filmstrip: "Winter Is Here," from the captioned filmstrip series *The Seasons* and "Winter Adventures," from the series *Seasons' Adventures* (Singer SVE).
6. Have a snow picnic.

teacher resources

Pictures and Displays

(See p. 79 for addresses of firms listed.)

1. Magnetic Seasons: magnetic visual aid (Instructo)
2. Seasons: flannelboard aids (Instructo)
3. Seasons: activity kits for "Fall" and "Winter" (Instructo)
4. Animals in Streams and Ponds, Animals in the Woods (Instructo)
5. Seasons: flannel aid (Milton Bradley)
6. Mini-Poster Cards: "Winter," 14 pictures, 10 inches by 13 inches in each set (Trend Enterprises)
7. Set out winter issues of, or mount pictures from, the *National Wildlife* or *Ranger Rick's Nature* magazines
8. In the Winter: eight pictures (Singer SVE)
9. Winter: set of three scenes each 18 inches by 23 inches (Hayes)
10. Winter Fun: seven bulletin board cut-outs from 3 inches to 26 inches (Trend Enterprises)
11. Post pictures of snow, frozen ponds, snowmen, bird or animal feeders and shelters, hibernating animals, winter sports like skiing, skating
12. Post the pictures: "Wintertime," "Winter Preparation," "Winter Hibernation," and "Winter Migration" from *Seasons;* "Snow" from *Science Themes No. 1;* and use the flannelboard aids for "The Snowman" from *Seasons and Weather* (David C. Cook)

13. Make a mobile of plastic snowflakes (available commercially where tree decorations are sold) or cut your own, using folded paper squares, circles, or hexagons, cutting only the folded edges. When opened they may be painted with glue and covered with glitter or artificial snow and then allowed to dry. Snowflakes may also be cut from heavy duty aluminum foil wrap. When opened, flatten these aluminum foil snowflakes between the pages of a book. Remember no two snowflakes are alike, so make yours different.

    NOTE: Snowflake stencils could be cut out of cardboard and designs stencilled on the windows using sponges and Glass Wax or Bon Ami. Commercial Christmas stencils are available at the grocery and department stores at Christmastime.

14. Decorate windows and walls with snowflakes cut as suggested above.
15. If you live where tumbleweed is available you can make a lacy (Christmas) tree by making a pyramid of tumbleweeds and spraying them white. A snowman can be made of tumbleweeds also and decorated appropriately with styrofoam balls painted the desired color. Buttons make good eyes and noses. A hat, scarf, and a small broom can be added if desired.
16. Doilies to put under the juice or milk cup at each place at snack or mealtime can be made from four-inch diameter circles as described in No. 13.
17. Miniature floating pine-cone candleholders make an interesting centerpiece for a winter birthday party. Saw off a half inch thick section of a pine cone. Glue this to a larger thin circle of wood or cork. Glue a small candle to the center of the cone. Float the candle base in water. Light candles. Several can be floated if a large enough container is available.
18. Make a snow scene: a mirror makes a good frozen pond. Surround the pond with cotton batting. Pine cones of various sizes and shapes can be used as trees. Paint green or white if you wish. Bare twigs can be the bare deciduous trees. Little figures of skiers, skaters, snowmen, birds, and rabbits or other small animals can be added to the winter wonderland.
19. If you have an artistic teacher, ask her to make some Jack Frost windows: cover the windows with commercial window cleaners. Let dry. With their fingernail or a cotton swab they can etch a frosty design.

Community Resources

1. Natural history museums: often exhibits are changed to reflect the change in seasons or there are different sections to the exhibits that show winter habitats
2. A frozen pond in a park nearby or an ice arena
3. Snow sculptures created by university or civic groups
4. A frozen food plant will sometimes give you "snow" scraped when defrosting units

19 spring

basic understandings

(concepts children can grasp from this subject)

Spring is a season of the year that comes after winter and before summer. There are many changes in nature in the spring.

Earth Changes

- In areas where there is ice and snow, these both melt.
- Days are longer (sunrise is earlier and sunset later than in winter).
- The temperature is usually warmer, the wind blows hard, and there are often thunderstorms.
- North, south, east, west, and central parts of the United States have very different types of weather within the period called spring. In some areas it is still quite cold; in others it may be a continuation of warm weather of the winter; or it may be rainy, windy, and warmer.
- The ground thaws as the rain warms and softens it. Spring showers and warm sunshine help seeds to sprout and begin to grow.
- There are often more storms (tornados and hurricanes) in spring when weather temperatures may change suddenly in some areas.
- The length of the season may seem longer or shorter depending on the weather where you live.

Plant Changes

- Seeds sprout and plants begin to grow.
- Leaf buds turn into leaves on trees and on bushes.
- Blossoms appear on some plants (fruit trees, spring bulbs, dandelions, and pussywillows).
- Grass turns green and starts to grow.
- Some indoor plants can be planted outdoors for the summer months, such as geraniums, ivies, cacti, rubber plants, begonias.

Animals

- Animals who hibernate (sleep during the winter) wake up and come out of their sleeping places.
- Most animals have new babies in the spring.
- Birds migrate to their summer homes and build nests.
- Birds and animals often get new coats of feathers or fur, to adjust to weather and new colorings of surroundings.

People

- We do not need to wear such warm clothing in spring.
- Farmers prepare ground for seed planting.
- Children and animals frolic outdoors.
- Spring is a time of beginning again: housecleaning, planting.
- Special celebrations in spring include: Easter, Pan-American Day, *Holi*, Passover, *Cinco de Mayo*, May Day, Mother's Day, Father's Day, Memorial Day.

Festivals

Spring festivals are celebrated all over the world. Some are related to religious holidays and others to the arrival of spring and the planting of crops. Two such special nonreligious festivals held in the United States are the tulip festivals held in Holland, Michigan, and Pella, Iowa. In South America, many countries' pre-Lent festivities occur during spring. Spring in the United States is also the season for basketball and hockey tournaments or play-offs and the beginning of outdoor track, baseball, golf, and tennis seasons.

Some holidays that are celebrated by young American children and their families during the spring months include:

Passover (PES-ah)

A yearly festival, celebrated by Jewish people for eight days every March or early April, Passover is the symbol of liberty, recalling the ancient Israelites' march to freedom from Egyptian slavery, as told in the biblical book Exodus. During Passover, Jews eat *matzo*, or unleavened bread, rather than bread made with yeast. It is eaten in memory of the fact that they had no time to leaven the bread when they fled from Egypt. *Matzo* is made from potato starch and *matzo* meal instead of flour.

On the first or second night a *Seder* (service) is held. At this service special foods are eaten that are not eaten at any other time of the year. Orthodox Jews use a special set of dishes, cooking utensils, and silver at this time, too. During the *Seder*, a special supper is served. A traditional platter is always placed on the Passover table beside the *Haggadah*, the book containing the story of Passover. The platter contains parsley, saltwater, a hard-cooked egg, a horseradish root, a lamb shank, *moror* (bitter herbs or horseradish sauce), and *haroset*, all symbolic in the Passover story, which is recited during the *Seder*. Close to this platter is a white napkin interleaved with three sheets of *matzo*. Two of the *matzo* are used in the ceremony and the third one, called the *afikomen*, is hidden. Whoever finds it gets a reward, and then it is divided so everyone can eat a piece for good luck.

Wine is an important part of Jewish feasts. At the *Seder*, a glass of wine that no one touches is poured for the prophet Elijah, who, the Jews expect, will come one day to announce the coming of the Messiah. After dinner the door of the home is opened and Elijah is invited to enter.

Vocabulary

freedom	*Seder*	*matzo*	cake
Passover	supper	macaroons	fruit

Extended Experiences

1. Invite a Jewish parent to visit the group and tell about the holiday, showing pictures or items of interest.
2. Prepare a Jewish food appropriate to the celebration.
3. Compare *matzo* and saltines: how they are alike and different in taste, color, texture, and shape.
4. Compare *matzo* and square sandwich bread made with yeast, as to shape, color, texture, and taste.
5. Compare two glasses of water, one of which has one teaspoon of salt added. Give each child a hard-cooked egg. Let each child dip the egg in the plain water and take a bite, then dip in the saltwater and take a bite.
6. Compare dried fruits with whole fruits if available. Soak dried fruits in water and compare with dried fruits as to texture, size, and taste.
7. Make a compote of dried fruits: simmer three cups of soaked dried fruit in 1½ cups water to which has been added ¾ cup sugar, thin slices of lemon, a stick of cinnamon, and 3 or 4 whole cloves tied in cheesecloth. Cook for 20 minutes or until tender. Discard spices and add 1 cup whole blanched almonds. Chill before serving.
8. Make Passover macaroons: beat 3 egg whites until they hold a stiff peak. Beat in 2 tablespoons superfine sugar until mixture is glossy. Fold in ⅔ cup sugar mixed with 6 tablespoons *matzo* meal and 1 cup ground almonds or coconut. Drop tablespoonfuls of the mixture on a cookie sheet lined with silicone paper. Bake in 300° oven for 20 minutes. Cool and peel off the paper.
9. Adapt the following games as noted:
   a. I See Something Square: show *matzo*. Look for square things.
   b. Chew, Lick, and Taste: use a variety of crackers including *matzo*.
   c. How Many?: count prune, peach, and apricot pits.
   d. Match-Them: use prune, peach, and apricot pits or pictures of these fruits.
   e. Grouping and Sorting by Association: use items in d. above.
   f. Alike, Different, and the Same: use items in d. above.
10. Play the record "Children Sing the Seder" (Tikva Records, 33⅓ RPM).

Book Center

Chanover, Hyman and Alice. *Pesah Is Coming!* New York: United Synagogue Book Service, 1956.

Morrow, Betty, and Lewis Hartman. "Passover, a Festival of Freedom." In *Jewish Holidays*. Champaign, Ill.: Garrard, 1967.

———. *Pesah Is Here!* New York: United Synagogue Book Service, 1956.

Simon, Norma. *My Family Seder*. New York: United Synagogue Book Service, 1961.

———. *Passover*. New York: Thomas Y. Crowell, 1951.

Easter

Easter is the most joyous Christian festival. It commemorates for the Christian the resurrection of Christ. Since this event is recorded in the Bible as occurring at the time of the Jewish Passover, it was originally celebrated at that time. But in 325 A.D., the Council of Nicaea determined that Easter would be the first Sunday after the first full moon which appears after the spring equinox (March 21st). Easter always occurs between March 22d and April 25th.

Basic Understandings for Children about Easter

- Easter Sunday is a special, joyful day celebrated in the Christian churches and their church schools.
- It is a day when Christian families are glad and remember Jesus and the first Easter.
- Many children go to church or attend sunrise services outdoors on Easter Sunday with their parents.

Teachers of young children in Christian day schools should consult their own denominational curriculum. Most religious concepts about this holiday are beyond the comprehension of very young children, except that Easter is a special celebration for remembering Jesus and that it is a most joyous day.

Churches are often decorated with white lilies, a symbol of purity and light. The cross reminds worshipers of the religious meaning of Easter.

Except for the association of Easter and what it means to Christians, with the potential for a new beginning, most child-related activities, including the Easter bunny, are not religiously oriented to this holiday. The new beginning might be shown in the new birth and renewal of life in springtime, such as the dormant bulb that grows into a new plant, the pupa that becomes a butterfly, and the earth coming to life again (for both plants and animals). However, the association is somewhat vague.

Other Nonreligious Customs Relating to Easter

Many Easter traditions and customs come from ancient pagan celebrations. The word "Easter" comes from the name of an Anglo-Saxon goddess, *Eostre*, who represented light or spring. The Anglo-Saxon tribes held a festival in her honor every April. Just as the earth is dressed in a new cloak of greenery, people often wear new clothes for Easter. In Europe, people take a walk through the fields. In America, there are Easter parades. Probably this custom originated with Emperor Constantine, who had his leaders don their most elegant robes on Easter to honor Christ's resurrection. There was an old belief that if a person wore a new article of clothing for the first time on Easter, he would surely have luck for the rest of the year.

The legend of the Easter bunny is definitely not religious. The legendary Easter rabbit or bunny, after a long winter nap, is supposed to hide brightly colored eggs in the new green grass. He may bring dyed eggs (see Color guide, p. 587), wooden eggs, even fancy sugar eggs. The idea of Easter eggs came to us from ancient Egypt and Persia. The eggs are a sign of new life. Newly hatched chicks and ducklings and baby rabbits are also associated with spring.

Extended Experiences

No special religiously significant activities have been noted here. However, any suggestions involving eggs, bunnies, and plants have been included under the various headings in this Spring guide, since they relate more to the season than to the Christian significance of the holiday.

A-ri-ni Nal (Ah-ree-nee Nal)

May 5th is a spring holiday set aside to honor children in Korea and is also the time of cherry blossoms. Children are wished happiness and prosperity. Usually, special privileges are allowed and elaborate plans made for children by their parents, such as picnics, trips to parks and mountains, and excursions to buy tea cakes or ice-cream treats. Schools invite parents and have special ceremonies and sports events. In Korea, bus rides are often free on this day as well as admission to the king's palace gardens.

In recent years, Japan has designated May 5th as Children's Day; it is known as *Kodo-mo-no-hi* (Koh-doh-moh-noh-hee).

Tan-go-no-sekku (Tahn-goh-noh-seh-koo)

Japanese Boys' Day, also called the Iris Festival, is a traditional holiday honoring boys in Japan. In both Korea and Japan, it is still considered lucky if a first son is born on May 5th. Carp kites are flown from bamboo flagpoles in almost everyone's garden. There is one kite for each son. Usually the oldest son has the largest and most beautiful kite; it may be up to fifteen feet long and it hangs highest on the flagpole. Boys are encouraged to be brave and strong like the carp struggling upstream and through waterfalls.

Fragrant iris leaves are put in the boy's evening bathwater by his mother. The sword-shaped iris leaf is symbolic of the spirit of brave warriors. Often boys receive gifts for their first Boys' Day celebration. In Hawaii, cloth and paper fish are flown from bamboo poles and displayed on this date.

Traditionally the family armor was unpacked and displayed on this day. If the family had no armor, a display of *samurai* (warrior) dolls was made. Similar to the March 3rd Festival of Dolls for girls (described in the Winter guide, p. 315), boys traditionally had a historical display of heirloom dolls, usually samurai or soldier heroes from the past, which belonged to an aristocratic family. These dolls are now extremely expensive because of the craftsmanship and artistry in the costumes, which are authentically duplicated.

Rice cookies covered with a bamboo leaf are one of the special foods served to friends.

Extended Experiences

1. Invite a Japanese friend or a Japanese boy who has a carp kite to bring it to show. (See photograph, p. 215.)
2. Buy a few Japanese paper kites for the children to fly. These kites are usually available from an Asian or import store in March or April.
3. If you live in a community where Japanese Americans live, ask if anyone has a collection of samurai dolls which might be displayed, or if this person would display them for the children to come and see. Take small groups and caution the children that they can only look and see, for these dolls are priceless.
4. If you are fortunate enough to have Japanese friends, ask them to come and share a doll, set of dolls, or pictures of such dolls.
5. You may wish to borrow or purchase the following for a display:
   a. *kokeshi* (koh-KAY-she), a wooden spool-like Japanese doll
   b. *daruma* (dah-ROO-mah), an egg-shaped wooden Asian doll

   NOTE: Color 'n Dress dolls and Bam-Beano wooden people from Uni-World Toys are similar to Asian dolls but are manufactured in America. Fisher-Price Weebles are also similar to the spool-like Kokeshi doll. It will be interesting for children to notice the similarities of dolls made and enjoyed by other children in different parts of the world.

6. Encourage the children to make their own carp kites by providing the necessary materials. (See illustrations and directions, p. 214.)
7. Make certain that some of the doll clothes in the doll center are for boy dolls. An addition of a new boy doll might be an occasion for sharing this Boys' Day festival.

Cinco de Mayo (Sin-koh day MY-yoh)

Mexican Independence Day, May 5th, is a holiday celebrating the day that the Mexican army under General Ignacio Zaragosa defeated an invasion of the French in Puebla, Mexico, and thus saved the nation.

Festivities include speeches, *mendudo* cookoffs, *mariachi* bands, dancing, crowning of a queen, and, of course, *piñatas* and treats for the children. If there are such celebrations in your area perhaps some of the children will attend.

Extended Experiences

1. Invite a parent who plays in a *mariachi* band to come and play his instrument for the children.
2. Find Mexico on a map or a globe. Ask if the children know anyone who has made a trip to Mexico.
3. Display a Mexican flag and a United States flag. Talk about the similarities and differences.
4. Make guacamole and serve with crackers or tortilla chips.
5. Display pictures of children in Mexico.
6. Have a fiesta: listen to a recording of a *mariachi* band. Dance using *maracas*. Make or purchase a *piñata*. (See *Las Posadas*, p. 278.)
7. Chocolate originated in Mexico. Make chocolate Mexicano. Melt 1 ounce of Mexican or other type of chocolate in 1 cup of milk. If you do not have Mexican chocolate, add a pinch of ground cinnamon. Beat with a *molinillo*, or eggbeater, until frothy.
8. Play the song "Cinco de Mayo" from the record *Holiday Songs and Rhythms*, Hap Palmer (Educational Activities, Inc., 33⅓ RPM).

Tu B'Shevat (Too-bish-vaht)

In Israel, this spring holiday in January or February is a special day for tree planting. It is on this day that the winter season ends. Since much of Israel is dry, trees help hold the soil in place and give shade. Symbolically, a tree often stands for nobility and utility; fathers therefore plant a cedar if a boy is born or a cypress if a girl is born. Children parade with gardening tools and later plant trees, sing, play outdoor games, and dance on this holiday.

In other countries on this day, Jewish families eat grapes, raisins, almonds, and the fruits of trees that grow in Israel, such as oranges, figs, dates, and *boksor* (fruit from the carob tree), as well as plant trees in memory of friends or relatives.

NOTE: If appropriate, on our Arbor Day (April 28th in most states), you might choose to plant a tree, bush, or plant in your yard and talk about how other people around the world have similar holidays because all people benefit from trees and plants.

Basanth (Buh-sahnth)

Usually this Muslim holiday for the first day of spring (lunar calendar) falls in late February or March and is heralded by the new moon. It is celebrated in some parts of Eastern Europe and Africa as well as Asia.

In Pakistan, Punjabi kites—special, elaborate, colorful kites without tails—are flown on this national holiday. Stout string stiffened or coated with starch and powdered glass allows boys to cut down each other's kites during competitions. Usually kites are flown from rooftops or high hills to avoid trees. Businesses and shops are often closed for the festivities.

NOTE: A simple kite might be made by the children. (See Chinese New Year guide, p. 214.)

Holi or Basaat (Hoh-lee or Buh-saht)

This is a spring festival and the gayest of the Hindu holidays. It usually occurs late in March or early April before the monsoon (big rain) begins. It is on the fifteenth day of the light half of the moon in the Hindu month of *Phalguna*. Children squirt colored water at each other. Water games sometimes involve teams of participants. Favorite Hindu colors, red, crimson, and saffron are most often used in water pistols or large pumps. In India, wreaths are often made to place around cows' necks or to be hung near windows and doors.

In Bengal, India, gifts are given and preparations made before eating special foods on this holiday, which is connected with Indian worship of Krishna, a Hindu god. Colored powders are used in the festivities. East Indian children who live in America enjoy throwing confetti when celebrating this holiday.

Extended Experiences

1. A special fun time for your children during this holiday might be to throw confetti, to make simple wreaths or necklaces with colored paper to hang near doors or windows, or to squirt water at each other when dressed appropriately (raincoats or swimsuits).
2. Children can squirt water and then sprinkle dry tempera on a mural laid on the floor, and watch colors run together.

Basanta (Buh-SAHN-tah)

This is another spring Hindu holiday celebrated three weeks earlier than Holi. In Sanskrit, *basanta* means yellow, which is the sacred color of the Hindus. In India, this festival is held in recognition of *Saraswati*, the Hindu goddess of sixty-four arts and sciences and also the wife of the god Brahma.

Extended Experiences

1. If you have East Indian friends, you might ask them to share some artifacts with the children, such as a beautiful silk sari, interesting pieces of ivory, silver, or clay, possibly

with mirrors embedded in them, or perhaps an exquisitely embroidered painting. Often ivory and wood are carved into elephants. Most young children are familiar with and fascinated by this animal and have seen it in picture books if not in zoos or circuses.

2. At Christmastime, charming clay elephants, bells, and camels made of mirror-faceted clay are available as tree ornaments at import shops. Other such items are available during the rest of the year.

3. Prepare and serve an Indian dish. Consult an international cookbook for recipes.

Sham Al Naseem (Shahm Ul Nah-seem)

In Egypt, this holiday welcomes spring for both Christians and Muslims. The name of this national holiday means literally "smell of spring," and the holiday often is celebrated by going outdoors on a picnic in the desert, to the beach at the Red or Mediterranean Sea, or for a boat ride up the Nile River.

Extended Experiences

1. Teach the children a common greeting for this day, Al Sal-a-mu-alaecum (Ehl Sahl-a-mo-uh-le-kum), which means "Peace be with you."

2. Prepare *midamis* (kidney beans) and *fasiyah* (dried fish), since they are often eaten on this holiday.

Now-Ruz (Noh-rooz)

This Iranian holiday celebrates three things: the beginning of the new year, spring, and Iran's national day. (See New Year's Day Around the World guide, p. 198.)

May Day

Young children in the United States and Europe make baskets from paper or recycled containers, fill them with flowers and sometimes popcorn and candy, and then hang them on the doorknobs of friends. Most often children leave their friendship baskets secretly, ringing the friend's doorbell and then hiding until the basket is discovered. This holiday is said to have come from a Roman festival of flowers.

Extended Experiences

1. Simple May baskets can be made by stapling a quarter-circle of wallpaper or construction paper into a cone-shaped basket. Plastic margarine tubs, berry baskets, or other small cartons can also be decorated with lick-and-stick forms or ribbons. Attach handles of pipecleaners, ribbon, and yarn.

2. May 1st is also Hawaii's Lei Day. Make simple leis by stringing paper forms (make some petal-like) and alternate with styrofoam bits on a piece of yarn or string, to celebrate this holiday.

Additional Facts the Teacher Should Know

In the northern hemisphere, spring is March 21st–June 20th. (In the southern hemisphere it is September 23rd–December 21st.) The equinox is the time of year when the center of the sun is directly over the equator. The word "equinox" means equal night. During an equinox the days are the same length as the nights all over the world. The sun appears to cross the equator twice a year, so there are two equinoxes. The spring, or vernal equinox occurs around March 20th as the earth tilts its northern hemisphere toward the sun. The autumnal equinox comes about six months later, around September 23rd, as the earth tilts back and the sun "moves" south. This change in the earth's position produces variations in the patterns of warm and cold air masses to such a degree that storms are frequent at the time of the equinoxes. As the sun "travels" north, its rays strike the northern countries more directly each day, and the weather grows steadily warmer. The time from the end of the vernal equinox to the beginning of the autumnal equinox is longer than the interval between the autumnal equinox and the following vernal equinox. This difference amounts to seven days each year, or six days in leap years. It is caused by the elliptical shape of the earth's path around the sun. The earth must move faster when it is nearer the sun.

NOTE: See Additional Facts the Teacher Should Know in the Day and Night guide for illustrations of the equinoxes. Other related guides are Animals, Water, and Color.

Methods Most Adaptable for Introducing This Subject to Children

- Talk about what happens in the spring: new leaves, flowers blooming, seeds sprouting, baby animals, birds returning, and nest building.
- Read a story about the change of seasons or spring. (See Book Center.)
- Let the children select pictures of spring and spring activities and put them on the bulletin boards. (They can do this easily with push-pins rather than thumbtacks.)
- Discovery table: a bird's nest or eggs, a blooming crocus which has been dug up and put in a pot, sprouting seeds, a tadpole or frog eggs in pond water.

  NOTE: Return these to pond when observation period is over.

- Force a flowering shrub or tree branch by bringing it inside late in February so that it will bloom early. Use the same procedure with a bulb.
- Children should be encouraged to watch for signs of spring: the first robin, a bulb sprouting, leaf or flower buds unfurling, the first dandelion, frogs croaking, grass turning green, a crocus blooming, snow melting.
- Care for a live bunny. (See Animal Charts.)

Vocabulary

rabbit	hunt	Easter	parade	dye	egg
kite	earth	tadpole	born	rain	wind
crocus	migrate	polliwog	dandelion	showers	seed
bulb	plant	spring	bouquet	bud	flower
sprout	robin	hatch	garden	blossom	leaf

learning centerf

Discovery Center

Plants

1. Provide child-size gardening equipment (real garden tools of small size are much more sturdy and satisfactory than toys) and, if yard space allows, plant a vegetable or flower garden. This can be a most educational and rewarding plant growing experiment. If the teacher plans extended experiences, children will be able: to observe plants' gradual growth, to learn the care needed, and to harvest, cook, and eat their crop, if vegetables, or pick and arrange, if flowers. You will need to plant early if your school ends by June 1st. Ideally, a plot in the play yard that can be easily cared for routinely by the children when they are outdoors is far better than a garden that must be maintained by a teacher until a crop can be harvested. Allow children to care for this garden by watering and weeding. Radishes and lettuce are rewarding because they mature quickly and are edible. Marigold seeds are fairly dependable for quick flowering.

   CAUTION: Careful supervision is necessary as tools have sharp edges.

2. Discover how seeds grow. Line the inside of a large straight-sided jar with brown blotting paper. Dampen this paper and place a variety of seeds of different sizes about halfway down the side of the jar between the jar and the blotting paper. The seeds will sprout at different times, which will help to maintain the children's interest. Radish seeds seem to sprout almost immediately. Bean sprouts are more likely than other seeds to mold before they have a chance to sprout. Carrot, lettuce, and corn seeds are also satisfactory. Just enough water should be kept in the jar to touch the bottom of the blotting paper. If the blotting paper dries out, the sprouts will die quickly.

3. Seeds may be placed in shallow pans and the corresponding vegetables or fruits displayed so that the children may see what grows from the seed: for instance, grapefruit seeds, a tiny grapefruit tree newly sprouted, and a grapefruit. The real object is better than a photograph or picture. **Variation:** Plant seeds or seedlings in peat pots. This allows plants to be taken home and placed directly into the ground there. If they are planted, however, in a paper or plastic cup without making a hole in the bottom, roots are more likely to rot from being overwatered even though maintenance may be supervised by a willing parent.

4. Grow grass by sprouting bent grass on a damp sponge or wet blotter. Before seeding, cut sponge or blotter in shapes such as a shamrock for St. Patrick's Day (March 17th).

5. Provide a magnifying glass for the close examination of buds, new leaves, tree seeds, and insects.

6. Force a hyacinth bulb: set several bulbs into the soil in a large pot and bury so that the tops of the bulbs are about eight inches below the surface of the ground. This may be done in late October or November. After ten or twelve weeks, bring inside and place in a cool, dark place until the sprouts are about four inches high—keep watered. Bring into the light occasionally and observe that the yellow sprouts turn green very soon, and the buds and blooms appear. Fertilize in sprout stage with Hyponex. You should have hyacinths blooming in February.

7. If children plant bulbs in the fall, they can watch the plants develop and bloom naturally in April. A lily bulb can be forced to bloom during the Easter season. This is more satisfactory than just buying one that is already blooming.

8. Watch a sweet potato sprout. (See Food guide, p. 549.) It is interesting to observe that the part of the potato in the water makes roots while the top produces sprouts with leaves.

9. Plant seeds in eggshells. Marigold or pumpkin seeds produce very gratifying results and may be taken home and planted by the children, by gently crushing the eggshell before putting it in the ground. The seeds are easily tended by placing the eggshells in an egg carton and keeping the lid on until the seeds sprout. Water with a teaspoon.

10. A spring walk will enable the children to find and observe many new and growing things. Take a magnifying glass and paper sacks in which to collect *treasures*.

Animals

1. Care for a baby animal such as a gerbil, guinea pig, or rabbit. Be sure there is a home that will welcome this creature when you no longer wish to keep it in the classroom. (See Animal Charts for care and feeding.)

2. Incubate and hatch an egg. Children need to learn to respect and care for living things. Make a calendar to check off days: twenty-one days for chicks and twenty-eight days for ducklings. Quail eggs are another possibility.

3. Obtain silkworm eggs in March. If carefully tended, these will hatch into tiny larvae which must be fed mulberry leaves (lettuce, chopped very fine, will substitute for a week until the mulberry leaves unfurl). The entire life cycle from eggs to eggs may be observed by the children before the end of May, and the new eggs may be stored in a cool place until the next spring.

4. Prepare and observe an ant house (commercially available through catalogs listing science supplies).

5. Earthworms may be housed in a jar of loose earth and fed on a small amount of minced lettuce.

   CAUTION: Do not drown them with too much water.

6. Provide insect cages for insects the children may catch. Observe for a day or so and then turn the insects loose. Many children seem to feel that "a bug is to squash"; careful handling and concern for these small creatures must be emphasized constantly. (See Insect guide, p. 435.)

7. Obtain praying mantis egg cases (Linwood Gardens, Dept. 743, Linwood, N.J. 08221). These hatch in May and emerge as tiny replicas of the adult insect. The process is fascinating to watch.

   CAUTION: Be sure to keep the case in a jar covered with gauze or you will have baby mantids everywhere.

8. Visit a farm to see new baby animals. (See Farm Animals, p. 389.)

9. Go to a pond or brook to find frog eggs or tadpoles. You might be just in time to watch the eggs hatch into tadpoles. Spring peeper tadpoles turn into frogs in one season and into bullfrogs in two seasons. The huge bullfrog tadpoles are great to observe. Be sure to keep these creatures in pond water. It is advisable to return them to their natural environment, since they are becoming an endangered species.

10. Display Plants and Seeds, picture fold-outs; Take a Walk in Spring, Life Cycle of a Frog, and Life Cycle of a Robin sequence charts (Child's World). The companion book *Spring Is Here* and cassettes provide additional experience in observing and listening.

Weather

1. On a windy day, fly a kite (see Chinese New Year guide, p. 214) or blow bubbles outdoors. (See p. 558.) The children could let milkweed seeds out of the pods. Make

paper pinwheels or fly paper airplanes or helicopters. (See Air Transportation guide, p. 467.) Release fluffy feathers into the air.

2. Go for a walk during a spring shower. Look for a rainbow.
3. Make a rainbow. (See Color guide, p. 586.)
4. Use a cardboard thermometer. (See Mathematics guide, p. 620.)
5. Make a weather calendar: each day in March, have a child check on the weather and paste the appropriate symbol on the day: sun, clouds, rain, or snow. There is usually quite a variety.

Senses

1. Listen for sounds of spring: bird and animal calls, thunder, wind, raindrops, insects buzzing.
2. Uniquely delightful spring smells are: fresh air, different flower fragrances, spring rain, the smell of soil, fresh-cut grass.
3. Create the opportunity to feel pussywillows, new grass, animal fur, blossoms, wind and air currents, seeds.
4. Look for all signs of spring. (See Methods Most Adaptable for Introducing This Subject.)
5. If you have access to a spotlight or a filmstrip projector, let children experiment with making shadow pictures. View-Master projectors are quite inexpensive.

Dramatic Play Centers

Home-Living Center

1. Replace some winter articles such as hats, scarves, and mittens with different spring hats, gloves, stoles, and rainwear.
2. Suggest that the house could be spring-cleaned or rearranged.
3. The doll clothes could be washed and hung out to dry.
4. Provide flowers, real or artificial, to make bouquets.

Block-Building Center

1. Block corner: set out unbreakable chicks, ducks, rabbits—suggest building pens, hutches, and fences. Include sets of mother animals and their young.
2. Inexpensive small plastic flowers could be used to lay out a park or garden by letting children insert into flat pieces of styrofoam to hold upright as if growing.

Other Dramatic Play Centers

1. Locate bunny, duck, chicken, or baby animal Halloween costumes for children to wear to pretend to be animals. Attaching a tail, wings, or ears will suffice. Appropriate face masks can be made from wire coat hangers, sacks, or paper plates. (See Halloween guide, p. 227.)
2. Commercial or homemade sock puppets can be used for a puppet show behind a box, three-way screen, or puppet stage.
3. Hand puppets can be made from small paper sacks, and the children can either paste on ears and faces or mark them with felt-tip pens. Children's white socks make nice puppets, too.
4. Arrange a hat store from hats children make in the Art Center or commercial hats available from Constructive Playthings.
5. Make available some commercially made Easter baskets, plastic eggs, stuffed animals, and other Easter items. Children like to hide their own eggs.

Learning, Language, and Readiness Materials Center

Commercially made games and materials for use at a table or a mat:

(See Basic Resources, p. 79, for manufacturers' addresses.)

1. Judy Puzzles: Animal Parents and Babies, series 6–11 pcs. each; Animal, series 4–14 pcs. each
2. Judy Puzzles: Humpty Dumpty, 13 pcs.; Little Bo Peep, 8 pcs.; Tulip, 6 pcs.; Parade, 20 pcs.; Boy with Pigeons, 6 pcs.; Valentine's Day, 19 pcs.
3. Judy See-Quees: Seasons, 4 pcs.; Seed to Flower, Robin Builds a Nest, Tadpole to Frog, Caterpillar to Butterfly, An Apple Tree Grows, Eggs to Chickens, Making Maple Syrup, all 6 pcs. each
4. Judy Reversible Puzzles: Tadpoles and Frogs, 5 pcs.; Caterpillars and Moths, 12 pcs.; Bees and Hive, 15 pcs.
5. Judy Circular Puzzles: Seasons, 21 pcs. with teacher's guide
6. Baby Animals: 7-18 pcs. (Playskool)
7. Animals and Their Young: poster cards (Milton Bradley)
8. Lotto: Farm, Zoo, World Around Us (Ed-U-Card)
9. Animal and Bird Dominoes (National Wildlife Federation)
10. Domestic Animals and Pets, Farm Animals, Seasons: flannelboard aids (Milton Bradley)
11. Spring: Mini-Poster Cards, 14 pictures, 10 inches by 13 inches per set (Trend Enterprises)
12. Seasons and Plant Growth: flannelboard aids (Milton Bradley)
13. Seasons: table top set, 40 illustrations (Instructo)

Teacher-made games and materials for use at a table or on a mat:

NOTE: For detailed description of Games, see pp. 50–59.

1. Children may cut out and paste spring pictures on pages, to be assembled into a book about spring or to put up on the bulletin board. Use pictures from seed and flower catalogs.
2. Make Match-Them or classification cards by mounting large gummed seals of birds, animals, flowers, butterflies, rabbits, or Easter eggs. Make Match-Thems of animals and their young or animals and what they eat.
3. How Many?: make circle counters for counting or sorting colors and other subjects by mounting the gummed seals listed in No. 2 on cardboard discs or octagons. (See p. 56 for illustration of discs.)
4. Grouping and Sorting by Association: sort plastic eggs by colors and put in Easter baskets, or precut Easter eggs from a variety of brightly colored construction paper to classify by color or size.

Art Center

** 1. Add interest to easel painting center by using pastel colors (add color to white paint).

** 2. Spatter-paint over animal or flower shapes. Children can make their own stencils by choosing or arranging geometric shapes cut from innertubes or plastic upholstery scraps.

** 3. Pastel soap painting: color Ivory detergent flakes with tempera to make pastel shades for painting. A little liquid starch added to this stiff mixture makes it less fragile when dry.

** 4. Blow painting (to illustrate wind): place spoonful of paint on paper and, using halves of drinking straws, blow on the paint for a splatter-type picture.

*** 5. Sponge-paint blossoms on crayoned tree trunks drawn on construction paper.

* 6. Mud-paint outdoors with bare feet.

** 7. Large kindergarten chalk used on pastel construction paper creates a lovely effect. Do this activity at the easel to avoid smearing. Spray with hair spray or fixative when finished.

** 8. Dipping pastel chalk in sugar water before applying to construction paper or brushing buttermilk on paper before using chalk makes a more permanent product.

*** 9. Make rainbows using flat sides of crayon stubs or Chunk-O-Crayons (Milton Bradley).

** 10. Use animal- or flower-shaped cookie cutters with play dough.

*** 11. Cut and paste pictures from flower and seed catalogs, wallpaper books, and old greeting cards.

*** 12. Tear free-form shapes from white construction paper (pieces as large as possible). Paste on blue paper. Just for fun, suggest that the children tell you what the picture looks like after it is finished. Make up their own *It Looked Like Spilt Milk* book with these pages. (See Book Center, p. 342.)

** 13. Color sawdust or rice with tempera or food coloring. Sprinkle on construction paper that has been brushed or squirted with white glue.

** 14. If you know of an office that uses computer cards, ask if they will save the tiny punched-out, pastel-colored pieces. Use these as in No. 13.

** 15. Make collages from seeds, twigs, and soft maple and elm pods.

** 16. Pastel styrofoam from egg cartons makes a lovely spring collage material.

** 17. Vegetable prints: save sliced ends of green peppers, celery, cabbage, lemons, limes, or apples. Dip in tempera (make stamp pad) and print on paper. Use sponge shapes or corrugated cardboard rolled across the paper (both ways) if more feasible than food scraps.

*** 18. Pressed flowers: use on spring mural or greeting cards.

*** 19. Draw two posts on paper, and paste a piece of string or yarn across between them. Children like to paste pieces of cloth on this line to look like clothes hanging on a clothesline in the wind.

** 20. Precut tissue paper circles. Children may wad these up, dip in paste, and fasten to paper to represent crocuses in green grass or blossoms on a tree.

*** 21. Individual pussywillows make tiny animals. Let children design their own "pussy-willow creatures" using other collage materials, crayons, or paint.

*** 22. Make egg carton caterpillars, paint green or another color. Add toothpicks with balls of playdough or small pipe cleaners for antennae. Children may paint or decorate with gummed paper according to their own imagination.

*** 23. Make a butterfly from a cylindrical clothespin: use precut rectangles of tissue paper for wings. Children may decorate with bits of gummed paper or other collage items. Birds can be made from Baggies stuffed with tissue; attach cut paper wings and tails with tape. Encourage children to explore insect, bird, and butterfly books.

*** 24. Make pinwheels or paper gliders. (See p. 467 for directions and illustrations.)

** 25. Make kites. (See p. 214 for illustrations.)

* 26. Paste precut colored-paper ovals in the center of a sheet of construction paper. Let children finish the picture by adding eyes, wings, bills, tails, and feet to make chicks and other animals.

** 27. Make bunnies, clouds, and lambs by pasting cotton balls on paper.

Book Center

NOTE: The book list in this guide has been divided into several sub-groupings for convenience. These groupings are listed alphabetically but not necessarily in any subject sequence.

Clouds and Rain

*** Fisher, Aileen. *I Like Weather.* New York: Thomas Y. Crowell, 1963.

  * Foster, Joanna. *Pete's Puddle.* New York: Harcourt Brace Jovanovich, 1950.

*** Gans, Roma. *Please Pass the Grass.* New York: David McKay, 1960.

  * Holl, Adelaide. *The Rain Puddle.* New York: Lothrop, Lee & Shepard, 1965.

 ** Keats, Ezra Jack. *A Letter to Amy.* New York: Harper & Row, 1968.

 ** Parsons, Ellen. *Rainy Day Together.* New York: Harper & Row, 1971.

 ** Scheer, Julian. *Rain Makes Applesauce.* New York: Holiday House, 1964.

*** Schlein, Miriam. *The Sun, the Wind, the Sea, and the Rain.* New York: Abelard-Schuman, 1960.

  * Shaw, Charles G. *It Looked Like Spilt Milk.* New York: Harper & Row, 1947.

*** Shulevitz, Uri. *Rain Rain Rivers.* New York: Farrar, Strauss & Giroux, 1969.

 ** Tresselt, Alvin. *Hide and Seek Fog.* New York: Lothrop, Lee & Shepard, 1965.

 ** ———. *Rain, Drop, Splash.* New York: Lothrop, Lee & Shepard, 1965.

*** Zolotow, Charlotte. *The Storm Book.* New York: Harper & Row, 1952.

Easter Bunnies, Eggs, Chicks

*** Anderson, Lonzo, and Adrienne Adams. *Zoo Rabbits.* New York: Viking Press, 1968.

*** Armour, Richard. *The Adventures of Egbert the Easter Egg.* New York: McGraw-Hill, 1965.

 ** Berg, Jean Horton. *The Little Red Hen.* New York: Harper & Row, 1963.

*** Boreman, Jean. *About Bantie and Her Chicks.* Chicago, Ill.: Childrens Press, 1959.

 ** Brown, Margaret Wise. *Little Chicken.* New York: Harper & Row, 1943.

 ** ———. *Nibble, Nibble.* Reading, Mass.: Addison-Wesley, 1959.

 ** ———. *The Runaway Bunny.* New York: Harper & Row, 1952.

  * ———. *The Golden Egg Book.* New York: Western Publishing, 1943.

  * Carroll, Ruth. *Where's the Bunny?* New York: Henry Z. Walck, 1962.

*** Duvoisin, Roger. *Easter Treat.* New York: Alfred A. Knopf, 1954.

*** Fisher, Aileen. *Listen Rabbit.* New York: Thomas Y. Crowell, 1964.

*** Foster, Marian Curtis. *Miss Flora McFlimsey's Easter Bonnet.* New York: Lothrop Lee & Shepard, 1951.

 ** Friedrich, Priscilla and Otto. *The Easter Bunny That Overslept.* New York: Lothrop, Lee & Shepard, 1957.

*** Garelick, May. *What's Inside?* Reading, Mass.: Addison-Wesley Co., 1955.

*** ———. *The Story of An Egg That Hatched.* New York: School Book Service, 1970 (paper).

 ** Grant, Bruce. *How Chicks Are Born.* Chicago, Ill.: Rand McNally, 1967.

*** Heyward, DuBose. *The Country Bunny and the Little Golden Shoes.* Boston: Houghton Mifflin, 1939.

*** Holl, Adelaide. *The Remarkable Egg.* New York: Lothrop, Lee & Shepard, 1958.

 ** Keats, Ezra Jack. *Jennie's Hat.* New York: Harper & Row, 1966.

  * Lenski, Lois. *Spring is Here.* New York: Henry Z. Walck, 1945.

*** Littlefield, William. *The Whiskers of Ho Ho.* New York: Lothrop, Lee & Shepard, 1958.

 ** Memling, Carl. *Hi! All You Rabbits.* New York: Parents' Magazine Press, 1970.

*** Milhous, Katherine. *The Egg Tree.* New York: Scribner's, 1950.

*** Peet, Bill. *The Pinkish, Purplish, Bluish Egg.* Boston: Houghton Mifflin, 1963.
*** Potter, Beatrix. *The Tale of Peter Rabbit.* New York: F. Warne, 1972 (paper).
 ** Schenk, Esther. *Eastertime.* Chicago, Ill.: Lyons and Carnahan, 1953.
*** Schloat, G. Warren, Jr. *Wonderful Egg.* New York: Charles Scribner's Sons, 1952.
 ** Seuss, Dr. (Geisel, Theodore). *Green Eggs and Ham.* New York: Random House, 1960 (an easy reader).
*** ———. *Scrambled Eggs Super!* New York: Random House, 1953.
 ** Steiner, Charlotte. *A Surprise for Mrs. Bunny.* New York: Grosset & Dunlap, 1945.
*** Thayer, Jane. *The Horse with the Easter Bonnet.* New York: William Morrow, 1953.
*** Tresselt, Alvin. *The World in the Candy Egg.* New York: Lothrop, Lee & Shepard, 1957.
  * Wiese, Kurt. *Happy Easter.* New York: Viking Press, 1962.
 ** Zolotow, Charlotte. *Mr. Rabbit and the Lovely Present.* New York: Harper & Row, 1962.
*** ———. *The Bunny Who Found Easter.* Berkeley, Calif.: Parnassus Press, 1959.

Seasons

  * Adelson, Leone. *All Ready for Summer.* New York: David McKay, 1955.
*** Birnbaum, A. *Green Eyes.* New York: Western Publishing, 1973.
 ** Burningham, John. *Seasons.* New York: Bobbs-Merrill, 1970.
*** Burton, Virginia Lee. *The Little House.* Boston, Mass.: Houghton Mifflin, 1969.
*** Clifton, Lucille. *The Boy Who Didn't Believe In Spring.* New York: E. P. Dutton, 1973.
*** Duvoisin, Roger. *The House of Four Seasons.* New York: Lothrop, Lee & Shepard, 1956.
 ** Gay, Zhenya. *The Nicest Time of the Year.* New York: Viking Press, 1960.
*** Lifgren, Ulf. *The Wonderful Tree.* New York: Delacorte Press, 1970.
*** Tresselt, Alvin. *It's Time Now.* New York: Lothrop, Lee & Shepard, 1969.
 ** Udry, Janice. *A Tree Is Nice.* New York: Harper & Row, 1956.
  * Zolotow, Charlotte. *Summer Is Here.* New York: Abelard-Schuman, 1967.

Seeds and Plants

*** Bulla, Clyde. *A Tree Is a Plant.* New York: Thomas Y. Crowell, 1960.
*** Goldin, Augusta. *Where Does Your Garden Grow?* New York: Thomas Y. Crowell, 1967.
*** Jordan, Helene. *How a Seed Grows.* New York: Thomas Y. Crowell, 1960 (paper).
*** ———. *Seeds by Wind and Water.* New York: Thomas Y. Crowell, 1962.
 ** Lubbel, Winifred and Cecil. *The Tall Grass Zoo.* Chicago, Ill.: Rand McNally, 1960.
 ** Selsam, Millicent. *Seeds and More Seeds.* New York: Harper & Row, 1959.
 ** Tresselt, Alvin. *Under the Trees and Through the Grass.* New York: Lothrop, Lee, & Shepard, 1962.
*** Watson, Aldren. *My Garden Grows.* New York: Viking Press, 1962.
 ** Weber, Irma E. *Up Above and Down Below.* Reading, Mass.: Addison-Wesley, 1943.

Spring

 ** Baum, Arlene and Joseph. *One Bright Monday Morning.* New York: Random House, 1962.
*** Chönz, Selina. *A Bell for Ursli.* New York: Henry Z. Walck, 1953.
 ** Francoise. *Springtime for Jeanne-Marie.* New York: Scribner's, 1965 (paper).
 ** Johnson, Crockett. *Will Spring Be Early?* New York: Thomas Y. Crowell, 1959.
*** Kay, Helen. *City Springtime.* New York: Hastings House, 1957.
*** Krauss, Ruth. *The Happy Day.* New York: Harper & Row, 1949.
*** Kuskin, Karla. *The Bear Who Saw the Spring.* New York: Harper & Row, 1961 (in rhyme).
  * Lenski, Lois. *Spring Is Here.* New York: Henry Z. Walck, 1945.

** Politi, Leo. *Juanita*. New York: Scribner's, 1948.

* Zolotow, Charlotte. *One Step, Two*. New York: Lothrop, Lee & Shepard, 1955.

Spring Creatures

** Brown, Margaret Wise. *The Dead Bird*. Reading, Mass.: Addison-Wesley, 1958.

*** D'Aulaire, Ingri and Edgar. *Don't Count Your Chicks*. Garden City, New York: Doubleday, 1943.

*** Duvoisin, Roger. *Two Lonely Ducks*. New York: Alfred A. Knopf, 1955 (counting book).

** Flack, Marjorie. *Tim Tadpole and the Great Bullfrog*. Garden City, N.Y.: Doubleday, 1959 (paper).

** Freschet, Berniece. *The Old Bullfrog*. New York: Scribner's, 1968 (paper, 1972).

** Friskey, Margaret. *Seven Diving Ducks*. Chicago, Ill.: Childrens Press, 1965.

*** Gans, Roma, and Franklyn M. Branley. *Flash, Crash, Rumble, Roll*. New York: Thomas Y. Crowell, 1964.

*** ———. *It's Nesting Time*. New York: Thomas Y. Crowell, 1964 (filmstrip, record, cassette).

** Garelick, May. *Where Does the Butterfly Go When It Rains?* Reading, Mass.: Addison-Wesley, 1961 (Scholastic Book Service, paper, 1970).

* Hawkinson, John. *Robins and Rabbits*. Chicago, Ill.: Albert Whitman, 1960 (a sightsaver edition is available).

** Ipcar, Dahlov. *The Song of the Day Birds and the Night Birds*. Garden City, N.Y.: Doubleday, 1967.

** Lionni, Leo. *Inch by Inch*. New York: Astor-Honor, 1962.

*** McCloskey, Robert. *Make Way for Ducklings*. New York: Viking Press, 1969 (paper).

** Miles, Miska. *Apricot ABC*. Boston, Mass.: Little Brown, 1969 (insects, animals).

*** Miller, Edna. *Mousekin Finds a Friend*. Englewood Cliffs, N. J.: Prentice-Hall, 1967 (paper).

*** Oppenheim, Joanne. *Have You Seen Birds?* Reading, Mass.: Addison-Wesley, 1968.

* Poulet, Virginia. *Little Blue Bug and the Bullies*. Chicago, Ill.: Childrens Press, 1971.

*** Tresselt, Alvin, *The Frog in the Well*. New York: Lothrop, Lee & Shepard, 1958.

*** ———. *Hi, Mr. Robin*. New York: Lothrop, Lee & Shepard, 1950.

** Victor, Joan Berg. *Where Is My Monster?* New York: Crown, 1971.

** Weil, Lisl. *The Wiggler*. Boston: Houghton Mifflin, 1971.

*** Zemanc, Harve. *The Speckled Hen*. New York: Holt, Rinehart & Winston, 1966 (paper).

Wind

** Ets, Marie Hall. *Gilberto and the Wind*. New York: Viking Press, 1963.

* Hutchins, Pat. *The Wind Blew*. New York: Macmillan, 1974.

*** Lund, Doris Herold. *Attic of the Wind*. New York: Parents' Magazine Press, 1966.

** Rey, Margaret. *Curious George Flies a Kite*. Boston, Mass.: Houghton Mifflin, 1958.

*** Tresselt, Alvin. *Follow the Wind*. New York: Lothrop, Lee & Shepard, 1950.

*** Yolen, Jane. *The Emperor and the Kite*. Cleveland, Ohio: Collins, Williams, & World, 1967.

** Zolotow, Charlotte. *When the Wind Stops*. New York: Abelard-Schuman, 1962.

planning for grouptime

NOTE: All music, fingerplays, poems, stories, and games listed here may also be used at other times during the session as appropriate. See Core Library, Basic Resources, p. 76, for publishers and addresses. Addresses for sources of records will be found on p. 81.

Music

Songs

FROM original songs in this book by JoAnne Deal Hicks
- ** "It's Spring," p. 351
- * "Raindrops," p. 352
- * "Bugs," p. 443
- ** "The Turtles down the Road," p. 422
- ** "Springtime" (a parody), p. 121
- ** "A Cloudy Spring Day," p. 580

FROM *Songs for the Nursery School*, MacCarteney
- * "Hop, Little Bunny," p. 30
- * "Pretty Little Bunny," p. 30
- * "The Ducklings," p. 33
- * "The Hen," p. 33
- * "Ducks," p. 35
- * "Fly Away, Little Birdie," p. 36
- * "Robin Song," p. 36
- *** "Tell Me, Wind," p. 56
- * "Windy Weather," p. 58
- * "It's Raining on the Town," p. 59
- * "'Tis Raining," p. 60
- ** "All the Birds Are Singing Again," p. 61
- * "Spring Is Here," p. 61
- * "Hot Cross Buns," p. 75
- * "Humpty Dumpty," p. 75

FROM *Songs for Early Childhood*, Westminster Press
- ** "Sweet Plum Blossoms," p. 19
- ** "Pretty Little Pussy Willow," p. 20
- * "Sleep, Little Seed," p. 21
- * "Lying on the Hillside," p. 26
- * "Sing a Song of Sunshine," p. 36
- * "Sing a Song of Gardens," p. 37
- ** "I Went Walking Outdoors Today," p. 40 (children may suggest things they saw or heard)
- * "Little Birds Are Singing a Song," p. 46
- ** "Go to Sleep Now, Little Bird," p. 47
- * "Our Bunny's So Funny," p. 51

* "Butterfly, Butterfly," p. 54
* "Walking in the Sunshine," p. 101
* "Springtime," p. 106

FROM *Music Activities for Retarded Children*, Ginglend and Stiles
** "It's Easter," p. 68
* "The Seasons," p. 94

FROM *Wake Up and Sing*, Landeck and Crook
*** "Little Seed," p. 92

FROM *Music Resource Book*, Lutheran Church Press
* "Listen to the Rain," p. 25
* "Isn't It Fun?" p. 46 (adapt to spring—rain, dig in the sand, etc.)
** "Six Little Ducks," p. 62

Records

"A Springtime Walk," *Lucille Wood Picture Song Book* (Bowmar, 33⅓ RPM or cassette)
"All About Spring" (33⅓ RPM, available from Lyons)
"Carnival of the Animals" (Golden Record, 33⅓ RPM)
"Easter" and "Maypole Dance," *Holiday Rhythms* (Bowmar, 33⅓ RPM)
"Indoors When It Rains" (Children's Record Guild, 45 and 78 RPM)
"Easter Time Is Here Again," *Holiday Songs and Rhythms*, Hap Palmer (Educational Activities, 33⅓ RPM)
"Muffin and Mother Goose"/"Muffin in the City"/"**Muffin in the Country**" (Young People's Record [YPR], 33⅓ RPM)
"My Playmate the Wind" (YPR, 78 and 45 RPM)
"Peter Cottontail" (Golden Records, 45 or 33⅓ RPM)
"Raindrops Keep Falling on My Head," B. J. Thomas, any recording
"**Rainy Day**"/"Building a City"/"What the Lighthouse Sees" (YPR, 33⅓ RPM)
"Spring" (Kimbo, 33⅓ RPM or cassette and filmstrip)
"The Carrot Seed"/"Eagle and the Thrush"/"Wait 'Til The Moon is Full" (YPR, 33⅓ RPM)
"The Rainy Day Record" (Bowmar, 33⅓ RPM)
"Another Rainy Day Record" (Bowmar, 33⅓ RPM)
"My Friend"/"A Visit to My Little Friend"/"**Creepy, Crawly Caterpillar**" (YPR, 33⅓ RPM)
"Train to the Farm," **All Aboard** (YPR, 33⅓ RPM)
"Singin' in the Rain" (Peter Pan, 33⅓ RPM)
"Whoa, Little Horses" (YPR, 78 or 45 RPM)

Rhythms and Singing Games

FROM *Music Resource Book*, Lutheran Church Press
"A-Tisket, A-Tasket," p. 91 (substitute "little Easter" for "green and yellow" basket)
"This Is the Way We Plant the Seeds," adaptation of "Mulberry Bush," p. 92

FROM *Songs for the Nursery School*, MacCarteney
"Heigh-ho, Daisies and Buttercups," p. 62
"See How I'm Jumping," p. 95
"Bouncing," p. 96
"Follow Me," p. 96

FROM appropriate music listed under Songs

Allow children to be waddling ducks, hopping rabbits, pecking chickens, and so forth.

"Bunny Hop": make headbands with paper rabbit ears and tails attached. (See p. 36 for tails.)

"Easter Parade": use hats the children have made in the Art Center.

FROM *Creative Movement for the Developing Child*, Cherry

"Crawling," pp. 18–20
"Creeping," pp. 22–28
"Walking and Running," pp. 29–35
"Resting Games," pp. 56–61

Fingerplays and Poems

FROM *Rhymes for Fingers and Flannelboards*, Scott and Thompson

"Ten Fluffy Chickens," p. 30
"Kitty and Bunny," p. 32
"Creepy, Crawly," p. 33
"Once I Saw a Beehive," p. 35
"Frisky's Doghouse," p. 36
"Little Rabbit," p. 41
"An Egg," p. 41
"On Easter Day," p. 73
"The Rabbits," p. 75
"Once There Was a Bunny," p. 76
"Houses," p. 86
"What the Animals Do," p. 88
"Eensie Weensie Spider," p. 91
"Sleepy Caterpillars," p. 91
"Dive, Little Tadpole," p. 92
"Things That Hop," p. 93
"I Am a Little Toad," p. 93

"Turtles," p. 94
"Five Little Robins," p. 95
"Here Is A Bunny," p. 96
"Two Blackbirds," p. 103
"Little Miss Muffet," p. 105
"Making Kites," p. 124
"The Wind," p. 125
"Raindrops," p. 125
"The Rain," p. 125
"Yellow Daffodil," p. 126
"The Flower," p. 126
"Relaxing Flowers," p. 126
"Flowers," p. 127
"Pretending," p. 128
"Five Little May Baskets," p. 128
"I Am a Top," p. 130

FROM *Let's Do Fingerplays*, Grayson

"Animal Antics," section, pp. 30–38
"Kitty, Kitty," p. 42
"Chickens," p. 42
"My Garden," p. 46
"Pitter-Pat," p. 46

"Raindrops," p. 47
"Five Little Froggies," p. 62
"Five Little Kittens," p. 64
"Two Little Ducks," p. 71
"Two Little Blackbirds," p. 73

FROM *Very Young Verses*, Geismer and Suter

"Birds, Beasts, and Bugs," pp. 1–42 (all poems)
"Rabbits," p. 17
"New Shoes," p. 55
"My Shadow," p. 61
"Lawn Mower," p. 79
"About the Seasons," pp. 112–17 (all poems)
"About the Weather," pp. 150–59

Stories

(To read, read-tell, or tell. See Book Center for complete list.)

  ** *One Bright Monday Morning*, Baum
  ** *Gilberto and the Wind*, Ets
  ** *Tim Tadpole and the Great Bullfrog*, Flack
  ** *Inch by Inch*, Lionni
 *** *Make Way for Ducklings*, McCloskey
 *** *My Garden Grows*, Watson
   * *The Golden Egg Book*, Brown
 *** *Easter Treat*, Duvoisin
  ** *The Easter Bunny That Overslept*, Friedrich
  ** *A Surprise for Mrs. Bunny*, Steiner
   * *Happy Easter*, Wiese

Games

(See Games, p. 50–58, and Teacher-Made Games in this guide for directions.)

1. Name It or Scramble: new leaf, bud, blade of grass, bird's nest, pussy willow, daffodil
2. I See Something That Tells It's Spring: outdoors or in the room
3. Reach and Feel: bag of spring items
4. Listen and Hear: sounds of spring outdoors or with window open
5. Who Am I?: riddles, simple descriptions of baby animals
6. Alike, Different, and the Same: use plastic models of young animals, eggs, flowers, or similar flannelboard figures.
7. Listening: "Hen and Chicks": mother hen (chosen child) leaves the room. One or more children are chosen to be a chick. When mother hen returns, they peep softly until she finds them by the sound.
8. Come, Chick, Chick, Chick: "Come, chick, chick, chick. Here's food for you to eat." Repeat these two lines as children pretend they are chicks and come to the teacher for food from teacher's hands. Substitute other animal names.
9. Pin the Tail on the Bunny (Pin the Tail on the Donkey): use circles of masking tape to stick tail on, or sew a magnet on a yarn pom-pom and put bunny on a metallic board or cookie sheet. (See p. 48 for description of magnetized flannelboard.)

Routine Times

1. Decorate the snack table with garden flowers or potted spring bulbs that have been forced.
2. Eat snacks or meals outside. Have a picnic.
3. Eat vegetables you have grown for snacks or at mealtime.
4. Use spring fingerplays at snack or mealtime.
5. Frost egg-shaped cookies with pastel frosting.
6. Bunny salad: make with a pear half, red-hot-candy eyes, marshmallow tail, carrot-strip ears on a lettuce leaf.
7. Eat eggs in different ways: deviled eggs, egg salad.
8. Use large egg-shaped paper placemats or spring placemats that children have made and decorated.
9. Easter baskets may be used for the snack table centerpiece.

10. Marshmallow bunnies are quickly made with red-hot-candy eyes, miniature marshmallow for tail, pink paper ears, and a large marshmallow for the body. These are nice party favors.
11. When dressing, talk about the weather and what clothing is needed.
12. Look for signs of spring while walking or busing.
13. Rest outside in suitable weather. Look at clouds; listen for birds, wind, thunder, insects.

Large Muscle Activities

1. Shadow Tag
2. Leap Frog
3. Follow the Leader
4. Fly a kite
5. Play with balloons
6. Encourage water play (See Water guide, p. 566.)
7. Dirt and Sand play (See Water guide, p. 569.)
8. Have an Easter Egg Hunt, outdoors if possible. Use eggs made of paper or plastic, or candy eggs wrapped in a plastic wrap.
9. Water-paint the cement walk or walls and equipment outside using large paintbrushes and buckets to hold water.

Extended Experiences

1. Visit a local greenhouse to see Easter lilies and other spring blooming plants.
2. Visit a local farm to see newborn animals, spring planting, or beehives.
3. Visit a hatchery and obtain chicken or duck eggs to hatch.
4. Visit a zoo that may have new baby animals or a pet farm section.
5. Go to a park on a nature walk or to an open field to fly a kite.
6. Visit a feed and seed store or a farm implement company.
7. Explore a "magic circle." Give each child or group a yard length of string to outline a circle on the ground. Let them use a magnifying glass to see what can be found in their area. Encourage them to look carefully under stones and in grass for items.
8. A small shallow stream of water is a safe place to observe water creatures like tadpoles, frogs, crayfish, and minnows.

teacher resources

Books and Periodicals

1. Blough, Glenn O. *Elementary School Science and How to Teach It.* New York: Holt Rinehart & Winston, 1974.
2. Buck, Margaret Waring. *In Ponds and Streams.* Nashville, Tenn.: Abingdon Press, 1955.
3. ———. *In Yards and Gardens.* Nashville, Tenn.: Abingdon Press, 1952.
4. ———. *Small Pets from Woods and Fields.* Nashville, Tenn.: Abingdon Press, 1960.

5. Cooper, Elizabeth K. *Science in Your Own Back Yard.* New York: Harcourt Brace Jovanovich, 1958.
6. McClung, Robert M. *All about Animals and Their Young.* New York: Random House, 1958.
7. Sterling, Dorothy. *Insects and the Homes They Build.* Garden City, N.Y.: Doubleday, 1954.
8. Teale, Edwin Way. *The Strange Lives of Familiar Insects.* New York: Dodd, Mead, 1964 (paper, 1968).
9. Spring issues of farm and garden journals or magazines.
10. Seed catalogs.
11. Brandwein, Paul E., and Elizabeth K. Cooper. *Concepts in Science.* Harcourt Brace Jovanovich, 1967.
12. Audubon Publications: bird calls, books, records. Audubon Society, 950 Third Avenue, New York, N.Y. 10022.
13. *National Geographic* magazine: National Geographic Society, 17th and M Streets N.W., Washington, D.C. 20036.
14. *National Wildlife* and *Ranger Rick* magazines: National Wildlife Federation, 1412 16th Street, N.W., Washington, D.C. 20036.
15. Cooper, Terry Touff, and Marilyn Ratner. *Many Hands Cooking, An International Cookbook for Boys and Girls.* New York: Thomas Y. Crowell, 1974. Holiday Date Bits (Israel), p. 37; Kaju (India), p. 39; Tofu Toss (Japan), p. 44; Ancient Day Salad (Egypt), p. 38.

Pictures and Displays

(See p. 79 for addresses of firms listed.)

1. Make a tree for all seasons: obtain an attractive bare tree branch and secure with sand or pebbles in a three-pound coffee can. Children may glue tissue paper blossoms on it in the spring and follow through the seasons with tree leaves in summer, fruit, nuts, colored leaves, or seed pods in autumn, and the bare branch for winter.
2. An "insect motel" to use on a collecting trip or for a temporary display can be made simply by cutting a 2 inch by 4 inch rectangular window from the side of a pint cylindrical ice cream carton. Roll a piece of screen wire to fit inside and cover the window. A string may be attached to the lid for carrying. This will save many an insect guest from too much handling. Nylon hose pulled over a milk carton from which two large windows have been cut is also useful. Another insect keeper can be made from a piece of screen rolled into a cylinder, with empty tuna cans placed on each end.
3. Picture Packets: Seasons; Seeds and Plants; Science Themes Nos. 1 and 2; A Trip to the Farm; Holidays (David C. Cook)
4. Singer Study Prints: In the Spring; Spring and Summer Holidays; Basic Science Series 100 and 200 (SVE)
5. Make frames for children's finger paintings by cutting ovals or rectangles from large white mat board or cardboard, and superimpose on the paintings. Reuse for other art works.
6. Signs of the Season: Spring Mini-Poster Cards (Trend Enterprises)
7. Three large tumbleweeds of graduated sizes wound with bathroom tissue make a magnificent Easter rabbit of heroic proportions; make pink posterboard ears.
8. Make a mobile of Easter eggs, either blown raw eggs or decorated crisp paper egg shapes made by children.

Community Resources

1. County extension offices
2. Dairy councils
3. Greenhouses or garden centers
4. Florist shops
5. Hardware stores: small-size, sturdy garden tools (not toys)
6. Local and state film lending libraries: check to see what films or filmstrips are available on subject of spring and spring activities.

It's Spring

JoAnne Deal Hicks

Raindrops

JoAnne Deal Hicks

One rain-drop falls up-on my nose.

Two rain-drops splash up-on a rose.

Three rain-drops dance up-on my hat. And

four rain-drops pit-ter pit-ter pat.

20 summer

basic understandings

(concepts children can grasp from this subject)

Summer is a season of the year that comes after spring and before fall. There are many changes in nature in the summer.

Earth Changes

- In some areas there is not much rain. It is hot or warm every day.
- When there is no rain in an area the ground gets very hard and cracks. In some places the earth dries out and becomes dust; then it is dusty when the wind or a breeze blows.
- Sometimes, in the summer, ponds, streams, and lakes dry up or become smaller.
- Breezes blowing across nearby ponds, oceans, lakes, or rivers help to keep people and animals cool.
- On very windy days dust storms may form.
- Cement, sand, and brick hold the heat from the sun and are hot to touch, walk on, or live by.
- In the United States, the daylight hours in summer are longer and there are fewer hours of darkness.
- In some parts of the United States, summer weather lasts a long time, while in other areas the hot weather period is very short.

Plants

- Many trees, flowers, and shrubs bloom and grow in the summertime.
- Fruit, nuts, and vegetables grow best in summer and ripen enough to eat.
- Often grass, trees, flowers, and other plants need to be watered if there is not enough rain.
- Some plants wither and dry up in the hot sun.
- Leafy bushes, trees, and vines offer shade for homes, people, and animals.

Animals

- Some animals shed their heavy coats of fur in summer. Sometimes people help their pets by cutting their hair to make them cooler; examples: sheep and poodles.
- Some animals change from lighter to darker colors in summer to match where they live; examples are birds, rabbits.
- In summer animals need water to drink and in which to bathe. They also need shade and places in which to cool off (ponds, streams, and lakes).
- Some animals and birds raise their young, feed them, protect them, and teach them to find food and defend themselves. (See Animal guides.)

People

- Because it is often hot we need to wear less clothing in summer.
- Some children go barefoot.
- People often lie in the sun to get suntanned. We must be careful, however, not to get sunburned.
- Children and adults like to swim, go boating, water-ski, and play in water in summer.
- We often go to parks, have picnics, go on hikes, and play games outdoors in the summer, such as baseball, tennis, miniature golf, ball.
- Often food becomes ripe and can be canned, preserved, frozen, stored, or eaten by people in summer.
- Many families go camping, go on vacations (take trips), or have more time to do things together in summer.
- We should not waste water in summer.
- We often need to turn on fans, water coolers, and air conditioners in the buildings where we live, work, and play in order to keep cool.
- We may turn on the air conditioners in cars, trucks, buses, and tractors in order to be more comfortable when traveling in the summer.
- Some communities in which we live have special programs or activities at schools, parks, pools, churches, or community centers. Children often go with families to county or state fairs that are usually held in late summer.
- Many schools close for the summer. Others stay open and offer special classes.
- Special celebrations in summer include Independence Day, Flag Day, the Chinese Dragon Boat Festival, Pueblo Indian corn dances, Hopi snake dances, Arapaho sun dances, and intertribal Indian ceremonials and Pow-wows.

Additional Facts the Teacher Should Know

Summer is one of the four seasons which in most of the United States is approximately from June 22 to September 22. Summer weather is not the same for all the states. The northern states do not have as high temperature readings for such a prolonged time as do the southern states where temperatures of 80° and above occur almost daily from the middle of April to the middle of October. Therefore, it is expected each teacher will keep in mind the uniqueness of his/her area when teaching about this season. It is difficult for young children to grasp the full meaning involved in the concept of summer but they can begin to understand some of the changes which take place at this time of year. They can also learn about some of the most common activities families enjoy together at this time and about some of the celebrations that take place during the summer.

Indian Religiouf Rites

Indian Religious Rites: Many are held in the summer months. Some of them are listed here.

In midsummer the Plains Indians, which include the Arapaho, Shoshone, and Cheyenne, perform an elaborate dance around the head of a buffalo mounted on a pole. They hope it will bring them good luck, rain, prevent accidental death, or heal a sick friend.

In August the Pueblo Indians of New Mexico have a corn dance that asks for rain and a good harvest of corn. The Hopi Indians of Arizona perform a snake dance to bring rain. The antelope priests shake rattles while one holds a snake in his teeth. Later the snakes are released in the desert to carry rain prayers to the gods.

One large such gathering, held annually in Gallup, New Mexico, sometimes includes up to 15,000 Indians who participate in an intertribal Indian ceremony. More than twenty tribes are represented. In the morning there are parades with many Indians riding on horseback. The afternoon is devoted to sporting events. Evenings are spent performing ceremonial dances (often eighteen different dances each night). However, these ceremonial festivities are no longer open to the public. Some of your school children may be attending these festivities with other members of their tribes and families. Other parents and children in your center should be encouraged to attend any cultural event related to a local Indian tribe such as special sporting events, dances, art shows, or places where Indian handicrafts might be on sale.

Pow-wows are held in many areas of the country where large groups of Indians live. These are primarily social gatherings. Often they include dances and sporting events that are open to the general public. Check with the local Chamber of Commerce regarding such events.

Also invite parents and children from your school to read and share books for children and adults that have been written by Indians. Children should develop a respect, appreciation, and understanding of Indians and their culture and should learn more accurately about Indian history and customs than that which has been misrepresented in movies and story-books in the past. If the children share a good book or the experience of having attended a pow-wow, you will wish to include some of the suggestions in the various learning centers, such as art and music activities relating to Indian culture. Otherwise, the suggestions in this guide may have little meaning. Note reference in the vocabulary that may help you correct previous stereotypes.

In selecting books for children avoid books that perpetuate stereotypes of the past regarding either Chinese, American Indian, East Indian, or any other group of people. See the guide on I'm Me, I'm Special. In the Thanksgiving guide see other background information about how Indians lived long ago. Please read the Additional Facts the Teacher Should Know in both of these guides before including any plans about the Indian culture in summer curriculum plans.

Dragon Boat Festival

On the 5th day of the 5th lunar month, many Chinese celebrate this holiday by racing long boats decorated to look like dragons with the head at the bow and the tail at the stern. The Chinese believe the dragon is the ruler of rivers, lakes, and seas, and is the giver of rain needed for crops. The Chinese dragon is a positive symbol in the Chinese culture. At one time it was a symbol of the emperor and it has always represented good fortune. It is often used in art forms, in parades, and on other occasions of celebration. At this festival, families stand on the banks and encourage the boat crews. The enthusiasm and team spirit shown is much like that shown at the crew races held by college and university students in the United States. Eating rice dumplings wrapped in reconstituted dry leaves is one of the special treats anticipated by all at the time of the Dragon Boat Festival.

Traditionally the Dragon Boat Festival was held in memory of Wu-Yuen, a courageous cabinet member of the emperor of Chu during the third century. This statesman had martyred himself by drowning in Mick-Lor Lake near where he had been exiled. When advising the emperor, Wu-Yuen had repeatedly given suggestions to improve the social conditions of the times. The emperor, however, did not listen and eventually banished Wu-Yuen to the distant lake area, where he continued to protest by writing poetry and articles until he drowned himself. In celebrating this festival, the people wrap rice in dry grape leaves in a special manner (like a package) and then drop it into the waters hoping to feed his spirit in memory of his concern for all the people. Rice dumplings wrapped like this are still a special treat for this holiday.

NOTE: If your children live near a boating area, river bay, or harbor, they may be introduced to this festival following publicity relating to a local boat race or following their sharing information about a boating experience. (If you decide to include this festival and wish to expand your children's understanding of Chinese culture, see the Chinese New Year guide, pp. 203–20.)

Kandy Perahera (Kahn-dee Pear-uh-hair-uh)

In Sri Lanka, once called Ceylon, there is the Festival of the Sacred Tooth, known as *Kandy Perahera*, which occurs in July at the time of the new moon. It is held in the city of Kandy. There is a torchlight procession led by costumed men cracking whips. Behind them are as many as 200 decorated elephants followed by priests in robes of silver and gold. One of the elephants is more elaborately decorated than the others and is called the Middle Tusker. Upon his back is a jeweled casket with Buddhist relics. It is said that long ago one of these caskets contained one of Buddha's teeth. There are also drummers, dancers, and flame throwers. The procession makes its way to the Mahawali River where the priests slash the water with swords. Four jugs are filled with river water and taken to the Temple of the Sacred Tooth, where they are kept until the next *Kandy Perahera*.

NOTE: Include this only if you have a resource person (parent, student, friend) from Sri Lanka or India who can introduce and share this festival with children, showing pictures and artifacts.

Flag Day

Flag Day (June 14th) is technically in spring, but since it occurs after most schools are out it is thought of as a summer celebration. Very young children cannot be expected to comprehend the history and heritage of our country. They can, however, begin to learn about some of our national symbols, such as the flag, the Statue of Liberty, the White House, the Capitol, and the Liberty Bell in Independence Mall. Recently, with the many celebrations planned for our country's Bicentennial, many children are learning much more about these symbols.

On June 14, 1777, Congress adopted the flag with thirteen alternate stripes of red and white representing the original thirteen states and the union represented by thirteen white stars on a field of blue. As each state was adopted another star was added to the field of blue. Our present flag has fifty stars. Betsy Ross made the first flag. Young children of three and four years of age should not be required to recite the pledge to the flag every day. However they can learn to respect the flag and learn how to hold and carry it without letting it touch the floor. Small individual flags are best for young children, as each wants to carry one. Simply remove flags from children who are not treating them with respect.

Independence Day

Independence Day (July 4th) is a national holiday. Many families go to parks for picnics, to swimming pools, beaches, amusement parks, and parades and often plan to view a fire-works display after dark. This commemorates the July 4, 1776, signing of the Declaration of Independence. Independence Hall was built in 1732 and was used as a statehouse for the colony of Pennsylvania. The Declaration of Independence was signed in this hall and is on display today for all to see. The first Continental Congress met there and chose George Washington to be the first commander-in-chief of the United States army. The Liberty Bell is now housed in the Liberty Bell Pavillion, one block from Independence Hall. It was rung for the first time on July 8, 1776, when the Declaration of Independence had its first public reading. It cracked shortly after it was hung and had to be recast. It cracked a second time in 1835. It has not been recast or rung since.

The Statue of Liberty stands on Liberty Island in New York harbor and is 150 feet high. This female figure holds a tablet in her left hand and a torch in her right hand. A symbol of freedom made by the French sculptor, Frederic Bartholdi, the statue was given to the United States by the French government in 1884. The money to build the 150-foot pedestal on which it stands was donated by thousands of Americans.

Other guides related to the subject of summer are Animals, Color, Food, Water, and Transportation.

Methods Most Adaptable for Introducing This Subject to Children

- Take a walk and look for some of the signs that tell us it is summer, such as lawn sprinklers turned on, dogs panting, people dressed in lightweight clothes, trees leafed out, flowers blooming, and noisy cicadas.
- Read a story about summer.
- Children may be talking about vacations or special activities their families are planning.
- Everyone is talking about how hot it is.
- Make lemonade to drink outside in the shade of a tree.
- Display pictures of summer activities, for instance, at the beach, in the swimming pool, boating, and picnicking.

Vocabulary

summer	fan	Indian	hose
sprinkler	lawns	elephant	cool
water cooler	leaves	plant	water
air conditioner	march	flower	shells
hot	flag	fruit	beach
ice	holiday	ripe	sand
dry	parade	shade	swim

If the children develop an interest in special American Indian-related activities add:

rattle	hogan	totem pole	warrior
leather	adobe	moccasins	wampum
feathers	chickee	reservation	hominy
canoe	bow and arrow	cradle board	
tepee	pow-wow	sign language	
wigwam	tom-tom	Indian horn	

NOTE: We have intentionally omitted brave, squaw, chief, and papoose. These terms are *not* used, except inappropriately by non-Indians.

learning centers

Discovery Center

1. A discovery table: children can bring in things they have found, such as flowers, shells, fruits and vegetables, a bird's nest, insects.
2. If you planted a garden in the spring continue to care for it. Check to see if the soil is hard or damp. If it is hard it should be hoed and watered. If you don't have a garden, check seed packages and see if there is still time to start a garden in your area.
3. A melon-tasting feast: bring in a watermelon, honeydew melon, and a cantaloupe. Cut each melon. Compare color, odor, taste, and texture. Compare seeds.
4. A berry tasting party: set out bowls of whole, washed blackberries, blueberries, raspberries, and strawberries. Compare size, color, shape, odor, and taste.
5. Set out fresh vegetable tray: include a potato, carrot, onion, tomato, celery, radish, cucumber (whatever is available and in season). Let children explore. Talk about color, shape, taste, odor, and texture. Let children help wash, slice, peel.
6. Listen for cicadas: they make a noisy, shrill sound when it gets hot. Try to find one.
7. Look for a rainbow after a sudden summer shower.
8. After several hours of rain look for worms on the sidewalks.

9. Insects and spiders are plentiful in summer and the children will discover many, especially butterflies and fireflies. Look under rocks. (See Insects and Spiders guide for related discovery activities.)

10. Plant and care for some flowers: marigolds and zinnias are very hardy and grow in almost all parts of the country.

11. Borrow or purchase several types of plants: see list below. Help children discover that different plants need different amounts of water and begin to understand the phrase "No plant likes wet feet!" by allowing them to water and observe several plants.
   a. Cactus or rubber plant: water once a week or every ten days.
   b. Boston fern: water every other day (needs to be root-bound).
   c. Philodendron: water every other day.
   d. Azalea (planted in peat moss): water daily.

   NOTE: Plants should never stand in water. It is better to water more often, and very little at one time. Feel soil; if dry it needs water. For a 4-inch pot with plant, add ⅛ to ¼ cup water. For a 6-inch pot with plant, add 1 cup every other day. Leaves do NOT need to be misted (leaves washed) because indoors there is no breeze or sun to dry and leaves can rot. To help the children remember, make a chart for watering plants that has symbols to identify which plants need attention on which days.

12. Make or buy a bird bath and put it in a quiet part of the play yard. Make certain the children can observe it from their classroom window.

13. Set out a View Master with appropriate reels: The American Indian, the U.S. Capitol Building, the White House, Independence Park, Statue of Liberty, and others about national parks, flowers, and marinelands.

14. Make strawberry or peach ice cream: use your favorite recipe.

15. Make lemonade: squeeze lemons. Taste with and without sugar.

16. Explore The Child's World Multi-Media Kit on summer: Let's Take a Walk in Summer fold-out chart; the companion book *Summer Is Here*, with a cassette with sounds of the season.

17. Set out The Child's World Picture Fold-Outs: Plants That Provide Food and Plants and Seeds.

18. Display a shell collection: provide a magnifying glass for closer viewing or hide some shells in a small box of sand and let the children find and arrange them.

19. If feasible, allow children to remove their shoes to walk in the grass, step on cement, walk on blacktop, or step on dirt or on a smooth board. Which is warmer? Cooler? Smoother? Rougher? Softer? Harder? **Variation:** Ask children to touch and compare the temperature of a metal bar, piece of wooden equipment, the ground, all in the sun. Which is cooler? Touch the same objects in the shade. What is different? Why?

   CAUTION: Make certain there is no glass or any sharp object where children will be walking or stepping.

20. If you have flowers or flowering bushes in the school yard, allow children to pick some buds with stems and place them in a container of water. Set them in a window where they can get sun. Observe what happens.

21. If some equipment such as a tire, wooden box, or a board has been left sitting over a grassy area for several days, move it and let the children discover what happened to the grass underneath that was without sun and air. Leave uncovered. Observe.

22. When busing children for an excursion in summer, turn on the air conditioner (if you have one) in the car and talk about what happens to the air in the car if we leave the windows closed.

Dramatic Play Centers

Home-Living Center

1. Set out beach hats, hats with visors, straw hats, beach towels, terry robes, thongs, sandals, and sunglasses.
2. Place travel folders, brochures on local parks, and road maps out on shelves to encourage planning of family trips.
3. Set out boxes of artificial flowers with a variety of containers and allow children to make floral arrangements.

Block-Building Center

1. Set out cars, campers, trains, ships, and planes to encourage travel play. (See Transportation guides.)
2. Set out farm equipment to encourage planting, cultivating, and harvesting of crops. Provide small plastic foods to carry to market. (See Food guide.)

Other Dramatic Play Centers

1. Set up a tent on the playground for the children to use for camping out.
2. Set up a water table, large tub with water, or tractor tire cut in half, forming two circular troughs for sailing boats or water play.
3. Add new equipment to the sandbox to increase interest in this area, e.g., sieves, funnels, pails, and shovels.

Learning, Language, and Readiness Materials Center

Commercially made games and materials for use at a table or on a mat:

(See Basic Resources, p. 79, for manufacturers' addresses.)

1. Judy Puzzles: Holiday Parade, 20 pcs.; Balloon Seller, 17 pcs.; The Hot Dog Vendor, 15 pcs.; Car, 11 pcs.; and Jet Airplane, 14 pcs.
2. Judy See-Quees: Tadpole to Frog, Robin Family, 6 pcs. each; and The Apple Tree in Seasons, Children and Seasons, 12 pcs. each
3. Judy Sequence Play Tray Card Set: Seasonal Activities
4. ETA Equilibrium Elephant Puzzle: to use for *Kandy Perahera* or circus interest
5. ETA Puzzle Animals: elephant to use for *Kandy Perahera* or circus interest
6. ETA Science Puzzle Assortment: The Four Seasons
7. ETA Perception Puzzles: boats, autos, 5 pcs. each
8. ETA Lacing Cards: sailboat, elephant to use for interest in *Kandy Perahera*
9. Judy Seasons Puzzle: 20-inch circular puzzle with teacher's guide
10. Four Seasons: 16 blocks produce 4 seasonal scenes (Childcraft)
11. Puzzles for All Seasons (Childcraft)
12. Decreasing Insets: (sail) boats (Childcraft)
13. Outdoor Puzzles (Childcraft)
14. Seasons and Weather: flannelgraph kit (David C. Cook)
15. Instructo Desktop Activity Kit (Seasons)
16. Seasons Flannel Aid (Milton Bradley)
17. Signs of the Seasons: Mini-poster cards (Trend Enterprises)
18. Scenes Around Us Story Posters: Summer (Milton Bradley)
19. Playskool Plaques: Fishing, 8 pcs.; Family Drive, 14 pcs.; Camping, 11 pcs.; Little Leaguer, 16 pcs.; Sand Box, 21 pcs.; Kiddie Pool, 17 pcs.

Teacher-made games and materials for use at a table or on a mat:

NOTE: For detailed description of Games, see pp. 50–58.

1. Look and See: use different-shaped and colored sea shells, a variety of plastic foods, transportation toys, or American Indian, East Indian, or Chinese artifacts.
2. Reach and Feel: use a swim mask, sunglasses, bathing cap, and sand shovel.
3. Match-Them: for Flag Day make two sets of flag cards by mounting gummed flag seals of different countries on 3″ × 5″ cards. Seals are available where stamp collectors' accessories are found.
4. Summer Fun: the children can make a picture book of summer by cutting out appropriate pictures and mounting on paper, punching, and fastening together.

Art Center

* 1. Summer is all colors! Move art media outdoors whenever possible. Feature a wide choice of colors at the easel especially if the group has been with you all year.

** 2. Sponge-paint blossoms on crayoned tree trunks; trunks and branches can be made by using the broad side of short crayons which have the paper wrappings removed.

*** 3. Spatter-paint a long line of elephants on a long sheet of paper for the 200 elephants in the *Kandy Perahera* parade. Put up on the wall as a mural. Let each child who wishes do one or more. Offer a variety of sizes and shapes of stencils or let children make their own elephant form from innertube shapes.

** 4. Blow-painting: drops of bright-colored paint blown with a straw over paper result in a fireworks bursting in air effect for Independence Day.

** 5. Sand-painting: sand can be washed, mixed with dry tempera, and dried in the oven. Child draws a design on paper with glue squeezed from tip of white glue bottle. Sprinkle colored sand over the glue. When dry, shake off excess. Sand should remain on glue. A brush can also be used to apply the glue.

** 6. Make wet-sand sculptures by using various containers as molds or mold with the hands.

** 7. Glue cupcake papers or crumpled tissue paper to green construction paper to simulate flowers in the grass; also let children tear, cut, or slash paper for grass.

*** 8. Burlap pictures: cut squares from burlap bags or colorful burlap material. Thread wide-eyed embroidery needles with brightly colored yarn. Let children sew a design on the burlap.

** 9. Simulated porcupine quill art: weave colored toothpicks into burlap squares.

* 10. Make drawing in sand or damp earth with a stick.

Book Center

** Alexander, Martha. *No Ducks in Our Bathtub*. New York: Dial Press, 1973.

* Burningham, John. *Seasons*. New York: Bobbs-Merrill, 1970.

*** Carrick, Donald. *The Tree*. New York: Macmillan, 1971.

*** Clark, Ann Nolan. *Tia Maria's Garden*. New York: Viking Press, 1963.

**** Dalgliesh, Alice. *The Fourth of July Story*. New York: Charles Scribner's Sons, 1966 (paper, read-tell).

** Deasy, Michael. *City ABC's*. New York: Walker & Co., 1974.

* Fisher, Aileen. *I Like Weather*. New York: Thomas Y. Crowell, 1963.

* Foster, Doris. *A Pocketful of Seasons*. New York: Lothrop, Lee & Shepard, 1960.

*** Goudey, Alice. *The Day We Saw the Sun Come Up*. New York: Scribner's, 1961.

** Grant, Sandy. *Hey, Look at Me! A City A.B.C.* Scarsdale, N.Y.: Bradbury Press, 1973.

**** Kessler, Leonard. *Last One in Is a Rotten Egg*. New York: Harper & Row, 1969 (read-tell).

*** Kinney, Jean. *What Does the Sun Do?* Reading, Mass.: Addison-Wesley Co., 1967.

* Krauss, Ruth. *The Growing Story*. New York: Harper & Row, 1947.

* Lenski, Lois. *On a Summer Day*. New York: Henry Z. Walck, 1953.

* Loree, Kate. *Pails and Snails*. New York: E. M. Hale, 1967.

** Lund, Doris. *The Paint Box Sea*. New York: McGraw-Hill, 1972.

*** MacDonald, Golden. *The Little Island*. Garden City, N.Y.: Doubleday, 1946 (paper, 1974).

*** Podendorf, Illa. *True Book of Seasons*. Chicago, Ill.: Childrens Press, 1972.

* Schick, Eleanor. *City in the Summer*. New York: Macmillan, 1969 (paper, 1974).

*** Spier, Peter. *The Star-Spangled Banner*. Garden City, New York: Doubleday, 1973.

** Tresselt, Alvin. *I Saw the Sea Come In*. New York: Lothrop, Lee & Shepard, 1965.

** ———. *Sun Up!* New York: Lothrop, Lee & Shepard, 1949.

** Udry, Janice. *A Tree Is Nice*. New York: Harper & Row, 1956.

** Wondriska, William. *The Stop*. New York: Holt, Rinehart & Winston, 1972.

planning for grouptime

NOTE: All music, fingerplays, poems, stories, and games listed here may be used at other times during the session as appropriate. See Core Library, Basic Resources, p. 76, for publishers and addresses. Addresses for sources of records will be found on p. 81. In parodies, hyphenated words match music notes of the song used.

Music

Songs

FROM original songs in this book by JoAnne Deal Hicks

"Going Fishing," p. 581   "Color Fun," p. 599
"Fruitbasket Song," p. 561   "Water Play," p. 582

SUMMERTIME FUN (a parody)
  (tune: "Pussy Cat, Pussy Cat")
  Adaptation by JoAnne Deal Hicks

I like to boat, and to ski is such fun.
I like to fish, then to lie in the sun.
I like to swim . . . and when I am done
I'm hap-py, so hap-py that sum-mer's be-gun.

FROM *Songs for Early Childhood*, Westminster Press
 ** "Apples Green and Apples Red," p. 18
*** "Sweet Plum Blossoms," p. 19
 ** "In My Little Garden Bed," p. 24
  * "Lying on the Hillside," p. 26
*** "I Have a Brook to Play In," p. 32
 ** "Gather Shells and Pebbles," p. 33
  * "The Waves Are Rolling Down the Shore," p. 33
 ** "O Seashell Sing of Rolling Waves," p. 34
 ** "Beautiful Wonderful Sights to See," p. 39
 ** "I Went Walking Outdoors Today," p. 40
  * "The Firefly," p. 51
 ** "Little Cricket in the Grass," p. 53
 ** "Butterfly Butterfly," p. 54
 ** "Buzz Buzz Buzz the Bees," p. 55
  * "Funny Little Grasshopper," p. 56
  * "Driving Along the Highway," p. 80
  * "When Friends Come to Our House," p. 89
  * "Let's Go Outdoors," p. 90
  * "Walking in the Sunshine," p. 101
  * "Hold On Tightly," p. 103
*** "See How I'm Jumping!," p. 104
  * "Riding in the Wagon," p. 109
 ** "A Window Box of Flowers," p. 112
  * "The Parade," p. 124

Records

"Circus Comes to Town"/"When the Sun Shines"/"Around the World" (Young People's Record [YPR], 33⅓ RPM)
"I Am a Circus"/"Castles in the Sand"/"Out of Doors" (YPR, 33⅓ RPM)
"Train to the Beach" (Children's Record Guild, 78 RPM)
"At the Beach," *Dance-A-Story* (RCA Victor, 33⅓ RPM)
"A Summer Day on the Farm" (Bowmar, 33⅓ RPM or cassette and songbook)
"The Harbor and the Sea" (Bowmar, 33⅓ RPM or cassette and songbook)
"Camping in the Mountains" (Bowmar, 33⅓ RPM or cassette and songbook)
"Patriotic Songs," edited by Lucille Wood (Bowmar, 33⅓ RPM)
"Animals and the Circus" (Bowmar, 33⅓ RPM)
"American Indian Dances" (Childcraft, 33⅓ RPM)
"Music of the Sioux and Navajo" (Childcraft, 33⅓ RPM)

Rhythms and Singing Games

Patriotic parade: for Flag Day have children march to any good patriotic song, each carrying a small American flag.

NOTE: Stress respect for the flag. Do not allow children to abuse their flags or let them touch the ground or floor. If this is difficult to do with your group, give the children instruments while an adult or one or two children you have selected can carry the flags.

Independence Day parade: march to patriotic band music playing rhythm band instruments.

Kandy Perahera procession: some children can be elephants, some priests, some drummers, some dancers, some flame throwers (let them use yellow orange scarves or crepe paper streamers). Use any slow tempo march or "elephant" music from your rhythm activity records.

American Indian celebrations: use drums; half the children may beat drums while the other half move creatively:

Walk to a drum beat
Run to a drum beat
Jump to a drum beat
Hop on one foot, land on both feet
Dance—bearing weight first on the toes of one foot, then heel of same foot. Alternate feet. (repeat: toe, heel, toe, heel)

Select appropriate action songs from *Songs for the Nursery School* (MacCarteney), *Songs for Early Childhood*, and original songs listed above involving animals, children, or vehicles moving in special ways.

Fingerplays and Poems

FROM *Rhymes for Fingers and Flannelboards*, Scott and Thompson
"Riding the Merry-Go-Round," p. 15

"Animals," p. 18
"Monkey See, Monkey Do," p. 18
"Creepy, Crawly," p. 33
"¿Que Colores Veo?," p. 45
"What Colors Do I See?" p. 45
"I Am a Little Toad," p. 93
"Things That Hop," p. 93
"Five Little Seashells," p. 94
"Little Birds," p. 95
"Here Is a Bunny," p. 96
"Two Blackbirds," p. 103
"My Balloon," p. 132
"Fun at the Playground," p. 133

FROM *Let's Do Fingerplays*, Grayson
"An Airplane," p. 22
"The Train," p. 22
"The Bus," p. 25
"Row, Row, Row Your Boat," p. 26
"My Turtle," p. 32
"There Was a Little Turtle," p. 33
"My Garden," p. 46
"Who Feels Happy?," p. 76
"The See Saw," p. 78
"The Window," p. 78

Stories

(To read, read-tell, or tell. See Book Center for complete list.)

  ** *Sun Up!*, Tresselt
   * *Seasons*, Burningham
   * *Pails and Snails*, Loree
 *** *Tia Maria's Garden*, Clark
  ** *I Saw the Sea Come In*, Tresselt
 *** *The Little Island*, MacDonald
   * *The Growing Story*, Krauss
  ** *The Paint Box Sea*, Lund

Games

(See Games, pp. 50–58, and Teacher-Made Games in this guide for directions.)

1. Guess What?: I like to do outside in summer. Describe swimming, going on picnics, going to zoos. Together think of summer-related activities.
2. What Am I?: describe our national symbols, the flag, the Statue of Liberty, the White House, the Liberty Bell, and the American eagle.
3. I'm Taking a Vacation: describe something you will put into your suitcase. "I need it after I eat and before I go to bed ... I use it in my mouth, with toothpaste" (toothbrush). Continue to give other hints until children guess. **Variation:** "I am going in something that ..." (describe airplane, car, bus).

Routine Times

1. At snack or mealtime use foods harvested from the children's garden. Also offer special summer treats like watermelon, strawberries, tomatoes, corn on the cob, and cherries.
2. If children have been to a pow-wow or other Indian celebrations use food sources which the Indians introduced to the pilgrims, such as for snacktime, pop*corn*, *peanut* butter on crackers, *strawberries*, *pineapple* chunks, *cocoa*, fresh or dried fruit. For mealtime, *corn*-bread cake with *maple* syrup, sweet *potatoes*, *nuts*, *squash*, *turkey*, barbecued meat, fish, pot roast, *succotash*, *fried bread*, pudding, or fruit.
3. At mealtime have a picnic in the park.
4. On Flag Day and Independence Day decorate the snack or lunch table with red, white, and blue. Serve red, white, and blue foods. (See Color guide, p. 595.)
5. At grouptime, sit cross-legged like Indians and talk about what you are going to do and decide things the way a tribal council does.

Large Muscle Activities

1. Walk a balance beam, log, or chalk mark drawn on the floor.
2. Run to a destination and back.
3. Take a hike.
4. Toss and catch a beach ball.
5. Have a parade outside. (See Rhythms and Singing Games.)
6. Run in the spray from a lawn sprinkler.
7. Jump the Stream: put two lengths of rope parallel and close to one another to outline a stream. Each child playing jumps over the stream. After each has jumped, move the ropes a little further apart, widening the stream. If a child lands in the stream he or she sits on the bank and watches the others jump to see if they made it across without getting their feet wet or falling in. Continue until all are sitting on the bank.
8. See Zoo guide for related circus activities.
9. Add some new homemade sand toys and tools to the sandbox accessories or purchase some new items, such as sand combs (Childcraft), or sand tools, pails, sifters, measuring cups and spoons, sprinkling cans, boats. See sand and water equipment section of most early childhood equipment catalogs.

Extended Experiences

1. Go to a park on a picnic.
2. Watch a parade.
3. Visit the zoo or a circus. (See Zoo Animals guide.)
4. If children have been to a pow-wow, invite an Indian to visit the center and share artifacts, paintings, jewelry, beadwork, or leatherwork, or tell a story (Indian legend) often told to very young children.
5. Have a parent, friend, university, college, or exchange student from Sri Lanka or a part of India tell about *Kandy Perahera*. Ask them to bring something of interest from their country to share.
6. See the filmstrips titled Play in the Park and Fun at the Beach (Bowmar).
7. See filmstrip set, Five Families (Scholastic), Circus Family, Yah-a-Tat (Indian), and China-town (Chinese).

teacher resources

Books and Periodicals

1. *Foliage, Plants for Modern Living.* Copy prepared by Mary Jane Coleman. Kalamazoo, Mich.: Merchants Company Publisher, 1974.
2. W. Ben Hunt. *Golden Book of Indian Crafts and Lore.* New York: Golden Press, 1961.
3. *International Wildlife, National Wildlife,* and *Ranger Rick,* summer issues. National Wildlife Federation, 1412 16th St. N.W., Washington, D.C. 20036.

Pictures and Displays

(See p. 79 for addresses of firms listed.)

1. Seasons: picture packet with resource sheets (David C. Cook)
2. Holidays: Independence Day with resource sheet (David C. Cook)
3. Seasons and Holidays (Singer, SVE, picture-story study prints); Set 2, In the Summer; Set 5, Spring and Summer Holidays
4. Children Around the World (Singer, SVE, picture-story study prints); Set 4, Children of North America: Little Star, a Navajo girl
5. Symbols of America: Set 2 (SVE)
6. American Indians, Yesterday and Today (David C. Cook)
7. Pictures of elephants, parades, the flag, the U.S. Capitol, the Statue of Liberty, Independence Hall, the Liberty Bell, summer flowers, and summer activities

Community Resources

1. Cherry or peach orchard; farm
2. American Indian, student, parent, or friend
3. Student, parent, or friend from Sri Lanka (Ceylon) or from India to tell about *Kandy Perahera*
4. A Chinese parent or friend to explain the Dragon Boat Festival

21 Fall

basic understandings

(concepts children can grasp from this subject)

Fall is a season of the year that comes after summer and before winter. Autumn is another word for fall. There are many changes in nature in the fall.

Earth Changes

- The daylight hours become shorter and the night (hours of darkness) longer because the sun rises later and sets earlier.
- The temperature slowly drops and the weather becomes cooler, especially at night.
- Frost may appear at night or in the early mornings. We can see our breath.
- The soil gets harder and sometimes freezes.
- There are usually more rainy or cloudy days than in summer.
- There are usually more storms, hurricanes, and tornadoes than there are in summer.
- By Thanksgiving many of the northeastern states in our country have snow while the southern states are still very warm.

Plant Changes

- Most leaves begin to change color; some trees remain green and are called "evergreens."
- Parts of some plants fall to the ground, such as leaves, apples, nuts, pine cones, and other seeds.
  - a. Some leaves change color but do not drop until replaced by new leaves in the spring, for example, pin oak.
  - b. Palms remain green all year round. Old leaves turn brown, wither, and fall off, while new leaves are continually blooming.
- In some areas grass and plants turn brown and wither.
- Some bulbs are dug up and stored and others are planted for spring blooming.

- Some plants are brought inside to prevent freezing, such as geraniums, ivy, cactus, rubber plants, and those in hanging baskets.
- In fall many foods ripen and are picked. This is called "harvesting." Examples are pumpkins, apples, cranberries, acorn squash, potatoes, and nuts.

Animal Changes

- Some birds and butterflies fly (migrate) south where they can find food more easily.
- Some animals get ready to sleep or rest a long time (hibernate) by eating much food or storing it in their homes.
- Some animals grow thicker fur or a special undercoating to help keep them warm.

People

- We begin wearing warmer clothes, such as sweaters and light jackets in most southern states and heavy jackets, caps, and mittens in northeastern states.
- In northern states people need to build fires or turn on heaters or furnaces, while those living in most southern states do not need to run their air conditioners as often.
- Many people set out bird feeders and food for the birds after the snow begins.
- In many areas farmers harvest many foods and sow winter crops.
- Activities include raking leaves, homecomings, football, and the World Series.
- Celebrations in fall include: Labor Day, Columbus Day, *Rosh Hashanah, Yom Kippur, Sukkot, Divali,* Halloween, Harvest Home Festival, and Thanksgiving. (See related guides.)

Additional Facts the Teacher Should Know

It is difficult for a preschool child to grasp the full meaning involved in the concept of fall because it is not something he/she can see, touch, or hold, except by various parts. However, children can learn that it is a time of year when various changes take place in the plants and animals in our environment.

Fall is one of the four seasons of the year; in most of the United States it occurs from approximately September 23rd to December 21st. (See p. 534.) The four seasons do not occur at the same time all over the world because the sun's rays are striking the earth differently at any one time, resulting in very different climates. Also countries with large geographic area, such as the United States, have a wide range of climates during a given season. For example, families living in southern states do not experience four seasons of equal length as do those in northeastern states. They have five months of summer (May 15th to October 15th), two months of fall (October 15th to December 15th), two months of winter without snow (December 15th to February 15th), and three months of spring (February 15th to May 15th). Washington and Oregon have seasons similar to the southern states, but they do not have temperatures as high. Hawaii has almost perpetual summer, while Alaska has almost perpetual winter with short, cool summers.

Squirrels are rodents or gnawing animals that are related to rats and beavers. They can be found in many parts of the world and in most parts of the United States, in woods and city parks. Their obvious activity of collecting seeds and nuts for the winter has long been a sign of fall. (For additional information, see Animal Charts.)

Chipmunks are like small squirrels, but they live in cleverly hidden burrows 6 to 8 inches under the ground. They make several passageways, storage rooms, and a large bedroom. There are several kinds living in North America, Canada, and Asia.

The most common are reddish or grayish brown with black and white stripes down their backs. They are about 10 inches long with flat, bushy tails. They eat seeds, nuts, berries, insects or grubs, and they hibernate from November until spring. However, chipmunks may come out of hibernation at intervals. The male and female chipmunk live together in the burrow. Three to five chippers are born by April.

In the fall the monarch butterfly, which is orange and black, hatches from a caterpillar which has black, yellow, and white stripes around its body. The monarch's larva can be found in the fields near milkweed, which it likes to eat and which, incidentally, gives the caterpillar a bad taste to birds. If you find one and wish to observe it, put it in a container or box with a screen over the top opening for ventilation. Place a stick in the container at a 45-degree angle for it to use to suspend its chrysalis. Provide it with fresh milkweed leaves daily. It will eat a good deal just before it spins a chrysalis of a lovely apple-green color, edged at the large end with gold. A monarch butterfly will emerge in less than two weeks and should be allowed to fly away. These butterflies migrate after they emerge and return in the spring to lay their eggs. The change from caterpillar to butterfly is called "metamorphosis." (See Insects and Spiders guide.)

Woolly bears are the caterpillars of the Isabella tiger moth and are found in almost all parts of the United States. They are black and reddish brown. They hibernate through the winter, then spin their cocoons in April or May. Near the end of May the moths are hatched. Some people say they are weather predictors. The thicker the fur or the wider the black bands, the colder the winter will be; but no one has ever proved it. Do not bring a woolly bear inside if you want to see it change into a moth; it is too warm inside. Build a small wire cage out of window screening about the size of a three-pound coffee can, leaving it open at one end. Place the open end down over a patch of clover or dandelions and put the woolly bear inside the cage. The children will then be able to watch without losing or disturbing the caterpillar. (See Insects and Spiders guide.)

Migration is the movement of animals from one place to another. Animals which migrate are birds, fish, and butterflies. In the fall, birds migrate from the north to the south, where they can find food. Some birds which migrate are Canadian geese, robins, swallows, and mallards. Not all birds migrate when it turns cold; cardinals, English sparrows, chickadees, juncos, and nuthatches are some examples of birds who remain during the winter months. These birds have a special snowsuit of soft down, which they grow when it turns cold to help keep them warm through the winter.

Hibernation is a sleep or half-sleep state many animals remain in during the winter months. At this time the animal's body functions slow down and it is able to live through the cold winter when it would not be able to find food. Some may lie in a deep sleep and others may move around on warm days. Animals do not grow during hibernation and may lose as much as one-third of their weight. Only those animals that can store up enough food to last through the winter are able to hibernate. Bears are said to hibernate but their body temperature does not drop as much as it does in a true hibernating animal. Certain frogs, turtles, toads, and lizards bury themselves in the earth below the reach of frost. The horseshoe crab sinks in the mud beneath deep water until May or June. Spiders and snails hibernate under rocks. The woodchuck (groundhog), raccoon, and praying mantis also hibernate. (See Animals of the Woods Chart and Zoo Animals Chart for more information about some of these animals.)

Trees are divided into three main groups. Those that lose their leaves are called "deciduous" trees. Most deciduous trees lose their leaves in the fall. The leaves of the pin oak turn brown in the fall but do not drop until spring. Some members of the oak family remain green throughout the winter, like the live oak. Conifers or cone-bearing trees remain green all year round and are called "evergreens." Palms constitute the third group of trees. They are found in southern California, Texas, and Florida. The most common ones are date palms, coconut palms, and Chinese fan palms.

Fruits that ripen in the fall are purple grapes, apples, papaws (custard apple or wild banana), Osage orange (hedgeapple), persimmon, bittersweet, beechnut, white oak, staghorn sumac, and milkweed.

Flowers that bloom in the fall are chrysanthemums, goldenrod, purple asters, barberry, heather, thistle, and wild sunflower.

Methods Most Adaptable for Introducing This Subject to Children

- Take a walk and look for things or changes that tell us it is fall, such as leaves, nuts, milkweed pods, woolly bears, birds flying south.
- A child brings in a pretty leaf, an apple, pine cone, or chrysanthemum and you can say, "This is one of the things (or signs) that tell us it is fall." Let the children take turns holding the item and help them to observe, describe, and compare it with other items.
- Read a book about fall or the four seasons.
- Set out a new fall puzzle or flannelboard-figure kit.

Vocabulary

fall	chrysalis	high, low	evergreen
autumn	change	warm, cool	red
hibernate	bird(s)	frost	orange
migrate	squirrel	thermometer	yellow
harvest	chipmunk	tree	green
caterpillar	woolly bear	leaves	brown
butterfly	chrysanthemum	nuts	
cocoon	temperature	pine cone	

learning centers

Discovery Center

1. Have a table where children can put things they bring in that tell us it is fall. There should be small boxes, an insect house, magnifying glass, pictures of fall, and resource books. October and November issues of *Ranger Rick's Nature* magazine and *National Wildlife* are especially suitable. Help the child identify the object he has brought in and discover its outstanding characteristics, such as color, shape, size, weight, texture, name, and use. If it is an animal or insect, add habits, what it eats, what it does, how it moves, sounds it makes, and safety precautions. Find these things in the pictures or resource books you have provided. (Use with Learning, Language, and Readiness Materials and Activities.)

2. Display: Take a Walk in the Fall picture charts with companion book *Fall Is Here* (The Child's World)

3. Display: Life Cycle of a Monarch sequence chart (The Child's World)

4. Display: How Seeds Travel from Plants and Seeds picture fold-outs (The Child's World)

5. Find a milkweed pod and open it. Talk about how seeds travel: wind, on clothing, animals' fur, mouth.

6. Apples can be cut in half crosswise to reveal a star-shaped seed case with seeds. Talk about the various parts, color, texture, and shape. Buy yellow, red, and green apples. Ask how they are alike and how they are different.

   CAUTION: Make a cardboard sheath for the paring knife and keep it in the sheath and out of the children's reach when not in use.

7. Make applesauce: the teacher should pare, core, and cut the apples in advance. Put apples, water, and sugar in saucepan and cook on a stove, electric skillet, or hot plate. The children can help with the measuring, stirring, and mashing. A dash or two of nutmeg, cinnamon, or ginger may be added. Serve warm or cool with a cookie or cracker or save until mealtime. Have whole apples available and talk about differences in size, texture, and appearance. Children may enjoy singing "Sing a Song of Applesauce," p. 562.

   CAUTION: High heat is required for cooking the apples. Extra supervision is necessary. Try to have extra help and then limit this center to three or four children at a time.

8. Buy and compare several kinds of corn: popcorn, corn on the cob, canned, frozen, and cream style. Compare the size, taste, and texture as appropriate. Pop some corn to serve as a snack. Use an electric popper with a glass lid or a wire basket popper so children can see corn popping. (See Sight guide for songs and other related experiences with popcorn.)

   CAUTION: High heat is required. Close supervision will be necessary.

9. Buy as large and as accurate a thermometer as you can. Indoor-outdoor models are excellent as children can see differences or similarities between the two. They can see that as it gets colder the mercury goes down and vice versa. (See also No. 11, p. 375.)

10. Obtain a kitchen food scale or balance pans so children can weigh nuts, apples, or pumpkins. Which weighs more, an apple or a nut? A pumpkin or five apples? Children may want to weigh themselves or other objects in the classroom. Of course other scales will be needed for this.

11. When outdoors watch for birds flying south, if you live in a migration pattern and have a good view of the sky. As a beginning experience you might simply announce, "Look, the birds are flying south, where it will be easier for them to find food." With children who have had more experience, you might use a compass to find north and then draw a directional cross on the sidewalk in chalk or paint it on a block of wood. Use N, E, S, W for the four points. Help children decide which direction is south from where they are. On a windy day, you could tie a scarf to a stick and hold it over the compass cross and see which way the wind is blowing.
12. Discover that wet leaves leave a print on the sidewalk.
13. Falling leaves, nuts, and apples may lead to an interest in gravity.

Dramatic Play Centers

Home-Living Center

1. Set out sweaters, coats, and blankets for dolls to indicate the change in the weather.

Block-Building Center

1. Set out farm animals. Suggest through conversation or pictures the need to build barns or buildings for the animals.
2. Make a barn of large hollow blocks or large cardboard boxes. Sing "Little Gray Ponies," on p. 22 of *Songs for the Nursery School* by MacCarteney, and let children act out this song.

Learning, Language, and Readiness Materials Center

Commercially made games and materials for use at a table or on a mat:

(See Basic Resources, p. 79, for manufacturers' addresses.)

1. Farm Lotto (Ed-U-Card)
2. Seasons, flannelboard aids (Instructo or Ideal)
3. Scenes Around Us, story posters (Milton Bradley)
4. Autumn, Halloween, and Thanksgiving (Dennison or Hallmark seals)
5. Seasons (Instructo activity kits); Fall and Winter; Spring and Summer. These sets each have two basic background scenes which can be changed by putting the appropriate environmental changes in front and dressing the figures with appropriate clothes. If both sets are available changes from summer to fall and fall to winter can be made as well as letting the children visualize all four seasons and making comparisons.
6. Playskool Puzzles: Squirrel, 6 pcs.; Butterfly, 15 pcs.
7. Difference Puzzles: Apples (Constructive Playthings)
8. Judy See-Quees: Seed to Pumpkin, 12 pcs.; Seasons, 4 pcs.; Squirrel Adventure and Caterpillar to Butterfly, 6 pcs. each
9. We Dress for Weather, flannelboard aid (Instructo)
10. Science Studies: flannelgraph set (David C. Cook)

Teacher-made games and materials for use at a table or on a mat:

NOTE: For detailed description of Games, see pp. 50–59.

1. What's Missing?: use several objects from the discovery table, such as a pine cone, nut, hedgeapple, or leaf.

2. Show Me: use a nut, yellow leaf, and apple. "Show me the one you eat." "Show me the one that is round."
3. Match-Them: "This leaf is yellow; each of you (or name one child) find me something in this room that is yellow." "This nut is round; find me something in this room that is round." Use sets of two cards with identical pictures of fall objects to match.
4. What Am I?: "I am thinking of something that is tall and green and has needles; what is it?" "I am thinking of something that has gray fur and likes to eat nuts; what is it?" "I am thinking of something that is big and round and orange; what is it?"
5. Reach and Feel: use fall objects.
6. Grouping and Sorting by Association:
   a. Buy several kinds of nuts in quantity or use those you find. Identify the nuts for the children and compare the size, color, and texture. Mix the nuts together in a large bowl or container and provide as many smaller bowls or containers as there are kinds of nuts. Let the children sort the nuts.
   b. Sort leaves by color or by shape. Use the ones you find or precut some from colored construction paper.
   c. Sort pine cones by size or type.
7. Alike, Different and the Same: make card sets with pictures of leaves, trees, birds, squirrels, chipmunks, fall fruits, and vegetables. Put out two cards that are alike and one that is different.
8. Count nuts, seeds, pine cones, or leaves. Beginning concepts are one to three and experienced children may count to ten with understanding.
9. Division: apples can be cut in halves or quarters for a snack.
10. Make a calendar for September, October, and/or November with large 2-inch square blocks for the days. Paste appropriate pictures on the square for each holiday you are planning to celebrate. Remember to highlight trips and birthdays. You might add to the decoration of the room and the children's understanding if you cut a large tree from brown construction paper and put it beside the calendar. Cut enough leaves of various colors to put on the tree to correspond with the number of days on the calendar. Each day take one of the leaves off the tree and cover up the day that is on the calendar. When the month is over the tree will be bare, coinciding with the way trees will look in your community. Choose to do this during the fall month when leaves usually drop in your area.
11. Make a large cardboard thermometer with movable elastic or ribbon mercury. (See Mathematics guide, p. 620.) Talk about the kinds of clothes we wear when the temperature is at various positions (or degrees) on the thermometer. Pictures of children wearing appropriate clothes can be cut from catalogs and pasted on the cardboard. Wider cardboard should be used for the thermometer to accommodate the pictures of clothing. Also you could set the temperature on the cardboard thermometer at the same degree as on the real thermometer. The next day you can look at the outdoor thermometer again, compare it with the cardboard thermometer, and help children decide if it is warmer or colder than yesterday.

Art Center

  * 1. All art media: feature the fall colors seen in your area in the easel paints, finger-paints, chalk, crayons, and playdough.
 ** 2. Spatter-painting: place a leaf that a child has found on a piece of paper. Let the child spatter-paint over the leaf, using a vegetable brush rubbed over wire screening fastened to a cigar box or wooden frame. When dry, remove the leaf.
 ** 3. Allow children to arrange various leaves, twigs, nutshells, and dried grasses on a

piece of construction paper. Spatter-paint the arrangement. When dry, remove the articles and an interesting design will remain.

** 4. Teacher may make a leaf stencil by tracing around a well-shaped leaf on cardboard and then carefully cutting out the leaf. The stencil can be used to make leaf designs by spatter-painting or daubing on paint with sponges. Upholstery plastic or rubber innertubing makes a washable, reusable stencil.

** 5. Roll-on painting: the teacher should cut out sleeves of various upholstry fabrics with deep cut designs. Wrap the fabric swatches around small rolling pins and fasten in place with two rubber bands. Drop small amounts of selected fingerpaint or thick poster paint on a piece of paper. Let the children choose the roller designs and colors they wish. There will be interesting blends of color. If they are ready, help the children to see the relationship between the colors put on and the ones resulting from the blending.

** 6. Crayon rubbings: fasten a nicely shaped leaf with a good vein pattern onto an easel using double-sided Scotch tape in at least two places. Thumbtack a sheet of newsprint over the leaf. Have child rub firmly over leaf with the flat side of a crayon (from which the paper has been removed). Leaf outline and vein pattern should appear.

* 7. Pasting leaves: use those that are found outside or teacher may precut leaves from colored construction paper. Paste leaves on paper as the children wish.

* 8. Tearing leaves: children may make their own leaves by tearing them out of tissue paper. These paper leaves could be used in pasting leaves, No. 7.

** 9. Hand printing leaves: children dip each hand, palm down, in separate fall colors and then press palms down on paper in different positions. Hands may be washed and two other colors chosen. When finished, the effect is like varicolored leaves.

* 10. Leaf printing: use any of the following methods to make leaf prints:
* a. Cut flat sponges into leaf shapes. Children dip them in selected paint and press on paper in desired pattern.
* b. Cut sponges into any small shape and let children daub paint with sponges on the paper desired. Use separate sponge for each fall color. Result looks like varicolored leaves.
*** c. Place leaves the children bring (or precut some from construction paper) on blue print paper. Expose to the sun for five to ten minutes. The outline of the leaf will remain when the leaf is removed.

*** 11. Caterpillar: remove the lid from an egg carton and cut the bottom portion in half lengthwise to make two caterpillars. Children may paint their caterpillars colors of their own choosing. Pipecleaners or hair curler picks make good antennae (feelers). For variation, cotton balls may be dipped in dry powdered paint and glued to the humps to give the caterpillar a fuzzy appearance.

*** 12. Fall mural: children first draw tree trunks by holding an unwrapped crayon sideways and using downward strokes. Branches can be added by a few upward strokes fanning out from the top of the trunk. Leaves may then be added to the trees by using the methods suggested in Nos. 5, 7, 8, 9, 10(a) or (b) above. A ground cover may be made by pasting on dried grasses, nutshells, and twigs.

Book Center

* Adelson, Leon. *All Ready for Winter.* New York: E. M. Hale, 1952.
* Bancroft, Henrietta. *Down Come the Leaves.* New York: Thomas Y. Crowell, 1961.
* Burningham, John. *Seasons.* New York: Bobbs-Merrill, 1970.

*** Duvoisin, Roger. *The House of Four Seasons.* New York: Lothrop, Lee & Shepard, 1960.
  * Fisher, Aileen. *I Like Weather.* New York: Thomas Y. Crowell, 1963.
  * Friskey, Margaret. *Johnny and the Monarch.* Chicago, Ill.: Childrens Press, 1946.
 ** Krauss, Ruth. *The Growing Story.* New York: Harper & Row, 1947.
 ** Kumin, Maxine. *Follow the Fall.* New York: G. P. Putnam's Sons, 1961.
  * Lenski, Lois. *Now It's Fall.* New York: Henry Z. Walck, 1948.
*** Marino, Dorothy Bronson. *Buzzy Bear's Busy Day.* New York: Franklin Watts, 1965.
 ** Miles, Betty. *A Day of Autumn.* New York: Alfred A. Knopf, 1965 (paper).
*** Podendorf, Illa. *True Book of the Seasons.* Chicago, Ill.: Childrens Press, 1972.
*** Tresselt, Alvin. *It's Time Now.* New York: Lothrop, Lee & Shepard, 1969.
 ** Udry, Janice. *A Tree Is Nice.* New York: Harper & Row, 1956.
  * Wing, Helen. *The Squirrel Twins.* Chicago, Ill.: Rand McNally, 1961.
  * Zion, Gene. *All Falling Down.* New York: Harper & Row, 1951.

planning for grouptime

NOTE: All music, fingerplays, poems, stories, and games listed here may also be used at other times during the session as appropriate. See Core Library, Basic Resources, p. 76, for publishers and addresses. Addresses for sources of records will be found on p. 81.

Music

Songs

FROM original songs in this book by JoAnne Deal Hicks
 * "What Foods Do You Like?" parody, p. 556
 * "Fruitbasket Song," p. 561
 * "Sing a Song of Applesauce," p. 562

FROM *Songs for Early Childhood,* Westminster Press
 * "Softly, Softly Floating Down," pp. 20–21
** "Popping Corn," p. 79

FROM *Music Resource Book,* Lutheran Church Press
 * "Leaves of Yellow, Red and Brown," p. 72

FROM *Wake Up and Sing,* Landeck and Crook
 * "The Wind Blows East," p. 95

FROM *Music Activities for Retarded Children,* Ginglend and Stiles
 * "The Seasons," p. 94
 * "Isn't It Fun?" p. 110

Records

"Emperor's New Clothes"/"Harvest Time" (Young People's Record [YPR], 33⅓ RPM)
"My Friend"/"Visit to My Little Friend"/"Creepy, Crawly Caterpillar"/"Merry Toy Shop" (YPR, 33⅓ RPM)
"Fun in Fall" (Golden Record, 33⅓ RPM)
"Autumn (November)" (Bowmar, 33⅓ RPM)

Rhythms and Singing Games

FROM *Songs for the Nursery School*, MacCarteney
 * "The Little Gray Ponies," p. 22
 * "Fly Away, Little Birdie," p. 36
 ** "Nutting," p. 63
 * "Falling Leaves," p. 63
 * "The Month Is October," p. 64
 * "Autumn Leaves," p. 64
 ** "Shake the Apple Tree," p. 66

NOTE: Dramatize falling leaves, migrating birds, shaking down apples with the songs above. Other activities might include crawling or tunneling to music, to simulate animals burrowing underground to hibernate for the winter.

Fingerplays and Poems

FROM *Let's Do Fingerplays*, Grayson
"This Little Squirrel," p. 35
"Little Bird," p. 37
"Falling Leaves," p. 47
"October," p. 47
"Whirling Leaves," p. 47

FROM *Rhymes for Fingers and Flannelboards*, Scott and Thompson
"Five Little Squirrels," p. 88
"Squirrel in a Tree," p. 89
"Sleepy Little Caterpillars," p. 91
"Striped Chipmunk," p. 96
"Little Leaves," p. 119
"Three Little Oak Leaves," p. 119
"Five Red Apples, p. 120
"In Wintertime," p. 120

BABY SEEDS

In a milkweed cradle, snug and warm,   (CLOSE FINGERS INTO FIST)
Baby seeds are hiding safe from harm,
Open wide the cradle, hold it high,   (OPEN HAND AND HOLD IT UP IN THE AIR)
Come along wind, help them fly.   (WIGGLE FINGERS)

WHISKY FRISKY

Whisky Frisky
Hippity hop,
Up he goes
To the tree-top.

Whirly, twirly,
Round and round
Down he scampers
To the ground.

Furly, curly
What a tail!
Tall as a feather,
Broad as a sail!

Where's his supper?
In the shell;
Snappy, cracky,
Out it fell.

CRUNCHY LEAVES

We make such a crunchy sound
In the leaves upon the ground.
Crunchy, crunchy, hear the noise
Made in leaves by girls and boys.

LITTLE SQUIRREL

I saw a little squirrel
Sitting in a tree;
He was eating a nut
And wouldn't look at me.

ROLY-POLY CATERPILLAR

Roly-poly caterpillar   (WALK FINGER ACROSS LEFT PALM)
Into a corner crept,   (FOLD UP FINGERS OF LEFT HAND OVER CATERPILLAR)
Spun around himself a blanket,   (MAKE WINDING MOTION AROUND HAND)
Then for a long time slept.   (PRETEND TO SLEEP; CLOSE EYES)

Roly-poly caterpillar   (PRETEND TO WAKE; OPEN EYES)
Wakening by and by,
Found himself with beautiful wings,   (PUT THUMBS TOGETHER; FLUTTER FINGERS LIKE WINGS)
Changed to a butterfly.   (FLY THE BUTTERFLY AWAY)

WALKING AROUND THE BLOCK

We went walking around the block together
Leaves were scarlet, leaves were brown
It was fun in sunny weather
Squirrels darting—squirrels scampering
Acorns dropping—brown birds chattering
Leaves were crunching with our feet
Smell of pine was sharp and sweet
We held pine cones in our hand
It was fun when we walked together
Walked around the block in autumn weather
Walked around the block in sunny weather
All of us liked it
All of us thought it was fun!

GRAY SQUIRREL

Gray squirrel, gray squirrel,
Whisk your bushy tail,
Gray squirrel, gray squirrel,
Whisk your bushy tail.

Wrinkle up your funny nose,
Hold a nut between your toes,
Gray squirrel, gray squirrel,
Whisk your bushy tail.

FROM *Very Young Verses*, Geismer and Suter
"About the Seasons," pp. 122–32

Stories

(To read, read-tell, or tell. See Book Center for complete list.)

 * *All Ready for Winter*, Adelson
 * *Down Come the Leaves*, Bancroft
 * *Seasons*, Burningham
** *The Squirrel Twins*, Wing

Games

(See Games, pp. 50–59, and Teacher-Made Games, p. 375, Nos. 1. 2. 3, 4, 5, 7 in this guide for directions.)

1. What's Missing?
2. Show Me
3. Match-Them
4. Reach and Feel
5. What Am I?
6. Alike, Different, and the Same

Routine Times

1. During snack or mealtime feature foods that are harvested in fall: popcorn, apple wedges (spread peanut butter on them for variation), nuts, applesauce, corn, squash, sweet potatoes, pumpkin pie, pumpkin custard, or pumpkin cupcakes. Use your favorite recipes.

   NOTE: Children who are deprived of food at home may find it difficult to use food as a cognitive medium as suggested in Discovery Activities and Teacher-Made Games and Materials. For these children, these activities might best be carried out in combination with snack or mealtime with the idea the food will be consumed immediately afterward. Sorting nuts or other similar use of foods may also be successfully offered as cognitive media after a mealtime. Otherwise, use pictures of food or plastic models.

2. While busing or walking children to and from school, look for signs that it is fall.
3. Before dressing to go outside you might talk about the weather. Look at the indoor-outdoor thermometer and talk about what we need to wear today.
4. Encourage resting by suggesting the children pretend to be hibernating animals getting ready to sleep through the cold winter.

Large Muscle Activities

1. Raking leaves: if your center is in an area where trees grow, you may wish to rake leaves into a pile and run and jump in them. If your play yard does not have trees that drop their leaves, you may plan a trip to a nearby park or to a child's home where there are some. Children enjoy scuffling through the leaves to hear the crunchy, crackling noise. Songs about leaves may be sung at this time. Leaves can be raked into a pile and jumped into. Child-size leaf rakes are desirable, or shorten handles of adult-size leaf rakes by cutting and sanding the edges.

2. Kicking football: children with above-average large muscle control may enjoy kicking a football off a tee. Using a whiffle football (plastic with holes cut in it), show the children how to set the ball on the tee and, if necessary, demonstrate how to kick.

   CAUTION: Be sure to place the tee so that the ball will be kicked away from where other children are playing. If a regulation-size football is used, do not inflate to its full extent.

Extended Experiences

1. Take a walk to look for things that show us it is fall. Collect leaves, nuts, milkweed, pine cones, caterpillars, and other finds. Bring back to the center for the science and nature table, creative arts activities, and learning games. Take sacks to collect pebbles, twigs, dry grasses or flowering weeds, seeds or hedgeapples. Also look for chipmunks or squirrels collecting nuts and try to spot migrating birds.
2. A trip to an apple orchard to pick apples.
3. A trip to a grocery to buy apples, gourds, nuts, popcorn, or pumpkins for the various planned activities.
4. Visit a farm or agricultural museum to see harvesting and planting equipment.
5. Visit a natural history museum showing animals in fall.
6. Show a filmstrip, "Autumn Is Here," "Fall Adventures" (SVE)
7. Show a filmstrip, "Things That Fall" (Constructive Playthings)

teacher resources

Books and Periodicals

1. Sterling, Dorothy. *Fall Is Here*. Garden City, N.Y.: Doubleday, 1966.
2. Zim, Herbert S. and Alexander C. Martin. *Trees*. New York: Western Publishing, 1952 (paper).
3. *National Wildlife* and *Ranger Rick* magazines, October, November issues. Published by the National Wildlife Federation, 1412 Sixteenth Street, N.W., Washington, D.C. 20036.
4. Weyerhauser, Box A-35, Tacoma, Washington 98401. Watch for their ads in magazines. Reprints of them are available if you write immediately.
5. St. Regis Paper Company, 150 East 42nd Street, New York, N. Y. 10017. Watch for their ads in your favorite magazine.

Pictures and Displays

(See p. 79 for addresses of firms listed.)

1. Mount pictures of trees in fall, squirrels, chipmunks, monarch butterfly, harvest fruits and vegetables, children in sweaters and coats, animals hibernating, birds migrating, Halloween, Thanksgiving, and other fall holidays and celebrations in appropriate places.
2. Place a bowl or vase of plastic or real fall flowers on a windowsill, snack table, or library table for the children to enjoy.
3. A basket or cornucopia of plastic or real fruits that ripen in the fall could be placed on a low table for the children to enjoy and talk about.
4. In the fall: Black Bear, Pheasants, Harvesting Corn, Roadside Stand, Indian Summer, Cycling in the Woods, Playing Football, Milkweed Seedpods. All are picture story prints, 13 inches by 18 inches in color (SVE).
5. Science Themes: Set 1, Monarch Butterfly; Set 2, Squirrels. Seasons: Fall Trees; Fall Harvesting; Winter Preparation; Hibernation; Migration (David C. Cook)
6. Fall: mini-poster cards, 14 pictures, 10 inches by 14 inches (Trend Enterprises)

Community Resources

1. County agricultural extension agent
2. 4-H club members
3. Department of Agriculture at a local college or university

PART FIVE

Animals

Introduction Animals

basic understandings

(concepts children can grasp from this subject)

- Anything that is alive and is not a plant is an animal.
- There are many different kinds of animals in the world (at present, approximately three million).
- Some of the different kinds of animals are: birds, fish, insects, worms, shell creatures, reptiles, amphibians, and mammals.
- All animals need food and water to live. Some animals eat plants; some eat other animals (meat); some, like people, eat both meat and plants.
- Animals get their food in many different ways and places:
  1. out of the air—frogs catch flying insects.
  2. in the water—ducks catch fish.
  3. on the ground—cows eat grass.
  4. out of the ground—birds eat worms.
  5. above the ground off bushes, plants, or trees—rabbits eat lettuce, raccoons eat berries.
  6. from their keeper or owner—lions in a zoo, pets in a home, chickens on a farm are given food.
  7. from their mother or father (parents)—baby kittens nurse from their mother.
- Some animals are born alive, while others are hatched from eggs.
- Most animals do not look like their parents at birth, but they change and grow up to look like them later.
- Animals differ from each other in color, in size, in body covering, in body parts, but they are similar to each other within family groups.
- Each animal moves about in its own special way. Some of the ways animals move are:

swim, float	jump, leap, or hop
fly	climb
walk, run, trot, gallop	swing
slither, slide, creep, or crawl	burrow or tunnel

- Each animal makes a different sound. Some of the sounds they may make are:

bark	growl	chatter	chirp
whinny	snort	squeal	whistle
grunt	bleat	honk	hiss
crow	quack	moo	purr
roar	mew	trumpet	

NOTE: Try to imitate actual sounds. See Additional Facts the Teacher Should Know.

- Animals have different kinds of coverings such as:

fur	hair	skins (hides)	feathers
shell	scales	plates	

- Animals are used by people in many ways:
    1. for pleasure—as pets to love and to play with; to observe their beauty or uniqueness; to ride.
    2. for protection—watchdogs; seeing-eye dogs.
    3. for work—to help man to carry, to push, to pull, or to lift something; to guard other animals.
    4. for clothing—wool and silk cloth; leather for shoes, belts, and purses; feathers for hats and decorations; fur for coats; yarn for sweaters and mittens.
    5. for food—eggs, meat, milk, cheese, or to feed other animals.

    CAUTION: Better to stress natural products rather than those requiring loss of the life of an animal.

- Some animals we hear about are make-believe, such as dragons and unicorns.
- Some animals, such as dinosaurs and dodo birds, are extinct.
- Each kind of animal is given a different name for the male, the female, the offspring, and the group. (See Animal Charts.)
- Animals need people to help them:
    1. by caring for them in captivity in zoos, homes, animal hospitals, or on farms.
    2. by helping them to live in their natural homes:
        a. by assisting wild animals to find food and water especially in times of hardship.
        b. by protecting them from other animals, from machines, from people, from enemies, and from weather.
        c. by building or fencing off special places for them to live.
        d. by having rules for fishers and hunters.
- Sometimes animals are referred to by the place where they live: farm animals, animals of the woods, zoo animals, and pets (animals we have at home).
- Many animals, especially birds, insects, and wild animals, are colored to look like the place where they usually live. Because they match tree bark, leaves, ground, rocks, or grass, other animals or hunters cannot find them easily and they are safe.
- Animals live in different kinds of homes: water, burrow, nest, or tree.
- A veterinarian is a doctor for animals.
- An animal hospital or clinic is a place where sick and injured animals can be taken to get help.
- The Humane Society (animal shelter) is a place where lost animals or animals without owners can be cared for until they are claimed or a home is found for them.

Additional Facts the Teacher Should Know

Most animals we have seen or heard about have backbones and are called *vertebrates*.

Insects and spiders, examples of animals without backbones, are called *invertebrates*.

Mammals are warm-blooded vertebrates that are born alive, covered with fur or hair. They feed (nurse) their babies with milk from their own bodies. The duckbill platypus and the spiny anteater produce their young as eggs, but they, too, nurse the young once they are hatched.

Reptiles and amphibians are cold-blooded vertebrates. Reptiles crawl on their bellies such as snakes or creep on very short legs such as lizards, turtles, alligators, and crocodiles. Reptiles are covered with dry scales, are not slimy, and most lay eggs on dry land. Four groups of reptiles now living are: lizards, snakes, turtles, alligators and crocodiles. Amphibians live both in water and on land. Their skins are bare and moist, with no scales, fur, or feathers. Most live just on land, but all return to the water to breed. Frogs, toads, and salamanders are amphibians. Cold-blooded animals must bury themselves underground or hibernate in a cave in cold weather. (See Fall and Winter guides.)

Most baby animals are cared for by their parents when young; some must take care of themselves from birth. Some baby animals eat the same kind of food that their parents eat; others get milk from their mother's body (nurse or suckle).

To avoid misinformation or misconceptions while teaching about the sounds animals make, try to imitate the sound the animal really makes. If possible, listen to good records and tapes with accurate reproductions of these sounds. (See Voice under Description and Characteristics in the Animal Charts.) Many stories and songs refer to animal sounds as "cock-a-doodle-doo," "bow-wow," and "meow." When reading stories or teaching songs, substitute the words "the rooster crowed," "the dog barked," or "the cat mewed," or do your best to imitate the sound by saying "the rooster sounds something like this . . ."

22 Farm Animals

basic understandings

(concepts children can grasp from this subject)

- A farm is a piece of land, usually larger than a city lot, used to raise crops or animals. It is ordinarily located outside a city or town.
- There are many kinds of farms: poultry, grain, dairy, livestock, and truck. At one time a farmer used to raise crops *and* animals. Some farmers still do. But more often only one main crop or one kind of animal is raised: cotton, nuts, beans, wheat, peaches, berries, sheep, turkeys, ducks, or hogs.
- Horses and cattle are sometimes raised on ranches. The people who work on ranches are called ranch-hands or cowboys.
- Animals usually raised on a farm are: cows, horses, donkeys, mules, sheep, goats, pigs, chickens, ducks, turkeys, and geese.
- Most farm animals need to be fenced into fields so they do not stray into a roadway or into another farmer's field. Fences prevent animals escaping to other fields where they might eat the wrong foods.
- To protect them from bad weather, farm animals usually have special houses, such as barns, sheds, stables, coops, or pens, to sleep in at night.
- Sometimes the farmer raises food for the farm animals: hay, alfalfa, corn, oats, milo, and barley.
- The farmer, family, and employees work long hours to care for their animals and their crops. At certain seasons of the year (during planting, cultivating, irrigating, harvesting, butchering, breeding, and marketing) they are much busier than at other seasons.
- A herd is a group of one kind of animal living together.
- Farm animals help the farmer:
  1. horses provide transportation; pull wagons
  2. chickens lay eggs
  3. cows and goats give milk
  4. cats catch mice; dogs guard other animals
  5. sheep supply wool
  6. bees make honey

NOTE: Stress products *without* loss of life.

- The farmer uses many tools and machines to take care of farm animals. (See Tools and Machines guide.)
- Some farm animals are pets as well as useful, such as horses, ducks, goats, donkeys, burros, and pigs.
- Many farm families like to show their best animals at state and county fairs or 4-H shows. Sometimes they win ribbons or prizes.
- At rodeos, cowboys show how well they can rope (lasso) calves and ride horses.

NOTE: Include understandings listed for Animals, p. 385, as appropriate.

Additional Facts the Teacher Should Know

See Farm Animal Chart for detailed information regarding their characteristics, habitats, handling, feeding, and reproduction.

Methods Most Adaptable for Introducing This Subject to Children

- At mealtime, discuss animal-food products from farms.
- Child takes a trip to a farm.
- Tell or read-tell a farm storybook like *Big Red Barn*.
- See a truck full of farm animals.
- Make a picture display of farm scenes.
- Visit of a parent who is a veterinarian or a farmer.
- Make a cake or cookies. This can lead to a talk about the original source of eggs, milk, butter, and cream.

Vocabulary

saddle	hayloft	poultry	field	hay
cowboy/cowgirl	feeder	livestock	dairy	silo
cattle	trough	harness	fence	stall
sheep	stable	pasture	farm	barn
brand	pig pen	corncrib	ranch	herd

Add to the above list words that pertain to farm animals observed by your group. Include the names, body parts, sounds, and foods eaten by animals you are observing.

learning centers

Discovery Center

1. Make butter. (See Food guide, p. 548.)
2. Churn butter using a butter churn.
3. Examine raw eggs; then poach, scramble, soft-cook, hard-cook, and bake them. Compare.
4. Make cottage cheese:

   > 1 quart of milk
   > 1 rennet tablet

   DIRECTIONS:

   > Heat milk to lukewarm.
   > Dissolve rennet tablet in a small amount of the milk.
   > Stir rennet mixture into remaining milk.
   > Let stand in a warm place until set.
   > Drain through a strainer lined with cheesecloth.
   > Bring corners of cloth together and squeeze or drain mixture.
   > Rinse mixture with cold water and drain again.
   > Add a little butter and salt.

5. Make pudding: pour hot milk into a plastic container. Add instant pudding mix. Seal container, then shake. Let pudding cool before eating.
6. Take a pony ride at a farm or in a park.

   NOTE: Must have adequate adult supervision and animals must be used to children. Do not insist any child ride who does not *wish* to.

7. Explore wool: examine wool clippings, lanolin, dyed yarn, yarn spun into thread, wool cloth, sheepskin, wool articles (mittens or scarves). Order a folder with attached samples from a wool company. (See Teacher Resources, p. 399.)
8. Explore a loom or other spinning and weaving equipment.
9. Examine feathers: note difference between tail or wing feathers and downy fluffs. See if feathers will float. Talk about why they float. What are feathers for? (To keep birds warm or cool, to help ducks float on water.) Use a magnifying glass to examine feathers.
10. Examine blown out or hard-cooked eggs: compare size, shape, and colors of chicken, duck, goose eggs. Put feathers with each kind of egg in a cigar box with a picture or model of bird so that children can make a proper association.
11. Various grains that farm animals eat can be examined under a magnifying glass or viewed in a sealed pill bottle.
12. Examine leather: identify an article's source, such as pigskin gloves, calfskin shoes, horsehide baseball, sheepskin coat or collar.

    CAUTION: Remember some animals are now protected by law against extinction.

13. Hatch an egg in an incubator.
14. Taste goat milk, cream, skimmed milk, whole milk, cottage cheese, sour cream, honey-butter, margarine, buttermilk. Smell sour milk.
15. Let children explore eating shredded wheat (like hay), dry cereal, candy corn without using their hands as suggested in Pet Animals guide, p. 404.
16. Display Animals That Help Us Picture Fold-Out (The Child's World).

Dramatic Play Centers

Home-Living Center

1. Post pictures of baking, showing eggs and milk next to a mixing bowl.
2. Show picture of a chicken with eggs or a cow being milked.
3. Mount on cardboard, pictures of fried eggs, bacon, meat for children to pretend to cook and to serve. Cover pictures with clear adhesive plastic for greater durability.
4. Display wooden eggs that are available through Montgomery Ward's farm catalog or can be made on a lathe by a skilled craftsman. Unbreakable plastic eggs are available through toy companies. Occasionally, colored plastic eggs are available at discount stores at Easter. Eggs may be put in refrigerator or cupboard. Cut or break egg carton in half.
5. Put "milk bottles" (bowling pins) or unbreakable juice containers that resemble milk bottles in a painted soft drink carrier. Carrier can be used by a child pretending to be a milk deliverer. Child may also wear a cap.
6. Add empty milk cartons and empty evaporated milk or pudding cans with "cut" edge taped for safety. If possible choose labels showing whole food in natural state. (See Food guide.)
7. Add pie tins, fry pans with spatulas, muffin tins, eggs, and dairy products for cooking.

Block-Building Center

1. Set out block accessories such as model farm animals (including cats and dogs), tractors, dump trucks, farm fences, trees, troughs, and people.
2. Hang pictures of farm activities including a farmer milking cows or harvesting crops to feed livestock. Also include pictures of hens, eggs, pigs, and other farm animals.
3. Set out a shoebox filled with excelsior for hay to "feed" farm animals.
4. Add some blue paper cut in free-form shapes to use as lakes and ponds.
5. Set out colored cubes and colored spools to be used for loading and unloading trucks and wagons.
6. Encourage use of large hollow blocks for building barns. Children may pretend to be animals.
7. Make silo from Christmas brick paper wrapped around a cardboard cylinder.
8. Add buckets, work gloves, old saddle or child harness, dishpans for feeding chickens, work hats, step ladders (to go to hayloft).
9. Purchase thin arches (Creative Playthings) to use as water tanks, ponds, and enclosures.

Other Dramatic Play Centers

1. Set out clothes and props for farmer or ranch hand. (See p. 20.)
2. Make paper sack costumes or hand puppets designed to look like farm animals (see p. 228); provide Halloween costumes of farm animals such as ducks, chicks, and rabbits. Appropriate coat hanger masks can be used. (See Halloween guide, p. 227.)

Learning, Language, and Readiness Materials Center

Commercially made games and materials for use at a table or on a mat:

(See Basic Resources, p. 79, for manufacturers' addresses.)

1. Animal Puzzle Dominoes, also Jumbo Puzzle Dominoes (Constructive Playthings)
2. Farm Lotto Game (Ed-U-Card)

3. Judy Puzzles: Duck, 8 pcs.; Tractor, 11 pcs.; Cow, 16 pcs.; Barn, 12 pcs.; Rooster, 15 pcs.; Kitten, 5 pcs.; Farmer, 10 pcs.; Puppy, 13 pcs.; Terrier, 6 pcs.; Horse and Foal, 7 pcs.; Sheep and Lambs, 10 pcs.; Pig and Piglets, 7 pcs.; Farm Animals, 5 pcs.; Cat and Kittens, 13 pcs.
4. See Inside Puzzles: Dairy Barn, 16 pcs. (Creative Playthings)
5. Playskool Puzzles: Horses, 15 pcs.; Farm, 15 pcs.; Farmer, 14 pcs.
6. Judy See-Quees: Story of Milk, 12 pcs.; From Seed to Pumpkin, 12 pcs.; An Apple Tree Grows, 6 pcs.; Eggs to Chickens, 6 pcs.
7. Ani-Space: 8 farm (Lauri)
8. Animals and Their Young: 30 poster cards (Milton Bradley)
9. Barnyard Animals: 7 pcs. pliable plastic (Practical Drawing Co.)
10. Farm Animals Flannel Aid: 25 pcs. (Milton Bradley)
11. Judy Animal story sets
12. Before and After Puzzle: 2 pcs. each (Holcomb's)
13. Play Family Farm: 21 pcs. (Fisher-Price)
14. Handpainted Farm Animals: 100 pcs. (ABC School Supply)
15. Handpainted farm set to scale, 21 pcs. (ABC School Supply)
16. Rubber Animal Sets: 7 pcs., farm animals (Constructive Playthings)
17. Giant Block Play Animals: 12 pcs., farm animals (Childcraft)
18. Farm Animal Set: 10 wood pcs. (available in most catalogs)
19. Table Block Farm: 18 pcs. (Childcraft)
20. Concepto-Sort: 225 picture-word playing cards, 45 animals (Educational Performance Associates)
21. Stand-up Puzzle: Farm, 20 pcs. (Childcraft)
22. Farm Animals and Babies: flannelboard set (Instructo)

Teacher-made games and materials for use at a table or on a mat:

NOTE: For detailed description of Games, see pp. 50–59.

1. Match-Them: Match farm animals with what they give us; parents with their babies.
2. Look and See: Homemade felt animal shapes or farm animal pictures mounted on felt are very satisfactory to use on a flannelboard. Use food with animal, mother with young, and so on.
3. Make cardboard Classification Cards at least 9 inches by 12 inches on which to place pictures of animals as children classify them. Decorate cards, each with a different picture or drawing in the center (house, lake, grass, and barn) or models of these. This activity may also be done by using appropriate pictures of houses, cages, or barns pasted on the end of shoe boxes.
4. Offer a box of geometric felt shapes with a square of dark felt flannelboard. Child may make into animal shapes.
5. Match-Them: Use homemade animal-word identification cards. Cut several cardboard rectangles about 5 inches by 5 inches. Glue picture of animal on upper half of the card. Letter name of animal beneath picture. Cut several more cardboard rectangles 1 inch by 4 inches. Letter animal name. Children can match lettered name on small card to that lettered on large card. Game may be varied for younger children by making "match" cards (these might be 2 inches by 4 inches) using the animal picture instead of the animal name. Check dimestores and shopping centers for sticker-picture books such as Farm Fun or Animal Homes for use in making game cards. School supply stores stock packages of gummed animal seals.
6. Count animal parts in pictures of animals or live animals in Discovery Center.

7. Grouping and Sorting by Association: Use plastic animals. Classify by their outer coverings, by their products, by their homes. Sort into boxes labeled with a picture of that animal. (See illustration.)
8. If you have enough staff or an assistant who can take shorthand, have the children dictate a story about a farm or what they saw on a visit to a farm. Then, write it down and post it with farm picture.

Art Center

* 1. Offer clay for modeling.
2. Collage pictures:
***   a. geometric-shaped construction paper collage: let children experiment several days prior with felt shapes or magnetic geometric shapes until they get the idea that everything is a shape or combination of shapes

**   b. yarn collage: include clipped yarn, yarn fluffs, and various lengths and colors of yarn

**   c. texture collage: be sure to include spotted fabric shapes

**   d. grain and seed collage: use grain seeds or other products gathered from a farm for a collage. Consider if appropriate to your group

**   e. scrap collage: dye eggshells and use in collage pictures

* 3. Buttermilk chalk picture: using hands or brush, cover paper or cardboard with two or three tablespoons of buttermilk. Dry hands and then paint with fat, colored chalk. It dries and does not rub off readily.

* 4. Complete the picture: let children mount a cut-out of farm animals, including cats and dogs, on plain paper or cardboard. Let them color in the rest of the picture for a background scene. Children may choose to cut out of wallpaper book. Introduce questions: "Where is your animal?" "What is it doing?" "When you finish the picture what will you know?"

Book Center

** Anderson, C. W. *Blaze and the Gray Spotted Pony*. New York: Macmillan, 1968.

** ———. *Lonesome Little Colt*. New York: Macmillan, 1961.

* Anglund, Joan. *Brave Cowboy*. New York: Harcourt Brace Jovanovich, 1959.

* Barton, Byrom. *Buzz, Buzz, Buzz*. New York: Macmillan, 1973.

* Brown, Margaret W. *Big Red Barn*. Reading, Mass.: Addison-Wesley, 1956.

* ———. *Country Noisy Book*. New York: Harper & Row, 1940.

*** Collier, Ethel. *I Know a Farm*. Reading, Mass.: Addison-Wesley, 1960.

** De Paola, Tomie. *Charlie Needs a Cloak*. Englewood Cliffs, N.J.: Prentice-Hall, 1973.

*** Einsel, Walter. *Did You Ever See?* New York: Scholastic Book Services, 1962 (paper).

** Flack, Marjorie. *Angus and the Ducks*. Garden City, N.Y.: Doubleday, 1939.

*** Galdone, Paul. *The Little Red Hen*. New York: Seabury Press, 1973.

**** Garelick, May. *What's Inside?* New York: Scholastic Book Services, 1968 (paper; information-photographs).

*** Greene, Carla. *Cowboys, What Do They Do?* New York: Harper & Row, 1972.

** ———. *I Want To Be a Dairy Farmer*. Chicago, Ill.: Childrens Press, 1957.

* Hawkinson, Lucy. *Picture Book Farm*. Chicago, Ill.: Childrens Press, 1971.

* Lenski, Lois. *Animals for Me*. New York: Henry Z. Walck, 1941.

*** ———. *Granja Pequena*. New York: Henry Z. Walck, 1968 (Spanish).

** ———. *Little Farm*. New York: Henry Z. Walck, 1965.

** ———. *Cowboy Small/Vaquero Pequeno*. New York: Henry Z. Walck, 1960.

** McCloskey, Robert. *Make Way for Ducklings*. New York: Viking Press, 1969.

* Merrill, Jean and Frances G. Scott. *Here I Come—Ready or Not*. Chicago: Whitman, 1970.

*** Petersham, Maud and Miska Petersham. *The Box with Red Wheels*. New York: Macmillan, 1973 (paper).

*** Provenson, Alice and Martin Provenson. *Our Animal Friends at Maple Hill Farm*. New York: Random House, 1974.

** Rojankovsky, Feodor. *Animals on the Farm*. New York: Alfred A. Knopf, 1967.

*** Selsam, Millicent. *All About Eggs*. Reading, Mass.: Addison-Wesley, 1952.

*** Sootin, Laura. *Let's Go to a Farm*. New York: G. P. Putnam's Sons, 1958.

* Tensen, Ruth M. *Come to the Farm*. Chicago, Ill.: Reilly & Lee, 1949.

* Tresselt, Alvin R. *Wake Up Farm*. New York: Lothrop, Lee & Shepard, 1955.

* Williams, Garth. *The Chicken Book*. New York: Delacorte Press, 1970.

planning for grouptime

NOTE: All music, fingerplays, poems, stories, and games listed here may be used at other times during the session as appropriate. See Core Library, Basic Resources, p. 76, for publishers and addresses. Addresses for sources of records will be found on p. 81.

Music

Songs

FROM original songs in this book by JoAnne Deal Hicks
* "Who Can Feed the Animals?" p. 400
* "Animal Nonsense Song," verses 2, 6, p. 412

FROM *Songs for the Nursery School*, MacCarteney
* "High-Stepping Horses," p. 20
** "Little Gray Ponies," p. 22
** "Barnyard Song," p. 31
* "Ducks," p. 35 (See also pp. 33–34.)
* "Baa, Baa, Black Sheep," p. 74
* "Mary Had a Little Lamb," p. 85
** "Little Bo Peep," p. 88

FROM *Wake Up and Sing*, Landeck and Crook
** "Three Pigs," p. 110

FROM *Music Resource Book*, Lutheran Church Press
** "Barnyard Song," p. 14
* "I Wish I Were a Windmill," p. 60
** "Six Little Ducks," p. 62

FROM *Music Activities for Retarded Children*, Ginglend and Stiles
** "I Have a Little Rooster," p. 64

FROM your favorite American folksong book for children
* "Old MacDonald"
* "Farmer in the Dell"
* "Little Boy Blue"

Records

"All Aboard: Train to the Zoo/**Farm**/Ranch" (Young People's Record [YPR], 33⅓ RPM)
"Chugging Freight Engine"/"**Little Gray Ponies**"/"Rhyme Me a Riddle" (YPR, 33⅓ RPM)
"Come to the Party"/"**Grandfather's Farm**"/"Song for Laughter" (YPR, 33⅓ RPM)

"Ride 'Em Cowboy"/**"Let's Go to the Rodeo"**/"Ship Ahoy" (YPR, 33⅓ RPM)
"Muffin and Mother Goose"/**"Muffin in the City"**/"Country" —(YPR, 33⅓ RPM)
"The Milk's Journey" (Children's Record Guild [CRG], 45, 78 RPM)
"Whoa Little Horses" (YPR, 45, 78 RPM)
"Can I Borrow Your Burro?" (Kimbo, 33⅓ RPM or cassette, guide included)
"Jungle Animals and Farm Animals" (Kimbo, 33⅓ RPM or cassette, guide included)
"Sizes and Sounds" (Kimbo, 33⅓ RPM or cassette, guide included)
"The Farm" (David C. Cook, 33⅓ RPM, record and flannelboard kit)
"Farmyard Fun Songs" (Happy Time, 33⅓ RPM)
"A Day on the Farm" (Golden Book/Record set, 45 RPM)

Rhythms and Singing Games

FROM *Creative Movements for the Developing Child*, Cherry
"Galloping Horses," p. 44

FROM original songs in this book by JoAnne Deal Hicks
"Animal Nonsense Song," p. 412, verses 2, 4, 5, 6, 8 (Follow activity suggestions on song
   sheet.)

Fingerplays and Poems

FROM *Rhymes for Fingers and Flannelboards*, Scott and Thompson
"The Farm," pp. 26–37

FROM *Let's Do Fingerplays*, Grayson
"When a Little Chicken Drinks," p. 36   "Two Little Ducks," p. 71
"This Little Calf," p. 38   "Two Mother Pigs," p. 72

Stories

(To read, read-tell, or tell. See Book Center for complete list.)

  * *Country Noisy Book*, Brown   * *Here I Come—Ready or Not*, Merrill
** *Make Way for Ducklings*, McCloskey   ** *Lonesome Little Colt*, Anderson
  * *Wake Up Farm*, Tresselt   ** *Charlie Needs a Cloak*, De Paola

Routine Times

1. Serve animal cookies and milk at snacktime.
2. At snack or mealtime, have the children eat scrambled, deviled, or hard-cooked eggs that
   they prepared earlier (in the Discovery Center).
3. Serve cheese wedges, cottage cheese, and a variety of milk and juice drinks at snacktime.
4. Talk about source of foods and make up guessing game as you eat.
5. If you have a rest period, encourage the children to curl up like a cat or a dog.
6. In dismissing children to leave the room or go outside, say "you can gallop like a horse,
   hop like a bunny, waddle like a duck . . ."

Large Muscle Activities

1. Allow wagons, trikes to be used as tractors for hauling (could clean up twigs on the farm).
2. Large hollow blocks, cardboard packing boxes, cylinders, or laundry barrels can be used for farm animal houses, barns, silos.
3. Ring-necked goose (plastic can be weighted by filling with water). Colored loops are tossed over neck and head (begin with largest loops and add smaller as children become more skillful). Available from Creative Playthings.
4. Using large balls, let children pretend to be goats and butt the balls with their heads.
5. Imitate how animals walk.
6. Allow digging and plowing in one area of yard.
7. Add water to sand and dirt and encourage the exploration of these elements that are so important to growing things.
8. Let the children pretend to be horses by providing stick horses.

Extended Experiences

1. Trips children can take:
   a. dairy (**CAUTION:** May be too much machinery for very young children)
   b. milk station if one is nearby
   c. ice-cream shop
   d. dairy section of the grocery store
   e. zoo (visit farm section to see most common farm animals)
   f. farm (turkey, sheep, dairy, pony, or chicken)
2. Visit of farm animal pets to school (turkey, lamb, or young goat)
3. Show a filmstrip.
4. Invite a milk carrier or milk route sales person to deliver ice cream or chocolate milk and talk with children.

teacher resources

Books and Periodicals

1. *How and Why Series:* Horses and Dogs. New York: Wonder-Treasure Books
2. Farm journals

Pictures and Displays

(See p. 79 for addresses of firms listed.)

1. Hang a mobile of shapes with a picture of an animal on one side and its products on the back. Mount pictures on circles, squares, or triangles for mobile.

2. Put out *Instructo Series*, Scott, Foresman, Society for Visual Education, or other pictures of food and animals (include farm animals only, at first).
3. Bulletin board ideas (each in a separate section):
   a. ranch, cowboy, cattle
   b. poultry farming
   c. grain fields
   d. dairy farm, swine farm, beef farm
   e. fruit orchards

   NOTE: Vary the choice of number of sections with pictures available and the size of the bulletin board and your focus of interest.

4. American Hereford Association (bull, cow, steer): 3 pictures, 11 inches by 14 inches. Write to the association at Kansas City, Missouri 64105. (Check with similar association or meat packing plant nearest you.)
5. Instructo Series: animal study prints, 32 pictures.
6. Sounds Around the Farm and Zoo: one of a series of 5 vols. including record, picture cards, photographs (Scott, Foresman).
7. SVE Picture Series: farm and ranch animals.
8. Pictures cut from farm journals.
9. A Trip to the Farm: picture packet (David C. Cook).
10. Write for catalog of materials available from National Dairy Council, 111 North Canal Street, Chicago, Illinois, or check with local dairy council representative.
11. Check with church school teachers for other pet animal pictures and related materials through their and your own denomination's press.
12. Write to the Pendleton Woolen Mills, Portland, Oregon, or any woolen mill near you, for the story of wool.
13. Picture fold-outs: Animals That Help Us (The Child's World).

Community Resources

1. Veterinarian
2. Dairy council representative
3. 4-H leaders
4. Agricultural extension agents
5. Farmer
6. Agri-business teacher or vocational agriculture teacher in the junior or senior high school

Who Can Feed the Animals?

A Question and Answer Song

JoAnne Deal Hicks

Teacher:

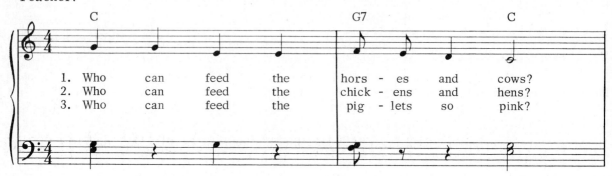

1. Who can feed the hors - es and cows?
2. Who can feed the chick - ens and hens?
3. Who can feed the pig - lets so pink?

Children:

1. I can,___ I know how! A buck-et of grain, a
2. I can,___ I know when! A pan___ of seeds, some
3. I can, I think, I think! Some yel - low corn, a

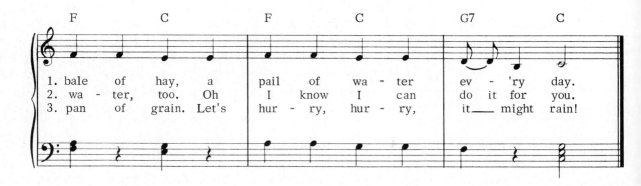

1. bale of hay, a pail of wa - ter ev - 'ry day.
2. wa - ter, too. Oh I know I can do it for you.
3. pan of grain. Let's hur - ry, hur - ry, it___ might rain!

NOTE: Teacher sings the question to the children, showing flannelboard pictures of the necessary food and feeding utensils to "help" the children with their answers. For the youngest children teach one verse at a time.

...ent and sleep	reproductive and life cycle	handling

ent and sleep

- , stalks, slinks, pounces, and jumps.
- on same side of body simultaneously.
- to string; rolling a ball; pouncing on a
- urls up to sleep.

reproductive and life cycle

- Can breed at 6 months. May have 3 to 5 kittens, 2 or 3 times a year. Gestation: 55 to 63 days; blind at birth, eyes open usually from 10 to 14 days. Mother licks kitten's belly to start breathing and bites off umbilical cord. Gets teeth at 8 weeks. Usually weaned from mother in 5 to 6 weeks. Mother housebreaks. Mother carries kitten by the nape of the neck.
- Lives to be about 14 years old.

handling

- Handle gently, p
- legs or tail.
- Dangerous. Will If claws are rem protected.
- Brush or vacuu vaccinated for 4 feline rhino-trac mixture to food.
- **Caution:** Child used by cats for
- See **Note** under

- s eyes to sleep.

- Gestation: around 63 days (varies with breed); can have as many as 16 puppies. Puppy is blind, deaf, and barely able to crawl, but it can smell, taste, and touch. Nurses within minutes after birth, weaned at 5 to 6 weeks. After two weeks eyes open. At 3 weeks it can hear, walk, and eat solids when its first teeth appear. Mother stays very close to puppies for the first 9 days.

- Handle like a kit people when it
- Brush regularly.
- Social, but will
- Should be vacci rabies, and lept
- **Note:** New ow veterinarian abo planned surgery

- mp, leap, run, and scamper. Stands on
- in ball in nest to sleep.

- Monogamous. Lives comfortably with a mate. Gestation: 24 days; average litter: 3 to 7; mating takes place 3 times a year. Can breed at 3 months. Newborn develop slowly; eyes open after 20 days. Can live in same cage with parents for 2 to 3 months. Then needs cage of its own.

- Handle gently. D
- **Caution:** Befor observation of b of gerbils or one provide homes t much a concern

---

- ns, burrows, good climber; prefers
- climbing back down. Provide ramps cise.
- ly sleeps days and is active at night. o sleep.

- Gestation: 16 days. Litter: average is 2 to 8; born helpless with eyes and ears closed, pink and hairless skin; nurses about a month. Eyes open in 15 days, ears open in 5 days. Can breed at 2 months of age. Hamsters multiply rapidly.
- Mother should have rest from mate at least one week after weaning young.
- One pair of hamsters may have children and grandchildren in one school year.
- Adult is 5 to 6 inches long. Life span: 2 to 3 years.

- Handle gently. D Move slowly (qu
- Has sharp teeth away. Pour cold puncture medic
- Keep father awa from babies (ma
- Males and fema mating.

- in open area may move faster.
- imber and does not jump. Will stay arring accidents).
- feet behind to sleep. Sleeps at night

- Gestation: 65 to 70 days. Females are mature at 9 months and can breed for 3 to 5 years. Litter: 1 to 6; good sow produces 5 litters a year. Young are vigorous, can take care of themselves very early. Born fully haired, eyes open, and with teeth. Within 2 or 3 days can eat solid food. Advisable to wean at 3 to 4 weeks.
- Mother can be returned to breeding pen 1 week after babies weaned. After 30 days, if pregnancy is evident remove female and place in hutch by herself.
- Mature adult weighs 34 to 42 ounces, 10 inches long. Life span is 8 years.

- Lift from behind its shoulder, fin scratches.
- To bathe: Disso lukewarm, wash Rinse in clean v
- Cage needs to t Fecal matter ha
- Protect from co contracts few di
- Needs protectio

- s. Climbs up and down and has a
- r protection, but they do not keep out ng to sleep, but it is good to cover draft and light.

- In nature, breeds in colonies. In captivity, can be encouraged to breed in any month. Must have quiet. After mating, will begin laying eggs on alternate days in nest box until it produces 3 to 5 eggs. Newly hatched chicks are weak and unfeathered. Fluffy down appears within a week. Well feathered in 4 to 5 weeks, then leave nest.
- Male is mature at 10 months; female is mature at 1 year.

- Can be handled quietly because alarm the bird.

cautions and special needs	relation to other animals and to world
ace hand under body for support. Do not lift by bite and scratch if scared, angry, or mishandled. ved, cat becomes vulnerable and must be hair often to prevent hairballs. Should be diseases—distemper, neumonitis, rabies, and eitis. Worms eliminated by adding special Flea powder or collar eliminates fleas. en may get pinworms from open sandboxes toilet area. dogs (applies to cats).	• On farm, valuable for killing rats and mice. • Seeks attention by meowing and rubbing against human's leg; likes to be petted. Some can live amicably with other cats and dogs in a household.
en. More easily handled if it has contact with 3 to 7 weeks old. Bathe when needed—dry well. ite to protect itself if scared or angry. ated for 4 diseases—distemper, hepatitis, -spirosis. The latter is a health hazard to people. ers of pets should consult their own t nutrition, deworming, inoculations, and a schedule (for spaying, ear trimming).	• Used as seeing-eye dog; for hunting; for caring for other animals, such as sheep; for protection. • Circus dog is trained to walk on hind legs, jump through hoops, leap. • As a pet, dog can be trained to sit, stand, heel, come, beg, roll over, and fetch a stick or newspaper. • Loyal companion and guardian of kind owners. Many have good homing sense. Some can live amicably with other dogs and cats in the household.
o not move quickly. Keep from drafts. planning to breed animals for classroom rth, consider the possibility of borrowing a pair that is pregnant. Otherwise you will need to or young. Today, overpopulation of pets is as as overpopulation of people.	• Wonderful pet for children. Usually does not bite or scratch. If escapes, may return to cage. • Because it is relatively free of disease in its natural habitat, it is very useful in scientific research.
o not handle first week or when first received. ck movements startle the animal). and can bite very hard. If it bites, do not pull water on hamster until it releases. Have a ly attended. from mother prior to birth of young and away y try to eat them). es fight readily, so keep separate except for	• Makes a good pet to observe. Used in scientific research laboratories. • Can possibly do damage if escapes. • Are gentle, trusting, and inquisitive pets.
one hand under body, other hand cupped over ers around side of belly. Rarely bites or e mild soap in boiling water. When water is thoroughly, loosening up all dirt and stains. ater and rub and brush coat till dry. cleaned every day if you have several pigs. strong odor. , damp, and drafts. If cared for properly, eases. from other house pets, such as dog or cat.	• Once used extensively in laboratories, but does not reproduce as rapidly or in as large a number as rabbits, hamsters, and mice. • Makes a cuddly and gentle pet. Can be taught to sit up and beg and even to whistle at arrival of owner.
often if it is done very gently. Move slowly and sudden movements or loud noises or voices may ick up from behind.	• Molting is a natural process. Conditioning food process is important. • As a pet it is fun to watch and cheerful to hear. Can learn small vocabulary if trainer repeats word over and over. Easier to teach tricks and to talk if you have a single bird.

23 Pet Animals

basic understandings

(concepts children can grasp from this subject)

- Any tame animal that is kept just for fun as a special friend is called a pet.
- Children should choose pets carefully because:
  1. pets have special needs due to their size, diet, need for exercise, and need for protection.
  2. some pets are more playful than others and therefore make better companions.
  3. some pets need more care than a child can give and parents may not wish to assume the responsibility.
- Sometimes you cannot keep a pet where you live:
  1. big pets, such as ponies, lambs, and goats, need large, fenced areas in which to exercise.
  2. some pets are noisy and need to live outside or where they do not need to be confined.
  3. some pets need special equipment, such as cages or tanks, in order to be kept in a house.
  4. sometimes motels and apartments do not allow people to keep pets.
  5. some pets are more dangerous than others (they may bite or scratch).
  6. an animal should not be kept in a cage if it cannot be happy there.
  7. some pets cost more money than others to feed and care for because their food may be hard to get or may be too expensive.
  8. we need permission from our families for most pets.
- All pets need to be loved and cared for.
- Sometimes pets get sick or injured. Doctors for pets are called veterinarians.
- Some common housepets are dogs, cats, gerbils, goldfish, parakeets, hamsters, guinea pigs, canaries, and turtles.
- Other pets include rabbits, crickets, chameleons, horned toads, white mice or rats, and guppies.
- Pets need to be handled gently and carefully.
- Pets often need baths, their hair brushed, their toenails clipped, and their eyes washed out. They also need opportunities to eat, sleep, and play much like children do.

- Some pets, like dogs and cats, have to wear a license tag, so if they are lost they can be returned to their owners.
- Some pets need to be immunized (have shots like children do) so they cannot give or get diseases from other animals or people.
- Sometimes children and parents exhibit their pets at pet shows. Prizes and ribbons are given for pets that are well mannered and well groomed (prepared for showing).
- Some pets can be trained to obey their owners and do tricks.

NOTE: Include understandings listed for Animals, p. 385, as appropriate.

Additional Facts the Teacher Should Know

See Pet Animal Chart for detailed information regarding pets' characteristics, habitats, handling, feeding, and reproduction.

Methods Most Adaptable for Introducing This Subject to Children

- A child brings a new or favorite pet to share with the group.
- As a result of a dog or cat "following" a child to school.
- A child shares news of birth of pet babies at home.
- Following a trip to a pet shop to purchase a pet and its food for the classroom.

Learning how to care for and handle a pet is an important part of a child's relationship with animals.

- Display pictures of children with pets showing the pets playing, sleeping, eating or the children caring for the pets. (See Pictures and Displays, p. 411.)
- Read a new pet storybook or poem, or teach a song about a pet.
- Present a new puzzle or game about pets. (See Commercially made games.)
- On the introduction of a new classroom pet by teacher.

Vocabulary

pet	supplies	love, care	fur	home
cage	feeding dish	pellets	coat	house
bone	biscuit	drink	claws	indoor
bed	water bottles	whiskers	paws	outdoor
tail	exercise wheel	feathers	born	feed

Include the names, sounds, body parts, and foods eaten by the pets you are observing. Also include breed or species of pet, such as collie, parakeet, or goldfish, as appropriate.

learning centers

Discovery Center

1. Questions to ask while observing a pet in the classroom:
   What kind of animal is it?
   What does it look like?
   What does it eat?
   How does it eat?
   How does it sleep?
   What is it doing?
   What sounds does it make?
   How does it move?
   How could it best be handled? Why?
2. Compare with another kind of pet. How are they different? How are they the same? Why?

   CAUTION: Be sure that when animals are brought to school they are used to children and are known to be friendly to them. If the animal will stay for half or all day, have a place for it to be safe from the children for periods of time. Also provide food, water, and a place to eliminate. Someone who knows the animal should be present to help handle it. If baby animals are considered, try to provide at least two of them. This prevents the overtiring of just one well-discovered and enjoyed baby animal. It also means less waiting for a turn.

If it is feasible, set up a pet animal center like the one above. All the children can share the responsibility of caring for the pets. This is particularly good for children who may not be able to have pets in their homes.

3. Set out a variety of food—plants, meat, human food—to discover which the animal will select. Talk about why? What body parts does it need to eat the food it chose? What body parts would it need to eat other food?

4. Experiment by having the children eat without hands. Let them eat prepared cereal from a napkin, plastic tablecloth, aluminum pie pan, styrofoam meat tray, or any similar container on the floor. This will show them that pets with long narrow noses, long or rough tongues, or beaks can do things we cannot do.

5. Compare animals by using toy animals or pictures and by grouping them into categories (big/brown/furry/hoofed or pets/farm/zoo/forest).

6. Make sugar cookies shaped like cats, bunnies, chickens. Decorate with colored frosting, or paint cookies with egg yolk and one tablespoon water with food coloring added to desired intensity. Use new, clean watercolor brushes to apply. Give each child one or two tablespoons of frosting in a plastic cup with a spreader. A coffee stirrer is great.

   CAUTION: Do not use same bowl of frosting or spreader for everyone. Children will want to taste.

7. Make a display of common pet supplies: an unbreakable pet feeding dish, pet toys (bone, ball, or rubber mouse), leash, license tags, brush, empty cage, cedar chips, and empty containers of cat, dog, fish, or bird food. Ask children which pet uses the various supplies (pictures on boxes will provide a hint). The pictures you post above the display of appropriate pets eating and sleeping or of children caring for pets may also suggest answers.

Dramatic Play Centers

Home-Living Center

1. Provide stuffed animals for "pets."
2. Include a pet bed, box, or basket with blanket or cushion in it. You may make it large enough for a child to be a pet.
3. Add a few pet toys: ball, rubber bone or mouse, ball on a string. Use unbreakable pet feeding bowls and plastic baby bottles for feeding "toy" pets.

Block-Building Center

1. Set out rubber, wooden, cardboard, or unbreakable plastic models of pets on the block shelf.
2. Hang pictures showing children with their pets' homes in order to encourage an interest in building homes, or fences for pets.

Learning, Language, and Readiness Materials Center

Commercially made games and materials for use at a table or on a mat:

(See Basic Resources, p. 79, for manufacturers' addresses.)

1. Animals and Young: 2 pc. puzzles (Trend Enterprises)
2. Match-Them: Animal Homes (Playskool)
3. Match-Ups: Animals (Playskool)
4. Farm Lotto: includes pets (Ed-U-Card)
5. Domestic Animals and Pets: 12 each (Milton Bradley)
6. Sewing Tiles (Playskool)
7. Instructo Study Prints: 32 prints of animals
8. Jumbo Animal Dominoes (Playskool)
9. Playskool Puzzles: Baby Animals Series, 6–9 pcs. each
10. Judy See-Quees: Choosing a Pet, 12 pcs.
11. Take Apart Wooden Animals: 78 pcs. (ABC School Supply)
12. Judy Puzzles: Pets, 5 pcs.; Terrier, 6 pcs.; Cat and Kittens, 13 pcs.; Bassett, 9 pcs.; Kitten, 5 pcs.; Fish, 6 pcs.
13. Lift-Up Puzzle: Guess Whose Feet/Ears/Tail (The Child's World)

Teacher-made games and materials for use at a table or on a mat:

NOTE: For detailed description of Games, see pp. 50–59.

1. Name It: use models or pictures of pets.
2. Who Am I?: describe various pets.
3. Which Is (Larger)?: change adjective, use pictures or toy animals.
4. Look and See: use pet pictures or models.
5. Match-Them: use on individual or large flannelboards; match pets with foods they eat, parent with its young, or pet with its home.
6. Guess What?: use recordings of animal sounds.
7. Count pets in a picturebook—how many cats? Count body parts of pets in classroom. Make counting discs or squares with gummed seals of pets on cardboard.
8. Use commercial game cards, such as Snap, Animal Rummy, or Kiddie Cards, for matching cards. Modify games to suit your group or a child's ability.

Art Center

* 1. Clay dough: do not set out rollers or cookie cutters, just set out clay and coffee stirrers or palate sticks for cutting or marking. This will allow for making forms rather than limit products to baked goods.

* 2. Use potter's clay: note preparation instructions on box or bag.

*** 3. Finish the picture: give children paper with circle or oval shape drawn or pasted to it and encourage them to use crayons to "finish" the picture. Ask them what it makes them think of: animal object, animal face? (This is better when it follows an experience with felt shapes.)

*** 4. Some five and five-and-a-half year olds can make representative picture books of animal drawings using crayons. It is wise for teachers to label the pictures with the names children supply in talking about their pictures so that their parents can identify them.

*** 5. Cut and paste: make a pet book. Teacher can add story line for a group book or children can mount pictures they like until they have enough for their own books. Staple pages together. Pictures are at a premium, so a group book may be necessary.

6. Make an animal picture collage:

***   a. geometric paper collage: encourage children to make a picture of their favorite pet or a pet they would like to own. (Make available precut geometric shapes for the inexperienced cutter.)

***   b. texture collage: be sure to include trays of clipped yarns, scraps of felt, fur, textured cloth, bits of rope or yarn for tails, and buttons for eyes.

***   c. yarn collage pictures: use a paintbrush to spread thinned glue over a page. "Draw" with yarn lengths, securing them as you go. Child can fill in with clipped yarn. Include the colors of most pets (black, brown, white, grey, or beige) so that the children will have available the colors of pets they know. Heavy cotton rug or ribbon yarn fluffs are the best.

** 7. Styrofoam sculpture: provide children with an assortment of precut styrofoam pieces (curved and square), styrofoam balls of various sizes, and decorations, such as pieces of yarn, bits of leather, felt, buttons, and colored toothpicks, to make their favorite pet animal (real or imagined).

Other Experiences in This Center Using Art Media

** 1. Encourage children to make Match-Them Game, which they can keep, using matching gummed animal seals with pictures of food they eat or match two seals of the same animal. Mount on circles or octagonal shapes as there is no up or down on either of them.

** 2. Bookmarks: children can cut out small pictures of pets boldly encircled with a magic marker, or they can lick and stick favorite gummed labels of pets on strips of cardboard (coverstock scraps from a printer) for a bookmark to share with group, or give as gift to a parent or older brother or sister.

** 3. Pull toy for a pet:
    a. tie colorful ends of bread wrappers or tissue into a pompon with about two feet of string attached (for kitten).
    b. dye spools using vegetable dye in pans; thread with string for pulltoy for a pet.

** 4. Stick puppets: let children cut out pictures of pets boldly encircled with a magic marker to avoid cutting difficult appendages. Then let them glue to oval or round shapes of cardboard. For a handle, slip tongue depressors between the picture and the cardboard. This can be made by younger children if the teacher precuts cardboard and picture.

***   **Variation:** make a collagelike face on a paper plate using styrofoam shreds, yarn, clipped yarn, and buttons. Use very thin packing paper strips or straws for whiskers and tail. Melt crayons into bottle lids to use as eyes, noses, or mouths; ruffled crepe paper for manes, clipped construction paper, tissue, or overlapping circles of velveteen or satin for scales or feathers. Glue plastic stick handle or staple stiff cardboard handle to back of plate. These puppets may be used as masks: children can grasp the handle and hold plate in front of their face.

Book Center

**   Alexander, Martha. *No Ducks in Our Bathtub.* New York: Dial Press, 1973.

***   Anderson, C. W. *Billy and Blaze.* New York: Macmillan, 1964 (paper, 1971).

*   Brown, Margaret W. *Home for a Bunny.* New York: Western Publishing, 1972.

***   Burch, Robert. *Joey's Cat.* New York: Viking Press, 1969 (sound filmstrip/record/cassette).

***   Cook, Gladys Emerson. *Big Book of Cats.* New York: Grosset & Dunlap, 1954.

**   de Regniers, Beatrice Schenk. *It Does Not Say Meow.* New York: Seabury Press, 1972.

***   Fisher, Aileen. *Listen Rabbit.* New York: Thomas Y. Crowell, 1964.

*   Flack, Marjorie. *Angus and the Cat.* Garden City, N.Y.: Doubleday, 1971.

*   ———. *Angus Lost.* Garden City, N.Y.: Doubleday, 1941.

**   Gag, Wanda. *Millions of Cats.* New York: Coward, McCann & Geoghegan, 1938.

***   Grabianski, Janusz. *Grabianski's Dogs.* New York: Franklin Watts, 1968.

***   Green, Margaret. *Big Book of Pets.* New York: Franklin Watts, 1966.

***   Greene, Carla. *Animal Doctors, What Do They Do?* New York: Harper & Row, 1967.

*   Hazen, Barbara. *Where Do Bears Sleep?* Reading, Mass.: Addison-Wesley, 1970.

*   Hoban, Tama. *Where Is It?* New York: Macmillan, 1974.

*   Keats, Ezra J. *Hi Cat!* New York: Macmillan, 1970.

****   ——— and Pat Cherr. *My Dog Is Lost.* New York: Thomas Y. Crowell, 1960.

*   ———. *Whistle for Willie.* New York: Viking Press, 1969.

**   Kellog, Steven. *Can I Keep Him?* New York: Dial Press, 1971.

*   Leichman, Seymour. *Shaggy Dogs and Spotty Dogs and Shaggy and Spotty Dogs.* New York: Harcourt Brace Jovanovich, 1973.

***   Lenski, Lois. *Animals for Me.* New York: Henry Z. Walck, 1941.

**   ———. *Debbie and Her Pets.* New York: Henry Z. Walck, 1971.

***   Newberry, Clare Turlay. *Smudge.* New York: Harper & Row, 1948.

**   Palazzo, Tony. *Animal Family Album.* New York: Lion Press, 1967.

****   Pape, Donna Lugge. *A Gerbil for a Friend.* Englewood Cliffs, N.J.: Prentice-Hall, 1973.

***   Parish, Peggy. *Too Many Rabbits.* New York: Macmillan, 1974.

***   Politi, Leo. *Saint Francis and the Animals.* New York: Charles Scribner's Sons, 1954.

*   Risom, Ole. *I Am a Puppy.* New York: Western Publishing, 1970.

*   ———. *I Am a Kitty.* New York: Western Publishing, 1970.

**   Selsam, Millicent. *How the Animals Eat.* New York: E. M. Hale, 1955.

**   Shura, Mary Frances. *Mary's Marvelous Mouse.* New York: Alfred A. Knopf, 1962.

**   Skaar, Grace. *The Very Little Dog.* Reading, Mass.: Addison-Wesley, 1949.

***   Skorpen, Liesel. *All the Lassies.* New York: Dial Press, 1970.

**   Steiner, Charlotte. *My Bunny Feels Soft.* New York: Alfred A. Knopf, 1967.

**   Thayer, Jane. *The Puppy Who Wanted a Boy.* New York: William Morrow, 1958.

*   Tresselt, Alvin. *Wake Up Farm.* New York: Lothrop, Lee & Shepard, 1955.

*   Wildsmith, Brian. *Birds.* New York: Franklin Watts, 1968.

*   ———. *Fishes.* New York: Franklin Watts, 1970.

  * Williams, Gweneira. *Timid Timothy*. Reading, Mass.: Addison-Wesley, 1944.
*** Yashima, Mitsu and Taro Yashima. *Momo's Kitten*. New York: Viking Press, 1961.
 ** Zion, Gene. *Harry by the Sea.* New York: E. M. Hale, 1965.
 ** ———. *Harry the Dirty Dog*. New York: Harper & Row, 1956.
 ** ———. *No Roses for Harry*. New York: Harper & Row, 1958.

planning for grouptime

NOTE: All music, fingerplays, poems, stories, and games listed here may be used at other times during the session as appropriate. See Core Library, Basic Resources, p. 76, for publishers and addresses. Addresses for sources of records will be found on p. 81.

Music

Songs

FROM original songs in this book by JoAnne Deal Hicks
 * "Animal Nonsense Song," p. 412, verses 2, 4, 5, 7, 8

FROM *Songs for the Nursery School*, MacCarteney
** "Chase Your Tail, Kitty," p. 25
 * "Warm Kitty," p. 27
 * "Hop Little Bunny," p. 30
 * "Ducks," p. 35
 * "Fly Away Little Birdie," p. 36

NOTE: These are all excellent action songs.

FROM *Wake Up and Sing*, Landeck and Crook
** "Long Time Ago," p. 108

FROM *Music Resource Book*, Lutheran Church Press
 * "Sweetly Sings the Pussycat," p. 61

FROM *Songs for Early Childhood*, Westminster Press
 * "I Love My Little Kitty," p. 48
** "My Dog Feels Soft and Silky," p. 52

Records

"Muffin and Mother Goose"/"Muffin in the City/Country" (Young People's Record [YPR], 33⅓ RPM)
"Muffin in the City" and "Muffin in the Country" (YPR, 45, 78 RPM)
"Doggie in the Window" (Happy Time and Golden, 33⅓ RPM; Golden, 45 RPM)

Rhythms and Singing Games

FROM *Songs for the Nursery School*, MacCarteney
Use appropriate actions with songs, pp. 25, 27, 30, 35, 36

FROM *Music Resource Book*, Lutheran Church Press
* "Six Little Ducks," p. 62

Rhythmic Activity: pretend to move like various pet animals. (See Pet Animal Chart.)

Fingerplays and Poems

FROM *Rhymes for Fingers and Flannelboards*, Scott and Thompson
"Counting Kittens," p. 30
"Little Kittens," p. 31
"Five Little Puppies," p. 36
"Frisky's Doghouse," p. 36

FROM *Let's Do Fingerplays*, Grayson
"Kitten Is Hiding," p. 32
"There Was a Little Turtle," p. 33
"My Rabbit," p. 34
"Golden Fishes," p. 35

FROM *Listen and Help Tell the Story*, Carlson
"This Little Cow," p. 23
"Five Royal Penguins," p. 24
"The Little Fish," p. 28
"The Toad's Song," p. 30
"Once I Caught a Fish Alive," p. 31
"The Puppy and the Kitty Cat," p. 36
"Five Little Chickens," p. 39

Stories

(To read, read-tell, or tell. See Book Center for complete list.)

** *The Very Little Dog*, Skaar
** *Can I Keep Him?* Kellog
 * *Angus and the Cat*, Flack
** *Harry the Dirty Dog*, Zion
*** *Too Many Rabbits*, Parish

Routine Times

1. Serve commercial animal cookies or those baked and frosted by children for snack or mealtime.

Large Muscle Activities

1. Set out boxes and barrels for children to crawl into and through to imitate animal behavior.
2. Play ball (roll or toss two or more).
3. Encourage children to do "tricks" like a pet animal. For safety, have them do "tricks" on a mat or on grass.
4. Play follow the leader: the group moves as directed, imitating ways pets move—hop, crawl, leap, run, walk, climb, slither. The children may take turns being leader and choosing actions. Teacher may suggest actions as necessary. This activity is best done with a small group.

Extended Experiences

1. Take a trip to teacher's home or a child's home to see a pet.
2. Visit pet store to view supplies as well as pets.
3. Visit a pet farm or pet library.
4. Visit pet section in variety store (in group of eight or less at a time). They often have baby gerbils or hamsters, fish, birds, and sometimes chameleons or lizards.
5. Invite a representative of the Humane Society or a veterinarian to bring an animal and talk to the children about the care of pets. Alert them to what the children may be able to understand or need to hear. Keep it simple.
6. View short filmstrip about a pet (no more than ten minutes). Edit it if it is too long to suit your group.

teacher resources

Books and Periodicals

1. *How and Why Series:* Dogs, Fish, and Horses. New York: Wonder-Treasure Books, 1962
2. *Nature Wonderland.* Britannica's Preschool Library
3. *Ranger Rick* magazine. Washington, D.C.: National Wildlife Federation

Pictures and Displays

(See p. 79 for addresses of firms listed.)

1. If children have access to magazines, encourage them to bring pictures of their favorite kind of pet or to share a book with a picture of pets that they like. Mount or group on a bulletin board. Set books out in book center. If they are not suitable for book center, share them at grouptime and highlight briefly without reading them entirely. Altruistic organizations or church groups may be enlisted to assist you in obtaining magazines with pictures of animals.

2. Group pictures of a specific kind or family of pets: all kinds of cats, black pets, furry pets, or caged pets. Sometimes a large, abstract-shaped, colored piece of paper or a small yarn circle can help group pictures on a bulletin board or wall display.
3. Snapshot display: Our Pets at Home. Encourage the children to bring snapshots of pets they have or have had. Label with child's name, name of pet, and kind of pet. You may need to begin the display with pictures of pets you have had. Post near Grouptime Area so children can point and share at that time. **Variation:** Let child select picture of a pet he or she would *like* to have. Let child cut or mount, label each with child's name.

   CAUTION: When returning the picture to the child, put in envelope and pin to outer garment to avoid loss.

4. The Child's World Picture Fold-Outs: Pets. Packet includes House Pets, Farm Pets, Pond Pets, Wild Pets, School Pets, People Who Care for Pets.
5. Basic Science Series I, No. 5 Pets—SVE Picture-Story Study Prints (Chicago: Society for Visual Education)
6. We Drink Milk Series—Dairy Council

Community Resources

1. Veterinarian
2. Humane Society
3. Animal clinic

Animal Nonsense Song
A Dramatic Play Song

JoAnne Deal Hicks

1. I am a lit - tle bun - ny, I'm sit - ting on a log. I
2. I am a lit - tle po - ny, I'm chew - ing on some hay. I
3. I am a lit - tle butter-fly, I'm sit - ting on a rose. I

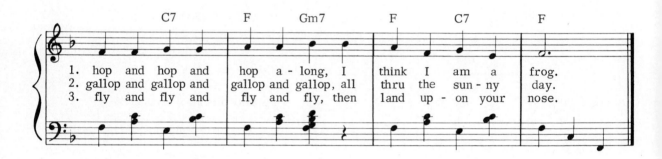

1. hop and hop and hop a - long, I think I am a frog.
2. gallop and gallop and gallop and gallop, all thru the sun - ny day.
3. fly and fly and fly and fly, then land up - on your nose.

Verse 4: I am a lit-tle kit-ten, I'm sit-ting on a rug,
I purr and purr and purr and purr, then curl up like a bug.

Verse 5: I am a lit-tle yel-low duck, I wad-dle down the road,
I quack and quack and quack and quack, and chase a hop-ping toad.

Verse 6: I am a lit-tle chick-en, I'm strut-ting through the weeds,
I peck and peck and peck and peck, I'm look-ing for some seeds.

Verse 7: I am a lit-tle tur-tle, I hide with-in my shell,
I creep a-long and creep a-long, and fall in-to a well.

Verse 8: I am a lit-tle dog-gie, I'm chew-ing on a bone,
I bark and bark and bark and bark, in-to the tel-e-phone.

NOTE: Children enjoy pantomiming the various actions.

24 Animals of the Woods

basic understandings

(concepts children can grasp from this subject)

- A woods or forest is an area of ground with many trees and bushes. It often has streams of water or a pond.
- Wild animals who live in this area are called animals of the woods or forest animals.
- The most common forest animals are rabbits, skunks, deer, foxes, bears, raccoons, opossums, chipmunks, turtles, and birds.
- Most animals of the woods are colored or marked to match the leaves, bark, rocks, or grass where they usually live.
- Small forest animals are often frightened by loud noises and people.
- Some animals, like snakes, may eat only once a week. Other animals, like birds, hunt and eat almost all day long.
- A wild animal often feeds and rests in its home.
- We should not throw glass, cans, paper, or garbage in ponds and streams because this pollution is killing the forest animals.
- We can sometimes see some animals of the woods in a zoo or a park.
- Animals often found in city parks are squirrels, frogs, birds, and insects.

  NOTE: Include understandings listed for Animals, page 385, as appropriate. See guides on the seasons regarding hibernation, migration, and other seasonal habits of forest animals.

Additional Facts the Teacher Should Know

See Animals of the Woods Chart for detailed information regarding their characteristics, habitat, handling, feeding, and reproduction. When teaching this subject, encourage children to observe and protect animals in their own surroundings. Frogs and toads have not been included as animals to be observed (captured) because pollution is decreasing these animals in number. Also, by bringing the eggs or polywogs into the classroom, you are further decreasing their chances to survive. Animals that have been in captivity for even a short time stand little chance of survival when returned to their natural habitat.

Snakes are not included in this guide because they bite, are hard to feed, and because it is difficult for the average person to tell the harmless ones from the poisonous ones.

Trying to catch wild animals is dangerous, as most animals will bite when they feel trapped or threatened, and may carry rabies.

Methods Most Adaptable for Introducing This Subject to Children

- Observe a bird, squirrel, toad, or turtle while on a walk or when these animals come to a feeding station.
- If the school is a country day school, you may possibly see a red fox, raccoon, opossum, or small deer near a stream in the woods.
- Occasionally in a small town or city, you may see a skunk or smell its characteristic odor after a rain.
- In winter, seeing footprints of an animal in the snow.

Vocabulary

forest	burrow	fur	odor	footprint	den	lodge
woods	nest	hide	wild	hibernate	cave	trees
stream	hole	hoofs	claws	pollution	log	rock

Include the names, sounds, body parts, and foods eaten by the most common animals of the woods that you observe.

learning centers

Discovery Center

1. Examine picture-information cards (a) and fold-outs packet (b):
   a. *Teach Me About North American Mammals* (Gelles-Widmer, 1968).
   b. *Animal Homes*, also *Pets* (Child's World, 1969).
2. Leaf through selected issues of *Ranger Rick*, *National Wildlife*, *International Wildlife*, and *National Geographic* magazines.
3. Display food that forest animals eat: acorns and other nuts, eggs, seeds, berries, and fruit. (Use artificial berries and fruit.)

4. Borrow a caged squirrel, a descented skunk, a raccoon, a snake, or any other animal for a short visit accompanied by its owner.
5. Take a walk to a park, a pond, a field, or a wood to see what animals live there. Observe them from a respectful distance. Older children may use binoculars or a telescope. Take paper sack for collecting litter.
6. Bring a boxed turtle or pet rabbit to school.
7. Display *Life Cycle of a Frog/Robin*, fold-out charts (The Child's World).
8. Look at View-Master reels: Smokey Bear, Fish Life, Birds of the World, The Balance of Nature, and other reels listed by specific names of state and national parks (Sawyer Inc.).

   NOTE: When doing 4, 5, and 6, see Discovery Activity No. 1, Pet Animals guide, p. 403.

Dramatic Play Centers

Block-Building Center

1. Add painted, model forest animals available in variety stores.
2. Provide small twigs and branch sections for use in building animal homes or environs.
3. Set out unbreakable plastic trees or bushes from commercial animal sets.
4. Children may tear or cut free forms of blue construction paper for lakes, ponds, or streams.
5. Provide strips or squares of green carpet or upholstery for grass.
6. Papier-mâché rocks or crumpled tan or grey construction paper may simulate rocky areas without the danger presented when using real rocks or stones.

   NOTE: Additional activities and materials may be found in the following guides: squirrels—Fall; birds—Fall, Winter, and Spring; rabbits—Spring.

Other Dramatic Play Centers

1. Animal sack masks or animal hand or face puppets may be used by older children with verbal skills. Animal faces may be made on large or small grocery sacks, depending on use. (See illustration, p. 228.)

Learning, Language, and Readiness Materials Center

Commercially made games and materials for use at a table or on a mat:

(See Basic Resources, p. 79, for manufacturers' addresses.)

1. Forest Animal Seals (Eureka Co., Dennison Co., or Scripture Press)
2. Judy Puzzles: Squirrel, 11 pcs.; Turtle, 14 pcs.; Rabbit, 11 pcs.; Frog, 10 pcs.; Duck, 8 pcs.; Fish, 6 pcs.; Owl and Owlet, 11 pcs.; Canada Goose and Goslings, 9 pcs.; Jay family, 9 pcs.; Birds, 6 pcs.
3. Playskool Puzzles: Life Cycle of the Frog, 14 pcs.; Rabbits (mother and babies), 13 pcs.; Squirrel, 6 pcs.
4. Animal Puzzles with knobs: Frog, Turtle, Snail (Childcraft)
5. Fish Puzzles (Creative Playthings)
6. Wild Animals: flannelboard aids (Milton Bradley)
7. Woodland Friends: flannelboard aids (Instructo)
8. Wildlife Concentration Cards (National Wildlife Federation)

9. Wildlife Old Maid Cards (National Wildlife Federation)
10. Animal Rummy and/or Snap Cards (available in variety store)
11. Animal Face Puppets (Instructo)
12. Hand Puppets: Fox, Rabbit, Bear (Community Playthings)
13. Judy See-Quees: Squirrel Adventure; Tadpole to Frog
14. Tadpoles and Frogs, reversible puzzle, 5 pcs. (Judy Puzzles)
15. Guess Whose Feet/Ears/Tail puzzle game (The Child's World)

Teacher-made games and materials for use at a table or on a mat:

NOTE: For detailed description of Games, see pp. 50–59.

1. Match-Them: use mounted forest animal seals or National Wildlife stamps
2. How Many?: use felt animal shapes, flannel-backed pictures of animals, or plastic models of forest animals
3. Grouping and Sorting by Association: group animals by their coverings, their actions, or their body parts (fur/fin/feather; flies/runs/swims; no legs/two legs/four legs)
4. Adapt games in Farm, Pets, or Zoo guides to forest animals

Art Center

* 1. Easel paint or crayons: offer green, yellow, black, tan, and brown
* 2. Model with dough or natural clay
** 3. Collage: yarn, paper, geometric cloth or paper shapes, fur, feathers, and assorted materials for creating animals

Bottom side

** 4. Collage turtle: precut turtle shapes from green, brown, or black construction paper. Set out empty halves of walnut shells, individual egg carton sections, paints, and glue. Children choose colors and materials they wish to use to make their own turtle. Dotted lines indicate positioning of nut shell on top side. Walnut shells can be cut in half with a sharp knife by following the seam line. Save meats for cooking.
** 5. Design arrangements: set out hammer and nail sets, magnetic or felt geometric shapes for creating "animals"

Book Center

** Alexander, Martha. *I'll Protect You from the Jungle Beasts.* New York: Dial Press, 1973.
** Brown, Margaret W. *Home for a Bunny.* New York: Western Publishing, 1975.
** ———. *The Dead Bird.* Reading, Mass.: Addison-Wesley, 1963.
* Cook, Bernadine. *The Little Fish That Got Away.* Reading, Mass.: Addison-Wesley, 1956.
**** Erickson, Phoebe. *True Book of Animals of a Small Pond.* Chicago, Ill.: Childrens Press, 1953.
** Ets, Marie Hall. *Play with Me.* New York: Viking Press, 1955.
** Flack, Marjorie. *Tim Tadpole and the Bullfrog.* Garden City, N.Y.: Doubleday, 1934.
** ———. *Ask Mr. Bear.* New York: Macmillan, 1932.
*** Freeman, Don. *Fly High, Fly Low.* New York: Viking Press, 1957.
** Freschet, Bernice. *Turtle Pond.* New York: Charles Scribner's Sons, 1971.
*** Gans, Roma. *It's Nesting Time.* New York: Thomas Y. Crowell, 1964 (filmstrip and record).
** ———. *Birds Eat and Eat and Eat.* New York: Thomas Y. Crowell, 1963 (filmstrip and record).

* Gay, Zhenya. *Look!* New York: Viking Press, 1957.
* ———. *Who Is It?* New York: Viking Press, 1957.
* Hamberger, John. *This Is the Day.* New York: Grosset & Dunlap, 1971.
** Hazen, Barbara. *Where Do Bears Sleep?* Reading, Mass.: Addison-Wesley, 1970.
*** Holl, Adelaide. *The Remarkable Egg.* New York: Lothrop, Lee & Shepard, 1968.
*** Humphreys, Dena. *The Big Book of Animals Every Child Should Know.* New York: Grosset & Dunlap, 1962.
** Jewell, Nancy. *The Snuggle Bunny.* New York: Harper & Row, 1972.
* Keats, Ezra Jack. *Over in the Meadow.* New York: Four Winds Press School Book Service, 1971.
**** Kohn, Bernice. *Chipmunks.* Englewood Cliffs, N.J.: Prentice-Hall, 1970 (reference only).
** Krauss, Ruth. *Happy Day.* New York: Harper & Row, 1949.
*** Langstaff, John. *Oh, A-Hunting We Will Go.* New York: Atheneum, 1974.
*** McCloskey, Robert. *Blueberries for Sal.* New York: Viking Press, 1948.
*** ———. *Make Way for Ducklings.* New York: Viking Press, 1941.
** Raskin, Ellen. *Who Said Sue, Said Whoo?* New York: Atheneum, 1973.
*** Rinkoff, Barbara. *Guess What Trees Do?* New York: Lothrop, Lee & Shepard, 1974.
* Risom, Ole. *I Am a Mouse.* New York: Western Publishing, 1974 (includes chipmunk, cricket, turtle, owl, fish, duck, bird, lizard).
* ———. *I Am a Bear.* New York: Western Publishing, 1967 (includes bird, beaver, mouse, bug, squirrel, moose, chameleon, fish).
** Rockwell, Anne and Harlow Rockwell. *Toad.* Garden City, N.Y.: Doubleday, 1972.
*** Schwartz, Elizabeth and Charles Schwartz. *When Animals Are Babies.* New York: Holiday House, 1964.
*** Tresselt, Alvin. *Beaver Pond.* New York: Lothrop, Lee & Shepard, 1970.
**** *White-Tailed Deer.* Washington, D.C.: National Wildlife Federation, 1973 (reference).

planning for grouptime

NOTE: All music, fingerplays, poems, stories, and games listed here may be used at other times during the session as appropriate. See Core Library, Basic Resources, p. 76, for publishers and addresses. Addresses for sources of records will be found on p. 81.

Music

Songs

FROM original songs in this book by JoAnne Deal Hicks
** "Animal Nonsense Song," p. 412, verses 1 and 7
** "The Turtles Down the Road," p. 422

FROM *Wake Up and Sing,* Landeck and Crook
*** "Bam Chi, Chi, Bam" p. 102

FROM *Songs for Early Childhood*, Westminster Press
** "Go to Sleep Now Little Bird," p. 47
 * "Our Bunny's So Funny," p. 51

FROM *Music Resource Book*, Lutheran Church Press
** "The Rabbit Song," p. 54

Records

"Birds, Beasts, Bugs and Little Fishes," Pete Seeger (Folkways, 33⅓ RPM and cassette)
"Six Little Ducks," *Another Rainy Day Record* (Bowmar)
"There Was a Little Turtle," *Another Rainy Day Record* (Bowmar)
"Rhythm Time," record 2, Bears, Frogs, Soaring Hawks, and Hopping Rabbits (Bowmar)
"Eastern Bird Songs"; "Western Bird Songs" (National Wildlife Federation)
"Noah's Ark"/"**Walk in the Forest**"/"How the Water Got to the Tub" (Young People's Records [YPR] 33⅓, 45, 78 RPM)
"Jump Back Little Toad" (CRG, 78 RPM)
"About Brave Hunter Who Stalks the Deer," *Dance-A-Story* (RCA, 33⅓ RPM/storybook)
"Teddy Bear's Picnic" (Happy Time/Candem, 33⅓ RPM)
"Bunny Hop" (Peter Pan, 33⅓ RPM)
"Peter Cottontail" (Golden and Candem, 33⅓ RPM; Golden, 45 RPM)
"Little White Duck" (Happy Time, Peter Pan, Columbia, 33⅓ RPM and Golden, 45 RPM)

Rhythms and Singing Games

FROM original songs in this book by JoAnne Deal Hicks
 * "The Turtles Down the Road." (See Note, p. 422.)

FROM *Music Activities for Retarded Children*, Ginglend and Stiles
** "I Wish I Was," p. 72

FROM *Creative Movement for the Developing Child*, Cherry
"The Bear," p. 28

NOTE: Choose appropriate piano or phonograph music for movements of animals, such as bunnies, squirrels, bears, foxes, mice, and birds. Use scarves for wings and tails. Sew a loop of elastic to a small chiffon colored square for a wristlet. It can be worn at wrist or fastened to strap or belt.

Fingerplays and Poems

FROM *Rhymes for Fingers and Flannelboards*, Scott and Thompson
"Rabbits," pp. 75–76
"In Fields and Woods," pp. 87–97 (includes squirrels, chipmunks, frogs, toads, mice, birds, and bunnies)

FROM *Let's Do Fingerplays*, Grayson
"Animal Antics," pp. 30–37
"Chickadees," p. 60
"Five Little Froggies," p. 63

"Five Little Squirrels," p. 63
"Telegraph Poles," p. 66
"Two Little Blackbirds," p. 73

NOTE: See Spring guide for rabbits and Fall guide for squirrels.

THE TURTLE
Unknown

The turtle crawls on the ground and makes a rustling sound.
He carries his house wherever he goes,
And when he is scared, he pulls in his nose and covers his toes!

FIVE LITTLE TURTLES
by Bonnie Flemming

One little turtle all alone and new,
Soon it finds another and then there are two.
Two little turtles crawl down to the sea,
Soon they find another and then there are three.
Three little turtles crawl along the shore,
Soon they find another and then there are four.
Four little turtles go for a dive,
Along swims another and then there are five!

NOTE: Use felt or flannelboard turtles.

ANIMAL HOMES
by JoAnne Deal Hicks

The cow has a barn, a chick has his pen,
The pony his stable, a fox his den.
The bear likes his cave, a guppy his bowl.
The rabbit his hutch, the wee mouse his hole.
The bee has a hive, a bird has its nest,
The spider his web, but *my* home is best!

IF A SQUIRREL COULD
by JoAnne Deal Hicks

If a squirrel could bark like a dog,
If a squirrel could hop like a frog,
If a squirrel could squirm, or if he could crawl,
Then he just wouldn't be a squirrel at all!

HERE IS A BUNNY

Here is a bunny with *ears* so funny,   (BEND 2 FINGERS OVER THUMB)
And here is a *hole* in the ground.   (MAKE HOLE WITH LEFT HAND ON HIP)
When a noise he hears, he pricks up his *ears*   (HOLD "EARS" STRAIGHT)
And *hops* into his hole so round.   (HOP BUNNY OVER AND POP IN HOLE)

Stories

(To read, read-tell, or tell. See Book Center for complete list.)

** *Ask Mr. Bear,* Flack
* *I Am a Mouse,* Risom
* *I Am a Bear,* Risom
* *Over in the Meadow,* Keats
** *I'll Protect You from the Jungle Beasts,* Alexander
*** *Oh, A-Hunting We Will Go,* Langstaff
*** *Make Way for Ducklings,* McCloskey

Games

(See Games, pp. 50–59, and Teacher-Made Games in this guide for directions.)

1. Look and See: use flannel-backed pictures of woods animals
2. Alike, Different, and the Same: use materials prepared for Match-Them
3. Reach and Feel: use fur, feather, acorn, twig, and grass

Routine Times

1. At snacktimes or meals offer nuts, peanuts in shell, sunflower seeds, toast squares, carrot or celery sticks, lettuce or cabbage leaves, raisins, apples, bananas, berries, animal crackers.
2. At naptime encourage children to curl up like sleeping animals.

Large Muscle Activities

1. Caves: packing boxes or barrels placed horizontally on the playground allow children to pretend to be animals in caves
2. Tree homes: laundry or fat fiber barrels with a hole sawed in one side, painted, and mounted vertically on wooden frames outdoors
3. Burrows or tunnels: Tunnel-of-Fun by Childcraft for indoor play or encourage digging outdoors in wet sand or dirt
4. Beaver dams: children can gather sticks (or use tongue depressors) to use in the sandpile; provide water
5. Gopher or rabbit holes: low cardboard boxes turned upside down with a hole cut in the top. Make up games using these on rainy days
6. Nuts: collect acorns or other nuts that have fallen from trees, or wad brown tissue paper for use by children pretending to be squirrels
7. Nests: allow children to use twigs and small branches in the sandpile to build animal homes; remove each day and store in a sack

    CAUTION: Do not use dead elm twigs because of Dutch elm beetles.

8. Forest animal models: place in or near the sandpile. Aid in developing creative play involving animals of the woods
9. Follow the Leader: imitate the way the various animals move or walk

Extended Experiences

1. Trip to a museum that has displays of forest animals.
2. Trip to a zoo or a park that has animals of woods and stream.
3. Trip to an aquarium or marina if group is interested in fish.
4. Trip to see a beaver dam. Avoid trip after a heavy rain as dams may be damaged. A naturalist or taxidermist may advise you where you may see one, or where to find squirrels, raccoons, and foxes.
5. Explore a stream or wooded area if one is nearby.
6. Woods party or picnic. Make name tags using forest animal stickers or wildlife stamps. Have children bring stuffed animals or puppets if they wish. Serve foods listed under Routine Times, No. 1.

7. Invite a park director or a forest ranger to tell your group how they can help forest animals. Two or three suggestions are best. Perhaps he could bring a Smokey the Bear poster to share.

teacher resources

Books and Periodicals

1. *How and Why Series:* Birds. New York: Wonder-Treasure Books, 1960
2. *Ranger Rick, National Wildlife, International Wildlife.* Washington, D.C.: The National Wildlife Federation
3. *National Geographic.* Washington, D.C.: National Geographic Society

Pictures and Displays

(See p. 79 for addresses of firms listed.)

1. Picture Series (David C. Cook)
   a. Science Themes 1: turtles, robins, frogs, toads
   b. Seasons: rabbits, squirrels, chipmunks
   c. Science Themes 2: rabbits, squirrels, birds
   d. Eco-Systems, Ecology, and Birds of Our Land
   e. Pets: chipmunks, raccoons, skunks, lizards, and turtles
2. Baby Animals of the Wild, Animal Homes, Kinds of Animals, Pets (wild and pond), The Child's World Color Study Prints and Picture Fold-Outs
3. Forest products companies often picture forest animals in their magazine advertisements
4. Display plastic forest animal models in a forest scene. Use as a table centerpiece for a forest party
5. Display stuffed forest animals children may share, such as teddy bears, rabbits, skunks, squirrels, chipmunks, and deer
6. Catchy Colors Mobile: 8 fish (Instructo)
7. Wildlife stamps (National Wildlife Federation)

Community Resources

1. Forest ranger
2. Game warden
3. Department of Biology or Zoology at a university
4. Taxidermist
5. Museum curator
6. City or state park director

The Turtles Down the Road

JoAnne Deal Hicks

NOTE: Children who wish may be "turtles." A timer could be set for a certain length of time and the children told to *slowly* crawl from one end of the room to the other. When the timer goes off, the distance each child has traveled could be measured. This could lead to a discussion on movement and distance.

25 Zoo Animals

basic understandings

(concepts children can grasp from this subject)

- A zoo is a place where people can safely see wild animals in captivity.
- At a zoo, animals from all over the world are kept in cages, in fenced off areas, or in special houses that are like their former homes (caves, hillsides, woods, or waterways).
- At zoos, certain families of animals are grouped near each other:
  1. cats (tigers, panthers, lions, cheetahs, leopards)
  2. monkeys and apes (gorillas, orangutans, chimpanzees, spider monkeys)
  3. bears (black, brown, grizzly, polar, panda)
  4. birds
  5. reptiles and snakes
  6. fish
- Animals found in most zoos are giraffes, elephants, lions, tigers, monkeys, zebras, bears, and hippopotamuses.
- Other animals sometimes included in a zoo are alligators, crocodiles, rhinoceroses, camels, goats, deer, seals, foxes, wolves, peacocks, ostriches, panthers, leopards, and tortoises.
- It is necessary to cage wild animals because most of them are not safe to play with. Also a cage offers protection for the animals and keeps them from straying.
- Tame animals are usually safe to play with (except when eating or sleeping). Wild animals are *not* safe to play with except by owners who have tamed and trained them.
- Some of the animals that we see in the zoo, such as elephants, seals, tigers, and monkeys, are taught by their trainers to do tricks. They are often used in circuses or in special shows at the zoo.
- We pay money to go into some zoos. This money helps to pay for the feeding, care, and purchase of the animals.

Grouping and Sorting by Association The children above are playing the game Grouping and Sorting by Association, using different animals. (See Basic Resources, p. 56.) The child at left is selecting zoo animals to place in one of the homemade cages, while the child in the center is placing her choices of pets around the house and yard. The child at right is reaching for a calf to place with other farm animals on the farmyard space.

- Many people work in a zoo to keep the animals healthy, safe, fed, and exercised. Other people sell tickets, food, and rides or care for the walks, roads, plants, and flowers.
- Some zoos have a pet farm or a children's zoo where children may pet, touch, feed, or ride the animals.

NOTE: Include understandings listed for Animals, p. 385, as appropriate.

Additional Facts the Teacher Should Know

See Zoo Animal Chart for information regarding the characteristics, habitats, feeding, and reproduction of some of these animals.

Methods Most Adaptable for Introducing This Subject to Children

- Set new model zoo animals out on the shelves or on a table.
- Read or read-tell a story about a zoo or zoo animals.
- Show a picture in a newspaper about a zoo or a zoo animal pet in the community.
- Bulletin board display. (See Pictures and Displays.)

Vocabulary

wild	cage	zoo	claws	cave	perform
tame	sharp	tour	hoofs	tank	striped
keeper	watch	gate	fur	fence	spotted
tricks	circus	pool	mane	arena	protect

Include animal names, sounds, body parts, and foods eaten by the zoo animals observed by your group.

learning centers

Discovery Center

1. Explore picture information cards: Teach-Me North American Animals, Flash cards. (Mab Graphic, Inc.)
2. Display some nonperishable models of foods that wild animals eat: hay, grass, leaves, bark, bananas. (See Zoo Animal Chart.)
3. Borrow from school, church, or public library a short zoo animal educational film or filmstrip.
4. Use View-Master reels: Wild Animals of Africa and Wild Animals of the World; Children's Zoo and San Diego Zoo; Lion Safari, Old Time Circus, and Circus—Ringling Brothers.
5. Make a lion out of peanut butter cookies. Frost with yellow frosting and add coconut dyed yellow for mane and red-hots for the tongue.
6. Decorate ripple cookies (shortbread with a chocolate rippled striping) into tigers by adding licorice strip cut thin for whiskers, Life-Saver eyes, red-hot tongue, gumdrop nose (to fill center hole).

Dramatic Play Centers

Home-Living Center

1. Post pictures to suggest family going to the zoo (children and their doll families).
2. Set out souvenir pennants, made in Art Center, to carry to the zoo.
3. Provide stuffed zoo animal toys, such as teddy bears, tigers, and pandas.

Block-Building Center

1. Set out rubber, plastic, or wooden models of zoo animals.
2. Place hay or excelsior in a box for children to feed or bed down animals.

3. Set out wooden snap clothespins for fences.
4. Hang pictures of animals in a zoo. These may suggest that children build enclosures for wild animals with the hollow or unit blocks.

Other Dramatic Play Centers

1. Use cartons as cages or caves for children to crawl inside. Cut cardboard to make barred windows.
2. Set out cable spools or nail kegs for platforms for performing animals and ruffled collars for clowns, performing seals or dogs. Let children pretend to be trained animals using balls and Hula Hoops. Offer balloons.
3. Set out home-made "top" hat, black felt hat, or plastic derby for master of ceremonies.

   NOTE: Teacher may need to become zookeeper or master of ceremonies if children become too hilarious.

4. Tour train: set up as described in Rail Transportation guide, p. 478. Post large pictures of zoo animals or outdoor scenes for passengers to see. Sell tickets.
5. Laminate pictures of raw meats for "pretend" feeding of zoo animals.
6. Have small buckets available for feeding and watering the animals.
7. Set out work gloves and a large ring with keys for opening cages (variety-store sheriff's lock and keys are great).
8. Allow children to use small rubber hose (discarded bathinette hose, dishwasher or sink hose, or hygienic syringe tubing) for washing elephants and cages.

Learning, Language, and Readiness Materials Center

Commercially made games and materials for use at a table or on a mat:

(See Basic Resources, p. 79, for manufacturers' addresses.)

1. Judy Puzzles: Zoo Animals, 5 pcs.; Circus Animals, 5 pcs.; Monkey and Baby, 6 pcs.; Panda and Cub, 10 pcs.; Penguin Family, 8 pcs.; Kangaroo and Joey, 6 pcs.; Circus Elephant, 10 pcs.; Tiger Through Hoop, 9 pcs.; Seal Balancing Ball, 7 pcs.; Lion in Circus Wagon, 10 pcs.; Skating Bear, 7 pcs.
2. Elly Elephant, 6 pcs.; Monkey Shines, 7 pcs. (Playskool)
3. Zoo Lotto Game (Ed-U-Card)
4. Building Zoo (Creative Playthings)
5. Fourway Blocks (Creative Playthings)
6. Jumbo Animal Dominoes (Constructive Playthings)
7. Ani-Space (Lauri)
8. Judy See-Quees: Trip to Zoo, 12 pcs.
9. Wild Animal Picture Dominoes (Educational Teaching Aids)
10. Animal Card Games: See Animals of the Woods, pp. 415–16.
11. Equilibrium Puzzles: Elephant, Camel, Lion, Bear (ETA)
12. Teddy Bear Counters (Milton Bradley)
13. Zoo Animals: flannelboard aids (Instructo)
14. Wild Animals: flannelboard aids (Milton Bradley)
15. African People N' Places (Creative Playthings)
16. Basic Cut Puzzles: Giraffe (Developmental Learning Materials and ETA)
17. Zoo Fence (Childcraft)
18. Vinyl Zoo Animals: Lion, Zebra, Giraffe, Elephant, Bear, Rhinoceros, Hippopotamus (Childcraft)

19. Rubber Zoo Set (Childcraft)
20. Zoo Animals: painted wooden zoo animals (Childcraft or Constructive Playthings)
21. Table Block Zoo: 15 zoo animals, fence, zookeeper, and palm tree (Childcraft or Constructive Playthings)
22. Miniature Wooden Animals: pairs of zoo animals (Childcraft)
23. Puzzle Stand Ups: Kangaroo, Monkey, Bears in a Tree (Childcraft)
24. Animal Cages (Constructive Playthings)
25. Puzzle Animals: 6 puzzles, 5 pcs. each (ETA)
26. New Wild Shapes Mobile (Instructo)
27. Guess Whose Feet/Ears/Tail (The Child's World)
28. Wildlife Lotto (Constructive Playthings)

Teacher-made games and materials for use at a table or on a mat:

NOTE: For detailed description of Games, see pp. 50–59.

1. Match-Them: zoo animal model with picture of the animal. Large size animal gummed seals may be glued to the backs of old playing cards for this purpose.
2. Alike, Different, and the Same: name animals that have similar characteristics, such as claws, teeth, tails, and fur. Have children separate small model animals into groupings of zoo, pet, farm animals. Compare animals by size, color, family to designate which are alike, which are different.
3. Grouping and Sorting by Association: by fur, feather, or fin or those that swim, fly, crawl, or walk, using models or pictures.

Art Center

* 1. Make pennants for zoo visitors. Put large paper triangles (pennant shaped) on easel with large edge at child's left. Children may staple to cardboard sticks when dry.
* 2. Make place cards with zoo animal stickers. Children may use magic markers to edge, stripe, polka dot, and letter name, if they can. Use for zoo party.
** 3. Crayon picture of favorite zoo animal.
*** 4. Make caged animal pictures: cut out and paste animal pictures on a plain piece of paper; cut strips and glue on picture as bars. Precut pictures are offered to youngest children. Wallpaper books and discarded picture books are good sources of pictures. Glue on bars by gluing only along top and bottom of page.
* 5. Collage picture: provide spotted and striped fabric for zoo animals, Easter basket grass, fur bits, yarn, rope, leather scraps, and cotton balls.
* 6. Yarn collage: provide yarns of various sizes and colors.
*** 7. Box sculpture: let children stack or fasten together small boxes for use in making animals. Attach with masking tape. Supply rope or yarn for tails, buttons for eyes, scrap leather or felt scraps for tongues.

Other Experiences in This Center Using Art Media

1. Puppets:
*   a. stick: see Pet Animals guide, p. 406.
***   b. sock: artistic child may use magic marker for eyes, nose, and mouth on a light colored sock.
**   c. paper sack: use the largest brown paper bags, cut hole in bottom for head, cut armholes, decorate like a zoo animal. (See illustration, p. 228.)

*** 2. Zoo cages: paint shoe boxes. Paste, glue, or draw a zoo animal picture on the inside bottom of each box. Then glue construction paper strips over opening or punch with nail holes along two opposite edges and thread pipe cleaners through. Put excelsior or straw in the bottom of the cage and small bottle caps for feeding dishes (glue to bottom of cage). Wheeled cages can be made by using milk bottle caps or other discarded items like plastic discs or wheels. (Teacher may make for display.)

3. Decorate reinforced nail kegs that are sturdy enough to climb and stand on. Use water base paints and paste ons. This is to be used by children in dramatic play areas when they are imitating wild animals performing.

Book Center

*** Bettinger, Craig. *Follow Me Everybody*. Garden City, N.Y.: Doubleday, 1968.
 ** Bridges, Will. *Zoo Babies*. New York: William Morrow, 1953.
 ** ———. *Zoo Pets*. New York: William Morrow, 1955.
  * Carle, Eric. *Do You Want to Be My Friend?* New York: Thomas Y. Crowell, 1970.
*** Conklin, Gladys. *Little Apes*. New York: Holiday House, 1970.
 ** de Regniers, Beatrice Schenk. *Circus*. New York: Viking Press, 1966.
  * Flack, Marjorie. *Ask Mr. Bear*. New York: Macmillan, 1971.
  * Freeman, Don. *Dandelion*. New York: Viking Press, 1964 (filmstrip and record).
 ** ———. *The Seal and the Slick*. New York: Viking Press, 1974.
*** Graham, Margaret Bloy. *Be Nice to Spiders*. New York: Harper & Row, 1967.
*** Greene, Carla. *I Want to Be a Zookeeper*. Chicago, Ill.: Childrens Press, 1957.
 ** Hader, Beda and Elmer Hader. *Lost in the Zoo*. New York: Macmillan, 1951.
  * Hoffmeister, Donald F. *Zoo Animals*. New York: Western Publishing, 1967.
 ** Ipcar, Dahlov. *Black and White*. New York: Alfred A. Knopf, 1963.
  * Krauss, Ruth. *Bears*. New York: Harper & Row, 1948.
  * Munari, Bruno. *Zoo*. Cleveland, Ohio: Collins and World, 1963.
  * Rojankovsky, Feodor. *Animals in the Zoo*. New York: Alfred A. Knopf, 1962.
  * ———. *The Great Big Animal Book*. New York: Western Publishing, 1950.
*** Schlein, Miriam. *Heavy Is a Hippopotamus*. Reading, Mass.: Addison-Wesley, 1954.
  * ———. *Big Lion, Little Lion*. Chicago, Ill.: Albert Whitman, 1964.
 ** Slobodkina, Esphry. *Caps for Sale*. Reading, Mass.: Addison-Wesley, 1957.
 ** Stewart, Elizabeth Laing. *The Lion Twins*. New York: Atheneum, 1964.
 ** Suba, Susanne. *The Monkeys and the Peddler*. New York: Viking Press, 1970.
*** Taylor, Mark. *Henry Explores the Jungle*. New York: Atheneum, 1968.
  * Wildsmith, Brian. *Circus*. New York: Franklin Watts, 1970.

planning for grouptime

NOTE: All music, fingerplays, poems, stories, and games listed here may be used at other times during the session as appropriate. See Core Library, Basic Resources, p. 76, for publishers and addresses. Addresses for sources of records will be found on p. 81.

Music

Songs

FROM *Songs for the Nursery School*, MacCarteney
** "The Bear Went Over the Mountain," p. 40
  * "Elephants," p. 42

FROM *Songs for Early Childhood*, Westminster Press
  * "Pretending," p. 111

A TRIP TO THE ZOO
(tune: "Frère Jacques")
Adaptation by JoAnne Deal Hicks

See the li-on, see the li-on, in his cage, in his cage.
Lis-ten to his roar-ing. Lis-ten to his roar-ing. . . . I can too, I can too!
(ALLOW CHILDREN TO ROAR)

See the mon-keys, see the mon-keys, in their cage, in their cage.
Hear them as they chat-ter, chit-ter, chit-ter, chat-ter. I can too, I can too!
(ALLOW MONKEY CHATTERING)

See the big bear, see the big bear, in his cage, in his cage.
He can stand on one leg. He can stand on one leg. I can too, I can too!
(CHILDREN STAND ON ONE LEG)

See the black snake, see the black snake, curled up small, curled up small.
He can be so qui-et. He can be so qui-et. So can I . . . so can I!
(CHILDREN CURL UP ON FLOOR)

Records

"**All Aboard: Train to the Zoo**"/"Farm"/"Ranch" (Young People's Record [YPR], 33⅓ RPM)
"**Circus Comes to Town**"/"When the Sun Shines"/"Around the World" (YPR, 33⅓ RPM)
"**I Am a Circus**"/"Castles in the Sand"/"Out of Doors" (YPR, 33⅓ RPM)
"**Noah's Ark**"/"Walk in the Forest"/"How the Singing Water Got to the Bathtub" (YPR, 33⅓ RPM)
"**Waltzing Elephant**"/"Penny Whistle"/"Shhhh . . . Bang!" (YPR, 33⅓ RPM)
"Noah's Ark" and "Balloons," *Dance-A-Story* (RCA, LP, storybooks)

"What's New at the Zoo," "Never Smile at a Crocodile," "Jungle Animals," "Farm Animals," "Houses and Sounds," "Guessing Sounds," "Funny Sounds," *Stories and Songs About* (Kimbo, 33⅓ RPM)

"A Visit to the Zoo" (Little Golden Book and Record set, 45 RPM)
"Wild Animal Safari" (ABC, 33⅓ RPM)

Rhythms and Singing Games

FROM *Songs for Early Childhood*, Westminster Press
"When I Went to See the Zoo," p. 120

FROM *Music Activities for Retarded Children,* Ginglend and Stiles
"Elephant Song," p. 46

FROM *Creative Movements for the Developing Child,* Cherry
"Kalamazoo, The Kangaroo," p. 37
"The Walk in the Jungle," p. 42

FROM your own rhythm record sets: select appropriate music for elephants, bears, monkeys

FROM your own favorite music book: choose appropriate music for giraffe stretching, kangaroo hopping, and so on.

Adapt "This is the Way We Wash Our Clothes" to: This is the way the elephant walks, the lion stalks, the monkey climbs, and so on.

Fingerplays and Poems

FROM *Rhymes for Fingers and Flannelboards,* Scott and Thompson
"The Circus and the Zoo," pp. 13–18

FROM *Let's Do Fingerplays,* Grayson
"The Alligator," p. 32

TWO LITTLE MONKEYS

Two little monkeys, jumping on the bed, *jump, jump, jump.*
    (USE TWO INDEX FINGERS DOING JUMPING MOTION)
One fell off and bumped his head.
    (ONE INDEX FINGER FALLS—OTHER HAND IS PLACED ON HEAD)
We took him to the doctor, and the doctor said:
    (WALK INDEX FINGERS TO DOCTOR)
That's what you get, for jumping on the bed.
    (SHAKE ONE INDEX FINGER—POINTING AT GROUP)

Stories

(To read, read-tell, or tell. See Book Center for complete list.)

   * *Ask Mr. Bear,* Flack
   * *Dandelion,* Freeman
   * *Bears,* Krauss
  ** *Caps for Sale,* Slobodkina
 *** *Henry Explores the Jungle,* Taylor
   * *Circus,* Wildsmith

Games

(See Games, pp. 50–59, for directions.)

1. Guess Who?: children cover faces, one child is chosen to be "it"—makes zoo animal sound—children guess
2. Reach and Feel: use model zoo animals in a bag
3. Who Am I?: describe zoo animal
4. Which Is Larger?: compare sizes of rubber or plastic animals or pictures of animals. For more accurate comparison, select pictures and models that are scaled to natural size.
5. Look and See: use model zoo animals, cut up old picture books or order zoo animal cut-outs

Routine Times

At snack or mealtime:
1. Have a zoo party with centerpieces of stuffed wild animal toys.
2. Eat animal cookies that are standing in green frosting and green coconut on bar cookies. Make bars or stripes by using thinned frosting applied with a squirt bottle.
3. Eat decorated cookies: lions or tigers. (See Extended Experiences.)
4. Let older children "sell" real popcorn at the zoo as snack for the day.

   CAUTION: Use soft kernel variety. Encourage children to chew it carefully and wash it down with a drink of water.

5. Popsicles: Freeze juice in cubes with coffee stirrers inserted for handles. Children may "buy" these as treats.

Large Muscle Activities

1. Add cartons to make zoo train cars.
2. Encourage "monkeys" to do tricks on climbing gyms using monkey grip for safety (thumbs under, fingers over).
3. Play May I? with several moving at once. Children may take three elephant steps, two lion leaps, three alligator glides, one kangaroo hop, and so on.
4. Play Teddy Bear: "Teddy bear, teddy bear turn around."
5. Pantomime a walk through a zoo: children choose an animal to pantomime; cages can be backs of school chairs; children crouch behind chair and if teacher is musical, the piano makes magnificent sound effects to accompany the children's pantomime of the animals.

Extended Experiences

1. Plan a trip to:
   a. zoo or circus
   b. museum that displays zoo animals
   c. pet farm
   d. home that has a pet monkey
2. Souvenir stand: sell pennants made in Art Center, No. 1, p. 427, or balloons.

3. Popcorn stand: sell sacks filled with popcorn for snack. Provide cash register, play money, vendor's hat and apron. (See Basic Resources, p. 22.)
4. Invite a zookeeper to visit the class with a zoo pet.
5. Places to See in the City Filmstrips: Children's Zoo, Animal Farm, City Zoo, Aquarium. (Educational Teaching Aids)

teacher resources

Books and Periodicals

1. *Ranger Rick, National Wildlife, International Wildlife*, Washington, D.C.: National Wildlife Federation.

Pictures and Displays

(See p. 79 for addresses of firms listed.)

1. Group pictures of zoo animals into families (cat family). Mount pet cat pictures on different color to differentiate from wild cats. Society for Visual Education, Picture Story Study Prints: Zoo Animals, Basic Science Series II, Set 6
2. Display A Trip to the Zoo (David C. Cook Picture Packet)
3. Display a group of stuffed toy wild animals
4. Display pictures of the Circus (Trend Enterprises)
5. Post pictures from A Day at the Zoo (Instructo Bulletin Board Kit)
6. Play and view Sounds Around the Zoo, one of a series of five volumes: records, pictures, cards, and photos (Scott, Foresman)

Community Resources

1. Museum curator
2. Zookeeper or zoo park personnel
3. Instructors of zoology from a nearby college or university

...ment and sleep	reproductive and life cycle	handlin...
...own bears can walk on hind feet. ...liberate in most movements but can ...ary. ...ult grizzly bear does not climb; black ...er. ...with young in caves. ...ned sleeper or dozer). New soles grow ...ong sleep. Polar bear lives in herd; ...lone.	• Mates in summer; cubs most often born in January or February. Born with eyes closed, toothless, and nearly hairless. • *Brown:* Mates every other year in summer. Both parents care for cubs. Gestation: 6 to 7 months. Litter: 1 to 3. Newborn weighs 1½ pounds; eyes open after 9 to 10 days. Life span: up to 40 years (in captivity), 20 years (in nature). • *Black:* Can reproduce once a year. Sociable during mating season. Gestation: 6 to 7 months. Litter: 1 to 5. Newborn weighs 6 to 12 ounces, eyes open in 40 days after weaning. Full grown is 7 feet tall, and weighs 200 to 475 pounds. • *Grizzly:* Gestation: average 7 months. Newborn about 8 inches long and weighs 1½ pounds. Grows to 8½ feet tall and weighs 900 to 1150 pounds.	• Should be hand... • European brow... roller-skate, and... • Unpredictable,... wounded. May... scratches with... • **Caution:** Huma... young, especial... • *Black:* Once tro... • *Brown:* At one... important sourc... settlers.
...or shuffles very softly with a rolling ...on feet. Can move 20 miles per hour. ...walk along riverbed, using trunk as a ...v: when trunk is held forward, hind ...can push. ...ually lies down to sleep. African ...naps standing up. Sleeps with ...over nostrils to keep out mice and	• Gestation period: 18 to 24 months. Single births. Calf is woolly at birth. Can walk within one hour after birth, after 2 days can walk with herd. Sheds milk tusks at 5 to 6 months. Weaning begins at 3 to 4 months though it may nurse to 2 years. • Reaches puberty at 8 to 16 years and continues to grow until 30 years. Adult can weigh 6 tons. Height: 7 feet to 11½ feet. Lives 50 to 60 years (maximum 70).	• Asian is more e... • Trunk is sensiti... captivity).
...pping gallop. Takes enormous strides. ...cking chair). Kneels forelegs first when ...d legs first. Cannot swim. Travels in ...nd neck as club and kicks with hind ...ng position with head lowered and ...ith head erect, forelegs tucked under	• Breeds all year round. Gestation: 14 to 15 months. Has single offspring. Nurses calf for 9 months. • Calf begins browsing when it is 2 to 3 weeks old. • Mature adult weighs 900 to 2600 pounds and often reaches a height of 18 feet. Lives 20 years (in nature), up to 28 years (in captivity).	• Mothers have w... and fathers pro... • Needs head roo... • May become int... trees, other gira... • Should be hand...
...pounces. Swims, but only when ...branches of low stout trees. ...rnal. Spends day in secluded spot after ... Active mainly at night.	• Female reaches puberty at 3 to 4 years old. Can breed at 2 to 3 years old. Breeds throughout year. Lion is polygamous. • Gestation: usually 105 to 113 days. Litter: 2 to 4 cubs in wild, 2 to 6 cubs in captivity. Newborn: furred, marked with spots and stripes, eyes closed, fully open in 8 days. Weaned at 3 months. • Mature by 4 to 5 years. Lives 20 to 25 years (in nature); may live up to 30 years (in captivity). Weighs 400 to 550 pounds; up to 9 feet long.	• Kills with swipe... and neck and b... Retractable cla... struggles, claws... • Should be hand...
...monkey is well coordinated after one ...yful, climbs with all four limbs, swings ...t seldom descends to the ground. ...n upright along tree branches with aid ...ove ground. ...d feet clench like fists around ...ned around branches to secure its	• Breeds at 4 to 5 years old. Gestation period: 17 weeks (spider monkey); 180 days (capuchin). Has single offspring. Born with eyes open. Weighs 1 pound at birth. • Mature monkey is 10 to 12 pounds, body 20 inches long, tail 30 inches long (spider), 20 inches long (capuchin). Lives about 25 to 30 years in captivity.	• Baby spider mo... limbs clasping... back except wh... • Mature male of... scratch if fright... • Sensitive to su... • Steals things, li... • Very unsanitary
...pounces, swims, does not ordinarily ...if necessary. Stalks prey with a silent ...nores, lies on side, or at ease near ...ghtly. Rests after eating.	• Gestation: 105 to 113 days. Litter: 2 to 3. Weighs 2 to 3 pounds at birth. Eyes open after 14 days. Not weaned until at least 6 months. Can breed at 2 years. When strong enough joins mother in hunt. • Full grown after 4 years. Three feet high at shoulders; 6 to 7 feet long; 3 foot long tail. Weighs 250 to 500 pounds. Lives 12 to 19 years (in captivity).	• Cub is like kitte... constantly wate... • Very sharp teet... or choking it.
...ed for protection. Has well-developed, ...ith powerful hooves. Like horse, it can ...hooves and forward with forefeet. Not ...Can run up to 26 miles per hour. ...ng and early evening. ...y also lie down to rest.	• Usually has single births. Gestation: 10 to 12 months. Foal quite strong when born. Will interbreed with horses and asses. Polygamous. Adult at 2 years can reproduce for 2½ to 4 years. • Adult stands 5 feet high at shoulder. Lives up to 20 to 30 years (in captivity).	• Not consistent • Best to maintai... but can withsta... for run if not to... • Defends itself b...

cautions and special needs	relation to other animals and to world
ed only by trainer. .can be tamed and taught to dance, ride a bike, .do other stunts. Best trained when young. specially when frightened, angry, hungry, or ttack or bite, has strong canine teeth, hugs or ont legs or claws. s should show respect for mother with new y while she is giving birth. ~hy for sportsmen; now needs man's protection. me was source of skin rugs and blankets. Was .for meat, fat, and hides for Indians and early	• Can be seen and enjoyed in zoos and circuses. • Sometimes kills livestock. Can be dangerous.
sily trained. Should be handled by trainer only. .e and delicate. Toenails need to be pared (in	• Tusks: source of ivory. Weight of one of African's tusks can vary from 55 to 205 pounds. • Excellent haulers; can fell trees. • Can be seen and enjoyed by the public in zoos and circuses. • Destructive feeders; destroy crops.
~ak maternal instinct. However, both mothers ~ct young from predators. .n and high feeder in captivity. ~sted with ticks. Needs to scratch on bushes, fes, or on ground. ~ed by trainer only.	• Africans eat giraffe flesh and prize the tail for adornment. • Can be seen and enjoyed by visitors in zoos. • Lion preys on giraffe in the wild.
of paw but also grasps paws around prey's head ~tes throat and neck. Has very sharp teeth. .s structured in such a way that when prey .sink in deeper. ~ed by trainer only.	• Once a danger to man. Now protected by man to prevent extinction. • Can be seen by public in zoos and circuses. • Greatest enemies are men, wild dogs, and elephants.
~key is first carried on mother's belly with all 4 ~other's fur. After a week it moves to mother's ~n nursing. Stays with mother for up to 2 years. ~n hard to control; stubborn, will bite and ~ned or threatened; unpredictable. ~den drop in temperature. ~es to play, good mimic.	• Used for food in some parts of the world. Hides used for drumheads. • As pet: unpredictable and quite mischievous and destructive. • Can be seen by public in zoos. • Used in laboratory experiments (rhesus monkey).
~. Can be trained by special trainer but must be ~ed. . Kills by leaping on victim and breaking its neck	• Keeps down number of wild pigs, which destroy crops. • In past, its pelt was highly esteemed for beauty and warmth. Sportsmen hunted it for trophies. Today, it needs protection of man to avoid extinction. • Can be seen by public in zoos and circuses. Noted for stripes and coloring.
~hen trained, not easy to handle. .shelter around 60 degrees Fahrenheit in winter, ~d cooler temperatures. Can be turned out daily .cold. .biting and kicking with feet.	• Has been known to be domesticated in South Africa. • Source of food for Africans and also lions. • Hides used to be valuable trophies. Needs protection of man to avoid extinction. • Used to pull carts or to ride. • In zoos, can be seen and enjoyed for rare beauty of design of coat.

26 Insects and Spiders

basic understandings

(concepts children can grasp from this subject)

- There are many kinds of insects (over half a million).
- Insects are found in nearly all parts of the world. Some even live in ice and snow.
- Insects differ in many ways: size, shape, color, kinds of eyes, mouths, and number of wings, as well as the food they eat.
- Insects have six legs (3 pair) and, if winged, four wings (2 pair).
- Bees, wasps, butterflies, moths, flies, grasshoppers, ants, dragonflies, ladybugs, mosquitoes, beetles, crickets, bugs, and fireflies are insects we often see.
- A spider is not an insect. It is called an arachnid.
- Spiders have eight legs (4 pair) and no wings.
- Most spiders spin webs for their homes, for their young, or to help catch insects for food.
- Insects and spiders live all around us in the grass, in the trees, on the flowers, and in the dirt.
- Some insects (bees, ants, termites, and certain wasps) live in big family groups.
- All insects and spiders come from eggs.
- When some insect babies hatch out of their eggs they are called larvae (caterpillars in the case of butterflies). Others, like grasshoppers, hatch looking like a grownup insect only smaller.
- Young spiders are called spiderlings.
- Some insects and spiders are beautifully colored (morpha butterfly, golden garden spider, harlequin cabbage bug).
- Some insects (mosquitoes) spread disease.
- Insects sometimes eat our food while it is growing in the fields. Farmers do not like this.
- Insects help us by making honey (bees) and pollinating fruits and flowers.
- Spiders help us by eating insect pests.
- Birds, snakes, frogs, and toads eat great numbers of insects.

NOTE: Include understandings listed under Animals, p. 385, as appropriate.

Additional Facts the Teacher Should Know

Insects:

Insects are invertebrates and have no backbone. There are more kinds of insects than any other kind of animal. They have a segmented body, jointed legs, and an external skeleton. They never have more than three pairs of legs, their body is divided into three parts (head, thorax, and abdomen), and the adults usually have two pairs of wings. Some insects are harmful. They may eat crops or cause the spread of disease. Many insects are helpful. They help pollinate fruits and flowers. Insects are food for birds, frogs, toads, and snakes. They provide us with many products including honey and medicinal substances.

Insects have two sets of jaws, but they do not move as ours do. They grind or move sideways. Some insects use their mouths for chewing and others for piercing and sucking. Some insects use their legs for more than walking. They use them for swimming, jumping, or digging. Some have forelegs that are adapted for grasping and holding prey. Others have legs with hairs or suction discs to help them walk on water. Other special leg structures are: combs for cleaning antennae or eyes; hearing organs and other special sensory structures, such as taste, smell, and chemical receptors; noise-making organs; silk glands.

Insects breathe although they require very little oxygen. They get oxygen through their body walls or through special openings for breathing. They can also get oxygen from their food.

An insect's blood can be colorless, pale yellow, green, or red depending on what it has eaten. One part of a tube that carries its blood pulsates and is called the heart. Insects have a central nervous system and a primitive kind of brain. They are more sensitive to touch than people are. They have touch receptors all over their bodies, and each has two "feelers." Insects can also hear. Some can hear sounds that humans cannot. They can taste. Insects have a keen sense of smell and use it to recognize other insects of their own kind, to find their way, to find a mate, and to locate food. Most insects have two kinds of eyes and in some ways can see better than humans. They mate to reproduce, and their reproductive organs are named similarly to humans: testes, ovaries, vagina.

Insects do not have a voice like humans, but they do make sounds with other parts of their bodies. Some tap their heads against the sides of their burrows. Others may hum or buzz by vibrating their wings or their thorax, or they may squeak by forcing air out through their breathing holes. Insects may also make a sound by rubbing one part of their body against another part. For example, some crickets and grasshoppers rub a "scraper" on one wing cover across a "file" on another wing cover.

Insects outgrow their skeletons. They shed the one that is too little and form a new, larger one. Insects come from eggs, and many can be seen by the human eye. Baby insects are usually called larvae. Most insects have a pupal stage. The pupae of butterflies are called chrysalises because they are studded with bright metallic spots. The pupae of many species are usually enclosed in a cocoon that the larvae make before they enter this stage. Most cocoons are made of silk, often with bits of leaves, wood, earth, or excrement worked into them. Some are waterproof and airtight, but others have valves, or openings, with lids at one end to help the emergence of the adult. Cocoons may be found in dirt, under tree bark, beneath stones, rolled up in leaves, hanging from twigs, or tucked into crevices. When an insect struggles free of the cocoon it may have to wait until its wings dry before it can fly away.

In order to observe the opening of a cocoon or a chrysalis, create a cage from a rectangular piece of wire mesh screen and two cylinder-shaped shallow cans or pans. For sides to the cage, select a piece of screen large enough to overlap 2 to 3 inches when coiled inside one of the two pans (or cans). Use the second pan or can as a lid. Cake pans or large tuna cans work well. Twigs with the cocoon or chrysalis should be placed in a vertical position inside the cage. A cocoon found during the cold months of the year and brought into a warm room will develop a month ahead of the regular season. It should be kept in a cool place, and then in the spring placed in the cage for observation. Sprinkle the cocoon occasionally with a little water to keep it pliable. If several cocoons of the same mother are placed in the cage at the same time and allowed to develop into adult moths, the eggs laid may hatch and grow into small caterpillars.

If the cocoon of a praying mantis is found, place it in a large, transparent container with tiny holes punched through the lid. Because large numbers of praying mantises are hatched at the same time, this is necessary if you do not want them all over the room. Children enjoy watching the actions of these young insects who are just like the adult except that they do not have any wings. They are absolutely harmless.

Any insect developed from a cocoon or chrysalis should be set free after a few days. Otherwise, when they try to fly they will break their wings on the cage and die.

Caring for caterpillars:

Children often find caterpillars at various times during the spring, summer, and early fall months. If found on a tree or bush, put some of the leaves of the plant in the cage with them. Different caterpillars eat the leaves of different kinds of plants. They also may not be ready to spin a cocoon. When they are ready to do this, they will leave the food alone and hunt for a suitable place.

NOTE: Children can be taught to handle caterpillars carefully. Too many children tend to destroy every tiny creature they see.

If the caterpillar of the tomato sphinx (tomato worm) is brought in, put it in a fruit jar with some dirt, as it burrows into the ground to pupate. The caterpillar of the polyphemus moth may be put in a glass jar containing twigs and leaves. Clean out the jar daily. When the caterpillar is ready to spin its cocoon, it will use the twigs and side of the jar as its foundation and spin the leaves into its cocoon. After it is spun, the cocoon may be removed from the jar and put in a cool place. It should be dampened from time to time. If placed in a warm place and kept moist you can force its development and it will come out as a full-grown moth.

Twigs should be placed in the jar with the cecropia and monarch caterpillars. With the monarch butterfly, the leaves from a milkweed plant should be placed in the jar. The caterpillar spins a pad of silk on a leaf or twig, hangs from it, and sheds its larval skin, leaving the green chrysalis. This is an extremely interesting stage of development to observe. The film *Under Ohio Skies*, obtained from your state film library, has an excellent sequence showing this process taking place. (Check with your state library to see if it is available.) Some woolly bear caterpillars hibernate in the larval stage under dead leaves and bark. They will spin a cocoon in the spring and a tiger moth will emerge in late May. Other varieties spin a cocoon in the fall. (See Fall guide for further information.)

NOTE: Silkworms are great to observe. The entire metamorphosis takes less than two months from hatching eggs to laid eggs. Earthworms are *not* a stage of insect development. They are annelids.

Spiders:

Spiders are not insects. They have no backbones and do not have antennae. They usually spin silken webs. They have four pairs of legs instead of three. The one pair of legs nearest the head is used primarily for holding and moving things. The other three pairs are used for walking. Spiders have only two body parts. Spiders are found in almost all parts of the world.

Most spiders have poison glands and fangs. They use them for defense or for killing prey. Generally, however, spiders are not dangerous to man because they usually do not attack human beings unless they are provoked or cornered. If they do bite, the wound is usually not serious.

CAUTION: Black widow and cinnamon brown spiders *are* poisonous! Children should be cautioned to observe spiders, not to touch them.

Silk is made in abdominal glands inside the spider's body and comes out of tubes called spinnerets. It hardens and forms strands that are fine but very strong and elastic. This silk is used to make webs to preserve food and protect the eggs it lays.

A spider's blood is clear. Its heart is like that of the insect. It can breathe through body openings like that of the insect or through book lungs. They are called book lungs because they look like an open book.

There are male and female spiders. All spiders come from eggs. Like insects, spiders have to shed the skeleton that is too small in order to grow larger. Many spiders lay eggs in a cocoon fastened to a twig, or a stone, or a web. Spiders hatch inside the cocoon. The baby spiders or larvae grow very rapidly and become spiderlings. If the temperature is warm, the spiderlings may tear their way out of the cocoons and almost immediately begin feeding.

Adult spiders spend much of their time seeking food. Some chase the insects they will eat, some spit sticky material on them to immobilize their victims, some wait in holes for the insects to fall in and be trapped, and some spin webs to catch the insects.

All spiders spin a dragline behind them and attach it at various intervals. Using the dragline, a spider drops from a surface, hangs suspended in midair, and then climbs back up or floats gently down. Draglines are also used to lay down the framework of webs. Webs come in many shapes.

Spiders can be put in a jar with holes in the lid (not big enough for them to get out of). Cover the bottom of the jar with soil. Place leaves and twigs on the soil, or lean a small branch with smaller branches coming off it against the jar or stick in the soil. These will provide food and will be a center of interest for the children to observe how this animal handles its food. Water is supplied by putting a piece of moist blotting paper or a piece of moist sponge in the jar.

Methods Most Adaptable for Introducing This Subject to Children

- Pictures of insects and spiders and their homes should be prominently displayed to encourage conversations between teacher and child about them.
- An ant farm could be prepared and put out for display. While outside, the children could look for ant hills and make closer observations with a magnifying glass.
- In the appropriate season, the children, with the help of the teacher, could collect insects or spiders and keep them as described earlier or in a plastic bug keeper for a day.
- Go on a walk to look for insects or spiders and their homes.
- Follow a child's discovery of a water bug or other bug outdoors with other discovery activities.
- Locate a cricket by its sound (in season).
- A child may bring in a specimen—look up in a book how to care for it.

Vocabulary

insect	grasshopper	moth	antennae (feelers)
larva	spider	wasp	butterfly
pupa	pollinate	beetle	ladybug
cocoon	spiderling	cricket	ant
caterpillar	mosquito	firefly or	bee
hatching	dragonfly	lightning bug	fly

Include the names, sounds, body parts, and foods eaten by the insects you are observing.

learning centers

Discovery Center

1. An insect or spider collection could be brought to school as well as books that help to identify the names of these animals.
2. Parents should be notified that the class is especially curious about spiders and insects in a particular week, and that they can do much to stimulate their children's interest and answer their questions.
3. Present a honeycomb and let the children taste the honey it contains.
4. Observe an ant farm (available from Childcraft and Constructive Playthings).
5. Find a caterpillar, care for it, and observe what happens.
6. Compare a moth and a butterfly. (See No. 7.)
7. Observe a dead fly or other insect under a microscope or magnifying glass (a Tripod Giant Magnifier is available from Constructive Playthings).
8. Listen to a cricket (if you have one) during quiet or rest time.
9. Observe an insect caged in a Bug Keeper (Constructive Playthings).

10. Observe Silk Factory (Childcraft).
11. Look at View-Master reels: Insect World and Butterflies.
12. Display picture fold-out series: Bees in "Animals That Help Us" and Insects in "Kinds of Animals" (The Child's World).

Learning, Language, Readiness Materials, and Activities

Commercially made games and materials for use at a table or on a mat:

(See Basic Resources, p. 79, for manufacturers' addresses.)

1. Butterfly: 10 pcs. (Childcraft Knob Puzzle)
2. Two Ladybugs: 4 to 9 pcs. (Childcraft Knob Puzzle)
3. Butterfly: 15 pcs. (Playskool)
4. Butterfly: 5 pcs. (Judy Deluxe Puzzle)
5. Judy See-Quees Story Board: The Butterfly
6. Butterflies: matching halves to wholes (Childcraft Puzzle)
7. Honeybee Tree: for 2 to 4 players (Childcraft Game)

Teacher-made games and materials to use at a table or on a mat:

NOTE: For detailed description of Games, see pp. 50–59.

1. Match-Them: sets of animals and foods they eat; include bugs for turtles and birds and flowers for bees.
2. Make Match-Them cards with butterfly or insect stickers. These can be used for counting and sorting.

Art Center

* 1. Teacher can cut easel paper in the shape of butterfly wings. Paint as usual.
* 2. While children are fingerpainting play the record "Flight of the Bumblebee." Suggest that they might pretend their fingers are bumblebees buzzing around bushes or chasing something (could be animal or person).
* 3. Fingerpaint creepy-crawly pictures.
** 4. Make insect bodies of clay or playdough. Use sticks, pine needles, pipe cleaners, or paper for legs and wings.
*** 5. Let children creatively arrange crayon shavings on a butterfly- or bug-shaped piece of wax paper, cover with a plain piece of wax paper, and press with an iron set at low heat. (Use iron with caution.) Alternative: mount melted crayon pictures under a butterfly- or bug-shaped mat opening.
*** 6. String beads, paper circles, and/or disc-shaped styrofoam packing pieces.
* 7. Allow children to use straws, toothpicks, and pipe cleaner segments for appendages if they make insects with their clay and need them.
** 8. Other bugs/spiders can be made from circles/ovals of corrugated cardboard and decorated. Pipe cleaners may be inserted through holes for legs. Single egg carton cups can also be similarly used for insect bodies. Allow children to lick and stick colored geometric gummed shapes on "bugs" or paint their "bugs" appropriately.
** 9. Make available half lengths of the bottom of egg cartons (elongated variety) for the children to paint. Set out appropriate colors of paint. Short lengths of pipe cleaners or hair-curler pins may be used as "feelers."

**10. Make thumb print insects. Let children crayon legs to make the thumb prints look like insects.

Book Center

** Adelson, Leone. *Please Pass the Grass*. New York: David McKay, 1960.
*** Allen, Gertrude E. *Everyday Insects*. Boston: Houghton Mifflin, 1963.
** Brinckloe, Julie. *The Spider's Web*. Garden City, N.Y.: Doubleday, 1974.
** Carle, Eric. *The Very Hungry Caterpillar*. Cleveland, Ohio: Collins and World, 1970.
*** Caudill, Rebecca. *A Pocketful of Crickets*. New York: Holt, Rinehart & Winston, 1964.
**** Chenery, Janet. *Wolfie*. New York: Harper & Row, 1969.
** Conklin, Gladys. *We like Bugs*. New York: Holiday House, 1962.
*** ———. *Lucky Lady Bug*. New York: Holiday House, 1968.
** ———. *I Like Caterpillars*. New York: Holiday House, 1958.
**** ———. *I Like Butterflies*. New York: Holiday House, 1960 (read-tell one page at a time).
*** Craig, M. Jean. *Spring Is Like the Morning*. New York: G. P. Putnam's Sons, 1965.
*** Freschet, Bernice. *The Web in the Grass*. New York: Charles Scribner's Sons, 1972.
* Garelick, May. *Where Does the Butterfly Go When It Rains?* Reading, Mass.: Addison-Wesley, 1961.
** Gold, Augusta. *Spider Silk*. New York: Thomas Y. Crowell, 1964 (record/filmstrip).
*** Goudey, Alice E. *Butterfly Time*. New York: Charles Scribner's Sons, 1964.
** Graham, Margaret Bloy. *Be Nice to Spiders*. New York: Harper & Row, 1972.
**** Griffen, Elizabeth. *A Dog's Book of Bugs*. New York: Atheneum, 1968.
*** Hawes, Judy. *Watch Honey Bees with Me*. New York: Thomas Y. Crowell, 1964.
** Kepes, Juliet. *Ladybird Quickly*. Boston: Little, Brown, 1964.
* Lionni, Leo. *Inch by Inch*. New York: Astor-Honor, 1962.
** Lubell, Winifred and Cecil Lubell. *The Tall Grass Zoo*. Chicago, Ill.: Rand McNally, 1960 (many excellent illustrations).
**** Mitchell, Robert L. and Herbert S. Zim. *Butterflies and Moths*. New York: Western Publishing, 1964 (paper, read-tell).
*** Mizumura, Kazue. *If I Were a Cricket*. New York: Thomas Y. Crowell, 1973.
** ———. *Way of an Ant*. New York: Thomas Y. Crowell, 1970.
* Nakatani, Chiyoko. *The Zoo in My Garden*. New York: Thomas Y. Crowell, 1973.
*** Packard, Andrew. *Mr. Spindles and the Spiders*. New York: Macmillan, 1961 (read-tell).
**** Piecewicz, Ann Thomas. *See What I Caught*. Englewood Cliffs, N.J.: Prentice-Hall, 1974.
*** Selsam, Millicent. *Terry and the Caterpillars*. New York: Harper & Row, 1962 (tell).
**** Sterling, Dorothy. *Caterpillars*. Garden City, N.Y.: Doubleday, 1961.
**** Stevens, Carla. *Catch a Cricket*. Reading, Mass.: Addison-Wesley, 1961.

planning for grouptime

NOTE: All music, fingerplays, poems, stories, and games listed here may also be used at other times during the session as appropriate. See Core Library, Basic Resources, p. 79, for publishers and addresses. Addresses for sources of records will be found on p. 81.

Music

Songs

FROM original songs in this book by JoAnne Deal Hicks
* "Bugs," p. 443
* "The Tiny Weaver" (a listening song), p. 444

FROM *Songs for Early Childhood,* Westminster Press
"Little Cricket in the Grass," p. 53
"Butterfly, Butterfly," p. 55
"Buzz, Buzz, Buzz, the Bees," p. 55
"Funny Little Grasshopper," p. 56

BUGS
(tune: "Frère Jacques")
Adaptation by JoAnne Deal Hicks

Big bugs, small bugs, big bugs, small bugs.
See them crawl. See them crawl.
Creep-y, creep-y, crawl-ing. Nev-er, nev-er fall-ing.
Bugs, bugs, bugs. Bugs, bugs, bugs.

Thin bugs, fat bugs. Thin bugs, fat bugs.
See them crawl, on the wall.
Creep-y, creep-y, crawl-ing. Nev-er, nev-er fall-ing.
Bugs, bugs, bugs. Bugs, bugs, bugs.

Records

"Birds, Beasts, Bugs, and Little Fishes," Seeger (Folkways, 33⅓ RPM or cassette)
"Shoo-Fly," *American Game and Activity Songs for Children* (Folkways, 33⅓ RPM, words sung slowly; repetitious)
"Flight of the Bumblebee," *Children's Concert Series,* Rimsky-Korsakov (Children's Record Guild, 78 RPM)
"**Eensie, Weensie Spider**"/"Skittery Skattery"/"Sleepy Family" (Young People's Record [YPR], 33⅓ RPM)
"Visit to My Little Friend"/"**Creepy, Crawly Caterpillar**"/"Merry Toy Shop" (YPR, 33⅓ RPM)

NOTE: The above songs are available singly from Young People's Records, 45 or 78 RPM.

"Spin, Spider, Spin" (Childcraft, 33⅓ RPM)

Rhythms and Singing Games

FROM *Creative Movement for the Developing Child,* Cherry
"Creep-Caterpillar," p. 58   "Winged Movements," p. 59
"Fuzzy Caterpillar," p. 58   "Flap Your Wings," p. 59
"Spinning My Cocoon," p. 59

FROM *Songs for the Nursery School,* MacCarteney
"Zum! Zum! Zum!," p. 37

FROM *Music Activities for Retarded Children,* Ginglend and Stiles
"Shoo Fly," p. 130

FROM original songs in this book by JoAnne Deal Hicks

"The Tiny Weaver," p. 444: creepy, crawly music. Pretend to be caterpillars. Play "fluttering" music for butterflies. Play a chromatic scale on the piano for bees (white note followed by black notes on upper register of piano keyboard).

Fingerplays and Poems

FROM *Let's Do Fingerplays*, Grayson

"Five Little Ants," p. 63   "Bumblebee," p. 73
"Grasshoppers," p. 65   "Eensie, Weensie Spider," p. 103

EENSIE WEENSIE SPIDER
Adaptation of Southern Folksong

The tiny, tiny spi der went up the water spout.   ("WALK" FIRST AND SECOND FINGERS UP ARM)
Down came the rain and washed the spi der out.   (BRUSH HAND DOWN ARM)
Out came the sun and dried up all the rain.   (MAKE CIRCLE WITH ARMS OVERHEAD)
And the tiny, tiny spi der went up the spout again.   ("WALK" TWO FINGERS UP ARM)

FROM *Rhymes for Fingers and Flannelboards*, Scott and Thompson

"Once I Saw a Beehive," p. 35   "Five Little Busy Bees," p. 97
"Ten Little Grasshoppers," p. 90   "Little Miss Muffet," p. 105
"Sleepy Caterpillars," p. 91

THE ANT HILL

(THE RIGHT HAND WITH THE THUMB CLOSED INSIDE IS THE ANT HILL. THE FINGERS WILL BE THE ANTS. LIFT EACH FINGER AS IT IS COUNTED, BEGINNING WITH THE THUMB)

Once I saw an ant hill, with no ants about.
So I said, "Little ants, won't you please come out?"
Then as if they had heard my call, one, two, three, four, five came out.
And that was all.

FROM *Very Young Verses*, Geismer and Suter

"Under the Ground," p. 9   "The Cricket," p. 12
"Little Black Bug," p. 10   "Fuzzy Wuzzy, Creepy Crawly," p. 14
"Little Bug," p. 11

Stories

(To read, read-tell, or tell. See Book Center for complete list.)

  * *Inch by Inch*, Lionni
*** *If I Were a Cricket*, Mizumura
 ** *Be Nice to Spiders*, Graham
 ** *The Very Hungry Caterpillar*, Carle
  * *Where Does the Butterfly Go When It Rains?* Garelick

Routine Times

1. Use fingerplays, poems, and songs about insects or spiders while children are coming to the table for lunch or snacks.
2. Serve honey and biscuits for snack or mealtime.

Extended Experiences

1. Go for a walk in a nearby park, around the block, or around the playground area to find bugs (under rocks, in cracks in sidewalks, in bushes—shake bushes into an open umbrella).
2. Have someone bring a butterfly collection to show.

teacher resources

Books and Periodicals

1. *Butterflies and Moths: A Golden Nature Guide*, Robert T. Mitchell and Herbert S. Zim, New York: Western Publishing, 1964 (paper).
2. *Cricket in a Thicket*, Aileen Fisher, New York: Scribner, 1963 (poems).
3. *National Merit Encyclopedia*
4. *Ranger Rick, National Wildlife,* and *International Wildlife*, Washington, D.C.: National Wildlife Federation.
5. *National Geographic* magazine

Pictures and Displays

(See p. 79 for addresses of firms listed.)

1. Display magazines with special articles on insects:
   a. *National Geographic* magazine
   b. *Ranger Rick* magazine
   c. *National Wildlife* magazine
2. Use the 3-D bugs and caterpillars made in Creative Art for table decor.
3. Put up pictures of spiders, caterpillars, moths, and butterflies from your own personal files.
4. Display and use commercial picture packets:
   a. Monarch Butterfly, Insects/Bees, Science Themes No. 1 (David C. Cook)
   b. Bees/Ants, Science Themes No. 2 (David C. Cook)
   c. Insects, Instructo Flannelboard Set, 12 prints
   d. Color Study Prints, Insects and Spiders (The Child's World)
   e. Sequence Charts, Life Cycle of Monarch Butterfly (The Child's World)
   f. Basic Science Series No. 1, Common Insects (SVE)
   g. Basic Science Series No. 2, Moths and Butterflies (SVE)

Bugs

JoAnne Deal Hicks

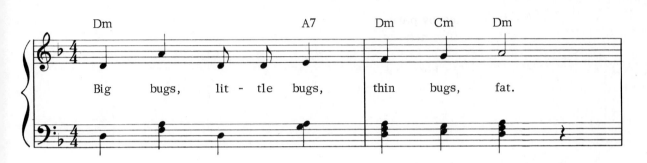

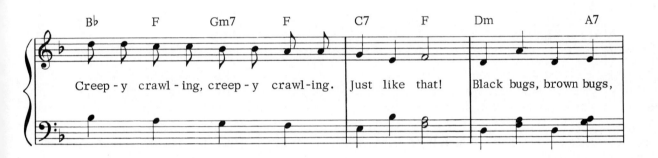

NOTE: This should be a pleasant, not a frightening, song. Talk about how insects move and how they help us. Choose one or two children to be "creepy, crawly bugs" and one or two children to be "leaping, jumping bugs."

The Tiny Weaver

A Listening Song or Dramatic Play Accompaniment

JoAnne Deal Hicks

Have you ev-er seen a spi-der on the wall? How it hangs up-on a thread and will not fall. How it dan-gles, how it spins, weav-ing out and weav-ing in, then it spins and spins to weave that thread a-gain.

NOTE: Teacher may wish to sing this song to the group after exploring the subject of spiders. Use pictures from *National Geographic* or *Ranger Rick* magazines. Allow children to join in singing the words as they become familiar with them.

PART SIX

Transportation

27 Many Ways to Travel

basic understandings

(concepts children can grasp from this subject)

- Transportation means moving people or things from one place to another.
- People can move from one place to another:
  a. by their own movements: walking, running, swimming, or crawling.
  b. by using an animal: riding one or being pulled by one in a wagon or carriage.
  c. by riding in or on a machine: car, train, plane, ship, or bus.
- Some machines that move or carry us need motors, wind, water, steam, gas, oil, or people to make them go.
- When we travel or transport things:
  a. we first decide what we need to move, people or things.
  b. we think about where we need to move them or ourselves.
  c. we decide the best way to move them or ourselves.
  d. we buy a ticket, pay a fare, or give instructions to the person or animal that is going to take us.
  e. we may turn a key or a switch or pull a throttle if we are to start the machine in which we are traveling.
- Machines most often used for moving people or things are cars, trucks, buses, taxis, trains, airplanes, ships, and boats.
- The person who steers most transportation machines is called the driver.
- A driver must have a license and follow certain rules. Drivers who break the rules may get a ticket from a law enforcement officer, pay a fine (money), or have their licenses taken away.
- We usually must pay money to transport people or things:
  a. people may buy tickets to ride on trains, airplanes, ships, or buses.
  b. people may pay fares (money) to ride in a taxi, bus, subway, ferry, or trolley car.
  c. people who own their own car (or other machine) must take care of it and buy gasoline and oil for it.

    d. sometimes drivers must pay a toll (money) to drive on roads or drive in tunnels or drive over bridges. The money collected is used to help build and care for the roads, tunnels, and bridges.
- We can travel or carry things on the ground, in the air, or through the water.
- When people walk on the sidewalks we call them pedestrians; when they cross streets they must be careful and obey the safety officer or traffic lights.
- People can do many things while traveling as passengers: eat, sleep, rest, talk, read, and sometimes stand, walk, or use rest rooms.
- Drivers must pay attention to their driving and passengers must be careful not to disturb or distract the driver.
- All drivers must follow signs and signals for safety. For example:
  - a. railroad engineer: semaphores, flags, and whistles.
  - b. pilot: windsocks, radar, and radio signals.
  - c. ship captain: whistles, buoys, flags, and radio signals.
  - d. safety officer: road signs and traffic lights.
- There are many specially trained people who help us with transportation, such as conductors and flight attendants. (See guides on Air, Rail, Road, Space, and Water Transportation.)

Additional Facts the Teacher Should Know

This Transportation guide will deal with concepts and activities that involve all methods of moving people or things from one place to another. It will deal with movements of self, use of animals to ride or pull, and transportation by air, water, road, rail, or in space. Supplementary guides dealing specifically with transportation by air, rail, road, water, and space have been developed for use where special interest in one form of transportation is indicated. First experiences with transportation should begin with ways the child can move and carry things. Use of wheel toys that can be pushed, pulled, or pedaled enlarge the concepts of moving things and people. Cars or buses used for transporting the children to and from the center would provide additional experiences with transportation. If your center is near a railroad track, beneath a flight pattern, or near a river you will have natural exposure to these means of transportation.

The basic concepts listed are understandably broad and are not intended to be taught outside of the children's opportunities to experience them. For example, you would not suggest activities involving toll booths, ferries, or trolleys if they do not exist in your community, unless a child in your group has had experience with them. Select those that will have the most meaning for your group.

Methods Most Adaptable for Introducing This Subject to Children

- A child or teacher at the center takes a trip.
- Read a story about transportation.
- Put up pictures or display scale models of trains, airplanes, ships, boats, cars, trucks, buses, or spaceships.
- Visitor: if one of the children's father or mother works for a transportation agency have him or her visit the classroom, dressed in working attire, and talk about the job. If possible, the visitor could bring something that he or she uses on the job to show the children.

Vocabulary

transportation	bus	driver	ride	run
passenger	ticket	train	walk	crawl
schedule	fare	carry	ship	drive
airplane	toll	suitcase	stop	truck
move	taxi	baggage	go	
carry	tourist	boat	start	
trip	travel	pack	car	

learning centers

Discovery Center

1. Help children discover that there are many ways to move things or people: carry by hand, animal, car, train, truck, airplane, or ship. Discuss the methods by which a product, like milk, is carried by people, animals, cars, trains, planes, and ships. If possible, have pictures of each mode of transportation used.
2. Encourage children to observe signs, safety officers, stop lights, and parking meter signs when taking a trip and crossing streets. Provide picture books, films, or license rule manuals to help children discover some of these signs and signals.
3. Display hats and pictures of people at work to help children discover that some people wear uniforms or special clothes when they work on their transportation job and some do not.
4. Display one each of a model train, car, truck, bus, ship, boat, and airplane on a table. Encourage discussion about transportation. Discuss likenesses and differences and why each is necessary.
5. Display pictures and/or models of animals used to carry people or things, such as horses, elephants, burros, dogs, camels. *Animal Friends and Neighbors* by Jan Pfloog, listed in the Book Center, has large pictures of some of these animals.

Dramatic Play Centers

Home-Living Center

1. Have several overnight bags available so they can be packed for a trip with dressup clothes or doll clothes.
2. Have several travel brochures with colorful pictures and timetables on a shelf for the children to look at.
3. Put play money in purses so tickets can be purchased or fares or tolls paid.
4. Hang travel posters here and in the Block-Building Center.

Block-Building Center

1. A steering wheel or dial panel, planks, and hollow blocks will all provide opportunities for many kinds of transportation play. A dial panel (see illustration, p. 478) can be made out of wood or a heavy cardboard box. See other Transportation guides for specific suggestions for its use.
2. Set out items to be transported in both large and small trucks, such as animals, blocks, cars, and containers full of buttons, beads, spools, twigs, and pebbles.
3. Commercial materials that will add to dramatic play with transportation are listed below:
   a. unit blocks to build roads, bridges, stations, garages, docks, and airports
   b. unit block transportation vehicles: cars, trucks, planes, taxis, boats, ships
   c. unit block people to transport and transportation helpers
   d. unit block animals to transport
   e. hollow blocks and building boards for larger-scale building
   f. fourway traffic light (Childcraft)
   g. traffic signs: unit block size and wheel toy size
   h. wheel toys: doll carriage, wagons, trikes, wheelbarrows
   i. oversize vehicles: trucks, planes, trains, and boats
   j. ride 'em vehicles
   k. cash register and play money (metal and paper)
4. Post pictures of highways, bridges, docks, airports, railroad stations, or launching pads in block-building area to encourage use of unit blocks as related to transportation.

Other Dramatic Play Centers

1. Two rows of chairs with an aisle between might suggest travel by bus, train, subway, trolley, or airplane. If space is limited one row may be sufficient. Provide money, tickets, and conductor's hat or make a hat using pattern on p. 496.

Learning, Language, and Readiness Materials Center

Commercially made games and materials for use at a table or on a mat:

(See Basic Resources, p. 79, for manufacturers' addresses.)

1. Concepto-Sort: 225 Picture Word Playing Cards (Educational Performance Associates)
2. Traffic: puzzles with small knobs, 14 pcs. (Childcraft)
3. Vehicle Puzzle: 9 vehicles, 2 pcs. each (Childcraft)
4. Mix 'n Match Puzzles: Transportation (Trend Enterprises)
5. Play Board Puzzles: Transportation, 5 standup pcs. (Childcraft)
6. Horse and Cart: First Jigsaws, 5 pcs. (Childcraft)
7. Coaster Seat/Coaster Sled (Constructive Playthings)
8. Transportation Fleet (Community Playthings)
9. Mini Puzzles: Transportation (Creative Playthings)

Teacher-made games and materials for use at a table or on a mat:

NOTE: For detailed description of Games, see pp. 50–59.

1. Look and See: use sturdy models of the various transportation vehicles.
2. Reach and Feel: use sturdy models of different types of transportation vehicles.
3. Can You Remember?: use transportation toys.

4. How Many?: how many ways can you get from one side of the room to the other? Get to school? From one city to another? Get a car across the river? Get across the ocean? (See the song "Ways I Can Move," p. 458.)
5. Who Am I?: describe someone who works for an airline, railroad, bus company, or trucking firm, for example, "I fly an airplane; who am I?"
6. Grouping and Sorting by Association: place several models of each type of transportation vehicle in a box or on a tray. Let children sort into appropriate groups. Label boxes or make an appropriate garage, hangar, or harbor into which vehicles can be sorted.
7. Alike, Different, and the Same: use scale models or sets of picture cards of the various transportation vehicles. Toy catalogs or model catalogs available at some hobby centers may provide you with the pictures for this game. Have children find two just alike. As children gain experience, add one that is different to pairs that are alike and ask child to "find the one that is different," such as two cars and a bus.
8. Color, Shape, Size, and Number: at every opportunity, when observing real transportation vehicles or using scale models, talk about the color, shape, size, and number characteristics as appropriate. Examples: "What *color* is the caboose?" "Put away the *big* truck." "How *many* propellers does your airplane have?" "*Count* the wheels on the car."

Art Center

*** 1. Pasting: children could help make a picture book of transportation for the Book Center by cutting pictures out of magazines, catalogs, or brochures and pasting them on colored construction paper. These pages could then be punched and placed in a three-ring notebook.

   NOTE: Cut one side and the bottom rectangle out of six large grocery bags. When all six are cut, stack and fold them to form a book. Staple at the folded edge to make a large flat scrapbook of twelve pages.

Book Center

*** Chaplin, Cynthia. *Wings and Wheels*. Chicago, Ill.: Albert Whitman, 1967.
  * Dawson, Rosemary and Richard. *A Walk in the City*. New York: Viking Press, 1960.
  * Keats, Ezra Jack. *Skates*. New York: Franklin Watts, 1973.
  * Lenski, Lois. *Davy Goes Places*. New York: Henry Z. Walck, 1961.
 ** Pfloog, Jan. *Animal Friends and Neighbors*. New York: Western Publishing, 1973.
*** Thomas, Ianthe. *Walk Home Tired Billy Jenkins*. New York: Harper & Row, 1974.
*** Zaffo, George. *Airplanes and Trucks and Trains, Fire Engines, Boats and Ships, and Building and Wrecking Machines*. New York: Grosset & Dunlap, 1968.
*** ———. *The Giant Nursery Book of Things That Go*. Garden City, N.Y.: Doubleday, 1959.

planning for grouptime

NOTE: All music, fingerplays, poems, stories, and games listed here may also be used at other times during the session as appropriate. See Core Library, Basic Resources, p. 76, for publishers and addresses. Addresses for sources of records will be found on p. 81. In parodies, hyphenated words match the music notes of the tune used.

Music

Songs

FROM original songs in this book by JoAnne Deal Hicks
** "Ways I Can Move," p. 458
** "Let's Take a Ride," p. 470

*** TAKE A TRIP (a parody)
(tune: "Twinkle, Twinkle, Little Star")
Adaptation by Wendy Flemming

Take a bus or take a train,
Take a boat or take a plane.
Take a tax-i, take a car,
May-be near or may-be far.
Take a space ship to the moon,
But be sure to come back soon.

NOTE: To add interest use pictures, figures, flannelboard, or models.

** GET ON BOARD

Get on board lit-tle chil-dren
Get on board lit-tle chil-dren
Get on board lit-tle chil-dren
There's room for many and more.
There's room for Bet-ty. There's room for Tom-my.   (and so on)

There's room for man-y and more.
There's room for man-y and more.

NOTE: Can be sung when playing train, plane, bus, or ship. It is a good way to in-volve those who may be watching.

FROM *Songs for the Nursery School*, MacCarteney
* "I'm Jumping," p. 2
* "Riding in a Wagon," p. 2
* "Bicycle Song," p. 17

Records

"My Friend"/"**A Visit to My Little Friend**"/"Creepy, Crawly Caterpillar"/"Merry Toy Shop" (Young People's Record [YPR], 33⅓ RPM)
"**Chugging Freight Engine**"/"**Little Gray Ponies**"/"Rhyme Me a Riddle" (YPR, 33⅓ RPM)
"Who Wants a Ride" (YPR, 45 and 78 RPM)
"Whoa! Little Horses" (YPR, 78 RPM)
"Sleigh Ride," Leroy Anderson
"On the Trail," *Grand Canyon Suite*, Ferde Grofé (sound of a donkey)

Rhythms and Singing Games

1. Hoofbeats can be imitated by using walnut or coconut shells or wooden tone blocks when records or songs about horses or donkeys are played.
2. Play a variety of tempos on the piano or from segments of action records that will encourage the children to walk, run, tiptoe, and jump.
3. The sounds made by airplanes, trains, cars, trucks, buses, or boats can be suggested by the music of certain records or piano music or appropriate rhythms. Allow children to respond creatively. (See Basic Resources, p. 42.)
4. Stick horses. Allow children to use stick horses when galloping or trotting music is used.

ROUND AND ROUND THE VILLAGE

Sing this song using different ways of moving around a village.

Let's fly a-round the vil-lage. (PRETEND TO BE AN AIRPLANE)
Let's walk a-round the vil-lage.   (ALSO USE JUMP, HOP, SKIP, OR GALLOP)
Let's drive a-round the vil-lage.   (PRETEND TO BE CARS, TRUCKS, OR BUSES)
Let's swim a-round the pool.   (PRETEND TO DO THE CRAWL)
Let's row a-round the lake.   (PRETEND TO ROW A BOAT)
Let's pad-dle down the riv-er.   (PRETEND TO PADDLE A CANOE)

AS I WAS WALKING DOWN THE STREET
   (*Adaptation of* "Rig-a-Jig-Jig")

As I was walk-ing down the street, down the street, down the street
A lit-tle friend I went to meet, hi-ho, hi-ho, hi-ho.

Skip-pet-y-skip and a-way we go, a-way we go, a-way we go
Skip-pet-y-skip and a-way we go, hi-ho, hi-ho, hi-ho!

NOTE: Change verse to include running, jumping, hopping, flying in the sky, rowing down a stream, and other action verbs.

FROM *Songs for the Nursery School*, MacCarteney
"Follow Me," p. 96

Change words to make different kinds of vehicles:

Toot, toot, toot, I'm a train.
Brrrrrrrrr, I'm a plane.
I can walk, yes, I can.   (run, hop, skip, jump)
I'm a horse, I can trot.

Fingerplays and Poems

FROM *Very Young Verses*, Geismer and Suter
"About Going Places," pp. 84–109

FROM *Let's Do Fingerplays*, Grayson
"Things That Go," pp. 22–26

FROM *Rhymes for Fingers and Flannelboards*, Scott and Thompson
"The Airplane," p. 21
"Five Little Sailors," p. 23

Stories

(To read, read-tell, or tell. See Book Center for complete list.)

** *Animal Friends and Neighbors*, Pfloog
* *A Walk in the City*, Dawson
*** *Airplanes and Trucks and Trains, Fire Engines, Boats and Ships, and Building and Wrecking Machines*, Zaffo

Games

(See Games, pp. 50–59, and Teacher-Made Games in this guide for directions.)

1. Look and See
2. Reach and Feel
3. Can You Remember?
4. How Many?
5. Who Am I?
6. Grouping and Sorting by Association

Routine Times

1. During snack or mealtime, talk about how the various foods you are eating were brought to the center.
   a. How does the food get from the kitchen to the tables?
   b. How does the food get from the store to the kitchen?
   c. How does the food get from garden, dairy, or canning factory to the store?
2. At snack or mealtime, ask children to help by *transporting* food, dishes, silver, water, and other food or utensils as needed.
3. At pickup time, point out to the children that carrying things in our hands and walking are forms of transportation. Suggest also the use of wagons and rolling platforms as means of transporting blocks and toys to shelves to be put away.
4. While riding or walking look for different kinds of *vehicles*, for example, cars, trucks, buses, trains, airplanes, boats.
5. When riding in a bus or car, talk about safety in a car or bus: use safety belts if available, lock the doors, be considerate of the driver; as appropriate, talk about traffic signals and rules.

Large Muscle Activities

1. An old discarded steering wheel from a junked car, remounted on a large wooden box big enough for three or four children to stand in, makes an excellent dramatic play vehicle. If built to look like no one vehicle it will be more versatile. A couple of broomhandle clips mounted on the side will allow for hanging a hose when it is a fire engine or a coil of soft rope for a lifeline or old bicycle tire for a life preserver when it is a boat.

NOTE: Set it up on cement blocks outside and drill a few drain holes in the bottom of the box so it will weather without rotting, and so termite infestation can be minimized.

2. Encourage use of wheel toys for transport of each other or things around the play yard. Add traffic signs and signals.
3. Remind children of traffic rules, such as one-way traffic or boundaries.

Extended Experiences

1. Visit a railroad station, bus terminal, or airport. Time your visit to see arrivals and departures.
2. Ride on a bus, trolley, train, or boat (whatever is possible in your area that would interest your group), considering safety factors involved.
3. Visit a park or other public site that may have a ship, locomotive, or airplane as a permanent display, with pieces of play equipment or mounted so that children are free to explore.
4. Have parents or other persons employed by transportation companies visit the classroom dressed in working attire. Invite them to talk about their jobs. Ask them to bring, if possible, something to show the children that is used on the job.
5. Visit a hobby shop that has a model car racetrack or model train on display.

teacher resources

Books and Periodicals

1. All of George Zaffo's books on transportation.

Pictures and Displays

(See p. 79 for addresses of firms listed.)

1. Pictures of trains, cars, trucks, buses, boats, ships, wheel toys, or children walking or running could be mounted and displayed on walls
2. Transportation packet (David C. Cook)

Community Resources

1. Travel agencies for posters, brochures, and timetables
2. Public relations personnel of various airlines, steamship lines, or railroad companies for pictures, calendars, brochures, and timetables
3. Hobby centers for models and catalogs

Ways I Can Move

JoAnne Deal Hicks

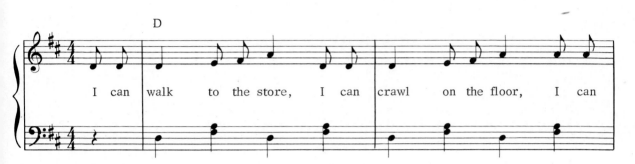

I can walk to the store, I can crawl on the floor, I can

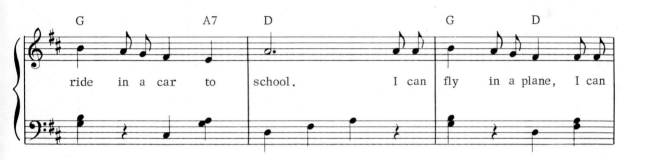

ride in a car to school. I can fly in a plane, I can

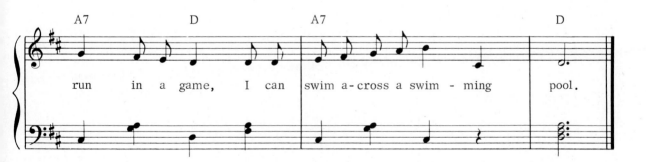

run in a game, I can swim a-cross a swim - ming pool.

NOTE: Use appropriate actions. Children who wish may crawl on the floor, pretend to swim, "fly" across the room, or "drive" their car to school.

28 Air Transportation

basic understandings

(concepts children can grasp from this subject)

- Airplanes carry people and things from one place to another by flying in the sky.
- Some airplanes are small and carry one or two people and some are very big and carry many, many people.
- Some people own their own private airplanes.
- People can buy tickets (pay money) to ride in an airplane.
- Most airplanes take off and land on runways at an airport.
  a. Sea planes take off and land on water.
  b. Ski planes take off and land on snow.
- The person who flies the airplane is called the pilot; his/her assistant is called the co-pilot.
- Flight attendants ride in the cabin on a passenger plane to help make the passengers comfortable and serve them snacks or meals.
- The air terminal is the building at the airport where people may buy tickets and wait for airplanes. It often has a lounge, rest rooms, restaurant, snack bar, telephones, car rental and ticket agents, gift shops, and news stands.
- The control tower is a tall building where a control officer sits who can view all the runways. It has equipment which helps the officer guide pilots in safe takeoffs and landings.
- Hangars are buildings at the airport that house airplanes when they are not in use.
- There are many different kinds of airplanes: passenger planes (airliners), cargo planes (for freight only), sea planes, helicopters, gliders, war planes, ski planes, and jets.
- Rockets and missiles carry people and things into outer space, to the moon, and to other planets. (See Space guide.)
- Windsocks tell pilots which way the wind is blowing.
- Each airplane has a number, symbol (logo), or flag so we know who owns it. International aircraft have the flags of their countries painted on the sides.
- Airplanes have seat belts for safety, just as automobiles do.

Additional Facts the Teacher Should Know

How can something that is heavier than air fly? An airplane flies because of the work done by the propellers, the wings, and the engine. A glider does not have an engine but is towed (lifted) into the air by another airplane to which it is attached by a cable. When the glider is at the proper height the cable is released and the glider flies (glides) back to earth. Airplanes are powered by gasoline engines, turbine engines, jet engines, or rockets. These engines provide power to turn the propellers or provide forward thrust for the airplanes. Forward thrust causes air to flow over the wings, which are curved on top and flat on the bottom. As airplanes are thrust forward, air flowing over the curved part of the wing has farther to go than air flowing across the flat underside. The air that has to go farther therefore goes faster to meet the slower air beneath. Because the air goes faster it does not push down as much as the slower air pushes up. The faster airplanes go forward, the greater the lift; therefore, airplanes fly.

Not all modern planes have propellers. Many jet planes do not, nor do rockets or missiles. Gases from burning fuel in the engine rush out from a hole in the rear of each engine (these can be seen in the pods under the wings) with terrific force and the plane is pushed forward. Forward thrust can be demonstrated by blowing air into a balloon and then letting the balloon go. As the air rushes out the open end the balloon goes in the opposite direction. Jet engines use the oxygen from air, but rockets must carry their own oxygen supply. The first plane to fly faster than the speed of sound was a jet. When a plane or rocket flies faster than the speed of sound an explosion is heard and the plane or rocket is said to be "breaking the sound barrier." Vibrations from the explosion may cause houses to shake, windows and dishes to break or rattle, and objects to fall.

Three controls are used in flying an airplane. They are the control stick, the rudder pedals, and the throttle. In smaller, older planes the control stick has a knob on the end for the pilot to grasp, but newer and larger craft have a small steering wheel. There are two ways to turn an airplane to the right and to the left—by moving the stick or turning the wheel to the left or right and by pushing the rudder pedals down. Usually a pilot works both the stick and rudder pedals together. There are two different ways to make an airplane go up or down. When the control stick is pushed forward the airplane moves toward the earth; if the stick is pulled back, the airplane climbs. The second way involves the throttle, which controls the speed of the engine. Pushing the throttle in makes the engine go faster, increasing the lift, and the airplane goes higher. If the throttle is pulled back, the engine slows down, increasing the downward force, and the plane descends.

Most takeoffs and landings are made by pilots with permission obtained by two-way radio communication with the traffic control officer in the tower at the airport. In good weather with good visibility pilots land planes under their own control. However, the control officer in the tower can bring in an airplane with the use of radar and other instruments when visibility is poor. Bringing a plane in by radar is called a ground control approach (GCA) and instrument landing systems (ILS) means a radio highway approach.

Airports range in size from small landing fields with one runway, a windsock, and no landing lights (no night service) to the huge international airports serving several airlines, including those flying to and from other countries. The largest airports have terminals built on a circular layout and are virtually mini-cities.

At the larger airports each airline has its own ticket counter, baggage claim center, boarding gates, and customer service staff. Tickets are now written and confirmed by computer. Tickets are presented by customers at customer service stations near boarding gates, where they receive boarding passes. When it is time for boarding a plane customers must go through a security checkpoint. Because of many recent hijackings and hidden bombs, all persons must walk through a magnetometer or scan-screen which detects the presence of metal. All coats, purses, and hand-carried luggage are checked by security guards or placed in a scan-ray machine to detect metal. Once through the security checks travelers walk through tunnels called "Jet-ways" or "Avio-bridges" to waiting planes.

Customers' baggage is placed on a conveyor belt which takes it out to a service area where it is placed on baggage tugs or luggage carts and taken to waiting planes. A ramp with a conveyor belt carries it up into the baggage compartment.

Airline terminals have restaurants, snack bars, cocktail lounges, rest rooms, gift shops, telephones, car rentals, and information desks. The largest terminals have mini-buses, limousines, or computerized transfer systems to carry passengers from one airline to another. Buses, taxis, and limousines are available for passengers to go to the downtown areas. Many air terminals have motels or hotels for people to stay overnight. Other accommodations are usually available within a mile or two. The motel or hotel will often provide a courtesy car.

All foods and drinks served on the airplane are catered by food services. The food is prepared in advance and brought to the airplane before takeoff. The small kitchens, or galleys, are used for preparing drinks and setting up trays which are taken to passengers in their seats by flight attendants. Special diet menus can be ordered by passengers if the airline has been alerted to their specific needs.

Helicopters cannot fly as fast as airplanes but they can take off and land straight up and down, making them excellent for rescue work in mountains and valleys where runways do not exist. They have two sets of propellers called "rotors." Most have one big rotor overhead and a smaller one on the tail. One set of rotors turns clockwise and the other set counterclockwise, keeping the airplane in balance.

Ski planes are equipped with giant skis that allow them to glide over snow. Sea planes are equipped with pontoons, allowing them to land and float on water. They both also have sets of wheels which can be lowered to allow them to land on runways.

Airplanes have many parts: wings, propellers, engine, control stick or steering wheel, tail, rudder, and wheels. The cockpit is where the pilot sits to fly the plane. The cabin is where the passengers sit. Transcontinental planes have galleys, rest rooms, and lounges. Some planes have seats that can be converted to upper and lower berths for sleeping.

Methods Most Adaptable for Introducing This Subject to Children

- A child or one of the teachers at the center takes a trip by airplane.
- Put up pictures or display scale models of various kinds of planes.
- Read a story about airplanes.
- Visitor: if one of the children's parents works for an airline have him/her visit and tell about the job.

Vocabulary

airplane	terminal	cockpit	fasten
airport	hangar	fly	control officer
runway	tower	jet	takeoff
flight attendant	baggage	wing	landing
airline	ski plane	pod	windsock
glider	sea plane	propeller	
pilot	helicopter	seat belt	

learning centers

Discovery Center

1. Display model airplanes of various kinds. Help children identify the airplanes and discover the uses made of each kind. Recognize likenesses and differences. Look for symbols (logos), numbers, and flags for identification. These should be models that would withstand manipulation. Demonstrate with models how airplanes take off and land.
2. Help children understand how a propeller works by providing pinwheels, either commercial or homemade. (See pattern on p. 467.)
3. Help children understand how a jet engine works by blowing up a balloon and letting it go. The escaping air pushes the balloon forward.
4. Make a windsock to take outside to find out which way the wind is blowing. Sew a tube of material or the sleeve of a man's shirt to a circle of wire or embroidery hoop. Fasten the hoop to a stick which can be used as a handle or stuck in the ground. Airplanes must take off and land into the wind. The windsock tells the pilot which way the wind is blowing.

NOTE: See Discovery Center in the Space guide for more activities related to aircraft.

Dramatic Play Centers

Home-Living Center

1. Have airline schedules and travel brochures in this center to encourage the planning of a trip by airplane. Suitcases should be available to pack and money placed inside the purses to be used for purchasing tickets.

Block-Building Center

1. Build a runway with long planks or unit blocks. Have wooden or unbreakable model airplanes available for takeoffs and landings.

2. Add cars, people, and baggage to various models and types of airplanes on shelves. These will suggest to children who may have had some experience with airplanes the idea of building an airport terminal, runway, tower, or hangar where they could be used.
3. Pictures of terminals, airplanes being loaded and boarded, or airplanes flying may also encourage an interest in air transportation in the Block Center.

Other Dramatic Play Centers

1. A walking board or plank laid across a wooden box or sturdy cardboard carton could make an airplane. Add a steering wheel or dial panel. (See illustration, p. 478.) Propellers can be cut out of cardboard and thumbtacked or taped to the edge of the plank. A step unit can be pushed up to the plane for passengers to get on or off the plane. A wagon or rolling platform can be used to take passengers' luggage to and from the plane.
2. Set up two rows of chairs with an aisle between. Section off a galley with a three-way play screen or other room divider. Provide TV dinner trays with laminated food cut-outs and paper cups for the flight attendants to serve to the passengers.
3. Set up two short rows of chairs with an aisle between for airport limousine or minibus. Driver can wear a chauffeur's cap. Sky-cap can manage luggage.

Learning, Language, and Readiness Materials Center

Commercially made games and materials for use at a table or on a mat:

(See Basic Resources, p. 79, for manufacturers' addresses.)

1. Transportation toys: Peg Bus, Airplane, Helicopter, Bus, Tractor, and Wagon (use as baggage tug) (Childcraft)
2. Wood Flyers: Transport Jet, Helicopter, and Super Jet (Childcraft)
3. Playskool Airport
4. Play Family Airport (Fisher Price)
5. Airplane: crepefoam puzzle (Lauri)
6. Playskool Puzzles: Airplane, 15 pcs.; Helicopter, 10 pcs.
7. Judy Puzzles: Airplane, 12 pcs.; Jet-Airplane, 14 pcs.; Helicopter, 14 pcs.
8. Planes Directionality Form Boards: (Ideal)

Teacher-made games and materials for use at a table or on a mat:

NOTE: For detailed description of Games, see pp. 50–59.

1. Look and See: use scale metal or unbreakable plastic models of different kinds of airplanes which show detail.
2. Can You Remember?: use different kinds of airplane models.
3. Alike, Different, and the Same: make two sets of each type of airplane available. Mix the sets together and have children find the ones that match. Put two matching planes and a different one together. Ask children to point to the one that is different.
4. Color, Shape, Size, and Number: at every opportunity when observing real planes or working with models or pictures, talk about size, color, shape, and number. Count wheels, pontoons, propellers, jet pods, wings, and tails.

Art Center

** 1. Make several different kinds of airplane stencils. Let children spatter-paint airplanes on blue construction paper, choosing colors and models they wish to use to make their airplanes.

* 2. Children could help make a picture book of airplanes by pasting precut pictures of different kinds of airplanes onto construction paper. The pictures could then be put in a colorful plastic three-ring binder.

*** 3. Gliders can be made by paper folding. (See illustration below.) The teacher may make some, showing the children how to make the folds. Once the children have the idea they will design some of their own.

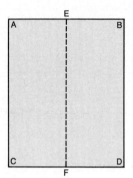

Start with paper 8½" × 11".
Fold paper in half lengthwise.
Unfold and label with letters.

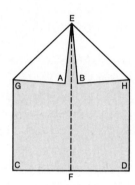

Fold A and B to within ½" of center line E–F.

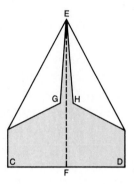

Fold G and H over A and B to within ⅜" of center line E–F.

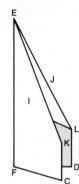

Fold I–K–C over J–L–D.

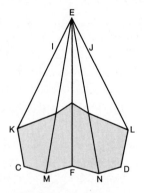

Fold E–I–K–C and E–J–L–D back to center line E–F, forming fold lines E–M and E–N.

Turn glider over. Fold E–L and E–K back to E–F.

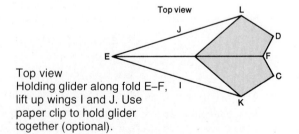

Top view
Holding glider along fold E–F, lift up wings I and J. Use paper clip to hold glider together (optional).

*** 4. At the woodworking table set out wheels (discs of wood cut from dowels, bottle caps, and plastic caps) and precut shapes of soft wood that children can nail together to make airplanes. Propellers can be precut from plastic lids or plastic bottles.

Book Center

*** Bendick, Jeanne. *The First Book of Airplanes*. New York: Franklin Watts, 1958.

*** Chapin, Cynthia. *Wings and Wheels*. Chicago, Ill.: Albert Whitman, 1967.

**** Colonius, Lillian, and Glen W. Schroeder. *At the Airport*. Chicago, Ill.: Melmont, 1967 (reference).

*** Greene, Carla. *I Want to Be a Pilot*. Chicago, Ill.: Children's Press, 1957.

**** Knight, Clayton. *The Big Book of Real Helicopters*. New York: Grosset & Dunlap, 1963 (good illustrations but adult text; read-tell).

*** Pope, Billy N. *Let's Take an Airplane Trip*. Dallas, Texas: Taylor Publishing, 1971.

**** Zaffo, George. *The Big Book of Airplanes*. New York: Grosset & Dunlap, 1966 (good illustrations but adult text; read-tell).

planning for grouptime

NOTE: All music, fingerplays, poems, stories, and games listed here may also be used at other times during the session as appropriate. See Core Library, Basic Resources, p. 76, for publishers and addresses. Addresses for sources of records will be found on p. 81. In parodies, hyphenated words match the music notes of the tune used.

Music

Songs

FROM original songs in this book by JoAnne Deal Hicks

* "Let's Take a Ride," p. 470 (first verse)

FROM *Songs for the Nursery School*, MacCarteney

* "Airplane Song," p. 10

FROM *Music Resource Book*, Lutheran Church Press

* "Airplane, Airplane," p. 49

** I'M A LITTLE AIRPLANE
(tune: "I'm a Little Teapot")
Adaptation by Bonnie Flemming

I'm a lit-tle air-plane;   (RAISE ARMS TO SIDE AT SHOULDER HEIGHT)
I can fly,   (TURN RIGHT ARM IN FRONT OF YOU FOR PROPELLER)
Here is my throt-tle;   (REACH HAND OUT TO INSTRUMENT PANEL)
Give me a try.   (PUSH THROTTLE IN)
When I get all revved up   (MAKE ENGINE NOISES)
Then I fly   (MOVE FORWARD DOWN RUNWAY)
Off the run-way   (KEEP MOVING FORWARD)
To the sky!   (GO UP ON TIPTOE RUNNING FORWARD)

Records

"Jet Plane," *Rhythm Time*, Record 1   (Bowmar, 33⅓ RPM)
"Trains and Planes"   (Young People's Record [YPR], 78 RPM)
"Little Airplane," *Songs for Children with Special Needs*, Record 1   (Bowmar, 33⅓ RPM)
"United States Air Force Song," U.S. Air Force Band   (RCA Victor, 33⅓ RPM)
"Larry's Airplane Ride," *Transportation*   (Bowmar, 33⅓ RPM or cassette)

Rhythms and Singing Games

FROM *Songs for the Nursery School*, MacCarteney
"Tiptoe Aeroplane," p. 10

FROM *Creative Movements for the Developing Child*, Cherry
"Airplanes," p. 35
"Helicopters," p. 35

Fingerplays and Poems

FROM *Rhymes for Fingers and Flannelboards*, Scott and Thompson
"The Airplane," p. 21

FROM *Let's Do Fingerplays*, Grayson
"An Airplane," p. 22

FROM *Very Young Verses*, Geismer and Suter
"There Are So Many Ways of Going Places," p. 85
"Riding in an Airplane," pp. 96–97
"Aeroplane," p. 98
"Taking Off," p. 99
"About Going Places," pp. 96–100

Stories

(To read, read-tell, or tell. See Book Center for complete list.)

*** *I Want to Be a Pilot*, Greene
*** *The First Book of Airplanes*, Bendick
*** *Let's Take an Airplane Trip*, Pope

Games

(See Games, pp. 50–59, and Teacher-Made Games in this guide for directions.)

1. Look and See
2. Can You Remember?
3. Alike, Different, and the Same

Routine Times

1. At snack or mealtime have children arrange chairs in two double rows. Use trays or paper plates shaped like trays. Have flight attendants put snacks or food on the trays and serve to passengers on the plane. Use finger foods for this snack or meal. Dried fruits can be used instead of fruit juices, and liquids should be omitted with younger children. If liquids are served fill glasses only half full. Try water first.
2. At pickup time if you have a ride 'em-type airplane children may taxi some of the toys back to the hangar (shelf).
3. When walking or riding to and from the center listen for airplanes.
4. At rest time suggest that the children be very quiet and listen for an airplane.

Large Muscle Activities

1. Use a packing box, lard barrel cut in half, or sturdy carton with a walking board across it for an airplane. Add a steering wheel or dial panel. (See illustration, p. 478.) A set of stairs pushed up to the packing box can be used for passengers to load. A wagon or wheeled platform can be used for a baggage cart.
2. Outdoors is the perfect place for action songs. (See Music.)
3. Provide the children with a paper pinwheel. (See illustration below.) Let them run, pretending the pinwheels are propellers and they are the airplanes.

Pinwheel pattern

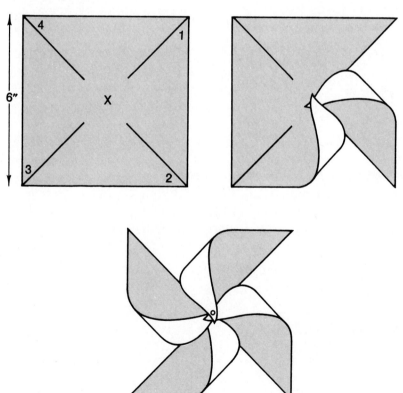

Pinwheel: From each corner, cut three inches toward the center. Place each A over the X and hold with thumb. When all are in place, fasten pinwheel to a dowel 6″ to 10″ long with a large-headed pin.

4. Paper gliders are fun to hold and run with or fly. (See pattern, p. 464.)
5. Paper helicopters are fun to drop from the top of the jungle gym, a ladder climber, or a packing box. (See illustration below.)

Helicopter pattern

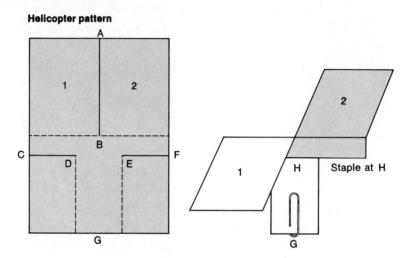

Helicopter: Cut an 8½″ x 11″ piece of construction paper into fourths. Each quarter sheet will make one helicopter. Following illustration, fold each in half and cut from A to B. Cut C–D and F–E. Fold F to D and C to E. Paper-clip together at G, staple at H. Fold down wings 1 and 2. Hold high, spin, and let go.

Extended Experiences

1. Visit an airport to see airplanes take off and land. For very young children perhaps a first visit to a small private airfield might be best. Jet engines are very noisy and may frighten young children. At a smaller field there would perhaps be a greater opportunity to take a closer look at the airplanes and visit a hangar. Perhaps permission could be obtained for the children to board one of the planes to see what one looks like inside. Older children who have more experience with airplanes may be able to comprehend the various parts that make up a large air terminal.
2. Invite a pilot and/or flight attendant to come to the center and talk briefly about his/her job. If possible ask that he/she wear the job uniform and bring a piece of equipment or tool that is used on the job.
3. Show slides of various airplanes and different buildings found at your local airport or one in a nearby larger community. Contact a local flying school or the manager or public relations director of a nearby airport or airline company for slides or names of persons who may have such collections.

teacher resources

Books and Periodicals

1. Knight, Clayton. *The Big Book of Real Helicopters*. New York: Grosset & Dunlap, 1963.
2. Zaffo, George J. *The Big Book of Airplanes*. New York: Grosset & Dunlap, 1966.

Pictures and Displays

(See p. 79 for addresses of firms listed.)

1. Transportation Packet (David C. Cook)
2. Display travel posters, airline tickets, baggage claim checks, airline schedules, and models of several kinds of passenger planes.
3. Display airplanes so they will be out of reach of children, using airplane models built by a hobby enthusiast.
4. Use sturdy model airplanes as a table centerpiece to encourage discussion about airplanes while children are eating.
5. Put up pictures from your file of different kinds of airplanes, an airport, a pilot, flight attendants, a control tower, and a windsock.

Community Resources

1. Airline companies: contact public relations directors for literature.
2. Airport: contact the manager of your local airport to arrange a visit.
3. Civil Air Patrol: ask the chamber of commerce if a CAP group exists in your community. Members may have slide collections, own their own airplanes, or be willing to talk to your group about airplanes.
4. Hobby centers: for catalogs of model airplanes that could be used to make required materials. Obtain the names of persons who have collections of model airplanes and who may be willing to lend them for display. These people may also have collections of slides that could be borrowed.
5. Flying school: contact the director about an instructor pilot coming to the center to talk to the children or about a visit to the flying school for a closeup view of an airplane, with permission to board one.
6. Strategic Air Command: for names of pilots who could talk to the children. Many members own airplanes, models, or slide collections.
7. Recruiting officer: contact the United States Air Force for literature and posters that could be used for display, showing men and women in uniform.

Let's Take a Ride

Jo Anne Deal Hicks

Variation: Let's take a ride in a sail-boat, let's take a ride on the lake.
Let's take a ride, let's take a ride, let's take a ride on the lake.

Let's take a ride in an au-to, let's take a ride down the road.
Let's take a ride, let's take a ride, let's take a ride down the road.

29 Rail Transportation

basic understandings

(concepts children can grasp from this subject)

- Some transportation machines run on rails, for example, railroad trains, subway trains, trolley cars, monorail trains, and cable cars.
- Most trains and trolley cars run on two rails called tracks; monorail cars run on one rail.
- You may find these rails or tracks in many places:
  - a. railroad tracks are laid on top of the ground.
  - b. trolley tracks are set into roads in a city.
  - c. a monorail is an elevated train which travels on a single rail above or below the vehicle.
- Trains take people or things from one city to another.
- Trolleys are like city buses; they take people from one part of the city to another part. However, they can move only where tracks are laid.
- There are different kinds of trains:
  - a. passenger trains carry people from one city to another.
  - b. commuter trains carry people to and from work.
  - c. subway trains carry people in tunnels under the ground from one part of the city to another.
  - d. freight trains carry things from one city to another. Some things they carry are animals, food, furniture, lumber, and oil.
  - e. work trains (maintenance-of-way trains) carry workers and machines to help repair track and trains.
- The locomotive or diesel engine pulls the train. Two or more diesel units are needed if the train is very long.
- There are different kinds of cars on a passenger train: coach, sleeping car, dining car, vistadome car, lounge or club car, baggage car, and observation car.
- There are many different kinds of cars on a freight train: tank car, box car, cattle car, gondola car, hopper car, autoveyor, refrigerator car, and caboose.

- Many people work for the railroads: ticket agents, engineers, brakemen, conductors, porters, cooks, waiters, and dispatchers.
- The trains stop at various stations so that passengers can get on and off and freight can be loaded and unloaded.
- A railroad station or terminal is a large building where passengers can buy tickets to ride on the train. Most stations have a snack bar or restaurant, magazine stands, waiting room or lounge, and toilet facilities.
- Many of the things you do at home may be done on a train:
  a. sit, talk, read, look out the window, walk, or eat snacks.
  b. eat a meal in the dining car.
  c. sleep in a pullman car in bunk-type beds called "berths" or in a small compartment.
  d. wash your hands and go to a toilet in the lavatory.
  e. you may take your pets but they must ride in the baggage car.
- There are special signals for drivers on roads to watch for that tell them a train is coming: two flashing red lights, a bell, or sometimes crossing gates are dropped across the road.
- The train blows its whistle when it is ready to start, is going to cross a road, or is coming into a station.

Additional Facts the The Teacher Should Know

Diesel or steam engines are called "locomotives." Diesel engines have almost entirely replaced steam engines. Therefore the coal-shoveling fireman's job has become obsolete and the diesel engineer is now assisted by a front brakeman who helps him check the road signals and other safety controls.

Passenger service has steadily decreased throughout the country while freight service has increased. Many companies have ceased passenger service and others have merged in an effort to survive. The National Railroad Passenger Corporation, known as Amtrak, has established a network of passenger service throughout the country in the hope of increasing passenger service, although some states and many major cities are not included. However, it has not proved successful. Amtrak and the other railroad companies are using existing railroad track which is in poor condition resulting in slow, uncomfortable rides, irregular schedules, and some accidents. Passenger service will continue to decline until faster, safer, more comfortable, and more dependable service is provided.

On the East Coast there are some high-speed passenger trains called Metroliners which can go over 100 miles per hour. They operate between Boston and New York, Philadelphia, and Washington, D.C. In Japan there is an excellent high-speed train called the Tokaido Express which travels 125 to 175 miles per hour. In Germany there is a high-speed train system that is computerized, safe, and comfortable.

The Postal Department no longer uses railway post-office cars on the railroad. Mail does travel in sacks in baggage cars on passenger trains or in box cars on freights. Individuals or businesses can send freight via the REA Express, which often uses trains to transport goods. If businesses wish to transport their products by rail they must contract to use an entire car —a refrigerator car, box car, or tanker. Some businesses, such as Swift, Wilson, Texaco, and Deep Rock, have bought their own cars and pay the railroads a fee for hauling them.

There are different kinds of trains and different kinds of cars used in making them. It is not appropriate to teach detailed definitions but you should use the correct names when talking to the children about trains. You may say, "This is a tank car. It carries milk." The following descriptions may aid you in identifying the various cars for young children:

Diesel or steam locomotive pulls cars on a freight or passenger train.

Switch engine is used in freight yards for switching railroad cars and making up trains.

Coach is a passenger car with rows of upholstered seats that usually recline. New high-level coaches have seats on an upper level and baggage and toilet facilities below.

Dining car has a kitchen (galley) and a dining room with tables and chairs where passengers may eat, just as in a restaurant. Some trains have a coffee shop.

Sleeping car has bedrooms and roomettes for people planning to sleep on the train.

Parlor, lounge, or club cars have chairs and small tables arranged like a living room where people may read, talk, write letters, play card games, or have a snack.

Baggage car is a box car that holds trunks, suitcases, animals in cages (dogs and cats), and other bulky things that passengers are taking with them.

Vistadome car has a glass ceiling and seats on two levels for passengers to enjoy the scenery. The first level is frequently a lounge.

Box car is a rectangular car with huge sliding doors that open to load or unload contents. It can carry furniture, tools, machines, and other nonperishable goods.

Refrigerator car is a box car built with refrigeration. It is used for transporting perishable goods such as flowers, fruit, vegetables, meat, and dairy products.

Tank car is a cylindrical-shaped car that carries liquids, such as milk, oil, gasoline, and some chemicals.

Gondola car is a rectangular box car without a top for carrying goods that are not damaged by rain or snow, such as pipe, steel, or concrete blocks.

Flat car is a rectangular platform for carrying large items "piggyback" that are not damaged by rain or snow, such as tractors, logs, or trailer trucks. Sometimes stakes are used on each side to keep things like pipes or logs from rolling off. Most items are tied down.

Autoveyor is a special triple-deck car that carries automobiles.

Cattle car is a box car made with wooden slats that are spaced so that air can get in, for carrying animals, such as cows, sheep, horses, pigs, and chickens.

Hopper car has slanting ends to help the coal or gravel flow out when it is time to unload. Some have covers for things that would be damaged by rain or snow.

Caboose is the last car on a freight train. It is an office for the conductor, bedroom and kitchen for the crew, and a storehouse for the rear brakeman. It has bay windows on the side or a cupola on top so he can watch the train. It has a telephone hookup to the engineer in the locomotive.

Maintenance-of-way cars are several cars that are equipped with special tools and machines for repairing track and cars.

Monorail cars or trains run on a single track. They are often used at world fairs or recreational areas.

Cable cars are used to cross waterways or deep valleys or to go up and down mountains or hills. They usually work in pairs. They are pulled on stationary tracks by a motorized cable.

Many Different People Work for the Railroad

Ticket agents sell tickets to people and make reservations on the trains.

Conductor is in charge of the freight or passenger train. On a passenger train, he is responsible for the safety and comfort of the passengers; he collects tickets and decides when the train is to stop and when it is ready to depart. On a freight train he keeps a record of all shipments and is responsible for delivering the goods to their correct destination.

Porter carries passengers' suitcases and trunks and helps make them comfortable. In the sleeping cars, he makes up the berths when it is time to go to sleep.

Dining car steward is in charge of seating people, supervising the waiters, and serving as cashier.

Chef has charge of the kitchen or galley and supervises the cooks who prepare the meals.

Waiters serve the passengers their meals in the dining car.

Engineer drives the locomotive.

Front brakeman rides in the cab of the locomotive with the engineer. He assists the engineer by checking road signals and other safety devices.

Rear brakeman assists the conductor on a passenger train and couples and uncouples the cars on a freight train.

Dispatcher is in an office in the station. He is in radio or telephone communications with the other stations, the engineers, and the yard. The dispatcher is responsible for the trains coming in and out of the station.

There are many different kinds of train signals used: lights, lanterns, semaphores, and whistles. Track signals for the engineer include red, amber, and green lights and semaphores. A semaphore is a wooden arm attached to a pole. Children who have had many experiences with trains may be ready to use some of the signals in their play, rather than tooting incessantly without meaning. See list below:

Whistles:

   One short toot = Stop

   Two long toots = Go ahead

   One long toot = Train approaching the station

   Three short toots = Stop at the next station

Lights for engineer include:

   Red = Stop

   Green = Go

   Amber = Caution

Lanterns:

   Swinging a lantern back and forth in front of knees = Stop

   Raising and lowering = Go ahead

Semaphores:

   Arm up = Track is clear—full speed ahead

   Arm half-way down = Caution

   Arm at right angles to pole = Stop

A freight yard contains many sets of track connected by switches. Some are incoming tracks, some are outbound, and some are classification tracks where cars are sorted and made up into trains by using a switch engine. There are storage tracks where cars are held until needed, riptracks where cars are given light repairs, and other tracks for freight to load and unload. At these freight-loading locations there are special ramps and equipment to help make the freight loading easier.

Some yards have a roundhouse, a semicircular building which holds many engines and cars for repair. A turntable is used to position the car or engine on the right piece of track. Engine houses are now replacing the roundhouse. Engines and cars are built in a railroad shop.

Many people work in the yards, the roundhouse, the railroad shop, and engine house. The towerman or yardmaster is very important to the smooth operation of the yards. He is responsible for directing the switch engineers and yard crew and for keeping the trains made up, safe, and on schedule. More and more of the yard work is being computerized. The titles for some of the railroad jobs, such as brakeman and towerman, have not yet changed, but there is at least one woman engineer.

Each railroad company has its own colors and a symbol called a "herald." The locomotives are painted with company colors and a unique design. For example, Amtrak has a red, white, and blue arrow design. The herald is painted on each of the company cars. Frequently the company's initials are part of the herald.

Wallace Sanders, a black train yard worker in Jackson, Mississippi, wrote the famous ballad "Casey Jones." It tells of the heroic engineer "Casey" (John Luther) Jones who died at the throttle on April 30, 1900. His train, the Cannon Ball Express, was going 60 miles per hour when it hit the rear of a freight train that had not quite cleared the main track.

Methods Most Adaptable for Introducing This Subject to Children

- A child or teacher in your group takes a trip on a train.
- There are tracks near your center and the children show an interest.
- Read a book about trains.
- Put up pictures of trains or set out authentic scale models.
- Have someone who works for the railroads visit the center and talk about his/her job.

Vocabulary

whistle	subway	vistadome	signal
freight	locomotive	cable car	switch
passenger	conductor	berth	track
monorail	engineer	upper	tank car
station	trolley	lower	flat car
engine	dining car	coach	box car
caboose	sleeping car	train	cattle car

learning centers

Discovery Center

1. Set out scale models of the different kinds of freight and passenger trains and let children discover the similarities and differences. Ask which are alike? Different? The same?
2. Display pictures of trains with the herald shown on each to help children discover the fact that each railroad company has a different symbol or herald on the various cars.
3. Display wall charts L-1, L-2, and L-3 available from the American Association of Railroads (AAR) (see Teacher Resources, p. 484) or use as follows:
   a. L-1, Railroad Alphabet—This chart could be cut up and each letter with its picture and verse could be pasted on a separate page and put in a three-ring notebook for the children to look at or for the teacher to read to a small group.
   b. L-2, Our Railroad Helpers—Cut up and make into a book or a series of mounts those most appropriate for your group. They will help children discover the many people who work for the railroad and what they do. Make them available when a parent who works for the railroad visits.
   c. L-3, Railroads in Our Daily Lives—This will help children discover how many things they use every day that are transported to their city by the railroads.
4. Put out the AAR Train Display Streamer. The freight train on one side and passenger train on the other help children discover the different cars that make up a train.

Display various transportation models. Try to use models that are the same scale.

5. Display the AAR Freight Train Cut-out (contains ten freight cars, a diesel locomotive, and a caboose in color). One side pictures the exterior of a car and the other side shows the interior of the car. You may wish to mount these on cardboard to help them stand up or insert a double-length unit block beneath to give it additional support. May be used for vocabulary "Name It" or "Scramble" game.

Dramatic Play Centers

Home-Living Center

1. Have several overnight bags available. These may be packed with dress up clothes and doll clothes for taking a trip by train.
2. Put several train schedules on shelves to be used in planning a trip by train.
3. Place play money in purses for use in purchasing tickets.

Block-Building Center

1. Encourage interest in trains by putting up pictures of stations and trains in the Block-Building Center.
2. Set out the interlocking train set, Child Guidance Railroad, or Skaneatles sets.

3. To simulate a train station set up a three-way play screen with tables or build a ticket counter with hollow blocks and boards. Use the ride-on type of train or allow the children to build a coach by using two rows of chairs with an aisle between. Provide engineer caps, bandana handkerchiefs to wear around the neck, conductor hats (see pattern, p. 496), paper punches, colored paper scraps for tickets, and train schedule sheets or folders for this Dramatic Play Center. A simple lantern (no glass) and a dial panel (see illustration) are other dramatic play accessories children may use. Encourage children to share hats. You may need to get a timer or suggest a defined reasonable time limit for a treasured prop. If not necessary, let children decide and choose.

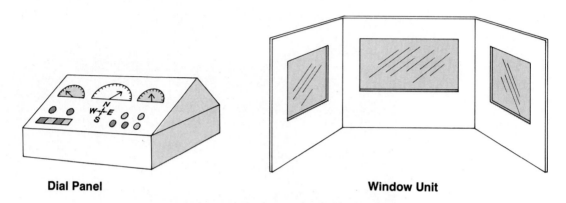

Dial Panel   **Window Unit**

Cut out "windows" or paste or paint pictures of appropriate scenery for the driver. Place around dial panel or a steering wheel unit. (Contributed by Janice Bailey.)

Learning, Language, and Readiness Materials Center

Commercially made games and materials for use at a table or on a mat:

(See Basic Resources, p. 79, for manufacturers' addresses.)

1. Judy Transportation Puzzles: Subway Train, 8 pcs.; Diesel Locomotive, 12 pcs.
2. Upright Insets: Train (Childcraft)
3. Playskool Plaques: Locomotive, 12 pcs.
4. Directionality Form Boards: Steam Engines (Ideal)
5. Railroad Station: Stand Up Puzzles, 18 pcs. (Childcraft)
6. Engine: Simple Puzzles, 5 pcs. (Childcraft)

Teacher-made games and materials for use at a table or on a mat:

NOTE: For detailed description of Games, see pp. 50–59.

1. Look and See: use scale model freight or passenger cars.
2. Reach and Feel: using a Feel It Box (see Touch guide, p. 155), put one model railroad car at a time in it to prevent damage and allow child to decide which kind of car it is, for example, box, tank, locomotive. Identify by name all the cars before selecting the one to hide. Choose those with very different physical characteristics.
3. Can You Remember?: use different kinds of railroad cars.
4. Who Am I?: describe the different people who work for the railroad: engineer, conductor, brakeman, porter.

5. Grouping and Sorting by Association: use model railroad cars or paste pictures onto cards, one car to a card. Let children group into a freight train or passenger train.

6. Alike, Different, and the Same: use model railroad cars or make picture cards with a car on each card. Put out two cars that are alike and one that is different, such as a tank car and a box car. If two complete sets of different kinds of cars are made children could first find the two that are alike.

7. How Many?: make up a passenger train or freight train using models or picture cards with a varying number of different kinds of cars. Ask "How many box cars?" "How many diesel units?" Be sure to omit one type of car and then ask "How many _____ cars?" to get the answer "None." How many altogether? Keep within ability level of your group.

8. Color, Shape, Size, and Number: at appropriate times when observing trains or working with scale models talk about these characteristics: "Show me a yellow car." "What shape is the box car?"

Art Center

** 1. Provide the children with circles and rectangles of various colors and sizes to paste on construction paper. Some may discover these shapes can be put together to resemble a railroad car, trolley, or subway train.

Other Experiences in This Center Using Art Media:

1. Shoebox train: a usable train with short-term durability can be made from combining two parts of several shoeboxes in various ways, painting them, and tying them together with nylon twine, plastic clothesline, or thin rope. With the lid left on it is a box car; the cover alone is a flat car; the box alone is a gondola car; an oatmeal or cornmeal carton glued to a box top makes a tank car; a long lid with a smaller box glued on it and another longer lid on top of the box makes a recognizable caboose; a long lid with an oatmeal box glued on and a small square box glued to the end of the oatmeal carton for the cab makes a locomotive. (See below.) Have parents save the necessary boxes for you or ask the assistance of a local Girl Scout, Boy Scout, or Camp Fire Girl group to make one for you. If you make your own, let each child who wishes paint one of the cars.

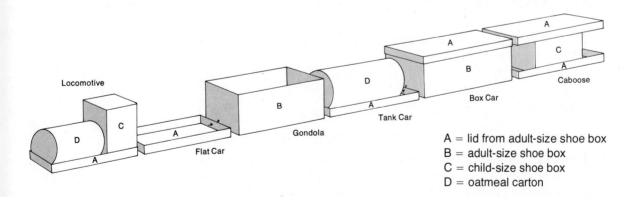

A = lid from adult-size shoe box
B = adult-size shoe box
C = child-size shoe box
D = oatmeal carton

2. Children could help make a picture book of trains. Those with cutting ability may cut the pictures out of magazines or model catalogs. Others can choose precut pictures they wish to paste onto construction paper and put in a colorful plastic three-ring notebook.

Book Center

*** Brown, Margaret Wise. *Two Little Trains*. Reading, Mass.: Addison-Wesley, 1949.

** Burton, Virginia Lee. *Choo, Choo, the Runaway Engine*. New York: Scholastic Book Service, 1971.

*** Elting, Mary. *Trains at Work*. Irvington-on-Hudson, N.Y.: Harvey House, 1962.

*** Greene, Carla. *Railroad Engineers and Airplane Pilots: What Do They Do?* New York: Harper & Row, 1964.

*** Kessler, Ethel and Leonard. *All Aboard the Train*. Garden City, N.Y.: Doubleday, 1964.

** Lenski, Lois. *The Little Train*. New York: Henry Z. Walck, 1940 (paper, 1973).

** Meeks, Esther K. *One Is the Engine*. Chicago, Ill.: Follet, 1972.

*** Piper, Watty. *The Little Engine that Could*. New York: Platt & Munk, 1954.

** Zaffo, George. *Big Book of Real Trains*. New York: Grosset & Dunlap, 1953.

planning for grouptime

NOTE: All music, fingerplays, poems, stories, and games listed here may be used at other times during the session as appropriate. See Core Library, Basic Resources, p. 76, for publishers and addresses. Addresses for sources of records will be found on p. 81.

Music

Songs

FROM original songs in this book by JoAnne Deal Hicks

** "Let's Take a Ride," p. 470. Sing these words:
Let's take a ride on a fast train, let's take a ride down the track.
Let's take a ride, let's take a ride, let's take a ride down the track.

FROM *Songs for the Nursery School*, MacCartney

* "We're Going on the Train," p. 11

* "Little Engine," p. 11

*** "The Switching Engine," p. 14

*** "The Railroad Train," p. 16

FROM *Music Resource Book*, Lutheran Church Press

* "I'm a Big Black Engine," p. 51

FROM *Songs for Early Childhood*, Westminster Press

** "The Little Red Choo-Choo," p. 110

* "The Train," p. 122

FROM *Wake Up and Sing*, Landeck and Crook

** "Rock Island Line," p. 64

FROM traditional songs in your favorite American folk song book
** "Down by the Station"
*** "I've Been Working on the Railroad"

Records

"All Aboard: **Train to the Zoo/Farm/Ranch**" (Young People's Record [YPR], 33⅓ RPM)
"Chisolm Trail"/"**Working on the Railroad**"/"There's Gold in California" (YPR, 33⅓ RPM)
"**Chugging Freight Engine**"/"Little Gray Ponies"/"Rhyme Me a Riddle" (YPR, 33⅓ RPM)
"Muffin and Mother Goose"/"Musical Mother Goose"/"Muffin in the City/**in the Country**"
 (YPR, 33⅓ RPM)

Above titles also available on Children's Record Guild (CRG) label, 78 RPM.

"Trains and Planes" (CRG, 78 RPM)
"Train to the Beach" (CRG, 78 RPM)
"Little Red Caboose" (Disneyland, 33⅓ RPM)
"Little Engine That Could"/"Casey Jones"/"John Henry"/"Submarine Streetcar" (Disneyland, 33⅓ RPM)

Rhythms and Singing Games

Sand blocks rubbed together can be used with songs or records to accent the rhythm of train wheels.

Trains: talk about how the children might become a train (each being a car), such as putting their hands on the shoulders of the person in front of them. Let children suggest ways.

Use music about a train on a record or the piano. Play "Goin' Down the Track," p. 486.

NOTE: It is better to let the children imaginatively imitate a train than make rhythm time a structured activity.

A wooden whistle would be another effective sound to accompany either of the other activities. (Needs to be washed between uses if used by more than one person.)

Fingerplays and Poems

FROM *Rhymes for Fingers and Flannelboards*, Scott and Thompson
"Here Is the Engine," p. 20.
"Railroad Train," p. 20.

FROM *Let's Do Fingerplays*, Grayson
"Down by the Station," p. 22
"The Big Train," p. 22
"The Train," p. 22
"Choo-Choo Train," p. 23

THE ENGINEER

I ride in the engine   (POINT TO SELF)
The whistle I blow   (PULL CORD)
I do all the things
That will make the train go.   (PULL THROTTLE; TURN DIALS)

Whoo! Whoo! Goes the whistle   (PUT HANDS TO MOUTH)
Clickety-clack go the wheels   (ROLL ARMS IN WHEEL MOTION)
I'm chief engineer   (PAT CHEST)
'Til I'm called for my meals!   (PRETEND TO EAT)

FREIGHT TRAIN
  by Bonnie Flemming

As the big locomotive moves slowly down the track
I wonder where it goes to and when it's coming back.

The engine needs a brakeman, it needs an engineer
It pulls so many cars of freight that come from far and near.

See the big red box car and there is an orange one too
Now see an autoveyor with cars of green and blue.

Next there are two long flat cars with tractors for the farm
You see, the wind and weather will do them little harm.

Refrigerator, tank, and flat cars go rolling down the track
All these cars have wheels of steel that go clickety-clickety-clack.

Look now at the very end a red caboose I see
And there is the friendly brakeman waving back at me.

NOTE: Use model railroad cars or pictures to illustrate the poem. If pictures are found they
could be mounted on colored construction paper and put in a three-ring notebook to
make a picture story.

Stories

(To read, read-tell, or tell. See Book Center for complete list.)

** *One Is the Engine,* Meeks
*** *Two Little Trains,* Brown
** *Big Book of Real Trains,* Zaffo (Read to p. 25 and count the cars as they are added on
the bottom edge of each page.)

Games

(See Games, pp. 50–59, and Teacher-Made Games in this guide for directions.)

1. Look and See
2. Reach and Feel
3. Can You Remember?
4. Who Am I?
5. How Many?
6. Alike, Different, and the Same

Routine Times

1. At pickup time, if you have a large ride-on train, encourage children to put appropriate-sized articles on the train as baggage or freight to be transported back to the shelves.
2. While riding or walking to and from the center look for trains and railroad crossings.
3. At snack or mealtime talk about those foods that may have come to your city by train and which kind of car would have been used, such as milk, tank car; fruits and vegetables, refrigerator car; packaged foods, box cars.
4. Suggest "Let's go to the dining car for snack or lunch." Put up a sign over the door: "Dining Car."
5. At rest time you might pretend that children's mats or cots are berths on a sleeping car and wake them up at the appropriate time by acting as a porter.
6. Transitions: announce you are making up a train to go (name a place). Call names of children in the order they are to be connected to the engine (leader). Hands can be placed on shoulders of person in front of each child or any way you or the children may choose for staying connected. Destination may be the Art Center, Discovery Center, and so on.

Large Muscle Activities

1. If a suitable surface exists, and weather permits, take the ride-on train outside. Make or buy a railroad crossing sign and set up a crossing with chalk-drawn tracks for the train and roads for the wheel toys.
2. Make a train with children as the cars (like Follow the Leader). Use a wooden whistle for sound effects. Have the engineer decide where the train is going to go and ask the children to follow. It could have stops at the swings, slide, sand box, water table. Passengers may get on and off at each stop. (See Rhythms and Singing Games.)
3. Combine a steering wheel and packing boxes or a dial panel for outdoor train play. (See p. 478.)

Extended Experiences

1. Visit a railroad station: time your visit to coincide with the arrival or departure of a freight or passenger train. Let the children explore the station and see what it contains. Point out the waiting room, ticket agent, snack bar or restaurant, rest rooms, and magazine stand. Let the children watch someone buying a ticket, checking baggage, or boarding a train. By calling the station agent in advance you may arrange for the children to board a train, caboose, or locomotive.

2. Take a train ride: unfortunately most local passenger train service has been discontinued, but if short trips are still available in your city try to take a train trip. Commuter and subway trains are also possibilities.
3. Some steam engine runs and narrow gauge railroads are maintained for recreational or historical purposes. You might also consider these as special excursion opportunities.
4. Ride a miniature train or monorail train in a nearby park or recreational area.
5. Inquire if a roundhouse with turntable is available in your area and if the children could watch it operate.

   CAUTION: Locomotives are very noisy when they are running, and very big. Children may become frightened by them. Adult supervision on these trips should be one adult to two children, one for each hand!

6. Take a small group of mature children who show an avid interest in trains to visit the home of a model railroader to see an H-O gauge layout. The model railroader can demonstrate how a freight or passenger train is made up, how a slower train is put on a siding to allow a faster train to pass, and how "Casey Jones'" accident occurred.
7. If parents of some of the children work for a railroad you might invite them to come and talk about their jobs. If possible, they should wear what their job requires and bring something of interest that is related to their job to show the children.

teacher resources

Books and Periodicals

Paperbacks are available on request by writing School and College Service, Association of American Railroads (AAR), American Railroads Building, Washington, D.C. 20036.
1. A list of train and engine books for children
2. Bibliography of railroad literature
3. Railroad film directory: this directory has the addresses and lists of materials available from major railroad companies
4. Teaching Aids on Railroad Transportation: a catalog
5. Tommy and Tess Take a Train Trip: available in quantities that you could give to the children to take home. It is a coloring book for the primary grades and a picture book for the younger child
6. Quiz Junior: Railroad Questions and Answers

Pictures and Displays

(See p. 79 for addresses of firms listed.)

1. Pictures of trains, stations, crossings, and train personnel from your own personal file
2. Most railroad companies put out calendars which are available on request. They usually have large pictures of trains on them.

3. Make a table display using model railroad trains. If possible have a passenger train, freight train, work train, trolley, and subway train. Include timetables and brochures with the display. Train crew hat, conductor's hat, rail spike, tickets, and lantern may be obtainable.
4. The items listed in No. 3 may be used for a centerpiece at snack or mealtime to encourage conversation about trains.
5. Teaching Aids on Railroad Transportation available free from AAR:
   a. Forty Railroad Pictures (Teacher's Kit)
   b. Classroom Wall Charts: L-1, L-2, and L-3
   c. Small Train Display Streamer
   d. Freight Train Cut-out
6. Freight Trains: Transportation Packet (David C. Cook)

Community Resources

1. Railroad companies serving your city: ask for timetables, calendars, brochures.
2. Travel agents: ask for posters, brochures, and schedules.
3. National Railway Historical Society: ask your local chamber of commerce if a chapter exists in your community. Sometimes a historical museum or model railroad layout is maintained from which you may borrow items for a table display. Members take frequent trips by rail and may have slides to share.
4. National Model Railroad Association: see No. 3.
5. Hobby Center: train catalogs would be a good source of pictures for readiness materials. The manager may also give you the name of some model railroaders who would be willing to lend or demonstrate model trains.

Goin' Down the Track

An Accompaniment for Dramatic Play

JoAnne Deal Hicks

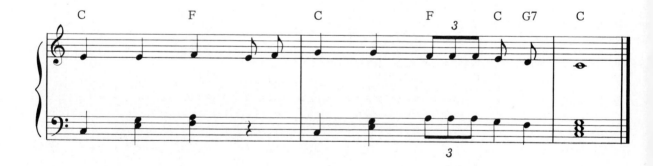

30 Road Transportation

basic understandings

(concepts children can grasp from this subject)

NOTE: The word "car" in the following statements is used to represent all road vehicles. If your group interest at the moment is "trucks" then use only that term in the basic statement instead of car. When car is used it would then refer only to automobiles.

- Cars (and trucks, buses, campers) are machines that we drive on roads (or the ground) to get people or things from one place to another.
- The person who steers a car is known as the driver and those who ride with him/her are known as passengers.
- Cars are made in different shapes, sizes, and colors.
- Cars have motors which are run by gasoline, diesel fuel, or batteries.
- Most families own a car which they use to go many places, such as to drive to and from work, school, shopping centers, the doctor, the laundry or dry cleaners, to visit friends or relatives, or to take trips to see interesting things.
- Cars are usually parked in garages or carports; buses and trucks are parked in large buildings known as barns.
- Cars get gasoline, oil, water, and air at a service station (gasoline station or filling station). Trucks get diesel fuel or gas at a truck stop.
- Cars are repaired in garages, body shops, and some service stations.
- Cars can be washed automatically in a car wash.
- Cars have safety belts and door locks to help keep us safely inside.
- The driver must pay attention to his/her driving and the passengers must be considerate (helpful) by sitting and talking quietly.
- A driver has to take special tests to get a driver's license.
- A driver must obey (follow) certain traffic rules or else he/she may get a ticket from a law enforcement officer and have to pay a fine (money) or have his/her driver's license taken away.

- Road signs, traffic lights, and safety officers help drivers drive safely.
- When we travel by car we can eat
  a. by taking a sack lunch and eating it in the car as we ride.
  b. by taking a picnic lunch and stopping at a roadside area.
  c. by stopping at a restaurant (diner, café) and buying a meal (food).
- When we travel by car we can sleep
  a. as we ride in the car because some models have reclining seats (not the driver's).
  b. at a roadside rest or campground and sleep in the car, a camper, a house trailer, or pitch a tent.
  c. by stopping and getting a room in a hotel or a motel.
- If a car has a wreck (accident) it is towed to the garage by a wrecker.
- There are different kinds of cars: sedan, convertible, station wagon, sports car, dragster, jeep, racing car, and van.
- Some cars are built and equipped to help do special jobs:
  a. Police cars have sirens and two-way radios. They are driven by patrol officers.
  b. Fire engines are red, yellow, or white and carry ladders, hoses, and fire fighters to fires.
  c. Ambulances are usually white and have sirens. They are equipped with first aid equipment and stretchers. They carry people who are sick or hurt to the hospital.
  d. Taxis have meters and two-way radios. People can pay the driver to take them where they wish to go.
- Trucks are specially built to carry things, animals, or people, for example, dump, pickup, fire equipment, moving van, concrete mixer, trash hauler, milk, mail, livestock, and gasoline.
- There are different kinds of buses: school, city, and transcontinental.
- Many cars can tow things: trailers, campers, boats, horse van, or other cars.
- A ferryboat carries cars and people across a river.
- Tunnels are dug under rivers and through mountains for cars.
- Bridges are built so cars can get across rivers and deep valleys.
- Sometimes drivers have to pay a toll (money) to drive on some roads, cross some bridges, or drive through some tunnels.
- Other names for a road are street, avenue, boulevard, drive, court, lane, freeway, thruway, expressway, turnpike, and highway.
- There are two-wheeled vehicles, such as bicycles, motor-bikes, and motorcycles.
- Some drivers like to enter car races, such as drag racing, the Indianapolis 500, stock car racing, or one of the Grand Prix races in Europe.

Additional Facts the Teacher Should Know

This transportation guide deals with those transportation machines which use roads (or the ground) as the surface on which they travel. There are many different kinds of cars, trucks, and buses being designed and manufactured today. They come in varying sizes, shapes, and colors. Most cars go by a brand name, such as Ford, Chevrolet, Oldsmobile, or Buick, which identifies its manufacturer. Each company produces several different models of cars and gives them names which indicate they are as fast and sleek as their animal namesakes—"Impala," "Jaguar," and "Mustang" or are as luxurious and expensive as implied by "Continental," "Riviera," and "LTD," or are exceptionally rugged Travel-Alls, "Ranchero," and "Bronco."

Two-wheeled vehicles which can be driven on roads are powered both by pedaling and by gasoline motor. All bicycles, except those with training wheels, can be ridden in the streets and bikers must follow the same rules that automobile drivers must follow. Most communities have a license requirement for two-wheeled vehicles. In addition, there is a national law requiring all motorcyclists to wear helmets while riding. Most bicycles are referred to as 20″, 24″, 26″, or 28″, referring to the diameter of the wheels. Some bikes have hand-powered brakes and special gear mechanisms which allow the driver to pedal at various speeds with less effort. If two-wheeled vehicles are driven at night they must have headlights and rear reflectors.

There are many different kinds of cars and trucks:
Familiarize yourself with them to identify them correctly for the children.

Sedans carry one to six people and may have two or four doors. Most cars have a trunk in the back where a spare tire is stored under the floor and suitcases or other luggage can be stored. Most cars have heaters, radios, clocks, air conditioning, and seat belts. Some seats recline or have head rests.

Coupe is a shorter, more compact car than a sedan. It may seat two to four people.

Convertible is similar to a sedan or coupe but has a roof which folds back or can be removed.

Station wagon is similar to a sedan but is longer, with a large floor area instead of a trunk for carrying things. Usually there is a luggage rack on the roof.

Sports car is a sedan or coupe with bucket seats (contoured), extra chrome trim, sidewall or mag wheels, and special custom paint jobs.

Racing car is a small one-seat car which is designed to go very fast for a long period of time.

Dragster is a small car designed to go very fast for a short distance from a standstill.

Jeep is an open car without sides or top; it is used primarily by the army for driving over open country and rough roads.

Van is larger than a sedan but smaller than a bus. It may have three or four rows of seats and carry up to twelve people. Vans can travel at a maximum speed of 50 to 60 miles per hour.

Taxi is a sedan with a time meter and a two-way radio which is used for transporting people for a set fee based on actual mileage.

Ambulance is specially designed to transport sick or injured persons. A stretcher, cot, or rolling table can be put into the back section. It has emergency medical equipment that varies, depending on the training of the attendant who rides with the patient. It is usually painted white and has a red cross on it. A siren and flashing red light warn of its coming.

Limousine is a long comfortable sedan used for transporting up to nine people to and from rail and air terminals. Some businesses provide free limousine service for their customers.

Police car (patrol car) is a sedan with a siren, a flashing light, and a two-way radio.

There are many different kinds of trucks used for the transportation of goods and people. The part of the truck that the driver sits in is known as the cab. The cab and the motor are usually mounted over the front wheels of the truck. Smaller trucks are molded onto a single frame like an automobile but most larger trucks are in two or more sections. The part that pulls is called the "tractor" and the section that is being hauled is called the "trailer." A flat bed trailer is a platform on wheels. Containerized freight can be lifted onto it using a crane, while some machines, like tractors and other farm equipment, can be driven up on ramps. Cylindrical or oval-shaped trailers are called tank trailers and rectangular, enclosed trailers are vans. Most trucks are powered by gasoline or diesel fuel. Those burning diesel fuel can be recognized by the vent pipe behind the cab.

Pickup truck is a small truck with an open bed with short sides for carrying small equipment, tools, and other supplies.

Dump truck is larger than a pickup and has higher sides. It is built with a hydraulic lift so the bed can be tilted to allow the contents to be slid out through the hinged tail gate or a special opening. It is used to haul dirt, coal, and gravel.

Tank truck is an oval trailer used to carry liquids, such as milk, chemicals, oil, or fuel.

Moving vans come in various sizes and are large, enclosed rectangular trailers used for moving household goods or office equipment. Many are padded and carry extra pads for protecting furniture while it is being moved. Dollies (wheeled platforms with handles) are used to help move heavier pieces to and from the truck. There is a ramp from the street up to the bed of the truck. Some vans have a tail gate that can be raised and lowered like an elevator for lifting heavy pieces onto the truck.

Refuse or sanitation truck is used for carrying trash and garbage to a city dump. Some have special devices for compressing trash so it will take up less space. In some cities people who work with these trucks are called "trash haulers" or "sanitation engineers."

Cement mixer is a specially built truck that has a round mixer tank which turns and mixes sand, gravel, and concrete. A tank holds water which is added as needed. The cement runs down a chute from the mixer tank.

Freight trailer has a rectangular van used for carrying food, clothes, equipment, tools, and manufactured goods.

Automobile carrier is designed to carry cars. The cars are driven on and off the trailer on tracks called "skids."

Livestock truck is a rectangular-shaped trailer with air spaces between the slats for transporting cattle, horses, pigs, chickens, and other animals.

Gooseneck trailer is a long flat trailer for carrying very heavy equipment like steam shovels or houses. The front of the trailer reaches over the wheels behind the cab and resembles the neck of a goose.

Fire truck carries ladders, hoses, fire fighters, and equipment to fight fires. There are several different kinds of fire trucks. A pumper truck carries hoses and pumps water for other fire trucks. A hook and ladder truck has specially designed ladders for reaching the tops of tall buildings. Fire trucks used at airports carry tanks of water and foam dispensers. Country fire trucks also carry their own water and are built to drive over fields and rough roads as well.

Canteen truck is designed like a small kitchen for the preparation of carry-out types of foods. Some are used to feed workers involved with emergencies or jobs in remote areas. Others are used as food-vending businesses.

Delivery truck is a small, enclosed truck used to deliver commercial products to homes; such trucks are operated by bakeries, florists, druggists, department stores, dry cleaners.

Milk truck is a rectangular-shaped truck with refrigeration for carrying milk, ice cream, and other dairy products to stores and peoples' homes. There is also an oval-shaped truck used to transport milk to pasteurization plants.

Mail truck is a truck used by the post office to transport mail and packages. Smaller trucks are used for picking up mail from deposit boxes or taking relays to storage boxes. Relays are sorted letters which have been arranged by mail carriers for delivery to houses or businesses. Larger mail trucks are used for carrying sacks of mail or packages to other cities or distribution points.

Mailster is a small, motorized, three-wheel unit for delivering mail to houses.

Camper is a small trailer designed with windows; it is equipped for home living.

There are many different kinds of buses:

School or church bus (usually painted yellow) is a rectangular-shaped vehicle that has a center aisle with eighteen to twenty seats, one behind each other on either side; it is used to transport people to and from school or churches or on educational trips. The gasoline engine of a school bus is located in the front.

Dreamliner or city bus is a vehicle that carries people from one part of the city to another. Such buses stop at special places called "bus stops." Sometimes there are small, roofed structures and/or seats where passengers may wait. These buses have two doors that open in accordion fashion. One is designated for passengers to enter and the other for them to exit. Passengers usually enter by a front door where there is a coin box by the driver's seat for depositing the fare. Some city buses sell tokens which can be used to ride the bus. These buses have butane motors in the rear of the bus. Usually they are air conditioned.

Transcontinental bus is sometimes called a "scenic cruiser." These buses are air conditioned and frequently have two levels of seats and domed windows for viewing scenery as they travel from one city to another. They usually have diesel engines in the rear and there is usually a section under the seats to which access (for storing passengers' luggage) is gained from hinged doors on the outside of the bus. There are also racks over the seats for passengers to put small suitcases and other luggage carried by hand. Many transcontinental buses have toilet facilities and can provide snacks or meals for passengers. The buses take on or discharge passengers at a bus station or terminal, which has a ticket agent who sells tickets and makes bus reservations. There is also a rest room, lounge, snack bar or restaurant, and magazine stand for passengers to use while waiting for buses or to be used as rest stops by passengers who are traveling in buses that do not have toilet facilities or meal service.

There are many people who work with cars, trucks, and buses:

Dealer or salesperson sets up a showroom or sells cars.

Body worker pounds out dents and repaints.

Wrecker or junker tears apart old cars and salvages reusable parts.

Parts dealer sells parts.

Tire dealer sells tires and repairs them.

Hauler moves cars from factory to dealer.

Factory worker assembles cars.

Clerk sells licenses and issues licenses for drivers.

Service station attendant sells gasoline, oil, and batteries and washes windshields. Some do repair work, wash and wax cars, lubricate, change oil, or repair a tire.

Safety officer directs traffic and patrols streets to see that drivers are following rules. He or she can issue tickets to drivers who break rules.

Truck driver is a person hired to drive a truck. Some drivers have special training for their jobs, such as plumbers, telephone linemen, movers, fire fighters, and mail carriers.

Bus driver is the person who drives a bus. He/she sometimes issues tickets and collects money from customers. Most of these drivers have taken first aid training.

Chauffeur is a person who is hired to be a driver. Some schools, businesses, and private homes hire chauffeurs. All drivers who transport people around for pay, such as taxi drivers, bus drivers, and ambulance drivers, must have a chauffeur's license.

Parking attendant parks cars and supervises them by the hour, day, or week for a fee.

Toll booth attendant collects tolls from drivers.

The various parts of the automobile are familiar to most people and need not be defined. It is important that you use the correct name for the various vehicles and their parts when talking to children even though you do not teach definitions. The functions of the dashboard, steering wheel, brake pedal, accelerator, windshield, windshield wipers, tires, and fenders are common knowledge. The speedometer tells how fast the vehicle is going and the odometer tells how far the car has been driven. If you are uncertain what the various parts are, ask a service station attendant or licensed driver to tell you.

Many books, records, songs, fingerplays, and poems still reflect the older titles for the community helpers now called mail carrier, milk carrier, fire fighter, and safety officer. No need to discard them; simply substitute the correct name as you use the material with the children. You may wish to make edited notes directly in your book. (See Families at Work guide for complete helper list.)

Methods Most Adaptable for Introducing This Subject to Children

- A child or one of the teachers at the center shares his or her experience of a trip taken by bus or car.
- Read a story about cars, trucks, or buses.
- Put up pictures of cars, trucks, or buses, or make a display of models of all kinds of road transportation vehicles.
- Visitor: if one of the children's parents drives a taxi, mailster, bus, or other vehicle have him or her visit the Center and tell about the job.

Vocabulary

traffic	car wash	parking lot	driver	meter
light	restaurant	gas	speed	steer
road sign	motel, hotel	oil	ticket	bridge
wreck	service station	air	license	tunnel
wrecker	safety officer	tow	race	garage
toll booth	fire fighter	key	haul	ferry
attendant	mail carrier	drive	park	taxi

kinds of cars, trucks, and buses   parts of cars

names of roads

learning centers

Discovery Center

1. Set up a display table with scale model cars, trucks, and buses. Help children understand that each vehicle is specifically designed to do a special job of carrying people or things from one place to another.
2. Show maps of your city, your state, and the United States. Talk about how different maps are used by drivers. Discuss different ways to ride around on the roads in your city, your state, and the country. Talk about how the children got to the Center: by car (kind), taxi, bus, van, or truck.
3. If the playground or windows in the Center overlook a busy street which the children can view easily, in safety, talk about the different kinds of vehicles that use the road. If the Center gets special mail or package deliveries, suggest this activity for a time when they are made.
4. Help children discover that every vehicle that drives on the road must have a license. Trucks that drive in many states have several. Start a collection of license plates from all the states and display them so that children can see the similarities and differences.

They sometimes have mottos, emblems, or state nicknames on them. Talk about the special features of your state's plates.

5. On a table display a driver's license, license plate from your county, road maps of your city and state, a model of a car, station wagon, camper, and house trailer, and brochures of parks or well-known land marks in or near your community. Encourage conversation about how families use their cars for fun and pleasure.

6. Use of brakes: use several blocks and two boards to make a little hill and a steep hill. Provide cars for the children to roll down the hills. Which car goes faster? Which driver would need to use the brakes the most?

Dramatic Play Centers

Home-Living Center

1. Make bus schedules and travel brochures available so a trip by bus or car can be planned. Suitcases and money in purses will increase the amount of travel play.
2. If one of the children volunteers to pretend sickness, suggest taking a car or taxi to the doctor's office or, if an emergency, call an ambulance. A wagon or castored platform makes a good ambulance.
3. Fill a lunch pail for an auto mechanic, a truck driver, or a bus driver to take to work.
4. A box of tools should be available that an auto mechanic might take to work or to fix the family car. This could be a trike if allowed indoors or a ride-on truck or car.
5. Set out hats for the different kinds of helpers who use vehicles.

Block-Building Center

1. Unit blocks: feature road accessories, such as scaled cars, people, and road signs, to encourage building of roads and transportation play. Have cans of small materials, such as buttons, pebbles, and twigs, for children to use as freight.
2. Encourage children with some road-building experience to construct bridges, tunnels, toll booths, garages, or bus stations.
3. Suggest with the aid of pictures and conversation that those with many road-building experiences may wish to make a network of roads, several buildings (restaurants, motels, a bus station, a bus barn, traffic signals, bridges, and tunnels), or a whole city. This kind of activity may last over several days if structures and roads can remain standing from day to day.
4. Occasionally when the children name a structure they have built you may wish to fasten a sign to it: "Mary's Motel" or "Steve's Service Station."
5. Gasoline pumps of the correct scale for use with unit blocks are commercially available or you can make your own with scraps of wood and paint, using plastic clothesline or rope for gas hose.
6. The Road Transportation Fleets (Community Playthings) line of toys is excellent.
7. Hollow blocks: build roads for larger trucks and cars by using blocks and ramps. Encourage the road-builders to make a garage, station, or parking lot. A gasoline pump for use with hollow blocks could be made from wood and garden hose. A less durable pump can be made from the hard cylindrical core around which newsprint is rolled. Two of these cylinders set in a large wooden box or sturdy carton with rope or garden hose attached make very usable gas pumps. Children can help paint them with water base paint. Two tall, corrugated boxes may be weighted by placing rocks in the bottom, painting them, and attaching rope or garden hose to make pumps. These are only sturdy enough for short-term use.

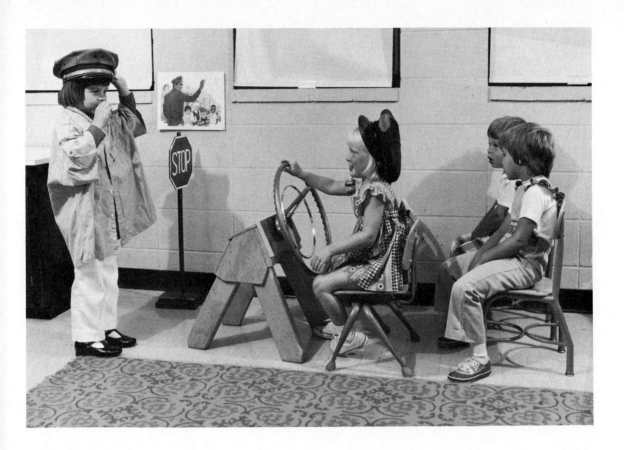

8. Miniature Traffic Signs: 10 signs, 7¼" tall; also Traffic Signs and Symbols, 6 in each set, 30" tall (Practical Drawing Co.)

Other Dramatic Play Centers

1. A bus can be made by lining up two rows of chairs with an aisle between. A commercial or hand-made steering wheel or dial panel (see p. 478) may be added for the driver to use. (See illustration above.)
2. A car or taxi can be made by putting two rows of three chairs one behind the other. The steering wheel or dial panel should be placed in front of the driver (left front seat). Add traffic signs to this dramatic play.
3. Set up a post office, using a multiplay screen or hollow blocks and boards. Provide a cash register or box, play money, postal scales, and sheets of stamps, such as Christmas Seals, Easter Seals, Wildlife stamps, or Boystown stamps. Shoeboxes or paper sacks may be used for sorting bins. A date stamp and ink pad may be used for canceling letters and a shoulderbag purse makes a good mailbag (or one could be made from a large grocery sack). (See Basic Resources, p. 22.) Paint tall, rectangular cardboard boxes red, white, and blue to resemble mailboxes (letter drops). Use old junk mail for letters. Provide mail carrier with a hat (see pattern, p. 496) and let him or her pick up the mail at the letter drop in a wagon or on a ride-on truck. Take mail to the post office for sorting and canceling. Send a Special Delivery letter or package to the Home-Living Center.
4. Encourage playing fire fighters by providing hats (see pattern, p. 496), ladders, and discarded garden hoses. A bicycle handle grip makes a good nozzle for the hose. A wagon or long, sturdy cardboard box would make a good fire engine. If you have a ladder box or climbing house children could pretend that it is the building that is on fire (the cleated ladders can safely be rested on the rungs for climbing).

5. Obtain discarded hats and uniform shirts from safety officers, bus and taxi drivers, or highway patrol officers. Less durable hats can be made of construction paper. (See patterns below.)

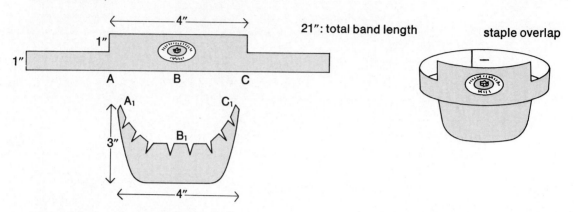

Letter Carrier or Conductor's Hat

Using blue construction paper, cut out a rectangle 21″ long and 2″ deep. As shown in diagram, top left, cut away 8½″ × 1″ at each side to leave peak 4″ × 2″ at center of hat. Notch visor as indicated in diagram, bottom left. Staple ends of headband together. Glue visor to band.

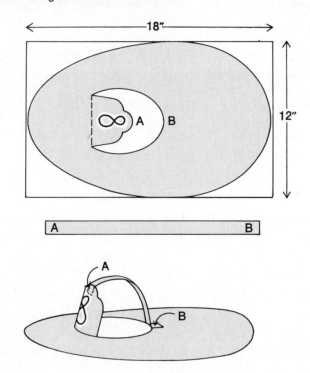

Firefighter's Hat

Cut hat shape out of a 12″ × 18″ piece of red construction paper according to illustration. Cut out the unshaded area for child's head. Cut strip A–B to define the crown of the hat. Staple A to the back of the flip-up (marked with the number 8) and B to the middle of the back opening. (See arrows.)

6. If adequate outdoor play space is available you might consider obtaining a small car (such as a Volkswagen) for the children to use. The doors may be removed permanently to avoid bruised fingers and other accidents. The upholstery should be removed so rats or mice do not nest in it, and all glass windows must be removed for safety.

NOTE: See Large Muscle Activities for additional ideas.

Learning, Language, and Readiness Materials Center

Commercially made games and materials for use at a table or on a mat:

(See Basic Resources, p. 79, for manufacturers' addresses.)

1. Signs and Symbols: flash cards (Milton Bradley)
2. Playskool Plaques: Schoolbus, 15 pcs.; Family Drive, 14 pcs.; Fire Truck, 15 pcs.; Camping, 11 pcs.
3. Lauri Crepe Foam Puzzles: Car; Truck
4. Active Play Puzzles: Traffic, 14 pcs.; Family Drive, 14 pcs. (Childcraft)
5. Judy Transportation Puzzles: Policeman, 12 pcs.; School Crossing Guard, 13 pcs.; Street Repairman, 11 pcs.; Fire Engine, 14 pcs.; Car, 11 pcs.; Diesel Truck, 11 pcs.; School Bus, 12 pcs.; City Bus, 13 pcs.; Delivery Truck, 12 pcs.; Transportation, 6 pcs.
6. Garage: a Stand-Up Puzzle, 18 pcs. (Childcraft)
7. Ideal Tell-a-Story: City Life
8. Judy See-Quees: Helping the Fire Fighters, Riding the Bus, 6 pcs. each
9. Directionality Form Boards: Cars, Trucks
10. ETA Puzzle Blocks: Automobiles
11. Landscape Peg Set (Playskool)
12. Guidance Town USA (Child Guidance)
13. Playskool Village
14. The Community: flannelboard set (Instructo)
15. Community Helpers/Workers (Instructo Flannelboard Aids)
16. Safety on Streets and Sidewalks (Instructo Flannelboard Aids)

Teacher-made games and materials for use at a table or on a mat:

NOTE: For detailed description of Games, see pp. 50–59.

1. Look and See: use scale models of a car, truck, taxi, bus, and camper.
2. Reach and Feel: use small, sturdy models of a station wagon, tank truck, pickup truck, and sedan.
3. Can You Remember?: use car, taxi, and pictures models of various drivers, such as safety officer, cab driver, bus driver, and milk carrier.
4. How Many?
   a. How many ways can you get to school using machines that drive on the roads?
   b. How many wheels does a bicycle have? a car? a bus? Supply models of these vehicles so children can count rationally.
   c. How many ways can a car get across a river? (bridge, tunnel, ferry)
5. Who Am I?: describe drivers of various vehicles, such as: "I drive a truck that carries milk to peoples' houses; who am I?"
6. Match-Them: make card sets of two each of different kinds of cars, trucks, and buses and two each of the drivers, such as taxi drivers, bus drivers, safety officers, and trash haulers. Mix the pairs up and have children find the two pairs that match.
7. Grouping and Sorting by Association: use the cards made in No. 6 and group them as cars, trucks, or drivers. Or have children match a driver with the kind of vehicle he/she drives. Suit the number of pairs offered to the ability of the child or group.
8. Alike, Different, and the Same: use the sets of cards made in No. 6.
9. Color, Shape, Size, and Number: at every opportunity when observing real road transportation vehicles or when using scale models talk about color, shape, size, and number, for example, "See the big truck." "What color is the car?" "The cylindrical tank truck carries gas."

Art Center

** 1. Pasting: provide the children with colored construction paper and precut rectangles, squares, and circles of various sizes and let the children make a design with them. Perhaps some will discover they can make trucks or wagons.

*** 2. At the woodworking bench set out wheels with various-sized discs of wood cut from dowels, bottle caps, or plastic lids and precut shapes of soft wood that children might use to make a transportation machine.

> **CAUTION:** Do not direct children as to what they should make, but instead offer assistance as needed to help them make what they have in mind. Shapes cut from colored plastic soap bottles (heat in hot water before cutting with scissors or use an Exacto knife) make colorful bumpers and stripes that are easily punctured by nails.

Other Activities in This Center Using Art Media:

** 1. If gasoline pumps have been made as suggested in Dramatic Play Center the children can help paint them with water base paint as it washes off hands and brushes!

Book Center

* Alexander, Anne. *ABC of Cars and Trucks.* Garden City, N.Y.: Doubleday, 1971.
*** Baker, Eugene. *I Want to Be a Taxi Driver.* Chicago, Ill.: Childrens Press, 1969.
*** Barr, Jene. *Mr. Zip and the U.S. Mail.* Chicago, Ill.: Albert Whitman, 1964.
* Brown, Margaret Wise. *The Little Fireman.* Reading, Mass.: Addison-Wesley, 1952.
* Cameron, Elizabeth. *The Big Book of Real Trucks.* New York: Grosset & Dunlap, 1970.
** Hitte, Katheryn. *A Letter for Cathy.* Nashville, Tenn.: Abingdon Press, 1953.
** Holl, Adelaide. *ABC of Cars, Trucks, and Machines.* New York: McGraw-Hill, 1970.
** Keats, Ezra Jack. *A Letter to Amy.* New York: Harper & Row, 1968.
* Kessler, Ethel and Leonard Kessler. *Big Red Bus.* Garden City, N.Y.: Doubleday, 1964.
* Lenski, Lois. *Policeman Small.* New York: Henry Z. Walck, 1946.
** ———. *The Little Fire Engine.* New York: Henry Z. Walck, 1946.
* MacDonald, Golden. *Red Light, Green Light.* Garden City, N.Y.: Doubleday, 1944.
**** Miner, Irene. *The True Book of Our Post Office.* Chicago, Ill.: Childrens Press, 1955.
*** Oppenheim, Joanne. *Have You Seen Roads?* Reading, Mass.: Addison-Wesley, 1969.
**** Penick, Ib. *The Pop-up Book of Trucks.* New York: Random House, 1974.
* Scarry, Richard. *The Great Big Car and Truck Book.* New York: Western Publishing, 1951.
** ———. *Cars and Trucks and Things That Go.* New York: Western Publishing, 1974.
* Shuttlesworth, Dorothy. *ABC of Busses.* Garden City, N.Y.: Doubleday, 1965.
* Zaffo, George. *The Great Big Book of Real Fire Engines.* New York: Grosset & Dunlap, 1958.

> **NOTE:** Look in the library for books by Carla Greene about people who want to be drivers of different kinds of cars and trucks.

planning for grouptime

NOTE: All music, fingerplays, poems, stories, and games listed here may be used at other times during the session as appropriate. See Core Library, Basic Resources, p. 76, for publishers and addresses. Addresses for sources of records will be found on p. 81. In parodies, hyphenated words match the music notes of the tune used.

Music

Songs

FROM original songs in this book by JoAnne Deal Hicks
** "Ways I Can Move," p. 458   *** "Color Fun," p. 599, verse 3
** "Let's Take a Ride," p. 470

FROM *Wake Up and Sing*, Landeck and Crook
* "Riding in My Car," p. 66

FROM *Songs for Early Childhood*, Westminster Press
** "Driving Along the Highway," p. 80 (can also adapt to air and rail transportation)

FROM *Music Resource Book*, Lutheran Church Press
* "The Wheels on the Bus," p. 50 (you could also add: The horn on the bus goes beep, beep, beep; wipers on the bus go swish, swish, swish; money on the bus goes clink, clink, clink; people on the bus go bump; babies go "wah"; driver says "please move back"; bell on the bus goes ding; buzzer goes buzz; brakes go rumph; and doors go shush.)

WATCHING TRAFFIC (a parody)
(tune: "Frère Jacques")
Adaptation by Bonnie Flemming (verse 1: Romona Ware)

Watch the cars go, watch the cars go,
Whiz-zing by, whiz-zing by.
Beep, beep, beep, beep, beep, beep,
Beep, beep, beep, beep, beep, beep,
That's like mine! That's like mine!

Watch the bus go   (REPEAT)
Roll-ing by   (REPEAT)
Stop for all the peo-ple   (REPEAT)
Get on board!   (REPEAT)

See the trucks go, see the trucks go
Down the street, down the street.
Gas and oil and milk trucks,
Mail and trash and dump trucks,
On their way, on their way.

THE FIRE FIGHTER (a parody)
 (tune: "The More We Get Together")
 Adaptation by Bonnie Flemming

Oh, hear the warn-ing si-ren
The si-ren, the si-ren
Oh, hear the warn-ing siren;
Get out of the way!

Oh, see the big red pump-er
The pump-er, the pump-er
Oh, see the big red pump-er
Go off to the fire!

Oh, see the brave fire fighters
Fire fight-ers, fire fight-ers
Oh, see the brave fire fighters
Put out the big fire!

Records

"Build Me a House"/"Silly Will"/**Milkman's Journey**" (Young People's Records [YPR], 33⅓ RPM)
"**Little Fireman**"/"Little Cowboy"/"Little Hero" (YPR, 33⅓ RPM)
"**Men Who Come to Our House**"/"**Let's Be Firemen**"/"**Let's Be Policemen**" (YPR, 33⅓ RPM)

NOTE: The above records are also available singly on 10-inch 78 RPM records on the Children's Record Guild label.

"Let's Take the Bus" (Golden Record, 33⅓ RPM)
"**Songs of Safety**"/"Manners Can Be Fun" (Vocalion, 33⅓ RPM)
"The Car Goes Beep Beep," *Developing Everyday Skills* (Kimbo, 33⅓ RPM)

Rhythms and Singing Games

A very fast chromatic scale (every black and white note) can be played on the piano and children may pretend to be firetrucks racing to the scene of a fire. To simulate a fire alarm, see p. 42.

The rapid repetition of two notes on the piano (C, D, C, D, C, D) simulates the sound of a car motor. This may be played while the children pretend to drive their cars around the room. Cars can run out of gas as the music slows down or get a flat tire when the music stops altogether.

Fingerplays and Poems

FROM *Very Young Verses*, Geismer and Suter
"About Going Places," pp. 84, 85, 86, 93–95

FROM *Let's Do Fingerplays*, Grayson
"The Windshield Wipers," p. 24   "Driving Down the Street," p. 25
"Auto Auto," p. 24   "The Bus," p. 25

WINDSHIELD WIPER

I'm a windshield wiper   (BEND ARM AT ELBOW WITH FINGERS POINTING UP)
This is how I go   (MOVE ARM TO LEFT AND RIGHT, PIVOTING AT ELBOW)
Back and forth, back and forth   (CONTINUE BACK AND FORTH MOTION)
In the rain and snow   (CONTINUE BACK AND FORTH MOTION)

Stories

(To read, read-tell, or tell. See Book Center for complete list.)

* *ABC of Cars and Trucks,* Alexander
* *Red Light, Green Light,* MacDonald
* *The Little Fireman,* Brown
* *The Great Big Car and Truck Book,* Scarry
* *The Great Big Book of Real Fire Engines,* Zaffo
** *ABC of Cars, Trucks, and Machines,* Holl

Games

(See Games, pp. 50–59, and Teacher-Made Games in this guide for directions.)

1. Look and See
2. Can You Remember?
3. Who Am I?
4. Alike, Different, and the Same
5. Grouping and Sorting by Association
6. Reach and Feel

Routine Times

1. Use scale model cars, trucks, and buses with scale model people, animals, and road signs as a centerpiece at mealtime to encourage conversation about road transportation.
2. During snack and mealtime talk about which truck or car brought the food.
3. At pickup time have children use ride-on trucks, wagons, or castored platforms to carry toys back to shelves.
4. While walking or riding to and from the Center look for cars, trucks, and buses. Talk about how to cross a street safely when walking.
5. When riding to and from the Center talk about safety in a car or bus:
   a. Always use seat belts if they are available.
   b. Always lock the doors and do not allow children to lean against them.
   c. Talk about being considerate of and not disturbing the driver.
   d. En route talk about traffic signals and rules as you see them on the street.
6. At rest time pretend you have been traveling for a long time and have decided to stop at a motel or hotel for the night.

Large Muscle Activities

1. Encourage use of trikes, wagons, and ride-on cars and trucks as transportation machines. Provide rope or commercially available plastic-link chains so that a trike can tow a wagon.
2. Make or buy some traffic signals and road signs. Set up certain traffic patterns. Draw lines on the sidewalk with chalk or use a length of rope for a highway divider. Have a safety officer who checks on drivers and issues tickets to those who break rules. Provide the safety officer with a hat, whistle, and keys for a jail, if you have one. A driver may need to lose his/her driver's license for a time.

   CAUTION: Whistles should be washed if shared.

3. Set up a garage or service station next to the highway where drivers can get gas, oil, water, and air. Provide gasoline pumps (see Dramatic Play), oil can, water and funnel, bicycle tire pump, tool box with rubber or plastic tools (commercially available) for a mechanic, and a pail (can be empty) and rag or chamois cloth to wash windshields.
4. Set up a parking lot where trikes can be parked while driver goes shopping. Provide stiff pieces of paper as checks and money and cash register for an attendant.

5. Set up a restaurant by the highway or a roadside stand where drivers can stop for a snack or meal. Chefs can wear white aprons and hats (Patterns, p. 22) in the kitchen, while those waiting on table can wear aprons and carry trays. If possible, take tables and chairs outside or use a packing box.

Extended Experiences

1. Take a walk to a nearby mailbox (letter drop) to mail a letter(s) and to watch the mail truck arrive and the letter carrier pick up outgoing mail.

   NOTE: Time your walk to coincide with regular pickup.

2. Visit a post office to see the mail trucks unload the mail to be canceled and sorted and then loaded to go to other cities or to storage boxes in the city.
3. Visit a fire station to see where the fire fighters eat, sleep, and care for the fire engines. Find out when they wash the trucks and hoses. If the station has a pole ask for a demonstration of sliding down the pole or jumping into a net. If they have a hook and ladder ask for a demonstration of how the ladder is put up.

   CAUTION: One adult for each two children is required on this trip because if an alarm is turned in while you are visiting, the children must be kept out of the way of the fire fighters and trucks. Explain to the children in advance that the alarm is very loud so all the fire fighters can hear it.

4. Visit a grocery store to see delivery trucks bringing food to the store. Check with the store manager in advance and find out when deliveries are made in greatest number and find a safe place to stand while watching. Arrange with the store manager to allow the children to go into the storeroom afterward so they can make the association between the delivery and the items on the shelf. Of course, plan to buy something that is needed like milk or bread.
5. If delivery trucks come to the center, allow the children to watch the unloading. Perhaps the driver will allow the children a closer look inside the door of the truck.
6. Take a bus ride or visit a terminal to see arrivals and departures of buses. If you cannot take a trip make arrangements with a bus company for children to board a scenic cruiser that is temporarily idle.
7. Ride a city bus if your city has buses. Allow each child to deposit his/her own fare.
8. View a filmstrip, Junior Safety Series (David C. Cook)
9. Fathers Work, a filmstrip series (David C. Cook): (a) My Dad Is a Moving Man (b) My Dad Works in a Service Station
10. Invite a safety officer to come to the center in a patrol car. Have the officer talk about the uniform and what things are carried or worn. Show the children how one talks to the control center and how the siren and flashing light are activated.
11. If one of the children or a staff member comes to the center in a taxi, ask if the children might look inside. Ask the driver to show the children the meter and the radio.
12. Invite a mail carrier to come to the center in uniform and bring a truck or mailster so the children may have a closer look inside the door of one. Perhaps they could have a Get-Well card, invitation to parents, or a Mother's Day card for the letter carrier to take to the post office. The children might send valentines or letters to each other to be delivered to the center, or the teacher could put a letter, Christmas card, or valentine for each child in a large manila envelope and address it to the center so that all will arrive together.

13. Invite a fire fighter to bring one of the fire trucks to the center. This is especially good for younger children and for those who show fear of fire engines or fire houses. There is also no worry about an alarm being turned in, and the children are freer to explore the fire engine and view it more closely. Show the children what is worn to put out a fire and show them where the ax and tools are kept. Listen to the siren.

teacher resources

Pictures and Displays

(See p. 79 for addresses of firms listed.)

1. Transportation Packet (David C. Cook)
2. Home and Community Helpers Packet (David C. Cook)
3. School and School Helpers Packet (David C. Cook)
4. My Community Packet (David C. Cook)
5. Community Helpers (SVE Picture Story Study Prints)
6. People Who Come to My House study prints (The Child's World)
7. Put up road maps of your city, state, and the United States.

Community Resources

1. Department of public safety: an education officer can provide you with information about safety officers and help arrange a visit of one to your center.
2. Fire department: a safety director or public relations officer can provide you with information about fire fighters and help arrange a visit to a fire station or for a fire fighter to visit the center.
3. Post office: a public relations director will help explain the workings of the post office and arrange for a mail carrier to visit your center or help arrange a visit to the post office. Many post offices do not allow children under six inside the post office working area.
4. Bus company: a public relations director will help arrange a bus trip or tour of a terminal and a bus.
5. Trucking firms in your community may cooperate in letting the children have a closer look at the trucks they use. They may have calendars with pictures of trucks on them.

31 Water Transportation

basic understandings

(concepts children can grasp from this subject)

- People or things can be carried across (through) the water in a boat or in a ship.
- The boat or the ship is made to float on the water.
- The boat or the ship moves through the water in different ways:
  - a. wind blowing the sails
  - b. people paddling, rowing, or poling
  - c. motors or engines
- There are many different kinds of boats: rowboat, canoe, motorboat, lifeboat, sailboat, fishing boat (trawler), ferry boat, houseboat, and tugboat.
- There are many different kinds of ships: ocean liners, cargo ships, tankers, cabin cruisers, warships, submarines, and sailing ships (long ago).
- People can cross the ocean in passenger ships (steamships or luxury liners) that have many stores and service personnel:
  - a. each passenger has his/her own room as in a hotel or a motel.
  - b. the passengers eat in a dining room as in a restaurant.
  - c. there are places to buy clothes, food, flowers, shoes, and medicine.
  - d. the ship has a doctor, nurse, dentist, and hospital (infirmary).
  - e. it has a dry cleaner, laundry, barber shop, and beauty parlor.
  - f. it has a ballroom, theater (movies), game rooms, lounges, and one or more swimming pools.
- The captain and the crew help the boat or the ship to move through the water.
- A dock or a pier is a platform where people can get on or off a ship.
- People get from the dock to the ship by walking up a ramp (gangplank) or steps.
- Ships and boats are given names, such as the *Mayflower*, the *Queen Mary*, and the *Nautilus*.
- The crew of a boat or a ship can talk to or signal the crew of another boat or ship by using whistles, flags, or lights.
- Buoys and lighthouses help the crew to know where to safely sail (steer) the ship.

- Most boats and ships move on the surface of the water.
- Submarines can submerge and move below the surface of the water.
- Ferry boats carry people and cars across rivers or bays.
- Many people enjoy boating, boat racing, or fishing from boats.
- Some people own their own boats; others rent them.
- Fishers are people who go out in boats to catch fish, lobsters, and crabs. They then sell their catch to canneries, markets, or the public.
- Some people live on boats called "houseboats."
- Some people own or rent cabin cruisers for vacations on the water. People can eat and sleep in cabin cruisers.

Additional Facts the Teacher Should Know

All boats may be known as ships and all ships may be known as boats. However, the term "boat" is usually used when you are referring to a small craft, and "ship" is used when referring to large craft. A boat floats because of the way it is built. Much of the boat is filled with air which is much lighter than water. Therefore, if the boat is constructed correctly, it will weigh less than the water that would take up the same space even when the boat is loaded with cargo, crew, and passengers.

There are many different kinds of boats with which you should be familiar so that you may use the correct term when identifying them for the children:

Rowboat is a small boat that is moved through the water by pulling on a pair of oars.

Sailboat is moved through the water by wind filling its sails.

Canoe is a small boat with two seats. It is moved through the water by the use of one or two paddles.

Motorboat is a small craft with seats much like a car. It has a steering wheel and is powered by a gasoline engine.

Ferry boat is a large craft with a wide flat deck that is even with the dock and open on either end to allow cars to drive on and off. It is used for carrying cars and people across a large body of water.

Fishing boat or **trawler** is equipped with nets and water tanks. The fish are caught in the nets and stored in the water tanks until the boat can reach shore.

Houseboat is a specially built boat with one or more rooms for a family to live for long periods of time.

Cabin cruiser is designed for family living for short periods and is usually used for short or long vacations.

Tugboat is a small, sturdy boat that has padded bows for pushing and guiding bigger vessels in a harbor. Tugboats are also strong enough to pull several barges.

Barge is a large, long, flat boat used for carrying coal, steel, and other materials.

Tanker is a large ship that carries oil or chemicals.

Cargo carrier is a large ship which carries materials from one port to another. Some cargo ships carry passengers but they travel slower and do not have all the services provided on passenger ships.

Passenger ship or **ocean liner** carries people and their baggage from one port to another. These ships are like floating cities in that they have the same shops and services one would find in a city. They also carry pets, automobiles, and some cargo. Each passenger is assigned a room (bedroom, stateroom) or suite of rooms for his/her use on the voyage. Passengers eat in the dining room and are given a menu choice and served as they would be in a restaurant. A passenger ship has stewards and stewardesses to assist in making the passengers comfortable and a social director who helps them get acquainted and plans social and recreational activities. There are a ballroom, theater, swimming pool, lounges, bars, and game rooms.

Submarine is a ship that is specially designed to travel under water. They have ballast tanks which are filled with seawater to make the ship heavy enough to sink (submerge). When the submarine is ready to come up (surface) the water is replaced by compressed air which makes it light enough to float. Older submarines were propelled by diesel engines but most of the newer ones have nuclear reactors to heat the steam that makes them go. A periscope allows the crew to see what is on the surface of the water while they are submerged. Submarines can remain submerged for many days and are provided with the basic services necessary for under-water living. Submarines are usually named for famous Americans or for fish.

Coast Guard cutter is a ship that is specially equipped to assist in the rescue of ships in distress, to police the waters for offenders of navigation laws, and to monitor weather so that they can issue reports to other ships about sailing conditions.

Fireboat is equipped to put out fires on ships, piers, or along the waterfront. These boats can deliver as much water to a fire as nine fire engines could on land.

Aircraft carrier is designed with wide decks and very short runways which allow airplanes to land and take off while at sea. The airplanes' wings fold up and they can be stored inside the ship. Planes are brought up to the flight deck on an elevator. There is a hook located near the tail. When a plane lands on the deck this hook is caught in what is known as the arresting gear, which helps stop the plane and prevent it from going off the flight deck into the water.

Boats and ships have many parts with which you should be familiar:

Bow is the front of the ship.

Stern is the rear of the ship.

Starboard is the right side of a ship, as you face the bow.

Port is the left side of the ship, as you face the bow.

Deck is the flat surface on the upper part of the ship where the crew and passengers can walk. Passenger ships have several decks.

Children in boat are fishing using cardboard tubes as fishing poles. Other children are "painting" the boat with used paint cans filled with water.

Hull is the lower part of the ship or boat.

Screw is the propeller that turns, pushing the boat through the water.

Galley is the kitchen on a ship.

Hatch is the door on a ship.

Anchor is the heavy weight at the end of a long rope or steel cable which is dropped or let out when the ship wishes to remain in one place and does not have a dock at which to tie up.

Hold is the large room(s) in a ship where cargo is stowed.

Mast is the slender vertical pole used to hold up the sails on a sailboat.

Boom is the horizontal pole used to hold the sail on a sailboat or is the pole on a cargo ship that sticks up and out and holds the ropes and pulleys used in loading cargo onto the ship.

Wheelhouse is located in the front, top part of the ship. It has windows all around to provide the captain with a view for operating the ship. The wheelhouse is equipped with many instruments which help sail the ship, such as compasses, very accurate clocks, weather instruments, radios, and radar. There is also communication and special equipment to connect the wheelhouse with the chief engineer in the engine rooms down inside the ship.

Many people are needed to run a ship:

Captain is in charge of the ship.

First mate or executive officer is the second in command.

Helmsman steers the ship.

Chief engineer is in charge of the engines.

Deckhands man the ropes, keep the decks clean, and ensure that equipment is in working order. These men or women are also known as sailors, gobs, crew.

The United States Navy maintains a fleet of ships for the purpose of protecting our country. They have special names for their officers and crew. If this information is needed ask the navy recruiting officer in your community.

The captain and crew can communicate with other ships and with land in many ways:

Telephones can be used and telegraph and radio messages can be sent while at sea.

Flags are used to represent letters and numbers. Messages are spelled out.

Morse code can be used by opening and closing the shutters on a large lamp.

Ships have whistles which can be blown in certain patterns of long and short blasts which carry special meanings. One short toot: turning to the right; two short toots: turning to the left; three short toots: backing up; four short toots: danger; one long toot: leaving the pier; three long toots: "hello."

On board ship, time is designated by bells. There are six tours of watch duty of four hours each, starting at 8 P.M. Each half hour of the watch is struck by using the bells. One bell: 8:30; two bells: 9:00; three bells: 9:30; and so on, until eight bells are struck at midnight, ending the first watch. At 12:30 one bell is struck and the pattern repeated for each four-hour watch.

Smaller craft are moved through the water by use of oars, paddles, sails, or small motors. Larger craft have diesel engines or nuclear reactors to turn the large propellers known as screws. When the propellers turn one way they push the water behind and the ship goes forward. When the propellers turn the other way the water is pushed ahead and the ship goes backward. The rudder can be turned to make the ship turn left or right.

Lighthouses and buoys help the captain and crew of a ship avoid shallow water and rocks or other obstructions. They have both lights and bells on them so they can be seen and heard at night or in a fog.

Fishing is a very important business, especially for people living by rivers and oceans. Fishermen are now called "fishers." Some commercial fishing is still done by hook and line but trawling and seining have largely replaced this method. Fishers either drag nets through the water (seining) or set out main lines to which shorter lines with baited hooks are attached (trawling). As many as 5,000 hooks are sometimes baited and set and the main line may run for miles. The line is marked with buoys or floats so it can be found again. Salmon, tuna, red snappers, and halibut are usually caught this way.

Lobsters and crabs are caught in slotted wooden traps called "lobster pots" which are baited with fish. The lobsters and crabs can get in but cannot get out. Lobsters are found along the northeastern shoreline, especially Maine. Shrimp are found primarily in the waters of the Gulf of Mexico.

Methods Most Adaptable for Introducing This Subject to Children

- Display pictures of boats or ships near Dramatic Play Centers and on bulletin boards.
- Read a story about boats or ships.
- While on another trip the children may see boats on a river or lake.
- Invite a parent who may be in the navy or may work for a shipping company to tell the children about his or her work.

Vocabulary

boat	paddles	deck	water	cargo
ship	captain	anchor	float	row
dock	sailor	life preserver	sink	tow
oars	crew	lifeboat	shore	rope
sails	cabin	lighthouse	steer	

learning centers

Discovery Center

1. Obtain authentic, sturdy, scale models of different kinds of ships and boats. Identify them and tell how they are useful and how they move through the water.
2. Some children may wonder how something as big and heavy as a boat can float. You might help their understanding of this by telling them the shape is important. The boat or ship must be made to hold a lot of air, which is lighter than water. The following demonstration might help. Have two pieces of aluminum foil of the same size. Have one of the children wad one of the pieces into a ball. Place it in the water. It should sink. Help the children make a little rowboat out of the other piece by turning up the edges and putting it on the water. It should float.
3. Show the children how sailboats move. Float a model sailboat in the water table or a tub of water. Let children blow on the sails. Ask what would happen if they were sailing and the wind stopped.
4. Submarines submerge: see Floating and Sinking in Water Around Me guide, p. 567.
5. Floating boats may lead to an interest in water. (See Water Around Me guide.)

Dramatic Play Centers

Home-Living Center

1. Put up pictures of boats and ships used for pleasure and travel. Set out brochures on traveling by ship to encourage the planning and taking of a trip on the water.
2. Have suitcases available for packing.
3. Put money in purses for purchase of tickets.

Block-Building Center

1. Make a dock with unit blocks. Set out small model ships and boats for encouraging this kind of play.
2. Have cans or boxes of small materials, such as sticks, stones, buttons, and cloth scraps, to use as cargo.
3. Build a boathouse for boats with unit blocks.
4. Outline a rowboat on the floor with hollow blocks lying on their long edges. Provide sailor hats.

Other Dramatic Play Centers

1. The rocking boat makes a good boat to row or paddle. Sing "Row, Row, Row Your Boat" as children rock. Make paddles or oars out of cardboard if you wish. Provide sailor hats.
2. The rocking boat can also be a fishing boat. Give the children upholstery-roll poles with string tied to a magnet. Stock the lake or river with paper fish which have a paper clip put on for a mouth. Let them fish. Supervise carefully. (See **CAUTION**, p. 570.)
3. Ask your church or florist to save you the large heavy cardboard boxes in which wedding flowers are delivered. These make fine boats. Almost any sturdy box will make a boat.
4. Piers for larger floor toy boats can be made from hollow blocks. Piers can also be used for fishing activities.

Learning, Language, and Readiness Materials Center

Commercially made games and materials for use at a table or on a mat:

(See Basic Resources, p. 79, for manufacturers' addresses.)

1. Steamship: simple jigsaw, 6 pcs. (Kiddiecraft)
2. Playskool Plaque: Fishing, 8 pcs.
3. Ships: Rubber Differences Puzzles (Childcraft)
4. Ship: First Jigsaw, 5 pcs. (Childcraft)
5. Judy Transportation Puzzle: Tugboat and Ship, 12 pcs.
6. Harbor: Stand-Up Puzzle, 17 pcs. (Childcraft)
7. Sailboats: shape discrimination (most catalogs)
8. Boats: shape and size puzzle (Constructive Playthings)
9. Lobster: knob puzzle (Childcraft)
10. Tug: Crepefoam Puzzle, 10 pcs. (Lauri)

Teacher-made games and materials for use at a table or on a mat:

NOTE: For detailed description of Games, see pp. 50–59.

1. Look and See: use models of different kinds of boats and ships.
2. Can You Remember?: use models of boats and ships.
3. Alike, Different, and the Same: make sets of two each of the different kinds of boats and ships. Mix them up and let the children find the ones that match. Use a matching pair and one that is different; ask child to point to the one that is not like the others.
4. Grouping and Sorting by Association: take one of each of the boats and ships used in No. 3 and mix with one each of trucks, airplanes, and railroad cars. Ask the child to find all the ones that go on water, on rails, on roads, or in the sky.
5. What Am I?: after the children are familiar with some of the boats and ships and their uses, describe one and ask children to identify, such as, "I am thinking of a boat that carries automobiles and people across a river. What am I?"

Art Center

* 1. Children could help make a picture book by pasting precut pictures of boats and ships on construction paper. The mounted pictures could then be put in a loose-leaf notebook. Children with cutting experience could help with the cutting.
*** 2. Precut a sailboat stencil. Let children spatter paint it on blue construction paper, choosing the color they wish. Allow to dry and spatter paint the sails white or paste on triangles cut from cloth or paper.
*** 3. Precut hulls and sails of different sizes and colors from fabric scraps or construction paper and let children paste on blue construction paper.
*** 4. At the Woodworking Center provide wooden precut shapes and scraps that would allow children to make boats and ships of their own design. Masts could be made of wooden dowels or plastic straws. Float boats in water.

   NOTE: Hand drills should be provided for drilling mast holes.

** 5. Styrofoam can be precut to take on the shape of a ship's hull. Provide toothpicks, straws for masts, and smaller styrofoam scraps to be used for a cabin or wheelhouse. Paper or cloth sails can be glued to the masts. Let children float the boats in a tub of water or at the water table.

Book Center

*** Flack, Marjorie. *Boats on the River*. New York: Viking Press, 1946.
*** Gramatky, Hardie. *Little Toot*. New York: G. P. Putnam's Sons, 1939.
*** ———. *Little Toot on the Mississippi*. New York: G. P. Putnam's Sons, 1973.
*** Greene, Carla. *I Want to Be a Fisherman*. Chicago, Ill.: Childrens Press, 1957.
** Lenski, Lois. *The Little Sailboat*. New York: Henry Z. Walck, 1937.
** Oppenheim, Joanne. *Have You Seen Boats?* Reading, Mass.: Addison-Wesley, 1971.
*** Swift, Hildegarde. *The Little Red Lighthouse and the Great Gray Bridge*. New York: Harcourt Brace Jovanovich, 1974 (paper).
**** Zaffo, George. *The Big Book of Real Boats and Ships*. New York: Grosset & Dunlap, 1972 (read-tell).

planning for grouptime

NOTE: All music, fingerplays, stories, and games listed here may be used at other times during the session as appropriate. See Core Library, Basic Resources, p. 76, for publishers and addresses. Addresses for sources of records will be found on p. 81.

Music

Songs

FROM songs in this book
* "Let's Take a Ride," p. 470
** "Lightly Row," p. 517
* "Michael Row the Boat Ashore," p. 518

FROM *Songs for the Nursery School,* MacCarteney
*** "My Boat Is Rocking," p. 44
* "The Tug Boat," p. 45

FROM *Wake Up and Sing,* Landeck and Crook
** "Ocean Go," p. 98

Records

"Building a City"/"**What the Lighthouse Sees**"/"Rainy Day"   (Young People's Record [YPR], 33⅓ RPM)
"**Fog Boat Story**"/"Music Listening Game"/"Do This Do That"   (YPR, 33⅓ RPM)
"Ride 'em Cowboy"/"Let's Go to the Rodeo"/"**Ship Ahoy**"   (YPR, 33⅓ RPM)

NOTE: Above titles are also available singly on 10-inch 78 RPM records on the Children's Record Guild label.

"Scuffy the Tugboat" (Golden Record, 33⅓ RPM)

Rhythms and Singing Games

FROM *Creative Movements for the Developing Child,* Cherry
"Tug Boat," p. 25
"Rocking Boat," p. 55

"Row, Row, Row Your Boat": have children sit on floor in pairs facing each other with hands joined and legs spread out in shape of a V, with soles of shoes touching. As you sing the song together have children pull each other forward on a rotating basis—first one, then the other, in time to the music.

Fingerplays and Poems

THE BOATS

This is the way, all the day long
The boats go sailing by,
To and fro, in a row,
Under the bridge so high.

(FORM A BRIDGE WITH LEFT ARM AND MOVE RIGHT HAND BACK AND FORTH UNDER IT)

ROW, ROW, ROW YOUR BOAT

Row, row, row your boat
Gently down the stream,
Merrily, merrily, merrily, merrily,
Life is but a dream.

(PUT FISTS TOGETHER IN FRONT OF YOU AND PRETEND TO ROW)

FROM *Very Young Verses,* Geismer and Suter
"About Going Places," pp. 101–09
"Bridges," p. 101
"Ferry-Boats," p. 102
"Freight Boats," p. 103
"Back and Forth," pp. 104–05
"The Fog Horn," p. 106
"Boats Sail on the Rivers," p. 107
"Where Go the Boats?" p. 108
"Fog," p. 166

Stories

(To read, read-tell, or tell. See Book Center for complete list.)

*** *Boats on the River,* Flack
*** *I Want to Be a Fisherman,* Greene
*** *The Little Red Lighthouse and the Great Gray Bridge,* Swift
**** *The Big Book of Real Boats and Ships,* Zaffo

Games

(See Games, pp. 50–59, and Teacher-Made Games in this guide for directions.)

1. Look and See
2. What Am I?
3. Can You Remember?
4. Alike, Different, and the Same

Routine Times

1. At snack or mealtime serve chocolate, cocoa, bananas, pineapple, or coconuts. Explain that these foods probably came to our country by cargo ship. Serve fish, lobster, or crab and talk about how they are caught in nets by fishers in fishing boats.
2. At snack or mealtime have a captain's table. Each day choose one child to be captain who in turn selects those who will dine at the captain's table. Make certain everyone gets included!
3. At pickup time have the children use the large floor toy boats to carry some of the toys (cargo) back to the shelves (port).
4. At rest time tell the children you will ring the ship's bell four times when it is time to get up. Use a bell with a clapper and ring as follows for four bells: strike bell twice, pause, strike bell twice more.
5. In busing children to and from the Center or on other trips in the community you may cross rivers, go around lakes, or by the ocean where boats or ships may be seen. Talk about the kinds of boats you see and what they do.

Large Muscle Activities

1. A packing box or other large, sturdy carton could be used for boat play. A cleated walking board could be used as a gangplank to the packing-box ship. Put a real rowboat on the playground. (See p. 508.) Combine with a steering wheel or dial panel. (See illustration, p. 495.) Provide sailor hats.
2. Float boats at a water table or other large container filled with water.
3. Have water available to fill the canals in the sandbox. Provide small boats to encourage water transportation play in this area.
4. See Other Dramatic Play Area for additional suggestions involving large muscles.
5. Slice a tire for a boat canal. (See Water Around Me guide, p. 577.)

Extended Experiences

1. Watch boats or ships on a nearby river, lake, or ocean.
2. Take a ferry boat ride.
3. Ride an excursion boat.
4. Go out in a sailboat, rowboat, or motorboat.

   CAUTION: All children should wear life jackets and one of the adults in the boat should have a current senior lifesaving certificate.

5. Watch a fishing boat or cargo ship unload.
6. Watch a boat race: sculling, a regatta, or a motorboat race.
7. Invite a Chinese parent, university student, or friend to visit your classroom and tell about the Dragon Boat festival in China. Perhaps this person would have, or could find, a picture of one of these boats. (See Summer guide, pp. 355, 356.)
8. Invite a sailor to come in uniform and tell the children about living and sailing at sea.

teacher resources

Pictures and Displays

(See p. 79 for addresses of firms listed.)

1. Transportation packet (David C. Cook)
2. Transportation Posters: Harbor, Lake (Trend Enterprises)
3. Catchy Colors Mobile: rowboat/fish (Instructo)
4. Display pictures from your personal file which might include different kinds of boats, persons who work with boats, buoys, a lighthouse, boat races, docks, fishers, fishing nets, lobster pots.

Community Resources

1. Shipping companies may have calendars or brochures with pictures of ships.
2. Marina for rental of boats
3. Navy recruiting officer for posters of navy ships and personnel
4. Fishing companies or fishers for permission to watch the unloading of fish
5. Regatta clubs for schedules of races or names of persons who may be willing to give the children rides in their boats

Lightly Row
(Alles Neu Macht Der Mai)

Traditional Tune ("Fahrathen")   German Folk Song

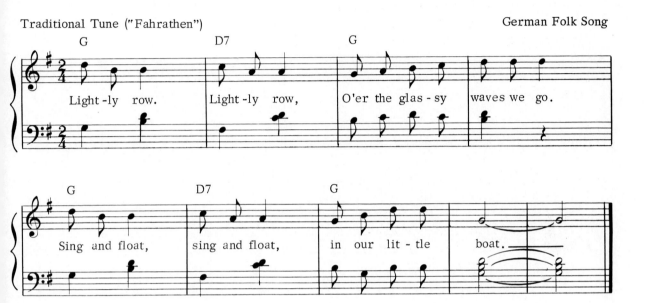

NOTE: Two lines (verses 2 and 3) have been omitted in this adaptation of the original tune to simplify it for use with young children.

Michael Row the Boat Ashore

(Original title: Michael Haul the Boat Ashore)

Traditional Negro Spiritual

Traditional

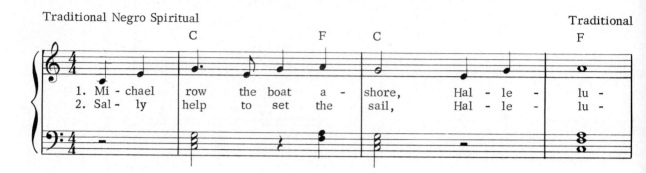

1. Mi - chael   row   the   boat   a - shore,   Hal - le - lu -
2. Sal - ly   help   to   set   the   sail,   Hal - le - lu -

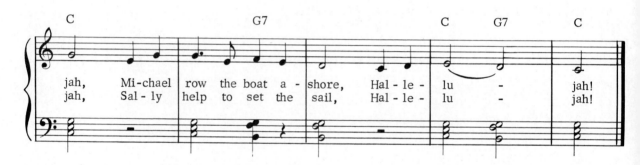

jah,   Mi - chael   row   the   boat   a - shore,   Hal - le - lu - jah!
jah,   Sal - ly   help   to   set   the   sail,   Hal - le - lu - jah!

Verse 3: Pe-ter pad-dle the can-oe, etc.
Verse 4: Mar-y fly the plane a-round, etc.
Verse 5: Moth-er drive the car to town, etc.
Verse 6: Fath-er ride the train to work, etc.

NOTE: The "Hallelujah" is optional. Phrases can be completed by repeating preceding refrain. For example, "row the boat!" "trim the sail!"

Adapted by Bonnie Flemming

32 Space Transportation

basic understandings

(concepts children can grasp from this subject)

- We live on a planet called "earth."
- It is the shape of a great big ball.
- The earth goes around the sun. The path it takes around the sun is called its "orbit."
- There are eight other ball-shaped planets that also circle the sun. They look like stars to us.
- Gravity pulls us toward the center of the earth and keeps us from falling off.
- Spaceships (capsules), missiles, rockets, and satellites have to go very fast and very high to get away from the earth's gravity.
- Space is very big; it never ends.
- Everything we see in outer space (moon, sun, and stars) is very, very far away.
- Planets are even farther away than the moon; that is why they look as small as stars.
- Some stars are as big or bigger than the sun, but they look small because they are so very far away.
- Traveling very fast, the way space capsules do, it takes about two and a half days without stopping to get to the moon; it would take three years to get to the sun, and millions of years to get to the nearest star.
- If a car could drive the distance to the moon, traveling at the rate usually used by cars on the highways, it would take about five months without stopping to get that far, and about 190 years to get as far as the sun.
- It is dark and cold in outer space.
- There is no air to breathe or water to drink in outer space.
- In the United States, people who travel in space are called "astronauts."
- When astronauts go into outer space they must wear special suits and take their own light, heat, air, water, and food in their space capsule (command module).
- Because gravity on the moon is much less than on earth, astronauts can jump higher and farther on the moon than they can on earth.

- Rockets are used at Cape Canaveral to fire spacecraft into the air.
- Retrorockets slow spacecraft down so they can land.
- Three big parachutes are used on individual spacecraft to slow them down even more before they land on the ocean.
- After splashdown helicopters pick up the astronauts and bring them to an aircraft carrier.
- Russia was the first country to put a spacecraft in orbit around the earth. It was called Sputnik I.
- Russia was the first country to put a man in orbit. He was known as a cosmonaut.
- The United States was the first country to put a man on the moon.
- No plants, animals, or water were found on the moon. There were only hills, valleys of rocks, and plains of light gray soil.
- Man-made satellites orbit the earth. They are used to relay pictures and information back to earth.
- The Russians and the Americans are exploring space together.

Additional Facts the Teacher Should Know

To a young child, the concepts of time, distance, and space are very difficult to grasp. A long time is until next summer. A great distance is one hundred miles away to grandmother's house. Therefore, this guide does not include much in space beyond the moon. The differences between stars and planets, the magnitude of the universe, and similar concepts are beyond the comprehension of a small child.

There are five classifications of space:

a. terrestrial space: starts at the earth's surface and extends up about 4,000 miles
b. cislunar space: the part of space between the earth and the moon
c. interplanetary space: begins where the sun's gravity becomes stronger than the earth's— about 50 billion miles from earth
d. interstellar space: space between the stars
e. intergalactic space: space between the galaxies (never ending)

Distances in space are measured in light years or the distance light travels in one year. Light travels 186,000 miles per second.

Space, which is infinite, is broken up by galaxies (large systems of stars) held together by mutual gravitation. Within each galaxy there are groups of stars known as constellations, other stars, and planets. A star is a fixed heavenly body which is gaseous and gives off heat and light. The sun is a giant star around which our earth and eight other natural planets orbit. It takes the earth 365¼ days to move around the sun in a slightly elliptical path.

The nine planets in order from the sun are Mercury, Venus, Earth, Mars, Jupiter, Saturn, Uranus, Neptune, and Pluto. Planets differ from stars in that they travel in an orbit, rotate on their axes, are not gaseous, and do not give off heat or light of their own but rather reflect the light from the sun. Asteroids are minor planets, from 1 to 480 miles in diameter, that orbit around the sun. Comets also move about the sun but in very erratic orbits; they consist of a central mass and a misty envelope which may extend into a stream called its "tail."

A meteorite is a mass of stone and metal, often a remnant of a comet, that flies through space. Sometimes one enters our atmosphere and is slowed by the dense air; the resulting friction eventually causes it to heat to a luminous glow which is visible from the earth. It is then called a "meteor" or "shooting star." Meteorites are a hazard to space travelers.

A satellite is any body which orbits a planet. The moon is a natural satellite. Our earth has one moon which has no life, water, wind, or heat, and which reflects light from the sun. (See Day and Night guide.) The earth has several manmade satellites now orbiting it. These satellites are unmanned but have instruments that take data and pictures which help us predict the weather, assist in navigation and mapping, and help us learn more about our earth, the moon, and the other planets. Some satellites are used to relay television pictures and telephone messages. The satellite batteries use sunlight instead of chemicals.

In the last two decades the United States and Russia have made remarkable progress in space exploration:

October 4, 1957: the first satellite, Sputnik I, was successfully launched by Russia.

April 12, 1961: Russia's cosmonaut Yuri A. Gagarin was the first man to orbit the earth.

February 20, 1962: John Glenn, an American astronaut, orbited the earth three times in "Friendship Seven."

June 3, 1965: Edward White was the first American to walk in space.

January 27, 1967: first Apollo crew, Virgil Grissom, Edward White, and Robert Chaffee, died in an electrical fire.

July 20, 1969: Americans Neil Armstrong and Edwin Aldrin first to land on the moon. Armstrong's words were "That's one small step for man, one giant leap for mankind."

July 17, 1975: Apollo-Soyuz docking. First American-Russian docking in space. Thomas Stafford, Vance Brand, and Donald Slayton represented the United States. Aleksei Leonov and Valery Kubasov represented the Soviet Union.

The National Aeronautics and Space Administration (NASA) was created by Congress in 1958 for the purpose of exploring space. Project Mercury existed from 1961 to 1963 and ended with the 22 orbits of Gordon Cooper. Then followed ten manned Gemini flights that proved the capabilities of our men and equipment. The purpose of the Apollo program was accomplished in 1969 when Armstrong and Aldrin placed an American flag on the moon and set up equipment that could relay information back to earth. Subsequent trips to the moon resulted in many more experiments, the collection of rocks and soil, and the use of a motorized vehicle, the lunar rover. The Apollo program ended with the Apollo-Soyuz mission.

Russia and the United States are continuing to work together on further space exploration. Probes have been sent to Venus and Mars. These satellites have been equipped to relay pictures and other data about the planets back to Earth.

The space capsules (command modules) and satellites are mounted on three-stage rockets. The first two stages provide enough power and speed to send them beyond the earth's gravitational pull; the third stage sends them into orbit around the earth. Other rockets are included in the systems to allow astronauts or ground crews to change direction as needed.

All the American manned flights were launched from Cape Canaveral, Florida, and were then monitored by the staff at the Mission Control Center at Houston, Texas, with the aid of radar tracking and communication stations around the world. Without the knowledge and work of thousands of persons our space program would not have been possible.

learning centers

Discovery Center

1. Gravity: jump from a box. Why do you go down? Why do you go down a slide? Why can't you slide up? Why does a swing go down each time? Why does a seesaw go down? Why does one end go up? Drop different objects—pebbles, leaves, feathers, a plastic sand shovel, or a flower from the top of a jungle gym. Do any go up? If so, why? Do some fall faster than others? If so, why? If a block building tumbles, use it to explain gravity. Ask the children to raise their arms to shoulder height and see how long they can keep them there. Tell them why their arms get tired. Ask the children to see how high they can jump. Discuss why they can't jump higher, and why they could jump higher on the moon.

2. Inertia: if one child is sitting in a wagon and another child starts to pull the wagon with a jerk, the first child tends to stay where he is and therefore falls backward. The opposite is true when in motion: if the wagon stops suddenly, his body tends to keep going and he falls forward. These are both examples of inertia. Also, once you are in motion on a tricycle or slide, you tend to keep going until stopped.

3. Centrifugal force: the water in a small plastic bucket swung around a person's head does not spill because it is pulling away from the center of the earth when moving in a circular path. Demonstrate and let children try.

4. Friction: talk about how friction slows you down on a slide. Let children run their hands along the slide and feel it get warm due to friction. Ask them if their hands get warm or cool.

5. Weightlessness: use the term when comparing the feeling they have when their end of the seesaw starts to go down or when the children reach the top of the arc and just before they start down when swinging. Talk about how astronauts might feel similarly.

6. Disorientation: use the term when children are whirling around and spinning rapidly or when they turn upside down on a swing or jungle gym.

7. Thrust: inflate a balloon, then let it go. Let the children discover how the air escaping from the open end of a balloon pushes it forward.

8. Demonstrate lighter-than-air craft by using a helium-filled balloon.

9. Demonstrate with a paper airplane the thrust and lift of a heavier-than-air craft. Let children try. (See illustration, p. 464.)

10. Use real binoculars to show how things can be brought closer. Use indoors or out with close adult supervision. Children's binoculars can be purchased that bring objects three times closer.

11. Telescopes can show how things far away, like the moon, can be brought much closer. If possible, let children look through a telescope. Adult supervision is needed.

12. Demonstrate how distance makes things appear smaller by having a child go to the end of a long hallway while the others watch. Outdoors, watch a car being driven away. Observe, as long as the children can continue to keep the vehicle in sight. Ask if the car seems to get smaller, larger, or stay the same size. Why?

13. To simulate the moon's surface half fill a cake pan with very soft clay or plaster of Paris. Throw several marbles of different sizes into it and then remove them. These look similar to moon craters. Form some mountains and plains. Let harden. Sprinkle with clay dust. This is what the surface of the moon looks like. Show actual pictures of the moon's surface. Take your "moon" into a darkened room and shine a flashlight on it from an oblique angle. This should show up the craters the way the sun shows the moon's

craters and mountains to us. Look at the surface of the sand in the box outdoors after a very hard, short rain with no wind. It will be pitted like the surface of the moon.

14. Rocket: paint a small paper bag to look like a space capsule. Blow up a balloon 8 inches long. Put the capsule on the tip and let the balloon go (described in *Funny Bags* by Betsy Pflug, J. B. Lippincott, Philadelphia, 1974). This works on the same principle as the capsules used by the National Aeronautic and Space Administration (NASA). The air rushing out the back of the balloon creates a force making the rocket move with equal force in the opposite direction. It takes a large rocket with several stages to launch a small capsule. Different sizes of capsules could be tried on the balloon.

15. Parachute: use a 12-inch square of plastic wrap. Tie an 18-inch piece of string to each of the four corners. Put the ends through a small spool and tie into a knot. These can be dropped from a jungle gym or slide, or thrown into the air. Paper napkins or square-neck scarves can be used the same way.

16. Set out copies of *Look, Ranger Rick, Life,* and *National Geographic*, which contain articles on outer space. Note also the four-starred books in the Book Center list.

17. View-Master reels: The Conquest of Space, Our Planet Earth, America's Man in Space, Moon Landing 1969, Kennedy Space Center, and Probing the Universe.

18. Display space postage stamps that show a capsule, a walk in space, a landing on the moon, and the Apollo-Soyuz docking.

19. Display color photographs of our earth taken from outer space and photographs of the moon. Discuss the likenesses and differences.

Dramatic Play Centers

Block-Building Center

1. Provide cylindrical and cone-shaped blocks for children who wish to build space stations and rocket ships. Display authentic space pictures on walls in this area.
2. Styrofoam cones, balls, wreaths, and sheets would provide some short-term exploration.
3. When block buildings fall, talk about gravity.

Other Dramatic Play Centers

1. Binoculars or telescopes may be made by the teacher for use by the group.

   Materials needed:

   a. rolls from paper towels, waxed paper, plastic wrap, or aluminum foil are used to make telescopes
   b. rolls from toilet paper are needed to make binoculars

   Procedure: the various tubes are of different diameters and some of them actually telescope. The teacher should find pairs that fit one inside the other (e.g., a wax paper roll and a paper towel roll). Let the children paint or decorate them. The teacher would also need to fasten the toilet paper rolls together in pairs for binoculars after they had been painted by the children.

2. Teacher may construct a rocket ship for the children to use indoors.

   Materials needed:

   a. cardboard cone
   b. cardboard fins
   c. spools
   d. wires, earphones
   e. large cardboard boxes of different sizes (large enough for a child to get into)
   f. wooden or metal knobs (handles from cupboard doors), old dials

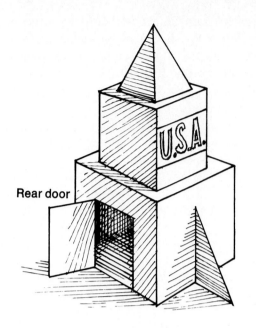

Rear door

Procedure: Using the illustration as a guide, the teacher cuts a door in the biggest box and a hole in the top of it. The next biggest box is fastened over this, open side down. A cone is made from a large sheet of posterboard and fastened to the top of the second box. Fins are made from a piece of posterboard, cut in two diagonally, and attached to the side of the lower box. Dials, knobs, spools, and wires are attached inside the boxes wherever the teacher wants. The children can paint each section with wide brushes and tempera, or the whole spaceship can be covered with silver paper or painted with gray or aluminum paint. Instead of standing upright, the rocket ship could be horizontal on the floor. A rocket ship can also be made by arranging large packing boxes on the playground and adding a nose cone, fins, and instruments as on the one for indoors.

3. Teacher may provide a homemade space helmet for children to use.

   Materials needed:

   a. Round ice-cream cartons, gallon plastic milk or water jugs, and gallon carton or paper sacks large enough to go on a child's head
   b. Discarded garden or vacuum cleaner hose which has been washed
   c. Paper cups, wire, electrical cord, pipecleaners, boxes, leather straps or canvas webbing, and plastic holders from pop cans

Procedure: Using the illustration as a guide, the teacher cuts the end and a face hole or eye holes from a plastic milk jug and smoothes edges, then cuts a hole for the hose. Children fix helmets any way they choose. They may be painted with tempera or colored with felt pens. A hose may be attached from a hole in the back or front of a shoebox, which is worn on the child's back and secured over his or her shoulders by means of straps.

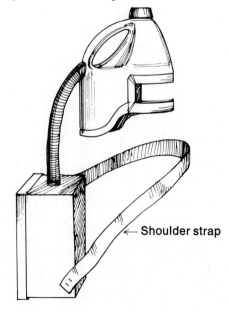

← Shoulder strap

Learning, Language, and Readiness Materials Center

Commercially made games and materials for use at a table or on a mat:

(See Basic Resources, p. 79, for manufacturers' addresses.)

1. Play Family Airport: helicopter (Constructive Playthings)
2. Airplane and Helicopter: with hardwood or plastic wheels (Creative Playthings)
3. Play Airport: 19 hardwood pieces (Childcraft)
4. Giant Magnet: helps explain gravity (Creative Playthings)
5. Giant Magnifier: lens in a stool (Creative Playthings)
6. Big I, Little I Lenses: telescope effect (Creative Playthings)
7. Six-inch prism (most catalogs)
8. Judy See-Quees: Man in Space, 12 pcs.
9. Gyroscope (Childcraft)
10. Space Rings (Creative Playthings)
11. Space Relationship Cards: 35 laminated cards (Milton Bradley)
12. Globe: 8 inches, 10 inches, or 12 inches (most stores and catalogs)
13. The Universe Transparencies (Instructo)
14. Space Pictures: transparencies; includes the first quarter, total solar eclipse, and more (Instructo)
15. Measurement Puzzles: height (Creative Playthings)
16. Judy Space Exploration Series: 6 puzzles, 10 to 17 pcs. each
17. Solar System Model: with scale models and teaching guide (Instructo)
18. The Solar System and Air Transportation: two sets of flannelboard aids (Instructo)
19. Space Exploration Series: set of puzzles, 10-17 pcs. (Childcraft)
20. Earth in Space: flannel aid (Milton Bradley)
21. Moonlife: Tell-a-Story (Ideal)
22. Space Explorers: cut-outs (Instructo)
23. Playskool Puzzle: the Solar System, 21 pcs.

Teacher-made games and materials for use at a table or on a mat:

NOTE: For detailed description of Games, see pp. 50–59.

1. Look and See: use flannel aids of the sun, earth, star, and moon or astronaut, lunar lander, rocket, and capsule.
2. Name It: use items named in No. 1.
3. Which Comes First?: series of pictures showing rocket on launch pad, rocket aloft, lunar lander on moon, splash down
4. Alike, Different, and the Same: use flannelboard aids or plastic models of items suggested in No. 1.
5. Match-Thems: the moon, earth, and other planets are round. Find other things in the room that are round.

Art Center

* 1. Offer silver and white tempera paint at the easels and at the tables. Use with black or blue paper.
*** 2. Offer wood scraps, nails, clothespins, tongue depressors, Popsicle sticks, toilet paper rolls, and other throw-aways which may be needed if children wish to make a wood sculpture rocket or lunar lander.

*** 3. Provide a variety of cardboard tubes, cones, and other cartons for box sculpture. Cut masking tape in lengths and hang pieces from the edge of the table or ruler, so the tape is more readily available to children.

> **NOTE:** Provide single sections of an egg carton near a supply of empty toilet paper rolls for the child who may need a tip end to complete a rocket. Children may wish to paint.

*** 4. Paint and add construction paper fins to thread cones which may be obtained free from manufacturers of uniforms or bags or from upholsterers.

** 5. Make available styrofoam balls and toothpicks, in varying shapes or styrofoam circles for children who may wish to make Sputnik or Vanguard satellites.

Other Experiences in This Center Using Art Media:

*** 1. Children may paint binoculars or spaceships made by the teacher for dramatic play or may make their own with help and supervision.

Book Center

** Carlson, Bernice Wells. "The Spaceman in the Rocket Ship." In *Listen and Help Tell the Story*. Nashville, Tenn.: Abingdon Press, 1965.

*** Chester, Michael and William Nephew. *Let's Go to a Rocket Base*. New York: G. P. Putnam's Sons, 1961.

** Freeman, Mae B. and Ira M. Freeman. *You Will Go to the Moon*. New York: Random House, 1971.

*** Greene, Carla. *I Want to Be a Space Pilot*. Chicago, Ill.: Childrens Press, 1961.

* Kuskin, Karla. *Just Like Everyone Else*. New York: Harper & Row, 1959.

** Lewis, Claudia. *When I Go to the Moon*. New York: Macmillan, 1961.

** Phleger, Frederick. *Ann Can Fly*. New York: Random House, 1959.

*** Ravielli, Anthony. *The World Is Round*. New York: Viking Press, 1963.

**** Schneider, Herman and Nina Schneider. *You, Among the Stars*. Reading, Mass.: Addison-Wesley, 1951.

** Ungerer, Tomi. *Moon Man*. New York: Harper & Row, 1967.

* Zacks, Irene. *Space Alphabet*. Englewood Cliffs, N.J.: Prentice-Hall, 1964.

* Zaffo, George. *The Giant Book of Things in Space*. Garden City, N.Y.: Doubleday, 1969.

> **NOTE:** Look in your library for books on space by F. M. Branley to read-tell.

planning for grouptime

NOTE: All music, fingerplays, poems, stories, and games listed here may also be used at other times during the session as appropriate. See Core Library, Basic Resources, p. 76, for publishers and addresses. Addresses for sources of records will be found on p. 81. In parodies, hyphenated words match the music notes of the tune used.

Music

Songs

FROM original songs and parodies in this book
* "Take a Trip," p. 452
* "Ways I Can Move," p. 458
* "I'm a Little Airplane," p. 465
* "Let's Take a Ride," p. 470. Sing these words (by Bonnie Flemming):
  Let's take a ride in a spaceship, let's take a ride out in space.
  Let's take a ride, let's take a ride, let's take a ride out in space.

FROM *Songs for Early Childhood*, Westminster Press
* "Lying on the Hillside," p. 26
* "Bright Stars, Light Stars," p. 27
* "Sailing High," p. 85

FROM *Wake Up and Sing*, Landeck and Crook
* "Sally Go 'Round the Stars," p. 90

FROM *Songs for the Nursery School*, MacCarteney
* "See the Sunshine," p. 7
*** "Moon, Moon," p. 92

FROM *Music Activities for Retarded Children*, Ginglend and Stiles
*** "Five Little Spacemen," p. 50

Records

"**By Rocket to the Moon**"/"Billy Rings the Bell"/"Lonesome House" (Young People's Record [YPR], 33⅓ RPM)
"By Rocket to the Moon" (Children's Record Guild, 78 RPM)
"Space Songs," *Ballads for the Age of Science* (Motivation Company, 33⅓ RPM)
Outer Space, 2 albums (Kimbo, 33⅓ RPM)
"He's Got the Whole World in His Hands," *Fun Activities for Fine Skills* (Kimbo, 33⅓ RPM)
"Journey to the Moon" (Golden Record, 33⅓ RPM)

Rhythms and Singing Games

"Bend and Stretch," *Romper Room Record* (Golden, 12 inch LP)

FROM *Songs for the Nursery School*, MacCarteney
"I'm Jumping," p. 2
"Sally Go Round the Moon," p. 81
"See How I'm Jumping," p. 95 (change word "fast" to "high")

WE'RE FLYING TO THE MOON (a parody)
  (tune: "The Farmer in the Dell")
  by JoAnne Deal Hicks

ALL CHILDREN WHO ARE INTERESTED MAY JOIN HANDS IN A CIRCLE IN A SQUATTING POSITION AND BEGIN THE COUNTDOWN

10, 9, 8, 7, 6, 5, 4, 3, 2, 1, 0, Ignition, BLAST OFF!

THE COUNTDOWN IS CHANTED LOUDLY AND CHILDREN SLOWLY RISE AS IT PROCEEDS. AT THE WORDS "BLAST OFF," ARMS SHOULD BE RAISED TOWARD THE SKY. AS THE SONG BEGINS, THE CHILDREN MOVE CLOCK-WISE UNTIL THE END OF THE FIRST VERSE.

VERSE 1: We're fly-ing to the moon, we're fly-ing to the moon, we've left the earth in our rocket ship, and we're fly-ing to the moon.

VERSE 2: We're tak-ing a walk in space, we're tak-ing a walk in space, we've left the earth in our rocket ship, and we're tak-ing a walk in space.

(DROP HANDS AND ALL BEGIN THE EXAGGERATED MOTION OF A "SPACE WALK." IF GROUP IS SMALL, THE TEACHER MAY LOOP A LONG PIECE OF YARN AROUND THE WAIST OF ONE CHILD, ALLOWING ANOTHER CHILD TO HOLD THE OTHER END OF THE YARN. TEACHER MAY ATTACH THE YARN TO A CIRCLE OF ELASTIC THAT COULD BE STEPPED INTO BY THE CHILD. ELASTIC WILL GIVE SOME ADDED FREEDOM TO THE EXTENSION OF THE YARN AS THE CHILD MOVES AROUND IN SPACE.)

CAUTION: Individual walks are not advisable in a large group as children who are waiting may become impatient.

VERSE 3: We're land-ing on the moon, we're land-ing on the moon, we've left the earth in our rocket ship, and we're land-ing on the moon.

(GROUP JOINS HANDS AND MOVES CLOCKWISE UNTIL END OF THIRD VERSE)

VERSE 4: We're walk-ing on the moon, we're walk-ing on the moon, we've left the earth in our rocket ship, and we're walk-ing on the moon.

(DROP HANDS AND ALL BEGIN THE LARGE LEAPS AND BOUNDS OF A WALK ON THE MOON)

VERSE 5: (COUNTDOWN IS REPEATED EXACTLY AS AT BEGINNING OF GAME, AS GROUP PREPARES TO "BLAST OFF" FROM THE SURFACE OF THE MOON)

VERSE 6: We're fly-ing back to earth, we're fly-ing back to earth, we've left the moon in our rocket ship, and we're fly-ing back to earth.

(GROUP MOVES COUNTERCLOCKWISE WITH HANDS JOINED)

VERSE 7: We're splash-ing down in the sea, we're splash-ing down in the sea, we've left the moon and outer-space, and we're splash-ing down in the sea.

(WITH HANDS AT SIDES CHILDREN SLOWLY FALL INTO THE SEA WHERE THEY AWAIT THE ARRIVAL OF THE RESCUE SHIP. A ROCKING MOTION MAY BE DONE AT THIS TIME TO SIMULATE ROLLING WAVES UNDER THE FLOTATION RING AND SPACE CAPSULE.)

Fingerplays and Poems

FROM Fingerplays and Poems in the Transportation guides
"We Go Traveling," p. 454

FROM *Listen and Help Tell the Story*, Bernice W. Carlson
"Space Rocket," p. 53

Stories

(To read, read-tell, or tell. See Book Center for complete list.)

** "The Spaceman in the Rocket Ship," Carlson
** *You Will Go to the Moon*, Freeman
*** *I Want to Be a Space Pilot*, Greene
 * *The Giant Book of Things in Space*, Zaffo

** *Ann Can Fly*, Phleger
** *Moon Man*, Ungerer
 * *Space Alphabet*, Zacks

Games

(See Games, pp. 50–59, and Teacher-Made Games in this guide for directions.)

1. Look and See
2. Alike, Different, and the Same
3. Which Comes First?

Routine Times

1. Snack or mealtime: serve an astronaut's meal, such as space food sticks, breakfast bars, dehydrated foods, pellets of food, such as raisins, carrot sticks, or puddings in squeeze bottles or plastic sacks.
2. Transitions or taking turns: use countdown method to go in or outdoors, to go to the bathroom, and so on. "10, 9, 8, 7, 6, 5, 4, 3, 2, 1, 0, John's turn!"

Large Muscle Activities

1. Discovery Center experiences 1 to 15 on pp. 512–13 may be explored at this time.
2. Build a space station outdoors using packing boxes or jungle gym.
3. Soak sandpile with a hose. Allow or encourage children to make moon mountains and plains. Drop solid heavy balls, such as golf balls or croquet balls, into the sand to make craters. Supervise closely.
4. Allow children to throw plastic lid flying saucers, which they can decorate with felt-tip markers.

Extended Experiences

1. Depending on community resources arrange a trip to an airport, planetarium, space center, rocket launching center, or a traveling NASA display.

2. Visit a playground or park that has a rocket slide or space capsule as part of the equipment. Youngest children should look at it only.
3. Have a pilot or astronaut visit your school and bring something he/she uses to show and talk to the children about space flights. Keep simple.
4. Have an amateur radio operator visit and demonstrate a radio key or tune in the amateur bands of a shortwave radio. Explain that this is the way we can keep in contact with astronauts in space.

teacher resources

Books and Periodicals

1. Asimov, Isaac. *Satellites in Outer Space.* New York: Random House, 1966.
2. Branley, Franklyn M. *Book of Flying Saucers for You.* New York: Thomas Y. Crowell, 1973.
3. ———. *Book of Outer Space for You.* New York: Thomas Y. Crowell, 1970.
4. ———. *Man in Space to the Moon.* New York: Thomas Y. Crowell, 1970.
5. ———. *The Moon, Earth's Natural Satellite.* New York: Thomas Y. Crowell, 1972.
6. Chappell, Russell E. *Apollo.* Washington, D.C.: Government Printing Office, 1974.
7. Darby, Gene. *What Is the Earth?* Westchester, Ill.: Benefic Press, Berkley-Cardy Co., 1961.
8. DePree, Mildred. *A Child's World of Stamps.* New York: Parents' Magazine Press, 1973.
9. Podendorf, Illa. *The True Book of Space.* Chicago: Childrens Press, 1972.
10. Sonneborn, Ruth A. *The Question and Answer Book of Space.* New York: Random House, 1965.
11. Wilford, John Noble. *We Reach the Moon.* New York: W. W. Norton, 1969.

Pictures and Displays

(See p. 79 for addresses of firms listed.)

1. Moon and Stars/Sun: Science Themes II packet (David C. Cook)
2. Helicopters: Transportation packet (David C. Cook)
3. Solar System/Space: Bulletin Board Cut-outs (Trend Enterprises)
4. Exploring Space (SVE Picture Sets)
5. Space Rings: can be hung as a mobile (Creative Playthings)
6. Teacher can make and hang a mobile consisting of the various bodies in the solar system.
7. Solar System Mobile: in scale (Ideal)

Community Resources

1. Planetarium
2. Parks with a capsule, missile, or rocket as a permanent display
3. University science department:
   a. geologist: for information about moon rocks and samples of other rocks and minerals found in your state
   b. astronomers: may have observatory or telescopes
4. Amateur radio operators

PART SEVEN

The World
I Live In

33 Day and Night

basic understandings

(concepts children can grasp from this subject)

- The sun gives off light and heat.
- It is lighter and warmer during the day because at that time our part of the earth is turned toward the sun.
- At night it is darker and colder because at that time our part of the earth is turned away from the sun.
- When it is day in our half of the world, it is night in the other half of the world.
- A whole day lasts twenty-four hours and consists of both the day (light) and night (dark).
- Sometimes the daylight lasts longer than the darkness (in summer), and at other times the darkness lasts longer than the light (in winter).
- Night is nice. (Stress pleasant aspects of night.) It is a good time to sleep and rest.
- The sun is a big star. Stars shine (give off light and heat) all the time.
- Clouds may hide the sun and stars from our view.
- Fog is caused by clouds forming close to the earth. It may hide the sun and stars from our view.
- The sun and the stars shine all the time. We do not see the other stars in the daytime because the sunlight is so bright we cannot see them.
- Most stars are so far away we see them as tiny dots of light.
- Some of the stars appear grouped together. These groups are called constellations.

Additional Facts the Teacher Should Know

The earth turns counterclockwise (from west to east) on its imaginary axis, which runs from the north to the south pole as it travels on an elliptical path around our sun. It takes twenty-four hours, or one calendar day, for the earth to turn completely around once on its axis.

A moon is a heavenly body that revolves around a planet. We have one moon that is about 240,000 miles away. It is 2,100 miles wide and about 80 times lighter than the earth. Therefore its force of gravity is much less. People weigh less on the moon. The moon's gravity exerts some pressure on our earth and causes large bodies of water to move, resulting in tides. The moon rotates on its axis as it orbits around the earth. It takes the moon 27 days and 8 hours to orbit around the earth and about the same time to turn around once on its axis. Therefore we always see the same side of the moon.

The moon gives off no light of its own. What we see is a reflection of the sun's rays off the surface of the moon. One-half of the moon is always lighted by the sun, but when the moon is almost between the earth and the sun, we do not always see the lighted half. The sun's rays are so bright, we do not often see the moon during the day. When we can see all of the lighted half we say we have a full moon. As the moon changes its position, less and less light is reflected off it toward the earth. Accordingly, it becomes less and less visible to humans on the earth. This is why sometimes the moon appears to be only a crescent or half moon shape, although its size does not actually change. The different positions are called phases.

An eclipse of the moon is when the earth is between the sun and the moon and the sunlight cannot shine on the moon. The moon gets very dull, and we can barely see it. An eclipse of the sun is when the moon is between the sun and the earth and we cannot see the sunlight.

CAUTION: It is dangerous to look directly at an eclipse of the sun. Permanent eye damage can result.

At certain times of the year, particularly in the autumn, the moon rises early and shines for a long time. This is often called a "harvest moon." It sometimes appears large and orange in color if there is dust in the air.

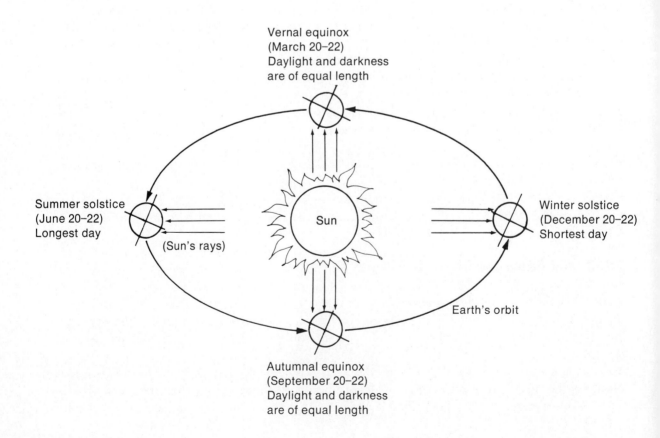

Twice during the year in the continental United States, we have approximately twelve hours each of daylight and darkness. One time is the vernal equinox on March 20, 21, or 22, and the second is the autumnal equinox on September 20, 21, or 22. The exact date is determined officially each year when the sun crosses the equator at noon. During the summer, our part of the earth is tipped toward the sun and we have longer days. In winter, we have the shortest days as our part of the earth is tipped away from the sun. (See illustration, p. 534.)

Many children are afraid of nighttime and the dark. Often, at about the age of four and one-half to five, children who have been perfectly willing to go to bed will begin to cry and want a light left on. Children should learn facts about light and dark, but also be encouraged to talk about their fears related to darkness or being away from home at night. They should learn about the beauty, goodness, and necessity of night. Dreams become important to children at about three and one-half years of age. The teacher should be prepared to listen to what the children say about their dreams and offer them reassurance.

Methods Most Adaptable for Introducing This Subject to Children

- Display pictures showing activities during the day and during the night.
- Say "good morning" when children arrive and "good night" if they leave in late afternoon.
- Darken room to simulate night at rest time.
- Put up a mobile of our solar system.
- Read a story, such as *Night's Nice*. (See Book Center, p. 538.)

Vocabulary

sun	stars	moon	awake	sunglasses	sunny
day	earth	cold	dream	flashlight	cloudy
hot	dark	sleep	shadows	nightmare	shine
fog	light	rest	prism	sundial	night

learning centers

Discovery Center

1. Shadows: call attention to the children's shadows and those of objects on the playground. Discover that shadows are caused by light.
   a. Measure children's shadows in the morning, at noon, and before they leave in the afternoon, all at the same spot.
   b. Have the children put one hand in the sun and one in the shade on a sidewalk. Discuss which is warmer and why.

c. Pound a long stick (four or five feet) into the ground in an open spot. Measure the length of its shadow from time to time during the day. Discuss.

d. Indoors, have the children look for their shadows. Use a flashlight as the sun and a stand-up doll as a person. Let each child discover how to make long and short shadows on all sides of the doll. How do you make the shadow disappear?

e. Use a bright light on a movie screen, sheet, or light colored wall and let the children make shadow pictures.

f. Make shadow silhouettes. (See Games, No. 3, p. 540.)

g. Display Chinese paper cuts. (See p. 220 for where to order.)

2. Make a sundial and mark the hours. Explain that this is how people told time before clocks were invented. Check an encyclopedia for instructions.

3. Day and night: on a globe, stick a small paper figure to the location of the city where the children live. Stick one on the opposite side also. Darken the room and use a flashlight to represent the sun. Turn the globe slowly. The children will observe what causes day and night. If you have no globe, use a ball instead. (See Clouds, below.)

4. Clouds: they can keep us from seeing the sun, stars, and moon. Cut out paper clouds or use a cotton ball to place between child's eyes and the sun (outdoors) or a lamp (indoors) or when looking at constellation boxes.

5. Heat of the sun: discuss how the sun burns us. Also stand in the sun and then stand in the shade. Which is warmer? Use thermometer to show changes of temperature in sun and shade. The teacher can demonstrate how the sun can burn a hole in a piece of paper with a magnifying glass.

   CAUTION: Watch children closely.

6. Absence of light: take brightly colored objects into a closet and slowly close the door. The colors will disappear.

7. Reflected light: shine a small flashlight on a circle cut out of white material in a dark closet. The object will appear to shine too. That is how the moon shines at night with the sun's reflected light. Our earth is especially bright when the sun shines on it because so many things reflect the sun's light, especially the dust in the air.

8. Light is made up of many colors. Use a prism to demonstrate this. (See Color guide, p. 586.)

9. Bake cookies: cut in shape of stars, moon (crescent), and sun (round). Frost yellow or white. Add silver dragées to moon and stars.

10. Constellation Box: teacher can poke holes to represent stars in a constellation in the bottom of a round salt box. (The Big Dipper is the most familiar.) Hold the box up to a light or a window and look through the hole where the pouring spout was. Or punch holes in the lid of an oatmeal box in the same manner. Shine a flashlight through it to project constellation onto the wall or ceiling of a dark room. Use a ten-penny nail or ice pick for punching holes.

    CAUTION: Be sure to mark the constellation *in reverse* on the outside of the box, so it will appear the way we see it in the sky.

Dramatic Play Centers

Home-Living Center

1. Darken this area of the room if possible by turning off the lights or partitioning off the area with screens and covering the windows with a dark material.

2. Set out night clothes and blankets for dolls.

3. Bring nightgowns, pajamas, robes, and slippers for dress up.
4. Bring a box big enough for a child to use as a bed or a cot; also provide some cuddly animals and crib blankets.
5. Simulate having the sun rise by lighting the area and removing coverings from windows. Family members get up and get ready for school, breakfast, and work.

Block-Building Center

1. Make available sturdy doll house furniture so that children can build a ranch-type house without a roof with the unit blocks and arrange furniture as they wish for eating, sleeping, and so on.
2. Set out commercial or homemade doll houses with open sides or top for children to arrange furniture and family models in various day and night activities.

Learning, Language, and Readiness Materials

Commercially made games and materials for use at a table or on a mat:

(See Basic Resources, p. 79, for manufacturers' addresses.)

1. Globe: 8 inch, 10 inch, or 12 inch (most stores and catalogs)
2. Magnifying glass: 4 inch wide lens set in a metal frame with a strong handle
3. Six inch prism: available from most catalogs
4. Doll house furniture: major catalogs; most variety stores
5. Family members: block accessories, multiethnic; major catalogs
6. Moon and Star: lacing cards (ETA)
7. Primary cut-outs: Stars, flannelboard aids (Instructo)
8. Flashlight: 3 colors with red warning blinker
9. Judy Puzzle: Owl and Owlet, 11 pcs.
10. Playskool Puzzles: Owl, two trays; Ursa Major, 7 pcs.

Teacher-made games and materials for use at a table or on a mat:

NOTE: For detailed description of Games, see pp. 50–59.

1. Look and See: use flannelboard figures of sun, moon, and star.
2. I See Something, What Do You See?: I see something round like the moon; black like the night; yellow like the sun; pointed like a star.
3. Who's Missing?: change to Who Went to Bed?
4. Match-Them: use sun, stars, and phases of the moon.
5. Alike, Different, and the Same: 2 suns and a star; 2 stars and a moon.
6. Make a calendar for the month. Each day paste a cut-out of a sun or a cloud on the appropriate square. Count the cloudy and sunny days.

Art Center

** 1. Spatter paint: teacher precuts star and moon stencils. Using a screen, children spatter dark blue or black tempera paint over the stencils and onto white paper.
2. Starry night: use an old window shade of a dark color or a night shade.
** a. Have children use white crayons or chalk on the dark side to draw the sky at night.
*** b. Have children punch holes in the shade with a bobby pin to form some "constella-

tions." When the window shade is placed in a sunny window, the "stars" will seem to shine.

* 3. Teacher precuts phases of the moon in pale yellow manila construction paper or silver or white gummed-back paper. Children paste these on sheets of black paper. Prepackaged star stickers may be added.

*** 4. Night and day pictures: join a light and dark piece of construction paper end to end or back to back. Children cut night and day pictures from magazines and paste on appropriate side, or draw pictures with chalk or crayons.

*** 5. Mural: in the center of a long sheet of brown paper, the teacher or one of the children can make a large yellow or orange ball for the sun. The rest of the children can color with paint, crayons, or felt pens, a figure (person, house, tree, animal) on one side or the other of this sun. Then they put a black shadow opposite the sun on their figure to show the relationship of light and shadow. Best following Discovery Center 1d. (See p. 536.)

Book Center

** Baum, Arline and Joseph. *One Bright Monday Morning*. New York: Random House, 1962.

* Brown, Margaret W. *Goodnight Moon*. New York: Harper & Row, 1947.

* ———. *A Child's Goodnight Book*. Reading, Mass.: Addison-Wesley, 1950.

** Bulla, Clyde R. *What Makes a Shadow*. New York: Thomas Y. Crowell, 1962.

* deRegniers, Beatrice S. and Isabel Gordon. *The Shadow Book*. New York: Harcourt Brace Jovanovich, 1962.

*** ———, and Leona Pierce. *Who Likes Sun?* New York: Harcourt Brace Jovanovich, 1961.

** Emberley, Barbara and Ed Emberley. *Night's Nice*. Garden City, N.Y.: Doubleday, 1963.

*** Fisher, Aileen. *In the Middle of the Night*. New York: Thomas Y. Crowell, 1965.

** Garelick, May. *Look at the Moon*. Reading, Mass.: Addison-Wesley, 1969.

*** Goudey, Alice E. *The Day We Saw the Sun Come Up*. New York: Scribner's, 1961.

*** Hazen, Barbara. *Frère Jacques*. Philadelphia, Pa.: J. B. Lippincott, 1973.

** ———. *Where Do Bears Sleep?* Reading, Mass.: Addison-Wesley, 1970.

** Hoban, Russell. *Bedtime for Frances*. New York: Harper & Row, 1965.

** Hurd, Edith T. *The Day the Sun Danced*. New York: Harper & Row, 1965.

** Kauffman, Lois. *What's That Noise?* New York: Lothrop, Lee & Shepard, 1965.

*** Kinney, Jean. *What Does the Sun Do?* Reading, Mass.: Addison-Wesley, 1967.

**** Mack, Stan. *Ten Bears in My Bed: A Goodnight Countdown*. New York: Pantheon Books, 1974.

** Mayer, Mercer. *There's a Nightmare in My Closet*. New York: Dial Press, 1968.

** Myers, Walter M. *Where Does the Day Go?* New York: Parents' Magazine Press, 1969.

** Schneider, Nina. *While Suzie Sleeps*. Reading, Mass.: Addison-Wesley, 1968.

* Shaw, Charles G. *It Looked Like Spilt Milk*. New York: Harper & Row, 1947.

** Showers, Paul. *In the Night*. New York: Thomas Y. Crowell, 1961.

*** Shulevitz, Uri. *Dawn*. New York: Farrar, Straus & Giroux, 1974.

*** Tresselt, Alvin. *The Hide and Seek Fog*. New York: Lothrop, Lee & Shepard, 1966.

* Zolotow, Charlotte. *Sleepy Book*. New York: Lothrop, Lee & Shepard, 1966.

* ———. *Wake Up and Good Night*. New York: Harper & Row, 1971.

*** ———. *When the Wind Stops*. New York: E. M. Hale, 1965.

NOTE: Check your library for books on the moon by Franklyn M. Branley.

planning for grouptime

NOTE: All music, fingerplays, poems, stories, and games listed here may also be used at other times during the session as appropriate. See Core Library, Basic Resources, p. 76, for publishers and addresses. Addresses for sources of records will be found on p. 81.

Music

Songs

FROM *Songs for Early Childhood*, Westminster Press
* "Sing a Song of Sunshine," pp. 36–37
* "Bye Low, My Baby," p. 82
* "All Day Long as I Play," p. 82
** "A Little Star Creeps O'er the Hill," p. 83
** "Sleep Golden Poppy," p. 84 (listening)

FROM *Songs for the Nursery School*, MacCarteney
*** "Moon, Moon," p. 92
** "Hush My Baby," p. 93

FROM *Wake Up and Sing*, Landeck and Crook
* "Wake Up," p. 10
** "Mary Ann," p. 23

FROM *Music Resource Book*, Lutheran Church Press
* "Are You Sleeping?" p. 28
* "Isn't It Fun?" p. 46

Records

"Night"/"Night's Nice"/"Who Likes the Dark?"/"In the Night"/"It Is Night"/"Sleepy Book"/ "Night Cat" (Bowmar, 33⅓ RPM)
"Follow the Sunset" (Folkways, 33⅓ RPM)
"Carrot Seed"/"Eagle and the Thrush"/**"Wait Till the Moon Is Full"** (Young People's Records [YPR], 33⅓ RPM)
"Circus Comes to Town"/**"When the Sun Shines"**/"Around the World" (YPR, 33⅓ RPM)
"Eensie, Weensie Spider"/"Skittery Skattery"/**"Sleepy Family"** (YPR, 33⅓ RPM)
"Fog Boat Story"/"Music Listening Game"/"Do This, Do that" (YPR, 33⅓ RPM)

NOTE: Above records also available singly on 45 or 78 RPM by Children's Record Guild or Young People's Records.

"Lullabies from Around the World" (Rhythms Production, 33⅓ RPM)

Rhythms and Singing Games

FROM *Songs for the Nursery School*, MacCarteney
"See the Sunshine," p. 7

FROM *Songs for Early Childhood*, Westminster Press
"Walking in the Sunshine," p. 101

Fingerplays and Poems

FROM *Rhymes for Fingers and Flannelboards*, Scott and Thompson
"Five Little Babies," p. 79
"This Little Boy," p. 80 (adapt for boy or girl)
"Wake Up, Little Fingers," p. 109
"Thumbkins," p. 115
"Resting Time," p. 117

FROM *Let's Do Fingerplays*, Grayson
"Sleepy Fingers," p. 43
"Bedtime," p. 101

Stories

(To read, read-tell, or tell. See Book Center for complete list.)

   * *Goodnight Moon*, Brown
  ** *Night's Nice*, Emberley
  ** *Bedtime for Frances*, Hoban
   * *Sleepy Book*, Zolotow
  ** *While Suzie Sleeps*, Schneider
  ** *In the Night*, Showers

Games

1. World game: to be played after Discovery Center 3, p. 536. Darken the room. Put a lamp or flashlight at one end of the room. Have the children form a circle to represent the earth. Divide into two halves. The half facing the sun (the light) do daytime activities, such as eating, jumping, running. The other half, not facing the sun, pretend to go to sleep. Then the circle re-forms and the earth rotates half way around. Again there are night and day activities but for the opposite half of the earth.
2. Night and Day: the teacher tells the children to close their eyes, then calls on a child to tell about one thing that happens at night. Then the teacher tells the children to open their eyes and calls on another child to tell about one thing that happens in the day. Repeat as long as there is interest or every child has participated.
3. Whose Shadow?: hang a sheet. Place a light behind it. Have children cover their eyes and put their heads on their knees. Teacher taps one child who goes behind the screen. Others open their eyes and guess whose shadow.

Routine Times

1. At snack or mealtime have day and night cookies: stars, moon, sun, which the children or a cook has baked.
2. At rest time always darken the room slowly. Pretend night is coming and the sun is going down. Also, brighten the room as slowly as possible at the end of the rest period to simulate the sun coming up.

Large Muscle Activities

1. Play shadow tag or just try to step on each other's shadows outdoors. Show children how you can avoid getting your shadow stepped on by squatting quickly or hiding it in the shadow of a building or a tree.
2. Sally Go Round the Stars. (See Circle Games, p. 59.)

Extended Experiences

1. Send home with the children notes requesting that their parents take them out at night to see the stars, the moon, and a sunset, or get up early to watch a sunrise.
2. Have a visit from a parent who works at night, and have the parent talk about his or her job, such as police officer, firefighter, security guard, nurse.

teacher resources

Books and Periodicals

1. Zim, H. and R. Baker. *Stars*. New York: Simon and Schuster, 1951.
2. Lewellen, J. *The True Book of Moon, Sun, and Stars*. Chicago, Ill.: Childrens Press, 1954.

Pictures and Displays

(See p. 79 for addresses of firms listed.)

1. Use pictures from magazines that show day or night, or activities that go on during the day or night.
2. Make two dioramas: one could be a day scene, the other a night scene.
3. Art Center 2–5 could be made entirely by the teacher and used in the room.

Community Resources

1. Astronomer at a nearby college, university, or observatory
2. A planetarium, if located in or near your city

34 Food in My World

basic understandings

(concepts children can grasp from this subject)

- All people (regardless of age) need food to eat and water to drink in order to live.
- Most animals and plants need food to eat and water to drink in order to live.
- The right foods give us energy and many other things we need to grow, work, and play.
- There are many kinds of food: milk and cheese, vegetables, fruit, meat, eggs, fish, poultry, bread, and cereals.
- We can enjoy food in many ways: its color, its taste, its texture, its odor (smell).
- Some things we eat are called "empty calorie foods" because they contain few or no vitamins, minerals, or protein and are not necessary for good health, for example, pickles, candies, potato chips, soda pop, spices, and some seasonings.

NOTE: See Additional Facts the Teacher Should Know, last paragraph.

- Some people cannot eat all foods because they have allergies or other physical handicaps, such as diabetes or high blood pressure.
- Some children do not eat certain foods because of their families' customs and religious beliefs.
- We taste (flavor) through parts of our tongue called "taste buds."
- Our nose (sense of smell) helps us to know the food we are eating or cooking.
- Each food has a different (special) taste or flavor. Some foods taste sour, sweet, salty, or bitter.
- Flavoring or seasoning is something we can add to food to change its taste; each spice is different, for example, salt, pepper, vanilla, curry, cinnamon, ginger.

Sources of Food

- Many babies (both human and animal) get their first food by nursing from their mother's breast or sometimes from a bottle.
- Many people help grow and prepare the food we eat.
- Much of the food we eat comes from farms (from both animals and plants, including trees).
- Some foods (like fish and shell food) come from rivers, lakes, or oceans.
- Food can be bought in many forms, such as fresh (carrots), frozen (peas), dried (raisins), canned (vegetables and fruit), packaged (bread/cookies), processed (cereals).
- Some food is manufactured, such as crackers, prepared cereals, packaged mixes.
- We buy most of our food at grocery stores or supermarkets.

Preparing, Serving, and Packaging Food

- Some foods can be eaten raw, cooked, or dried, such as apricots.
- Some foods have different textures depending upon how they are prepared or eaten. (Some are hard, crisp, soft, rough, smooth, liquid, or solid.)
- Some foods can be eaten only when cooked, such as pork or popcorn.
- We can eat different parts of foods.

   a. With vegetables we sometimes eat the leaves, roots, tubers, flowers, or stems. Seldom do we eat more than one part of any one vegetable. (See chart, p. 547.)
   b. We eat the flesh of the fruit around the seed. Sometimes we can eat the skins of fruit (like dates, apricots, prunes, figs, cherries, apples, and pears). Some skins we do not eat (for example, bananas or grapefruit skins). Some skins, such as oranges and lemons, we eat only when using as a flavoring, as in marmalade or as a garnish.

- Food can be eaten in several ways: drinking, using fingers, using forks, spoons, or chopsticks, and sometimes using a straw.
- Foods we drink are known as beverages.
- The same food can be served and eaten in many ways, for instance, raw pineapple, canned crushed pineapple, canned chunks, canned halves, broiled on meat, cooked in cake, as juice, as sauce on ice cream, as jam, jelly, in ice cream, in sherbet, and as flavoring in icing or candy.
- We prepare special foods for babies (at home or in processing plants).
- Babies and older people without teeth or with stomach problems can eat special foods prepared for them that do not require chewing. They are often puréed or strained and mildly seasoned.
- We can eat food in different places:
   a. at tables in kitchens or dining rooms at home
   b. in bed when sick at home or in a hospital
   c. from snack trays or plates held in the hand while sitting in the living or family room
   d. in backyards or parks during picnics or barbecues
   e. in restaurants, hotels, or motel dining rooms, cafeterias, lunch counters, snack bars
   f. while traveling in cars, trains, airplanes, and boats (See Transportation guides.)
   g. in theaters when we eat snacks
- Most foods are prepared in kitchens (whether at home, in bakeries, in restaurants, by manufacturing companies, or by laboratories).
- Food is sold in many different kinds of containers, jars, boxes, cans, and glasses and is often wrapped in plastic, aluminum, cardboard, or paper.

Additional Facts the Teacher Should Know

Vitamins, minerals, and protein, along with enough carbohydrate for energy, are necessary for vitality and health.

The National Dairy Council's guide *Good Eating for Children* recommends the following diet daily:

1. milk (three or more glasses). Foods made with milk can supply part of this.
2. meat and eggs (two or more servings)
3. vegetables and fruits (four or more servings. Include some dark green or yellow vegetables and tomatoes or one citrus fruit)
4. bread and cereals (four or more servings)
5. cut down on sweets between meals

Spices and seasonings, along with additives like pickles, nuts, and onions, are often added to foods to improve their flavor and taste. However, foods cooked with little or no water or baked, broiled, or roasted retain their natural flavor and require fewer additives to make them delicious. They are more nutritious *and* as filling and enjoyable.

Good food habits:

1. help children to reach their maximum development physically and mentally.
2. allow them to have opportunities for social development.
3. permit children to enjoy food and eating.
4. prevent or delay diseases.
5. assist in care of their teeth and gums.
6. allow regular and normal elimination of waste.

If you serve food in your Center, check with your local county home economist regarding United States Department of Agriculture (USDA) food program guidelines. Although you are not required to follow them, their suggestions are excellent!

Usually very young children like (it varies with different ethnic groups):

1. mildly flavored foods rather than strongly flavored or highly spiced
2. fruits more than vegetables, although melons and berries should not be included that often
3. raw vegetables but may get tired of chewing
4. plain foods rather than casseroles, stews, or creamed foods
5. firm-textured food rather than soft, such as hard-cooked eggs rather than poached or scrambled
6. carrots more often than celery because of the strings in celery
7. sweets and rich foods; however, fried foods or very sweet foods can irritate the intestinal tract and reduce appetite
8. desserts, such as raw or cooked fruits, milk pudding, sherbet, ice cream, plain cookies, or cakes

Young children can become tired of chewing and inadequately chewed food can cause gastrointestinal irritation. Therefore, chopped vegetables, ground or bite-size meat, and diced or minced vegetables are easier to digest.

Encourage children to chew their food more slowly and completely before swallowing. It is necessary to chew, chew, and chew some more because digestion begins in the mouth with the enzyme action in the saliva. The esophagus carries food to the stomach. Hydrochloric acid is secreted into the stomach from its walls as well as more enzymes in gastric and pancreatic juices which continue the digestion process.

Valves control the entrance and exit of the stomach so food can remain until partially digested before allowing it to move on to the intestines. In the intestines intestinal fluid and bile continue the digestive process. The part of the food we eat that cannot be digested is discarded as solid waste in fecal matter.

When food is properly digested it becomes liquid and then can be absorbed into the blood and carried to the body through the cells.

Usually active children require more food for energy than less active children but size and functioning of the thyroid can be a varying factor. Consult parents if you feel one of your children has a special need. An overweight child should be encouraged to eat balanced meals and to participate in more active play. A very thin child needs to have opportunities for rest or quieter play.

The taste buds for bitterness are in the middle of the back of the tongue; the sour taste buds are in the middle of the tongue on the sides; the sweet taste buds are on the tip of the tongue; and the salt buds are between the sour and the sweet buds.

The palatability and acceptability of food are the result of a combination of factors: taste, smell, texture, temperature, appearance, the place where the food is eaten, the time and people with whom it is eaten, and the emotional state of the individual eating.

Other factors include the utensils used, ability to chew, variety of food offered, example of others present, and general level of health (for example, whether a child is well, tired, or ill).

Some children may not be able to eat certain foods because of dietary limitations, such as high blood pressure, allergies, celiac disease, nephritis, phenylketonuria (PKU), lacto intolerance, a hyperkinetic or diabetic condition, or the religious discipline of some ethnic groups. Foods most commonly associated with allergies are eggs, oranges, lemons, nuts, berries, chocolate, tomatoes, wheat, spices, and milk. If children in your group have special nutritional needs or limitations, consult the child's parents and/or physician before undertaking activities involving foods.

Young children should be encouraged to try a variety of tasty snack foods. Sweets that cling to the teeth should not be served. The residue particles of such food left after eating may ferment with bacteria and cause tooth decay. When giving foods such as raisins or dried fruits to the children, finish with "detergent" foods that are hard, firm, or crisp. These act like a toothbrush in helping to clear such food debris. Raw vegetables and fruits are examples of nutritious detergent-type foods. Encourage children to brush and floss teeth whenever possible.

Consult your local county home economist for more information about "empty calorie foods." Such foods as pickles, candies, potato chips, and soda pop may occasionally give children a few calories for energy, but they have a filling effect so that children may have little or no appetite for foods with the vitamins, minerals, and proteins necessary for good health.

VEGETABLES AND THEIR EDIBLE PARTS

Leaves	Flowers	Roots	Tubers	Stems	Seeds
chicory	broccoli	beets	potatoes	broccoli	peas
kale	cauliflower	onions	sweet potatoes	asparagus	string beans
endive	artichoke	salsify	peanuts	rhubarb	corn
watercress	(French)	carrots	artichokes	(has poisonous	pumpkin seeds
dandelion		parsnips	(Jerusalem)	leaves)	(can be roasted)
swiss chard		turnips		celery	eggplant
beet greens		radishes		kohlrabi	lima beans
lettuce		rutabagas			wax beans
cabbage					okra
spinach					
chard					
parsley					
celery					
(if dried)					
salsify					

NOTE: Botanically, tomatoes are considered a fruit or berry but are often called fleshy-fruited vegetables. Others include cucumbers, musk melons, pumpkins, squash, and watermelons.

Methods Most Adaptable for Introducing This Subject to Children

- Prepare a favorite food.
- Introduce a story about food like *Carrot Seed.*
- Have a tasting party. (See Taste guide, p. 141.)
- Take a trip to a grocery store to buy some fruit or vegetables to fix for a snack.
- Follow an interest in farms by taking a trip to see a vegetable garden or a fruit orchard or by tasting a food commonly eaten in another country.
- Set out a display of fresh vegetables and fruits.
- Visit the center's cook to see food prepared (snacks or lunch) for your facility. (You may wish to take the children in small groups.)
- Ask a parent or student from another country to prepare and serve a special native snack for the children.

Vocabulary

cereals	cheese	milk	spices
breads	seasonings	coffee	sacks, bags
vegetables	meal	pop	fresh
fruits	breakfast	beverage	cooked
meat	lunch	tea	canned
farm	dinner	picnic	baked
crops	snack	restaurant	frozen
garden	supper	cafeteria	containers
supermarket	salad	kitchen	aluminum
groceries	dessert	dining room	plastic
grocery store	cake	jars	waxed
fish	pie	cans	glass
poultry	cookies	boxes	
eggs	drink	cartons	

learning centers

Discovery Center

1. Explore foods, such as peas and carrots. Feel, smell, taste, compare. Include raw, frozen, cooked, canned, baby foods.
2. Cut open an apple, section an orange, peel bananas, or peel carrots or cucumbers with a peeler or scrub clean with a vegetable brush. Compare appearance, taste, and texture.
3. Make gelatin. Add a grated vegetable or fruit. Observe change in texture and taste.
4. Bake cookies. (You may use cookie mix and vary by adding raisins, or chocolate chips, coconut, nuts. Frosting them is fun too!) (See **NOTE**, p. 404.)
5. Make applesauce. (See recipe, p. 373.)

   NOTE: A cracker or square of toast or bread may make the cooked soft texture of apples more acceptable.

6. Make meatballs, cook, and eat. (Consider cost; use electric skillet.)
7. Make butter. Use baby food jars with screw lids filled half full with whipping cream.

   Procedure:
   Step 1: Let children take turns (one jar for every two children) shaking (about 5 minutes) until the cream separates. At first it appears like whipped cream, then like overwhipped cream, and finally, when ready, it shows an obvious separation.
   Step 2: Pour off liquid and taste. Wash butter in cold water in a bowl several times. Drain off milky liquid each time, taste, and then wash again until liquid is

nearly clear. Work the butter in the water with a wooden spoon as you wash. Step 3: Add salt to taste and let children spread on crackers or bread.

CAUTION: Remind the children periodically to check the screw lids to make sure they are tight.

8. Cook fresh vegetables and compare with uncooked. Include any of the following: carrots, celery, cauliflower, or peas. You might make vegetable soup.
9. Make a nutritious snack.
10. Cut carrot tops, beet tops, or pineapple tops and place in a shallow bowl of crushed stones or pebbles covered with water. Watch them grow from day to day.

NOTE: The stones supply minerals necessary for growth.

11. Cut off the top third of a sweet potato (or can be left whole) and set it in water, allowing sprouts to vine at the top.

NOTE: Make a cardboard collar to hold a whole potato from dropping into a wide-mouth container, or put toothpicks into the potato around its center to make a ledge to support it as it rests on the rim of the container.

12. Plant seeds, such as grapefruit, orange, avocado, or bean, to show graphically what happens as seeds grow. Plant some points up, some points down, and some sideways to discover which is best. For observing the complete plant cycle, plant lettuce, carrots, or parsley outside or in a window box. These grow rapidly and can be eaten.
13. Arrange with your Center's cook to watch him or her bake, prepare meat or poultry, or prepare vegetables by scrubbing or peeling, boiling, steaming, mashing, or creaming.
14. Examine a coconut. Ask children what they think is inside. Break open and taste. Ask the cook to prepare something with coconut that day.

NOTE: Check with the cook before planning visits to the kitchen or before using the oven or kitchen.

15. Make a box containing goose, duck, chicken, and pullet eggs (blown) with corresponding feathers for children to identify and match or compare.
16. Display: Plants That Provide Food and Animals That Help Us, picture fold-outs (The Child's World).
17. Divide foods in parts (halves, quarters, thirds). Explain that these are parts of a whole. Use graduated measuring cups to illustrate halves, thirds, and quarters to prepare children for measuring when cooking. Double check with a lined cup measure: two halves make a whole, three thirds make a whole.
18. Help prepare food for freezing; later help center's cook or observe cook preparing frozen food for snack or lunch.
19. Pop popcorn in a corn popper.

NOTE: See pp. 209, 238, 261, 263, 269, 329 for ethnic food recipes for nutritious snacks.

Dramatic Play Centers

Home-Living Center

1. Mount pictures of a parent and child preparing food or baking pastries, of families eating, and of shopping in a grocery store. Hang the pictures in the doll corner or on an adjacent bulletin board to encourage dramatic play with food.

2. Mount pictures of foods on heavy cardboard for use on plates; laminate or cover with adhesive clear plastic. Also use TV dinner carton cut-outs for pretend food.

   NOTE: If small plastic food that tends to depress easily is filled with a mixture of sawdust and glue and resealed it will last indefinitely. Add sawdust first and stir in glue and work around before sealing.

3. Buy some new plastic foods, such as a whole baked chicken, a meat roast, a dozen eggs, a ham, doughnuts, as well as fresh vegetables and whole fruit, and set out other plastic foods for children to pretend to cook, serve, and sell in the grocery store (see next section). Instead of plastic eggs, wooden eggs (nesting eggs) can be made by an adult on a lathe or ordered from the Montgomery Ward farm catalog.

4. Collect small empty cartons of cereal, salt, Jell-O, and cake mixes, and small cans of vegetables, fruits, and soups that can be placed in the home-living center cupboard for the children to use in meal preparation.

   NOTE: Open cans from the bottom and they will appear to be unopened when placed right side up on shelf.

5. Stuff bread wrappers with newspapers and tape shut.
6. Add measuring cups, funnel, and large wooden spoons with mixing bowls and cornmeal.
7. Add an eggbeater to use with water. Provide soapflakes and occasionally a little chocolate to the mixture to add aroma. The soap discourages sampling and tasting.
8. For a special activity allow playdough in the doll corner with cookie cutters and cookie sheets, cake pans, and muffin tins.

Block-Building Center

1. Make available a large plastic or wooden farm animals' set, farm helpers, tractors, and trucks. These may suggest growing food and raising animals to take to market.
2. Add a wooden barn. Available in most catalogs.

   NOTE: See Farm Animals guide for other activities related to raising food and farm animals.

Other Dramatic Play Centers

Grocery Store:
1. Add an area adjacent to the doll corner for grocery store play. Set up plank and hollow blocks for counter and shelves. Add a cash register, money, and grocery store aprons and caps.
2. Fill shelves with empty cartons and cans to be used for stock.
3. A three-way play screen makes an excellent store front. (See illustration, p. 551.)
4. Fasten large price signs to the store front (or use chalk to put prices on blackboard surface of three-way play screen).
5. Set out a food scale and plenty of small grocery sacks and small corrugated boxes for carrying out groceries. (Shipping bags are tough and durable.)
6. Help children set up a check-out counter. Remember they may need pad and pencil for figuring the bill and a telephone for call-in customers.
7. Before children arrive, make sure money is divided into all purses and billfolds so that everyone has money to purchase groceries.
8. Encourage children to sell back groceries as if they were wholesale dealers in order to restock shelves after they have purchased all the store items. They should be able to go to the back door of the grocery store. One child is needed to restock the shelves.
9. If possible, obtain a grocery cart from a neighboring grocery store's manager. (They sometimes will donate an old or damaged cart.)

Grocery Store For this dramatic play center, provide small shopping bags, laminated paper money, empty food cans (opened at bottom), plastic meat, fruit, vegetables, unbreakable eggs, and empty food cartons. See facing page for detailed suggestions. See p. 22 for patterns of clerk's hat and apron.

10. Set out milk carrier accessories (hat, milk bottles, and carrier) and ice-cream man props (hat, apron, scoop, and cone and ice cream cartons).

Learning, Language, and Readiness Materials Center

Commercially made games and materials for use at a table or on a mat:

(See Basic Resources, p. 79, for manufacturers' addresses.)

1. Farm Lotto (Ed-U-Card)
2. Judy Puzzles: Fruits, Vegetables, Farm Animals, Apple, 5 pcs. each; Pig and Piglets, 7 pcs.; Duck, 8 pcs.; Chicken and Chicks, 9 pcs.; Sheep and Lambs, Table Setting, 10 pcs. each; Tractor, Grocery Cashier, Farmer, Cow, 11 pcs. each; Rooster, 15 pcs.
3. Judy See-Quees: Baking a Cake, 4 pcs.; Eggs to Chicken, The Apple Tree in Seasons, Johnny Growing, Baking Cookies, 6 pcs. each; From Seed to Pumpkin, At the Supermarket, Story of Milk, 12 pcs. each
4. Cashier, Truck, Tractor, Farm, 11 to 15 pcs. each; Standup Puzzles: Farm, 20 pcs. (Childcraft)
5. Plastic Play Foods (Childcraft)
6. Balance Scale (Childcraft)

7. Play Store and Puppet Stage (Childcraft)
8. Cash Register (available in most catalogs)
9. Sculptured Rubber Animals: Farm (Constructive Playthings)
10. Farm Fence (Childcraft)
11. Table Block Farm (Childcraft and Constructive Playthings)
12. Nutrition: bulletin board aids (Instructo)
13. Food/Animals/Vegetables and Fruit: flannel aids (Milton Bradley)
14. Farm Animals Set (Fisher-Price)

Teacher-made games and materials for use at a table or on a mat:

NOTE: For detailed description of Games, see pp. 50–59.

1. I See Something. What Do You See?: refer to food in center of table or on tray.
2. Look and See: use plastic models, real food, or food flannelboard aids.

Child at left is placing food discs into a sorting tray. Picture cards at back of tray are a guide for division of discs. Numeral cards provide a more difficult task for a child with greater skill and ability. Child at right is matching food can labels mounted on masonite squares.

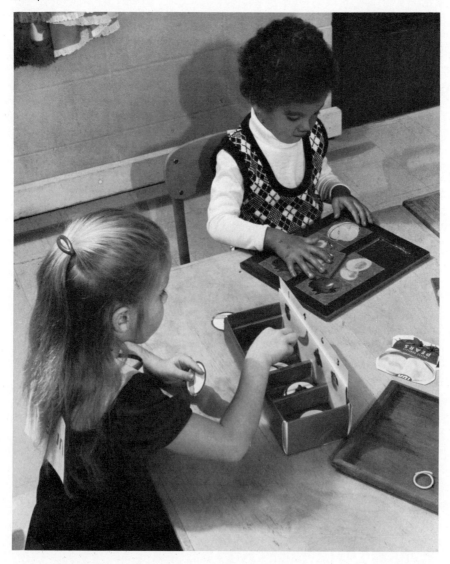

3. Sniff and Smell: use real food or film cans filled with seasonings.
4. Chew, Lick, and Taste: provide tasting party. (See Taste guide, p. 141.)
5. Can You Remember?: use props as for No. 2.
6. Guess What?: describe foods by color, shape, texture, size.
7. How Many (ways can you eat a single food)?: apples, bananas, for example.
8. Which (food do you eat raw, need to cook, need to peel)?
9. Farm Lotto (or make your own, using pictures of fruits and vegetables).
10. Match-Them: animal/product, vegetable/vegetable, and fruit/fruit, such as raw with cooked or whole with sections.
11. Alike, Different, and the Same: for example, a. apples both the same color but different size, b. different in color or form such as applesauce, c. two identical apples.
12. Sequence (you can find some examples in food ads for jams, biscuits, coke, juice): also use "before and after," "which came first . . ."
13. Directions (use plastic food).
14. Grouping and Sorting by Association: sort pictures of plastic models of food into card tuck charts, yarn circles, or cartons. Sort: a. food from other subjects, b. fruit from vegetables, c. drinks from meat. **Variation:** Let children select their favorite food from a pile of pictures on a table and tape their choice to a chart labeled Vegetables, Meat, Desserts, Fruit. Be sure to deemphasize empty calorie foods.
15. Reach and Feel: use plastic or real food in a bag or set out in front of the group. (See p. 53 for illustration.)
16. Make a little-to-big card series (animal pictures from farm journals).
17. Compare sizes big, bigger, biggest, using empty cans or cartons of various sizes.
18. Count: nuts or mounted decal pictures of food.
19. Play supermarket, using four sacks, each labeled with a picture suggesting each of four basic food groups: milk, meat and eggs, vegetables and fruit, bread and cereals.
20. Name It or Scramble: use real food, models, or flannelboard aids.
21. Make Match-Them Lace Boards (alike, different, same, or for association matching). Make each board with two columns as noted below. Punch holes by each item on each column to lace colored or black yarn from one side to the other. Vary arrangement so that lacing is diagonal as well as horizontal.

Column 1	Column 2
circle of one color	fruit of same color
black outline shape of corresponding fruit (or vegetable)	fruit of same shape
large decal or cut-out (can be outline or solid) of fruit	identical decal or cut-out of vegetable, fruit, meat, or other
animal	product we eat
animal	food it eats

22. Number Readiness:
    a. Use counting rhymes.
    b. See also Grocery Store, Nos. 4, 5, and 7, p. 550, and use here for an individual child or small group.

23. Discrimination and Classification:
    a. smelling, feeling, tasting in groups
    b. exploring textures (soft avocado, crunchy carrot or celery, slippery banana, squirty orange). Group citrus fruits separately (citrus fruits have sections).
24. Ring It: mount colored pictures of fruit or vegetables on a sheet of x-ray film. Cut out the center of a potato chip canister lid leaving a ½ to ⅓ inch rim. Wrap with bright-colored yarn. Children can use these yarn rings to circle pictures on their boards when the teacher calls a color or a fruit; or it is a self-correcting game if children use it independently.

Art Center

NOTE: Use of foods for creative art activities may be considered inappropriate by children whose families may have a greater need to prepare it for eating.

1. Tempera painting with a brush at easel or at table: you may add whole eggs to dry tempera and brush paint, or children may sprinkle broken eggshells on painting or on top of a monoprint. **Variation:** Add coffee grounds to easel paint for interesting texture.
2. Fingerpainting: use yellow, red, green (add salt for texture; pickling salt is more crystalline). One color is enough for youngest child.
3. Make playdough to use: explain to children it is made from salt (halite), flour (wheat), and water. Let them measure and mix. Talk about other uses for salt and flour. (See recipes, p. 27.)
4. Make food books:
    Meat We Eat
    Vegetables I Like
    Fruits I Like
    Desserts
    Drinks
    Breads
    Food Animals Eat (paste animal opposite picture of food it eats or on same page)
    a. Let children look through home magazines for pictures of food to cut out to paste.
    b. For younger children prepare pictures from magazines to be ready for cutting and pasting. It helps to circle or draw an abstract free-form shape around the picture as a cutting guideline if edges of pictures are too intricate.
    c. For the very youngest you may precut pictures and let it be a classification, preference selection, and pasting operation only.
5. Drawing tray: place a dark sheet of paper on the bottom of an edged tray. Cover paper with a thin layer of cornmeal or salt. Children can use a finger to draw. Then erase drawing by shaking the tray.

CAUTION: Any food used for an art medium must be stored in airtight containers because of the danger of attracting bugs, roaches, or mice. Use the food within a week or two and discard any remaining portion.

6. Seed collage: use watermelon or pumpkin seeds saved, or weed seeds.
7. Rice and felt collage (you may color rice).
8. Straw collage: paste straws on heavy paper to make a picture. **Variation:** Older children may wish to paint too.
9. Vegetable and fruit printing: use ends or discarded sections of carrots, cabbage, onions, potatoes, apples, green peppers, cauliflower.

Book Center

*** Balet, Jan. *The Fence*. New York: Delacorte Press, 1969.

**** Beck, Barbara. *The First Book of Fruits*. New York: Franklin Watts, 1967.

**** Bendick, Jeanne. *First Book of Supermarkets*. New York: Franklin Watts, 1954.

*** Brown, Myra B. *Company's Coming for Dinner*. New York: E. M. Hale, 1959.

**** Buckheimer, Naomi. *Let's Take a Trip to a Bakery*. New York: G. P. Putnam's Sons, 1956 (reference).

*** Buckley, Helen. *Too Many Crackers*. New York: Lothrop, Lee & Shepard, 1966.

** Carle, Eric. *The Very Hungry Caterpillar*. Cleveland, Ohio: Collins-World, 1970.

*** Curry, Nancy. *An Apple Is Red*. Glendale, Calif.: Bowmar, 1967 (also record).

**** Fenton, Carrol K. *Plants We Live On*. New York: John Day, 1971.

*** Floethe, Louise and Richard Floethe. *Blueberry Pie*. New York: Scribner's, 1962.

* Francoise, Charles. *Thank You Book*. New York: Scribner's, 1947.

*** Freeman, Mae Blacker. *Fun with Cooking*. New York: Random House, 1947 (cookbook).

*** Greene, Carla Baker. *I Want to Be a Dairy Farmer*. Chicago, Ill.: Childrens Press, 1957.

*** ———. *I Want to Be a Farmer*. Chicago, Ill.: Childrens Press, 1959.

*** ———. *I Want to Be a Fisherman*. Chicago, Ill.: Childrens Press, 1957.

*** ———. *I Want to Be a Restaurant Owner*. Chicago, Ill.: Childrens Press, 1959.

*** ———. *I Want to Be a Storekeeper*. Chicago, Ill.: Childrens Press, 1958.

*** Ipcar, Dahlov. *Ten Big Farms*. New York: Alfred A. Knopf, 1958.

**** Johnson, Hannah Lyons. *Let's Bake Bread*. New York: Lothrop, Lee & Shepard, 1973.

** Jordan, Helene J. *How a Seed Grows*. New York: Thomas Y. Crowell, 1960.

* Krauss, Ruth. *Carrot Seed*. New York: Harper & Row, 1945.

* ———. *The Growing Story*. New York: Harper & Row, 1947.

*** Le Sieg, Theodore. *Ten Apples Up on Top*. New York: Beginner Books, 1961.

** McCloskey, Robert. *Blueberries for Sal*. New York: Viking Press, 1948 (paper, 1968).

*** Mannheim, Greta. *The Baker's Children*. New York: Alfred A. Knopf, 1970.

** Miner, Irene. *True Book of Plants We Know*. Chicago, Ill.: Childrens Press, 1953 (information).

*** Rockwell, Anne and Harlow Rockwell. *Molly's Woodland Garden*. Garden City, N.Y.: Doubleday, 1971.

*** Scheib, Ida. *The First Book of Food*. New York: Franklin Watts, 1956 (information only).

*** Schroeder, Glenn W. *At the Bakery*. Chicago, Ill.: Melmont, 1967.

*** Selsam, Millicent. *All about Eggs*. Reading, Mass.: Addison-Wesley, 1952.

**** ———. *Play with Plants*. New York: William Morrow, 1949 (reference).

**** ———. *Play with Seeds*. New York: William Morrow, 1957 (reference).

**** ———. *The Carrot and Other Root Vegetables*. New York: William Morrow, 1971 (information and photographs).

**** ———. *Vegetables from Stems and Leaves*. New York: William Morrow, 1972 (photographs).

** ———. *Seeds and More Seeds*. New York: Harper & Row, 1947.

**** ———. *The Plants We Eat*. New York: William Morrow, 1955.

**** Shannon, Terry. *About Food and Where It Comes From*. Chicago, Ill.: Melmont, 1961.

* Shaw, Charles G. *It Looked Like Spilt Milk*. New York: Harper & Row, 1947.

** Steiner, Charlotte. *The Hungry Book*. New York: Alfred A. Knopf, 1967.

**** Uhl, Melvin John, and Madeline Otteson. *How We Get Frozen Dinners*. New York: Noble & Noble, 1965 (reference).

**** Webber, Irma. *Bits That Grow Big*. Reading, Mass.: Addison-Wesley, 1949.

** ———. *Up Above and Down Below*. Reading, Mass.: Addison-Wesley, 1943.

planning for grouptime

NOTE: All music, fingerplays, poems, stories, and games listed here may be used at other times during the session as appropriate. See Core Library, Basic Resources, p. 76, for publishers and addresses. Addresses for sources of records will be found on p. 81. In parodies, hyphenated words match the music notes of the tune used.

Music

Songs

FROM original songs and parodies in this book by JoAnne Deal Hicks
* "Popcorn" (a parody), p. 121
* "Fruitbasket Song," p. 561
* "Sing a Song of Applesauce," p. 562

WHAT FOODS DO YOU LIKE? (a parody)
   (tune: "Oats, Peas, Beans")
   Adaptation by JoAnne Deal Hicks

TEACHER SINGS SONG TO THE CHILDREN:

Eggs and milk and ba-con strips.
Eggs and milk and ba-con strips.
Do you, do you, do you, do you?   (POINTS TO INDIVIDUAL CHILDREN)
Like eggs and milk and ba-con strips?

(CHILDREN MAY THEN RESPOND BY NODDING HEADS IN AFFIRMATION OR VERBALLY EXPRESSING THEIR LIKE OR DISLIKE OF THE FOOD)

Many combinations of food may be used, for example:

dan-ish rolls and or-ange juice
pea-nut but-ter, jel-ly, too
ap-ples, grapes, and can-ta-loupe
cheese and pie with cold ice cream
corn and peas and broc-co-li
car-rots (or let-tuce, spin-ach) and po-ta-toes?
milk and fruit and ce-re-al

NOTE: This is a good opportunity to talk about trying new foods or about contrasts, such as eating soft food with crisp food to make the experience more pleasurable. (See p. 544 for other suggestions.)

FROM *Music Resource Book*, Lutheran Church Press
** "Oats, Peas, Beans, and Barley," p. 57
* "Mulberry Bush," p. 92

FROM *Wake Up and Sing*, Landeck and Crook
*** "Green Corn," p. 46
 ** "Solas Market," p. 85

FROM *Songs for Early Childhood*, Westminster Press
 ** "Apples Green and Apples Red," p. 18
  * "For Health and Strength and Daily Care," p. 75 (if you are allowed to use religious music)
 ** "Oats, Peas, Beans," p. 107
  * "Here We Go 'Round the Mulberry Bush," p. 108
    "Do You Know the Muffin Man," p. 118

FROM *Songs for the Nursery School*, MacCarteney
  * "Hot Cross Buns," p. 75
  * "Little Jack Horner," p. 77
  * "Peas Porridge Hot," p. 79
 ** "Polly, Put the Kettle On," p. 86
*** "Sing a Song of Sixpence," p. 87
*** "Bake a Cake," p. 107

Records

"**Gingerbread Boy**"/"Billy Goats Gruff" (Phoebe James, 78 RPM)
"The Donut Song" Burl Ives (Columbia Records, 33⅓ RPM)
"The Little Red Hen," *The Best in Children's Literature*, Series II (Bowmar, 33⅓ RPM)
"Golden Goose"/"**Hot Cross Buns**"/"Where Do Songs Begin" (Young People's Record [YPR], 33⅓ RPM)
"All Aboard! Train to the Zoo/**Farm**/Ranch" (YPR, 33⅓ RPM)
"Build Me a House"/"Silly Will"/"**Milk's Journey**" (YPR, 33⅓ RPM)
"Muffin and Mother Goose"/"Musical Mother Goose"/"Muffin in the City"/"**Muffin in the Country**" (YPR, 33⅓ RPM)
"**Carrot Seed**"/"Eagle and the Thrush"/"Wait 'Till the Moon Is Full" (YPR, 33⅓ RPM)
"Emperor's New Clothes"/"**Harvest Time**" (YPR, 33⅓ RPM)

Rhythms and Singing Games

FROM *Wake Up and Sing*, Landeck and Crook
"Congo Tay," pp. 82–83

FROM *Creative Movement for the Developing Child*, Cherry
Dance: children improvise movements for popcorn popping, pp. 39–40

See also Circle games in Basic Resources, p. 58.

Fingerplays and Poems

FROM *Rhymes for Fingers and Flannelboards*, Scott and Thompson
"Five Red Apples," p. 120

FROM original fingerplays in this book
"Apples," pp. 144

FROM your favorite edition of *Mother Goose* (Select action poems that have been set to music.)

Hot Cross Buns	*Pat-a-Cake*
Little Jack Horner	*Pease Porridge Hot*
Little Tommy Tucker	*To Market, to Market*
Muffin Man	*Old Mother Hubbard*

Stories

(To read, read-tell, or tell. See Book Center for complete list.)

** *Blueberries for Sal*, McCloskey
 * *It Looked Like Spilt Milk*, Shaw
** *The Very Hungry Caterpillar*, Carle
 * *Carrot Seed*, Krauss
*** *The Fence*, Balet
*** *Ten Big Farms*, Ipcar
*** *Molly's Woodland Garden*, Rockwell

Routine Times

1. At snack or mealtime serve food prepared earlier in the Discovery Center.
2. Serve a different raw fruit or vegetable each day for snacktime.
3. Talk about texture, color, and taste of foods while children are eating.
4. Prepare food at the table: pop corn in a popper, scramble eggs or meatballs in an electric skillet, prepare deviled eggs, or make finger snack foods. (See Discovery Center.)
5. Play What Is It?, I'm Thinking Of, or make up other guessing games about foods you are eating at snack or mealtime.
6. If you are allowed to use a table prayer you may wish to learn:

   Dear God,
     We thank you now for food to eat
     For fresh, clear water we can drink
     We thank you too for rest and care
     And little children everywhere.
                  Amen

   NOTE: Vary to match menu, meat to eat, good, fresh juice, and so on.

7. Plan with the Center's cook for introducing a variety of vegetables and fruits in snacks and mealtime.
8. Allow children to help set the table with flatware and glasses and napkins. Explain why they are placed as they are.
9. Children should brush teeth after each meal (show how, using pink tablets from the dentist after a meal one day).
10. Practice washing hands: children often do not wash the backs of their hands. (Boys' wrist movements are not as developed as girls'.) Encourage children to shake hands with themselves with soapy hands or to catch a fish (other hand). Teachers can also make bubbles by rubbing a bar of soap in water; they then can give children a handful of lathered bubbles to encourage soaping hands while washing.
11. Offer a choice of snack. Hang a restaurant sign over the lunchroom door.

Large Muscle Activities

THE FARMER PLANTS HIS SEED
  (tune: "The Farmer in the Dell")

(USE APPROPRIATE ACTIONS WITH HANDS AND ARMS)
VERSE 1:   The farmer plants his seed, the farmer plants his seed,
                 Hi-ho, the dairy-o, the farmer plants his seed.
VERSE 2:   The rain begins to fall, . . . (REPEAT AS IN FIRST VERSE)
VERSE 3:   The sun begins to shine, . . . (REPEAT AS IN FIRST VERSE)
VERSE 4:   The wind begins to blow, . . . (REPEAT AS IN FIRST VERSE)
VERSE 5:   The food begins to grow, . . . (REPEAT AS IN FIRST VERSE)

Extended Experiences

NOTE: See p. 72 for cautions about trips and excursions. Remember that official health standards may not allow visitors where food is prepared.

1. Trip to a bakery.
2. Trip to a grocery store or a supermarket. (Do not take children into the butchering section—they are too young.)
3. Trip to see a garden and see food growing.
4. Visit a restaurant and kitchen.
5. Visit a dairy store.
6. Visit a hatchery.
7. Watch delivery trucks unload at the school.
8. Invite your local county home economist to prepare a tasty or nutritious snack food for (or with) the children. Have him/her tell the children about empty calorie foods and the foods that help us grow.
9. Visit a truck farm or a large farm and see the equipment for planting and harvesting.
10. Invite a parent or student native to another country to visit and bring a special food to share or to help the children prepare a food enjoyed by children in his/her country. Demonstrate how best to eat the unusual food, whether it is Chinese, Mexican, soul food, Scandinavian, German, Italian.

teacher resources

Books and Periodicals

1. Cooper, Terry Touff, and Marilyn Ratner. *Many Hands Cooking, An International Cookbook for Girls and Boys.* New York: Thomas Y. Crowell, 1974.
2. Ferreira, Nancy J. *Mother-Child Cookbook: An Introduction to Educational Cooking.* Menlo Park, Calif.: Pacific Coast Publishers, 1969.
3. *Foods for Little People.* City of Berkeley Public Health Department, 2121 McKinley Ave., Berkeley, California 94703.
4. Croft, Karen B. *The Good for Me Cookbook.* 741 Maplewood Place, Palo Alto, Calif. 94303.
5. Robinson, Corinne H. *Normal and Therapeutic Nutrition.* New York: Macmillan, 1972.

Pictures and Displays

(See p. 79 for addresses of firms listed.)

1. Get large posters and signs from the grocery store to use as is with a pretend grocery store, to cut up for bulletin boards, or for use with games or props.
2. Check with outlet for the local Dairy Council (your local county home economist will know) for pictures and pamphlets and punch-out food models. Many times a model farm and large model cow are available on loan from your nearest Dairy Council office.
3. Food and Nutrition, Health and Cleanliness, A Trip to the Farm, Plants and Seeds: picture packet sets (David C. Cook)
4. Arrange a display of related food pictures which can be changed with the activities planned for each day, for example:
   a. a grapefruit, grapefruit juice, sectioned grapefruit, grapefruit in a salad (as a grouping of a fruit in many forms)
   b. a group of pictures showing whole fruits in relative sizes
   c. a series of familiar vegetables
   d. a series of pictures of desserts, meats, breads
   e. a food mobile showing the basic four food groups.
   f. a group of pictures showing outside and inside of fruits or vegetables, such as whole pea shell–tiny round peas or whole orange–orange sections
5. Order teachers' guides that accompany the following materials from the Dairy Council closest to you or from the National Dairy Council, Chicago, Ill. 60606.
   * *My Friend the Cow*, Lois Lenski
   ** *Let's Make Butter*
   ** *More Milk Please*
   *** *Your Health*, Marjorie Pursel
   We Like Milk Too, Picture Series
   What We Do All Day, Picture Series food models
   **** *Where We Get Our Food*
6. Plants and Foods, Nutrition: flannelboard sets (Instructo)
7. Visiting the Farm: Desk Top Activity Kits (Instructo)

Community Resources

1. Dairy Council representative (home economist)
2. County home economist specialist
3. Any food-processing plant in your city, town
4. Dairy store, grocery store, locker plant
5. Garden center (to buy seeds to plant)
6. Milk sales personnel (if deliveries are still made in your community)
7. Bakeries
8. A city market (farmers come in daily during harvest in spring, summer, and fall)
9. Parents: ask them to:
   a. Save some boxes and cans for the children to bring to school to use in the grocery store. (Tape boxes shut and make sure can edges are taped smooth and safe.)
   b. Save and send paper sacks and shopping bags for the school grocery.
   c. Request small shopping bag from parents (often available at Christmas time in specialty shops). Otherwise, children clear store shelves on first shopping trip. Smaller bags deter spending.

Fruitbasket Song

JoAnne Deal Hicks

NOTE: Continue singing, using any fruit the children might suggest. Remember: the song does not necessarily have to rhyme.

Sing a Song of Applesauce

JoAnne Deal Hicks

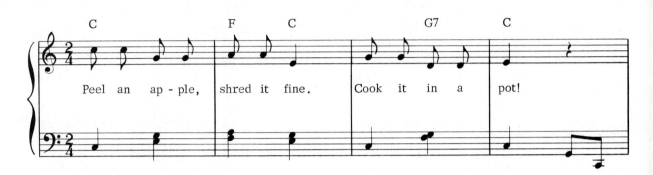

Peel an ap - ple, shred it fine. Cook it in a pot!

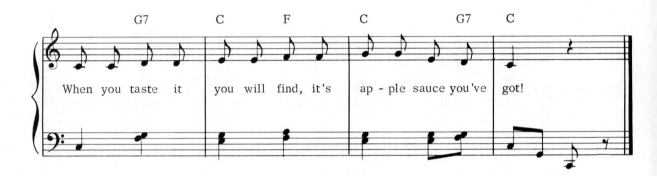

When you taste it you will find, it's ap - ple sauce you've got!

NOTE: Fun to sing while actually making applesauce.

35 Water Around Me

basic understandings

(concepts children can grasp from this subject)

> **NOTE:** Most statements below refer to water as a liquid unless identified by another term, such as ice, snow, fog, mist.

- Water is necessary to all living things.
- Water is all around us, in the air and in the ground. It is in milk, vegetables, fruit, meat, leaves, trunks, roots, and branches of a tree; it is even in stones.
- Water is used for many things:
  a. to drink: toads drink through their skin, birds tip their heads back, horses suck, cats and dogs lap, and other animals drink in their own ways
  b. to wash things: dishes, cars, clothes, ourselves
  c. to cook things in (eggs, vegetables); to use in things we cook (cakes, soup)
  d. to put out fires
  e. to play in: pools, ponds, lakes, oceans; or to play with when using hoses
  f. to water plants, lawns, trees, bushes
  g. to transport cargo and people on ships or boats
- Water is wet when it is a liquid. Scientifically it must be stated that it is dry when ice or vapor.
- Pure water is colorless. It often appears blue in ice or in a clear lake or green or brown in a river because it contains or reflects other matter.
- Water that has mineral salts (calcium and magnesium) is called "hard water." Rainwater is most often soft water. Well water or water from streams flowing over gypsum, limestone, or dolomite is more likely to be hard.
- Water is heavier than air.

- Ocean water is salty.
- More plants and animals live in water than on land (some in saltwater and some in fresh water).
- There is much more water than land on the earth's surface.
- Water pours (or flows): it will run from a high place to a lower place and seek the lowest possible level.
- Water takes three forms:
  a. it is a liquid in lakes, oceans, or when it comes from faucets
  b. it is a solid when it is ice or snow
  c. it is a gas when it is steam, clouds, air, fog, mist, or vapor
- Water comes to the earth as rain or snow. Most of it goes back into the air. Fog or mist is a cloud on the ground.
- Ice is very strong. It holds you up when you skate on it if it is thick enough. Some Eskimos used to build temporary houses from blocks of snow and ice. If water gets into bottles, iron pipes, or cracks in rocks or pavements it can break them when it turns into ice because it expands when frozen.
- Cold water from our faucets comes from many sources: surface run-off stored in reservoirs behind dams, deep wells, springs, streams, and rainwater collected in concrete basins.
- Hot water from our faucets is the same water as the cold but it is heated and stored in a hot water tank in our homes before we use it.
- Water needs to be saved if we are to have enough. We can help by turning off dripping faucets and by pouring excess drinking water on plants or in the garden instead of down sink drains.

  CAUTION: Do not overwater plants.

- Many things mix with water: sugar, salt, soap. Some things do not, such as sand or oil.

  NOTE: See Animal guides for uses and needs of water by animals and the Water Transportation guide for information about water as a waterway. See Basic Resources, p. 70, for rainy day ideas and pp. 199, 324, and 365 for holiday water fun.

Additional Facts the Teacher Should Know

Pure water is composed of the elements hydrogen and oxygen (two parts of hydrogen to every part of oxygen). When these two invisible gases combine to form a liquid (water) or solid (ice), we can see them. When they remain in a gaseous form, such as steam or vapor, they are not always visible. The earth's surface is about 75 percent water and 25 percent land. The human body is about 70 percent water. Many compounds contain water. Foods hold a lot of water: milk, 87 percent; peaches, 89 percent; eggs, 74 percent, steaks, 60 percent; watermelons, 92 percent.

Water is used in great quantities in industrial and power applications, such as electricity and steam. This level of information is usually hard for very young children to understand, so it has not been highlighted in the basic concepts.

Water is the most precious material on earth, more than gold, diamonds, or oil. One-quarter of all water is used for industry. It takes 10 gallons of water to prepare 1 can of lima beans and 500 gallons to make 1 gallon of gasoline! One-quarter of the water is used to make electricity with steam power. Two-fifths is used for irrigation, and less than one-tenth for houses and public buildings. We are using so much water that unless we learn to reuse it, there will not be enough for the next generation of people.

The three worst sources of water pollution are:
a. sewage: poured by communities into major streams
b. industrial wastes: loaded with chemicals dumped back into streams
c. agricultural use: pesticides washed into streams kill fish and hence poison birds and animals that prey on them

Three ways to stop water pollution:
a. build treatment plants for sewage
b. have industries build plants to treat their wastes
c. control use of dangerous pesticides

To control erosion by rain and water we can:
a. contour farms
b. build dams and reservoirs
c. build irrigation ditches
d. build canals

Clouds are water vapor that contain billions of tiny droplets of water. They can be several miles high. Rain occurs when these droplets in a cloud combine and get too heavy to float, so they fall to earth. Water keeps traveling from sky to earth to ocean, and back again to sky. This constant movement is called the "water cycle" and has been going on for billions of years. Water gets into the air by evaporation and transpiration from the leaves of plants. An apple tree will lose as much as 40 gallons of water from its leaves on a hot day. As raindrops ("soft" or nearly pure water) fall to earth, they pick up tiny particles from the air and the ground to become impure or "hard." Boiled-off frozen water becomes clean again. Water becomes a solid when it is frozen into ice at 32° F. It becomes a gas when it boils into steam at 212° F. Hailstones are frozen raindrops. When water freezes, it expands. Ice floats on water and fish can live below it.

NOTE: Some children will know about soft and hard water because they have automatic water conditioners in their homes and their parents may require that they drink water only out of a specific faucet (usually a kitchen faucet because of cooking).

Water is a natural air conditioner. Water in the thick layer of air around the earth absorbs the hot rays of the sun; if it were not there, it would be too hot on earth for life. At night it is the opposite. The damp air holds in the heat that has been absorbed during the day. Otherwise, the earth would freeze every night. Air is never completely dry; there is always a blanket of moisture around the earth.

Water and most other liquids weigh approximately one pound per pint. "A pint's a pound the world around" is a good way to remember this. Therefore, a quart would weigh about 2 pounds; a gallon, 8. Water is colorless. The deep blue or green color of lakes or oceans comes from light. The blue of the sky also comes from light rays reflected by water molecules. In space, the sky is black because there is no moisture.

All plants and animals began as simple forms in the ocean. The ocean has always been a great source of food. Our ancestors speared fish before they killed land animals. Amphibians, such as frogs and turtles, can get oxygen from the water through their skins and from the air by means of their lungs. Warm-blooded animals and man cannot breathe without mechanical assistance under water. The average adult loses about 2½ quarts of water every day through his skin, lungs, and body wastes. It is replaced by eating and drinking. The water lost in perspiring cools you off by evaporation.

For years, explorers used water routes for transportation, and later added canals for this purpose. See related guides Water Transportation, Winter (snow), and Spring (rain).

Methods Most Adaptable for Introducing This Subject to Children

- When children notice the weather on a rainy, snowy, or foggy day, relate it to water.
- On a cold day, the children might notice their breath outdoors; they are making their own clouds but they fade quickly.
- On the science table have a globe of the earth and two pitchers of water, one salty and one fresh. Point out the oceans on the globe and let the children taste the saltwater. Then point out the lakes and rivers and let them taste the fresh water. Notice how much of the earth's surface is covered with saltwater. Use disposable paper cups or plastic spoons for tasting purposes.
- Have picture books with children playing in water and books of animals in or near water.
- Have magazine pictures of lakes, rivers, and oceans around the room. Have an aquarium in a prominent place.

Vocabulary

water	ice	lake	ocean	dew	damp
wet	snow	stream	cloud	freeze	wash
pond	fog	river	mist	melt	spray
swim	rain	drops	moist	drip	sprinkle

learning centers

Discovery Center

Water is very inexpensive and readily available as a material for play. If you don't have water in the classroom, place a large metal or plastic tub, tank, plastic baby bath, or small wading pool on an old throw rug, blanket, bedspread or towels on the floor. Older children could help to partly fill container by carrying pitchers, buckets, or cups of water from the nearest source. Have lots of wiping-up materials handy, such as mops, sponges, and rags. If plastic aprons are available, use them. When weather permits, use waterplay outdoors. Unadulterated water can be poured on the ground.

A bathroom with a wall removed allows this area to become a water play center. It can readily be used with no extra supervision if the area is visible from a classroom area. Note rules on the wall. No. 3 is "Wipe up spills on the floor" and No. 4 is "Only teachers turn on the faucets."

1. Pouring and measuring: start out with plastic or metal measuring cups. Each day add something else, such as squirt bottles, funnels, plastic or rubber tubing, straws, short lengths of hose, sponges, eggbeaters, strainers, wire whips, cooking spoons (metal and wooden), measuring spoons, clothes sprinklers. Be sure all utensils are unbreakable and will not rust. Use eye or medicine droppers of different sizes and count how many drops they hold. Also do this with a baster. Use measuring spoons and cups to count how many of each in each.

2. Floating and sinking: use water to try floating and sinking objects, such as nails, rocks, wood, cork, styrofoam, polyethylene objects, spools, cups, and floating and sinking soap. Try a small glass bottle with the lid off; then screw the lid on tightly and try again. Next put some sand in the bottle, cap it, and try again. Keep adding more sand until it sinks. Do the same with water. Explain that when a submarine's air tanks are full of water, it floats; but when filled with water it sinks. As the water is pumped out and replaced with (compressed) air again it will rise to the surface. Air helps things float, such as balloons, corks, wood, and our lungs.

3. Washing: add detergent or soap to the water and use it to wash toys that are dirty *and* washable, such as cars, trains, tabletops, cupboard shelves, doll furniture and clothes. Experiment to see whether hot or cold water dissolves soap more quickly.

4. Mixing: let children mix different things with water, such as soap powder, sand, salt, flour, sugar, oil, baking soda, and cornstarch. Using three jars of water, put sand in one, dirt in one, and salt in one. Shake all three and notice how fast they clear up.

5. Evaporation: pour water to the same level in two similar jars. Put a rubber band around the outside of both at the water level. Cap one but leave the other uncapped. Observe the change in level from day to day. Notice the residue. Put a salt-and-water

mixture in a flat dish. Note the residue after evaporation. Taste it. Iron a damp cloth until dry. To watch evaporation, put some water on a warm sidewalk on a sunny day. Soon the sidewalk will be dry. Indoors, wipe a blackboard with a wet sponge and watch it become dry. Blow on it or turn a fan on it and observe.

6. Hot and cold: fill one jar with water, one with packed snow, and one with ice cubes or chips. After they have all become water, compare volumes and cleanliness of contents. Fill a glass bottle full of water and cap it tightly. Put it outdoors in below-freezing weather or in the freezer. The bottle will break when the water expands while turning into ice. Use a magnifying glass to see snowflakes. Watch them turn into water in your warm hand. Blow on a cold window to see the water vapor from your breath. Heat a small piece of ice to water and then to steam. Heat water to steam, then turn it back into water on a mirror or a metal pan. Water will take the shape of any container it is put into. Freeze water in a balloon, milk carton, pie pan, or paper cup (cone-shaped, if possible). Notice the shapes when the containers are removed. Spill some water on a flat table and notice the shape it takes. Fill a glass with hot water and another with cold. Measure the temperatures with a thermometer, if you wish. Put a finger in each glass. Put some water from each glass into a third glass. Feel it and measure the temperature. Put some ice cubes into a glass of water. Feel and notice its temperature. Also observe drops of water formed on the outside of the glass.

7. Absorption and Displacement: weigh a dry sponge; soak it with water and weigh it again. Show how water soaks into a paper towel but forms drops or runs off waxed paper. Show how water magnifies by dropping a penny into a glass of water. Suck on a straw in a glassful of water to show how you can lower the water level. Put your finger on the top end of the straw full of water. Then release your finger. Observe what happens.

8. Put some cut flowers or pussywillows in a jar of water and more in a jar with no water. Observe what happens. Keep a green plant watered, and a similar one unwatered.

9. Observe displacement by partly filling a jar with water. Put a rubber band at the water level. Lower several nails on a thread to the bottom, one at a time, and notice the water level.

10. Fill a glass jar with water. Punch two holes in the lid and screw it on tightly. Put your finger over one hole. Invert. Notice how the water comes from only one hole.

11. Punch holes in a vertical line from top to bottom of a can. Fill with water and observe that the water spurts farther from the bottom holes.

12. Put the top end of a dry towel in a pan of water on a table and the bottom end in a pan on the floor. See what happens.

13. Demonstrate how a siphon works with rubber tubing or a hose.

14. Make small waves by blowing on a flat pan of water.

15. Demonstrate the use of a level. Check to see if tables and shelves are level or not.

16. In the summer, supply a bowl of soapy water (do not use detergent) for each child and wooden spools and plastic straws for each. Let the children blow bubbles. Bubbles will show rainbow colors in the sun and be blown around by the wind, providing real enjoyment.

17. Using five pans, fill one with dirt; one, clay; one, sand; one, coarse sand; and one, pebbles. Slowly pour water on each and notice which pan the water sinks into fastest.

18. Make rainbows in the sun with water from a hose. Notice how waterdrops sparkle on grass.

19. Watch a street sweeper, if possible, to see how water is used in its operation.

20. On a hot day, wear swimming suits and run through a sprinkler or set up a water fight with squirt bottles and hoses, if possible. If no hose is available, use a large water cooler with rubber tubing and a pinch clamp on the spigot.

21. Let each child put out a lighted candle using a spray bottle filled with water.
22. While it is raining, listen for the thunder, watch for lightning, listen for the sounds of cars going by and of rain on the windows or on a metal roof. Use umbrellas and boots. Go outdoors in the rain (if it is not an electrical storm), in raincoats, or if it is warm enough, in swimming suits.
23. In the winter: see Hot and Cold in the Winter guide for related activities.
24. After a rain: look for worms, rainbows, how clean the leaves, grass, and street have become. See how dust has settled . . . how birds are bathing or drinking from a puddle . . . how clouds are blowing away. Look for a deep groove where rainwater came off a roof or washed out from a rainspout. Measure the amount of rain in a transparent tube or gauge. Watch water evaporate from wet sidewalks after rain.
25. Squirt a hose straight up. Also squirt it on the ground, turned on full force to show what water pressure can do. Squirt it on a metal roof or barrel, on the sidewalk, grass, a tree, or a window. Listen to the different sounds and watch the different ways it dissipates.

> **NOTE:** Draw no conclusions from the above-mentioned activities. Observe and comment only . . . *let the children discover.*

Dramatic Play Centers

Home-Living Center

1. Let children wash dolls in a plastic tub. Provide soap, powder, and lots of towels.
2. Let children wash and dry play dishes in this center.
3. Let children wash doll clothes and hang them to dry. This activity can take place outdoors if the weather is nice.
4. Ask the children to do some of the actual cleaning in the classroom (see Discovery Center), such as mop up spills and clean paintbrushes and other creative art materials. If you have a glass door, a child on each side, washing it at the same time, can be hilarious. Washing a mirror can also be fun.
5. Provide rainy or snowy day dressup clothes, such as rain hats, coats, boots, umbrellas, mittens; also fire-fighting hats, boots, and hoses. (See patterns, pp. 21, 496.)
6. Practice pouring: use real water, colored with food coloring, if you wish, for tea parties.

> **NOTE:** Disposable paper cups should be used unless dishes are washed with soap after the party.

Block-Building Center

1. Suggest using blocks to build canals, bridges, and dams for toy boats to use.
2. Show how a marina is made.
3. Suggest a car-wash building for toy cars to go through.
4. Suggest building fire stations for fire engines and build houses which have pretend fires to put out.

Other Dramatic Play Centers

1. Sandpile: use a hose in the summer to make a stream, dams, or a reservoir. Make a channel and let water from the hose flow in it. Sail wooden boats made from scraps at the workbench.

2. Set up a car wash outdoors. Use hose and wash wagons and tricycles. Supply rags and sponges.

3. Use wet sand for cooking with jelly molds, muffin pans, custard cups, and other aluminum or wooden utensils.

4. After a heavy rain, notice how water pushes aside fine sand, and exposes coarse pebbles and leaves trails of dirt.

5. Flood the sandbox and watch the rivers running off, the ponds that are left, and the dirt and sticks that are washed to a pile by the side.

6. Outdoors, arrange packing boxes like a boat or fleet of boats. Add fishing poles with magnets and paper fish with paper clips for fishing.

   CAUTION: Careful supervision is needed so that a magnet or pole does not hit anyone.

7. Paint outdoors with water. Provide buckets, large paintbrushes, old paint rollers and trays, and squirt bottles for spray painting. Also supply a painter's hat and overalls. Paint seesaws, boxes, slides, sidewalks, and toys with water. Use water to paint the outside wall of the building if it is one of the play yard boundaries.

8. Use mud dough: mix dirt and sand with water to the correct consistency. Mud dough makes good pancakes and cookies. Sprinkle sand on the products for sugar or add leaves and grass. Let dry and bake in the sun.

Learning, Language, and Readiness Materials Center

Commercially made games and materials for use at a table or on a mat:

(See Basic Resources, p. 79, for manufacturers' addresses.)

1. Water Play Kit (Childcraft)
2. Sand Toys (variety available in most catalogs)
3. Sand and Water Play Tables (most catalogs)
4. Water Play Trough (Childcraft)
5. Five Boat Fleet and Cargo Boat (Childcraft)
6. Boat Harbor Set, Wooden Lobster Boat, Wooden Fishing Dinghy, Sailboat Fleet: all-wood boats (ABC School Supply)
7. We Dress for the Weather: flannelboard cut-outs (Instructo)
8. Weather Flannel Aid (Milton Bradley)
9. Storybuilder (includes rain overlay) (Childcraft)
10. Decreasing Insets: Boats, Swan, Fish (Childcraft)
11. Perception Puzzles: Boats (Childcraft)
12. Ducks: 12 pcs.; Firemen: 17 pcs.; Hippo: 7 pcs.; Duck: 8 pcs.; Firetruck: 15 pcs. (Playskool Puzzles)
13. Knob Puzzles: Goldfish, Frog, Turtle, Lobster, Seahorse, Three Fish, Four Ducks, Snowmen (all 4 to 10 pcs.) (Childcraft)
14. Animal Mothers and Babies, Hippo: 7 pcs.; Duck: 12 pcs. (Childcraft)
15. Beginner Wood Inlays: When It Rains, 4 pcs. (Childcraft)
16. Let's Go Fishing Game: 12 fish, 2 poles, 36 stick-ons (Mead)
17. Fire Hydrant: plus four wrenches (Constructive Playthings)
18. Waterproof Apron and Armlets (Constructive Playthings)
19. Playsink: molded basin (Constructive Playthings)
20. Judy Puzzles: Rain, 4 pcs.; Frog, 10 pcs.; Fish, 6 pcs.; Duck, 8 pcs.; Splashdown, 15 pcs.; Black Firemen, 11 pcs.; Firemen, 13 pcs.; Firetruck, 14 pcs.
21. Judy Reversible Puzzles: Tadpoles and Frog, 5 pcs.; Whale and Fish, 6 pcs.

22. Splashtimers: cylinders, tubes, and other (Creative Playthings)
23. Water Cycle: for flannelboard (Instructo)
24. Fish Puzzles: 9 parts, plastic (Creative Playthings)
25. Beginners' Floor Play Block Vehicles: Steam Boat, Sail Boat, Nesting Boats, Motor Boat (ABC School Supply)

Teacher-made games and materials for use at a table or on a mat:

NOTE: For detailed description of Games, see pp. 50–59.

1. Name It: use objects we use with water, such as a toy boat, a plastic glass, straw, scrub brush, ice cube tray, and hose. **Variation:** Use objects we use with water to get ready for bed, such as soap, washcloth, toothbrush, towel.

Art Center

* 1. Paint with dry tempera on wet paper, dipping into water, then into dry tempera.
*** 2. Let the children mix their own tempera with water. Show how the color gets lighter with additional water and darker with more paint added.
** 3. Paint with water colors as a change from more opaque tempera.
** 4. Wet a sheet of light-colored construction paper. Drip paint from a brush or squeeze bottle.
** 5. Drop paint onto a sheet of paper and blow through a straw on each drop.
* 6. Make blotto prints by pressing out a design by blotting paint between two pieces of paper.
* 7. Crayon with bright colors on a large sheet of white construction paper. Then do a wash over the entire paper with thin gray, blue, or purple tempera or water color.
*** 8. Try to crayon on wet paper; then try chalk on wet paper.
*** 9. Draw with colored chalk: decorate with drops of water from eye dropper or squeeze bottle.
* 10. Use water-soluble felt pens. Show how dry ones can be used again if dipped into water.
* 11. Paint on a blackboard with wet brushes, sponges, or rags.
*** 12. Let children mix dry, powdered clay with water to a modeling consistency.
** 13. Make a rain-and-clouds collage: use blue construction paper and paste on absorbent cotton for clouds, gold or silver rick-rack for lightning, Christmas tree icicles for rain, and offer other appropriate collage materials.
** 14. Wet paper for easy tearing in torn paper designs.
** 15. Make walnut shell boats: stick a round toothpick through a piece of white paper cut in the shape of a right triangle. Attach the other end of the toothpick to the bottom of the walnut shell at the pointed end with any kind of playdough that dries hard. (See p. 27 for recipe.) Let dry before using.
** 16. Make wooden boats at the workbench out of scrap lumber.
*** 17. Make paper boats by paper folding (see Chinese New Year guide, p. 212) and milk carton boats.

Outdoors

* 1. Paint with water on sidewalks and climbing equipment. Use buckets of water, old paintbrushes, and paint rollers.
* 2. Draw in wet sand with sticks.

* 3. If you have a muddy place on the playground after a rain, make mud handprints and footprints. When fairly dry, make plaster casts of them.
* 4. Use mud dough; also try mud and sand mixtures.
** 5. Draw on a dry sidewalk with a squirt bottle of water.

Book Center

*** Branley, Franklyn. *Floating and Sinking*. New York: Thomas Y. Crowell, 1967.
* Brown, Margaret W. *The Little Fireman*. Reading, Mass.: Addison-Wesley, 1952.
* ———. *Two Little Trains*. Reading, Mass.: Addison-Wesley, 1949.
** Duvoisin, Roger. *Two Lonely Ducks*. New York: Alfred A. Knopf, 1951.
*** Flack, Marjorie. *The Boats on the River*. New York: Viking Press, 1946.
* Foster, Joanna. *Pete's Puddle*. New York: Harcourt Brace Jovanovich, 1950.
*** Gans, Roma. *Icebergs*. New York: Thomas Y. Crowell, 1964.
*** Golden, Augusta. *The Bottom of the Sea*. New York: Thomas Y. Crowell, 1966.
*** Gramatky, Hardy. *Little Toot*. New York: G. P. Putnam's Sons, 1939.
* Keats, Ezra J. *The Snowy Day*. New York: Viking Press, 1962.
**** Kessler, Leonard. *Last One in Is a Rotten Egg*. New York: Harper & Row, 1947.
* Klein, Leonore. *Mud, Mud, Mud*. New York: Alfred A. Knopf, 1962.
** Lehr, Lore. *A Letter Goes to Sea*. New York: E. M. Hale, 1970.
* Lionni, Leo. *Swimmy* also *Nageot* (French version) and *Suimi* (Spanish version). New York: Pantheon, 1963.
** ———. *On My Beach There Are Many Pebbles*. New York: Ivan Obelensky, 1961.
** Lund, Doris. *The Paint Box Sea*. New York: McGraw-Hill, 1972.
* Mayer, Mercer. *Bubble Bubble*. Chicago, Ill.: Parents' Magazine Press, 1973.
*** McCloskey, Robert. *One Morning in Maine*. New York: Viking Press, 1952.
** Parson, Ellen. *Rainy Day Together*. New York: Harper & Row, 1971.
** Raskin, Ellen. *And It Rained*. New York: Atheneum, 1969.
* Shaw, Charles. *It Looked Like Spilt Milk*. New York: Harper & Row, 1941.
* Shulevitz, Uri. *Rain, Rain, Rivers*. New York: Farrar, Straus & Giroux, 1969.
** Spier, Peter. *The Erie Canal*. Garden City, N.Y.: Doubleday, 1970.
** Tresselt, Alvin. *Rain Drop Splash*. New York: Lothrop, Lee & Shepard, 1964.
*** ———. *The Frog in the Well*. New York: Lothrop, Lee & Shepard, 1958.
*** ———. *Hide Seek Fog*. New York: Lothrop, Lee & Shepard, 1965.
** ———. *White Snow*. New York: Lothrop, Lee & Shepard, 1964.
*** ———. *It's Time Now*. New York: Lothrop, Lee & Shepard, 1965.
** Udry, Janice M. *Mary Ann's Mud Day*. New York: Harper & Row, 1961.
** Walter, Marion. *Make a Bigger Puddle, Make a Smaller Worm*. New York: J. P. Lippincott, 1971.
*** Yashima, Taro. *Umbrella*. New York: Viking Press, 1958.
*** Zolotow, Charlotte. *The Storm Book*. New York: Harper & Row, 1952.
** ———. *Summer Is Here*. New York: Abelard-Schuman, 1967 (all seasons).

planning for grouptime

NOTE: All music, fingerplays, poems, stories, and games listed here may also be used at other times during the session as appropriate. See Core Library, Basic Resources, p. 76, for publishers and addresses. Addresses for sources of records will be found on p. 81

Music

Songs

FROM original songs in this book by JoAnne Deal Hicks
"Raindrops," p. 352
"Summertime Fun," p. 363 (a parody)
"A Cloudy Spring Day," p. 580
* "Going Fishing," p. 581
** "Water Play," p. 582

FROM *Songs for Early Childhood*, Westminster Press
* "Lying on a Hillside," p. 26
** "The Rain Is Raining All Around," p. 28
** "Hark! Thunder Growls," p. 29
** "Pitter Patter," p. 31
** "I Have a Brook to Play In," p. 32
** "The Waves Are Rolling Down the Shore," p. 33
** "O Seashell Sing of Rolling Waves," p. 34

FROM *Songs for the Nursery School*, MacCarteney
* "The Goldfish," p. 47
*** "Little Pool," pp. 52–53
* "This Is the Way We Wash Our Hands," p. 100

FROM *Music Activities for Retarded Children*, Ginglend and Stiles
* "Little Fish," p. 69

FROM *Wake Up and Sing*, Landeck and Crook
* "All the Fish Are Swimming in the Water," p. 100

FROM *Music Resource Book*, Lutheran Church Press
* "Listen to the Rain," p. 25
* "Row, Row, Row Your Boat," p. 28
* "This Is the Way We Wash Our Hands," p. 53
** "Six Little Ducks," p. 62

NOTE: See also Songs in the Spring and Water Transportation guides.

Records

"Building a City"/"**What the Lighthouse Sees**"/"**Rainy Day**" (Young People's Records [YPR], 33⅓ RPM)

"Train to the Beach" (Children's Record Guild [CRG], 45, 78 RPM)

"Indoors When It Rains" (CRG, 45, 78 RPM)

"The Rainy Day Record"/"Another Rainy Day Record" (Bowmar, 33⅓ RPM)

"Indoor Play for a Rainy Day" (Golden Record, 33⅓ RPM)

"Little White Duck," Burl Ives (Columbia, 33⅓ RPM)

"Singin' in the Rain" (Peter Pan, 33⅓ RPM)

"Raindrops Keep Fallin' on My Head" (any recording)

Rhythms and Singing Games

Reproduce tone:

a. Add water of varying amounts to a set of eight glasses that are alike. With care you can get a one-octave range of notes when the glasses are tapped with a rhythm stick. Let the children experiment with the pouring also. Simple tunes such as "Mary Has a Little Lamb" can be played.

b. String up a set of various-shaped bottles by their necks, add water to varying depths, and tap with a rhythm stick.

c. Put different amounts of water in stemware. Wet your finger, hold the stem of the glass, run your finger around the rim of the glass, and a clear note can be produced. Close supervision is necessary! If you look closely at the surface of the water, you can actually see tiny ripples that the sound vibrations make. Put different amounts of water in bottles and blow across the tops. Listen to the variations. Dramatize: wash doll clothes to music. Scrub tables to music. Wash hands to music. Fingerpaint to music.

Fingerplays and Poems

FROM *Let's Do Fingerplays*, Grayson

"Windshield Wipers," p. 24

"The Boats," p. 26

"Row, Row, Row Your Boat," p. 26

"Golden Fishes," p. 35

"When a Little Chicken Drinks," p. 36

"Pitter Pat," p. 46

"My Garden," p. 46

"Raindrops," p. 47

"Snowflakes," p. 48

"Snow Men," p. 48

"Two Little Ducks," p. 71 (See "Six Little Ducks" under Games.)

FROM *Rhymes for Fingers and Flannelboards*, Scott and Thompson

"Snowflakes," p. 122

"The Snowman," p. 123

"I Am a Snowman," p. 123

"Raindrops," p. 125

"The Rain," p. 125

FROM *Very Young Verses*, Geismer and Suter
"About Going Places," pp. 101–09
"About the Seasons," pp. 118, 119, 126, 133–36, 138–44
"About the Weather," pp. 151–53, 155–59, 166

Stories

(To read, read-tell, or tell. See Book Center for complete list.)

   * *Pete's Puddle*, Foster
 *** *The Sun, the Wind, the Sea, the Rain*, Schlein
   * *Rain, Rain, Rivers*, Shulevitz
  ** *Rain Drop Splash*, Tresselt
 *** *Umbrella*, Yashima

Games

1. "Mulberry Bush" (using such variations as wash our hands, face, teeth; wash the car; scrub the floor, stairs)
2. "Row Your Boat" by sitting in pairs on the floor with feet together and holding hands. Rock back and forth, keeping in rhythm with the tune as you sing.
3. "London Bridge": sing and play with older children
4. "Six Little Ducks": Follow the actions suggested in the song. Each child has a feather to hold in his/her hand for a tail.
5. Musical Chairs: variation, using puddles instead of chairs (See Games, pp. 50–59.)

Routine Times

Snack or lunch

1. Let children mix a powdered drink with water or make their own lemonade.
2. Let children make gelatin, measuring water and powder and stirring.
3. Taste different kinds of water: distilled, well water, tap water, rainwater, saltwater, and sugar water.
4. Invite children to drink cold, warm, and hot water.
5. Demonstrate what happens when you boil an egg, spaghetti, a carrot. Taste before and after cooking.
6. Try eating some kind of fish at snacktime and discuss where it came from.
7. Bake a cake mix for which you add only water, such as gingerbread. See how it changes in cooking.
8. Lick ice cubes.
9. In the summer make popsicles in the refrigerator. Cover and try to make them outdoors in freezing weather. Use juice.
10. Make crushed-ice confections. (See Winter guide.)
11. Float a flower (or candle) in a fairly flat bowl for a centerpiece at snacktime.

Toileting

1. Notice how much water is used in the bathroom, where it comes from, and where it goes. Follow the water pipes to their source, if possible.

2. Find the hot water tank.
3. Stress the importance of water for cleanliness and the need not to waste it.

Cleanup

1. Wash tables with a sponge before and after eating. Wash dishes used for snacks a few times.
2. Wash easels and shelves with sponges.

Children, wearing plastic smocks to protect their clothes, are discovering how water follows channels that have been formed in concrete basin. Child at left is floating boats in the pool formed by the flow of water.

3. Water plants, add water to fish tank, and be sure any small pets such as gerbils have adequate water supply. Talk about exact amount of water needed.
4. Wipe up spills with mops or sponges.

Rest

1. On hot days, try damp washcloths on foreheads.

Large Muscle Activities

1. Use a rocking boat both indoors and outdoors as a fishing boat.
2. Sail all the boats made in creative art activities in a play pool or water table, or have a tractor tire split crosswise to form two circular water-filled troughs in which to sail toys and other objects.
3. On hot days set up a play pool.
4. Let a hose trickle for drinks.
5. Play under a sprinkler.
6. Blow bubbles outdoors. (See Discovery Center, No. 16, p. 568.)
7. Plant a garden and water it regularly with a sprinkling can or hose.
8. On a hot day when the children are in swimming suits, run the hose down a slippery slide. Supervise carefully.
9. Fill balloons with water and drop them from a height such as a slide or jungle gym. Discuss how the heavy water broke the balloon.
10. Dig up earth and turn it over. Notice that it is damper underneath.
11. Set out a chunk of damp earth to dry in the sun. Feel and look at it later.
12. Water the grass.
13. Wash a car.
14. Put out a fake fire with water. Play fire fighter. (See Road Transportation guide.)
15. Make wet footprints on a dry sidewalk.
16. Crawl through or climb over large sewer pipes.
17. Play "Jump the Brook": two ropes are laid parallel to jump over. After each child has had a turn, increase the distance between the ropes.
18. Have a digging spot or hole where mud can be made. You will need shovels that really dig, big rocks to push around for stepping-stones, boards for bridges, boxes or tubs for boats and houses, and a handy hose or faucet nearby to rinse off with. If children are allowed to go barefoot be sure there are no sharp objects such as glass, tin cans, or pointed rocks in the hole.

Extended Experiences

1. Go for a walk and find sources of water outdoors, such as hoses, fire hydrants, puddles, drainage canals, and sewers. Notice clothes drying on a clothesline.
2. Take a walk indoors to try to locate water pipes, sewer pipes, and the hot water tank.
3. If possible, visit a house or building under construction to see how the plumbing is installed. Get permission and plan for adequate supervision.
4. Visit a plumbing shop, laundromat, or take a group through a car wash in a car.
5. Visit street construction where underground sewer pipes are exposed or are being laid.
6. Go to see a water tower or water storage tank on the ground.

7. If you visit a farm, notice the water tanks for livestock, the windmills to pump water, and a hand pump, if such is still in use.
8. If there is an aquarium in your area, take the children there.
9. If snorkel or scuba diving is taught in your area, arrange to have the children see a demonstration.
10. Visit an indoor and an outdoor swimming pool.
11. Watch a street sweeper washing and sweeping the street.
12. If you are lucky enough to live near a lake, river, or ocean, take a trip to watch boats of all kinds, water skiing, sailing. Extra supervision will be necessary if the children are allowed to wade or play in the sand or at the water's edge.
13. Visit an area where water is used for beautification, as where there are fountains, waterfalls, swans and ducks, boating, a waterlily pond, fish ponds.
14. Stand on a small bridge and watch the water flow under it on one side; cross to the other side and watch the water flow out from under it. Drop a small floating object (stick, pinecone) over the first side and watch it come out on the other side. Try a nonfloating object, such as a small rock.
15. Visit a small pond on a still day, if possible. Look at reflections in the water. Then disturb it and look again. (This can be done in a play pool in the yard.)
16. Throw pebbles into water and notice how they form concentric circles. On a hot day take off shoes and socks and wade.
17. Encourage children to play in dry and wet sand. Offer them a water source and sand tools.

The following activities would not be used every day, but at the teacher's discretion:
18. Invite the owner of a pet shop to visit and bring a pet turtle or fish and explain its care.
19. Ask a plumber to visit your school facility.
20. Invite a scuba diver to visit.
21. Borrow a globe and maps from a parent for finding water areas and streams.

teacher resources

Books and Periodicals

1. Rosenfeld, Sam. *Science Experiments with Water*. New York: E.M. Hale, 1966.
2. Podendorf, Illa. *Things to Do with Water*. Chicago: Children's Press, 1971.
3. Freeman, Mae Blocker. *Do You Know about Water?* New York: Random House, 1970. (Explains the water cycle simply and with good illustrations. Also describes the uses of water, such as drinking, bathing, swimming, fishing, and skating.)
4. *National Wildlife* and *Ranger Rick*. National Wildlife Federation, Washington, D.C.
5. *National Geographic*. National Geographic Society, Washington, D.C.
6. *Natural History*. The journal of the American Museum of Natural History, Central Park West at 79th St., New York, New York 10024.
7. Sootin, Harry. *Easy Experiments with Water Pollution*. New York: Scholastic Book Services, 1974.

Pictures and Displays

(See p. 79 for addresses of firms listed.)

1. Use posters from travel agencies showing lakes, ski areas, or the seashore.
2. Some calendars have excellent water pictures.
3. Make large posters to show clothing which is to be worn for rainy days, for snowy days, or for playing in the water on hot days.
4. Float a flower (or candle) in a fairly flat bowl.
5. Signs of the Season: Mini-Poster Card Book, fourteen 10″ × 13″ posters (Trend Enterprises).
6. Monthly Posters: ten 21″ × 29″ seasonal situations (Trend Enterprises).
7. Seasons: flannel aids, 31 figures, scenes, and objects (Milton Bradley).
8. Animal Homes: Picture Fold-Out Chart (The Child's World).
9. Life Cycle of a Frog: Sequence Chart (The Child's World).
10. Fall Fun Figures: for bulletin board range to 27″ (Trend Enterprises).
11. Let's Take a Walk: Chart Season Series (The Child's World).

Community Resources

1. Marina or aquarium
2. Aquarena, Sea-rama, Marineland
3. Fish hatchery
4. Plumber
5. Scuba diving school

A Cloudy Spring Day

JoAnne Deal Hicks

NOTE: This song will help to make a sudden storm less frightening for young children. Invite children to watch approaching clouds, lightning, rain, or sleet from a window. Turn on the lights as clouds cover the sun. Simulate the thunder and crack of lightning with drums and other percussion instruments. Let children select instruments they think sound like storm sounds. Triangles and finger cymbals may be used to simulate raindrops. Keep informed for a weather alert. If you must, move to a safer place away from the classroom. Play games, tell stories, sing songs, and in other ways be supportive and reassuring until the alert is over.

Going Fishing

JoAnne Deal Hicks

NOTE: Sing during a fishing activity or to recall such an activity.

Water Play

JoAnne Deal Hicks

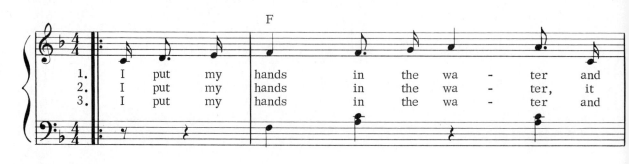

1. I put my hands in the wa - ter and
2. I put my hands in the wa - ter, it
3. I put my hands in the wa - ter and

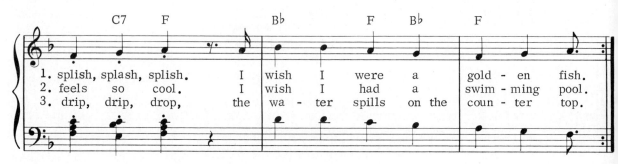

1. splish, splash, splish. I wish I were a gold - en fish.
2. feels so cool. I wish I had a swim - ming pool.
3. drip, drip, drop, the wa - ter spills on the coun - ter top.

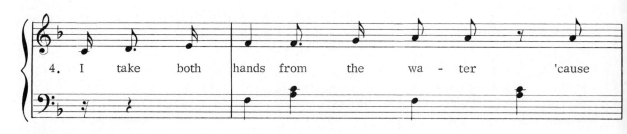

4. I take both hands from the wa - ter 'cause

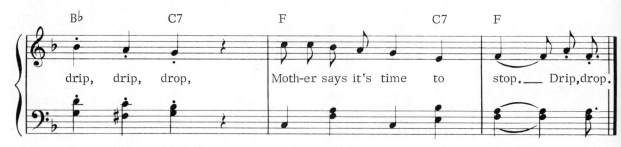

drip, drip, drop, Moth-er says it's time to stop.__ Drip, drop.

NOTE: Sing song using appropriate actions: weaving hands while held vertically like a fish swimming, shaking hands jerkily as if to dry when dripping, and finally showing surprise or sadness when "Mother says it's time to stop."

36 Color in My World

basic understandings

(concepts children can grasp from this subject)

- Color is a word used to describe an object.
- Colors are everywhere that we can see: in flowers, clothes, food, cars, and so on.
- Colors have names: red, orange, yellow, green, blue, and purple.
- We cannot see colors without light (in a dark place). If we cover our eyes we cannot see colors.
- Some rocks, minerals, and paints change color under special lights (fluorescent, ultraviolet, and "black" light) or glow in the dark.
- Sunlight (which we see as yellow or white) can be split into a rainbow.
- Some colors are used to depict certain things: yellow—sunshine, green—grass, blue—sky. However this does not mean these colors must always be used for these things.
- Colors are used for safety symbols that everyone recognizes, such as stop signs, traffic lights, school zones, and railroad crossings.
- Some colors (or pigment) can be mixed together to make other colors.

  blue + red = purple (violet)
  blue + yellow = green
  red + yellow = orange

  red + yellow + blue = brown
  white + color = tint
  color + black = shade

- We cannot make red, yellow, blue, black, or white by mixing paints.
- White can be made by spinning a color wheel but not by mixing paints.
- Each person has a skin, hair, and eye color that is just right for them. Each may differ from ours.
- Sometimes we have favorite colors or consider some colors prettier than others and therefore prefer to use these more often than others.

- Almost everything has a color except clear glass, clear plastic, pure air, and pure water.
- If we can see through something clearly, it is transparent.
- Colors look bright on a sunny day and dull on a cloudy day or when in the shade.
- There are paint colors that look like some metals we use: gold, silver, copper, and brass.
- Wood comes in different colors and has different names. Wood is usually named for the tree from which the lumber comes: maple, walnut, oak, white or yellow pine, cedar, ebony, and redwood.

Additional Facts the Teacher Should Know

Light, the source of all color, is white when it reaches us from the sun. Each color wave in the white ray of light has a different wave length, and each wave length, as it passes through a prism, is deflected at a different angle due to its velocity (rate of speed) in passing from one medium to another. Thus the complex white ray of light is dispersed into its many-colored wave lengths (a rainbow). The longest ray is red; the shortest is violet. The longer wave lengths of light are called warm colors—red, orange, yellow. The shorter wave lengths are called cool colors—blue and violet. Green falls between the warm and cool colors.

The primary colors for paint pigment are red, yellow, and blue. Secondary colors of orange, green, and purple are produced by mixing two of the primary colors together. The easiest way for children to get brown is by mixing red, yellow, and blue. Brown can also be obtained by mixing orange and black. Children may discover this method at the Art Center when using these paints during Halloween observance.

Hue is the name of a color. Value means the lightness or darkness of a color. Intensity means the saturation or purity of the color. A hue may vary in intensity when it is mixed with white to make a tint (be sure to add the color to the white); mixed with black to produce a shade (add black to the color); mixed with black and white to produce a tone; and mixed with its complement to form gradations of greyed tones.

The primary colors of light are red, green, and blue. They are used in stage lighting and window displays. If we take red, green, and blue spotlights into a darkened room and shine them on a white screen we will get the following secondary colors: red light + green light = yellow color; red light + blue light = magenta or red-violet; and blue light + green light = cyan blue or blue-green. Red, green, and blue light shining on the screen produces white.

Children and adults express their feelings by the use of color. Color may transmit an emotion or symbolic meaning to the beholder of an artwork. For many Americans, red may signify danger or bloodshed; yellow depicts happiness, cheerfulness, and brightness; blue means peacefulness, coolness, tranquillity; green, freshness and neutrality. Various cultures attach different meanings to color. To the Chinese, red means happiness and good luck; to the Irish, green is lucky, and to the Afro-Americans "black is beautiful."

Many words in the English language have meaning because of color. For example, we see "red" when we are angry, we are "green" with envy, we are "yellow" when we lack courage, we have the "blues" when we are sad. These concepts are on an adult level and only produce confusing ideas for the preschooler.

Some young children seem much more color-conscious than others. Children tend to be aware of color distinction and to be able to classify objects by color before they can attach a name to their groupings. The teacher must understand that children can experience color activities and enjoy them, but may not be ready for real recognition of the concepts involved. The teacher should avoid forcing these concepts on a child who is not ready.

When using color in art media, begin with the three primary colors. As any two or all three of these are mixed, other good colors are produced. Secondary colors may be added later for variety and for more brilliant hues. Pastel tints are delightful for a change of scene in the spring. Be sure to offer a choice of colors when children might wish to depict skin color in their art work. Remember that dark colors are as attractive and pleasant to look at and are associated with good things (such as chocolate pudding) just as the brighter, more vivid colors are.

The visual disorder of color blindness could be the cause for persistent color confusion by a child. There are simple tests to detect this condition. Consult an eye doctor for assistance. More boys show this tendency than do girls.

Methods Most Adaptable for Introducing This Subject to Children

- Go for a walk and observe colors.
- Read a simple story about pure colors, such as *My Slippers Are Red.*
- Explore a color module. (See Discovery Center, No. 15.)
- Seasonal activity: red, Valentine's Day; orange and black, Halloween; white, winter; and on other such occasions. (See related guides.)
- Daily activity: color in food at mealtime, discuss color of skin, hair, eyes at routine times, or color of cars, trucks, houses, trees, and flowers while in transit.
- Color Days: a total experience with color. (See Discovery Center, No. 1.)

Vocabulary

shadow	brass	color	pink
silver	orange	light	transparent
maple	red	dark	reflection
brown	blue	gold	violet (purple)
iron	yellow	white	shiny
sun	copper	black	glow
bright	walnut	rainbow	rust
dull	green	prism	ebony

learning centers

Discovery Center

1. Color days: explore a color for a certain time period. We recommend one week per color for a beginning experience, three to five days for those with previous experience, and one to three days for those with many color experiences. The following is an example of a red day:

   On the day preceding the first red day, send each child home with a note explaining the color days or week with a square of pure red paper pinned to the child's clothing. The child is told to come to school wearing some article of red clothing or to bring an object or a picture showing the color red. Both parents and children can become very involved in this project. Teachers, of course, should wear the color of the day. They may add a surprise element at special times during the day by pinning a "color book" on their smock or jacket. (Fold pages of appropriate colored paper into a small book 4 inches by 5 inches. Paste colored objects on each page.)

   NOTE: Have scarves, hankies, or colored yarn loops for children who forget to bring or wear something for the color day.

   Display a poster of red objects at the door or in a conspicuous place and put red objects on the discovery table. Feature the red media in the Art Center. Use a red fingerplay and read stories or books to the children that emphasize the color red. Serve red foods at snack or mealtime. Sing red songs and use red games and other activities. Feature fire fighters in dramatic play. After all the color days have been presented, all colors are stressed and rainbows are considered. It is often appropriate to culminate color days at Easter time with its multicolor activities. A suggested color sequence could be: red, yellow, blue, green, orange, and violet. (St. Patrick's Day is an obvious choice for green.) After violet, could be brown, then black and white, and finally rainbow days featuring all the colors.

2. Make a rainbow: a serendipitous event would be a real rainbow after a rain.
   a. A rainbow can be created by placing a small mirror in a glass of water, with the mirror tilted against the glass.
   b. If a prism is held up close to the eyes on a bright day, all objects viewed will be outlined in rainbows.
   c. The sun shining directly through the water in an aquarium makes a rainbow.
   d. Observe how a drop of oil in a puddle produces a rainbow of colors.
   e. Observe how a fine water spray with the sun shining through produces a rainbow.

   NOTE: Always have the sun in back of the child holding the hose. The sun must fall on the water to make a rainbow.

   f. Discover how a prism bends light to make a rainbow. The teacher can find different prisms—beads, chandelier pendants, diamonds, beveled glass.
   g. Commercial soap bubbles have rainbow colors. (Or make your own. See p. 27.)
3. Observe difference in the brightness of colors in sun and in shade.
4. The children may experiment in making the color brown by squeezing drops of primary food colors into water in a clear plastic glass.
5. Encourage children to mix primary colors to obtain secondary colors:
   a. tissue paper of primary colors may be superimposed and held against a window.
   b. overlay sheets or cut out shapes of colored plastic or cellophane.

c. easel paint or finger paint may be mixed to discover secondary colors.

d. water colors brushed and crossed on a large sheet of white paper.

e. use commercially made color paddle, rainbow box, and tri-color viewer.

6. Try on tinted glasses of different hues to observe same colored items.

7. Set out kaleidoscopes for examination by the children.

8. Explore a mirror to see how it reflects images.

9. Set out objects you can see through and those you can't: glasses, binoculars, fishbowl, clear plastic tumblers, and magnifying glass; rocks, wood, metal, china, construction paper.

10. Children may explore a colored flashlight. (Some have two or three colors.)

11. Older children may enjoy dyeing materials and seeing how things of the same color differ in shade. (See Thanksgiving in America guide, p. 246, for detailed suggestions.)

12. Dye white eggs that have been hard cooked.

13. Have samples of different kinds of wood and, if possible, pictures of the trees from which they come. Let children sand wood to make it smooth. Notice the different grains.

14. Display rocks and minerals of various colors. Provide hand-held and tripod magnifying glasses. Look at fluorescent minerals under a "black" light if one is available.

15. Color modules: furnish a large carton or wooden box (big enough to crawl inside) with nature items, food, upholstery and textured cloth, toys, and equipment to create a Color Saturation Mini-Room. You could, instead, set up a corner or enclose an area with a 3-Way Play Screen. Appeal to all of the child's senses! Invite the child to interact to this special color environment. Be sure to make the outside intriguing enough to entice the child inside. Prints of good paintings focusing on the color, windows to peek through, and a rug leading to the door will enhance this area. Equip your room or area in such a way that props can be interchanged to introduce new colors. Use hooks on the walls to hang a roller drop of drapery, wallpaper, plastic, or carpeting. Example: yellow —bananas, daffodils, yellow velvet upholstery, lemon incense, bamboo bug keeper, balloons, yellow cab, sponges, low watt yellow bulb, straw hat, lemon scented soap, yellow plastic or cellophane on the windows.

Dramatic Play Centers

Home-Living Center

1. Make available a full-length mirror and as many brightly colored objects, toys, and articles of dress-up clothes as possible. Reinforce color awareness in conversation that arises naturally with the children. Example: "The fire fighters that we visited had red hats, ours are red too."

2. Dress dolls or paper dolls in variously colored articles of clothing—use scraps of material or construction paper.

3. Emphasize color in foods (see Food guide) and table service.

4. Talk about metals: copper bottom and aluminum pots and pans, stainless steel utensils, silverware, and iron.

Block-Building Center

1. Emphasize color in cars, trucks, road signs, and other block building accessories.

2. Property lines could be drawn on the floor with colored chalk.

3. Teachers can identify each child's building with a colorful sign.

Other Dramatic Play Centers

1. Set out traffic signs and signals for use with wheel toys:
   a. those that are 30 inches tall are available in most catalogs.
   b. make traffic signals using Dennison Bulletin Board aids packaged as Traffic Safety.
   c. make your own signs and signals. A traffic light can be made by pasting red, green, and yellow circles on an egg carton lid.
2. Go fishing. Cut out paper fish of various colors. Attach paper clip for a mouth. Let children fish with cardboard tube pole and string line with magnet attached. Appropriate during or following this activity would be the song "Going Fishing," p. 581.

   CAUTION: When working with hyperactive children or those with little self-control, do not use magnets. Instead, the child drops a line on the fish he or she wants and an adult, or another child, who is sitting in or near the pond, attaches the line to the paper clip mouth. The child hauls in his or her fish, removes it from the line by sliding the line from under the clip, and drops it in the boat or bucket.

3. Dramatize *Caps for Sale* by Slobodkin, listed in Book Center. Props needed: red, green, yellow, and blue caps for the monkeys and one brown cap for the peddler.

Learning, Language, and Readiness Materials Center

Commercially made games and materials for use at a table or on a mat:

(See Basic Resources, p. 79, for manufacturers' addresses.)

NOTE: Set out puzzles and other cognitive materials featuring the color of the day.

1. Montessori Color Tablets (ETA)
2. Parquetry Blocks (Playskool)
3. Candyland (Milton Bradley)
4. Twister (Milton Bradley)
5. Winnie-the-Pooh game (Parker Brothers)
6. Color Lotto (Judy)
7. Tri-Color Viewer: red, yellow, and blue (Creative Playthings)
8. Pyramid Puzzles: 9 pattern cards and colorful matching strips (Ideal)
9. Color Pattern Board: 27 cubes in 9 colors (Constructive Playthings)
10. Color Chrominoes: color matching dominoes (Constructive Playthings)
11. Balloon Game (Childcraft)
12. Overlay Patterns: 60 transparent overlays (Childcraft)
13. Color Matching Board: 4 squares with knobs, 4 colors (ETA)
14. Color Garage: 4 cars, 4 colors, for handicapped (ETA)
15. Color Train Puzzle: color and shape for handicapped (ETA)
16. Color Paddles: red, yellow, blue (Childcraft)
17. Kaleidoscope: removable colored inserts (Steven)
18. Color Steps Set: 7 loose steps, 7 colors (ETA)
19. Kaleidoscope Puzzles: 12 puzzles 6 inches by 6 inches, 4 pcs. each (Ideal)
20. Honeybee Tree (Childcraft, Constructive Playthings)
21. Hexagonal Floor Mosaics: 30 pcs., 10 colors (ETA)
22. Color Cards: 11 colors, 2 cards each (Ideal)
23. Play Squares/Play Rings: slotted translucent rings in five colors—when overlapped other colors are created (Childcraft)

24. Mosaic: 27 pcs., primary colors (Creative Playthings)
25. Color Gradation Cards: 5 gradations of 7 colors; 2 inches by 2½ inches (Ideal)
26. Color Pattern Boards: 27 cubes, 9 colors, 12 pattern cards, 10 templates, and 1 tray (Ideal)
27. Intarsio: 144 colorful pieces to create designs (Childcraft)
28. Color Stacking Disks (Playskool)
29. Mr. Sketch: 8 bright water-color makers (Childcraft)
30. Prism (most catalogs)

Teacher-made games and materials for use at a table or on a mat:

NOTE: For detailed description of Games, see pp. 50–59.

1. Many inexpensive, unbreakable, small colored objects can be used in interesting color sorting games. For example: small plastic sports cars (usually red, blue, yellow, and green) can be parked in the matching colored construction paper parking lots. Cars or airplanes can be sorted into milk carton garages or hangers that have been painted different colors.
2. Spools may be painted pure colors and used as beads to string on long boot strings, or made into a sorting device on graduated lengths of dowel rods.
3. Match-Them: match paint chips, spools of thread, rug samples, or swatches of fabric.
4. Colored rubber bands of various widths and lengths can be stretched between pegs on a pegboard.
5. Color Lotto game: make duplicate sets of colored cardboard squares. Glue one set to Lotto Boards, making sure the same color squares are placed in a variety of positions on the various cards.
6. How Many?: use colored-paper geometric shapes, color chips, or other small colored objects like Teddy Bear Counters.
7. Play Sequence: make a row of colored squares or objects.
8. Match-Them: make two or more color envelopes. Enclose in each a red square, a yellow circle, a green triangle, and a blue rectangle. Ask children to take their envelope and remove matching shapes and match theirs with the teacher's.
9. Alike, Different, and the Same: children select the colored piece that does not belong with a group of like colored objects or pieces of paper.
10. Match-Them: match colored paper to pictures or objects in the room.

NOTE: Any conversation with a child about color helps to make the child more color conscious. Always include the name of the object that you are distinguishing by the color adjective. For example: "Do you want the red paint?" Otherwise, the child may think "red" is the object if you only say "Do you want red?"

Art Center

NOTE: In the art suggestions listed below, sometimes only one color example is given. Substitute other colors as you wish.

* 1. The featured color is used at the easel. If a secondary color is being emphasized, also offer the two primaries that produce the secondary.

   CAUTION: To keep paints from getting muddy, use small amounts of paint in junior baby food jars with screw lids. Change as needed. Use one brush for each jar.

**   2. Red: blotto pictures or string painting.

**   3. Blue: sponge painting on light blue paper.

**   4. Violet: finger paint. Start with uncolored finger paint. Let children sprinkle dry red tempera and paint with it for awhile. Then sprinkle on blue tempera from a small shaker to discover violet (purple).

**   5. Brown: spatterpaint brown animals on pastel paper, or make brown crayon rubbings over pennies.

*** 6. Make a rainbow using either water colors brushed onto a large white sheet of paper with a wide brush or use the long side of peeled crayons.

**   7. Scribble paintings: children scribble many colors on a large sheet of white paper pressing hard with wax crayons in bright colors. Then paint over entire paper lightly with either black water color or thin black tempera.

**   8. Offer bright tempera paint and brushes to children to paint their woodworking creations. Liquid detergent added to paint makes it stick better.

**   9. Roller painting: use small rolling pins or heavy cardboard tubes covered with upholstery, and roll across paint drops on wet surface. (See illustration, p. 30.)

* 10. Use spool brayers to make stripes and plaids of different colors.

* 11. Sort out crayons for the color of the day.

* 12. Use big kindergarten chalk for writing on the blackboard.

* 13. Vividly colored kindergarten chalk may be used on dark papers.

* 14. Orange: start with uncolored playdough. Sprinkle yellow dry tempera in a depression in the dough and work in with fingers, then add red tempera. Children will be able to discover orange. Some may make pumpkins or carrots.

* 15. Yellow: crumple precut yellow tissue circles and paste on green paper to represent yellow flowers in the grass.

*** 16. Multicolored tissue paper in irregular shapes that children may cut or tear easily can be overlapped and glued on rice paper with thinned white glue and used as transparencies in windows. A spectra of art tissue is available from the Practical Drawing Company, Dallas, Texas.

* 17. Black and white: collage made by gluing shavings of white styrofoam (as in packing boxes) on black paper, or make shadow pictures of the children's heads.

  18. Multicolor Days:

***   a. decorate eggs dyed in Discovery Center

**   b. make collage of crushed dyed eggshells by gluing on black paper with thinned white glue

*   c. sawdust mixed with thick tempera paint and spread to dry may be glued to paper later as a collage tray item

*   d. rock salt or coarse pickling salt, dyed and sprinkled in glue gives a sparkling effect

     e. sponge paint/stamp printing allows child to explore overlapping color

* 19. Collage from colored yarns, gift ties, sequins, and glitter. Children can ask for the colors they wish to use.

* 20. Collage of thin wood scraps and shapes glued together. This may be painted.

* 21. Green: sponges cut in various shapes can be used to make designs. Dip them in dark green paint and press them on light green paper.

*** 22. Fingerprints: sponges in flat dishes make stamp pads. Use one color (red, blue, yellow, green) per dish. Children use two fingers on each hand (one for each color) to print on white paper (requires coordination).

*** 23. Make multicolored wire sculptures from many colored, covered wires found in short ends of telephone cable (free for the asking!).

Other Experiences in This Center Using Art Media:

1. Origami (paper folding): See p. 212 for examples. Two-tone paper, available from the Practical Drawing Company, Dallas, Texas, is especially effective.

Book Center

** Adelson, Leone. *Please Pass the Grass!* New York: David McKay, 1960.

* Anglund, Joan Walsh. *What Color Is Love?* New York: Harcourt Brace Jovanovich, 1966.

*** Becker, Edna. *900 Buckets of Paint.* Nashville, Tenn.: Abingdon Press, 1949 (all colors).

** Birnbaum, A. *Green Eyes.* New York: Western Publishing, 1973.

** Bond, Carey. *Brown Is a Beautiful Color.* New York: Franklin Watts, 1969.

** Bright, Robert. *My Red Umbrella.* New York: William Morrow, 1959.

*** Campbell, Ann. *Let's Find Out about Color.* New York: Franklin Watts, 1969.

*** Church, Vivian. *Colors Around Me.* Chicago, Ill.: Afro-American Publishing, 1971.

*** Emberley, Ed. *Green Says Go.* Boston, Mass.: Little, Brown, 1968.

** Fenton, Edward. *The Big Yellow Balloon.* Garden City, N.Y.: Doubleday, 1967.

** Freeman, Don. *A Rainbow of My Own.* New York: Viking Press, 1966 (paper, 1974).

*** ————. *Mop Top.* New York: Viking Press, 1955.

*** Friskey, Margaret. *What Is the Color of the Wide, Wide, World?* Chicago, Ill.: Childrens Press, 1973.

** Gill, Bob. *What Color Is Your World?* New York: Astor-Honor, 1962.

*** Grossman, Barney and Gladys Groom. *Black Means . . .* New York: Hill & Wang, 1970.

**** Hirsh, Marilyn. *How the World Got Its Color.* New York: Crown Publishers, 1972 (tell).

* Hoffman, Beth G. *Red Is for Apples.* New York: Random House, 1966.

** Ipcar, Dahlov. *Black and White.* New York: Alfred A. Knopf, 1963.

** ————. *Brown Cow Farm.* Garden City, N.Y.: Doubleday, 1959.

** Johnson, Crocket. *Harold and the Purple Crayon.* New York: Harper & Row, 1955.

*** Juhl, Jerry. *The Big Orange Thing.* Scarsdale, N.Y.: Bradbury Press, 1969.

** Keats, Ezra Jack. *Peter's Chair.* New York: Harper & Row, 1967 (blue and pink).

*** Kessler, Leonard. *Mr. Pine's Purple House.* New York: Wonder-Treasure Books, 1965.

** Krauss, Ruth. *I Want to Paint My Bathroom Blue.* New York: Harper & Row, 1956.

** Lionni, Leo. *Little Blue and Little Yellow.* New York: Astor-Honor, 1959.

* Lipkind, Nicolas Mordvinoff. *The Two Reds.* New York: Harcourt Brace Jovanovich, 1958.

** McDonald, Golden. *Red Light, Green Light.* Garden City, N.Y.: Doubleday, 1944.

*** McGovern, Ann. *Black Is Beautiful.* New York: Four Winds Press, 1969.

*** Miles, Miska. *Apricot ABC.* Boston, Mass.: Little, Brown, 1969.

** Morrow, Elizabeth and René D'Harnoncourt. *The Painted Pig.* New York: Alfred A. Knopf, 1942 (all colors).

*** Nakagawa, Rieko. *A Blue Seed.* New York: Hastings House, 1967.

*** Parkin, Rex. *The Red Carpet.* New York: Macmillan, 1967 (paper, 1972).

** Purdy, Susan. *If You Have a Yellow Lion.* Philadelphia, Pa.: J. B. Lippincott, 1966.

** Reiss, John L. *Colors.* Scarsdale, N.Y.: Bradbury Press, 1969.

* Shaw, Charles G. *It Looked Like Spilt Milk.* New York: Harper & Row, 1947.

** Slobodkina, Esphyr. *Caps for Sale.* Reading, Mass.: Addison-Wesley, 1947.

* Steiner, Charlotte. *My Slippers Are Red.* New York: Alfred A. Knopf, 1957 (paper, all colors).

** Swift, Hildegard H. and Lynd Ward. *The Little Red Lighthouse and the Great Gray Bridge.* New York: Harcourt Brace Jovanovich, 1942 (paper, 1974).
*** Thayer, Jane. *Andy's Square Blue Animal.* New York: William Morrow, 1962.
** Zacharias, Thomas and Wanda Zacharias. *But Where Is the Green Parrot?* New York: Delacorte Press, 1968.
** Zion, Gene. *Harry, the Dirty Dog.* New York: Harper & Row, 1956 (black and white).
*** Zolotow, Charlotte. *The Sky Was Blue.* New York: Harper & Row, 1963.

> **NOTE:** Look in the library for a series of books on color by Robert Jay Wolff (New York: Scribner's).

planning for grouptime

> **NOTE:** All music, fingerplays, poems, stories, and games listed here may also be used at other times during the session as appropriate. See Core Library, Basic Resources, p. 76, for publishers and addresses. Addresses for sources of records will be found on p. 81.

Music

Songs

FROM original songs in this book by JoAnne Deal Hicks
* "Going Fishing," p. 581
** "The Color Song," p. 598. For the youngest child, teach one verse at a time.
** "Color Fun," p. 599. For the youngest child, teach one verse at a time.

FROM *Songs for the Nursery School,* MacCarteney
* "Falling Leaves," p. 63
* "Baa! Baa! Black Sheep," p. 74

FROM *Songs for Early Childhood,* Westminster Press
** "Apples Green and Apples Red," p. 18
*** "Snow Makes Whiteness Where It Falls," p. 44

FROM *Wake Up and Sing,* Landeck and Crook
* "Mary Was a Red Bird," p. 15

Records

"Chugging Freight Engine"/"**Little Gray Ponies**"/"Rhyme Me a Riddle" (Young People's Records [YPR], 33⅓ RPM)
"Little Red Wagon" (Children's Record Guild [CRG] 45, 78 RPM)
"Mod Marches" (Hap Palmer, 33⅓ RPM)
"**Baa, Baa, Black Sheep**"/"**Little Boy Blue**"/"**Two Little Blackbirds**," *Nursery and Mother Goose Songs* (Bowmar Records, 33⅓ RPM)

"Colors/If You Are Wearing a —————— Shirt, Stand Up," *Learning Basic Skills Through Music*, Vol. 1 (Hap Palmer, 33⅓ RPM, also available in Spanish)
"Color Me a Rainbow" (Melody House, 33⅓ RPM)

Rhythms and Singing Games

FROM *Songs for the Nursery School*, MacCarteney
"Heigh-Ho, Daisies and Buttercups," p. 62 (use brightly colored scarves)

FROM *Music Resource Book*, Lutheran Church Press
"A Tisket, a Tasket," p. 91

FROM *Music Activities for Retarded Children*, Ginglend and Stiles
"Stodola Pumpa," p. 100. **Variation:** green is the grass, yellow the leaves (Fall); red is the rose, and so on.

FROM any record in march tempo
Children could carry brightly colored flags of solid colors.

NOTE: Balloons, chiffon scarves, and crepe-paper streamers of different colors are good dance props. (See p. 33.)

Fingerplays and Poems

FROM *Rhymes for Fingers and Flannelboard*, Scott and Thompson
"Five Brown Pennies," p. 12
"What Colors Do I See?" p. 45 (English and Spanish)
"Five Little Easter Eggs," p. 73
"Little Boy Blue," p. 106
"Five Red Apples," p. 120
"The Yellow Daffodil," p. 126
"Purple Violets," p. 127

FROM *Let's Do Fingerplays*, Grayson
"Hair Ribbons," p. 17
"Old Shoes, New Shoes," p. 18
"Driving Down the Street," p. 25
"Two Little Blackbirds," p. 73

FROM *Childcraft*, Field Enterprises
"Clouds," Rossetti, p. 86
"Taxis," Field, p. 201

Come Along! Collection of poetry by Rebecca Caudill. New York: Holt Rinehart and Winston, 1969.

Hailstones and Halibut Bones. Poems about color by Mary O'Neill. Garden City, N.Y.: Doubleday, 1961.

MY PUSSY WILLOW

I have a little pussy
Her coat is soft and gray;
She lives down in the meadow
And she never runs away.

Although she is a pussy,
She'll never be a cat;
For she's a pussy willow!
Now what do you think of that?

COLORS IN MY FOOD
by Bonnie Flemming

Colors, colors, what colors do I see
In the food the farmer grows for me?
Orange carrots and ripe, red tomatoes,
Green string beans and nice brown potatoes.
Yellow butter is to spread on my bread,
Cold, white milk and an apple so red,
Yes, these are the foods that are best, I know,
Because they help me to grow and grow!

NOTE: Use flannelboard props of foods. Teacher or children may place foods on flannelboard as poem is read. Use real foods at snacktime and allow children to eat them when finished.

Stories

(To read, read-tell, or tell. See Book Center for complete list.)

   * *My Slippers Are Red*, Steiner
  ** *The Big Yellow Balloon*, Fenton
  ** *A Rainbow of My Own*, Freeman
 *** *A Blue Seed*, Nakagawa
 *** *Black Is Beautiful*, McGovern
 *** *Mr. Pine's Purple House*, Kessler
  ** *Brown Is a Beautiful Color*, Bond
  * *Red Is for Apples*, Hoffman
  ** *But Where Is the Green Parrot?* Zacharias
 *** *The Big Orange Thing*, Juhl

Games

(See Games, pp. 50–59, and Teacher-Made Games in this guide for directions.)

1. Name It or Scramble
2. I See Something or I Spy

3. Look and See
4. Guess What?
5. What Am I? (riddles)
6. Match-Them
7. Alike, Different, and the Same
8. Color Lotto

Routine Times

1. Snacktime/Mealtime: Do have a conference with the school cook and gain his or her imaginative cooperation in providing foods to match your color days.
   Suggestions:

Red Days
cranberry juice
tomatoes
red apple slices
cherry gelatin
strawberry tarts
cherry tarts
bing cherries

Blue Days
blue popcorn balls
blue milk (food coloring)
tint cream cheese blue
   and spread on crackers
blueberries

Yellow Days
pineapple juice
lemonade
yellow apple slices
½ unpeeled banana
scrambled eggs
custard
lemon gelatin

Green Days
lime gelatin
lime drink
lettuce
green grapes
celery
green peppers
pickles

Orange Days
carrot coins
orange juice
cheese crackers
orange slices
orange gelatin
mandarin oranges

Purple Days
grape juice
purple grapes
purple plums
grape jelly
grape gelatin

Brown Days
chocolate pudding
peanut butter
brown bread
hot chocolate
graham crackers
gingerbread children

Black and White Days
chocolate/vanilla cookies
milk
white bread
popcorn
marshmallows
prunes/raisins

a. Let children color their milk with drops of food coloring. Use colored cellophane straws to match color of the day. Children may choose a favorite color straw on multicolor days.

b. Use real or artificial flowers or fruits in appropriate colors to decorate the tables.

c. Make place mats from shelf paper or paper towels in the color of the day.

2. When it is time to get up from rest time, write child's name on the blackboard with chalk in the color of the day.

3. Designate which child should get up from rest time by saying, "Anyone who has on red shoes may get up now."

4. In transit: look for the featured color along the way.

Large Muscle Activities

1. Use balls of different colors for ball play.

2. Bean bag toss: use bean bags of different colors.

3. Blow and chase bubbles: make wire loop for giant bubbles. Dip loop into a shallow cake or pie pan that has commercial bubble liquid in it. (See bubble recipe, p. 27.)

4. Color songs (see Hap Palmer records): give each child a small object of red, blue, yellow, or green color. Child stands up or sits down as the words indicate, or when the color of child's clothing is called.

5. A Tisket, a Tasket: use green and yellow berry baskets; place behind one child instead of a handkerchief.

6. Two Little Blackbirds: children sit on the floor in two rows. First pair get up, "fly around," and come back and sit down at the end of the row as song is sung. Repeat until all who wish have had a turn.

7. Hot Potato (for Brown Day): see Games, p. 59.

8. Fly, Little Bluebird: see Games, p. 58.

Extended Experiences

1. Visit a paint store, fabric shop, or carpet mart.

2. Visit a furniture store. Notice different woods, metals, and fabrics.

3. A lapidist or "rock hound" may come and bring colorful rocks and minerals to show, especially those that change color under black light.

4. An artist might enjoy showing the children how to mix paints on a palette and several ways to use the paint.

5. If you know people who do stage lighting perhaps they would demonstrate how lights and gels are used for different effects.

6. This Is Color series (no sound, loop film): This Is Blue, This Is Red, This Is Yellow, This Is Green, This Is Purple, This Is Orange (Bailey Films Inc.).

7. Color Is Fun, and Things That Are Red. Each contains: 2 filmstrips, 2 records or 1 cassette, 6 color posters 18 inches by 24 inches, 6 Child Art Visuals in color, and Teachers Illustrated Guide (Bowmar Artworlds Multi-Media Program).

teacher resources

Pictures and Displays

(See p. 79 for addresses of firms listed.)

1. A bulletin board may be sectioned off into a color area for pictures. Objects that the children bring may be displayed on a color table.
2. Pictures illustrating the fingerplays add interest. Be sure to include pictures of rainbows, Easter eggs, and foods.
3. Grocery stores will often give teachers big pictures of fruits and vegetables that can be displayed.
4. Large posters can be made from pictures that are all one color including objects familiar to children. These posters can be used to show the featured color of the day and are mounted on the classroom door or in a conspicuous place where children may discuss them.
5. Display creative artwork made during the color week.
6. Display clear plastic glasses or vases of water tinted with food coloring on the window sills.
7. Learning Colors: 10 color posters 11 inches by 17 inches, Spanish and English words for color (Vanguard Visuals Co.).
8. Safety on Streets and Sidewalks (Instructo Flannelboard Sets).
9. School and School Helpers: Crossing Guard (David C. Cook).
10. Any pictures from other commercial packets or your personal file on other subjects that depict the color of the day.

Community Resources

1. Drapery, upholstery, and rug dealers for color samples
2. Paint stores for paint sample cards and formica samples
3. Grocery stores for colorful display media such as foods, flowers, butterflies
4. County home economist will have current information about color
5. Lapidist in a jewelry store
6. Rock hound: collector of rocks and minerals
7. Geologist in a nearby college or university

The Color Song

JoAnne Deal Hicks

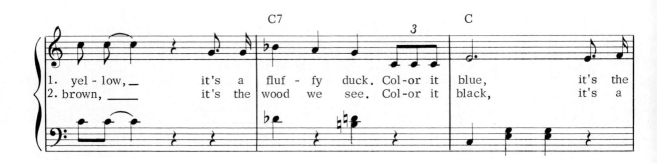

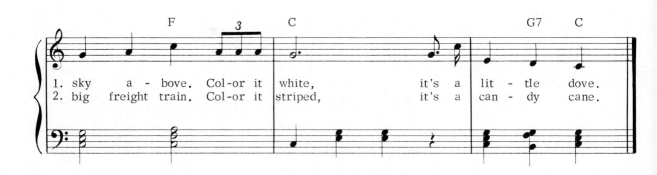

NOTE: Use this syncopated melody with appropriate flannelboard figures or colorful pictures as teaching aids. Teach the youngest children one verse only.

Color Fun

JoAnne Deal Hicks

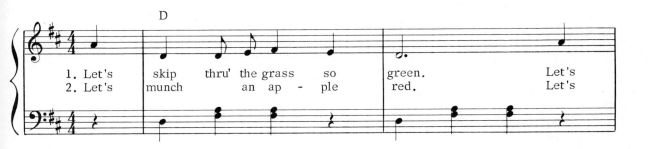

1. Let's skip thru' the grass so green. Let's
2. Let's munch an ap - ple red. Let's

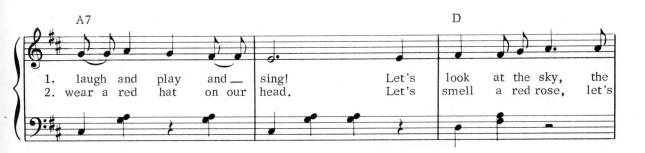

1. laugh and play and ___ sing! Let's look at the sky, the
2. wear a red hat on our head. Let's smell a red rose, let's

1. sky ___ so blue. Oh I want to do it, do you?
2. wrin - kle our nose. Oh I want to do it, do you?

Verse 3: Let's suck on a lem-on sour.
Let's pick a yel-low flower.
Let's ride in a cab, a yel-low cab.
Oh, I want to do it, do you?

Verse 4: Let's swim in the blue, blue lake.
Let's bake a blue-ber-ry cake.
Let's wish on a star, a twin-kling star.
Oh, I want to do it, do you?

NOTE: Pretend to take the children on a walk through the park. Use appropriate actions.

37 Tools and Machines to Use in My World

basic understandings

(concepts children can grasp from this subject)

- A tool is an instrument held in the hand and used to help do a job easier and faster.
- A machine is an object made up of two or more moving or unmoving parts used for doing some kind of work; it may or may not be operated by the hand or hands.
- A machine usually makes work easier.
- Tools and machines cannot work by themselves; they need people or some kind of power (heat, air, water, chemicals, and electricity) to make them work.
- A power tool is a kind of tool that was once operated by hand and is now operated by electricity, batteries, gas, or other sources of energy. We often need to turn a switch or control the tool by hand.
- A tool can also be a machine.
- Some tools are not machines, for example, pencils, erasers, rulers, drinking straws, cups, bowls, and magnifying glasses.
- Some of the tools we use at home are screwdrivers and screws, hammers, saws, pliers, scissors, brooms, hand eggbeaters, can openers, pulleys, ladders, and files.
- Tools we may use in the garden are rakes, hoes, spades, and trowels.
- Some of our toys and play equipment can be tools, such as slides, teeter-totters, swings, skates, wagons, tricycles, wheelbarrows, and other wheel toys.

- Some machines used in our homes are run by electricity, such as vacuum cleaners, food mixers, can openers, washing machines, clothes dryers, and sewing machines.
- Some machines used outdoors use chemicals, fuels, or motors to make them run, such as cars, lawn mowers, trains, and airplanes. (See Transportation guides.)
- Machines which help farmers do their work are known as farm machines—corn shellers, tractors, combines, seeders, cultivators, balers, milking machines, as well as simple tools like shovels and pitchforks.
- Machines which help us get from one place to another are transportation machines. (See Transportation guides.)
- Tools and machines are used in factories to make cars, furniture, toys, and other products.
- Tools and machines are used in offices to help do the work. Office tools often include pens, erasers, rulers, staplers, punches, and pencils. Some office machines used are adding machines, typewriters, Xerox machines, and telephones.
- Machines and tools are used to help build houses and buildings, using tools such as screwdrivers, saws, hammers, nails, and drills and machines such as cement mixers, bulldozers, and power saws.
- Machines are also used for road building and heavy construction, such as trenchers, steamrollers, road graders, steam shovels, bulldozers, pipe diggers, and cement mixers.
- Some tools and machines make loud noises, such as power mowers, electric drills, and hammers.
- Some tools and machines are quiet, such as pencils, screwdrivers, clocks, wristwatches, and metal tape measures.
- Although machines can help do work, they can also be dangerous if we get in their way or use them the wrong way.
- Most musical instruments are a kind of machine.

Additional Facts the Teacher Should Know

A machine is any device, simple or complex, by which the intensity of an applied force is increased, its direction changed, or one form of motion or energy changed into another form. It usually is made of two or more fixed or movable parts. All complex machines are combinations of six simple machines. These are further divided into (a) primary: lever, pulley, inclined plane, and wedge, and (b) secondary: wheel and axle, and screw.

A tool is a machine which is operated by hand. Complex machines use combinations of simple machines and may be run by various kinds of energy: heat, chemicals, electricity, atomic, oil, gas, and steam. In machines, a small force can be applied to overcome a much larger resistance or load.

A screw is actually an inclined plane wound around a straight central core. A wedge is another example of inclined plane. It is really two inclined planes joined together at a point. A needle and a nail are examples of a wedge. Tongs, scissors, and a crowbar are simple lever machines.

NOTE: Other related guides are: Transportation, Families at Work, Animals, and Food.

Vocabulary

TOOLS

Workbench
nail
screwdriver
pliers
wrench
ruler
tape measure
saw
crowbar
drill
wheel
axle
pulley
screw
wedge

tool
lever
inclined plane
hammer
Household
scissors
brush
can opener
rolling pin
nutcracker
rotary eggbeater
spoon
broom
tongs
needle

Office
stapler
punch
pen
pencil
eraser
typewriter
Gardening
rake
hoe
shovel
spade
trowel
wheelbarrow

MACHINES

Construction
excavation
cement mixer
road grader
pipe digger
concrete
vehicle
bulldozer
trencher
electric motor
energy
power
gear
switch
machinery
Farm
disker (harrow)
baler
combine

milking machine
tractor
seeder
cultivator
mower
Household
grinder
sewing machine
refrigerator
electric saw
vacuum cleaner
electric drill
electric mixer
blender
shaver
dryer
washer
clock

Transportation
bicycle
automobile
train
bus
boat, ship
airplane
wagon
Yard
electric lawn
    mower
snowblower
electric hedge
    clippers
fertilizer
    spreader
sprinkler

Methods Most Adaptable for Introducing This Subject to Children

- Display pictures of tools and machines.
- Read a story about a community helper and his/her tools or machines.
- Let children prepare soapflakes for soap painting using different tools. (See Discovery Center, No. 20, p. 605.)
- Have a display of simple tools and machines on the discovery table.
- Visit the site of a building or road being repaired or any similar work going on nearby and watch workmen using tools and machines. Talk about the machines being used and how they make work easier.

learning centers

Discovery Center

1. Toss scraps of paper on the floor. Let the children pick up scraps by hand or by using a broom, a handsweeper (Bissell type), and an electric vacuum cleaner. Talk about the help given in each case by the machine.
2. Make a Feel It Box (see illustration, p. 53) of simple tools to identify. Include a hammer, screwdriver, pliers, and scissors. Talk about how they help us.
3. Let the children beat an egg with a fork, a rotary beater, and an electric beater. Discuss the work involved.
4. Ask the children to try to pull a nail from a block of wood; then use a claw hammer.
5. Put blocks in a big box. Have the children try to lift it, push it; then put it on a dolly or wagon and move it. Discuss.
6. Use a single pulley fastened to a ceiling or a rope over a tree. Ask a child to lift a tricycle by himself or herself; then tie it on the rope and have him or her pull the other end. Ask, "Which is easier?"
7. Tie a string around a heavy box. Have the children try to lift it. Then fasten the box on a broomstick; put the broomstick across a chair or sawhorses and have children push down the other end. This illustrates the principle of the lever.
8. Have screws started in soft wood. Let children use screwdrivers. Also nails and hammers.
9. Let the children explore and use an old typewriter.
10. Let the children examine an old windup clock to see wheels and gears.
11. Wind a music box and let the children watch the gears move.
12. Provide a child's sewing machine; thread it and let the children sew small pieces of cloth. (Be sure to supervise this.)
13. Provide a science table with tools and machines (old radios, clocks, machines of any kind).
14. Let the children find as many wheels as they can in the room. Help them identify dials and faucets as wheels and to note gear wheels in toys and clocks.
15. Identify the number of wheels on various vehicles.
16. Use a magnet to pick up nails.

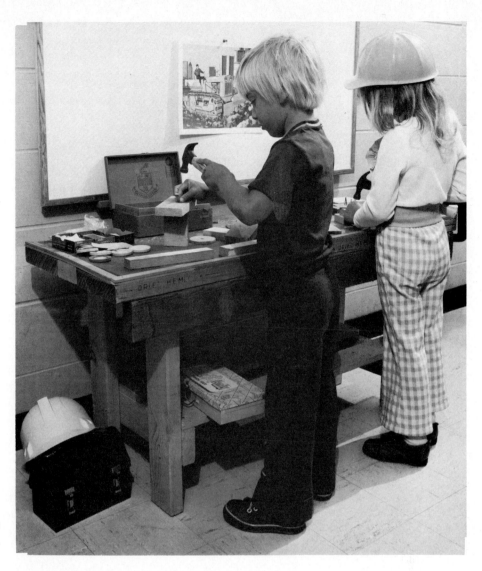

Carpenter's
Workshop.
See page 606.

17. Use a battery and wires to ring a buzzer or light a bulb.
18. Display "People Who Come to My House" and "People in the Neighborhood," picture fold-outs that show tools (The Child's World).
19. Encourage the children to explore instruments. Talk about how they help a person change sound to music.
20. Tell the children you want them to help make whipped soapflakes for fingerpaint. (See recipes, p. 28.) Give some of the children a fork, some a rotary eggbeater, and let some (with supervision) help operate an electric mixer. Talk about the time and work needed in each case. Ask the children to think of other machines and tools that help us.
21. Use tools and machines when cooking and preparing food. Here are some specific suggestions:

Machines

Electric blender:
a. Make milk shakes or eggnog.
b. Make applesauce. Cook apples, beat in blender, and add sugar.
c. Make peanut butter. Combine 2 cups shelled peanuts, 2 tablespoons salad oil, salt to taste.

Electric mixer:
a. Whip gelatin.
b. Make meringue or frosting.
c. Make cookies or cupcakes.
d. Make marshmallows. Combine 1 package (3 oz) of gelatin, ⅔ cup boiling water, 1 cup of sugar, and 3 tbsp light corn syrup.

Dissolve gelatin in water, stir in sugar, and blend in corn syrup. Chill until slightly thickened. Beat on highest speed until soft peaks form (15 minutes). Pour into pan lined with wax paper and greased with butter. Refrigerate overnight. Dust pastry board with powdered sugar. Cut into squares and roll in powdered sugar.

Hand Tools

Rotary beater:
a. Make meringues.
b. Whip Jell-O.
c. Make scrambled eggs.

Can opener: open a can of juice or other food.

Hand grinder: make cranberry relish. Combine 2 cups of cranberries and 2 oranges, whole (including rind). Put through a food chopper and add about 2 cups of sugar. Serve with crackers for snack.

Dramatic Play Centers

Home-Living Center:

1. Provide housekeeping tools, such as cleaning brushes, dustpans, dustcloths, brooms, mops, spray bottles. Supervise. Children may also be allowed to clean mirrors, windows, or lavatories.
2. Let children beat soapflakes in water.
3. Use playdough, rollers, and cutters with tongue depressors for slicing.
4. Encourage use of doll carriages and strollers or wagons to take dolls on an outing.
5. Talk about tools used in preparing, cooking, and eating foods, such as bowls, rolling pins, spatulas, potato masher, measuring cups, knives, forks, spoons. Discuss how tools make work easier.

Block-Building Center

1. Call attention to use of ramps, cranes, pulleys, levers, wheels, gears.
2. Provide rubber or soft plastic tools for use in this area.
3. Have some hard hats, tool aprons, and tool kits.

   NOTE: It is helpful to hang helper pictures from Community Worker Picture Sets above appropriate center to suggest constructive activities relating to real work situations.

Other Dramatic Play Centers

1. Carpenter's workshop: set up workbench and provide nails, screws, hammers, sandpaper blocks, and other tools as well as carpenter hats and tool aprons. (See illustration, p. 605.)

2. Painter's workshop: encourage children to pretend to paint using dry painter's brushes, empty paint buckets, and wearing painter's caps. Caps are often free at a paint store. Supply the painters with sample paint cards or swatches to show to customers. **Variation:** Outdoors, allow water to be used for paint. Invite painters to paint walls and toys.

3. Plumber's center: set out real sets of pipes (elbows, nipples, T's, faucets with adapter couplings, and a variety of pipelengths) for children to fit together. Include a wrench. Used pipe is often available from plumbing companies but it needs to be cleaned with steel wool and lubricated with Vaseline before using. Children will enjoy actually connecting their plumbing pipes to an outdoor faucet. This quickly becomes a discovery experience when water does or does not flow as expected. (See illustration on this page.)

Learning, Language, and Readiness Materials Center

Commercially made games and materials for use at a table or on a mat:

(See Basic Resources, p. 79, for manufacturers' addresses.)

1. Playskool Wood Toy Builder Set: wood with plastic nuts and bolts
2. Toymaker: wood girders, wheels, nuts, bolts (Childcraft and Creative Playthings)
3. Toycraft: durable plastic snap-together parts that make a variety of toys or vehicles that actually roll (Childcraft)

4. Lego Gear Set (listed in most catalogs)
5. Nuts and Bolts: brightly colored plastic parts (Child Guidance)
6. Playskool Puzzle Box: people and their jobs
7. Hammer and Nail Sets: workbench (Playskool)
8. Sand Tools and Sandbox Accessories (listed in most catalogs)
9. Gears in Action (Childcraft)
10. Tectonic Set: 152 pcs., rods, axles, wheels, wrenches (Mead)
11. Bilotoy (Denmark): nuts, bolts, screws (ABC School Supply)
12. Housecleaning Sets (listed in most catalogs)
13. Gardening Tools (listed in most catalogs)
14. See-Through Music Box (Creative Playthings)
15. Put-Together Toolbox (Creative Playthings)
16. Playskool Match-Ups: occupations, with tools used (2-pc. puzzles)
17. Simple Machines: set of 6 working models of simple machines (ABC School Supply)
18. Woodworking Tools (most catalogs)

Teacher-made games and materials for use at a table or on a mat:

NOTE: For detailed description of Games, see pp. 50–59.

1. Name It: use vocabulary list for suggestions for pictures or objects.
2. Grouping and Sorting by Association: sort pictures or plastic models of tools and machines used for various purposes into boxes labeled with pictures relating to farm, house, building, office, transportation, road work.
3. How Many: count the number of wheels on vehicles.
4. Match-Them: pair tool with association picture for its use, such as rake with leaves, eggbeater with eggs or bowl, or hammer with board. **Variation:** pair tools with helpers who use them from flannelboard aids or picture cards.

Art Center

* 1. Easel paint: offer different-width brushes.
** 2. Gadget printing: use gears, toy car wheels, nuts and bolts, and other such parts of tools, or items such as sponges, corks, pieces of wood molding, or rolled cardboard.
* 3. Paint with rollers: use small painting rollers or foam hair rollers.
* 4. Use tools, such as rollers, sticks, or cutters with clay or playdough.
*** 5. Use spool brayers to make stripes and plaids. (See p. 29.)
* 6. Use empty roll-on deodorant dispensers filled with thinned paint as markers.
* 7. Use paste sticks, brushes, or Q-tips to apply paste, and squeeze bottles to apply glue.
*** 8. Cut paper with scissors. Children might like to cut and paste a Tools and Machines book.
** 9. Let children hammer, saw, sand, and paint to make wood sculpture pieces.

Book Center

** Adler, Irving. *Machines.* New York: Abelard-Schuman, 1965.
** Beim, Jerrold. *Tim and the Tool Chest.* New York: William Morrow, 1951.
*** Branley, Franklyn, and Eleanor Vaughn. *Mickey's Magnet.* New York: Thomas Y. Crowell, 1956.

** Brown, Margaret Wise. *The Diggers*. New York: Harper & Row, 1960.

* Buehr, Walter. *The First Book of Machines*. New York: Franklin Watts, 1962.

** Burton, Virginia Lee. *Mike Mulligan and His Steam Shovel*. Boston, Mass.: Houghton Mifflin, 1959.

** ———. *Katy and the Big Snow*. New York: Houghton Mifflin, 1959.

*** Chapin, Cynthia. *Wings and Wheels*. Chicago, Ill.: Albert Whitman, 1967.

*** Kessler, Leonard. *Mr. Pine's Purple House*. New York: Wonder-Treasure Books, 1965.

*** Leavitt, J. *The True Book of Tools for Building*. Chicago, Ill.: Childrens Press, 1961.

* Lenski, Lois. *Davy Goes Places*. New York: Henry Z. Walck, 1961.

*** Notkin, Jerome. *How and Why Wonder Book of Machines*. New York: Wonder-Treasure Books, 1960.

** Petersham, Maud and Miska. *The Box with Red Wheels*. New York: Macmillan, 1949.

** Pine, Tillie. *Simple Machines and How to Use Them*. New York: McGraw-Hill, 1956.

** Rey, H. A. *Curious George Rides a Bike*. Boston, Mass.: Houghton Mifflin, 1952.

** Rockwell, Anne and Harlow Rockwell. *Machines*. New York: Macmillan, 1972.

* ———. *Tool Box*. New York: Macmillan, 1971 (paper, 1974).

*** Saunders, F. W. *Machines for You*. Brownwood, Tex.: Brown Press, 1967.

** Sharp, Elizabeth. *Simple Machines and How They Work*. New York: Random House, 1959.

*** Zaffo, George. *The Big Book of Real Building and Wrecking Machines*. New York: Grosset & Dunlap, 1951.

*** Zim, Herbert. *What's Inside of Engines*. New York: William Morrow, 1953.

planning for grouptime

NOTE: All music, fingerplays, poems, stories, and games listed here may be used at other times during the session as appropriate. See Core Library, Basic Resources, p. 76, for publishers and addresses. Addresses for sources of records will be found on p. 81.

Music

Songs

FROM original songs in this book by JoAnne Deal Hicks

** "Machine Sounds Around the House," p. 614

** "Now It's Time," p. 634

NOTE: See also original songs in the Transportation guides.

FROM *Music Resource Book,* Lutheran Church Press

** "The Wheels on the Bus," p. 50

* "I'm a Big, Black Engine," p. 51

FROM *Songs for the Nursery School*, MacCarteney

* "Transportation Songs," pp. 10–18
* "Digging in the Sand," p. 52
* "My Top Is Big," p. 99
** "Merry-Go-Round," p. 101
** "The Clock," p. 104

** "The Broom," p. 105
* "Cymbals," p. 109
* "The Bugle," p. 110
* "Scissors," p. 114
*** "The Steam Shovel," p. 116

FROM *Wake Up and Sing*, Landeck and Crook

** "Pretty and Shiny," p. 22
** "Riding in a Car," p. 66
** "Bling-Blang" ("You Get a Hammer, I'll Get a Nail"), p. 74

FROM *Songs from Early Childhood*, Westminster Press

** "Song of the Grandfather Clock," p. 81
* "The Little Red Choo-Choo," p. 110

FROM your own traditional songbook

** "Johnny Works with One Hammer"
** "I've Been Working on the Railroad"
** "Round and Round the Village" (See parody, p. 455.)

Records

"Building a City"/"What the Lighthouse Sees"/"Rainy Day" (Young People's Records [YPR], 33⅓ RPM)

"Drummer Boy"/**"Let's Play Together"**/"I Wish I Were" (YPR, 33⅓ RPM)

"The New House"/**"How Honey Helped"** (Folkways, 33⅓ RPM)

"Grandfather Builds a Table," *Creative Movement and Rhythmic Exploration* (Hap Palmer, 33⅓ RPM)

"Mechanical Rhythms," *Rhythm Time*, Record 1 (Bowmar, 33⅓ RPM)

Rhythms and Singing Games

"Rhythm Time No. 1" (mechanical rhythms including jet plane, mechanical toys, and clocks; Bowmar, 33⅓ RPM)

FROM *Music Resource Book*, Lutheran Church Press

"March of the Toy Soldiers," p. 38. (Teacher should pretend to wind up the mechanical toys before their march. Music from *The Nutcracker Suite*)

"Clocks," p. 31. (Let children swing their arms in rhythmic imitation of a pendulum.)

Fingerplays and Poems

FROM *Rhymes for Fingers and Flannelboards*, Scott and Thompson

"Here Are Mother's Knives," p. 80
"Ten Little Clothespins," p. 83
"I Am a Top," p. 130
"Jack in the Box," p. 132
"Fun at the Playground," p. 133
"See-Saw," p. 133

FROM *Let's Do Fingerplays*, Grayson

FROM *Very Young Verses*, Geismer and Suter

THE DIGGER

I'm a digger, big and strong   (PUFF OUT CHEST AND PAT)
Here's my arm, it's very long.   (EXTEND BOTH ARMS OUT STRAIGHT)
Here's my scoop, and with a spurt   (FORM SCOOP WITH HANDS AND SCOOP ARMS TO FLOOR)
I clutch the ground and bring up dirt.   (SCOOP UP DIRT AND RAISE ARMS)
I turn and drop it in the truck   (TURN WHOLE BODY AND OPEN HANDS LETTING DIRT FALL)
Then start all over—chuck, chuck, chuck.   (SWING BODY BACK TO STARTING POSITION)

THE CLOCK

Tick-tock, tick-tock,
Tick-tock says the clock.
Little boy, little girl,
Time to wash our hands.
        (put the blocks away)
        (go outside)
        (ride the bus)

Stories

(To read, read-tell, or tell. See Book Center for a complete list.)

** *Mike Mulligan and His Steam Shovel*, Burton
** *Tim and the Tool Chest*, Beim
 * *Tool Box*, Rockwell

Routine Times

1. Eat food prepared earlier at snack or mealtime.
2. Use a rolling cart to bring food to tables at snack or mealtime.
3. Call attention to tools and machines as you use them: doorknobs, light switches, levers, stairs, utensils, faucets, hand or nail brushes.
4. At pickup time use wagon or rolling platform to return toys to shelves.
5. When out walking or riding watch for use of machines and tools by others.
6. At mealtime talk about utensils as tools, including those used to prepare food.

Large Muscle Activities

1. Use wheel toys with ramps.
2. Use wheelbarrows for moving blocks.
3. Use pulleys for lifting pails of sand.
4. Oil the tricycles and wagons.
5. Bring out garden tools (spring).
6. Shovel snow (winter).
7. Rake leaves. Use wagons to collect the leaves (fall).
8. Add a variety of sand tools to the sandbox play area, such as sand combs, sifters, sand wheels, and a scoop 'n' scrape.
9. Water lawn with sprinkler or hose (summer).

Extended Experiences

1. Visit a building construction site if the builder will allow children there.
2. Attend a school band rehearsal.
3. Visit a gasoline station that has a lift and a car wash.
4. Go to a hardware store to show the children where tools and small appliances are sold. Buy some nails or screws, a pulley, a hammer, a screwdriver, some garden tools, or pipe fitting.
5. Invite parent community helpers to come on different days and show children the tools they use, how to use them, and when and why their tools are necessary, such as: a fix-it repairman might actually repair a playground vehicle while children watch, a carpenter might build a bird feeder or a simple tote tray to be used at school. Encourage children to help sand, stain, or paint.

   NOTE: If the carpenter has access to a crosscut section from a tree or perhaps a piece of lumber that shows an edge of bark, children can better associate the original source of lumber to trees.

6. Let children watch when a plumber comes to fix the plumbing. **Variation:** watch the custodian using tools to clean the school building.
7. Children will enjoy attaching their plumbing pipes (see Other Dramatic Play Centers, p. 607) and fittings to an outdoor faucet so that they can see what happens. This is an excellent cause-and-effect discovery experience.

teacher resources

Books and Periodicals

1. *The How and Why Library*. Vol. 9, "Make and Do." Chicago: Childcraft, 1964.
2. Pine, Tillie S. and Joseph Levine. *Simple Machines and How to Use Them*. New York: McGraw-Hill, 1965.
3. Most farm journals or implement catalogs.
4. Sears, Montgomery Ward, Spiegel, and other mail-order catalogs.
5. Mallinson et al. *Science I*. Morristown, N.J.: Silver Burdett Co., 1965.
6. Meyers, Jerome S. *Machines*. Cleveland, Ohio: Collins-World, 1972.

Pictures and Displays

(See p. 79 for addresses of firms listed.)

1. A Trip to the Farm and Community and Home Helpers: Teaching Picture Packets, 12 pictures in each set (David C. Cook).
2. People Who Come to My House and People in the Neighborhood: Picture Fold-Out Charts (The Child's World).
3. Musical Instruments: 18 flannelboard aids (Instructo).
4. Display mounted pictures of kitchen tools and machines from magazines.
5. Display mounted pictures of construction machines and tools in the Block Building Center.
6. Set out catalog sections showing gardening or yard tools or other tools and machines to be used around the home. Sale catalogs or advertisements are excellent sources of colored pictures. These can be cut out to make picture books, games, and puzzles.

Community Resources

1. A neighboring building site. Make certain it is safe to visit.
2. Parent community helpers, such as a carpenter, a plumber, or a road grader.
3. Implement dealers, automobile dealers, hardware dealers, television and radio dealers, and others who retail tools or machines might give you out-of-date catalogs or illustrative materials to be used for flannelboard aids, games, or sources of pictures for children to cut and paste.

Machine Sounds Around the House

JoAnne Deal Hicks

NOTE: Verse 1 is fun to use during a cooking activity—it could be sung during the time the children are waiting their turn to beat the batter.

38 Mathematics in My Everyday World

basic understandings

(concepts children can grasp from this subject)

- A group of objects is called a "set,", such as a set of blocks or a set of dishes.
- We count to find how many objects we have in a set: one to three, one to five, one to ten.
- Objects can be grouped in sets in many ways, such as by kind (family), size, color, use, weight, and shape (**classification**).
  - a. Objects that are grouped together because they are similar are alike or are the same.
  - b. Objects that are not like the others in some way are not alike or are different.
  - c. Two objects that are alike or are used together are known as a pair (socks, mittens, shoes) or twins (boys, girls, lambs, squirrels).
- We compare objects (**comparison**):
  - a. By size: small, large; big, little; tall, short; fat, thin; wide, narrow
  - b. By location: near, far; in front of, behind; over, under; in, out; up, down; above, below; inside, outside
  - c. By quantity: few, many; a lot, a little; more, less; some, none
  - d. By weight: heavy, light
- We can arrange objects in order (**seriation**):
  - a. By size: smallest to largest; largest to smallest; shortest to tallest; thinnest to thickest
  - b. By location: nearest to farthest; farthest to nearest
  - c. By position: first, second, third; next to last, last
- If we add an object to a set we have more than we did before (**addition**).
- If we take an object away from a set we have less than we did before (**subtraction**).

- If we remove all the objects in a set we have none left or an empty set.
- Objects or sets can be divided into subsets or parts (**division**).
  a. Sets are divided into two equal parts or are divided in half.
  b. Objects or sets can be divided into two or more unequal sets or subsets.
- If each child has one of the same thing we have just enough, for example, each child has one cookie or one chair (one-to-one correspondence or **equivalence**).
  a. If each child does not have a chair or a cookie we do not have enough or we have too few.
  b. If we have more chairs or cookies than children we have more than enough or too many.
- Objects have different shapes.
  a. Two-dimensional:
     1. circle: round
     2. triangle: three sides
     3. rectangle or square: four corners and four straight sides
  b. Three-dimensional:
     1. spherical: ball, globe, orange
     2. triangular: triangular block, rhythm band triangle
     3. rectangular: rectangular blocks, boxes, books
     4. conical: funnel, party hat
  c. Other shapes include stars, cylinders, arches, crescents, hearts, and diamonds.
- Many things help us measure.
  a. A clock tells us what time it is (the hour of the day).
  b. A thermometer tells us temperature (how hot or cold something is).
  c. A ruler (yardstick, measuring tape) tells us how long, high, or wide something is.
  d. A calendar tells us what day (week, month, year) it is.
  e. Scales tell us how much something weighs.
  f. Measuring cups and spoons help us measure food or other materials.
- A numeral represents a number rather than a letter or other symbol or character. Children can learn the correct names for numerals, such as one, 1; two, 2; three, 3. Children who speak other languages have other words for these numerals.
- We use numbers in many ways:
  a. on our house so our friends or the letter carrier can find us
  b. on the telephone so we can call someone
  c. on a cash register to find out how much we should pay the store clerk
  d. on money to help us know how much it is worth
  e. on stamps to help tell us how much they are worth
  f. on book pages so we can tell someone where to find a story or picture
  g. on license plates so we can tell who owns a car
- We use money to buy things, such as food, clothes, house, car, toys.
  a. We have coins and dollars to use as money.
  b. Our coins have names: penny, nickel, dime, and quarter. Many children do not have a clear concept of exact value.
- We use the word "time" to talk about when things happen. Children begin to understand:
  a. Today or day is the time between when we get up in the morning and the time we go to bed at night.
  b. Night is the time when it is dark and we go to sleep.

    NOTE: See Day and Night guide for additional concepts.

  c. Tomorrow is the time it will be when we wake up after we go to bed tonight.
  d. Yesterday is the day it was before we went to bed last night.

e. Morning is between breakfast and lunch.
f. Afternoon is between lunch and dinner (supper).
g. Evening is between supper and the time you go to bed.
h. The days have names: Sunday, Friday (children do not always know the correct order).
i. Several days make a week (children do not know how many).
j. The months have names: January, June (children do not always know correct order).
k. A year is a very, very long time. Children do not know how many days or weeks.

Additional Facts the Teacher Should Know

Mathematics, which involves concepts about numbers, measuring, money, spatial relationships, time, and problem solving, can be presented to young children in some form that is understandable to them; math, therefore, belongs in the curriculum for young children. The activities and materials suggested in this guide will serve to direct your attention to some of the potentials in the classroom environment for teaching mathematic concepts. You will certainly find many more ways of helping children discover some of the basic understandings.

Very young children can discover that we use numbers in many ways, have many ways of measuring, can classify things in many ways, can compare things in many ways; and can begin to understand some of the mathematic skills of counting, adding, subtracting, and dividing. However, very young children have difficulty realizing that objects can have more than one property and can belong to several classes—a red pencil can be grouped with red things, hard things, long things, and wooden things. This realization is acquired by grouping and regrouping according to different traits. At first the young child may need to group by traits suggested by the teacher, but the child with more experience should be encouraged to decide for himself the traits that make certain things go together. Grouping in different ways encourages flexible thinking.

The very young child's concepts of money are mainly confined to the knowledge that we earn it by working and then use it to buy the things we need or want. (See Families at Work.) They are beginning to know the names of some of the coins but do not know their exact value. A very young child will most likely think a nickel is worth more than a dime because it is bigger in size.

Time is one of the most difficult understandings for young children. They can learn that a clock tells us what time it is but they will be much older before they can tell the actual time for themselves. In the meantime it is helpful if the teacher verbalizes the use of the clock to familiarize the child with telling time. For example, he/she can point to the clock on the wall and say, "It is ten o'clock, time for juice," or looking at a wristwatch, can say, "My wristwatch says it is eleven thirty, time to go outside." The passage of time from one day to the next, one week to the next, and one year to the next develops slowly. Through conversation and the use of the calendar in the classroom children can come to understand that days of the week have names, that several days (one line of numbers on most calendars) make a week, several weeks (several lines or one page of the calendar) is a month, that the months have names, and that a year is a very long time. Children become most aware of the concept of a year when they hear much discussion about this around New Year's Day and on their birthdays. Children are usually five before they realize that holidays and birthdays recur on a regular basis. Some calendars read vertically and some have put Monday in the first space. It is best to use those which read horizontally.

Many different approaches to teaching math to very young children are being used today and many commercial materials are now available. This guide represents a potpourri, or a little bit of everything. A brief explanation of some of the methods follows to aid you in understanding their inclusion.

The new math being taught in many public schools today emphasizes understanding of how and why the mathematical processes work rather than demanding rote learning or acceptance on faith for many of the steps in problem solving. This basic philosophy of seeing, doing, and understanding has long been used on the preschool level. The new math, however, has a new vocabulary with "set" (a group of one or more) as its basic unit. It is appropriate to use this term with young children as they are already familiar with a set of dishes or set of blocks. However, use the term when referring to other things not normally referred to as sets, such as a "set of hats."

The extensive study done by Piaget of children's understanding of mathematical concepts is being given renewed attention in many early childhood centers. While his labels of "equivalence," "conservation," and "seriation" are not widely used, the activities basic to understanding the concepts are appropriate.

Montessori's major contribution to the teaching of math to young children is her ingenious self-teaching materials. They are all designed on the metric system and are self-teaching in that they vary in only one dimension at a time. Thus, if children order them incorrectly, the errors will be obvious and can be corrected. Montessori's sets of graded cylinders which vary in only one dimension (length, diameter) are excellent materials for teaching Piaget's concept of seriation. Thus, in these statements, we are suggesting the blending of many different approaches to the teaching of math to young children.

The United States is on the English measuring system while most of the other countries of the world are on the metric system. The metric system uses centimeters, meters, and kilometers as units of length while the English system uses inches, feet, yards, and miles. The metric system uses grams instead of ounces and liters instead of quarts and gallons. In the near future it is expected that Congress will pass a law putting the United States on the metric system. Many businesses are already converting, but it is anticipated that for ten years after the law is passed people will continue to use both systems. The following table shows English/metric equivalents.

English		Metric	
One inch	=	25.4	millimeters
One inch	=	2.54	centimeters
One yard	=	.914	meter
One mile	=	1.6	kilometers
One ounce	=	28.35	grams
One pound	=	453.6	grams
One quart	=	.94	liter

English		Metric
.039 inch	=	1 millimeter
.394 inch	=	1 centimeter
1.094 yards	=	1 meter
.621 mile	=	1 kilometer
.035 ounce	=	1 gram
2.2 pounds	=	1 kilogram
1.06 quarts	=	1 liter

NOTE: Other guides related to mathematics are: Families at Work, Food, Color, Road Transportation, and Day and Night.

Child is counting puppies on an apron flannelboard before choosing the corresponding numeral at the bottom of the flannelboard.

Methods Most Adaptable for Introducing This Subject to Children

- Cooking activities involving the measuring of ingredients and the use of various-sized utensils and pans
- Dramatic play: a grocery store where children can talk about and handle different-sized containers, sacks, and money (See Food guide, p. 550.)
- Flannelboard story emphasizing quantity and size, such as *The Three Bears* (great big daddy bear, middle-sized mother bear, wee little baby bear; various-sized bowls, chairs, and beds) (See illustration above.)
- Number readiness materials: commercially or teacher-made (See Learning, Language, and Readiness Center.)

Vocabulary

numbers	time	different	divide	circle
count	thermometer	match	half	square
measure	yardstick	less	empty	triangle
shape	calendar	more	set	star
scales	birthday	enough	pair	
ruler	same	none	twin	
clock	alike	add	both	

learning centers

Discovery Center

1. Make cookies, pudding, no-cook candy, Jell-O, or other dishes that require the use of measuring spoons and cups and various sizes of pans, bowls, utensils. Talk about full, half full, and empty; big, little, in, out, and measuring.
2. Measure and weigh children: if done at beginning of year repeat at a later time or end of year to tell them how much they have grown. Who is shorter, taller, heavier, lighter, the same? Tape plain paper, a tree, or giraffe picture chart to the wall and mark off in inches. Write children's names by the marks for their heights. With older children make a graph of the weights using one square equals one pound or 453.6 grams.
3. Balance scales: let children experiment with how many beans will balance a bolt or how many acorns (in terms of many or few) will balance a pebble. Talk about heavy and light.
4. Thermometers: have a large, accurate one in the room and on the playground. Talk about the weather and if it is hot or cold. Help children to see that as the weather gets warmer the mercury goes up, and as it gets colder, the mercury goes down. An indoor-outdoor thermometer is nice so the children can see the similarity or difference between the two.
5. Make a large cardboard thermometer with markings from −30 to 130° F. Make two horizontal slots ½ inch long at the highest and lowest markings. Cut a length of ⅜ inch wide elastic that is twice the distance between the slots, plus ¼ inch for overlap. Thread the elastic through the slots from the front and overlap elastic ¼ inch on the back and sew securely. Run the overlap down to the bottom slot. Color all the elastic that is showing on the front of the thermometer with a red felt tip marker. To lower mercury, pull the elastic down. To raise the mercury, pull it up. The elastic can be moved up or down by the child or teacher to help the child understand the concept of temperatures' rising and falling.
6. At a water or sand table or in a large pan provide measuring cups, containers of various sizes and shapes, measuring spoons, pitchers, and funnels. Let children experiment with pouring water or sand into the various containers and making comparisons. Watch for

opportunities to help children who are ready for it to discover that objects or liquids do not change in amount (number and quantity) when they are put in a smaller or larger container (conservation). Have child fill a 1-cup measuring cup (with handle and spout) to the 1-cup mark. Then have the child pour the contents into a tall narrow container. Notice the contents go higher. Ask if there is more in the new container than in the old one. Let child pour the contents back to check the answer.

7. Count body parts on animals: "How many feet?" "Ears?" "Tails?"
8. Count trees, leaves, flowers, petals, and seeds.
9. Count pebbles, pieces of coal, or seashells.
10. Classifying: children can group items of various kinds as to type, color, shape, weight, or texture. Use real objects from nature or pictures. Beginning experiences should include two or three different types of items with three to five in each group. Increase number and type as children gain skill. Let children decide on the groupings and explain their reasons for doing so.
11. Look for and identify shapes, indoors and out.

Dramatic Play Centers

Home-Living Center

1. Talk about sets of dishes and flatware and their sizes; sort by size and shape: saucers, cups, plates, glasses, knives, forks, and spoons.
2. Include plastic or metal measuring cups, spoons, mixing bowls, and beaters to bake with. Sometimes allow water or sand for measuring.
3. Talk about equivalence or one-to-one correspondence: "Are there enough cups and saucers for everyone? Too many? Too few? How many do we need?"
4. Put a discarded telephone book by the toy telephone to encourage looking up a number and calling someone. Underline the names of families in your center. Remind children that they need parental permission to use the phone at home.
5. Put a bathroom and/or kitchen scale in this center so children can weigh food, themselves, or their dolls. If possible, obtain a baby scale. Metric scales are now available.
6. Put up a calendar on the wall in this center.
7. Put out a toy clock with movable hands or an old alarm clock.
8. Talk about portions of food being served. Talk about more or less. Have child put food in two dishes. "Your doll is hungrier; will you give him/her more?"

Block-Building Center

1. Call attention to taller or shorter buildings, long or short roads. If a yardstick is handy you could help children measure their buildings or roads. "Who has more blocks?" "Do you need more blocks to make yours as tall as Joan's?" Count blocks used to make a road or bridge. Many and few: "Jimmy used many blocks to build a tower."
2. Call attention to shapes used: rectangular, triangular, or square. Help children see spatial relationships: up, down, above, below, under, beside; help children discover that two triangles can make a square, two squares together make a rectangle, two rectangles equal one longer rectangle. If a good set of unit blocks is available, ask for a specific number of blocks by name. "Please give me one square block." "Give me two arches."
3. Encourage older children to build a parking lot. Have one child park the cars and another collect the fees.
4. Encourage older children, who are familiar with them, to add toll bridges and tunnels to their block building.

Other Dramatic Play Centers

1. Set up a grocery store. (See Food guide, p. 550.) Emphasis should be on pricing (putting up signs with prices displayed, such as "2/50¢"). Scales for weighing produce, sizes and shapes of containers, a dozen is twelve, use of cash register (or divided box for coins), paying for food, and making change should be emphasized.

Learning, Language, and Readiness Materials Center

Commercially made games and materials for use at a table or on a mat:

(See Basic Resources, p. 79, for manufacturers' addresses.)

1. Liquid Measures: aluminum and plastic in English/metric (most catalogs)
2. Balance Scales: elementary wooden scale with pans (most catalogs)
3. Miniature Balance Beam Scale: English or metric (ETA)
4. Calendar, Day by Day (Milton Bradley, Judy, Playskool, Ideal)
5. Color Cubes (Playskool, Ideal)
6. Clock (Judy, Playskool, Creative Playthings, Ideal)
7. Color Stacking Disks (Playskool)
8. Coordination Board: Geometric Forms (Playskool)
9. Counting Stairway (Constructive Playthings)
10. Montessori Cylinders: natural wood or color coded (ETA)
11. Montessori Cylinders in Blocks with Knobs: 4 graded sets (ETA)
12. Instructional Scale (Mead Educational Services)
13. Equalizer Balance Scale (Mead Educational Services)
14. Difference Puzzles: same object in varying sizes (most catalogs)
15. Jumbo Color Dominoes (Playskool); Jumbo Tactile Dominoes (Ideal); Picture Dominoes (Milton Bradley, Judy); Money Dominoes (DLM)
16. Lauri Crepe Foam Puzzles: Fit-a-Shape, Fit-a-Clock, Fit-a-Number
17. Fraction Circles and Squares (Ideal)
18. Fractions Are as Easy as Pie (Milton Bradley)
19. Dry Measures/Liquid Measures (Practical Drawing Company)
20. Montessori Geometric Solids and Geometric Insets (ETA)
21. Jumbo Beads on Post: 1 to 5 concepts (Constructive Playthings)
22. Giant Blocks (Constructive Playthings)
23. Giant Mosaics (Childcraft)
24. Flannelboard Cut-Outs: shapes and numbers (Instructo, Milton Bradley)
25. Weather Board (Childcraft)
26. Jumbo Numerals: 5-inch numbers from 0 to 9 (Ideal)
27. Montessori Long Stair and Broad Stair: metric (ETA)
28. Abacus and Counting Frame (most catalogs)
29. Numberite: Judy; Locking Numbers (Ideal); Matchmates (Creative Playthings)
30. Number Post Cards (Milton Bradley)
31. Montessori Number Rods: 10 metric rods, each is one unit longer (ETA)
32. Number Learner Match Pegs (Judy); Number Sorter (Creative Playthings)
33. Parquetry Blocks (Playskool, Ideal, Milton Bradley)
34. Peg Boards (Playskool, Milton Bradley, Ideal)
35. Montessori Pink Tower: 10 metric stacking cubes (ETA)
36. Geo Blocs, Number Blocs, and Ten Blocs, with study guide (Meade Educational Services)
37. Play Store (Creative Playthings)

38. Play Money, Cash Register (most stores and catalogs)
39. Stepping Stones: kinesthetic math, numbers, and shapes (Instructo)
40. Postal Station (Playskool)
41. Apex Learners Ruler and Yardstick: English and metric (most catalogs)
42. Sorting Box: 4 shapes, 4 colors; 10 each (Playskool)
43. Judy See-Quees Puzzles: series of 4 to 6 sequential pictures that tell a story or event
44. Manipulative for Coordination Training Materials: teach seriation (ETA)
45. Shape Form Boards and Graded Geometrics (most catalogs)
46. Size Sorting Boxes (Playskool, Creative Playthings)
47. Multi-Sensory Letters and Numbers: beaded cards (Ideal)
48. Multi-Sensory Cubes and Spheres: 3 colors; 2 sizes each (Ideal)
49. Teddy Bear Counters (Milton Bradley)
50. Thermometer: local hardware store; Indoor-Outdoor, Large Wall (Constructive Playthings); cardboard thermometer with movable mercury ribbon (Ideal)
51. Unifix Math Materials (ETA)
52. Number Poster Cards; Match Plaques; Number Match Cards (Childcraft)
53. Weather Station (Milton Bradley)
54. Walk on Number Line (Instructo)
55. Weaving Mats: teaches concepts of over and under (Ideal)
56. Metric Lollipop Tree for measuring children in centimeters (Ideal)

Teacher-made games and materials for use at a table or on a mat:

NOTE: For detailed description of Games, see pp. 50–59.

1. Counting: rational counting of any objects the child is using during free choice period, such as blocks, beads, feathers, pegs, or scissors.
2. Classification: children can be given objects to group or classify, such as beads, cubes, buttons, and plastic lids of various sizes.
    * Children are asked to put those together that are alike.
    ** Let children decide how objects should be grouped, such as color, size, texture.
    *** After the first groupings by children ask if they can group objects another way. This encourages flexible thinking and the concept that there is more than one way to do things.
3. Number Stair: collect fifteen or fifty-five spools of identical size. Find doweling that will allow the spool to slide down easily. The spindles should be of graded height so that the first one holds one spool, the second holds two, and so on. Paint the spools that represent each number a different color with nontoxic paint. Fifteen spools will make a 1 to 5 number stair and fifty-five spools will make a 1 to 10 number stair. Let the children discover there are different pattern arrangements possible with this number stair.
4. Talk about shape, size, weight, and location of objects that children are working with during their free choice activity (as appropriate).
5. Use flannelboard with geometric or animal shapes allowing child to group things by shape which may be different in size or color. Later children can regroup by color or size, illustrating that objects can belong to different groups.
6. To establish one-to-one correspondence or equivalence (just enough for everyone): use spools to represent people and pop bottle caps for hats; let children pick out enough hats for all of them. Discover the meaning of just enough, not enough, too many, too few.
7. Use of Numbers: look for meaningful ways to use the calendar, clocks, scales, thermometer, telephone, money, stamps, and measuring sticks.

8. Look and See:
   a. Use different coins and bills.
   b. Use different stamps.
   c. Use thermometers, alarm clocks, foot rulers, measuring cups, desk calendars, and seamstress tape.
9. Reach and Feel: use items in (c) above.
10. Match-Them: match objects by shape, size, weight, location.
11. Cover-Ups (variation of Match-Them.)
12. Alike, Different, and the Same: use geometric shapes, coins, stamps.
13. Which Comes First?: use items of current interest.
14. How Many?: set out varying numbers of objects.
15. Block Form Board: on a large piece of cardboard trace around one of each of the shapes in your set of unit blocks. Let children match blocks with the shapes on the form board.
16. Object Form Board: trace around familiar objects and let children find the matching objects and place on the form board.
17. Make sand paper, felt, or flocked number cards.

Art Center

* 1. When painting give children a choice of one or two colors. Talk about the jars being empty or half full.
* 2. When molding and sculpting talk about the size of the ball of clay or dough being worked with. A large ball can be divided into two small balls.
** 3. Paste geometric shapes of various sizes on colored construction paper to make different designs. **Variation:** Use gummed paper or pieces of fabric.
** 4. Cut geometric shapes out of sponges. Let children use them to print designs on colored construction paper.
*** 5. At the woodworking table provide a ruler for measuring the boards to be cut. Provide nails of different lengths. Show children how to measure and how to decide the right-length nail to use.

Other Experiences in This Center Using Art Media:

*** 1. Cutting: show children with cutting skills how to cut a valentine (heart shape). Fold a square of paper in half. (This paper could be one of their fingerpaintings or easel paintings.) Teacher would, starting at fold, draw half of a valentine on the paper with a magic marker. Children should be instructed to start cutting at the bottom point on the fold and cut up and around and back to the centerfold top point.

Book Center

NOTE: The Book Center list has been divided into subgroups for convenience.

Numbers

* Baum, Arline and Joseph Baum. *One Bright Monday Morning*. New York: Random House, 1962 (paper).
*** Elkin, Benjamin. *Six Foolish Fishermen*. Chicago, Ill.: Childrens Press, 1957 (paper).

Geometric forms on the display shelf, as well as color cones, give children an opportunity to explore the concept of geometric forms as solids. Pictures on the display board show shapes from children's everyday experiences. Child at right is arranging a shape picture from geometric forms.

  * Feelings, Muriel. *Moja Means One.* New York: Dial Press, 1971 (Swahili Counting Book).
*** Françoise. *Jeanne-Marie Counts Her Sheep.* New York: Charles Scribner's Sons, 1963.
  * Friskey, Margaret. *Chicken Little Counts to Ten.* New York: Childrens Press, 1946.
*** Hoban, Tana. *Count and See.* New York: Macmillan, 1972.
  * Kredenser, Gail. *One Dancing Drum.* New York: S. G. Phillips, 1971.
*** Langstaff, John. *Over in the Meadow.* New York: Harcourt Brace Jovanovich, 1956 (paper, 1973).
 ** Leonni, Leo. *Inch by Inch.* New York: Astor-Honor, 1962.
 ** Sherman, Diane. *My Counting Book.* Chicago, Ill.: Rand McNally, 1963.
*** Slobodkin, Louis. *Millions, Millions, Millions.* New York: Vanguard Press, 1955.
 ** Stanek, Muriel. *One, Two, Three for Fun.* Chicago, Ill.: Albert Whitman, 1967.
*** True, Louise. *Number Men.* Chicago, Ill.: Childrens Press, 1962.
  * Wildsmith, Brian. *Brian Wildsmith's 1, 2, 3's.* New York: Franklin Watts, 1965.
  * Zolotow, Charlotte. *One Step Two.* New York: Lothrop, Lee & Shepard, 1955.

NOTE: Look in your library for the *Twins* book series by Helen Wing, New York: E. M. Hale, 1960–1966, and *The Sesame Street* books on numbers.

Time

*** Abisch, Roz. *Do You Know What Time It Is?* Englewood Cliffs, N.J.: Prentice-Hall, 1968 (paper).

** Balian, Lorna. *I Love You Mary Jane.* Nashville, Tenn.: Abingdon Press, 1967.

**** Bannon, Laura. *Manuela's Birthday.* Chicago, Ill.: Albert Whitman, 1972 (read-tell).

** Barrett, Judy. *Benjamin's 365 Birthdays.* New York: Atheneum, 1974.

** Buckley, Helen. *The Little Boy and the Birthday.* New York: Lothrop, Lee & Shepard, 1965.

*** Françoise. *What Time Is It Jeanne-Marie?* New York: Charles Scribner's Sons, 1963.

* Green, Mary McBurney. *Is It Hard? Is It Easy?* Reading, Mass.: Addison-Wesley, 1960.

** Hawkinson, John and Lucy. *Days I Like.* Chicago, Ill.: Albert Whitman, 1965.

** Hoban, Russell. *A Birthday for Frances.* New York: Harper & Row, 1968.

*** Hutchins, Pat. *Clocks and More Clocks.* New York: Macmillan, 1970 (paper, 1973).

*** ———. *Changes, Changes.* New York: Macmillan, 1971 (paper, 1973).

* Krasilowsky, Phyllis. *The Very Little Girl.* Garden City, N.Y.: Doubleday & Co., 1958 (paper).

* ———. *The Very Little Boy.* Garden City, N.Y.: Doubleday, 1962 (paper).

* Krauss, Ruth. *The Birthday Party.* New York: Harper & Row, 1957.

*** Schatz, Letta. *When Will My Birthday Be?* New York: McGraw-Hill, 1962.

** Schlein, Miriam. *Fast Is Not a Ladybug.* Reading, Mass.: Addison-Wesley, 1953.

*** ———. *It's About Time.* Reading, Mass.: Addison-Wesley, 1955.

*** Slobodkin, Louis. *Dinny and Danny.* New York: Macmillan, 1951.

*** Spier, Peter. *Fast-Slow, High-Low.* Garden City, N.Y.: Doubleday, 1972.

*** Watson, Nancy Dingman. *When Is Tomorrow?* New York: Alfred A. Knopf, 1955.

** Zolotow, Charlotte. *Over and Over.* New York: Harper & Row, 1957.

Space, Shape, and Size

*** Berkley, Ethel. *Big and Little, Up and Down.* Reading, Mass.: Addison-Wesley, 1950.

*** Brenner, Barbara. *Mr. Tall and Mr. Small.* Reading, Mass.: Addison-Wesley, 1966.

*** Kessler, Ethel. *Are You Square?* Garden City, N.Y.: Doubleday, 1969.

**** Kettlekamp, Larry. *Spirals.* New York: E. M. Hale, 1964 (photographs).

** Kohn, Bernice, *Everything Has a Shape and Everything Has a Size.* Englewood Cliffs, N.J.: Prentice-Hall, 1966.

** Marino, Dorothy. *Edward and the Boxes.* Philadelphia, Pa.: J. B. Lippincott, 1957.

** Mendoza, George. *Sesame Street Book of Opposites.* Bronx, N.Y.: Platt & Munk Pubs., 1973.

*** Schlein, Miriam. *Heavy Is a Hippopotamus.* Reading, Mass.: Addison-Wesley, 1954.

*** ———. *Shapes.* New York: E. M. Hale, 1952.

**** Walter, Marion. *Make a Bigger Puddle, Make a Smaller Worm.* Philadelphia, Pa.: J. B. Lippincott, 1971 (discovering the concepts of big and little with a mirror).

NOTE: Look in your library for books by Tana Hoban.

planning for grouptime

NOTE: All music, fingerplays, poems, stories, and games listed here may also be used at other times during the session as appropriate. See Core Library, Basic Resources, p. 76, for publishers and addresses. Addresses for sources of records will be found on p. 81.

Music

Songs

MEASURING
  (tune: "Pussy Cat, Pussy Cat")
  Adaptation by JoAnne Deal Hicks

Meas-ure your hand, and then meas-ure your nose,
Meas-ure your feet and then meas-ure your toes,
Meas-ure your head, then your ears, and your chin,
You're smil-ing, you're hap-py! Let's meas-ure your grin!

(Teacher may supply tape measure; children love to see how big they are. Children might also enjoy measuring the body parts of toy animals.)

FROM original songs in this book by JoAnne Deal Hicks
** "Bugs," a parody, p. 440 (stresses concepts large, small, thick, thin)
 * "Now It's Time," p. 634. Repetitive melody (teach one verse at a time when working with youngest children)

FROM *Songs for the Nursery School*, MacCarteney
** "Growing Up," p. 3
 * "Cobbler, Cobbler, Mend My Shoe," p. 4
** "One, Two, Three," p. 9
 * "Baa, Baa, Black Sheep," p. 74
 * "Hot Cross Buns," p. 75
*** "This Old Man," p. 83
 * "Swing High, Swing Low," p. 110

FROM *Wake Up and Sing*, Landeck and Crook
 * "Tap Your Foot," p. 14
** "Mo' Yet," p. 50 (teacher may sing to group)

FROM *Music Resource Book*, Lutheran Church Press
** "What Time Is It?," p. 30
 * "One Finger, One Thumb," p. 55

FROM *Music Activities for Retarded Children*, Ginglend and Stiles
** "Angel Band," p. 26 (substitute "instruments" for "angels" and the proper day of the week for "Sunday")
*** "Take Away Song," p. 99 (for younger children start with five objects)
"Grandfather's Clock" (find a picture of a grandfather's clock and modern clocks. Talk about the differences. Have children stand and swing arm like a pendulum as you sing this song. When singing this song you may wish to add a second verse.)

Records

"**Every Day We Grow-I-O**"/"**Big Rock Candy Mountain**" (Young People's Records [YPR], 33⅓ RPM)
"Counting Games and Rhythms for the Little Ones," Ella Jenkins (Folkways, 33⅓ RPM or cassette)
"Learning About Numbers" (David C. Cook, 33⅓ RPM) Includes flannelboard aids and resource sheets.
"Learning to Tell Time is Fun" (Disneyland, 33⅓ RPM)
"It's About Time" (Peter Pan, 33⅓ RPM)
"All About Days, Months, and Seasons"/"Time"/"Numbers and Counting"/"Money" (Miller-Brody, 33⅓ RPM or cassette)

NOTE: Many record album series have songs and activities involving counting, time, space, and shapes, such as Hap Palmer, Kimbo, Sesame Street, Bowmar, Captain Kangaroo.

Rhythms and Singing Games

FROM *Songs for the Nursery School*, MacCarteney
"Activities for Two-Year Olds," p. 1 (concepts of up, down, and around)
"I'm Jumping," p. 2
"I'm Running," p. 2
"See How I'm Jumping," p. 95

FROM *Music Activities for Retarded Children*, Ginglend and Stiles
"Elephant Song," p. 46
"One, Two, What Shall I Do?," p. 88

Fingerplays and Poems

FROM *Rhymes for Fingers and Flannelboards*, Scott and Thompson
"Birthdays," pp. 8–12
"Fun with Numbers," pp. 48–57

NOTE: Many fingerplays in the other sections of this book involve number concepts. Select those that are of current interest to your group.

FROM *Let's Do Fingerplays*, Grayson
"Ten Fingers," p. 3
"Right Hand, Left Hand," p. 9
"Point to the Right," p. 11

"Five Fingers," p. 11
"Two Little Hands," p. 12
"Five Little Girls," p. 20
"Clocks," p. 27
"I Have a Little Watch," p. 27
"The Metronome Song," p. 28
"People," p. 50
"The Stilt Man," p. 50
"Counting and Counting Out," pp. 59, 60, 62–68, 70–74
"Five Years Old," p. 101

GREAT BIG BALL

A great big ball   (ARMS MAKE CIRCLE OVER HEAD)
A middle-sized ball,   (MAKE BALL WITH BOTH HANDS IN FRONT)
A little ball I see.   (MAKE BALL WITH THUMB AND FOREFINGER)
Now let's count the balls we've made; 1—2—3   (MAKE EACH BALL AGAIN AS YOU COUNT)

HICKORY, DICKORY, DOCK

Hickory, dickory, dock,   (STAND, SWING ARM LIKE PENDULUM)
The mouse ran up the clock.   (BEND OVER; RUN HAND UP BODY)
The clock struck one,   (CLAP HANDS OVER HEAD ONCE)
The mouse ran down,   (RUN HAND DOWN TO FEET)
Hickory, dickory, dock.   (STAND; SWING ARM LIKE PENDULUM)

TWO LITTLE BLACKBIRDS

Two little blackbirds sitting on a hill,   (PLACE A FIST ON EACH KNEE)
One named Jack and one named Jill.   (MOVE EACH FIST A LITTLE)
Fly away Jack, fly away Jill,   (FLING EACH HAND OVER YOUR SHOULDER)
Come back Jack, come back Jill.   (BRING EACH HAND BACK TO KNEE)

Stories

(To read, read-tell, or tell. See Book Center for complete list.)

*** *Big and Little, Up and Down*, Berkley
 ** *Everything Has a Shape and Everything Has a Size*, Kohn
 ** *My Counting Book*, Sherman
*** *Shapes*, Schlein
 * *One Step Two*, Zolotow

Games

(See Games, pp. 50–59, and Teacher-Made Games in this guide for directions.)

1. Look and See: use thermometer, clock, timer, measuring cup, and ruler.
2. How Many?: count objects. (Avoid using melody to "Ten Little Indians" as it reflects insensitivity to American Indians.)

Routine Times

1. At snack or mealtime talk about whether there are enough napkins, cups, plates, or spoons for each child.
2. At snack or mealtime talk about the size of a serving. Would you like a big serving or a small serving? Tell children a specific number of crackers or snacks to eat. "Today you may have two square crackers."
3. At snack or mealtime, what happens to the level of juice or milk as it is poured from a pitcher into individual cups? (See-through containers are best for this.) What can you say about all the plates, the cups, and the pitcher when the food or juice is gone? "They are empty!"
4. At snack or mealtime serve sandwiches cut in half; fill juice or milk glasses each half full; serve bananas or apples cut in half.
5. Use an alarm clock, timer, or clock-radio to signify the end of rest time.
6. At the end of rest time you could say, "I am going to slowly count to ten and then I want you to get up slowly and walk slowly over to ————— ."
7. As you walk or ride call attention to the use of numbers on houses, stores, road signs, clocks, and thermometers. "Here we are at 215 Chestnut Street, Johnny's house."
8. Talk about tall and short buildings; things that are near and far; big trucks and small cars, while walking or bussing.
9. Count familiar objects while in transit.
10. Call attention to basic concepts involved while dressing, for example, we need a pair of mittens, socks, shoes (one for each hand or foot) or count how many children have blue coats, brown shoes, red mittens.
11. At pickup time ask for a specific number of objects. "Please give me two blocks to put on this shelf."
12. Comment on child's ability at pickup time: "You put many books on the shelf."

Large Muscle Activities

1. Walking, running, or hopping can be done fast or slow. Call attention to how long each method takes.
2. Throwing or rolling a ball can be done fast or slow. Did the ball go a long or a short way with each method?
3. Taking turns on the equipment requires that the children understand that there are not enough trikes, swings, or teeters for everyone and they must wait. If a piece of equipment is in big demand you could use a timer, a clock, or counting as a means of regulating length of turns.
4. Use of outdoor equipment offers opportunities to use basic concepts. Swings: swinging high or low, swinging fast or slow; jungle gym: "Peter reached the top of the jungle gym first." (This is made as a statement of fact, not the result of a teacher-inspired race.) Sandbox: "I see Mary and Edith sitting beside each other in the sandbox." Teeter: up and down; balancing each other's weight; heavy and light.
5. "Two Little Blackbirds." (See variation under Fingerplays and Poems, p. 629.)
6. When playing circle games talk about who is in the middle; who is beside or next to someone else; between, behind, in front of, as appropriate.
7. Skill Games (see Basic Resources):
   a. Beanbag Toss: use five beanbags. Talk about the results: "The first one got in; the second one didn't go far enough; the third one was close"; "You have two more to throw"; "Count how many you got in."

b. Johnny Can You Jump Over the Puddle: use measuring stick to see how far each child jumps.
c. Bowling: count how many are knocked down and how many are left standing.
d. Balls: use different-sized balls; talk about shape and texture.

Extended Experiences

1. Take a ride on a bus and let each child deposit his/her own fare in the box. Look for uses of numbers as you ride around your community.
2. Take a trip to a store to buy something needed for the classroom or a special activity. Notice use of numbers to mark prices of items and the use of scales, cash register, and money.
3. Take a trip to the post office to buy stamps or to mail letters or invitations.
4. Take a walk and look for uses of numbers on houses, stores, street signs. Talk about things that are far and near, tall and short, high and low. Talk about directions: "turn right," "turn left." Count objects you see or find.
5. Birthday celebrations should be kept simple:
   a. The normal routine should be maintained.
   b. If food will be served, recognize birthday at snack or mealtime.
   c. Special birthday plates, napkins, and cups may replace usual ones.
   d. Avoid noisemakers and favors because they are overstimulating.
   e. The birthday child may be recognized in the following ways:
      (1) Provide child with a special birthday chair. It may have a cushion, bow tied to it, or be placed at the head of the table.
      (2) Child may wear a crown or birthday button.
      (3) Child may blow out candles on a cake, cupcake, or frosted cookie. **CAUTION:** An adult should supervise the candle ceremony.
      (4) Cake (or substitute treat) may be placed in a wooden birthday ring (cut from thick plywood, with a center space to hold a cake on a plate) or on a pedestal cakeplate that plays "Happy Birthday" as the cake revolves.
      (5) When "Happy Birthday" is sung, you may wish to add the following verses: verse 2—"How old are you?" verse 3—you may wish to help the birthday child respond with "I'm ———— years old (REPEAT); "I'm ———— today; I'm ———— years old!"
      (6) Allow child some special privileges such as choosing a story, record, or song, feeding the pets or fish.

      NOTE: Large centers may find decorated sheet cakes or cupcakes the easiest to handle.

Utilizing wall space: This display of numbers from 1 to 10 with the equivalent number of objects next to each one is on a well-traveled stairway. As the children use the stairs to go from one area to another, they can pause to study the relationship between the numbers and the objects.

teacher resources

Books and Periodicals

1. DePrees, Mildred. *A Child's World of Stamps.* New York: Parents' Magazine Press, 1973.
2. Hear, Ida Mae. "Number Games with Young Children," *Young Children,* 24:3 (Jan. 1969).
3. Feigenbaum, Kenneth. "Activities to Teach the Concept of Conservation," *Young Children,* 24:3 (Jan. 1969).
4. Lavatelli, Celia. *Piaget's Theory Applied to an Early Childhood Curriculum.* Boston: Boston American Science and Engineering Inc., 1970.

5. Leeper, Sarah. *Good Schools for Young Children*. New York: Macmillan, 1974.
6. Pollach, S., and Juliana Gensley. "When Do They Learn Geometry?" *Young Children*, 20:1 (Oct. 1964).
7. Sharp, Evelyn. *Thinking Is Child's Play*. New York: E. P. Dutton, 1969 (paper, Avon, 1970).
8. Todd and Hefferman. *The Years Before School*. New York: Macmillan, 1968.

Pictures and Displays

1. Clock display: set out different kinds of clocks on a low table, windup, alarm clock, electric alarm, clock radio, cuckoo clock, cooking timer, egg timer (sandglass), kitchen wall clock, and a clock that strikes on the quarter hour. On wall above table put pictures of clocks that you are not able to obtain, such as grandfather's clock, a sunburst or other decorative clock, or a clock in a church or tower.
2. Display of scales: set out English and metric scales, postal scales, bathroom scales, balance scales, kitchen scales, baby scales. Pictures of those you cannot obtain like health and produce scales could be put up.
3. Thermometer display: different kinds of thermometers, indoor-outdoor, deep fat, candy, meat, fever. Pictures of hot and cold objects could be put on the wall behind the table. (Use English and metric.)
4. Display various kinds of measuring devices: foot ruler, yardstick, folding rule, metal roll-up tape, seamstress tape (English and metric).
5. Display a stamp collection: talk about the shape, size, color, or subjects. Find the numbers telling how much they are worth. Have different sizes of envelopes and different shapes: square, rectangular, large, medium, and small. Show postal cards with and without pictures and post cards and envelopes with stamp printed on and with stamps glued on.
6. Display your coins and dollar bills: talk about shape and size and identify by name. Talk about the fact that the presidents' pictures are on the money. February is a good time to talk about money (and stamps) because both have special meaning around Valentine's Day, George Washington's Birthday, and Lincoln's Birthday. Use only with older or experienced children.
7. Make a calendar to mount on the wall near your grouptime area. Use one sheet of construction paper for each month. Make squares at least 1½" × 1½" for each day. Dennison or Hallmark stickers can be used to mark special days and birthdays. You can also put on appropriate pictures or symbols to show trips or other special group discoveries that were made or will be made.
8. Rearrange your room so that a post office or grocery store can be set up between the Home-Living Center and the Block-Building Center to encourage interaction between these two groups.
9. Show pictures of subjects that can be counted or will lead to discoveries about some of the basic concepts in this guide, such as a bridge over water, an empty vase and one filled with flowers, a picture that shows things close up and at a distance.

Community Resources

1. Bell Telephone Company: telephone teaching kit
2. Post office: for stamps and posters of stamps
3. Stamp collectors

Now It's Time

JoAnne Deal Hicks

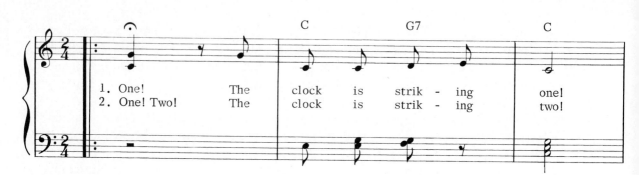

1. One!   The clock is strik - ing one!
2. One! Two!   The clock is strik - ing two!

1. Now it's time to go out - side and have some fun.
2. Now it's time for me to play a game with you.

Verse 3: The clock is strik-ing Three!
Now it's time for you to sing a song with me.

Verse 4: The clock is strik-ing Four!
Now it's time to go in-side and close the door.

NOTE: In second and succeeding verses, count each strike as you repeat the first note the appropriate number of times.